KW-492-822

EDITED BY PETER COWIE

VARIETY INTERNATIONAL FILM GUIDE 1997

LONDON
ANDRE DEUTSCH

HOLLYWOOD
SAMUEL FRENCH TRADE

UNITED INTERNATIONAL PICTURES

A Paramount • Metro Goldwyn Mayer • UNIVERSAL COMPANY

DISTRIBUTORS OF

THE GHOST AND THE DARKNESS
FIRST WIVES CLUB
THE SAINT

BOND 18
SUPERNOVA
HOODS

THE LOST WORLD
DANTE'S PEAK
LIAR, LIAR

UIP HOUSE, 45 BEADON ROAD, HAMMERSMITH, LONDON W6 0EG
TELEPHONE: 0181 741 9041 FAX: 0181 748 8990

The world's second oldest international film festival - founded in 1946.
Piazza Grande: our 7,000 seat capacity open-air cinema - Europe's largest screen.

Locarno 1996: vital statistics

- 150,000 audience
- 3,500 accredited professionals
- 1,000 journalists
- over 200 films screened

The 1997 Anniversary Edition:

- Clint Eastwood: director / producer / actor - a complete retrospective
- International Competition
- Out of Competition Special Screenings Piazza Grande
- Film-makers of the Present
- Cinema/cinemas
- Swiss Perspectives
- Leopards of Tomorrow
- Critic's Week

50th Locarno International Film Festival. August 6-16, 1997

MANFRED
DURNIOK
PRODUKTION
FÜR FILM UND
FERNSEHEN
International Motion Picture
and Television Productions,
Co-Productions and Film Distribution.
Hausotterstraße 36, D-13409 Berlin,
Germany, Phone (030) 491 80 45
E-Mail 100722.2445@compuserve.com
Fax (030) 491 40 66

CONTENTS

VARIETY INTERNATIONAL FILM GUIDE 1997

WORLD SURVEY

Editor: Peter Cowie
Managing Editor: Richard Combs
Consulting Editor: Derek Elley
Assistant Editor: Steve Pemberton
Advertising Co-ordination: Sandrine Bentata
Cover Design: Stefan Dreja
Book Design: John Harmer
Photo Consultants: The Kobal Collection

Editorial and Business Offices:
Variety
34-35 Newman Street,
London W1P 3PD
Tel: (0171) 637 3663
Fax: (0171) 580 5559

ISBN 0-233-99023-2
British Library Cataloging in Publication Data
Variety International Film Guide 1997
1. Cowie, Peter
011.37

Published in the U.S. by
Samuel French Trade
U.S. Library of Congress Catalog Card No: 64-1706

Copyright © 1996 by Reed U.S. Publishing Ltd

Photoset/Origination by Avonset, Bath
Printed and bound in Great Britain by Cromwell Press Ltd

SEAWELL FILMS

Jeannine Seawell

International Sales Representative for Quality Films to All Media

45 rue Pierre Charron 75008 Paris Tel: 47 20 18 73 Fax: 47 20 15 43

The Leading Worldwide Production Guide

1997 edition published in April.
Separate UK and USA editions also available.

Kemps Film, TV & Video Handbook provides you with complete coverage of the world's major markets, and contains essential information about all stages of the production process.

Invaluable for both International and National information
40,000 entries   53 countries   200 classifications

To order, contact Sara Tyler:
Tel: +44 (0) 171 637 3663   Fax: +44 (0) 171 580 5559

CONTENTS

INTERNATIONAL LIAISON

Africa: Roy Armes
Argentina: Alberto Tabbia
Australia: David Stratton
Bosnia: Rada Šesić
Brazil: Luis Arbex
Bulgaria: Ivan Stoyanovich
Canada: Gerald Pratley
Chile: Hans Ehrmann
Croatia: Tomislav Kurelec
Czech Republic: Eva Zaoralová
Denmark: Ebbe Iversen
Egypt: Fawzi Soliman
Estonia: Jaan Ruus
Far East: Derek Elley
Finland: Matti Apunen
France: Michel Ciment
Germany: Jack Kindred
Greece: Yannis Bacoyannopoulos
Hungary: Derek Elley
Iceland: Thorfinnur Ómarsson
India: Uma da Cunha
Indonesia: Marselli Sumarno
Iran: Jamal Omid
Ireland: Michael Dwyer
Israel: Dan Fainaru
Italy: Lorenzo Codelli
Japan: Frank Segers
Latvia: Andris Rozenbergs
Lithuania: Grazina Arlickaite
Luxembourg: Jean-Pierre Thilges
Malaysia: Baharudin A. Latif
Mexico: Tomás Pérez Turrent
Netherlands: Pieter van Lierop
New Zealand: Peter Calder
Norway: Trond Olav Svendsen
Pakistan: Aijaz Gul
Peru: Isaac León Frías
Philippines: Agustin Sotto
Poland: Wanda Wertenstein
Romania: Cristina Corciovescu
Russia: Michael Brashinsky
Serbia & Montenegro: Goran Gočić
Slovakia: Hana Cielová
Slovenia: Milan Ljubić
South Africa: Martin Botha
Spain: Peter Besas
Sri Lanka: Amarnath Jayatilaka
Sweden: Git Scheynius
Switzerland: Christoph Egger
Syria: Rafik Atassi
Thailand: Anchalee Chaiworaporn
Turkey: Atilla Dorsay
U.K.: George Perry
U.S.A.: William Wolf
Venezuela: Luis Sedgwick Báez

Miranda Richardson (right) in SWANN, directed by Anna Benson Gyles
photo: Michael Gibson

Kris Kristofferson in Sayles's LONE STAR
photo: Alan Pappe/Castle Rock

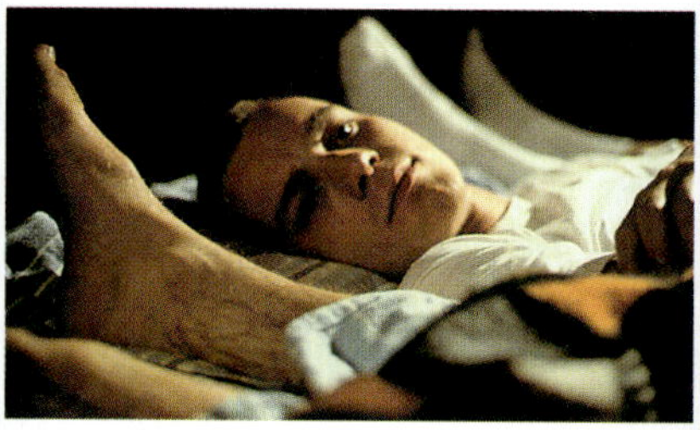

Still from TRAINSPOTTING
photo: Liam Daniel/PolyGram Int'l

NEW AND COMING

Top left: Emma Thompson and Kate Winslet in SENSE AND SENSIBILITY
photo: Clive Coote/Columbia TriStar

Above: Jeremy Irons and Liv Tyler in Bertolucci's STEALING BEAUTY

NEW AND COMING

Above: Christopher Eccleston and Kate Winslet in Winterbottom's JUDE
photo: Pierre Vinet/PolyGram Int'l

Below: Max von Sydow and Ghita Nørby in Troell's HAMSUN
photo: Nordisk Fil

Award-winner Anouk Grinberg (right) in Blier's MON HOMME

Cameron Diaz and Harvey Keitel in HEAD ABOVE WATER
photo: L . Sebastian/Fine Line

Helen Mirren in SOME MOTHER'S SON, a prize-winner at Edinburgh
photo: Denis Mortell/Castle Rock

Susan Sarandon, Best Actress at the Academy Awards, for DEAD MAN WALKING *photo: PolyGram*

U.S. Academy Awards: 1996

Best Film: *Braveheart.*
Best Direction: Mel Gibson for *Braveheart.*
Best Actor: Nicolas Cage for *Leaving Las Vegas.*
Best Actress: Susan Sarandon for *Dead Man Walking.*
Best Supporting Actor: Kevin Spacey for *The Usual Suspects.*
Best Supporting Actress: Mira Sorvino for *Mighty Aphrodite.*
Best Original Screenplay: Christopher McQuarrie for *The Usual Suspects.*
Best Adapted Screenplay: Emma Thompson for *Sense and Sensibility.*
Best Cinematography: John Toll for *Braveheart.*
Best Costume Design: James Acheson for *Restoration.*
Best Art Direction: Eugenio Zanetti for *Restoration.*
Best Editing: Mike Hill, Dan Hanley for *Apollo 13.*
Best Original Music or Comedy Score: Alan Menken, Stephen Schwartz for *Pocahontas.*
Best Original Dramatic Score: Luis Bacalov for *Il Postino.*
Best Original Song: "Colors of the Wind" from *Pocahontas.* Music by Alan Menken, lyric by Stephen Schwartz.
Best Sound: Rick Dior, Steve Pederson, Scott Millan, David MacMillan for *Apollo 13.*
Best Make-up: Peter Frampton, Paul Pattison, Lois Burwell for *Braveheart.*
Best Visual Effects: Scott E. Anderson, Charles Gibson, Neal Scanlan, John Cox for *Babe.*
Best Sound-Effects Editing: Lon Bender, Per Hallberg for *Braveheart.*
Best Foreign-Language Film: *Antonia's Line* (Netherlands).
Best Documentary Feature: *Anne Frank Remembered.*
Best Documentary Short: *One Survivor Remembers.*
Best Animated Short: *A Close Shave.*
Best Live-Action Short: *Lieberman in Love.*
Honorary Academy Awards: Kirk Douglas, Chuck Jones.
Special Achievement Award: John Lasseter.
Gordon E. Sawyer Award: Donald C. Rogers.

British Academy of Film and Television Arts Awards: 1996

Best Film: *Sense and Sensibility.*
Best British Film: *The Madness of King George.*
Best Direction: Michael Radford for *Il Postino.*
Best Actor: Nigel Hawthorne for *The Madness of King George.*
Best Actress: Emma Thompson for *Sense and Sensibility.*
Best Supporting Actor: Tim Roth for *Rob Roy.*
Best Supporting Actress: Kate Winslet for *Sense and Sensibility.*
Best Original Screenplay: Christopher McQuarrie for *The Usual Suspects.*
Best Adapted Screenplay: John Hodge for *Trainspotting.*
Best Original Film Music: James Horner for *Braveheart.*
Best Foreign-Language Film: *Il Postino* (Italy).
Fellowship Award: John Schlesinger.

European Film Awards: 1995

Best Film: *Land and Freedom* (U.K.).
Best Young Film: *La Haine* (France).
FIPRESCI Award: *Ulysses' Gaze* (Greece).
Documentary Award: Jens Meurer.
Lifetime Achievement Award: Marcel Carné.

French César Academy Awards: 1995

Best Film: *La Haine.*
Best Foreign Film: *Land and Freedom* (U.K.).

Best Director: Claude Sautet for *Nelly et Monsieur Arnaud.*
Best Actor: Michel Serrault for *Nelly et Monsieur Arnaud.*
Best Actress: Isabelle Huppert for *La Cérémonie.*
Best Supporting Actor: Eddy Mitchell for *Le bonheur est dans le pré.*
Best Supporting Actress: Annie Girardot for *Les Misérables.*
Best Upcoming Actor: Guillaume Depardieu for *Les apprentis.*
Best Upcoming Actress: Sandrine Kiberlain for *En avoir (ou pas).*
Best First Film: *Les trois frères.*
Best Screenplay:* Josiane Balasko, Telche Boorman for *Gazon maudit.*
Best Cinematography: Thierry Arbogast for *Le hussard sur le toit.*
Best Editing: Mathieu Kassovitz, Scott Stevenson for *La Haine.*
Best Original Score: Zbignew Preisner, Serge Gainsbourg, Michel Colombier for *Elisa.*
Best Sets: Joan Rabasse for *La cité des enfants perdus.*
Best Sound: Pierre Gamet, Dominique Hennequin, Jean Goudier for *Le hussard sur le toit.*
Best Costumes: Christian Gasc for *Madame Butterfly.*
Best Short: *Le moine et le poisson*
Best Producer: Christophe Rossignon for *La Haine.*

Italian Donatello Awards: 1996

Best Film: *August Vacation.*
Best Direction: Giuseppe Tornatore for *The Star Maker.*
Best Producer: Pietro Innocenzi, Roberto Di Girolamo for *Palermo Milan – No Return.*
Best First Feature: Stefano Incerti for *The Meter Reader.*
Best Actor: Giancarlo Giannini for *Celluloid.*
Best Actress: Valeria Bruni-Tedeschi for *The Second Time.*
Best Screenplay: Furio Scarpelli, Ugo Pirro, Carlo Lizzani for *Celluloid.*
Best Actor in a Foreign Film: Harvey Keitel for *Smoke.*
Best Actress in a Foreign Film: Susan Sarandon for *Dead Man Walking.*

Australian Film Awards: 1996

Best Film: *Angel Baby.*
Best Direction: Michael Rymer for *Angel Baby.*
Best Actor: John Lynch for *Angel Baby.*
Best Actress: Jacqueline McKenzie for *Angel Baby.*
Best Supporting Actor: Ray Barrett for *Hotel Sorrento.*
Best Supporting Actress: Amanda Douge for *The Eye, the Sky.*
Best Young Actor: Jamie Croft for *The Eye, the Sky.*
Best Original Screenplay: Michael Rymer for *Angel Baby.*
Best Adapted Screenplay: Richard Franklin, Peter Fitzpatrick for *Hotel Sorrento.*
Best Cinematography: Ellery Ryan for *Angel Baby.*
Best Foreign Film: *Once Were Warriors* (New Zealand).
Byron Kennedy Award: Jill Bilcock.
Raymond Longford Award: George Miller.

Independent Spirit Awards of Independent Feature Project/West: 1996

Best Film: *Leaving Las Vegas.*
Best Foreign Film: *Before the Rain* (Macedonia).
Best Director: Mike Figgis for *Leaving Las Vegas.*
Best Actor: Sean Penn for *Dead Man Walking.*
Best Actress: Elisabeth Shue for *Leaving Las Vegas.*
Best Supporting Actor: Benicio Del Toro for *The Usual Suspects.*
Best Supporting Actress: Mare Winningham for *Georgia.*
Best Screenplay: Christopher McQuarrie for *The Usual Suspects.*
Best First Feature: *The Brothers McMullen.*
Best Début Performance: Justin Pierce for *Kids.*
Best First Screenplay: Paul Auster for *Smoke.*
Best Cinematography: Declan Quinn for *Leaving Las Vegas.*

NORSTAR

A NEW VISION

ONE OF CANADA'S LEADING PRODUCTION AND DISTRIBUTION COMPANIES
AND A KEY PLAYER IN THE WORLD MARKETPLACE

NORSTAR ENTERTAINMENT INC.
86 BLOOR STREET WEST, 4TH FLOOR, TORONTO, CANADA M5S 1M5 TEL: (416) 961-6278 FAX: (416) 961-5608

This edition of IFG is dedicated to the memory of Krzysztof Kieślowski, who died in early 1996

DIRECTORS of the year

Theodor Angelopoulos

by Raymond Durgnat

Has the Golden Age of the art-house film ended, and the Silver, or Tinsel, Age begun? Though a few auteurs maintain the serious humanity of the Old Masters, from Renoir through Bergman to Antonioni, they seem outshone by a generation of Minor Decadents (Almodóvar, Jarman, Greenaway) whose gross-out tabu-bustings have brought critical taste down to the level of Tarantino, a sharply clever comic writer with a lager-lout soul. Yet the old Western visions of Man (Classical, Christian, rationalist, Socialist, Marxist) aren't quite dead, and still inspire a dogged and desperate Old Guard. Of whom Angelopoulos, in Greece, is almost the last. For Tarkovsky and Kieślowski have gone, alas; the Tavianis seem more head than heart; Makavejev works too rarely.

Strange, that these 'last humanists' link with Socialisms, East European-style. Perhaps those embattled peasant lands breed tougher, earthier, harder kinds of thinking than the West's dreaming spires and TV antennae. Tarkovsky's 'science-fiction' throbs with old-fashioned Russian Christian mysticism. Kieślowski plugs the Ten Commandments into EuroSocialist norms. The icily formalist Tavianis somehow yearn for family warmth. Makavejev's fantasies can seem jazzily post-modernist, but they're really gallows humour, about love and libido, topics complemented by Angelopoulos' darker, dourer themes. Though these inspirations dwell on Socialist societies, or faiths, their gloomy honesty strikes chords in us all.

Once upon a time, and not so long ago, Marxists pinned their hopes, and bet their lives, on Social History. But now they feel it has abandoned them, as other true believers have felt abandoned by their simpler faiths (in the gods, or the nation, or the state, or bureaucracy, or ethnicity). For years, Marxism debunked and despised the older loyalties and causes, and the communal forces they represented. But they've lurked and loomed ever larger in Angelopoulos' recent films, enriching their still basically Marxist frame. His latest, *Ulysses' Gaze*, harks back to Homer's *Odyssey* (850 B.C.). His social materialism pines to incorporate the more physical, more poetic responses and attitudes of peasants, intellectuals, bourgeois children. But now Marxism, too, can seem just another, equally alienated structure of the imagination, a mere aspiration as noble yet tragic as religion – or as humanist faith in Man. No, you don't have to be Marxist to share the pains of these pilgrims after meaning.

THEODOR ANGELOPOULOS was born in Athens on April 27, 1935, and grew up in

Still from RECONSTRUCTION *photo: The Kobal Collection*

a "politically divided" family (propitious formation for a political thinker!). He was five when the Nazis invaded, nine when the savage Civil War broke out. Later, he studied law, published poetry, lived in Paris. He entered fully into Communism at the Sorbonne (that erstwhile temple of Western humanism – but also *alma mater* to Pol Pot and friends). But he fell in love with film, studied with Jean Rouch, and became a film critic on an Athenian newspaper. The military junta, on seizing power in 1967, closed the paper, but they also introduced TV (perhaps to placate the masses). Thus they destabilised the movie industry, and unwittingly encouraged a Greek New Wave of low-budget art films aiming at a more international, art-house public, via the film festivals. This small but sufficient market niche enabled Angelopoulos' films to win ever more impressive prizes, until in 1995 *Ulysses' Gaze* won the Cannes 'double' (the Grand Prix and the International Critics' Prize). With Harvey Keitel as star, it could in theory bid for a wider English public – characteristically uncompromising though it is.

Missed Opportunities

Angelopoulos' first two films were made under, and against, the Colonels' régime. *Reconstruction* (1970) traces the disturbing social ramifications of a murder hunt. *The Days of '36* (1972) centres on a political execution and the dictatorship of an earlier 'Colonel', Metaxas, from 1936 to 1941. Both films bristle with political overtones, too oblique to be censored without embarrassment, but easily divined by Greek and 'progressive' spectators. In 1974, the junta collapsed, and Angelopoulos could paint two more panels of his triptych in Greek history. *The Travelling Players* (1975) summarises, in visionary, achronological fashion, Greek history 1941 – 1949, i.e., from the German invasion to the end of Civil War (between the Monarchists, whom Britain re-established, and the Communists, whom Stalin and Tito abandoned). In *The Hunters* (1977), upper-class huntsmen discover the bodies of Communist guerrillas, slain presumably in 1949. But here the murder-mystery form of *Reconstruction* gets a fourth dimension, as witnesses, suspects and the dead move back and forth between past and present, brooding over the guilts, failures and complicities, including those of the dead men's 'false friends', as if to accuse, or lament, the moderate politicians who ruled the roost from the Communists' defeat until – or right through? – the junta's rise and fall.

These films seem haunted by regrets, that Greek Communism missed its post-war 'window of opportunity', since when grassroots Communism has been fading away. His next two films contemplate, mournfully, two failures of popular radicalism. In *Alexander the Great* (1980), a turn-of-the-century bandit briefly personifies peasant resistance, but then alienates the people. In *Voyage to Cythera* (1984), an old peasant, a Civil War veteran, returns from his long exile in the Ukraine, only to find that 'you can't go home again' – for home has changed, and become a strange land, all the stranger since old friends, old surroundings, keep *promising* familiarity. The old peasant's son, an urbane film director, is alienated too, in his more intellectual, Antonioni-like, way. A scene which in Makavejev would have been a hoot, here chills the bones. A crowd of dockworkers well-meaningly sing the one or two militant songs whose words they half remember, but then switch to one they all know – 'As Time Goes By' from *Casablanca*.

Solitary Wanderers

The subsequent films focus on solitary wanderers, lost in a world made strange by failed hopes. As *The Beekeeper* (1986), Marcello Mastroianni, ageing, lonely, cherishes his beehive, venerable symbol for a utopian society. In *Landscape in the Mist* (1988), two children doggedly pursue their truant quest, from Greece to Germany, in search of a vanished father. The personal eclipses the political in this search for – History?, as the Father?, or the Law we long for? In *The Suspended Stride of the Stork* (1991), the young author of a book about the new *fin de siècle* renounces fame and friends to become a hermit. Why? The

Still from THE WANDERING PLAYERS *photo: The Kobal Collection*

Still from VOYAGE TO CYTHERA
photo: The Kobal Collection

mystery suggests a political *and* a personal despair, a shift from Marxist activism to social diagnosis (a more passive, acquiescent, pessimistic activity) into an ivory tower. Thus lapsed Marxism rejoins a kind of bourgeois decadence, in which history dissolves into memories and 'what ifs'.

In *Ulysses' Gaze* (1995), Keitel is a film director called "A" (for Angelopoulos? or one aspect of him?). Briefly returned from America, and revisiting his Greek roots, he embarks on a quest for some early, beautiful reels of film, long lost. The trail zig-zags through Greece, Albania, Bulgaria, Romania and Yugoslavia. The changing landscapes, the encounters with old friends, new companions, lost refugees, customs officials, taxi-drivers, whoever, provoke memories, fantasies, reveries, hallucinations, even an eerie identification with dead family. Thus geography becomes History (cultural or national, or social or personal, in a weave defying simple logic). A's journey ends where it begins, in Sarajevo (like our century of wars – 1914, 1995). The shots of city ruins, terrible beyond anything seen on TV, show all the difference between even the best TV journalism, and the heavier, richer gaze of the Art of the Film.

Angelopoulos brings his painter's eye to landscapes (arid, purple-tipped mountains), crowdscapes (human forms fading in fog), and roomscapes (opulent, chilly or charred black). They're never mere pictures, they're solid, physical, lived-in structures. Some are structures of property, labour and production, as in *Cythera*, the old peasant marking the boundaries of his fields. Others are structures of meaning, as in *Ulysses' Gaze*, the sandbagged cinema whose sombre interior weirdly evokes a cathedral (and hints at a temptation: art as a private religion, outside historical action?). It plays with a heretical idea: that nostalgia for one's childhood family, that Proustian, bourgeois emotion, may have its place. The long sequence-shots are so powerfully rhythmed, with their deliberate, quietly restless zooms, and slowly or briskly changed positioning of people, that aspiring film directors will want to study them forever. *The Travelling Players'* expertise is epitomised by one very long take, through a fixed camera, which telescopes a family's five successive Christmas reunions into one shot, as if they were one continuous event. Each year, the local Communist cadres pop in to confiscate more furniture: first the piano stool, then the piano, not overlooking a vase and the fresh flowers in it.

The Working Eye

Angelopoulos' elaborate zoom-and-camera-movements achieve a balance, or rather fusion of distance and communion, objectivity and sympathy. His camera-eye, like Ulysses' gaze, contemplates the world, not voyeuristically, nor just to reflect a man's own meanings back to him, but to discern the world's realities, to enter into a working relationship with them. To see is to grasp, it's manual labour with the eye. It's not voyeurism but sharing and belonging. The idea of seeing as participating feeds into Angelopoulos' interest in theatre

Reunion in THE SUSPENDED STRIDE OF THE STORK *photo: The Kobal Collection*

and in little rituals (which 'fix' the spiritual as material). And it drives A's quest for those early, primitive, in a sense innocent, reels of film.

A's voice-over, spare, considered, opens a third dimension of mental space. As it's kept clear of self-centred, introverted detail, it opens not into the little spaces of individual psychology, but on to wider, more basic, and therefore mythic issues (of family, friendship, quest, alliance). The film's fourth dimension is a web of cultural references, ranging from tersely suggestive asides like, 'It's all Hegel's fault, for influencing Marx', to a long, wordless visual poem, as a Lenin statue, huge but fragmented, prone on a motor-barge, moves through green countryside. The four women whom A encounters are (avowedly) modern counterparts of Homer's Penelope, Nausicaa, Circe and Calypso. But with a modernist twist: they're all played by the same, leonine actress.

Two of Angelopoulos' collaborators mark the link with the Golden Age. His co-scriptwriter, the poet Tonino Guerra, worked with Antonioni (on *L'Avventura* and *L'Eclisse*, earlier 'landscapes of alienation'), Fellini, the Tavianis and Tarkosvky. The film archivist is played by Erland Josephson, a strong, recurrent face in Bergman and Tarkovsky. Keitel, that ever-adventurous talent, so explosive in Scorsese, responds wonderfully to this opposite, implosive, intensely quiet style. His usual admirers, more accustomed to Hollywood's in-your-face histrionics, may take some time to adapt to this slower, figures-in-a-landscape non-emphasis. But it gradually elicits a quietly attentive mix of contemplation (at a distance . . .) and communion (thinking with . . .). It draws you in gradually, steadily; its sadness lacerates yet ennobles you.

Harvey Keitel in ULYSSES' GAZE
photo: The Kobal Collection

Angelopoulos Filmography

Unfinished Feature
1965
I ISTORIA TON FORMINX (The Forminx Story)

Direction: TA. Players: "Forminx" Pop Music Group.

Features
1970
ANAPARASTASSI (Reconstruction)

Script and Direction: TA. Photography: Giorgos Arvanitis. Editing: Takis Davlopoulos. Players: Thoula Stathopoulou (*The Woman*), Yannis Totsikas (*Gamekeeper*), Thanos Grammenos (*The Brother*), Petros Hoidas (*Prosecutor*), Mihalis Fotopoulos (*Husband*), Alexander Alexiou (*Policeman*), Iannis Balaskis (*Gendarme Officer*). Produced by Giorgos Samiotis. 110 mins.

1972
MERES TOU 36 (The Days of '36)

Script and Direction: TA. Collaboration: Petros Markaris, Thanassis Valtinos, Stratis Karras. Photography: Giorgos Arvanitis. Editing: Vassili Siropoulos. Art Direction: Mikes Karapiperis. Players: Petros Markaris (*1st Assassinated Trade Unionist*), Christos Kalavrouzos (*2nd Assassinated Trade Unionist*), Kostas Pavlou (*Sofianos*), Petros Zarkadais (*Sofianos' Accomplice*), Vassilis Tsaglos (*Prison Governor*), Iannis Kandilas (*Kriesis*), Kostas Mandilas (*British Ambassador*). Produced by Giorgos Papalios. 120 mins.

1974-5
O THIASSOS (The Travelling Players)

Script and Direction: TA. Photography: Giorgos Arvanitis. Editing: Takis Dovlopouios. Production Design: Mikes Karapiperis. Music: Loukianos Kilaidonis. Players: Eva Kotamanidou (*"Electra"*), Aliki Georgouli (*Her Mother*), Stratos Pachis (*Her Father*), Maria Vassiliou (*Her Sister*), Vanguelis Kazan (*The Informer*), Petros Zarkadis (*Orestes*), Kostas Mandilas (*British Officer*), Iakovos Pairidis (*The Communist*). Produced by Giorgos Papalios. 240 mins.

1977
I KYNIGHI (The Hunters)

Script and Direction: TA. Photography: Giorgos Arvanitis. Editing: G. Triandafillidis. Music: Loukianos Kilaidonis. Players: Venghelis Kazan (*Hotel Owner*), Giorgos Danis (*Businessman*), Ilia Stamatiou (*Editor*), Stratos Pahis (*Contractor*), Nikos Kouros (*Colonel*), Cristoferos Nezer (*Politician*), Mary Chronopoulou (*Wife*). Produced by Angelopoulos-INA. 165 mins.

1980
O MEGALEXANDROS (Alexander the Great)

Script and Direction: TA. Photography: Giorgos Arvanitis. Production Design: Mikes Karapiperis. Players: Omero Antonutti (*Alexander*), Eva Kotamanidou (*His Daughter-in-Law*), Grigoris Evanguelatos (*Teacher*), Mikhalis Yannatos (*The Guide*), Toula Stathopoulou (*Village Woman*), Christophoros Nezer (*Mr. Zelepis*). Produced by RAI/ZDF/Angelopoulos. 210 mins.

1984
TAXIDI STA KITHIRA (Voyage to Cythera)

Script: TA, Th. Valtinos, Tonino Guerra. Direction: TA. Photography: Giorgos Arvanitis. Editing: Giorgos Triantayllou. Production Design: Mikes Karapiperis. Music: Helen Karaindrou. Players: Manos Katrakis (*The Old Man*), Mary Chronoloulou (*Voula*), Dionyssis Papayannopoulos (*Antonis*), Dora Volanski (*The Old Woman*), Giorgos Nezos (*Panayotis*), Guilo Brogi (*Alexandros*). Produced by Greek Centre for Cinema/ ZDF/Channel 4/RAI/Greek TV/Theo Angelopoulos. 137 mins.

1986
O MELISSOKOMOS (The Bee Keeper)

Script: TA, Dimitris Nollas, Tonino Guerra. Direction: TA. Photography: Giorgos Arvanitis. Editing: Takis Yannapoulos. Art Direction: Mikes Karapiperis. Players: Marcello Mastroianni (*Spyros*), Serge Reggiani (*Sick Man*), Nadia Mourouzi (*The Girl*), Jenny Roussea (*Spyros' Wife*), Dinos Iliopoulos (*Spyros' Friend*). Produced by the Greek Film Centre/Theo Angelopoulos/ERTI (Athens)/MK2 Productions (Paris), French Ministry of Culture. 122 mins.

1988
TOPIO STIN OMICHLI (Landscape in the Mist)

Script: TA, Tonino Guerra, Thanassis Valtinos. Direction: TA. Photography: Giorgos Arvanitis. Editing: Giannis Tsitopoulos. Art Direction: Mikes Karapiperis. Music: Helen Karaindrou. Players: Tania Paleologou (*Voula*), Michalis Zeke (*Alexandre*), Stratos Giorgioglou (*Oreste*), Vassilis Kolovos (*Lorry Driver*), Dimitris Kaberidis (*Children's Uncle*), Yerassimos Skiaderesis (*Soldier*). Produced by Theo Angelopoulos OE/ Paradies Film (Germany)/ Générale d'Images/La Sept. 127 mins.

1991
TO METEORO VIMA TOU PELARGOU (The Suspended Stride of the Stork)

Script: TA, Tonino Guerra, Petros Markaris, with Thanassis Valtinos. Direction: TA. Photography: Giorgos Arvanitis, Andreas Sinanos*. Editing: Giannis Tsitopoulos. Production Design: Mikis Karapiperis. Music: Helen Karaindrou. Players: Marcello Mastroianni (*Politician/Disappeared Man/ Refugee*), Jeanne Moreau (*Woman*), Gregory Karr (*Reporter*), Ilias Logothetis (*Colonel*), Doira Chrysikou (*Girl*). Produced by Arena/Theo Angelopoulos/Greek Cinema Centre/Vega/Erre Produzioni. 140 mins.

1995
TO VLEMMA TOU ODYSSEA (Ulysses' Gaze)

Script: TA, Tonino Guerra, Petros Markaris, adapted by TA, Giorgio Silvagni. Direction: TA. Photography: Giorgos Arvanitis. Editing: Yannis Tsitopoulos. Production Design: Giorgos Patsas, Miodrac Mile Nicolic, Yannis Tsitopoulos. Music: Helen Karaindrou. Produced by Theo Angelopoulos/Greek Cinema Centre/Mega Channel/Paradis Film/La Générale d'Images/La Sept Cinéma. With the participation of Canal Plus, Basic Cinematografico Instituto Luce, RAI, Channel 4, Tele Muenchen/ Concorde Films/Herbert Kloiber. 177 mins.

Shorts

1968
I EKPOMBI (The Broadcast)

Production, Script and Direction: TA. Photography: Giorgos Arvanitis. Players: Theodor Katsadramis, Lina Triandafillou, Nicos Mastorakis. B&W. 23 mins.

TV

1981
HORIO ENA, KATIKOS ENAS (One Village, One Inhabitant).

1983
ATHINA, EPISTROFI STIN AKROPOLI (Athens, Return to the Acropolis).

Michael Mann

by Richard Combs

Is Michael Mann's *Heat* the *Greatest Story Ever Told* of crime movies? Is it the final statement on its genre that risks tipping over into inflated portentousness? There's more than a hint of religiosity about this project, from the hushed, ritualistic way it takes nearly three hours to tell its cops and robbers story, to the reverential tone with which it has been treated by some reviewers. Here, it seems, is a transcendental genre piece, an elevation and exaltation of the crime thriller. It ends with a familiar enough scene when supercop-nemesis Al Pacino reaches out for the dying hand of superthief Robert De Niro. Except that in *Heat*, the scene plays like a truly Sistine Ceiling moment.

Of course, this is to take a Devil's advocate position, secularly speaking. *Heat* deserves all the praise it has received as an action movie, for both the visceral punch and the high style of the armoured van heist that opens it, and the bank robbery that explodes into a messy street battle that ends it. And reservations about its extreme length can't diminish the fact that this is a superbly articulated film, incorporating microscopic detail about the jobs pulled by De Niro's 'crew' within a bold and expansive frame that assumes modern lives are as deserving of epic treatment as historical ones.

But it is *Heat*'s most famous scene that really crystallises reservations about how far Mann can push this form. Although they track each other, electronically survey each other, and intuit each other's qualities,

Exorcising the demon of THE KEEP *photo: Graham Attwood/The Kobal Collection*

De Niro and Pacino are kept apart until nearly the end of the film. Then a casual invitation from Vincent Hanna (Pacino) to Neil McCauley (De Niro) leads to their sitting down over a cup of coffee to discuss their business and their dreams. The meeting and mating of cop and criminal is a generic standby, but in *Heat* this scene really has no work to do because the epic form, the transcendental mode, already assumes the merging of one man with the other. Hanna and McCauley are stuck, two genre heroes trying to become the heroes of those greater psychic adventures which are the true measure of Mann: *The Last of the Mohicans* and *Manhunter*.

MICHAEL MANN was born in Chicago in 1943 and was educated at the University of Wisconsin and the London Film School. His early work as a writer in television established the urban crime thriller as his domain: he wrote episodes of *Starsky and Hutch* and *Police Story*, and directed an episode of *Police Woman*. The unique thing about Mann's career is that he didn't simply learn his trade in workaday TV crime and then graduate to the big-screen league, but returned after two films to reinvent the TV genre, with the designer-hip *Miami Vice* (1984-89) and the epic-in-the-making series *Crime Story* (1986-88). Being a producer is part of the style and stamp of Mann's personality as a director, and his reach can be as extensive in TV as in the cinema: *Heat* itself draws on a pilot Mann directed in 1989, *L.A. Takedown*, for a TV series that didn't materialise.

Family Support

The media first become confused with *The Jericho Mile* (1979), which Mann directed for television but which was released theatrically outside the United States. It's an off-shoot of the crime genre, a prison melodrama, and probably the first clear indication of Mann's intention not to play by the letter of the genre anyway. This will take him in two, often contradictory, and often not too well reconciled directions. One is a distinctive visual style, both an abstraction and a detailed itemisation, an isolation, of the elements of the crime film.

It is both an aestheticising tendency and a stocktaking one. Mann's feature film début, *Thief* (1981), gives us a political economy of the independent jewel thief (James Caan), the lone wolf as both businessman and artisan: how he chooses his tools as well as his targets.

In the other direction, Mann is the great romantic, even sentimentalist, of his generation. It's not the visual inventories that hold his films together but the bonding of couples and families. In *The Jericho Mile*, even the prison authorities are a kind of loving support group for the existentially self-made hero (Peter Strauss). In *Heat*, of course, family problems on both sides of the law take up much of that daunting running time.

There's a curious corollary to this with regard to Mann's women. Being an equal opportunities film-maker, he gives the same chic styling, the same hip existentialism and post-modern macho dialogue to both his male and female characters. But since the latter remain quite traditionally fixed, within the couple or the family, this results only in their becoming something like existential housewives.

Robert De Niro and Amy Brenneman in HEAT
photo: Warner Bros/Frank Connor

Let Evil Speak unto Evil

The ways in which Mann is trying to distort and expand the crime movie are suggested most clearly by his films outside the genre. He explicitly abandoned it after *Thief* to make *The Keep* (1983), a horror film in which he wanted to 'go beyond traditional three-act narrative

Daniel Day-Lewis falls foul of the colonial struggle in THE LAST OF THE MOHICANS
photo: Morgan Creek/Warners/Frank Connor

into something more expressionistic, something with more enchantment'. Based on a novel by F. Paul Wilson, this is about evil meeting evil: a contingent of Nazi troops, billeted in a Romanian castle in 1941, find themselves being attacked by something monstrous within.

The film has the story and the setting – a wonderfully intimidating haunted castle, so alien in scale and design, built at England's Shepperton Studio where the film was made – for a dark romantic epic. But it doesn't have the dramatic space – hindered no doubt by its many production problems – to differentiate a confusing number of spiritual antagonists.

These problems Mann would resolve – after a break to create *Miami Vice* – in his next film, *Manhunter* (1986). There are elements here of *The Keep* in modern dress – it replaces a special-effects monster with the chilliest psychopath ever acted on screen – and it's a more successful epic, Mann having discovered how much physical space and spiritual scope a clean designer look can give.

The pity is that one of Mann's best films has more or less been eclipsed by *The Silence of the Lambs*, the second and less significant adaptation of a Thomas Harris novel featuring the fearsome Dr. Hannibal Lecter. Mann's Lecter (Shakespearean actor Brian Cox) is not as all-devouring as Anthony Hopkins', but is somehow more threatening. He's finely attuned to the internal circuitry of Mann's film, and the seductive, soothing compositions in blue, green and white that suggest the whole film is some kind of forensic experiment.

The point of *Manhunter* is not that the good guy, investigator Will Graham (William Peterson), contains the same psychopathic impulses as the bad guy, Francis Dollarhyde (Tom Noonan). It's more that they can't help communicating with each other; they're in touch through those circuits, as we all are. Cinema, too, is part of the network, and *Manhunter* contains as many reflections on the sweet communion, the transmission of desire and dis-ease through looking and filming as, say, Michael Powell's *Peeping Tom*.

Radical Focus

Manhunter is a wonderful modern film – or as post-modern *and* as sentimental as Mann ever gets, while still looking all of a piece.

Tuesday Weld and James Caan in THIEF

But it says something about the nature of his film-making, and his ambition, that his masterpiece to date may be *The Last of the Mohicans* (1992). For all his chic sheen, Mann takes an atavistic view of human nature, and *Mohicans* is his most atavistic form, a throwback to the romanticism of the pre-anguished Western (cf. *Unforgiven*).

Or it may simply be Mann's most successful invention of his own form: an eighteenth-century pre-Western that uses some startling changes of focus to accommodate both the boundless wilderness and the close-up, close-order political and military forces that have arrived to fight over it. The film also accommodates his most unabashed treatment of the romantic couple (Daniel Day-Lewis and Madeleine Stowe).

Heat (1995) stretches to accomplish something similar within the genre that Mann knows best. It's impressive as a summation, though it's possible that the TV series *Crime Story* goes at least as far against greater odds. *Heat*'s shifts of focus between the microcosm of the job and the social macrocosm of its cop and criminal families are beguiling. But they're not as radical as the cultural vistas locked together by the changes in focal length of *The Last of the Mohicans*.

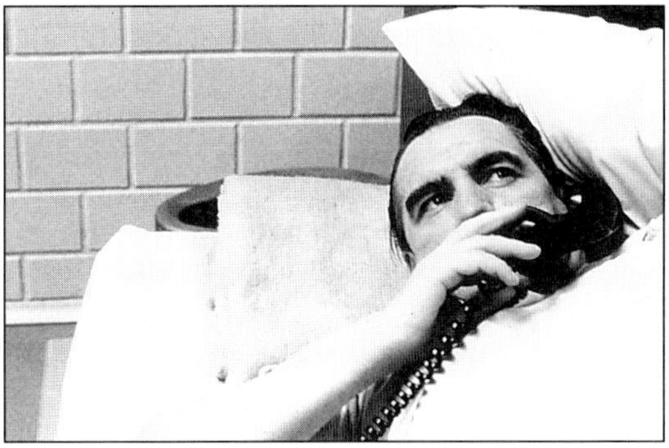

Brian Cox as Hannibal Lecter in MANHUNTER

Mann Filmography

1979
THE JERICHO MILE

Script: Patrick J. Nolan, MM. Direction: MM. Photography: Rexford Metz. Editing: Arthur Schmidt. Art Direction: Stephen Berger. Music: Jimmie Haskell. Players: Peter Strauss (*Larry "Rain" Murphy*), Richard Lawson (*R.C. Stiles*), Roger E. Mosley (*"Cotton"*), Brian Dennehy (*"Dr.D."*), Geoffrey Lewis (*Dr. Bill Janowski*), Billy Green Bush (*Warden Earl Gulliver*), Ed Lauter (*Jerry Beloit*), Beverly Todd (*Woman posing as Wylene Stiles*), William Prince (*OAU Chairman*), Miguel Pinero (*Rubio*). Produced by Tim Zinnemann for ABC Pictures International. 97 mins. TV film.

1981
THIEF

Script: MM, based on the novel *The Home Invaders* by Frank Hohimer. Direction: MM. Photography: Donald Thorin. Editing: Dov Hoenig. Production Design: Mel Bourne. Music: Tangerine Dream. Players: James Caan (*Frank*), Tuesday Weld (*Jessie*), Willie Nelson (*Okla*), James Belushi (*Barry*), Robert Prosky (*Leo*), Tom Signorelli (*Attaglia*), Dennis Farina (*Carl*), Nick Nickeas (*Nick*), W.R. (Bill) Brown (*Mitch*), Norm Tobin (*Guido*), John Santucci (*Urizzi*), Gavin MacFadyen (*Boreksco*). Produced by MM for Michael Mann Company/Caan Productions. 123 mins.
(a.k.a. *Violent Streets*).

1983
THE KEEP

Script: MM, based on the novel by F. Paul Wilson. Direction: MM. Photography (scope): Alex Thomson. Editing: Dov Hoenig, Pamela Power. Production Design: John Box. Music: Tangerine Dream. Players: Scott Glenn (*Glaeken Trismegistus*), Alberta Watson (*Eva Cuza*), Jurgen Prochnow (*Captain Woermann*), Robert Prosky (*Father Fonescu*), Gabriel Byrne (*Kaempffer*), Ian McKellen (*Dr. Theodore Cuza*), Morgan Sheppard (*Alexandru*), Royston Tickner (*Tomescu*), Michael Carter (*Radu Molasar*), Phillip Joseph (*Oster*), John Vine (*Lutz*), Jona Jones (*Otto*). Produced by Colin M. Brewer, Gene Kirkwood, Howard W. Koch Jnr. for Paramount. 93 mins.

1986
MANHUNTER

Script: MM, based on the novel *Red Dragon* by Thomas Harris. Direction: MM. Photography (scope): Dante Spinotti. Editing: Dov Hoenig. Production Design: Mel Bourne. Music: Michael Rubini, The Reds. Players: William Peterson (*Will Graham*), Kim Greist (*Molly Graham*), Joan Allen (*Reba McClane*), Brian Cox (*Dr Hannibal Lecter*), Dennis

Farina (*Jack Crawford*), Stephen Lang (*Freddie Lounds*), Tom Noonan (*Francis Dollarhyde*), David Seaman (*Kevin Graham*), Benjamin Hendrickson (*Dr. Frederick Chilton*), Michael Talbott (*Geehan*), Dan E. Butler (*Jimmy Price*), Michele Shay (*Beverly Katz*). Produced by Red Dragon Productions for De Laurentiis Entertainment Group. 120 mins.

1992
THE LAST OF THE MOHICANS

Script: MM, Christopher Crowe, based on the novel by James Fenimore Cooper and the screenplay (1936) by Philip Dunne. Direction: MM. Photography (scope): Dante Spinotti. Editing: Dov Hoenig, Arthur Schmidt. Production Design: Wolf Kroeger. Music: Trevor Jones, Randy Edelman. Players: Daniel Day-Lewis (*Hawkeye*), Madeleine Stowe (*Cora Munro*), Russell Means (*Chingachgook*), Eric Schweig (*Uncas*), Jodhi May (*Alice Munro*), Steven Waddington (*Major Duncan Heyward*), Wes Studi (*Magua*), Maurice Roeves (*Colonel Edmund Munro*), Patrice Chereau (*General Montcalm*), Edward Blatchford (*Jack Winthrop*), Terry Kinney (*John Cameron*), Tracey Ellis (*Alexandra Cameron*), Justin M. Rice (*James Cameron*). Produced by MM, Hunt Lowry for Morgan Creek. 122 mins.

1995
HEAT

Script and Direction: MM. Photography: Dante Spinotti. Editing: Dov Hoenig, Pasquale Buba. Production Design: Neil Spisak. Music: Elliot Goldenthal. Players: Al Pacino (*Vincent Hanna*), Robert De Niro (*Neil McCauley*), Val Kilmer (*Chris Shiherlis*), Jon Voight (*Nate*), Tom Sizemore (*Michael Cheritto*), Diane Venora (*Justine*), Amy Brenneman (*Eady*), Ashley Judd (*Charlene*), Mykelti Williamson (*Drucker*), Wes Studi (*Casals*), Ted Levine (*Bosko*), William Fichtner (*Van Zant*), Natalie Partman (*Laureen*), Tom Noonan (*Kelso*), Kevin Gage (*Waingro*), Hank Azaria (*Marciano*). Produced by MM, Art Linson, Arnon Milchan, Pieter Jan Brugge for Monarchy Enterprises, a Forward Pass production. 171 mins.

Nanni Moretti

by David Rooney

While Nanni Moretti's films have played to a devoted coterie of admirers in Italy and France for more than a decade, it was his 1993 feature *Dear Diary*, in which the director comes of age as a "splendid 40-year-old", that brought him to a wider international audience.

An intimate recap of an eventful year in the life of Italy's most idiosyncratic auteur, *Dear Diary* is both an autobiography and a succinct career summation, capturing Moretti's unrelenting restlessness and his quest for ideological perfection in himself and others. Most of all, it is an act of peaceful resignation from his youthful struggle against the world.

Significantly, in *Dear Diary*, Moretti abandons the character Michele Apicella, the alter ego who has been his voice in all but two features. Instead, he opens himself up for public inspection. Combining sincerity with cynicism, he offers a wry chronicle of his own life and that of a generation that has witnessed both the disintegration of society and social values, and the moral degradation of politics.

Born in 1953 in Brunico, in the north of Italy near Bolanzo (but a citizen of Rome by adoption), NANNI MORETTI has become one of the most influential figures in contemporary European cinema. In Italy, he has acquired a kind of guru status over the years with a small but stimulating body of films that communicate in simple, direct, uncompromising terms, eloquently and amusingly expounding his unapologetically arrogant world view.

That world view was first put on display in *Io sono un autarchico*, shot on Super-8 in 1976. Following in 1978 with *Ecce Bombo* and in 1981 with *Sogni d'oro*, Moretti quickly established an edgy, neurotic, tirelessly questioning attitude to the direction Italy was taking, and the compromises being accepted by his less exacting contemporaries.

An Uncertain Future

Critical reaction initially pigeonholed Moretti with a group of young Italian comedy actor-directors emerging at the time – such as Carlo Verdone and Massimo Troisi. But it soon became apparent that his frame of reference was wider, his sense of irony more intellectual than comical, and his humour considerably more acerbic, at times characterised by a bitter anger toward his targets.

His early, affectionate portraits of articulate young urbanites, with the rebelliousness of '68 behind them and an uncertain future ahead of them, in many ways were the precursors of the introspective generational films that were to flourish in Italy at the start of the 1990s. They depict a blank generation suffering from a profound disengagement from politics, the establishment, family, friends and the opposite sex.

While the fragmented structure and relatively static camerawork of Moretti's early work makes it appear somewhat dated now, the importance of these first features within the Italian film-making climate of the time should not be underestimated. Few, if any, other voices in Italian cinema so clearly delineated the dissatisfaction and frustration of the 1970s; the profound but often futile attempts at self-analysis, and the painful awareness of being part of a time that was creating no significant cultural legacy.

Not surprisingly for a film-maker who so directly addressed a specific generation, Moretti's stock as a spokesman for the hip, leftist intelligentsia grew rapidly. This

Nanni Moretti indulges in some impromptu singing in DEAR DIARY *photo: Artificial Eye*

Laura Morante with Moretti in SOGNI D'ORO
photo: The Kobal Collection

stature advanced further with his 1984 release, *Bianca*, and its successor, *La messa è finita* (1985), both of which began to take a much more caustic view. Both films also benefited from a more robust narrative structure thanks to scripts co-authored with Sandro Petraglia.

In *Bianca*, which is playfully structured as something approaching a murder mystery, a high-school teacher confesses to multiple killings. At the same time, he admits his unwillingness to accept the contradictions and compromises of his friends' lives, and his terror at becoming part of a couple. Eventually, he renounces his almost spiritual quest to create the ideal existence in order to carve out a normal life.

Perfectionism & Powerlessness

Much darker in tone, *La messa è finita* is a more confrontational, disenchanted enterprise, with Moretti as Don Giulio, a priest who returns to his family and friends in Rome to find them unaccountably changed during his absence. Like the schoolteacher protagonist of *Bianca*, the clergyman is unable to come to terms with these imperfections, leaving him no choice but to accept his own powerlessness. The perfectionist side of Moretti's on-screen characters appears to bear a more than casual resemblance to his own off-screen persona. This perhaps accounts for his output having become increasingly less prolific – his last three features have come at intervals of four years – as his reputation has grown in Italy and beyond.

When *Palombella Rossa* (1989) was rejected by the Venice Film Festival, either in or out of competition, it created a film industry uproar. The feature eventually screened as the special event in the independently programmed Critics' Week section. Some pundits, however, defended the logic of Venice's rejection, pointing out that the film's analysis of the collapse of Italian Communism was unlikely to mean much to audiences outside of Italy – only, at a stretch, in France, which shared a not dissimilar political legacy. But *Cahiers du Cinéma* selected the film as one of 100 must-have titles for the essential videothèque, helping to inspire the international discovery of Moretti that was to come.

Moretti plays the leading role of a water polo player (the director was formerly a champion of the sport) and Communist Party deputy suffering from amnesia. It's a bleak account of political, sporting and personal defeat that is both his most complex and least coherent film. The cruel accuracy of the director's attacks is as sharp as ever, but much of the film smacks of sanctimoniousness and a sense of moral superiority.

Unguardedly Personal

In *Dear Diary*, Moretti's characteristic disdain is tempered by humour and self-irony, a mellowing that won him international acclaim and a Best Director prize at the 1994 Cannes Film Festival.

The film is comprised of three episodes: "On My Vespa", which sees him tooling around a semi-deserted, height-of-summer Rome admiring the architecture; "Islands", which takes him to the Aeolian islands off Sicily to weigh up the consequences of the lapsed ideals of his generation while on a futile quest for peace and quiet; and "Doctors", which pursues an unnerving quest through the Italian medical system to diagnose and treat a malignant tumour. This last section is the most unguardedly personal of all Moretti's work.

Moretti's trademark anger is exchanged

for what appears to be a Zen-like calm, coloured none the less by an acute awareness of the inadequacies of the society around him. In one of the film's most telling scenes, Moretti steps into an empty Roman movie house to watch a (fake) new Italian release. While the characters on screen punish themselves for having grown old and complacent, Moretti shouts, "I'm not guilty! You all shouted awful things in demonstrations and now you've grown old. I shouted the right things, and I'm a splendid forty-year-old".

Days of Sacher Torte

In 1986, Moretti formed his own production company, Sacher Film, with producer Angelo Barbagallo, and in 1991, they took over management and programming of a Roman cinema, dubbed the Nuovo Sacher. A cozy art-house theatre in Rome's rustic Trastevere quarter, the venue is known for its superlative presentation quality; rumour has it that Moretti's pursuit of excellence has compelled him to upgrade the screen three times in the cinema's short life span. Naturally, the coffee bar serves sacher torte, a dessert associated with the director since his Michele Apicella character first eulogised its qualities in *Bianca*.

Moretti's influence as a cultural figure is evident from the Nuovo Sacher's uncommonly high success rate, obtaining long runs for commercially difficult films by directors like Derek Jarman, Abbas Kiarostami and Ken Loach, and making a surprise theatrical hit of Edgar Reitz's *Heimat* series. A release at the theatre is widely perceived as a critical endorsement in itself.

As producers, Moretti and Barbagallo have also been instrumental in launching the directorial careers of film-makers Daniele Luchetti, Carlo Mazzacurati and, more recently, Mimmo Calopresti, whose début feature, *La Seconda volta*, had its international première in competition at the 1996 Cannes Film Festival.

Moretti Filmography

In addition to his own films, Moretti has appeared as an actor in the Taviani brothers' *Padre Padrone*, in Daniele Luchetti's *Domani accadr* and *Il Portaborse*, and in Mimmo Calopresti's *La Seconda volta*. He has also directed several short films, including *Il Giorno della prima di 'Close Up'*, which screened at Cannes in 1996, and an episode of *L'unico paese al mondo*, a protest film made by nine Italian directors during Silvio Berlusconi's 1994 electoral campaign. Politics were also at the centre of his hour-long 1990 documentary *La cosa*, about then Communist Party leader Achille Occhetto's radical reform proposals.

1976
IO SONO UN AUTARCHICO

Script and Direction: NM. Photography: Fabio Sposini. Editing: NM. Music: Franco Piersanti. Players: NM (*Michele Apicella*), Simona Frosi (*Silvia*), Andrea Pozzi (*Andrea*), Fabio Traversa (*Theatre Director*), Giorgio Viterbo (*Giorgio*), Paolo Zaccagnini (*Paolo*), Guido Valesini (*Doctor*), Beniamino Placido (*Theatre Critic*). Produced by NM. 95 mins.

1978
ECCE BOMBO

Script and Direction: NM. Photography: Giuseppe Pinori. Editing: Enzo Meniconi. Art Direction: Massimo Razzi, Music: Franco Piersanti. Players: NM (*Michele Apicella*), Luisa Rossi (*Mother*), Glauco Mauri (*Father*), Lorenza Ralli (*Valentina*), Lina Sastri (*Olga*), Fabio Traversa (*Mirko*). Produced by Filmalpha/ Alphabeta. 103 mins.

1981
SOGNI D'ORO

Script and Direction: NM. Photography: Franco Di Giacomo. Editing: Roberto Perpignani. Art Direction: Giovanni Sbarra, Music: Franco Piersanti. Players: NM (*Michele Apicella*), Piera Degli Esposti (*Mother*), Laura Morante (*Silvia*), Alessandro Haber (*Gaetano*). Produced by Operafilm/RAI-1. 105 mins.

1984
BIANCA

Script: NM, Sandro Petraglia. Direction: NM. Photography: Luciano Tovoli. Editing: Mirco Garrone. Art Direction: Giorgio Luppi, Marco Luppi. Music: Franco Piersanti. Players: NM (*Michele Apicella*), Laura Morante (*Bianca*), Roberto

Vezzosi (*Commissioner*), Remo Remotti (*Siro*), Vincenzo Salemme (*Massimiliano*), Enrica Maria Modugno (*Aurora*), Claudio Bigagli (*Ignazio*). Produced by Faso Film/Reteitalia. 95 mins.

1985
LA MESSA E FINITA

Script: NM, Sandro Petraglia. Direction: NM. Photography: Franco Di Giacomo. Editing: Mirco Garrone. Art Direction: Amedeo Fago, Giorgio Bertolini. Music: Nicola Piovani. Players: NM (*Don Giulio*), Margarita Lozano (*Mother*), Ferruccio De Ceresa (*Father*), Enrica Maria Modugno (*Valentina*), Marco Messeri (*Saverio*), Roberto Vezzosi (*Cesare*). Produced by Faso Film. 94 mins.

1989
PALOMBELLA ROSSA

Script and Direction: NM. Photography: Giuseppe Lanci. Editing: Mirco Garrone. Art Direction: Giancarlo Basili. Music: Nicola Piovani. Players: NM (*Michele Apicella*), Silvio Orlando (*Rari Nantes Monteverde*), Mariella Valentini (*Reporter*), Asia Argento (*Valentina*). Produced by Sacher Film/Banfilm, in association with SOFINA and RAI-1. 89 mins.

Moretti with Laura Morante in BIANCA *photo: The Kobal Collection*

1993
CARO DIARIO (DEAR DIARY)

Script and Direction: NM. Photography: Giuseppe Lanci. Editing: Mirco Garrone. Art Direction: Marta Maffucci. Music: Nicola Piovani. Players: NM (*Himself*), Renato Carpentieri (*Gerardo*), Antonio Neiwiller (*Mayor of Stromboli*), Raffaella Lebboroni, Marco Paolini, Claudia Della Seta, Lorenzo Alessandri, Conchita Airoldi, Riccardo Zinna, Moni Ovadia, Jennifer Beals, Alexandre Rockwell. Produced by Sacher Film/Banfilm. 100 mins.

Moretti with Valeria Bruni-Tedeschi in LA SECONDA VOLTA

Paul Verhoeven

by Derek Elley

When *Showgirls* opened in the U.S. in September 1995 to howls of critical disapproval, you could almost hear the gods laughing. Beneath the barely concealed vein of xenophobia that a foreigner had dared to portray Las Vegas as an unethical, money-fixated town ran a shocked tone of moral outrage at the unredeemable characters and copious sleaze on display.

For anyone with a passing knowledge of Verhoeven's career prior to *RoboCop*, it would have been more surprising if he had not outraged puritan sensibilities. Rather than being just a cheap shot at an easy target, *Showgirls* is on every level a consistent entry in the Dutch director's oeuvre: visually extrovert, centred on a protagonist who goes through the mill, exploits it and survives, quietly romantic beneath its cynical front, and a hell of a cinematic ride.

The characters in his most typical films are driven, frequently cynical opportunists who undergo a kind of spiritual crucifixion and resurrection – though, to the outrage of those who like moral pay-offs, not necessarily to become better persons, more to go on to the next challenge. On an ethical level, there's precious little difference between the Catherine Tramell of *Basic Instinct*, Nomi Malone of *Showgirls* and Murphy of *RoboCop*, and the Erik Vonk of *Turkish Delight*, Martin of *Flesh & Blood*, and anyone in *Spetters*. Working regularly with writers (Gerard Soeteman, Joe Eszterhas, Ed Neumeier) and producers (Rob Houwer, Alan Marshall) who delight in transcending stereotypes, and cameramen (Jan de Bont, Jost Vacano) who can supply the necessary visual punch, Verhoeven remains the bane of the serious-minded critic – a gut-level auteur working in the commercial industry whose greatest fear is to be considered "boring".

PAUL VERHOEVEN was born in Amsterdam in 1938, the son of a school-teacher, and was raised in The Hague to the sound of Allied bombing of the German rocket base nearby. After secondary education, he studied mathematics at the University of Leiden, the Netherlands' oldest and most conservative seat of learning. While there, he made a prize-winning student film, the visually stylised *A Lizard Too Much* (*Één hagedis teveel*, 1960), a simple story of a student who has an affair with

Characteristic in-your-face imagery from Verhoeven in THE FOURTH MAN *photo: The Kobal Collection*

two women that's told in a surrealist style Verhoeven admits shows his early fascination with directors like Luis Buñuel and Alain Resnais, and also the painter Salvador Dali. (Prior to film-making, Verhoeven's initial interest had been painting.) On the basis of that work, he won a grant from the Culture Ministry for the 28-minute short *The Party* (*Het feest*), about a diffident schoolboy attracted to a girl in another class, which travelled to festivals.

After getting his doctorate in maths, Verhoeven did national service during 1965-66, managing to work in the navy's film department. It was a lively colour documentary, *The Dutch Marine Corps* (*Het korps mariniers*), that he made during this period that attracted the attention of the TV community. Following a long documentary on Dutch Nazi leader A. Mussert, Verhoeven was asked to make a mediaeval adventure series for children, the Ivanhoe clone *Floris* (1968). It was on this that he first worked with writer Gerard Soeteman, who was to script all his Dutch features, and the actor Rutger Hauer, whom the series launched as a leading man.

After making the government-sponsored 22-minute short *The Wrestler* (*De worstelaar*), about a man who learns his son is having an affair with a wrestler's wife, Verhoeven finally entered features with *Business Is Business* (1971), a series of rumbustious sketches about two prostitutes' various clients. The modest film was a sleeper hit locally, outgrossing *Love Story* and seen by one in three of the population.

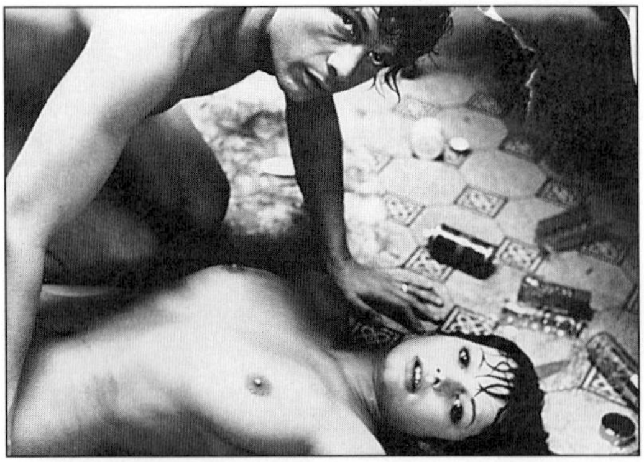

Still from TURKISH DELIGHT

Pushing the Envelope

The early 1970s was a time in Dutch cinema when feature-length films were still rare; for years the country had been more renowned for government-funded shorts by directors like Bert Haanstra. Verhoeven was one of a vocal but disparate group of directors who were convinced there was room for a feature industry. *Business Is Business* was the first 100% Dutch feature backed by Rob Houwer, a Dutch-German producer based in Munich, and its success forged a partnership that was to extend over four more features. Verhoeven's next film, *Turkish Delight* (1973), based on a local bestseller by Jan Wolkers, created a sensation with its frank and unblinking view of sexuality, its nihilistic hero, and its ridiculing of staid Dutch traditions.

Though the film starts with young sculptor Erik (Hauer) copulating his way through Amsterdam in an attempt to forget an as-yet nameless woman, the film gradually develops a more romantic tone as the story flashbacks two years and charts his relationship with Olga (Monique Van De Ven). Throughout the film, Verhoeven neatly switches from moments of tenderness between the pair to exuberantly sexual episodes leavened with spirited humour. As a work hurled in the face of the establishment (as well as the country's self-consciously arty, serious directors), *Turkish Delight* is virtually a declaration of war.

Verhoeven's next feature, *Katie's Passion* (1975), was based on three books of memoirs written in French by Neel Doff (born in 1858). The film follows Keetje (Monique Van De Ven), a young woman from a poor background, who passes through prostitution and an affair with a bank clerk to find eventual happiness with a rich notary's son. Verhoeven's third feature with cameraman Jan de Bont, the film has a striking look on its $1 million budget and, like *Turkish Delight*, balances its romantic moments with more unsettling sequences showing the hardship and squalour of the period (the 1880s). For many, this is Verhoeven's finest work, and the closest he has come to an 'art-house' movie.

Still from SPETTERS *photo: The Kobal Collection*

Three years later, Verhoeven pushed the local production envelope even further with the most expensive Dutch film ever, *Soldier of Orange* (1978), a World War II story of how events and history impact on the friendship of six Leiden University students. Though the film features plenty of crowd-pleasing action sequences, excellently staged, it is more about the individual characters' growth into self-knowledge, their response to events, and the ties of friendship that are tested by events. On an industry level, Verhoeven had finally proven that it was possible locally to make a blockbuster that was on a par with anything from a larger film-making country. The Dutch public flocked to see it, and Verhoeven himself still considers it his most personal film.

Last Blasts & Wrong Notes

Verhoeven returned to the more realistic style of *Turkish Delight* with his next film, *Spetters* (1980), about a group of youngsters in the Rotterdam suburbs united by a common interest in sex and motorcycles. Though the film recovered its $1.7 million budget locally, it created an uproar among special-interest groups, especially for its unvarnished depiction of gay-bashing. Locally, the film even spawned an Anti-*Spetters* Action Group (NASA), with Verhoeven berated on TV and in the press.

With government money (an integral part of Dutch film financing) increasingly difficult to find, Verhoeven and Soeteman pulled their cheekiest stunt to date, *The Fourth Man* (1983). Specifically designed, in Soeteman's words, "to fuck the Dutch critics" who lauded serious, symbol-laden works, the film can now be seen as almost a parody of an art-house movie, the portrait of a gay writer (Jeroen Krabbe) in a constant state of emotional and sexual delirium over a woman (Renee Soutendijk) and her boyfriend (Thom Hoffman).

Based on a slim novel by the bestselling author Gerard Reve, a flamboyant, openly homosexual, stridently right-wing local celebrity, the movie was voted one of the best Dutch films of all time by local critics, despite what Verhoeven now admits is "a completely ridiculous story" told in surrealist style. Sumptuously shot by Jan de Bont and moodily scored by Loek Dikker, it was to be Verhoeven's parting shot to the land of his birth.

Instead of taking the plunge and moving straight to the U.S. to make English-language films, Verhoeven settled on the compromise of using American finance (Orion Pictures) but shooting in Europe (Spain) with a mixed Dutch-U.S.-Australian cast for his next film, *Flesh + Blood* (1985). A 16th-century tale of a mercenary, Martin (Rutger Hauer), who kidnaps Agnes (Jennifer Jason Leigh), the future bride of a corrupt nobleman, the film offers only scattered pleasures, with the multi-national cast striking discordant notes and the script never achieving a consistent tone.

Showtime

It was Verhoeven's wife, Martine, who persuaded him to accept the script of *RoboCop* (1987), seeing opportunities way beyond the seemingly straightforward s-f action story of a Detroit cop who is reborn as the ultimate crimefighter, the semi-android RoboCop. Verhoeven came to see the figure as a kind of "American Christ" – preaching fine values but still resorting to the gun when words don't do the trick. The picture is essentially a European's sardonic view of a society dominated by the twin evils of have-a-nice-day TV and corporate values, through which the robotic hero cuts a ruthless swathe untroubled by notions of correctness, a true Verhoeven protagonist.

Peter Weller in ROBOCOP
photo: Orion/The Kobal Collection

Stone picks ice in BASIC INSTINCT
photo: Guild/The Kobal Collection

But again, beneath the apparently cynical front, the picture beats with a romantic heart, notably in scenes where RoboCop's human memories start to impinge on his computerised objectivity.

Though *Total Recall* (1990), Verhoeven's first chance at directing a big-star, mega-budget picture, seems his least personal movie, the central cogs are still there: a typically pragmatic hero (Arnold Schwarzenegger) who elbows his way past the norms of expected behaviour and gets a second chance at his life by revisiting earlier characters on a ruthlessly corporatised Mars. Freely expanded from a 1966 Philip K. Dick short story entirely set on Earth, the film is an exuberant ride on all levels, from Jerry Goldsmith's driving score, through regular collaborator Rob Bottin's special effects and William Sandell's flashy production design, to the muscular performances by Schwarzenegger, Rachel Ticotin, Sharon Stone and villains Ronny Cox and Michael Ironside.

By the time Verhoeven's path crossed with that of Joe Eszterhas, the director seems finally to have gained the measure of his newly adopted industry. Beneath its pulp-level characters and plot (which is illogical on closer examination), there is a confidence and assurance to *Basic Instinct* (1992) that succeeds in suspending the viewer's analytical faculties. Catherine Tramell (Sharon Stone) is the typical self-serving Verhoeven protagonist to the power of ten – bisexual, totally irredeemable and offering a glimpse of pure evil that is both shocking and seductive to the cop (Michael Douglas) caught in her web.

Though he claims not to have seen *The Fourth Man* until after writing *Basic Instinct*, Eszterhas has noted the "huge consonances of theme and meaning" between the two films, and Verhoeven's fascination with the aura and origin of evil. As Olga was enraptured by Erik in *Turkish Delight*, Agnes by Martin in *Flesh + Blood*, and Gerard by his illusions in *The Fourth Man*, detective Nick Curran finds in *Basic Instinct* that there's a darker side to everyone that can be tapped in the right circumstances.

In Eszterhas and Verhoeven's subsequent *Showgirls* (1995), it's a whole city (Las Vegas) rather than just a single character that exerts its effect on the protagonist: ambitious, small-town dancer Nomi (Elizabeth Berkley) finally abandons her principles, works the system to her own advantage, and at the end is shown moving on (in the film's most ironic joke) to Los Angeles. As the plastic-looking, unsympathetic protagonist, Berkley is cleverly cast, and Verhoeven manages to make the film's copious nudity seem an everyday, non-erotic event, totally appropriate to a town dedicated to the packaging of sanitised flesh. Like all Verhoeven's movies, *Showgirls* is entirely guided in tone and look by the milieu in which it is set.

Verhoeven Filmography

1971
WAT ZIEN IK (Business Is Business/Memoirs of a Streetwalker)

Script: Gerard Soeteman, from the novel by Albert Mol. Direction: PV. Photography: Jan de Bont. Players: Ronnie Bierman, Sylvia de Leur. Produced by Rob Houwer. 85 mins.

1973
TURKS FRUIT (Turkish Delight)

Script: Gerard Soeteman, from the novel by Jan Wolkers. Direction: PV. Photography: Jan de Bont. Editing: Jan Bosdriesz. Art Direction: Ralf van de Elst. Music: Rogier Van Otterloo. Players: Monique Van De Ven (*Olga Stapels*), Rutger Hauer (*Erik Vonk*), Tony Huurdeman (*Mrs Stapels*), Wim Van Den Brink (*Mr Staples*), Hans Boskamp (*Baboon*), Dick Scheffer (*Accountant*), Manfred de Graaf (*Henny*), Marjol Flore (*Tineke*), Marijke Frijlink (*Moniek*), Olga Zuiderhoek (*Gonnie*), Maartje Seijferth (*Josje*). Produced by Rob Houwer. 107 mins.

1975
KEETJE TIPPEL (Katie's Passion)

Script: Gerard Soeteman, from the memoirs *Jours de famine et détresse, Keetje and Keetje Trottin* by Neel Doff. Direction: PV. Photography: Jan de Bont. Editing: Jane Sperr. Art Direction: Roland de Groot, Dick Schillemans. Music: Rogier Van

Elizabeth Berkley in the underrated SHOWGIRLS *photo: Chargetex/Murray Close*

Otterloo. Players: Monique Van De Ven (*Keetje*), Rutger Hauer, Eddie Brugman, Hannah de Leeuwe, Andrea Domburg, Jan Blaaser, Peter Faber, Walter Kous, Fons Rademakers. Produced by Rob Houwer. 104 mins.

1978
SOLDAAT VAN ORANJE (Soldier of Orange/Survival Run)

Script: Gerard Soeteman, Kees Holierhoek, PV, from the memoirs by Erik Hazelhoff Roelfzema. Direction: PV. Photography: Jost Vacano, Peter de Bont. Editing: Jane Sperr. Art Direction: Roland de Groot. Music: Rogier Van Otterloo. Players: Rutger Hauer (*Erik*), Jeroen Krabbe (*Gus*), Peter Faber (*John*), Derek de Lint (*Alec),* Eddy Habbema (*Robby*), Lex van Delden (*Jacques*), Edward Fox (*Col. Rafelli*), Belinda Meuldijk (*Esther*), Susan Penhaligon (*Susan*), Andrea Domburg (*Queen Wilhelmina*). Produced by Rob Houwer. 165 mins. Dutch and English dialogue.

1980
SPETTERS

Script: Gerard Soeteman. Direction: PV. Photography: Jost Vacano. Editing: Ine Schenkkan. Art Direction: Dick Schillemans. Music: Ton Scherpenzeel & KAJAK. Players: Hans van Tongeren (*Rien*), Renee Soutendijk (*Fientje*), Toon Agterberg (*Eef*), Maarten Spanjer (*Hans*), Marianne Boyer (*Maja*), Hugo Metsers (*Angel*), Kitty Courbois (*Doctor*), Rutger Hauer (*Witkamp*), Jeroen Krabbe (*Henkhof*). Produced by Joop Van Den Ende for VSE. 115 mins.

1983
DE VIERDE MAN (The Fourth Man)

Script: Gerard Soetman, from the novel by Gerard Reve. Direction: PV. Photography: Jan de Bont. Editing: Ine Schenkkan. Art Direction: Roland de Groot. Music: Loek Dikker. Players: Jeroen Krabbe (*Gerard Reve*), Renee Soutendijk (*Christine*), Thom Hoffman (*Herman*), Dolf de Vries, Geert de Jong, Hans Veerman. Produced by Rob Houwer. 92 mins.

1985
FLESH + BLOOD

Script: Gerard Soetman, PV, from a story by Soeteman. Direction: PV. Photography (Technovision): Jan de Bont. Editing: Ine Schenkkan. Art Direction: Felix Murcia. Music: Basil Poledouris. Players: Rutger Hauer (*Martin*), Jennifer Jason Leigh (*Agnes*), Tom Burlinson (*Steven*), Jack Thompson (*Hawkwood*), Susan Tyrrell (*Celine*), Ron Lacey (*Cardinal*), Fernando Hillbeck (*Arnolfini*), Brion James (*Karsthans*), John Dennis Johnston (*Summer*), Simon Andreu (*Miel*), Bruno Kirby (*Orbec*), Kitty Courbois (*Anna*), Marian Saura (*Polly*), Hans Veerman (*Father George*), Jake Wood (*Little John*), Hector Alterio (*Niccolo*), Blanca Marsillach (*Clara*), Nancy Cartwright (Kathleen). Produced by Gys Versluys for Riverside Pictures/ Orion Pictures. 126 mins.

1987
ROBOCOP

Script: Edward Neumeier, Michael Miner. Direction: PV. Photography: Jost Vacano. Editing: Frank J. Urioste. Production Design: William Sandell. Music: Basil Poledouris. Players: Peter Weller (*Murphy/ RobCop*), Nancy Allen (*Lewis*), Daniel O'Herlihy (*The Old Man*), Ronny Cox (*Jones*), Kurtwood Smith (*Clarence*), Miguel Ferrer (*Morton*), Robert DoQui (*Sgt. Reed*), Ray Wise (*Leon*), Felton Perry (*Johnson*), Paul McCrane (*Emil*), Jesse Goins (*Joe*), Del Zamora (*Kaplan*), Calvin Jung (*Minh*), Rick Lieberman (*Walker*). Produced by Arne Schmidt for Orion Pictures. 103 mins.

1990
TOTAL RECALL

Script: Ronald Shusett, Dan O'Bannon, Gary Goldman, from a screen story by Shusett, O'Bannon and Jon Povill, inspired by Philip K. Dick's short story "We Can Remember It for You Wholesale". Direction: PV. Photography: Jost Vacano. Editing: Frank J. Urioste. Production Design: William Sandell. Music: Jerry Goldsmith. Players: Arnold Schwarzenegger (*Quaid/ Hauser*), Rachel Ticotin (Melina), Sharon Stone (*Lori*), Ronny Cox (*Cohaagen*), Michael Ironside (*Richter*), Marshall Bell (*George/ Kuato*), Mel Johnson Jr. (*Benny*), Michael Champion (*Helm*), Roy Brocksmith (*Dr. Edgemar*), Ray Baker (*McClane*), Rosemary Dunsmore (*Dr. Lull*). Produced by Buzz Feitshans, Ronald Shusett for Carolco Pictures. 109 mins.

1992
BASIC INSTINCT

Script: Joe Eszterhas. Direction: PV. Photography (Panavision widescreen): Jan de Bont. Editing: Frank J. Urioste. Production Design: Terence Marsh. Music: Jerry Goldsmith. Players: Michael Douglas (*Det. Nick Curran*), Sharon Stone (*Catherine Tramell*), George Dzundza (*Gus*), Jeanne Tripplehorn (*Dr. Beth Garner*), Denis Arndt (*Lt. Walker*), Leilani Sarelle (*Roxy*), Bruce A. Young (*Andrews*), Chelcie Ross (*Capt. Talcott*), Dorothy Malone (*Hazel Dobkins*), Wayne Knight (*John Correli*), Daniel von Bargen (*Lt. Nilsen*), Stephen Tobolowsky (*Dr. Lamott*), Benjamin Mouton (*Harrigan*). Produced by Alan Marshall for Carolco Pictures/Le Studio Canal Plus. 127 mins. (Overseas version: 128 mins.)

1995
SHOWGIRLS

Script: Joe Eszterhas. Direction: PV. Photography (Clairmont widescreen): Jost Vacano. Editing: Mark Goldblatt, Mark Helfrich. Production Design: Allan Cameron. Music: David A. Stewart. Players: Elizabeth Berkley (*Nomi Malone*), Kyle MacLachlan (*Zack Carey*), Gina Gershon (*Cristal Connors*), Glenn Plummer (*James Smith*), Robert Davi (*Al Torres*), Alan Rachins (*Tony Moss*), Gina Ravera (Molly Abrams), Lin Tucci (*Henrietta Bazoom*), Greg Travis (*Phil Newkirk*), Al Ruscio (*Mr. Karlman*), Patrick Bristow (*Marty Jacobsen*), William Shockley (*Andrew Carver*), Michelle Johnston (*Gay Carpenter*), Dewey Weber (*Jeff*), Rena Riffel (*Penny*). Produced by Alan Marshall, Charles Evans for United Artists/Chargeurs. 131 mins.

1997
STARSHIP TROOPERS

Script: Edward Neumeier, from the novel by Robert Heinlein. Direction: PV. Players: Dina Meyer, Jake Busey, Neil Patrick Harris, Michael Ironside. Produced by TriStar/Walt Disney. In production spring 1996, budgeted at $95 million.

Wayne Wang

by Philip Strick

With the launching at Cannes 1996 of a new production company, Chrome Dragon Films, the unpredictable career of film-maker Wayne Wang has taken a fresh turn. Teamed with Francis Ford Coppola, with whom he has had links since the days of *Dim Sum* (1985), he is set to operate as producer for six action movies, to be made in different Asian cities by six new Asian directors. The project could yet turn out, of course, to be one of those schemes that never gets much further than a Festival announcement. But probably its chief significance is as confirmation that Wayne Wang is now a major player in the peculiar politics of film production, although – by his own preference – decidedly not in the Hollywood playground. It also suggests that previously unremarked affinities can be sought between his films and Coppola's, in which immigration, eating, and family fortunes are similarly recurring themes.

The films of WAYNE WANG derive much of their appeal from his acute visual sense, which tellingly reflects the oscillations of his background. A man of two worlds, two cultures and two traditions, he has paid tribute to two extremes in his work and achieved a kind of equilibrium between them. Born (1949) and raised in Hong Kong, his English-speaking Jesuit schooling was offset by his father's devotion to American cinema (with particular emphasis on Audie Murphy, Frank Capra and John Wayne, inspiration for the boy's Christian name). He came to California in 1967 at the age of 18 to study painting, film and television and ran straight into an identity problem. "I thought", he says now, "that I was very American from the movies I'd seen, but I was very Chinese and very Hong Kong. I didn't know what to do with myself".

What Isn't There

The first answer, in film terms, was suicide. At the California College of Arts and Crafts, Wang's early ventures into photography and video were often pseudo-documentaries of his own death, a cathartic series of self-portraits which he claims to have donated, with unimaginable consequences, to the Salvation Army. Resurrected with the help of fellow-student Terrel Seltzer, who became his wife and screenwriter, he watched innumerable European films at the newly established Pacific Film Archive and co-directed a graduation feature in the style of Polanski, *A Man, a Woman and a Killer*, "about one of our friends who was a drug addict. It was very, very strange, self-obsessed and narcissistic, although there were things about the way the narrative was handled that got to be quite interesting".

After gaining technical experience from work both in California and back in Hong Kong, including Chinese television soap operas that were "basically propaganda about impoverished families enjoying great happiness", Wang's training process entered its most valuable phase with a film-free four years in San Francisco's Chinatown as community worker and English teacher. Almost by accident, an experimental film project emerged and steadied itself into *Chan Is Missing* (1981). With an amiably piecemeal story about a Chinatown taxi driver's hunt for a colleague who has disappeared with $4,000, it reflects a range of influences from Antonioni to *cinéma vérité*, with Hitchcockian use of music and locations (the *Vertigo* bridge), and a Godardian affection for the disguised-thriller format.

While making an ironic attempt to decipher the contradictions of Chinese-American society, *Chan Is Missing* reveals a respect not so much for actors (about whom Wang had reservations: "their work is sometimes simpler than they make out") as for *non*-actors, their eloquent faces studied in long-held candid-camera scrutiny. At the same time, Wang has a remarkable eye for images of nothing in particular, such as a car gliding out into traffic, patterns on the surface of water, a girl combing her hair in the street, window blinds being pulled down at night – moments which acquire an unexpected relevance. His concluding sequence, which he describes as "almost totally abstract", is a fragmented portrait of Chinatown illustrating his narrator's observation that "this mystery is appropriately Chinese: what's not there seems to have just as much meaning as what *is* there".

On Dangerous Ground

Based on the rigours of structuralist theory, this formal use of non-narrative images became a major strength of Wang's next film, *Dim Sum – A Little Bit of Heart* (1985).

SMOKE: Harvey Keitel in hot pursuit *photo: Artificial Eye*

Still from DIM SUM

Suggested by the relationship between Chinese-American Laureen Chew (who played the cab driver's niece in *Chan Is Missing*) and her stubbornly Chinese mother (who agreed to perform the same role on film), *Dim Sum* is a fascinating correlation of shapes and patterns that pays conscious tribute to the minimalist style of Japanese director Yasujiro Ozu and owes as much to the American painter Edward Hopper.

Set in the Chews' own home, the film dwells on furniture, photographs, and the interplay of light: the importance of windows and curtains is one of many sub-texts. None of this, though, detracts from the delicate account of the girl's dilemma: whether to get married as is expected of her or to remain as companion to her introverted parent. Beautifully performed, particularly by Cora Miao (who became Yang's second wife) as a family friend coping with the loss of her own mother, and by Victor Wong as a genially unsuitable suitor, the film captured the Chinese-American predicament so successfully that Wang found he was already at risk of being typecast.

Offered the script of *Slam Dance* (1987), he jumped at the chance to demonstrate his versatility: "I told myself not to get too involved, rather to make a good commercial action thriller that is also

Tom Hulce and Virginia Madsen in SLAM DANCE
photo: Island/Zenith/Warner Bros.

funny. But I *did* get involved". Clustered with high-profile players (Mary Elizabeth Mastrantonio, Tom Hulce, Harry Dean Stanton, Virginia Madsen), *Slam Dance* resembles *Chan Is Missing* in the sense that its plodding hero, a Los Angeles cartoonist implicated in a murder cover-up, spends most of the time trying to work out what's going on. Otherwise, with its aggressive contrasts of light and darkness, the film is somewhere in the noir-ist territory of *Diva* or *The Conformist*. Probably less interesting in its final form than in Wang's first cut, which shook his producers to the core, the film is nevertheless unjustly maligned: it has a richness and complexity of design, along with an off-beat line of humour, that is strikingly staged and edited. There are all kinds of canny references (to Hockney, for example), and the use of music – always prominent in Wang's work – is a special pleasure.

Retreating smartly to safer ground, Wang made *Eat a Bowl of Tea* (1989), based on Louis Chu's novel about the relaxation of the Exclusion Laws in 1949, a modest period piece set in New York's Chinatown. A study of the strains endured by Chinese newly-weds under the pressure of parental ambition, it proves a slight and sentimental case history, shot with moody elegance and much redeemed by Cora Miao's perky resilience. It was shot in Hong Kong, which turned out, after all, to be less than safe territory for filming purposes – to such a degree that Wang decided on revenge with a recklessly anarchic documentary-comedy, "a really crazy movie" written by Laureen Chew's husband Spencer

Harvey Keitel and Jim Jarmusch in BLUE IN THE FACE

Nakasako, who also took the central role. Scathingly titled *Life Is Cheap . . . But Toilet Paper Is Expensive* (1990), it used a collision of Western and thriller genres to comment on the unnerving prospect of Hong Kong's return to Chinese administration. Its multiple shocks and amputations, and not least its exhausting chase sequence using a hand-held camera, were so poorly received that Wang took a year (his mid-life crisis, he said) to recover.

The Godfather of Chinatown

The break was the making of him. With his film of Amy Tan's best-selling novel *The Joy Luck Club* (1993), Wang not only found the ideal synthesis of his earlier Chinatown themes but also – thanks to the complex four-story structure – a new discipline of style. Unobtrusively framed, with an intensity that recalls the precision (as well as the relationships) of Bergman's later works, the film may on reflection seem a touch glib and more than a touch contrived, but its visual restraint is immaculate. Inevitably evoking the historical melodramas of Chen Kaige and Zhang Yimou, with a hint of Oliver Stone (the landscapes of *Heaven and Hell* reappear), both the costume sequences and the spectacular crowd scenes are admirably handled. Chiefly, Wang gives the eight main actresses of his cast the chance to make the most of the recycled mother-versus-daughter contest – and they all prove to be winners.

"I *see* you", says one of the *Joy Luck Club* parents to her mixed-up offspring, and it is this appreciative perception that links Wang's recent double bill to his previous output. Set in a Brooklyn cigar shop, *Smoke* (1995) is derived from a story by novelist Paul Auster, centred on an unusually benevolent Harvey Keitel. With a camera that hardly moves from the middle distance (a whole scene is done in only four shots) and gets, in consequence, greater mileage out of the moments when it *does* shift (as when a past girlfriend, superbly played by Stockard Channing, receives a gift of much-needed cash), Wang has created a New York comedy-store film as if, China were somewhere in another galaxy. "He and I are basically humanists", he says of Paul Auster, "and we love to see the better side of people". They enjoyed the prospect so much that when *Smoke* finished ahead of schedule, they carried on shooting and made *Blue in the Face* (1995) in just six days. While retaining Keitel as the central figure, continuing the romance (with the effervescent Mel Gorham) he began in *Smoke*, this "escapade into modern-day vaudeville" involves appearances from Jim Jarmusch, Madonna, Lily Tomlin, Lou Reed and others, in the Brooklyn equivalent of a Joy Luck Club party.

Having established, like Coppola, that he can actually handle anything, his budgets having alternated over twenty years between a few thousand dollars and several million, Wayne Wang in fact now looks too good to waste on the producer's administrative chores of collating cash and talent. Taking the hint from *Blue in the Face*, for which he cheerfully shared the director's credit, the Chrome Dragon project could be interpreted as another step towards detachment from hands-on film-making, a Cormanesque retreat into Godfatherly supervision that would be greeted with mixed feelings by Wang's admirers. For preference, they would probably encourage him to concentrate on his special skill at visualising more personal interests on the screen. But he will, of course, go his own way.

Wang Filmography

1974
GOLDEN NEEDLES

(Assistant Director, Hong Kong sequences).

1975
A MAN, A WOMAN AND A KILLER

(Co-writer and co-director with Rick Schmidt and Richard R. Richardson).

BELOW THE LION ROCK

(Hong Kong TV series; WW directed several episodes).

1979
NEW RELATIONSHIPS

(45-minute documentary made solely from stills).

1981
CHAN IS MISSING

Script: WW, Terrel Seltzer. Direction: WW. Narration: Isaac Cronin, WW. Photography (b&w): Michael Chin, Kathleen Beeler. Editorial Consultant: Rick Schmidt. Music: Robert Kikuchi-Yngojo, Sam Hui. Players: Wood Moy *(Jo)*, Marc Hayashi *(Steve)*, Laureen Chew *(Amy)*, Judy Nihei *(Lawyer)*, Peter Wang *(Henry)*, Roy Chan *(Mr Lee)*, George Woo *(George)*, Ellen Yeung *(Mrs Chan)*, Emily Yamasaki *(Jenny)*, Presco Tabios *(Presco)*, Frankie Alarcon *(Frankie)*. Produced by Wayne Wang Productions, with a grant from The American Film Institute, in association with The National Endowment for the Arts. 76 mins.

1985
DIM SUM – A LITTLE BIT OF HEART

Script: Terrel Seltzer. Story: Terrel Seltzer, Laureen Chew, WW. Direction: WW. Photography: Michael Chin. Editing: Ralph Wikke. Music: Todd Boekelheide. Players: Laureen Chew *(Geraldine Tam)*, Kim Chew *(Mrs. Tam)*, Victor Wong *(Uncle Tam)*, Ida F. O. Chung *(Auntie Mary)*, Cora Miao *(Julia)*, John Nishio *(Richard)*, Amy Hill *(Amy Tam)*, Keith Choy *(Kevin Tam)*, George Wu *(Bar Patron)*. Produced by Project A Partnership for CIM Productions. 87 mins.

1987
SLAM DANCE

Script: Don Opper. Direction: WW. Photography : Amir Mokri. Editing: Lee Percy, Sandy Nervig. Production Design: Eugenio Zanetti. Music: Mitchell Froom. Players: Tom Hulce *(C.C. Drood)*, Mary Elizabeth Mastrantonio *(Helen Drood)*, Adam Ant *(Jim Campbell)*, Don Opper *(Buddy)*, Virginia Madsen *(Yolanda Caldwell)*, Harry Dean Stanton *(Detective Smiley)*, John Doe *(Gilbert)*, Robert Beltran *(Frank)*, Millie Perkins *(Bobby Nye)*, Rosalind Chao *(Mrs Bell)*, Judith Barsi *(Bean)*, Herta Ware *(Mrs Raines)*. Produced by Sho Films for Zenith Productions and Island Pictures. 101 mins.

1989
EAT A BOWL OF TEA

Script: Judith Rascoe, from the novel by Louis Chu. Direction: WW. Photography: Michael Chin. Editing: Richard Candib. Production Design: Bob Ziembicki. Music: Mark Adler, Todd Boekelheide. Players: Victor Wong *(Wah Gay)*, Russell Wong *(Ben Loy)*, Cora Miao *(Mei Oi)*, Eric Tsang Chi Wai *(Ah Song)*, Lau Siu Ming *(Lee Gong)*, Wu Ming Yu *(Mei Oi's Mother)*, Hui Fun *(Ben Loy's Mother)*, Law Fan *(Aunt Gim)*, Lee Sau Kee *(Bok Fat)*, Yuen Yat Fai *(Public Letter Writer)*, Wong Wai *(Chuck Ting)*, Philip Chan *(Henry Wang)*. Produced by American Playhouse Theatre for Columbia. 104 mins.

Peter Wang in CHAN IS MISSING

1990
LIFE IS CHEAP . . . BUT TOILET PAPER IS EXPENSIVE

Script: Spencer Nakasako. Story: Amir M Mokri, Nakasako, WW. Direction: WW. Photography: Amir M. Mokri. Editing: Chris Sanderson, Sandy Nervig. Editorial Consultant: Lee Percy. Music: Mark Adler. Narrator: Dennis Dun. Players: Spencer Nakasako *(The-Man-with-No-Name)*, Chan Kim Wan *(The Duck Killer)*, Victor Wong *(The Blind Man)*, Cheng Kwan Min *(Uncle Cheng)*, Cora Miao *(Money)*, Lam Chung *(Red Guard)*, Allen Fong *(Taxi Driver)*, John K. Chan *(Son-in-Law)*, Bonnie Ngai *(Daughter)*, Lo Wai *(Boss)*. Produced by Forever Profit Investments Ltd/Far East Stars. 89 mins.

1993
THE JOY LUCK CLUB

Script: Amy Tan, Ronald Bass, from the novel by Amy Tan. Direction: WW. Photography: Amir M. Mokri. Editing: Maysie Hoy. Production Design: Donald Graham Burt. Music: Rachel Portman. Players: Kieu Chinh (*Suyuan*), Tsai Chin (*Lindo*), France Nuyen *(Ying Ying)*, Lisa Lu (*An Mei)*, Ming-Na Wen *(June)*, Tamlyn Tomita *(Waverly)*, Lauren Tom *(Lena)*, Rosalind Chao *(Rose)*, Victor Wong *(Old Chong)*, Mei Juan Xi *(Lindo's Mother)*, Russell Wong *(Lin Xiao)*, Yu Fei Hong *(Ying Ying, age 16-25)*, Andrew McCarthy *(Ted)*, Christopher Rich *(Rich)*, Diane Baker *(Mrs Jordan)*. Produced by Buena Vista Pictures/ Hollywood Pictures. 139 mins.

1995
SMOKE

Script: Paul Auster. Direction: WW. Photography: Adam Holender. Editing: Maysie Hoy. Production Design: Kalina Ivanov. Music: Rachel Portman. Players: Harvey Keitel *(Auggie Wren)*, William Hurt *(Paul Benjamin)*, Forest Whitaker *(Cyrus Cole)*, Stockard Channing *(Ruby McNutt)*, Giancarlo Esposito *(1st OTB Man/Tommy)*, José Zuniga *(2nd OTB Man/Jerry)*, Stephen Gevedon *(3rd OTB Man/Dennis)*, Jared Harris *(Jimmy Rose)*, Daniel Auster *(Book Thief)*, Harold Perrineau *(Rashid Cole)*, Erica Gimpel *(Doreen Cole)*, Ashley Judd *(Felicity)*, Victor Argo *(Vinnie)*. Produced by NDF/Euro Space for Miramax Films, in association with Peter Newman/ Interal. 108 mins.

BLUE IN THE FACE

Script: improvisation, in situations created by WW, Paul Auster. Script Supervisor: Karen Kelsall. Direction: WW, Paul Auster; (video segments): Harvey Wang. Photography: Adam Holender. Editing: Christopher Tellefsen, Maysie Hoy. Music: John Lurie, Calvin Weston, Billy Martin. Players: Harvey Keitel *(Auggie Wren)*, Roseanne *(Dot)*, Michael J. Fox *(Peter)*, Lily Tomlin *(Derelict)*, Mel Gorham *(Violet)*, Jared Harris *(Jimmy Rose)*, Giancarlo Esposito *(Tommy)*, Victor Argo *(Vinnie)*, Madonna *(Singing Telegram Girl)*, Keith David *(Jackie Robinson)*, Mira Sorvino *(Blonde Woman)*, Jim Jarmusch, Lou Reed. Produced by Peter Newman/Interal in association with NDF/Euro Space for Miramax Films. 84 mins.

LASER DISCS

Introduction

This has been an excellent year for LD enthusiasts, and for those in the U.K. in particular. The threat from DVD is evaporating by the week, and the British firm Encore Entertainment has surged ahead with an exciting parade of releases (as many as a dozen a month), culled primarily from the riches of Fox and Columbia TriStar, but also from a wide variety of foreign-language and independent libraries.

Two handicaps seem likely to hobble DVD from the start. One concerns quality: DVD aims to replace run-of-the-mill videocassettes, not LD, and so perfection of sound and image are no longer paramount. The other concerns format: widescreen editions will not appear as they do on LD, thus alienating the fastidious collector.

Add to these disadvantages the chaotic software situation provoked by the Studios' refusal to sanction a universal playing system. Once again, PAL and NTSC will rule our purchasing rights and habits, while the music industry sails blithely on with a universal standard for compact discs.

So the film buff should relax and continue accumulating software, in the full knowledge that nothing out there yet matches the LD standard for depth of image and authenticity of sound. Some studios (notably Paramount) still drag their feet in restoring and re-releasing classic titles others like Warners, for example, are improving their output with refurbished gems such as *The Wild Bunch* and *Bonnie and Clyde.*

Voyager's Criterion Collection has published some excellent entries this year, from *Seven* to *Amarcord* (see reviews below), and the U.K.'s Encore has exploited the ultra-sharpness of the PAL format with *First Knight*, *Bad Boys* and *Braveheart* (which it sent to the shops the very week that Gibson's epic took home the Academy Award for Best Picture). Pioneer continues to do the LD community a significant service by providing the best hardware – and the installed base in the U.K. has doubled in the process over the past two years. Pioneer LDCE has also scored high marks for its discs of *Apocalypse Now*, *Stargate* and *Scarface.*

NTSC Banned in Britain

As from April 30, 1996, it became an offence to supply NTSC discs to the public in the U.K. The ostensible reason was "classification" (i.e. censorship), with certain discs being slightly different to their cassette counterparts because they were imported *intacta* from the States. Yet

The Encore disc cover for John Woo's A BETTER TOMORROW

even the most stalwart supporter of PAL will concede that it will take many years for the catalogue to match the sheer size and scope of the NTSC universe. There are approximately twenty times as many feature films in print on LD in the States as there are in Britain. What the authorities don't realise is that by pushing the NTSC buying habit below ground they are also restricting the acceptance of LD as a medium. Thank God for Encore and its determination to fill the racks with PAL releases that will attract the cognoscenti as well as a new generation of LD enthusiasts.

Peter Cowie

Stephen Haynes Talks About ENCORE ENTERTAINMENT

When the history of the PAL laserdisc market comes to be written, U.K.-based Encore Entertainment will get at least a chapter to itself. Though Pioneer was largely responsible in the early 1990s for keeping the market going (in the face of huge indifference from many film distributors, hardware manufacturers and journalists), Encore came out of nowhere to become the biggest issuer of PAL discs – and with a breadth of repertoire PAL collectors could only have dreamed of a couple of years ago.

Run by a tiny, dedicated team from offices in a converted farmhouse in the rural wilds south of Birmingham, Encore has grown in 2¼ years to a present catalogue of some 150 movies, still growing at the rate of some 4-8 titles a month. While other PAL issuers have stood still or withdrawn from the market, Encore has snapped up rights from 20th Century Fox, Columbia/TriStar, and specialist U.K. distributors Electric Pictures, Metro Tartan, MIA and Artificial Eye. In a first for a PAL LD company, Encore announced in June 1996 a licensing deal with BBC Video for classic TV series.

Managing director Stephen Haynes is actively seeking other distributors to join the Encore fold, though Warners (one of two big U.S. distributors, along with Buena Vista, which refuses to get into PAL LDs) is committed to DVD. Haynes claims he isn't worried about the supposed threat of DVD to traditional 12" LDs. "They say they want to make DVD mass-market, but it's taken 16 years or so to get LDs to this stage. And they have no plans to do widescreen issues, which is the prime draw for LD collectors."

From the beginning, Haynes has been convinced that the only way to create a viable PAL market is to keep pumping out new issues as fast and as cheaply as possible, to get people into the buying habit. Though the NTSC market has effectively been driven underground (to mail order) by recent legislation in the U.K., Haynes realises it is never going to go away and presents "no threat" to titles unlikely to be issued on PAL.

"I'm not against NTSC and I don't object to mail order – only to companies selling titles we own the PAL rights to." (They make much more profit selling an NTSC disc than a PAL one.) "As a collector myself, I don't want to lose the right to buy NTSC discs!"

Reverse Selling to the U.S.

Like several in the U.K., Haynes is even considering reverse selling NTSC discs to the U.S. "Two major holes in the NTSC catalogue are classic British films and foreign art-house. We're looking at setting up an NTSC operation, based here but with the discs going out through a U.S. distributor." In April, Encore already announced a distribution deal for its PAL

BEST RELEASES ON PAL: 1995-96

Braveheart (Encore)
Apocalypse Now (Pioneer)
Bad Boys (Encore)
First Knight (Encore)
The Madness of King George (Encore)
Stargate (Pioneer)
Glory (Encore)
E.T. The Extra Terrestrial (Pioneer)
The Battle of Algiers (Encore)
Waterworld (Pioneer)

Editor's Selection

BEST RELEASES ON NTSC: 1995-96

The Big Country (Image and MGM/UA)
Goldfinger – THX edition (MGM/UA)
Alice in Wonderland (Disney)
The Complete *Showboat* (MGM/UA)
The Virgin Spring (Voyager)
Wuthering Heights (Pioneer)
GoldenEye (MGM/UA)
The Old Dark House (Image)
Belle de Jour (Voyager)
Prokofiev: War and Peace (Philips)

Sedgwick Clark

catalogue in Australia (a still-nascent market with some 10,000 players), through local distributor DIA Multimedia.

Unlike some U.K. companies that tried to bully customers into supporting PAL over NTSC, Encore has put its money where its mouth is, adopted a more user-friendly approach, and made a determined effort to address five of the root problems that have held back PAL LD development: keeping up a regular flow of product; building loyalty by letting buyers know what is coming down the track; reducing prices to levels where a disc purchase is no longer a special event; getting discs out as fast as possible, alongside the video rental release (its success with *Braveheart* at Oscar time in early '96 paid dividends here); and building a broad spread of old, new and foreign repertoire.

Encore is the first sizeable PAL issuer run by people from the grassroots rather than drafted over from some division of a multinational. The team – who even operate their own website (http://www.compulink.co.uk/-encore), rightly figuring that many LD buyers are also techies – have so far shown that they know what their public wants and pride themselves on being a listening company. "In a niche market like LD, you can't afford to lose the trust of your buyers," stresses Haynes.

Haynes himself is a film buff who decided one day that if others could do it so could he. "I'd always been into films, and even wanted to make them. Then, after reading about the durability of laserdiscs and realising my own video collection was slowly decaying, I put together a business plan, got Barclays Bank to back it [in June '93], bought an off-the-shelf company, and in February '94 put out *Howards End*. I'd signed up (art-house distributor) Electric Pictures, and over the next few months issued *Henry . . . Portrait of a Serial Killer, Orlando, Delicatessen, Mean Streets* and (in August) *Leon, the Pig Farmer*."

With such a high end start, cashflow was "horrendous" in the early days, and it soon became clear Haynes would need a sizeable backer. The distributor Laser UK was interested, but then came along wealthy entrepreneur Richard Gabriel, who in February 1995 recapitalised the company with a £600,000 loan. It officially became known as Encore Entertainment, and Haynes (who'd sunk his own savings into the business at the start) remains the major shareholder. He's since been joined by his brother-in-law, Karl Evans, who now runs the company's new video label.

Barclays' loan has already been paid off, says Haynes, and the company moved into the black for the first time in February '96. Current turnover is around £1.2 million a year, and Haynes is looking for the company to be debt-free by February 1997.

But is there room for another sizeable company in the current PAL market? "I think so," says Haynes, "as the collectors will always buy the discs they want. We've luckily managed to make art-house titles a success – from my gut feeling for the market – but we realised we needed blockbusters to pay for them."

Stephen Haines

Pressing and Pricing Strategies

Encore divides its releases into four categories and determines pressing and pricing strategies accordingly. An "AA" category release (blockbusters such as *Braveheart, Speed, The Abyss*) will get an initial pressing of 2,000-3,000 units; an "A" (*Alien 3*) 1,000; a "B" (*Conan the Barbarian, Ricochet*) 750; and a "C" (mostly art-house, Hongkong movies) 500.

Art-house titles generally take at least 6-12 months to break even, whereas *Braveheart*, helped by lucky timing, has already made a profit and is into its second pressing after an initial 3,000. "B" titles will generally break even after three months. *Howards End* has so far clocked up a steady 500 or so units; *Battle of Algiers* and *Black Rainbow*, however, were notable flops, with microscopic sales. Haynes puts the current cost of pressing 500 doublesided discs at almost £5,000, translating to a retail cost of between £31.99 and £36.99 (Encore's highest).

Haynes says his ultimate aim is to bring popular titles down to £14.99 a disc – thereby putting LD on an equal price footing with video – though he admits that would only be possible at present if the company reverted to mail order, cutting out distribution costs. For boxed sets (which Encore pioneered on PAL, with *Jason and the Argonauts*), Haynes says the minimum pressing has to be 1,000, "otherwise the economics don't add up". Encore recently issued a Hammer set, and Haynes would like to do a John Wayne box.

Haynes' tastes are catholic. "I like lots of types of films – Hong Kong action films, foreign movies, classics, the whole range. One reason I wanted the 20th Century Fox catalogue was because of their sc-fi titles. Our research has shown that 28% of our buyers want these."

Looking at the changes over the past five years in the U.K. market, Haynes says the base in far more grassroots than was imagined at the start, and not just comprised of A/Bs. After starting off with a hard core of buffs, he senses more general consumers are now getting into LD, purely for "the sound and picture experience". The fact that the market is almost exclusively male, aged around 25-40, plays a major part in some of his buying decisions.

Haynes believes laser will always be a niche market – "but a nice niche!" He estimates the U.K. installed base at the end of 1995 at around 32,000-35,000 players, growing to some 50,000 by end-1996. In about three years, he reckons, "it should top out at around 100,000-150,000 players. If we can make a living now out of a 30,000-odd base, we should do very nicely on 100,000 or so."

RECENT ENCORE HIGHLIGHTS

Angel Enforcers (EE10161) – a clean, resubtitled version of the cult 1989 Hong Kong female actioner (*Dir:* Godfrey Ho), with its famous ice-block-and-grenades setpiece. Final 35 mins. in CAV.

**Bad Boys* (EE1073) – see main reviews

**Braveheart* (EE1078) – see main reviews

**Dolores Claiborne* (EE1086) – detailed, but not fully letterboxed, transfer of the 1995

LA SCORTA, typical of the adventurous LD release line-up from Encore

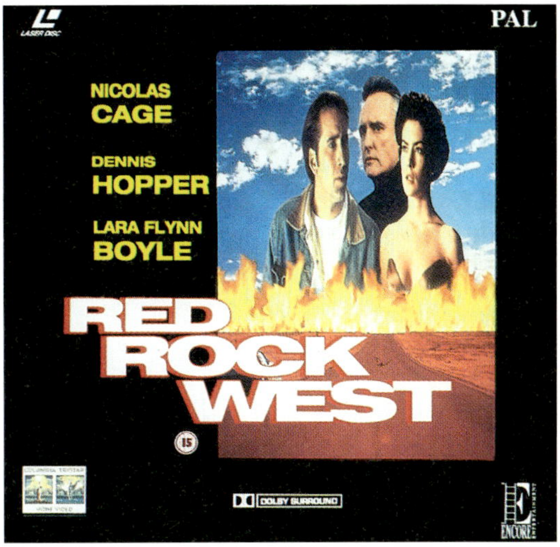

RED ROCK WEST, released on PAL by Encore

Taylor Hackford-Stephen King melodrama, with a fine performance from Jennifer Jason Leigh.

**Fantastic Voyage* (EE1060) – see main reviews

**The Guns of Navarone* (EE1031) – see main reviews

**The Madness of King George* – see main reviews

**Matador* (EE1019) – okay transfer of Pedro Almodóvar's first fully realised movie, a moody sex-and-death melodrama with Assumpta Serna and a young-looking Antonio Banderas.

**Princess Madam* (EE1028) – clean print of another Hong Kong female action classic from Godfrey Ho, a showcase for actress Yeung Pan-pan that really delivers in the last 25 mins, here in CAV.

**The Red Squirrel* (EE1027) – a contrasty, but otherwise okay version of Julio Medem's critically-acclaimed psychological brain-teaser, with favourite actress Emma Suarez as the maybe amnesiac woman.

**Subway* (EE1098) – a less than ideally sharp, but nicely letterboxed transfer of the Luc Besson romantic thriller, with a bonus of the French trailer to *Nikita* at the end.

Reviews

AMARCORD

Dir: Federico Fellini. *With* Magali Noël, Bruno Zanin, Pupella Maggio, Armando Brancia. NTSC. Widescreen (1.85:1, 1.76:1 captured). CLV. 2 discs. 127 mins. Criterion CC 1422L.

Not many nations guard their cinematic achievements so well as Hollywood, and the Criterion foreign catalogue must often rely on faded, flecked, and even incomplete materials. *Amarcord,* however, looks pristine, better even than on theatrical release when it won the Academy Award for Best Foreign Film of 1974. The digital transfer was created from a 35mm interpositive, and the English and Italian tracks were mastered from a 35mm magnetic audio master. Those who resent subtitles can flick their remote control to analogue, and hear the American-dubbed version (a useful alternative furnished by Criterion with many foreign-language discs). Peter Bondanella's jacket essay illuminates the film's political context.

Peter Cowie

APOCALYPSE NOW

Dir: Francis Ford Coppola. *With* Marlon Brando, Robert Duvall, Martin Sheen, Frederic Forrest. PAL. Widescreen (2.35:1, 2.10:1 captured). CLV. 2 discs. 147 mins. Pioneer PLFEC 33751.

Applause for the PAL version of *Apocalypse,* which has been available on NTSC in the States from Paramount in an "anamorphic widescreen" version. Pioneer opt for the 'scope format, which conveys the epic quality of Coppola's masterpiece, but the U.S. disc is supervised by cinematographer Vittorio Storaro, who feels that more "information" is captured with a slightly taller image. PAL has in-built advantages such as a basically sharper picture and a less fiery palette of colours and flesh-tones. Thanks to the Zoetrope engineers, sound on both releases is state of the art. As a demonstration disc, the Pioneer *Apocalypse Now* should convert anyone to laser.

Peter Cowie

BAD BOYS

Dir: Michael Bay. *With* Martin Lawrence, Will Smith, Tea Leoni, Tcheky Karyo. PAL. Widescreen (1.85:1, 1.66:1 captured). 1 disc. 118 mins. Encore Entertainment (EE1073).

As in its single-disc issue of *Fantastic Voyage,* Encore again pushes the CLV format to the limit, with a first side running 62 minutes; the sidebreak is comfortable, and there's still room for a (full-screen) trailer on the end of side two. This Simpson-Bruckheimer action movie about two fast-talking black cops makes exceptionally fine home viewing, not least because of the disc's terrific soundtrack in which showy effects are used sparingly but powerfully. The transfer is gorgeous, with the full brightness range, from deep blacks to rich, sunset oranges. The streetwise repartee between the two blacks becomes a little tiresome halfway through, but Tea Leoni's sexy, sassy performance as the girl in the middle is a major bonus.

Derek Elley

THE BIG COUNTRY

Dir: William Wyler. *With* Gregory Peck, Jean Simmons, Charlton Heston, Burl Ives, Carroll Baker, Charles Bickford. NTSC. Widescreen (2.35:1). CLV. 2 discs (including extras). 166 mins. Image-MGM/UA ID7352MG.

For years Wyler's epic western was available only on a faded, panned-and-scanned VHS tape. Rumour was that ownership disputes and lack of good elements prevented a laserdisc. It was genuinely delayed while Image hunted for a stereo track of Jerome Moross's magnificent score – the primary reason, some believe, that this film will, retain its classic status. Which is nonsense, for Wyler's final word on this genre is unerringly cast and acted, breathtakingly photographed, and knowingly paced to allow characterisations and tensions to develop to the full. Whether or not one cares about the director's stupidity-of-war subtext, *The Big Country* holds its own among *High Noon, Shane,* and *The Searchers* in the man-against-his-environment sweepstakes.

While Image finally gave up on locating stereo parts (the soundtrack album was artificially rechannelled), the mono presentation on this laserdisc sounds superb; moreover *all* the music composed and recorded for the film – not merely what was included in the final cut – is isolated on the second analogue track at natural concert volume. The widescreen transfer is gorgeous except for the mistimed day-for-night fight scene between Peck and Heston, which jarringly occurs in broad daylight. Also, was Saul Bass's credit sequence originally shot in a mud-brown tint rather than in colour? Newly recorded "remembrances" by Heston, an audio documentary on Moross's music, and various filmed interviews are included, as well as stills, the complete shooting script, and excellent annotations.

Sedgwick Clark

BRAVEHEART

Dir: Mel Gibson. *With* Mel Gibson, Sophie Marceau, Patrick McGoohan, Catherine McCormack. PAL. Widescreen (2.35:1, 2.1 captured). CLV. 2 discs. 177 mins. Encore Entertainment EE1078.

Encore was admirably rapid in getting this PAL version into the marketplace to capitalise on the Oscar publicity, and was rewarded with brisk sales and a profile-raising exercise in the U.K. Gibson's thirteenth-century historical saga about Scottish freedom fighter William Wallace still works well on home viewing, especially in this sharp transfer with a fine, unshowy Dolby Surround soundtrack that captures the savagery of hand-to-hand combat. Randall Wallace's literate script, and terrific performances by the four leads (and a host of supports), make this de facto Celtic *Spartacus* a moving as well as viscerally exciting experience, and the three-hour length never drags.

Derek Elley

THE BRIDGES OF MADISON COUNTY

Dir: Clint Eastwood. *With* Clint Eastwood, Meryl Streep, Annie Corley, Victor Slezak. NTSC. Widescreen (1.85:1, 1.80:1 captured). 2 discs. CLV. 135 mins. Warner Home Video 13772.

Eastwood's accomplishment in rendering Robert James Waller's saccharine novelette into a moving screen experience is accentuated to the full on disc. A glorious transfer captures each blade of Iowan grass, each troubled line in Eastwood's face, each beat of silence that inhabits the pared-down dialogue of this *amour fou* for which the Anglo-Saxon languages have no adequate equivalent. The disc also allows one to appreciate the skill of Lennie Niehaus, as he spins and weaves his variations on Eastwood's own haunting little piano theme.

Peter Cowie

D'ARTAGNAN'S DAUGHTER

Dir: Bertrand Tavernier. *With* Sophie Marceau, Philippe Noiret, Claude Rich, Sami Frey. PAL. Widescreen (1.85:1, 1.76:1 captured). CLV. 1 disc. 124 mins. Encore EE 1099.

The first Tavernier available on PAL LD, and all the more welcome for that. This rousing imbroglio, set in seventeenth-century France and reviving the legend of the Three Musketeers, features the swashbuckling Sophie Marceau. She performs all her own stunts, whether galloping bareback through misty forests or wielding a foil with impressive dexterity. The locations come over beautifully on disc, and if some of the

Sophie Marceau in D'ARTAGNAN'S DAUGHTER
photo: Artificial Eye

interior sequences look a little hazy, that's not the fault of the transfer. Surround sound is limited to the use of Philippe Sarde's evocative score, but this is one movie where the dialogue affords its own special satisfaction.

Peter Cowie

DOCTOR ZHIVAGO

Dir: David Lean. *With* Omar Sharif, Julie Christie, Alec Guinness, Tom Courtenay, Rod Steiger. NTSC. Widescreen. (2.35:1, 2.2:1 captured). AC-3 Digital. 4 discs (side 7 CAV). 193 mins. MGM/UA (ML103138).

MGM/UA's 30th anniversary edition of David Lean's 1965 classic is ideal in almost all respects, lacking only a running analogue commentary by some of the film-makers involved. That aside, however, the film is presented in a wonderful, digitally remastered version, the colours sharp and vivid (especially in the striking use of Soviet red) and the soundtrack clean, if a little lacking in stereo presence. The movie is spread across four sides, with the intermission halfway through the third. Especially thorough are the two sides of supplementals, with background on the original novel and the film's production plus four fascinating short promos and filmed press interviews. To its credit, the supplementary material does not downplay the contribution of cameraman Nicolas Roeg, who was replaced halfway through shooting by Freddie Young: his name can clearly be seen on several clapperboards and, for the first time, his artistic differences with Lean are explained. The film does not stand the test of time as well as Lean's *Lawrence of Arabia* or *The Bridge on the River Kwai*: its '60s youth slant can now be clearly seen, and Julie Christie and Tom Courtenay's performances (plus Maurice Jarre's bland score) are fatal flaws. At its best, however, with Alec Guinness and Rod Steiger, the movie still has some magical moments.

Derek Elley

DODES'KA-DEN

Dir: Akira Kurosawa. *With* Yoshitaka Zushi, Kin Sugai, Junzaburo Ban, Kiyoko Tange. NTSC (1.66:1). CLV. 2 discs. 140 mins. Criterion CC1443L.

Bravo to the Criterion Collection for reviving this 1970 masterpiece by Kurosawa. Thanks to the excellent transfer, Kurosawa's painterly compositions can be appreciated to the full, and *Dodes'ka-den* recognised as one of his most experimental works. A wry, poignant tragi-comedy, the film offers vignettes from the lives of some squatters living on a wasteland outside the big city. Flights of fantasy provide some escape from the turgid round of daily existence, and the young man, Rokkuchan, and his mother deserve a place in Kurosawa's pantheon of great characters. The release is presented in a gatefold sleeve, with an informative essay by Barbara Scharres.

Peter Cowie

FANTASTIC VOYAGE

Dir: Richard Fleischer. With Stephen Boyd, Raquel Welch, Edmond O'Brien, Donald Pleasence. PAL. Widescreen (2.35:1, 2.1:1 captured). 1 disc (side 2 CAV). 100 mins. Encore Entertainment (EE1060).

It's a delight finally to have this very '60s movie in a widescreen transfer: although the special effects now look creaky, Richard Fleischer's use of CinemaScope is an integral part of the enjoyment of this campy classic about a group of miniaturised scientists injected into a dying boffin's body to perform brain surgery. Thanks to amazing engineering by Encore, with a mind-boggling 63:59 on the first side, the rest of the picture is presented in CAV (ideal for perusing the effects), and there's even room for a fullscreen trailer at the end. The sidebreak is okay, and picture quality up to that of the original, in which the colours were never natural. A groundbreaking issue.

Derek Elley

FIRST KNIGHT

Dir: Jerry Zucker. *With* Sean Connery, Richard Gere, Julia Ormond, Ben Cross. PAL. Widescreen (1.85:1, 1.76:1 captured). CLV 2 discs. 129 mins. Encore EE 1065.

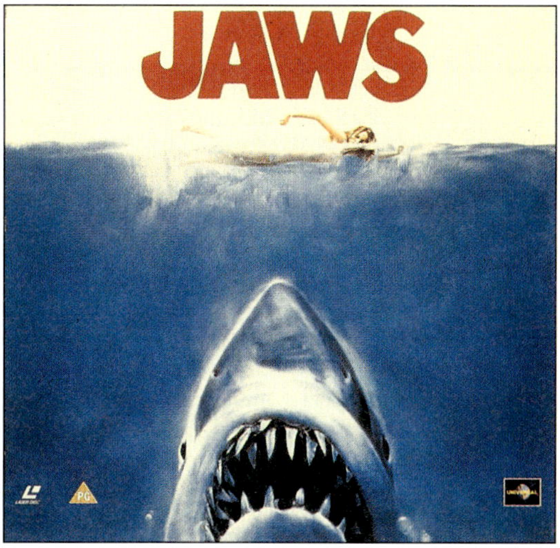

Pioneer released JAWS on PAL in 1996

Once again, a timely issue from Columbia via Encore – and a transfer made in heaven. Production designer John Box will be delighted with the rendering of his predominantly jet-black and dark blue colour scheme, something that could never occur in NTSC. Although Richard Gere still seems miscast as Lancelot in this Arthurian action drama, Connery remains as stalwart as ever, and Ben Cross exudes satanic glee as the evil Malagant. Check the "Beating the Gauntlet" chapter for some startling sound effects. Credit to Encore for again including the trailer.

Peter Cowie

GLORY

Dir: Ed Zwick. *With* Matthew Broderick, Denzel Washington, Cary Elwes, Morgan Freeman. PAL. Widescreen (1.85:1, 1.76:1 captured). CLV. 1 disc. 117 mins. Encore EE 1034.

Including a production brochure that gives background details about the shooting and the historical circumstances, TriStar's underrated *Glory* explores a byway of the Civil War, when a white colonel shapes and inspires a regiment of black men to feats of courage on the battlefield at James Island and Fort Wagner. The disc deserves the highest praise. Meticulous attention to visual detail (especially in long shots) and to the Dolby surround track show that Encore can explore the potential of the PAL format the maximum when they have the right elements. Trailer included.

Peter Cowie

THE GUNS OF NAVARONE

Dir: J. Lee Thompson. *With* Gregory Peck, David Niven, Anthony Quinn, Anthony Quayle. PAL. Widescreen (2.35:1, 2.0:1 captured). 2 discs (side 3 CAV). 157 mins. Encore Entertainment (EE1031).

This PAL issue of the UCLA Film & Television Archive's "restoration" (from the original picture negative and four-channel mag stereo master) generally scores over the Columbia Classics four-sided NTSC version (79596), despite having only one side in CAV and not letterboxing the trailer. The image is sharper and colours closer to the original's grubby khaki look, typical of films of the period (1962). The main improvement, however, which makes it such an exciting home cinema experience, is the soundtrack, which is sharper and with much more body and presence, paying dividends in the resonant climax inside the gun chamber. Unfortunately, Encore hasn't replicated Columbia's fine sleeve notes or gone for more fuller letter-boxing. This is one CinemaScope movie that benefits from the fullest aspect ratio.

Derek Elley

JAWS

Dir: Steven Spielberg. *With* Roy Scheider, Robert Shaw, Richard Dreyfuss, Lorraine Gary. PAL, Widescreen (2.35:1, 2.05:1 captured). CLV, 1 disc. 120 mins. Pioneer PLFEB 34291.

There's no way Pioneer could hope to compete with MCA/Universal's splendid CAV version (with supplementals in its Signature Collection (42583), but for anyone wanting a good, single-disc PAL widescreen version, this is very fine, though the letterboxing is fractionally less than on the NISC set (2.2:1 captured), the transfer is just as good despite being in CLV, with hard, saturated colours. As with many PAL versions, the soundtrack has more presence and immediacy than on the softer, more diffused NTSC disc, giving real bite to the bass-ier moments of John Williams' score. The trailer included here at the start of the disc is the re-release one – the last of the four in MCA's boxed set – and the chapter stops are identical.

Derek Elley

LEAVE HER TO HEAVEN

Dir: John M. Stahl. *With* Gene Tierney, Cornel Wilde, Jeanne Crain, Vincent Price. NTSC. Full screen . CLV. 1 disc. 110 mins. FoxVideo 8623-80.

This Technicolor restoration of John Stahl's 1945 classic – often called the first 'colour noir' – fractionally surpasses even MGM/UA's recent issue of *The Band Wagon* on a technical level, though it lacks the latter's extras and FoxVideo has not even bothered to unearth a trailer. That apart, this is a treasurable issue, with a pin-sharp transfer, full brightness range that complements Leon Shamroy's richly chiaroscuro photography, and monaural sound that has been cleaned up but not modernised in any way. Informative sleeve notes are a bonus, and the central drama, with Gene Tierney as the muderously possessive wife of writer Cornel Wilde, still works with its *echt*-1940's blend of criminality and spirituality wrapped around a family-values core, all economically summed up by Alfred Newman's score.

Derek Elley

THE MADNESS OF KING GEORGE

Dir: Nicholas Hytner. *With* Nigel Hawthorne, Helen Mirren, Rupert Everett, Ian Holm. PAL. Widescreen (1.85:1, 1.76:1 captured). CLV. 1 disc. 110 mins. Encore EE 1083.

So often a film seems enhanced by the LD format. *The Madness of King George* looked admirable in the cinema, but its plastic beauty and subtly nuanced screenplay come to the fore in this magnificent Encore release. Colour gradations are impeccable, the sound deploys all manner of ambient effects, and the supporting performances (Amanda Donohoe, Ian Holm, Rupert Graves) contribute more than they did on first release. Encore have included some bonus material, such as both the U.S. and the U.K. theatrical trailers, as well as a brief "featurette".

Peter Cowie

THE RIVER WILD

Dir: Curtis Hanson. *With* Meryl Streep, Kevin Bacon, David Strathairn. PAL. Widescreen (2.35:1, 2:15 captured). CLV. 1 disc. 111 mins. Pioneer LDCE (PLFEB 33431).

This *Deliverance*-style white-water thriller doesn't have quite the physical impact in home viewing that it had on the big screen, but Pioneer's sharp PAL transfer still works as a tense thriller, nicely paced. Though not very directional, the stereo sound is good and solid, and (as often in laser disc versions) the dialogue is actually clearer in noisy effects sequences. Meryl Streep's performance as the expert rafter who finally turns the tables on the villains who hijack her family is one of her very best, not least because of her lack of mannerisms, and she makes a surprisingly fine, in-shape action heroine. The colours on the PAL version are rather weak, but otherwise it's a good disc. The full-screen trailer is worth seeing for its pure awfulness.

Derek Elley

STAR!

Dir: Robert Wise. *With* Julie Andrews, Richard Crenna, Michael Craig, Daniel Massey. NTSC. Widescreen (2.2:1, 2.0:1 captured). 2 discs (side 4 cav). 176 mins. Foxvideo 1180-85.

Robert Wise's blighted 1968 bio-pic of Gertrude Lawrence (rightly described here by its star, Julie Andrews, as the last of the big studio musicals) gets a Special Edition worthy of its cult reputation, with a full side of CAV supplementals that chart every stage of production, presentation and subsequent recutting, plus audio commentary from the principals and the film's soundtrack on the analogue channels. The transfer, from the 65mm camera negative and six-track mag soundtrack, is very good, though the sound only blooms at a high level. In its original three-hour roadshow version, the movie creaks at times (mostly in its early stages, with Andrews playing a chirpy Cockney), and William Fairchild's script rarely equals the subject's ambitions, but in sheer production values and star performances (Andrews, Richard Crenna, and Daniel Massey's Noël Coward), it's still a delight to watch. Three numbers – 'Star', 'Someone to Watch over Me' and 'The Saga of Jenny' – are worth the price of the discs alone.

Derek Elley

STARGATE

Dir: Roland Emmerich. *With* Kurt Russell, James Spader, Jaye Davidson, Viveca Lindfors. PAL. Widescreen (2.35:1, 2.10:1 captured). CLV. 1 disc. 122 mins. Pioneer PLFEB 33861.

Stargate paved the way for *Independence Day* in Emmerich's meteoric career in America, and shows the German's talent for elevating the B movie formula into the apotheosis of kitsch. Absurd though the premise of *Stargate* may appear (transporting men and munitions through a time warp to some neo-Egyptian civilisation in the desert), the terrific Pioneer transfer makes home viewing an escapist delight. The Dolby Surround could hardly be bettered, and a trailer forms part of the attractively-packaged release.

Peter Cowie

THE USUAL SUSPECTS

Dir: Bryan Singer. *With* Stephen Baldwin, Gabriel Byrne, Chazz Palminteri, Kevin Pollak. NTSC. Widescreen (2.35:1, 2.1:1 captured). CLV 1 disc 106 mins. Polygram Video 0704.

Polygram have done Bryan Singer's brainteasing thriller proud with the original idea of a single disc at normal price complete with audio commentary on the analogue tracks. Though it disappointingly lacks a trailer, this is effectively a budget 'special edition'. The transfer is excellent, if a fraction lighter than the theatrical print, and the sound discreet and unshowy. More surprisingly, the film works both as a home cinema experience and on repeated viewings: with the ending no longer coming as a surprise, the mind is free to concentrate on small details and the complexity of the plot itself. The commentary by Singer and scriptwriter Christopher McQuarrie is ideal: relaxed, jokey (with both pointing out and laughing over continuity errors), and highly informative.

Derek Elley

W.C. FIELDS: 6 SHORT FILMS

Pool Sharks (1915, silent); *The Golf Specialist* (1930); *The Dentist* (1932); *The Fatal Glass of Beer* (1932); *The Pharmacist* (1933); *The Barber Shop* (1933). NTSC. (1.33:1). CLV. 1 disc. 112 mins. Voyager (no number).

Presumably these classic W.C. Fields shorts have never been gathered on disc before because the sound material (all 35mm, dutifully identified on the jacket) is not in pristine condition, although I've never

Julie Andrews in STAR!, restored with care and affection for laserdisc in 1996.
photo: Twentieth Century Fox/courtesy Kobal Collection

seen cleaner, higher-contrast prints than these. None of the occasional jump splices is destructive to pace or story line, and only the poorly recorded dialogue – often difficult to make out even when amplified through a stereo system – is frustrating. The comedian's Vaudeville pool and golf skits are documented in the first two shorts, but it was in the four Mack Sennett two-reelers that the misanthropic Fields character found full flower on the screen. The hilariously sadistic shaving and tooth-pulling scenes, his "child abuse" of Babe Kane, and his ill-concealed contempt for small-town folk are vintage Fields. Once again, thanks Voyager.

Sedgwick Clark

WUTHERING HEIGHTS

Dir: William Wyler. *With* Merle Oberon, Laurence Olivier, David Niven. NTSC. (.33:1). CLV. 1 disc. 103 mins. Pioneer Special Edition PSE95-64.

THE HURRICANE

Dir: John Ford. With Dorothy Lamour, Jon Hall, Mary Astor, Thomas Mitchell, Raymond Massey. NTSC. (1.33:1). CLV. 1 disc. 103 mins. Pioneer Special Edition PSE95-61.

Pioneer Special Edition has done well by the Samuel Goldwyn collection, most recently these two classics. The brilliance of these new transfers, especially that of the 1939 *Wuthering Heights*, totally surpasses the low-contrast textures of the mid-1980s discs, with their dizzying *moiré* patterns and tinny sound. Alfred Newman's evocative scores sound more richly romantic than ever on the new discs, but the only drawback to unqualified endorsement of both issues is the Chace Audio botch of *The Hurricane* (1937) track, which distractingly confines the dialogue to the left channel and most of the sound effects to the right, with the music given left and right stereo spread. Those whose playback equipment has a mono/stereo switch may be able to counteract this stupidity. But even then, while the increased sonority is undeniably impressive, the music sometimes overwhelms the dialogue and jumps into the foreground unnaturally (e.g., side 1 at the reel change at 41:46 and at 54:11). And figure this: the most thunderous sound during the hurricane scene is hidden on the left channel rather than on the LD player's regular audio track, the digital stereo channel.

Sedgwick Clark

LaserDisc ENTERPRISES
2516 Cobb Parkway
Smyrna, GA 30080
USA
24 Hr FAX | All Charge Cards Accepted
Ph (USA Code) 770-955-8909
Fx (USA Code) 770-984-2173
Friendly Service
U.S.A.'s Best LaserDisc Source
1,000's of Titles to Choose From

Specialist LaserDisc Stores

U.S.A.

Laser Blazer
2518 Overland Ave., Los Angeles, California 90064. Tel: (1-800-488 3472 – orders outside California). Fax: (310) 558 3255

Every available NTSC disc held in stock. Same-day shipping. Friendly atmosphere and convenient location not far from LAX.

Dave's Video/The Laser Place
12144 Ventura Blvd., Century City, California 91604. Tel: (818) 760 3472. Fax: (818) 760 3818

Immaculately-displayed full range of NTSC discs. Sales and rentals.

Ken Crane's
15251 Beach Boulevard, Westminster, California 92683. Tel: (714) 892 2283. Fax: (714) 892 8369

Huge stocks, and mouth-watering sales.

Disc-o-Rama
8 Hadco Road, Suite 8c, Wilmington, Delaware 19804. Tel: (302) 999 7581. Fax: (302) 999 7586

New and used discs available, both NTSC and imported.

LaserDisc Experience
7421 Douglas Blvd #E, Douglasville, Georgia 30135. Tel: (770) 947 1158.

Dallas Digital Video
Tel: (214) 987 4744. Fax: (214) 987 3544. Good prices on pre-releases and Japanese imported discs.

Laserland
200 Glen Cove Road, Carle Place, NY 11514. Tel: (516) 746 3147

Discs available for both purchase and rental

Sight and Sound
27 Jones Road, Waltham, Massachusetts 02154. Tel: (617) 894 8633

Specialists in imported animation and French films

Laser Island
1810 Voorhies Avenue, Brooklyn, NY 11235. Tel: (718) 743 2425. Fax: (212) 582 2634

Discounts on discs; excellent mail order service, plus catalogue, "Spinning Tales"

Laser Video West
12420 Santa Monica Blvd., Los Angeles, California 90025. Tel: (310) 571 0829. Fax: (310) 571 0863.

Modest stock. Domestic and foreign orders welcomed

LaserDisc Enterprises
2436 Cobb Parkway, Smyrna, Georgia 30080. Tel: (404) 955 8909. Fax: (404) 984 2173

Same day shipping, and 15% discount on many titles

The LaserDisc Division
12115 Magnolia Blvd., Suite 139, North Hollywood, California 91607-3709. Tel: (818) 766 2334. Fax: (818) 766 6799

New, used, rare, and out-of-print discs

LE Video
1239 9th Street, San Francisco, California 94122. Tel: (415) 566 3606

Over 5,000 discs to rent. Also vast range of video-cassettes

The Laser Outlet
366 N. Allen Avenue, Suite 250, Pasadena, California 91106. Tel and Fax: (818) 797 4484

Heavily discounted range of discs. Free UPS shipping when ordering 3 or more titles in the U.S.

U.K.

Thames Valley Laser
9 Crown Walk Shopping Centre, Bicester OX6 7HY. Tel: (01869) 320 550, (01869) 322 944

Players and discs stocked. Mail order service (fully insured)

Laserdisc House
110 West Street, Faversham, Kent ME13 7JB. Tel: (01795) 534403. Fax: (01795) 535498.

Monthly new release magazine issued. New discs in stock, but used LDs exchanged or purchased.

A & N Entertainment
75 Catholic Lane, Sedgley, West Midlands DY3 3YE. Tel: (01902) 665 309

Competitively priced discs

Derann
99 High Street, Dudley, West Midlands DY1 1QP. Tel: (01384) 233191. Fax: (01384) 456488

Mail-order, catalogue available of over 6,000 discs

Esprit Laserdiscs
21 Stone Street, Gravesend, Kent DA11 0NP. Tel: (01474) 567 900. Fax: (01474) 537 137

Laser Enterprises – L.C.D.
P.O. Box 345, Wickford, Essex SS11 8BT. Tel: (01268) 571686. Fax: (01268) 572420

Large catalogue available. Buy and sell all types of disc

Croydon Laservision
35 Lower Addiscombe Road, Croydon, Surrey CR0 6PQ. Tel: (0181) 688 5551. Fax: (0181) 688 5806

Mail order, second-hand, part exchange, Karaoke discs

The Cinema Store
46 Monmouth Street, London WC2H 9EJ. Tel: (0171) 379 7838.

Magazines, posters, stills, laser discs, etc

Gladden LaserDisc Entertainment
166 Pixmore Way, Letchworth, Herts SG6 1QS. Tel: (01462) 483847

Always a good source of special offers on PAL and NTSC

The Laserdisc Shop
15 Needham Road, London W11 2RP. Tel: (0171) 243 3142

More than 1,500 discs in stock, with special emphasis on pop music titles

The Laser Library
P.O. Box 145, Ipswich IP8 4LQ

Approval service available throughout the U.K. Membership advantages

Movie Boulevard
5 Cherry Tree Walk, Leeds LS2 7EB. Tel: (0532) 422 888. Fax: (0532) 438 840.

Catalogue. All discs available in a self-styled "Megastore", plus hardware and accessories

Laser House
4 Rupert Road, Southminster, Essex CM0 7AN. Tel and Fax: (01621) 773159

Mail order only. No postal charges.

LVS
18 King's Park, Primrose Hill, Langley, Herts WD4 8ST. Tel: (01923) 267060. Fax: (01923) 260078

NTSC, PAL and Japanese imports available. Free monthly supplement.

Spain

Forbidden
Citomelloso 51, Y-C, 28026 Madrid.

Good range of discs available in various languages.

Sweden

Lasermania
Box 4111, 102 62 Stockholm. Fax: (46 8) 642 9582.

New and used NTSC and Japanese imports.

Switzerland

LaserZone
Kasernenstr. 15, 8004 Zürich. Tel: (41 1) 291 0212. Fax: (41 1) 291 0405.

Discs and other movie memorabilia available.

Dedicated Magazines

Laser Disc Newsletter
P.O. Box 420, East Rockaway, NY 11518-0420. Tel: (516) 594 9304. Fax: (516) 594 9307

Far and away the best English-language guide to LD, as a labour of love by Douglas Pratt who seems to have viewed literally every disc ever released. The lengthly reviews are admirably balanced and sympathetic. $50.00 for 12 issues

Laser Classics
12122 Aero Drive, Garden Grove, California 92641. Tel: (714) 530 3543

Review publication. $24 for 12 issues domestic, $45 foreign

Laserdisc Gazette
Road 2, Box 654-LDN, Harpers Ferry, West Virginia 25425

Monthly journal. $20 for 12 issues domestic, $35 foreign

The Cinema Laser
P.O. Box 198, Commack, NY 11725-0198.

$10 for 4 issues, $20 foreign

Laser Marquee
P.O. Box 1615, Thomasville, Georgia 31799

Bi-monthly glossy magazine, leaning towards a fan's view of the movies rather than the quality of particular discs

The Spinning Image
P.O. Box 20094, Floral Park, NY 11002-0094.

In-depth reviews, articles and stills. Monthly.

CAM ORIGINAL SOUNDTRACKS
CAM®
NINO OLIVIERO AND RIZ ORTOLANI
MONDO CANE
LA DOLCE VITA
AMARCORD
GIUSEPPE TORNATORE
MARCELLO MASTROIANNI
STANNO TUTTI BENE
MILESTONES FROM THE GOLDEN ERA OF ITALIAN CINEMA
Rota, Trovaioli, Rustichelli, Lavagnino, Fusco, Piccioni, De Masi, Ferrio, Ghiglia, Cipriani, Carpi, Paris
MASTERPIECES FROM THE NEW ITALIAN CINEMA
Morricone, Bacalov, Siliotto, Lurie, Donaggio, Badalamenti, Crivelli, Di Pofi, Horowitz, Venosta
CAM® Original Soundtracks
VIA COLA DI RIENZO, 152 - 00192 ROME (ITALY) - FAX:(+39-6) 687.4046

Film Music Annual Roundup

by Andy Klein

Thanks to Hollywood's resources - in both talent and money – there have been many years when, despite a dip in the quality of the overall product, the big studios have still managed to turn out the lion's share of the best film music. 1995 was not such a year.

Forget that two of the most memorable scores – Akira Senju's *The Mystery of Rampo* and Angelo Badalamenti's *City of Lost Children* – were for foreign productions. Simply consider that even the clannish and self-congratulatory members of the Academy of Motion Pictures Arts and Sciences gave Luis Enrique Bacalov the award for Best Score for *Il Postino* – the first time that music for a foreign-language film has been so honoured. Bacalov was essentially an unknown in Hollywood, most of his work never having been released here.

He had several factors working in his favour: Miramax mounted a terrific promotional campaign for both film and score; Academy members partial to James Horner may have split their votes between his two nominated films, *Braveheart* and *Apollo 13*; and there was a general sense that *Il Postino* deserved *something*.

All that being said, the *Postino* score (released on CAM COS 700-038) was the most memorable of the nominated works. Bacalov's sweet main theme immediately evoked the story's tone; and the composer's restraint throughout was crucial in keeping the movie from sinking into bathos.

Of course, Bacalov won in the category entitled "Music, Original Dramatic Score" – as opposed to the new "Music, Original Musical or Comedy Score" competition. To judge by its history of rule changes, the Academy's music division is perhaps the most byzantine of a generally irrational lot. The number and nature of the awards is changed at least once a decade, to reflect shifts in the industry. But why would anybody separate "Dramatic Scores" from "Comedy Scores"? The Oscar crowd looks down on the Golden Globes for precisely this sort of categorising; but at least the Golden Globe folks use such distinctions for performance and writing awards – which makes a good deal more sense.

Songs vs. Music

The explanation requires some history. The old award for musicals was discontinued in 1985 when that genre had practically disappeared – and right before the Disney animation department's comeback. Be-

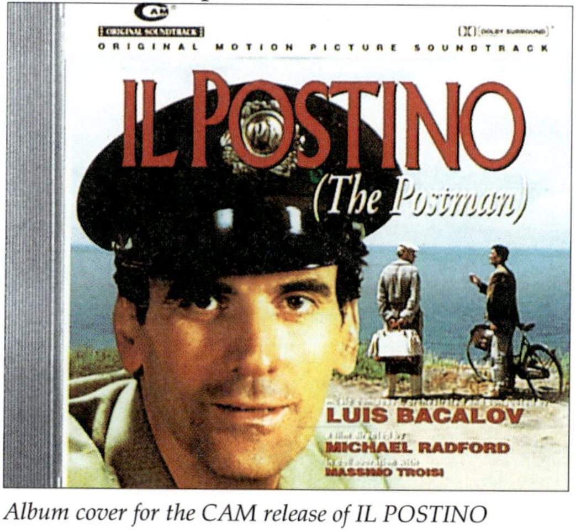

Album cover for the CAM release of IL POSTINO

tween 1989 and 1994, animated Disney musicals won the "Best Score" award four out of six years, despite the fact that the voters were *supposed* to exclude the songs in their deliberations. (There has always been a separate citation for "Best Original Song".) None the less, it's hard to believe that the voters meant to honour Alan Menken's underscore for *Aladdin, Beauty and the Beast* and *The Little Mermaid* minus the songs. So this year it was decided to revive the category for musicals.

Unfortunately, since there still aren't enough musicals to field a full slate of nominees, "Comedy" was senselessly lumped in with "Musical". And – surprise – Alan Menken won for *Pocahontas,* probably the worst recent Disney animation score. As the years pass since the death of Menken's lyricist, Howard Ashman, the latter's contributions look increasingly important.

Part of the general quality problem among composed scores may be due to the increase in the use of pre-existing source music. While Hollywood has always used recognisable pop tunes as a shorthand to set time and place, such tracks are usually a supplement to a traditional score. Woody Allen, who has used original music only twice in the last twenty years, has long been the exception. But Quentin Tarantino's success with all-pop scores for *Reservoir Dogs* (1992) and *Pulp Fiction* (1994) – the latter sparking a revival of surf music – is taking the industry even further from the fully composed score.

Play It Again

Martin Scorsese pushed the trend yet one more incestuous step this year: *Casino*'s brilliantly eclectic, wall-to-wall underscore of pre-existing music included not only Bach and the Rolling Stones, but excerpts from Georges Delerue's score for Godard's 1963 *Contempt*. To a large extent, this trend is driven by marketing considerations. Soundtrack albums don't get airplay unless they include pop tunes; and most of the time, it's cheaper to license old pop tunes than to write new ones.

Now and again, such scores are aesthetically satisfying as well: like *Casino*, Carl Franklin's *Devil in a Blue Dress* owed much of its atmosphere and period authenticity to its late-40s jazz and R 'n' B tracks. Elmer Bernstein's occasional underscore included some of the year's most flavourful film music; without enough material to justify its own CD, it was reduced to two brief tracks on the soundtrack release. Likewise, Mike Figgis, who was a professional musician before becoming a writer/director, wrote some excellent music for his acclaimed *Leaving Las Vegas*, supplementing a group of torchy standards.

Double Duty

Figgis wasn't the only notable hyphenate composer in 1995. Occasional actor Patrick Doyle provided a lively traditional accompaniment for *Sense and Sensibility;* and John Lurie, originally more famous for his roles in Jim Jarmusch films than for his music, gave *Get Shorty* one of the year's most effective scores. The wry, pared-down funk sound of Booker T. & the MG's perfectly matched the film's hip tone; Lurie filled out the score with more in a similar vein.

There are precedents for actor/composers and director/composers, but John Ottman must surely be the first editor/composer. Having served both functions on Bryan Singer's low-budget 1993 *Public Access*, he was enlisted by the director for double duty on the considerably higher-profile *Usual Suspects*. Whether his work in the editing room affects his composition is an interesting and unanswered question, but there can be no doubt that Singer's surprise hit had the most notable thriller music of the year.

Sequels frequently require the reworking of material from the original. Elliot Goldenthal ran Danny Elfman's *Batman* theme through a number of amusing changes; and Eric Serra came up with some remarkably inventive variations on the old James Bond theme. James Newton Howard made extensive use of Henry Purcell snippets and the Spanish melody "La Folia" in *Restoration*, integrating these authentic period melodies with the most beautiful original love theme to emerge from Hollywood in 1995.

Angelo Badalamenti must be the most underused composer in American cinema. It could be that his notoriously successful collaboration with David Lynch on all the director's works since *Blue Velvet* has typecast him, or scared other film-makers away. Whatever the reason, it's a shame. His occasional non-Lynch scores have been no less interesting; and his work on Jeunet and Caro's *City of Lost Children* is exquisite.

The only score even more exquisite this year was *The Mystery of Rampo*. Released in Japan in 1994, Kazuyoshi Okuyama's surreal mystery/romance/bio-pic only made it to the West in 1995. The fractured story denies us many of the comforts of standard narrative; what holds the film together are the gorgeous visuals and Akira Senju's extraordinary Mahleresque themes.

ANDY KLEIN is currently the cinema editor/chief critic for the *Los Angeles Reader*. He is a member of the National Society of Film Critics, and the Los Angeles Film Critics Association and has written extensively for *Variety*, the *Los Angeles Herald-Examiner*, *Movieline*, *American Film*, *Empire*, and others.

Luis Enrique Bacalov, Composer

When, at the 1996 Oscar ceremony, Luis Bacalov's music for Mike Radford's romantic comedy *Il Postino* won the Academy Award for Best Original Dramatic Score, the composer's name can have been familiar to few of those present. But the award crowned a prolific film career that dates back to 1960 and includes scores for Fellini, Pasolini, Petri and Lattuada. The 1996 event wasn't even Bacalov's first Oscar ceremony: back in 1965, his score for Pasolini's *Il Vangelo secondo Matteo* (*The Gospel According to St Matthew*) was nominated for an award. But until now the South American-born composer has been little known outside his adopted country of Italy.

Born in 1933 in Argentina, Bacalov was intended from early on for a musical career. His mother hoped he would dedicate himself to classical music; it was his cousin, the Hollywood composer Lalo Schifrin (whose successes include scores for *The Cincinnati Kid*, *Dirty Harry*, *Charley Varrick*, and the famous TV theme for *Mission Impossible*), who introduced him to jazz – and through jazz to the popular music of Latin America. Not that Bacalov ever abandoned his love of classical music; he remains an admirer of Wagner, though one would hardly guess it from the transparent textures of his music for *Il Postino*.

Moving to Italy at the end of the 1950s, Bacalov embarked on a productive career of writing music for films and television, providing scores for anything up to eight films a year. Among leading Italian film composers perhaps only Ennio Morricone can rival him for sheer output, and between the two of them they seem to have scored the bulk of the spaghetti westerns: Bacalov's filmography includes the original *Django* (Sergio Corbucci, 1966). Morricone, says Bacalov, 'is the greatest of us all. I'm a little jealous of him, but not too much – not as much as Salieri was of Mozart.'

Involved from the Script Stage

By far the greater part of Bacalov's film scores have been written for Italian movies, although during the 1980s he began to make a name for himself in France, starting with Diane Kurys's *Coup de foudre* (1982). Whenever possible he likes to be involved in a film right from the script stage, 'to enter into the spirit of the story . . . to follow the shooting, have plenty of time at your disposal.' Which make it all the more remarkable that he should have composed his most successful score to date after being called in at the last minute, with the film already in the can. Bacalov, in fact, wasn't the first choice to provide the score for *Il*

Luis Bacalov with some of the awards for his score for IL POSTINO (Globo d'Oro, Nastro d'Argento, BAFTA Award, and the Academy Award) *photo: CAM s.r.l.*

Postino. The original composer had walked out after a row with the musicians; Radford, who had heard the score Bacalov created for *Anni rebelli* (directed by the Italo-Argentine Rosana Polizzi), invited him to step in.

Despite this, says Bacalov, 'the miracle took place just the same,' and the score is one of the few where he feels he achieved all that he intended. 'I completed the score knowing that I had given 100%. It's a rare feeling, both in this profession and in life.' His sole regret is that the circumstances deprived him of the opportunity of working on *Il Postino* with its lead actor, Massimo Troisi – who, as is well known, made the film while mortally ill and died the day after it was completed. 'Massimo gave his life to this film,' Bacalov announced after receiving the Oscar. 'This film had been an act of love. An act owed to Massimo, who transmitted to it all his passion.'

Rapport with Radford

Bacalov established a good rapport with Michael Radford who deserves, he says, 'three-quarters of the statuette.' It was Radford's idea to incorporate in the score a tango, 'Madreselva,' sung by the great Argentinian artist Carlos Gardel. Bacalov readily acquiesced, since he now considers himself 'half-Argentinian and half-Italian,' and saw a chance to make the score 'a tribute to my first homeland, blended with the music of an Italian country band such as may be found in the smallest village.' In this, the score not only reflects the relationship that springs up between the Italian postman played by Troisi and Neruda, the exiled South American poet (Philippe Noiret), but glances at *Il Postino*'s bi-national origins: an Italian film co-scripted and directed by an Englishman.

Some purists have objected to the Argentinian element in the score, pointing

Continued on page 100

MUSICA & CINEMA
PREMIO ROTA 1996

The
NINO ROTA
award

1995 Premio Rota Recipient:
ENNIO MORRICONE
for lifetime achievement and contribution
to music for cinema.

CAM® Original Soundtracks

CAM • THE WORLD LEADER IN CINEMA SOUNDTRACKS

For further information on the 2nd Annual PREMIO ROTA AWARD, contact Alessandra Balzano at CAM Original Soundtracks in Rome, Italy - (Fax +39-6-6874046)

Neo-Realism: Play It Again!

While the highlight of the year at CAM may have been the Academy Award for Luis Bacalov's score of *Il Postino,* the most rewarding of their publications has been **The Italian Neo-Realism, Music and Cinema** (CVS 900-010).

CAM have resurrected the scores for twenty films of the postwar period, and re-recorded them as short suites. Listening to these two CDs, with the Digitally recorded, Dolby Surround sound swirling through the room, one is transported back to the magic of those neo-realist masterpieces to an infinitely greater degree than when hearing the original records (if any still exist).

The discs are housed in a handsome book-like album, with a four-colour spread on each of the films (including credits) in English and Japanese. Carlo Lizzzani writes a foreword about neo-realism and its significance and the producer of the album, Paolo Ruggeri, provides some useful background information about the composers involved.

Album cover for book and discs issued by CAM

And what a bunch they were! Alessandro Cicognini, Mario Nascimbene, Carlo Rustichelli, Renzo Rossellini, Giovanni Fusco, and a young (and prolific) Nino Rota.

Cheek and Dignity

Each of the tracks exerts its own particular appeal. The delicate xylophone rendering of Rota's score for *Sotto il sole di Roma* (Castellani, 1948). Cicognini's cheeky piano and xylophone accompaniment to *Due soldi di speranza* (Castellani, 1951). The dignity of Carlo Rustichelli's score for *Il cammino della speranza* (Germi, 1950).

Fusco combines harsh, declamatory chords on trumpet and piano for *Cronica di un amore,* to suggest the dislocated boredom of Antonioni's world. Rota invokes "Ol' Man River" and Western themes for his dramatic, bustling score for Lattuada's *Senza pietà* (1948).

There's the rollicking optimism of Cicognini's music in *Miracolo a Milano* (De Sica, 1950). Or the trombone in Rossellini's expectant theme for *Paisà*, giving way to an ominous bass line for piano. Most poignant and evocative of all, the jostling of mighty bells that heralds Willy Ferrero and Luchino Visconti's score for *La terra trema* (1948), surrendering to the collapsing of waves on the shore.

As a tribute to both the centenary of film, and to a now unfashionable period in European cinema, this album fills a huge space on the shelf. Paolo Ruggeri deserves much praise for his careful production of each suite, along with Andrea Ridolfi, who arranged and conducted the music with the Symphony Orchestra of Sofia, in the CAM studios in Rome.

Peter Cowie

ANIMATION

The Year in Review

by Bob Swain

This was the year that computer animation really came of age – in the shape of *Toy Story*, the first ever 100 percent computer-generated movie. "*Toy Story* is a breakthrough on the level of *The Jazz Singer* or *The Wizard of Oz* – 79 minutes of totally synthetic animation", says Steve Jobs, chairman of Pixar – the computer animation company which made it. "The computer graphics community has been climbing the walls of the castle in the past 20 years. Finally with *Toy Story* we are inside the castle. We have now pioneered the next major off-shoot of motion pictures".

Digital technology has become such a fundamental part of film-making that very few movies are made these days which don't feature some element of computer graphics. This is mostly in the shape of digital compositing, editing and special effects. Computers have also played an increasing role in the production of 2D cartoon animation, with the computer departments now a major component of studios such as Disney and Warner Bros. Many are aiming to apply the traditional human skills of character animation to the new world of 3D computer models.

One film that attempted to do just this in the past year was *Casper*. Industrial Light and Magic is the best-known computer animation company in the world, contributing effects to everything from *The Abyss* and *Terminator 2* to *Jurassic Park*, *Jumanji* and *Twister*. But for *Casper*, it was asked to create a leading character for the first time – and one that would be on screen for much of the movie. This has been followed up more recently by Draco the Dragon, who gets 22 minutes of screen time in *Dragonheart*. We recently also saw a couple of completely computer-animated television series, with Alliance's *ReBoot*, made at the Mainframe facility in Vancouver, and *Insektors*, created by Fantôme in Paris.

In the Beginning

But Pixar's John Lasseter was always the person who those in the industry expected to bring the medium to life on the big screen. He started out his career as a Disney animator, working on the 1981 release *The Fox and the Hound* before joining a group working on the studio's first computer animation test sequences. He then joined computer technology company Pixar in 1984 as the in-house creative talent, working alongside the software engineers to produce an annual short film to demonstrate the latest technical developments. The simple tale of two table lamps in 1986's *Luxo Junior* remains one of the best and most entertaining pieces of 3D character animation ever created.

Lasseter won the Oscar for best animated short in 1990 with *Tin Toy*. This eventually led to the three-year process of directing *Toy Story* – and a Special Achievement Oscar in 1996. *Toy Story* was the first product of a three-picture deal between Pixar and Disney; the second film, *Bugs*, is already on the way. Pixar and Lasseter's phenomenal success with their computer-animated movie has led others in the industry to consider going down the

Still from JAMES AND THE GIANT PEACH photo: Guild Pathe Cinema

Plasticine rules in Nick Park's Oscar-winning A CLOSE SHAVE

Dennis Quaid and a somewhat disguised Sean Connery, in DRAGONHEART *photo: ILM/Universal*

same path, with many more projects now in the pipeline. DreamWorks SKG, the new studio set up by Steven Spielberg, Jeffrey Katzenberg and David Geffen, recently bought into the market by taking a 40% stake in Pacific Data Images.

One of the most established computer animation facilities in the business, this Paolo Alto company has been producing work for commercials, television titles and feature film special effects since 1980. A three-picture deal has now been struck with DreamWorks and a first – but so far untitled – computer-generated movie is already in production. In the meantime, DreamWorks is already well into its stride in the production of *The Prince of Egypt* – the first 2D animated feature to be created at its new high-tech animation studios. Although the movie will have the feel of a traditionally animated film, its production has been handled almost entirely on computerised systems.

A Digital Dawn

The animation division is DreamWorks' first step in building Hollywood's first all-digital studio, with systems such as those for production and asset management also set to be applied to other fields. Although it is using some 3D animation systems, the principal animation software is Animo – developed by British company Cambridge Animation Systems.

This is the most popular computer package for traditional animation companies, with hundreds already sold to the likes of DreamWorks, Warner Bros, Nelvana and DIC. Although a fully automated system is also available, the most popular version still makes use of artists' key frames drawn on paper. These are then scanned into the system, where in-between frames can be generated, combined with backgrounds and other elements and automatically coloured.

Disney has also been evaluating the same software, although it has used its own CAPS system – jointly developed with Pixar – since introducing it for one scene in the 1986 film, *The Great Mouse Detective*. Computers have played an increasing role in Disney features ever since, with more and more three-dimensional scenes incorporated which could never have been created traditionally.

The ballroom scene from *Beauty and the Beast* featured a stunning computer-generated 3D environment. The wildebeest stampede from *The Lion King* used computer techniques to reproduce digitally thousands of running animals. The latest *Hunchback of Notre Dame* uses the technology to model the streets of Paris and give an imposing sense of scale to the cathedral.

One completely computer-animated film was nominated for a 1996 Oscar in the animated short category. *The End* was created by Chris Landreth at software company Alias|Wavefront, where he acts as an in-house animator testing the technology – much as John Lasseter did in the early days at Pixar. *The End* provided an impressive demonstration of a technology which is likely to play a significant role in the future of animation – motion capture. This allows computers to store data describing the movements of live actors and then apply the same information to computer-generated models. The result is the automatic creation of a natural-looking motion.

The World Remade

The special effects category of the Oscars has come to be seen as the award for computer animation in recent years. But this year it was shared between an animatronics specialist – the Henson Creature Shop – and a computer animation company – Rhythm & Hues – for their efforts in persuading us that pigs can talk for *Babe*. More fancied in advance of the award – and later going on to take the BAFTA for special effects – was Digital Domain for its work on *Apollo 13*. The space epic required plenty of computer tricks alongside some more traditional model shots to simulate realistically the launch and recovery of the fated mission.

Both Digital Domain and Rhythm & Hues have joined many other computer animation specialists in expanding their expertise into the adaptation of feature film hits as theme park attractions. With high budgets and running times of only a few minutes, it is possible to pack in far more impressive material than for any cinema or television production.

Digital Domain was set up and is jointly owned by Jim Cameron – director of the *Terminator* films. He recently used the facility to make *Terminator 2 – 3D* – a three-screen, 65mm true 3D experience for the Universal Studios Tour in Florida. Based on the established characters from *Terminator 2,* it takes the story forward still further with a brand new creature and more impressive computer animation than ever before.

The entire computer animation business is going through an incredible period of growth. From its beginnings in television and commercials, it now has a major part to play throughout an increasingly integrated multimedia world – from feature films to computer games to theme park attractions.

And some of the latest developments mean it is also becoming an increasingly global industry. The biggest concentration of facilities in the past has been in California, with easy access to the Hollywood studios. But there have also been significant centres based around the advertising industry capitals of New York and London, plus a French hub in Paris. All of these are now coming together with the advent of high-speed data transfer networks, allowing directors on one continent to work directly with animators on another. The digital revolution is bringing a new look to our screens but it is also creating a smaller world for film-makers.

Woody the cowboy in Walt Disney's TOY STORY, released through Buena Vista Int'l

JAMES AND THE GIANT PEACH

Script: Karey Kirkpatrick, Jonathan Roberts, Steve Bloom. Based on the novel by Roald Dahl. Direction: Henry Selick. Photography: Pete Kozachik, Hiro Narita. Editing: Stan Webb. Production Design: Harley Jessup. Conceptual Design: Lane Smith. Songs and Music: Randy Newman. Players: Simon Callow, Richard Dreyfuss, Jane Leeves, Joanna Lumley, Miriam Margolyes, Pete Postlethwaite, Susan Sarandon, Paul Terry, David Thewlis. Produced by Denise Di Novi, Tim Burton. 79 mins.

Talk of "a new Golden Age of Disney animation" may be dismissed as so much studio hype, but there's no denying that the release, within a few months, of *The Hunchback of Notre Dame* (traditional cel animation), *Toy Story* (the first computer-animated feature) and *James and the Giant Peach* (3D stop-motion) shows the Mousedom embracing a healthy and invigorating diversity of techniques.

Of the three, stop-motion would until recently have been by far the least expected candidate for big-budget exploitation. Cel has long been the dominant mode, and computer-animation was a natural for Disney the moment it became advanced enough; but stop-motion, even at its most sophisticated, retains something hand-crafted and (in the phrase of animator Trey Thomas, who worked on *James*) "rough around the edges" that harks back to the earliest pioneers of the technique, like Ladislaw Starewicz and J. Stuart Blackton.

James, of course, rides in on the success of Henry Selick's previous film, *The Nightmare Before Christmas*, the first stop-motion feature produced by a Hollywood major. Not that Selick got due credit for *Nightmare*; it was billed as *Tim Burton's The Nightmare Before Christmas*, even though Burton neither wrote nor directed it. Selick, while acknowledging Burton's contribution in terms of the film's original concept and characters, feels understandably slighted: "I was the guy who made the film for close to three years of my life, whereas he came to San Francisco for about five days, total, the entire time". It's fair to add, though, that without the power of Burton's name attached, the project would probably never have got the go-ahead.

The enabling name on *James* may well have been that of Roald Dahl, still, six years after his death, one of the world's most widely-read children's authors. But this time round, Selick should be sure of getting the credit he deserves. Where *Nightmare*, for all its spiky ingenuity, felt at times overdriven by Burton's personal obsessions and Danny Elfman's hyperactive score, *James* moves at its own pace, taking time out for moments of soaring lyrical joy as the peach sails serenely across the sky with its human/insect crew.

Yet the film doesn't lack excitement or menace, being at once darker and less dark than its predecessor. Though the *Nightmare* characters looked ghoulish, they were essentially harmless; but *James* – respecting the tone of Dahl's original – features episodes of genuine danger. Highlights include a deftly choreographed battle with underwater skeletons (combining a homage to Ray Harryhausen with a cameo from *Nightmare*'s Jack Skellinton) and the attack of the giant shark, a fearsome mechanical monster with rotary teeth that seems to have evolved from Captain Nemo's Nautilus in *20,000 Leagues Under the Sea*.

Dahl purists will object to some of the liberties taken, but the episodic, bedtime-story structure of the novel would have made a broken-backed screenplay. Something of Dahl's gloriously off-hand callousness has been lost: the odious aunts are merely battered, not squashed relishably flat, and the rhino that disposed of James' parents is given the dollar-book Freud treatment and inflated into a recurrent trauma. But by way of compensation, the film is rich in characterisation both visual and verbal.

James' insect companions are vividly delineated: fastidious, patrician grasshopper (voiced by Simon Callow), brash Brooklyn centipede (Richard Dreyfuss), motherly ladybird (Jane Leeves), twitchy

Scouse earthworm (David Thewlis), cool Parisian spider (Susan Sarandon), and dowagerly glow-worm (Miriam Margolyes). In the ultra-stylised live-action sequences that bookend the animated story, there's some spirited ugly-sisters mugging from Margolyes again and Joanna Lumley as the aunts from hell.

But ultimately what makes the film is the quality of the animation: flowing, intricate, textured, lovingly detailed. By restricting Randy Newman's songs (tuneful and instantly forgettable) to five, as against the dozen or so crammed into *Nightmare,* Selick gives us space to savour some delectably crafted moments: as when the spider, having fashioned a web-cocoon for James to sleep in, tucks him in solicitously with wittily co-ordinated movements of all eight legs.

3D stop-motion isn't used exclusively; there's a nightmare interlude that exploits the flatness of cut-out animation to create a sense of entrapment, and certain elements (notably the giant shark) are computer-created. All these techniques mesh seamlessly together, just as the film skilfully negotiates its shifts in tone from poignant to funny to scary. *James* consolidates the achievement of *Nightmare* and builds on it. On the basis of these two films alone, Henry Selick has surely earned his place as one of the great creators in the pantheon of stop-motion animation.

Philip Kemp

THE HUNCHBACK OF NOTRE DAME

Animation Script: Tab Murphy, Irene Mecchi, Bob Tzudiker, Noni White, Jonathan Roberts. Based on the novel *Notre-Dame de Paris* by Victor Hugo. Directors: Gary Trousdale, Kirk Wise. Editing: Ellen Keneshea. Art Direction: David Goetz. Visual Effects: Christopher Jenkins. Layout: Ed Ghertner. Background: Lisa Keene. Music/Songs: Alan Menken, Stephen Schwartz. Players: Tom Hulce, Demi Moore, Tony Jay, Kevin Kline, Paul Kandel, Jason Alexander, Mary Kay Bergman. Produced by Don Hahn for Disney Enterprises.

In support of the precarious EuroDisney adventure which, against all odds, resolutely continues to provide magical theme-park attractions on the outskirts of Paris, the latest full-length animated feature from the Disney studios (their 35th) firmly declares what fun it is to be French. Deftly packaged within the explosive panoramas of *The Hunchback of Notre Dame* is a spiky message about the skills, joviality, and sheer good-heartedness of outsiders who dare to challenge the mean-spirited and bring carnival happiness to the average Parisian.

Quasimodo the hunchback has always been a usefully symbolic figure. Victor Hugo's novel *Notre-Dame de Paris,* first published in 1831, was as much about the cathedral itself as about Quasimodo's love for the threatened gypsy girl Esmeralda, but it was the romantic melodrama that caught the imagination even if its conclusion (the girl is hanged and the hunchback entombed with her body) was on the grim side. Screen adaptations – there were at least four prior to the Lon Chaney classic of 1923 – found more positive endings: in the Theda Bara version, *The Darling of Paris* (1917), Esmeralda and her ungainly admirer were even united in marriage.

But whatever his fate, Quasimodo is intriguingly akin to other such popular sufferers as the Phantom of the Opera, Dracula, and Edgar Allan Poe's Roderick Usher. Like them, he is the guardian of an elaborate mansion, and his surveillance of the outside world is both a warning and a cry for help. Thanks to his role as bell-ringer, Quasimodo is also a recluse with a difference: his activities regularly punctuate the city's routine with reminders of religious obligation. Gazing down from the cathedral towers with his gargoyle friends at the streets below, he could

Quasimodo cavorts in THE HUNCHBACK OF NOTRE DAME

The gargoyles, Esmeralda and Quasimodo in THE HUNCHBACK OF NOTRE DAME
photos: Buena Vista International

imagine an almost supernatural control over their inhabitants – and indeed he creates, as puppetmaster, a table-top model on which the people of Paris are positioned as he wishes.

The new Disney rendition, as well as giving due weight (with the help of a French unit of animators) to Hugo's admiration for the cathedral's buttresses, spires, windows and statuary, picks up on these hints of theological debate with considerable zest. Having been saved by the Church's intervention when the racist Judge Frollo was about to kill him as a baby, Quasimodo is now tempted to emerge from the sanctuary of the cathedral despite Frollo's efforts to keep him there, a reversal of motivation rendered the more complex by their mutual passion for the free-ranging Esmeralda.

It is by relinquishing her that Quasimodo finds public acclaim, while Frollo, who is prepared to kill what he cannot have, plummets in flames to his doom. But like many of the jokes that go hustling by, such intricacies are there for the film's adult audiences to chew on. At a more junior level, the Disneyfied hunchback with his enviable acrobatic skill, the lightly sketched features beside which his gargoyle friends look far uglier than he does, and his eagerly youthful tones (voiced by Tom Hulce, whom he curiously resembles on occasion), is appealingly in the tradition of Dumbo and Pinocchio, a mild misfit whose adolescent disadvantages may yet make him into something special.

Woven into his story are the customary Disney pronouncements, as repeated by much the same team of contributors for the past decade and through much the same characters - the wilful heroine, the British-accented, villain, the attendant coterie of clownish companions, even (through the unwilling Frollo) the weary parent figure and mentor facing extinction as his pupil learns self-sacrifice, tolerance, courage, and other laudable qualities. No surprise to find that the *Hunchback* producer, Don Hahn, also guided *Beauty and the Beast* and *The Lion King,* that the *Hunchback* co-writer, Jonathan Roberts, also wrote *The Lion King* (and, as it happens, the screen adaptation of *James and the Giant Peach*), and that the *Hunchback* directors, Gary Trousdale and Kirk Wise, were responsible for *Beauty and the Beast,* in which so much of the Esmeralda/ Quasimodo story is anticipated.

Designed in far wilder colours than last year's *Pocahontas,* which made up in delicate forest shades for what it signally lacked in narrative substance, *The Hunchback of Notre Dame* is more in the style of *Aladdin,* influenced by at least two supervising animators from the earlier film – David Pruiksma, who attends to the gargoyles, and Tony Fucile, who makes of Esmeralda a wonderfully green-eyed liberationist, the kind whose sunglasses, if she had any, would always be in her hair.

Much of the film is a romp of inventive, witty artwork. And as well as being fascinating to watch, *Hunchback* is rendered soaringly operatic by Alan Menken's score and Stephen Schwartz's lyrics: it offers renewed and rewarding confirmation that the Hollywood musical is alive and well and living in Disneyland.

Philip Strick

Creatures Great and Small: The Henson Organisation

Post-traumatic shock can affect companies no less than people – especially creative companies. The sudden, appallingly unexpected death of Jim Henson in May 1990 knocked the organisation he had founded off its course: and for two or three years, it visibly floundered, uncertain and unhappy. Morale suffered, and work on some creatively indifferent films (*Neverending Story III, The Flintstones*) didn't help.

But now, it seems, the Henson organisation has found its soul again. At its London headquarters, the atmosphere is buoyant and fizzing with activity. The past year has been exceptionally successful, with a near-unbroken string of hits – starting off with *Babe*, the tale of a sheep-herding piglet that had audiences delighted – and pork butchers despondent – the world over. Besides giving Disney's mega-budget *Pocahontas* a run for its money, the film picked up a well-deserved Best Visual Effects Oscar for the Henson Creature Shop at the 1996 Academy Awards.

The box-office triumph of *Babe* mirrors the film's technical achievement: a seamless meshing of animatronics, computer-generated imaging (CGI), puppeteering and real live animals. Watching the film, it's impossible to tell which system or systems is being used at any one time. The joins don't show. But then, according to John Stephenson, Creative Supervisor of the Creature Shop, that's just how it should be.

"What's happening is that the various systems are starting to overlap: animatronics, CGI, they're all running off the same hardware and software. So the director may not even know – doesn't need to know – which system he's getting. And that's fine because all that matters is that we're giving him what he wants. How we get there is our worry, not his".

Monsters Go Real Time

Since *Babe*, there has been *Loch Ness*, with its Henson-created monster; the fifth Muppet movie, *Muppet Treasure Island*; the multiple Emmy-nominated *Gulliver's Travels*, a three-hour TV four-parter; *Muppets Tonight!*, the first new Muppet series for 15 years; and most recently, the live-action remake of *Pinocchio*, with Martin Landau playing Gepetto and the puppet played by . . . a puppet. (Landau reportedly observed that has "worked with far more wooden actors".) Plus a slew of other TV programmes, commercials, pop videos and the like.

Loch Ness marked a further break-through: "real-time CGI" – computer-generated creatures that 'act' alongside their human co-stars, live on set. This allowed Ted Danson, as the scientist hero, to react directly to the monster instead of having to emote into a void (as in *Jurassic Park*), with the creature being matted in

Henson's latest creation, PINOCCHIO

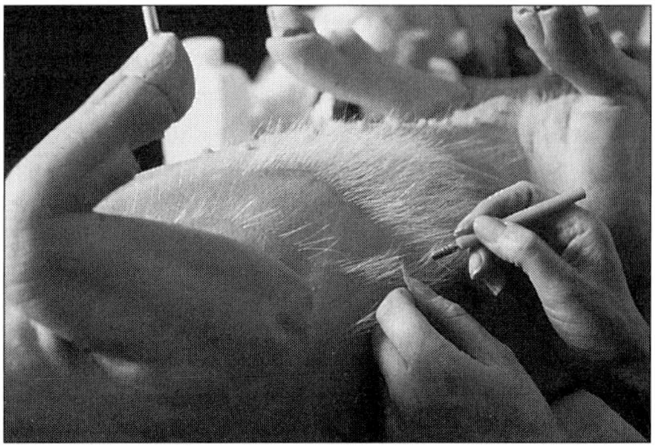

BABE, a triumph for subtle effects
photo: Kennedy Miller Pictures

later. The technique also meant that the director, John Henderson, was able to direct the monster as if it were a live actor, getting it to change its performance from take to take in infinitely subtle ways.

Henson's London base (the company also has offices in New York and Los Angeles) dates back to 1976, when Jim Henson's proposal for *The Muppet Show* was turned down by every US network. Lew Grade, then running ATV, was the only media boss to see the show's potential, and all five series were produced in London. The Muppets were largely worked by traditional puppeteering skills, albeit taken to a high degree of sophistication.

But the Creature Shop was eagerly pioneering animatronic technology, and in 1982, Henson released the first all-animatronic film, *The Dark Crystal*, co-directed with his associate, Frank Oz. Its successor, *Labyrinth* (1986), combined animatronics with human actors. Though technically impressive, both films were commercial disappointments.

Creatures Touched by Anarchy

Since then the Creature Shop has developed increasingly complex and sophisticated techniques, providing creatures for such productions as Gavin Millar's *Dreamchild* (1985), Nicolas Roeg's *The Witches* (1990), and the first two *Teenage Mutant Ninja Turtles* movies, as well as for television series like *Fraggle Rock* and *Dinosaurs*. The Shop's creations range from the ultra-realistic (not all the bears in Jean-Jacques Annaud's *The Bear* were the real thing) through semi-realistic (the animals in *Babe*, to pure cartoon. All but the most realistic tend to display elements of the quirky, off-beat humour and touches of anarchy that always characterised Jim Henson's own creations.

Long established on the slopes of Hampstead Hill, the Creature Shop recently moved downhill into new premises: a 19th-century railway building fronting the Regent's Canal, a stone's throw from the colourful tumult of Camden Lock. From the outside, the building is solid, foursquare in its Victorian self-confidence. The refurbished interior is spacious, light and airy, buzzing with a sense of quiet excitement. Besides the Creature Shop, the building also houses another branch of the increasingly labyrinthine Henson empire, the London offices of Jim Henson Productions.

Broadly, the division of labour is that Henson Productions produces films and TV programmes for the organisation, often in co-production with other companies, while the Workshop makes creatures and special effects on commission for other clients, as well as acting as the workshop for Henson Productions. By way of further complication, in 1995, Jim Henson Productions set up a new company in partnership with Sony Entertainment, called Jim Henson Pictures, to produce films for release through Columbia TriStar.

Creations Divide and Multiply

The first fruit of the Sony deal can be seen all over the London workshop: gorillas and parts of gorillas, from new-born to massively full-grown, strewn across benches and worksurfaces or strung up on rudimentary frameworks. These are in preparation for *Buddy*, a film to be directed by Caroline Thompson (*Black Beauty*), based on the true story of an eccentric L.A. socialite who raised a gorilla as her son. The film, starring Rene Russo, is due for release in 1997.

Other forthcoming cinematic projects include *Into the Woods*, an adaptation of Stephen Sondheim's musical; a film version of C.S. Lewis' classic children's fantasy, *The Lion, the Witch and the Wardrobe*, to be directed by John Boorman; *The Seven Deadly Sins*, an adult fantasy directed by Anthony Minghella; *The Deptford Mice*, the adventures of a group of heroic mice who save London from takeover by rats; and prosthetic work on Ralph Fiennes in the title role of *The English Patient*, adapted from the novel by Michael Ondaatje. Henson's have also optioned five more titles by Dick King-Smith, author of "The Sheep Pig" on which *Babe* was based.

Next up, though, and due for release for Christmas 1996, is the live-action remake of *101 Dalmatians*, produced for Disney and starring Glenn Close as Cruella de Vil. This, according to John Stephenson, will be "totally realistic", with "no cartoon element to it at all". As with *Pinocchio*, comparison with the original animated version will be inevitable. It says a lot for the sanguine mood currently reigning at Henson's that they're prepared to go head-to-head against two of Disney's best-loved films – with confidence that their creations won't suffer by comparison.

Philip Kemp

Profile of Nick Park

If awards count for anything, Nick Park is the world's greatest animator – ever. All his films have walked off with top prizes at international animation festivals, and the 1996 Academy Awards saw him pick up his third Best Animation Oscar for his latest tour de force of plasticine model animation, *A Close Shave*. Of his four films so far (barring some apprentice work), the only one *not* to win an Oscar was the first in the Wallace and Gromit trilogy, *A Grand Day Out*. And even that had managed to be nominated for an Oscar and won a BAFTA award.

It's a singular achievement for any animator whose work is not just thoroughly English, but specifically and unabashedly provincial. Park hails from Preston, Lancashire, and the humour of his films is flat-accented, straight-faced and self-deprecating, blending outlandish plots with mundane homely detail in a way that harks back to his fellow Lancastrian, George Formby. Yet Park's work exerts an international appeal to rival that of Disney or Hanna-Barbera. His two best-known characters – Wallace, the ingenious but naive inventor of eccentric devices, and his faithful and ultra-smart dog Gromit – have met with acceptance and affection wherever they've been shown, which by now takes in virtually everywhere in the world.

Protected Environment

The affection Park's films inspire is clearly a response to the affection with which they're made. At Aardman Studios in

Bristol, where he's worked ever since leaving the National Film and Television School in 1983, Park is notoriously protective towards his characters, loath to relinquish control over them even when – as in his two most recent films, *The Wrong Trousers* and *A Close Shave* – the increasingly ambitious production values and storylines make it essential to share animation work with collaborators.

And, unusually for an animator, Park seems to lack sadism; the world of his films is essentially good-natured, its humour quirky but never cruel, and even such ferocious creations as the *Terminator*-style cyborg bulldog of *A Close Shave* are granted last-reel redemption. The gleeful mayhem of a Švankmajer or a Tex Avery is beyond his compass.

Inherent in Park's devotion to his work is his meticulous attention to detail. His films are endlessly rewatchable, not just for the exuberance and fluent pacing of their storylines, but for the richness with which every frame is packed with details and incidental gags. The décor of Wallace's two-storey terraced house is lovingly observed, right down to the chintz patterning on the sofa and the prize cucumber framed on the wall, and Gromit's highbrow reading matter is invariably aptly chosen: Pluto's *Republic* or, when wrongfully imprisoned, *Crime and Punishment* by Dostoievsky.

This visual richness extends to the production values: Park prefers to regard himself as a 'film-maker' rather than an 'animator', and his films are framed and lit as carefully as for live action. The more sinister episodes of *A Close Shave* borrow the visual vocabulary of *film noir*, all tilted camera angles and encroaching shadows.

With String and Nails

Not surprisingly, Park's work is nothing if not labour-intensive. (Rather to his relief, computers have not yet to make much headway in the world of stop-motion

Nick Park and his creations

model animation.) *A Grand Day Out*, the film that introduced Wallace and Gromit to the world, took six years to make, partly because it was started – as a graduation film – while Park was still completing his course at the NFTS, and completed while he was working on other projects at Aardman. It also represented a learning process; Park describes it as "done virtually with string and nails, including the story". But even with all the resources and sophisticated back-up now available to Aardman's star performer, the two most recent films only progressed at the rate of some two seconds completed per day.

Park's perfectionism wasn't the sole reason. He also loves to use a highly mobile camera – an expensive preference in stop-motion animation since the camera, like the models, can be moved only a frame at a time, with alarming consequences for both schedule and budget. In his case, the investment paid off, as can be seen from the spectacular set-pieces that round off each film with such fluid energy: the intricate model-train chase of *The Wrong Trousers* and, in *A Close Shave*, an assault on the cyborg's lair that involves, *inter alia*, an airborne Gromit, and a flock of sheep poised in inverse-pyramid formation on a hurtling motorbike.

Such wild extravaganzas may obscure the fact that Park gets some of his funniest effects from the most economic means. Gromit has no mouth and an inexpressive blob of a nose; his emotions are vividly conveyed by his ears and the set of his eyebrows. The villain of *The Wrong Trousers*, a larcenous penguin, has even fewer facial features, just an immobile beak and boot-button eyes, yet its whole shape and stance radiate malignity.

In the film that brought him to fame, *Creature Comforts* (from which there spun off a much-loved series of television commercials for electricity), Park put pre-recorded interview tracks into the mouths of animated zoo animals. Much of the humour derived, not only from the witty matching (or mismatching) of voice and species, but from the throwaway background detail such, as a nearby animal scratching or having a crap. Even Gromit, ultra-civilised creature that he is, will occasionally and rather endearingly revert to basic canine behaviour.

Though his films are enjoyed by adults no less than children, there's an engaging innocence about Park's world. For all their technological wizardry, Wallace and Gromit inhabit a reassuringly cosy, late 40's time-warp, and the nearest any Park film has so far come to sex (Wallace's stammering, tongue-tied wooing of wool-shop owner Wendolene Ramsbotham in *A Close Shave*) isn't even adolescent, but pre-adolescent in its diffidence. It's this combination of highly sophisticated animation technique with the unpretentious naivety (even gormlessness) of the characters that gives his films their distinctive flavour and appeal.

Though Nick Park may now be the most famous animator since Disney, he shares none of Disney's empire-building ambitions and shows no inclination to set up on his own, evidently happy to remain with Aardman. His current project, his first ever feature-length film (to be co-produced by Jake Eberts' Allied Film-Makers), is being written and animated in collaboration with Aardman's co-founder, Peter Lord. The project is still in its earliest stages, and nothing is known about it – except that it won't star Wallace and Gromit. A disappointment for their fans, no doubt, but intriguing for anyone eager to see Park's idiosyncratic talent exploring fresh fields.

WORLD SURVEY

ALGERIA

Roy Armes

The breakdown of the state-controlled structure of film production, set up thirty years ago when the National Office for Film Commerce and Industry (ONCIC) was established, combined with the country's current political uncertainties, have severely restricted Algerian film production. Virtually the only film in the current season to be exported and shown at foreign film festivals (and also to obtain a commercial cinema release in Paris) is the Belgian-trained Belkacem Hadjadj's first feature, after a number of well-received shorts, **Once Upon a Time . . .** *(Machaho)*. This is the first Algerian feature to be released in which the characters speak Berber (Abderrahmane Boughermouh's adaptation of Mouloud Mammeri's *The Forgotten Hillside* was shot in 1992, but still awaits release). The Berber language was banned from the screen until the recent political upheavals, so the production of *Machaho* is in itself a political act. Hadjadj, who plays the lead himself, takes the opportunity to offer a critical examination of traditional attitudes and beliefs, particularly the male concept of honour. Cleanly shot in the Kabyle mountains and with an emphatic musical score, the film traces a simple narrative trajectory leading inexorably to confrontation and death.

Now Algeria is represented in the wider world largely by features made by its film-makers working abroad: those who have established themselves in France only during the last few years (such as Merzak Allouache, born in Algiers in 1944, who moved to Paris after the completion of *Bab el-Oued City* in 1994), those who came to France in their twenties (such as Abdelkarim Bahloul, born in Rebahia, Algeria, in 1950), and those who were born in France of Algerian descent (such as Rachid Bouchareb, born in 1953).

Merzak Allouache's sixth feature in a twenty-year career of feature film production is **Salut, Cousin!** Told with the director's customary humour, this is the story of two cousins. Mok, a second-generation immigrant and Parisian through and through, leads a hectic city life, trying to make ends meet. His cousin Alilo, newly arrived from Algiers and supposed to return there with a suitcase he cannot in fact track down, is amazed by all he sees. The film makes clear the vast differences in life-style between Paris and contemporary Algeria, and its conclusion is ironic.: while Alilo misses his plane back to Algiers, Mok is bundled off there, expelled from France for undesirable activities.

Merzak Allouache directing SALUT COUSIN!

Still from THE HAMLET SISTERS

In Abdelkrim Bahloul's **The Hamlet Sisters**, all the main characters still have links with the Maghreb, but the dichotomy between France and Algeria is no longer the key focus of attention. The film tells the story of two adolescent girls who are trapped in Paris when their escort is taken ill and all the trains have stopped. They are befriended by Allel, an elderly Algerian, who comes briefly to stand in for their absent father (a Berber who divorced their mother eleven years before). He tells them the meaning of their name: in Berber, 'hamlet' is the term applied to a man who supports, or to a woman who carries, a child. This meaning is itself only part of a general pattern of lives crossing and recrossing in night-time Paris, as the film unfolds in both a hymn to the city and a plea for tolerance and understanding.

If some of Rachid Bouchareb's earlier features, such as *Cheb* (1900), or *Shattered Years* (1992), deal with characters caught between Algeria and Europe, and so fit comfortably into an expected pattern for emigrant cinema, **Living Dust**, which in 1996 was nominated for an Oscar as Best Foreign Film, does not. This is a story of divided lives, but not those of France's North African communities. Instead, it tells the story of Son, the child of a black American officer who abandoned his Vietnamese family on the fall of Saigon in 1975. Son, the film tells us, is one of 40,000 such abandoned children, left to fend for themselves and, in his case, arrested and sent to a re-education centre in the mountains. There life is harsh and cruel but the boys make friendships, try to build their lives, struggle to escape. Son survives, helped by his intelligence, his will and the diary of prison camp life which he keeps.

Whether a film shot in Malaysia dealing with Vietnam and made by a director born in France can meaningfully be considered a part of Algerian cinema is questionable (though it did figure among the films fêted at the 1996 Biennale of African Cinemas in Paris). What is certain is that *Living Dust* is a powerfully emotive piece which draws attention to suffering too often ignored and fully deserves the acclaim it has received.

The documentary films by directors in exile from Algeria – particularly those shown at the Biennale – exhibit the same kind of questioning and disorientation which was characteristic of the Algerian-made feature films reviewed in last year's IFG: Zemmouri's **The Honour of the Tribe**, for instance, or Chouikh's **Youssef The Legend of the Seventh Sleeper**. The most articulate and revealing of them is Ahmed Lallem's **Algerian Women Thirty Years On**. Here Lallem, a well-established documentary film-maker, who made two features in the 1970s, looks back to a film he shot in 1966: *Elles*. This focused on the experiences, dreams and ambitions of a group of college students. Now Lallem has tracked down some of these women thirty years later, and four of them look at the images of themselves in 1966 and tell of their lives since then. The story is one of women returned to their place in a patriarchal society after the seeming liberation of the independence struggle. Lallem's film is an eloquent testimony both to the current situation in Algeria and to the harshness of exile.

Recent Films

MACHAHO (Once Upon a Time)

Script and Dir: Belkacem Hadjadj. Phot: Georges Lechaptois, Rachid Merabtine. Players: Meriem Barbes, Hadjira Oul Bachir, Belkacem Hadjadj. Prod: Les Films sur la Plage (France)/Imago Productions/ENPA/CAAIC (Algeria).

SALUT COUSIN! (Hello, Cousin!)

Script: Merzak Allouache, Caroline Thivel. Dir: Allouache. Phot: Pierre Aïm. Players: Gad el-Maleh, Messaoud Hattou, Magaly Berdy, Ann Gisel Glass, Jean Benguigui. Prod: JBA Production (France).

LES SŒURS HAMLET (The Hamlet Sisters)

Script and Dir: Abdelkrim Bahloul. Phot: Georges Lechaptois. Players: Emilie Altmayer, Bérénice Bejo, Mouloud Tadjer, Colette Nucci. Prod: Films sur la Place (France).

POUSSIÈRES DE VIE (Living Dust)

Script: Rachid Bouchareb, Bernard Gespert, from the novel *La colline de Fanta* by Duyen Ahn. Dir: Bouchareb. Phot: Youcef Sahraoui. Players: Daniel Guyant, Gilles Chitlaphone, Jéhan Pages, Léon Outtrabady, Siu Lin Lam, Eric Nguyen. Prod: 3B Productions (France).

Useful Addresses

Cinémathèque Algérienne
rue Larbi-Ben-M'Hidi
Algiers
Tel: 638 301

CAAIC
(Centre Algérien pour l'Art et l'Industrie Cinématographique)
Immeuble les Asphodeles
16030 Ben Aknoun
Algiers
Tel: 781 657
Fax: 784 104

ENPA
(Entreprise Nationale de Production Audiovisuelle)
3 avenue de l'Indépendence
BP 76
Didouche Mourad
Algiers
Tel: 665 140
Fax: 662 520

ANAF
(Agence Nationale des Actualitées Filmées)
12 rue Ali Bedjaoui
El Biar - Algiers
Tel: 791 029
Fax: 788 349

ARGENTINA

Alberto Tabbia

The INCAA (Instituto Nacional de Cine y Artes Audiovisuales) has once more changed director and policy. Julio Maharbiz (well known as a folklorist under the name Julio Márbiz), who carried out a well-publicised 'clean up' campaign of national radio, will now presumably do a similar job on the web of corruption surrounding subventions and credits from the Instituto. This is a subject that has long been gossiped about but never been taken as far as substantial legal action.

After rumours that the Instituto itself was going to be closed, state protection of any kind being anathema in this era of rampant privatisation, the film law, passed a year-and-a-half ago and slow to get moving, is finally taking effect. Most of the films that opened this year are either co-productions with the Instituto or have had credits from it. An old cinema in the centre of Buenos Aires has been leased by the Instituto and transformed into a three-theatre showcase of Argentine cinema where most new films open. Even the Mar del Plata film festival, which had been internationally recognised in the late 50s and early 60s, is going to be resurrected. A new society (ADECAA), in which directors, independent producers, unions and almost every branch of the film industry is represented, has been created to see that the film law functions properly, and as a kind of permanent consulting board for the Instituto.

If all this makes for a lively and fluid situation, the films themselves have proved the real disappointment. The past season has marked one of the lowest periods in recent Argentine film history. A majority of the new films are a rehashing of worn-out narrative formulas and subject

Martín Karpan (right) in YELLOW FLOWERS IN THE WINDOW

matter. It is as if old, comforting political attitudes were being invoked to avoid looking frankly and candidly at the changed social reality. This failure of observation is coupled with a still more deadening failure of imagination. Most of the films under review seem to be born old and tired, and show an utter lack of any original film sense in their makers.

Pablo Alarcón (right) and Héctor Bordoni in THE GOLDEN CONDOR

ALBERTO TABBIA is an Argentine film critic and cultural journalist. He co-edited the film series *Flashback* and is a regular contributor to the main Buenos Aires and Montevideo dailies, their literary supplements and other magazines as well.

Recent Films

LOLA MORA

Script: Mónica Ottino, J. Torre, Alejandro Margulis. Dir: Javier Torre. Phot: Willy Behnisch. Players: Leonor Benedetto, Alberto de Mendoza, Victor Laplace, China Zorrilla, Iván González, Noemi Frenkel. Prod: Javier Torre and the INCAA.

This bio-pic of the Argentine sculptress Lola Mora (1866-1936) follows her from her arrival in Rome at the end of the last century and her early success there to her return to Argentina, where she finds only an ambiguous notoriety – sexual discrim-

TOP TEN GROSSING FILMS IN ARGENTINA: 1995

The Mask
Pocahontas
Caballos Salvajes (Argentine)
Batman Forever
Casper
Dumb and Dumber
Forrest Gump
Die Hard 3
Disclosure
Legends of the Fall

ination, commissions for patriotic monuments, and public slander on account of her marriage to a man twenty years her junior. She becomes with age something of a visionary inventor and an explorer, dying in poverty and oblivion. Cameos by well-known local actors appearing as, for instance, D'Annunzio and the Queen of Italy, may be fun for Argentine audiences but contribute to a general lack of focus. Leonor Benedetto's intense physical presence does not convey an inner urge to create.

EL VERSO (Slick Talk)

Script and Dir: Santiago Carlos Oves. Phot: Jorge Ruiz. Players: Luis Brandoni, Virginia Lago, Hugo Arana, Marcos Zucker, Tincho Zabala, Andrea Tenuta. Prod: SCO Producciones/Aleph Producciones.

Juan has a way with words – he cheats on his customers, wife and mistress, even on his best friend, and all the people he cheats adore him. The day he loses confidence, this web of false relationships collapses around him. Through his main character, the author-director tries a sociological but affectionate analysis of a typical Buenos Aires character, but his film, suffering from a fatal lack of narrative drive, sheds no new light on its well-worn stereotypes.

CARLOS MONZÓN EL SEGUNDO JUICIO (Carlos Monzón: The Second Trial)

Script: Daniel Ginhson, Anibal Uset. Story: Dr Pamela Bisserier. Dir: Gabriel Arbos. Phot: Juan Carlos Lenardi. Players: Norma Aleandro, Carola Reyna, José Luis Alfonzo, Elio Marchi. Prod: Daniel Ginhson/Jorge Hartfiel Producciones/INCAA.

Described by the producers as a "docudrama", this film is the only one to have been produced after many attempts to deal with the life of Carlos Monzón met with opposition from his deceased wife's family. (Monzón, a boxing idol and occasional film star, killed his wife, was sentenced to eleven years in prison and died shortly before the shooting of this film started, in a car crash during a Sunday parole.) The contradictory and dramatic personality of Monzón, though served by the honest interpretation of José Luis Alfonzo, seems larger than this courtroom drama frame can contain. In its effort to avoid legal problems while touching on very delicate subject matter, the film becomes tame and loses its grip on its really wild lead character.

EL DEDO EN LA LLAGA (Finger in the Wound)

Script: Daniel Romañach, Alberto Lecchi. Dir: Alberto Lecchi. Phot: Hugo Colace. Players: Dario Grandinetti, Karra Elejalde, Juanjo Puigcorbé, Luisina Brando, Mario Pasik, Federico Olivera. Prod: Mandala Films/Kompel Producciones.

Two Spanish actors (one Basque, the other Catalonian), on tour in the Argentine provinces, meet an old friend and returned exile, now a disillusioned secondary school professor. The trio embark on a Quixotic unmasking of the local political mafia, supported by a bunch of non-conformist students. This is a crafty mixture of elements from recent money-makers such as the 1992 *Un lugar en el mundo* (*A Place in the World*), co-written by Alberto Lecchi, and the 1995 hit *Caballos salvajes* (*Wild Horses*). As a socially-minded thriller, it allows comforting identification for both young and middle-aged audiences and its traditional storytelling smacks less of classical models than marketing surveys.

CAZADORES DE UTOPIAS (Utopia Hunters)

Script: Ernesto Jauretche. Dir and Prod: David Blaustein.

Almost two and a half hours of interviews illustrated with archive material about the Montoneros, the self-appointed left-wing guerrillas of Peronism in the blood-soaked Argentine of the 1970s. Made by a militant, the film's declared attempts at historical perspective, and the occasional self-appraisal by some fighters, are pathetic in their mixture of high-minded paternalism and utter incapacity to assess the political project the movement tried to impose. Intended as a whitewashing group portrait, the film instead achieves, for the critical, non-partisan spectator, a total demolition job.

OTRA ESPERANZA (Another Hope)

Script and Dir: Mercedes Frutos, based on a short story by Adolfo Bioy Casares. Phot: Julio Lencina. Players: Pepe Soriano, Héctor Bidonde, Constanza Maral, Héctor Calori. Made in 1984-85.

Bioy Casares' story is a metaphysical fable – the inmates of a clinic-factory are made to suffer in order to transform their pain into energy. This first film, finally released after a long decade of production problems, translates the fable into social criticism, as a metaphor for capitalist exploitation. The concept could have been interesting but the uncertain grasp on narrative and characterisation (the "heavies" are caricatured without a shade of humour) contributes to the desultory results.

EL CONDOR DE ORO (The Golden Condor)

Script: Francisco D'Intino. Dir: Enrique Muzio. Phot: Alberto Basail. Players: Pablo Alarcón, Ulises Dumont, Blanca Oteiza, Gogo Andreu, Carlos Estrada, Luis Medina Castro, Alberta Banegas. Prod: Francisco D'Intino.

Two friends, one of them Indian, embark on a search for three rings as promised to an old Indian sage. Rescuing and losing them, escaping thugs and policemen, helped by a lighthouse keeper and a young girl, they travel – 'scenic railway' style – across every Argentine landscape: Iguazú falls, Patagonian glaciers, Jesuit mission ruins, beaches, mountains and plains. The Indiana Jones inspiration is weighed down by a pompous folkloristic, traditionalist moral.

HUNDAN AL BELGRANO (literally *Sink the Belgrano!*; intended English title: *Rule Britannia*)

Script and Dir: Federico Urioste. Editor: Miguel Pérez. Music: Luis Maria Serra.

A lumbering montage of newsreels and interviews on the Malvinas/Falklands war. Its political correctness recalls editor Miguel Pérez's *La república perdida* (*The Lost Republic*, 1984-85), a survey of Argentine political upheavals since 1930 from the point of view of the tepid Radical party then in power. The new film relies on the impact on local audiences of British 'revelations' (mostly by Labour MP Tom Dalyell) and plays down Ronald Reagan's double-dealing in the affair as well as totally omitting the crowds cheering the military junta in Buenos Aires at the beginning of the war.

HISTORIAS DE AMOR, DE LOCURA Y DE MUERTE (Stories of Love, Madness and Death)

Script and Dir: Nemesio Juárez, inspired by the life and work of Horacio Quiroga. Phot: Alberto Basail. Players: Victor Laplace, Ingrid Pelicori, Ulises Dumont, Inés Estévez, Fabián Vena.

This evocation of a complex character, the writer Horacio Quiroga (1878-1937), mixes biography and adaptation of his short stories in an attempt to make the work and the life mutually illuminating. The results are both confused and flat – no minor feat when dealing with a writer whose taste both for the macabre and wild life earned him comparison with Poe and Kipling. The actor Laplace had already played the role in a TV mini-series, and here he looks less anguished than irritated at the remake.

Forthcoming Films

FLORES AMARILLAS EN LA VENTANA (Yellow Flowers in the Window)

Script: Beda Docampo Feijóo, J. Ruiz, based on the latter's story. Dir: Jorge Ruiz. Phot: Carlos Torlaski. Players: Arturo Bonín, Katja Alemann, Carolina Fal, Martín Karpan, Victor Manso, Fabiana Garcia Lago, Marcelo Piraino. Prod: Sabina Sigler.

In 1921, a young girl arrives on a Patagonian 'estancia', an isolated property belonging to an expatriate German whom her mother, an ex prostitute, has married. She falls in love with a young 'peón', but when a mining strike erupts further south, the mother disposes of her daughter's unsuitable lover with a false accusation. A first film, entirely shot in the province of Chubut, this low-key chamber drama promises to reveal new possibilities for shooting in the far south.

GEISHA

Script: Maria José Campoamor, E. Raspo. Dir: Eduardo Raspo. Adapt: Javier Petit. Phot: Marcelo Iaccarino. Players: Ana Alvarez, Manuel Banderas, Jorge Marrale, Germán Palacios, Arturo Maly, Eleonora Wexler. Prod: Aleph Producciones (Buenos Aires)/Cartel (Madrid).

A woman refuses to accept that her best friend may have committed suicide and sets out to investigate, only to discover the dead woman had been a very peculiar 'geisha' – for her husband, for his partner and for the investigator's own husband. Shocked at first, she gradually takes the place of her dead friend in all these relationships.

LA REVELACIÓN (The Revelation)

Script: Mario David, Oscar Yedaide, based on Yedaide's short story. Dir: David. Phot: Maria Inés Teyssie. Players: Daniel Kuzniecka, Maria Valenzuela, Emilia Mazer, Gustavo Garzón, Lorenzo Quinteros. Prod: Rosebud.

A young man believes he is immortal and finds this an almost unbearable predicament. His quest for happiness leads him to a guru – a stockbroker who promises to show him "the real face of God".

AL CORAZÓN (To the Heart)

Dir: Mario Sábato. Prod: Estudios San Miguel.

An essay on the tango, illustrated with fragments of old Argentine movies, with actor-director Sergio Renán and singer Adriana Varela as hosts.

MUCHAS GRACIAS, MAESTRO (Many Thanks, Maestro)

Script: Lucho Schuarman, Luis Segura. Dir: Juan Bautista Stagnaro. Phot: Alberto Basail. Players: Osvaldo Pugliese, Arturo Bonin, Luis Brandoni, Marta Blanchi, Victor Laplace, Ulises Dumont, Enrique Pinti. Prod: M & M.

Between fiction and documentary, a portrait of the distinguished tango musician Osvaldo Pugliese.

LA DAMA REGRESA (The Lady Returns)

Script: Rodolfo Hermida, Polaco. Story: Humberto Ceferino Rivas. Dir: Polaco. Players: Isabel Sarli, Edgardo Nieva, Golde Flami, Federico Klemm. Prod: Fernando Sokolowicz.

BUENOS AIRES VICEVERSA

Script and Dir: Alejandro Agresti. Phot: Ramiro Aisenson. Players: Vera Fogwill, Nicolás Pauls, Fernan Mirás, Mirtha Busnelli, Carlos Roffe, Axel Harding. Prod: Agresti, Harding.

In Production

EL SUEÑO DE LOS HÉROES (The Dream of Heroes)

Script: Jorge Goldenberg, Sergio Renán, based on the novel by Adolfo Bioy Casares. Dir: Renán. Players: Fabián Vena, Soledad Villamil, Germán Palacios, Damián De Santo, Lito Cruz, Fernando Fernán Gómez.

DE MI BARRIO CON AMOR (From My Neighbourhood, with Love)

Script: Jacobo Langsner, José Santiso. Dir: Santiso. Phot: Alberto Basail. Players: Luis Brandoni, Roberto Carnaghi, Fabián Vena, Alicia Bruzzo, Mario Pasik.

BESOS EN LA FRENTE (Kisses on the Brow)

Script: Jacobo Langsner, Carlos Galettini, Irene Ickowicz, based on a play by Langsner. Dir: Galettini. Players: China Zorrilla, Leonardo Sbaraglia, Mabel Manzotti.

DESPABÍLATE, AMOR (Wake Up, Love)

Script and Dir: Eliseo Subiela. Players: Dario Grandinetti, Soledad Silveyra, Juan Leirado.

SOL DE OTOÑO (Autumn Sun)

Script: Santiago Carlos Oves, Eduardo Mignogna. Dir: Mignogna. Players: Norma Aleandro, Federico Luppi, Jorge Luz, Cecilia Rossetto, Gabriela Acher, Roberto Carnaghi.

EL MUNDO CONTRA MÍ (The World Against Me)

Script: Beda Docampo Feijóo, Daniela Bajar. Dir: Feijóo. Players: Paulina Rachid, Luis Brandoni, Mirtha Busnelli, Daniel Fanego, Jorge Marrale.

Producers

Aleph Producciones S.A.
Maipú 853 – 3° piso
1006 Buenos Aires
Fax: (54-1) 312 4150

Argentina Sono Film
Lavalle 1973/75
1051 Buenos Aires
Fax: (54-1) 814 4063

Imagen Satelital S.A.
Avenida Melián 2752
1430 Buenos Aires
Fax: (54-1) 546 8001

Jorge Estrada Mora Producciones
Esmeralda 570 – p. 13 of. 48
1007 Buenos Aires
Fax: (54-1) 393 9814

Kompel Producciones
Costa Rica 5882
1414 Buenos Aires
Fax: (54-1) 777 9250/53

Mandala Films
Carlos Pellegrini 739 – 10° B
1012 Buenos Aires
Fax: (54-1) 322 8631

Oscar Kramer Producciones
Libertad 1213
1012 Buenos Aires
Fax: (54-1) 311 4498

Distributors

Artistas Argentinos Asociados
Lavalle 1977/79
1051 Buenos Aires
Fax: (54-1) 811 5016

Buena Vista Columbia Tristar Films of Argentina S.A.
Ayacucho 533
1026 Buenos Aires
Fax: (54-1) 954 3819, 952 9168

Filmarte S.R.L.
Ayacucho 595
1026 Buenos Aires
Fax: (54-1) 476-1739

Lider Films S.A.
Lavalle 2086
1051 Buenos Aires
Fax: (54-1) 953 7355

UIP (United International Pictures) S.R.L.
Ayacucho 520
1026 Buenos Aires
Fax: (54-1) 111303

Warner Bros.
Tucumán 1838
1050 Buenos Aires
Fax: (54-1) 111191

Useful Address

INCAA (Instituto Nacional de Cine y Artes Audiovisuales
Lima 319
1073 Buenos Aires
Fax: (54-1) 112559

Leonor Benedetto as LOLA MORA

AUSTRALIA

David Stratton

If last year was something of a low point in terms of quality for Australian cinema, the current season has more than made up for it. Indeed, it's hard to recall, even in the vintage years of the late 70s, a year in which so many significant Australian films were made; it only remains to be seen how many of them can attract substantial audiences at home and abroad.

Of the 19 feature films completed since July 1 1995, seven were débuts, including by far the most popular film of the year, Chris Noonan's **Babe**. This was an international success, but a phenomenon in Australia where it seems to have become mandatory viewing for people of all ages. Noonan, backed by Kennedy-Miller (producers of the *Mad Max* trilogy) produced a timeless fairytale from British author Dick King-Smith's *The Sheep-Pig* (many Australians did, however, quibble at the Americanisation of many of the characters). The eponymous Babe is a charming porker whose ambitions to be a sheepdog provide a pungent allegory about not being pigeonholed. Noonan never allows the actors, including James Cromwell (son of Hollywood director John Cromwell), as the farmer, to be overshadowed by the scene-stealing quadrupeds, whether real or animatronic.

Noah Taylor in SHINE

Identity Issues

At the other end of the budget scale, the modest comedy **Love and Other Catastrophes**, by 23-year-old Emma-Kate Croghan, is almost equally astonishing. This story of the everyday lives of a group of Melbourne students, many of them studying film, is unaffected, relaxed and often very funny – and no issue is made about the gay life-style of two of the principal female characters. Funded independently for about $45,000, with extra money later injected by the Australian Film Commission to allow completion and a soundtrack full of songs, the film was sold around the world, starting with a $1 million deal with Fox Searchlight for North America, the U.K. and France. Any film which contains characters who worship *Calamity Jane* (one character's thesis is entitled "Doris Day – Feminist Warrior") deserves support.

Australian film-makers often have a problem when trying to sell films to America because of the changes demanded, and (if it's a pre-sale) the often unpalatable demands of casting. So there were wry smiles in January when reports from the Sundance Festival described a fierce bidding war over Scott Hicks' **Shine**, a film about a real-life character, pianist David Helfgott, who spent many years in a mental institution. This co-production with the U.K. centres on an astonishing trio of performances from the actors who play Helfgott at different stages during his life: Alex Rafalowicz (as a child), Noah Taylor (as a teenager) and Geoffrey Rush (as an adult). Armin Müller-Stahl, as David's monstrously protective father, and Lynn Redgrave as the understanding woman who marries the deranged but brilliantly talented man, are also memorable.

Coincidentally, **Lilian's Story**, directed by Jerzy Domaradzki, tells about a woman – again based on a real character – who was driven to the point of madness by a terrible father (Barry Otto). Ruth Cracknell plays the adult Lilian, free at last after years in an institution, while Toni Collette (of *Muriel's Wedding* fame) plays Lilian as a teenager, suffering beatings and worse at the hands of a violently disturbed man. Otto and Collette also had meaty roles in Mark Joffe's exuberant **Cosi**, in which a dedicated young social worker (Ben Mendelsohn) is bullied into staging a production of Mozart's *Così Fan Tutti* in a state mental hospital. Otto plays the most deranged of the inmates, Collette the most controlled (and proves she has a lovely singing voice). Joffe's brisk adaptation of Louis Nowra's hit play is fiercely funny, despite the arguably questionable subject matter.

Cops, Gurus and Exiles

Funny, too, is first-time writer-director Peter Duncan's **Children of the Revolution**, in which Rachel Griffiths appears as Anna, a sexy mounted policewoman who looks great in black leather and sporting handcuffs. She catches the eye of the son of Joseph Stalin, no less – young Joe (Richard Roxburgh) was conceived when his mother, Joan (Judy Davis), a dedicated member of the Communist Party, travelled to Moscow in 1953 and proved to be the Great Dictator's final sexual partner when he died in her arms. Geoffrey Rush and Sam Neill are also involved in this clever satire.

Black comedy is the style of a veteran practitioner on the Australian film scene, Paul Cox. His latest, **Lust and Revenge**, is a sardonic but rather bitter critique on the funding of the arts in the 90s. It could have been (and probably is) about the film industry. The story involves a wealthy pharmaceutical manufacturer (Chris Haywood) who commissions a statue (of a nude man) to be given, as a tax deduction, to the national gallery. He places his daughter (Claudia Karvan) in charge of commissioning the work, and the film

SHOWTIME™
Your Premier Movie Channel

encore™
Your All-Time Favourite Movies

Australia's premier Pay TV Movie Channels bring you the best movies from 20thCentury Fox, Paramount Pictures, Columbia TriStar and Universal Studios as well as independent and Australian film-makers.

First run, 24 hours a day, commercial free

The Premium Movie Partnership
55 Pyrmont Bridge Road, Pyrmont, NSW 2009 Australia
Ph: 61 2 9775 2525 Fax: 61 2 9776 5747

Acquisitions: Marion Pilowsky Programming: David Keg

SHOWTIME Your Premier Movie Channel is a Trademark of Showtime Networks Inc. All Rights Reserved. The Premium Movie Partnership Authorised User.

Matthew Dyktinski, Alice Garner, Radna Mitchell, and Frances O'Connor in LOVE AND OTHER CATASTROPHES
photo: Beyond Films Ltd.

revolves around the lustful affair between the daughter and the artist's model (Nicholas Hope), and the revenge taken by the model's wife (Gosia Dobrowolska). Though there are quite a few laughs, and odd cameo appearances by past Cox regulars Wendy Hughes and John Hargreaves, the latter in his final screen appearance, the film is oddly tentative in its approach to the 'lust' side of the equation.

Sam Neill in CHILDREN OF THE REVOLUTION

In the Cox film, the Dobrowolska character is a member of a religious cult, and the photos of her guru – seen everywhere in her house – are actually of Rolf De Heer, the talented director who, like Cox, emigrated to Australia from the Netherlands. Following the prestige success of *Bad Boy Bubby* (1993), which introduced actor Hope, De Heer made the ambitious s-f environmental film, **Episilon**, which, at the time of writing, is still awaiting completion after private screenings in an unfinished version. Meanwhile, De Heer made **The Quiet Room**, which competed for Australia in Cannes. Though not to everyone's taste, this is a sublimely beautiful film about childhood which takes the viewer into the world of a little girl whose parents are separating. The performance of the child, Chloe Ferguson, is quite astonishing.

Another rather cerebral film to achieve critical success during the year has been **What I Have Written**, by director John

Hughes, which represented Australia in Berlin. Angie Milliken stars as Sorrel, the wife of Christopher (Martin Jacobs), a Melbourne university lecturer. Sorrel travels to France with her husband and their travels are intercut with a series of potent still frames (evidently inspired by Chris Marker's *La Jetée*) in which the same actors take part in another story set in Paris in which the husband has a passionate affair with another woman. Back in Australia, with Christopher crippled by a stroke, Sorrel is approached by one of his colleagues (the excellent Jacek Koman), who reveals the existence of an autobiographical book – which proves to be the parallel story. Hughes' film is an elliptical, intellectually satisfying puzzle.

Milliken also makes a considerable impression in another exciting film, **Dead Heart**, which was co-produced by its leading actor, Bryan Brown. The first feature from writer-director Nick Parsons, *Dead Heart* is set in Wala Wala, a tiny community in the desert several hours' drive from Alice Springs. Brown plays the local cop who becomes involved in a case to do with traditional aboriginal tribal law, while Milliken is riveting as the bored wife of schoolteacher Lewis Fitz-Gerald; her affair with a young aborigine (Aaron Pedersen), and their defiling of a sacred site, leads to a murder which inevitably draws white law into murky areas of tribal pay-back and tradition.

Shirley Barrett's Cannes Camera D'Or winner, **Love Serenade**, is also set in a small community, but Sunray looks like a metropolis when compared to Wala Wala. In this one-horse town, sisters Dimity (Mirando Otto) and Vicki-Ann (Rebecca Frith) share a house and are both smitten by the arrival of Ken (George Shevtsov), an ageing hippy who has come to town to run the local radio station. Beautifully observed, and full of witty comments about small-town life, the film is also stylishly shot with precise wide-screen compositions by cinematographer Mandy Walker. A striking vision illuminates Hong Kong director Clara Law's first Australian film, **Floating Life**, which deals with a family who come to live in the outer suburbs of Sydney. The film is not so much about the problems facing new arrivals in Australia as it is about the way exile disrupts a family when it's cut off from its traditional roots. The actors, all cast from the Australian-Chinese community, give natural, unaffected performances.

Paul Cox directs Claudia Karvan in LUST AND REVENGE

Exiles also feature in **To Have & to Hold**, John Hillcoat's rather surprising follow-up

Bryan Brown in DEAD HEART

to his prison picture, *Ghosts of the Civil Dead*. This delirious melodrama, which deploys themes from *Rebecca* and *Vertigo* in a jungle setting (some of it was filmed on the Sepik River in Papua-New Guinea), stars Tcheky Karyo as a widower who finds a new bride (Rachel Griffiths) who reminds him of his late wife. In **Zone 39**, grief is the theme of an interesting attempt at an intellectual s-f film by director John Tatoulis. Set in a *1984*-ish future, the film deals with the crisis faced by a man (Peter Phelps) whose wife was murdered when he was posted to frontier territory where the state has tried to conceal a fatal pollution which is gradually destroying life.

True Lies

Two established directors came up with strong entries during the year. Richard Franklin's **Brilliant Lies**, based on a hit play by David Williamson, explores with intelligence and humour a case of sexual harassment involving a sexually active young woman (Gia Carides) and her married boss (Anthony La Paglia). Matters are complicated by the fact that no one's really telling the truth. Nadia Tass' **Mr. Reliable** is the second film based on events which occurred in the western suburbs of Sydney in 1968 when Wally Melish, an ex-convict, and Beryl, his girlfriend, became involved in what is reported to have been Australia's first police siege. Colin Friels is superb as the beleaguered Wally, as is Jacqueline McKenzie as Beryl. The film successfully evokes a time when anti-war sentiment had created an anti-Establishment mood in the community which led to Sydneysiders celebrating Wally's stand against the forces of authority.

Only three of the films mentioned above have been distributed in Australia at the time of writing, and all of them have done reasonably well (*Babe* exceptionally so). But one of the biggest commercial disappointments of last year was the engaging, but awkwardly titled, **Dad and Dave on Our Selection**, which first-time director George Whaley had also directed on stage. This is the third film version of the famous Steele Rudd stories (previously handled by Raymond Longford in 1920 and Ken G. Hall in 1932), and the film boasted inspired casting with Leo McKern as the crusty Dad, a fiercely independent

George Shevtsov with Miranda Otto and Rebecca Frith in LOVE SERENADE *photo: Beyond Films Ltd.*

squatter, and Joan Sutherland as his wife. With Geoffrey Rush as their gormless son, Dave, and Noah Taylor as the equally gormless Joe, plus Barry Otto as the villain, the film didn't lack popular and talented players. But its turn-of-the-century characters struck no chords with contemporary audiences.

Life, another filmed play, starred John Brumpton as a man doing time in the AIDS section of a big prison; a grim subject leavened with black humour by talented début director Lawrence Johnston. And Megan Simpson Huberman came up with an avowedly commercial, but rather slight, comedy in **Dating the Enemy**. Claudia Karvan and Guy Pearce give bold performances in a *Vice Versa*-style farce in which warring lovers swap bodies with predictable results.

Mention must also be made of three excellent documentary features produced during the year. Bob Connelly and Robin Anderson, who made a celebrated trilogy of films about tribal conflicts in Papua-New Guinea, returned home for **Rats in the Ranks**, an astonishing, suspenseful film about a local council election for mayor, which has almost Shakespearean characters and deals with the most basic betrayals and treacheries. Tom Zubrycki's **Billal** explores the effect on an Arab-Australian family when their 16-year-old son is brain-damaged after being deliberately hit by a car driven by an Anglo-Australian neighbour. And Gillian Armstrong, in **Not Fourteen Again**, returns to the three Adelaide women she first filmed in *Smokes and Lollies* in 1977, to find that the girls who were 14 then now have teenage children of their own.

Audiences continue to flock to cinemas in Australia, and multiplexes are still opening around the country. This year, though, there has been concern that the censorship office, which has virtually confined itself to classifying films for the past 25 years, may now be taking a more active and conservative interest. There was a ham-fisted attempt to cut the Jim Jarmusch Western *Dead Man*, on the grounds of sex and violence, and at the time of writing, the Sean Connery-Nicolas Cage blockbuster, *The Rock*, is being 'modified' by its distributor, Roadshow, to avoid an R (18) classification.

Peter Phelps in ZONE 39 *photo: Beyond Films Ltd.*

It's too early to tell if the election of the Liberal-National Party coalition to government in March will lead to cuts in funding for the film industry, but it's quite clear that any cuts would have a very significant effect on all sections of an industry which, in 1996, is holding its collective head very high.

DAVID STRATTON was Director of the Sydney Film Festival (1966-1983) and divides his time between writing for *Variety* and *The Australian*, and presenting movies on the S.B.S. TV network in Australia.

Angie Milliken and Jacek Koman in WHAT I HAVE WRITTEN *photo: Beyond Films Ltd.*

Industry Survey

At last estimate, Australia's cultural industries contributed just under two per cent of the nation's gross domestic product, the equivalent of around $AU13 billion. The film and television sector accounted for perhaps $AU2 billion of this and employed some 15,000 people. Impressive when you recall that 40 years ago there was no Australian television and only foreign films on our movie screens.

Government support for motion picture production is still enviable by international standards. The Australian Film Finance Corporation invested around $AU6.5 million in feature films, documentaries and adult and children's television drama in '95/'96. More money came from the Australian Film Commission. And film offices in five states contributed to script development and production.

This year the shop window has looked especially bright with the stunning success of *Babe* and the good showing by Aussie films at Cannes. Australian directors such as Baz Luhrman and Jocelyn Moorhouse maintained a distinctive expatriate presence in Los Angeles. And older directors with established international reputations (Bruce Beresford, Gillian Armstrong and Richard Franklin, for example) returned to direct major films at home.

But, inevitably, there are stresses and strains. "The FFC has not examined the effects of its policies on ordinary workers in the industry," says Stephen Wallace, President of the Screen Directors' Association. He's referring to the whittling down of fees for directors and producers in budgets approved by the Corporation in the six years of its existence. Total production actually slipped in '95/'96 and the fact is you have to be very quick on your feet, or very lucky, to make a decent living in the movie business. "I'd hate to be an independent producer in Australia," adds Michael Lake, CEO of Warner Roadshow Movieworld Studios on the Gold Coast. At the same time he professes satisfaction with the $150 million worth of production which passed through his studio this year, including *The Phantom* and the Japanese feature *Acri*.

"If the industry makes it impossible for producers to live, the whole thing falls down," states Alan Finney, newly-appointed Managing Director of Australian Production for Village Roadshow Limited. With nine local films to distribute in the next nine months, Finney is quick to praise their diversity and strength while acknowledging the paucity of blue sky for Australian producers. Not much money is trickling down to them.

Ironically, some of the biggest successes in recent years including *The Piano, Muriel's Wedding* and *Babe* have been financed overseas – meaning the profits stay in foreign hands. This is set to continue with more big players – 20th Century Fox and Miramax – for example, getting into the act.

The lack of non-government Australian capital investment in film and television production is a perennial problem with no wide agreement on a solution. And following the election of a conservative Federal government in March, the arts community generally is jumpy about the future, fearing savage cuts into funding in line with Prime Minister John Howard's economic rationalism. But while in opposition, Howard floated the idea of tax concessions for film profits. Movieworld's Michael Lake thinks this a positive move. Tristram Miall, producer of *Strictly Ballroom* and the new *Children of the Revolution* starring Judy Davis, believes the key to a sustainable industry is keeping budgets tight and guaranteeing film-makers a share in those profits.

In past years, one of the problems has been lack of competitive distribution for Australian films, but in the last 12 months many companies previously handling only imported films have picked up local titles. Small independents such as Newvision and Globe are new, energetic players. PolyGram, the Becker Group, Fox Searchlight and even Universal International Pictures are all actively involved.

Other major developments in the last year have been the launching of pay TV in Australia, the commitment by Rupert Murdoch's Fox to build a big studio complex in Sydney (with substantial federal and state assistance) and the gearing up of a multimedia industry with international ambitions. One of the last initiatives of the outgoing Keating administration was to pump a one-off injection of $AU50 million into Australian Multimedia Enterprises, an emphatic bid to seize a large chunk of a rather uncertain future.

Peter Thompson

PETER THOMPSON is a well-known broadcaster on film in Australia.

Producers

Anthony Buckley Prods.
27A Johnston Crescent
Lane Cove 2066
Tel: 428 2344
Fax: 427 0247

Barron Films
7/85 Forrest Street
Cottesloe 6011
Tel: 9385 1551
Fax: 9385 2299

Colosimo Film Production
22 Hanover Street
Fitzroy 3065
Tel: 9417 1241*
Fax: 9416 1779

Daniel Scharf Prods.
117 Wellington Street
Windsor 3181
Tel: 9510 1666*
Fax: 9510 6757

Entertainment Media
157 Eastern Road
South Melbourne 3205
Tel: 9690 1044
Fax: 9690 1764

Film Australia
Eton Road
Lindfield
Tel: 413 8777
Fax: 416 9401

Generation Films
111 Nott Street
Port Melbourne 3207
Tel: 9646 1033*
Fax: 9646 2158

House & Moorhouse Films
117 Rouse Street
Port Melbourne 3205
Tel: 9646 4025
Fax: 9646 6336

Jan Chapman Prods.
P.O. Box 27
Potts Point 2011
Tel: 331 2666
Fax: 331 2011

Kennedy Miller
30 Orwell Street
Kings Cross 2011
Tel: 357 2322
Fax: 356 3162

Latent Image
82 Glenmore Road
Paddington 2021
Tel: 331 4155
Fax: 331 4135

Meridian Films
117 Rouse Street
Port Melbourne 3207
Tel: 9646 4025
Fax: 9646 6336*

Palm Beach Pictures
P.O. Box 409
Paddington 2021
Tel: 365 1043
Fax: 365 1380

Phillip Emanuel Prods.
24 Herbert Street
Artamon 2064
Tel: 9901 4400
Fax: 9901 4356

Smiley Films
33 Riley Street
Wooloomooloo 2011
Tel: 361 4164
Fax: 332 3427

Southern Star Entertainment
Level 10
8 West Street
North Sydney 2060
Tel: 202 8555
Fax: 9925 0849

Village Roadshow Pictures
P.O. Box 1411M
Melbourne 3001
Tel: 9667 6666
Fax: 9663 1972*

Distributors

Beyond Films
53-55 Brisbane Street
Surry Hills 2010
Tel: 281 1266
Fax: 281 9220

Dendy Films
19 Martin Place
Sydney 2000
Tel: 233 8558
Fax: 232 3841

Globe Film Co.
505/127 York Street
Sydney 2000
Tel: 261 3334
Fax: 261 3312

New Vision Films
254 Bay Street
Port Melbourne 3207
Tel: 9646 5555*
Fax: 9646 2411

TOP TEN GROSSING FILMS IN AUSTRALIA: 1995

	US$
Batman Forever	14.0
Casper	13.2
Dumb and Dumber	13.0
Forrest Gump	10.3
Apollo 13	9.8
Die Hard 3	9.4
Braveheart	9.3
Babe	8.6
While You Were Sleeping	8.3
Ace Ventura: When Nature Calls	8.2

US$=AU$1.28
Source: Motion Picture Distribs Assoc. of Australia.

Palace Entertainment Corp.
233 Whitehorse Road
Balwyn 3103
Tel: 9817 6421*
Fax: 9817 4921

REP Films
P.O. Box 130
St Leonards 2065
Tel: 438 3377
Fax: 439 1827

Roadshow Film Distributors
P.O. Box 1411M
Melbourne 3001
Tel: 9667 6666
Fax: 9663 1972
*=for Melbourne

Ronin Films
P.O. Box 1005
Civic Square ACT 2608
Tel: (06) 248 0851
Fax: (06) 249 1640

Sharmill Films
4/20 Toorak Road
South Yarra 3141*
Tel: 9826 9077
Fax: 9826 1935

Southern Star Film Sales
Level 10
8 West Street
North Sydney 2060
Tel: 202 8555
Fax: 9959 3632

Useful Addresses

Australian Film Finance Corp.
G.P.O. Box 3886
Sydney 2001
Tel: 268 2555
Fax: 264 2663

Australian Film Commission
150 William Street
Wooloomooloo 2011
Tel: 951 6444
Fax: 959 6403

BOSNIA

Rada Šešić

Before war broke out in the former Yugoslavia, Sarajevo, the capital of Bosnia and Herzegovina, was a lively and important centre of national film production. Although directors from Sarajevo had always depended on technical equipment from Belgrade and Zagreb studios, in the last ten years they had made their own distinctive contribution to film production. The Bosnian-born director Emir Kusturica produced his first three feature films in Sarajevo, and before that, documentary film-makers from Bosnia and Herzegovina had won high praise. The main characteristic of their films was the focus on social issues and on people's everyday lives. These films have won first prizes at festivals in Kraków, Leipzig and Oberhausen.

With the outbreak of war, only four out of sixteen production companies continued to work. Equipment was either destroyed or removed by its owners. The building of the Bosnian film archive was also devastated and many historically important films have disappeared. In the first months of the war, most of Sarajevo's cinemas were heavily shelled (two of them had been founded in 1913), and for almost a year there were no cinema performances in Sarajevo. At the beginning of 1993, in the Academy for Film and Theatre, the first wartime cinema was launched – named "Apollo", after the very first cinema in Sarajevo. The ticket price was equivalent in value to one cigarette. Screenings have been held using VHS tapes, mostly of American films. Later, well-organised programmes and retrospectives from film festivals (Locarno, Edinburgh) were mounted, and at the end of 1993, an international film festival was held in Sarajevo. In 1994, one cinema began regular 35mm shows, but the repertoire was not extensive.

The Time of a Return

During the same period, film production in Sarajevo achieved an astonishing quality and quantity. The main production company, Saga, a group of film-makers, which had been highly active shortly before the war, began making small, personal films about the current situation. Each documentary is a kind of confession, whether it describes how the film-maker deals with the war's circumstances or comments on the experiences of other people, from both sides of the conflict. Notable among them is **Confession of a Monster**, directed by Ademir Kenović, a leading figure within Saga. This is an account of a young Serb who confesses to the rape of numerous Muslim women. In a very simple interview format, the prisoner confesses his crimes to the camera, and also describes his view of other people, his attitude towards life, his understanding of what he has done, and his ideas about crime and punishment.

One of the strongest and most disturbing of Saga's productions is **I Burnt Legs**, made by Srdjan Vuletić. The director as narrator tells how he finds the wartime city much more satisfying than he did in peacetime, how its emptiness matches the emptiness in his soul. Vuletić was at that

Still from ECCE HOMO

time a student of film-making who worked in one of Sarajevo's hospitals, burning amputated legs, during a siege. Zlatko Lavanić, one of Bosnia's best documentary film-makers, who unfortunately passed away last winter in Sarajevo, made his most intimate film, **A Letter to My Friends**, during the war. In just five shots, the film subtly captures the state of mind of someone living in the destroyed city.

The only film-maker who has managed to continue on 35mm, Vesna Ljubić, was able, with the help of a women's organisation from Bologna, to have the negative of her new film developed in Italy and then returned to Sarajevo for editing. In **Ecce Homo**, Ms Ljubić describes the war through the true account of a small boy whose younger brother has been killed. There is no voice-over commenting on the horrors – only images, supported by fragments of religious and other music, and the harsh calling of crows.

Advertisements for the End

The Planet Sarajevo, by Šahin Šišić, was also shot on negative, but on 16mm. Almost every day for the first two years of the war, the director shot all kinds of material on Sarajevo's streets. In 1989, Šišić won the first prize for his first documentary film in Cannes. He has created a very sophisticated, silent film essay that is a meditation on the destiny of his tragic city. **Mizaldo – the End of the Theatre**, by Semezdin Mehmedinović and Benjamin Filipović, tells the story of besieged Sarajevo and the attitude of the rest of the world towards the city. It plays like a television commercial, for the images coming out of Sarajevo are also part of an international television spectacle.

The one professional film that wasn't made in Sarajevo, *To Europe with Love*, was shot in Tuzla, in central Bosnia, by the distinguished documentary maker, Mirjana Zoranović. Just before the war, she completed *They*, about patients in a mental institution, and in her next film she dealt with people who were kept in completely inhuman conditions in a mental asylum during the war. **The Death in Sarajevo**, directed by Haris Prolić, shows Susan Sontag and other artists and intellectuals visiting Sarajevo to express their opposition to the war. The film takes a close look at the history of the city, its multi-ethnicity and the presence of different religions, the horror of concentration camps, of families split apart and childhoods destroyed. The scriptwriter, who is also the film's narrator, is the respected novelist Tvrtko Kulenović.

Nenad Dizdarević, who shot **The Years of Donkeys** on the eve of the war, organised its première in Sarajevo in 1994. The post-production was done in Paris, so this apparently will be the first feature film of the new state of Bosnia and Herzegovina. Last spring, Ademir Kenović began shooting **A Perfect Circle**, the first feature that will be completely made in the state of Bosnia and Herzegovina. The scriptwriter, Abdulah Sidran, is a respected Sarajevo poet and the scriptwriter of Kusturica's first feature films. The film relates the pain of people separated from their families by the war, and is partly autobiographical for both director and scriptwriter. This will be a co-production with many European countries.

Starvation Rations

Many important films have also originated on television in Bosnia and Herzegovina. **The Crucifying Path**, by Vlatko Filipović, a well-established cinéaste for the last twenty-five years, follows two Catholic priests who take two different routes to the same mass. One reaches his destination and the other is killed.

Almost every film made in Sarajevo in the last four years is extremely low-budget, often technically inadequate and semi-professional. During the war, crews would keep working on starvation rations, on petrol supplied from military sources, and row stock from the leftovers of pre-war productions or donations from friends and from abroad. At present, there is no basis for professional film production whatsoever, so the future is entirely dependent on foreign participation.

One of the extraordinary things in the cinema history of occupied Sarajevo is the continuous publication of the film magazine *Sineast*. Even before the war, this thirty-year-old magazine was the oldest of its kind in the former Yugoslavia. The editor-in-chief, Milan Cvijanović, managed to come out with two war issues, printed in black and white and on a low quality paper. But it kept up its best pre-war traditions, with coverage of films made in Sarajevo or destroyed during the war.

Unfortunately, many film-makers passed away during the war. Hajrudin "Šiba" Krvavac was a prestigious director in the former Yugoslavia, known particularly for his war movies. Emir Šećibović, a cameraman, and Damir Šabić, a managing producer, were killed in the war. Žika Ristić, one of the pioneers of documentary film-making, died in the first year of the war, as did cameraman and film director Jan Beran.

Sarajevo's cinemathèque has recently resumed screenings and the collecting of films. Most of the films from Bosnia and Herzegovina are still held by the ex-National Cinemathèque in Belgrade. Hopefully, they will soon be making their way to the archive in Sarajevo.

RADA ŠEŠIĆ was born in the former Yugoslavia (Croatia), and studied at Sarajevo University. In 1979, she began a career in radio journalism and has broadcast mostly on film. Her articles have appeared in major national newspapers and magazines, and for three years she had her own film programme on Television Sarajevo. She currently works in the Netherlands.

Useful Addresses

Saga Production Company
Fax: +1 412 339 47 24
Sarajevo

Cinema Apolo - Obala Art Centar
Obala, Sarajevo
Tel: 387 71 664 547

Ton & Lihgt Production Company
Sarajevo
Zadarska 3
Tel: 387 71 617 302

Igman Production Company
Sarajevo
Tel: 33 14 7000 610

Kinoteka Bosne i Herzegovine
Sarajevo

Film Magazine Sineast
Strossmajerova 1
Tel: 387 71 643 645
Fax: 387 71 47 00 29\
Sarajevo

Radio Televizija Bosne i Herzegovine
Bulevar Mese Selimovica 4
Tel: 387 771 455 124
Fax: 387 71 455 104 or
1 412 339 4265
Sarajevo

BRAZIL

Luis Arbex

Brazilian cinema underwent an extraordinary boom in 1995. The new signs of life – consolidation, revitalisation, and a sharp rise in the number of films and projects – have been impressive. After some radical changes, the economy is now showing signs of greater stability. A landmark has been the implementation of laws (Rouanet-Mendonca-Audiovisual) to provide for and increase the amount of state support.

The Secretariat of Culture, municipal departments, state governments, city halls and recently TV Cultura (a state-owned company) remain the basic co-producers. The Secretariat pays 80% of the budget for approved projects: 45 films due to be released will have received an average of R$200,000 each. TV Cultura as a co-

Still from THE GIRLS, directed by Emiliano Ribeiro

producer will finance, distribute and market new films. Other commissioning sources are Riofilme, INCE, Paris Filmes, the Sundance Institute, the Rockefeller Foundation, UGC International, Lumière Films, Sony Pictures Entertainment, Columbia Tri-Star, Gaumont, Warner Bros.

The Riofilme interunion workshop and the Sundance Institute are working together to operate an intensive course for native scriptwriters. Riofilme will première ten of the most ambitious features of the season. Film-makers who emerged from the ECA and FAAP cinema schools have become part of a new and talented generation, encouraged by the cheap cost of shooting outside the big cities and inspired by American independent film-making. Among those attracting critical acclaim are some promising and versatile women directors: T. Amaral, Camurati, Solberg, Gardenberg, Lamarca, Caffé.

Forty-seven features are currently ready for release, with 41 in the post/pre-production stages. Over 38 million tickets were sold in 1995 (a rise of 37%); with its 155 million inhabitants, the country ranks first in the Latin-American market and is the eighth best market for American films. Multiplexes are booming, though statistics rank them among the worst as far as image-sound comfort is concerned. Espaço Unibanco de Cinema and CINESESC art theatres, not located in shopping centres, figure among the best with the highest audience attendances. São Paulo-Rio account for 70% of the box-office.

DR. LUIS ARBEX won a scholarship to the U.S. for post-graduate medical training and remained there for eight years. Now retired, he dedicates his time to cinema research and travelling as a movie buff.

Recent Films

CARMEN MIRANDA – BANANAS IS MY BUSINESS

Script and Dir: Helena Solberg, David Meyer. Players: Letícia Monte, Erick Barreto, Cynthia Adler. Prod: Riofilme. *Documentary.*

UM CEU DE ESTRELAS (Sky Full of Stars)

Script: Roberto Moreira, Márcio Ferrari, Jean-Claude Bernadet. Dir: Tata Amaral. Players: Alleyona Cavalli, Paulo Vespúcio Garcia, Lígia Cortez.

CINEMA DE LÁGRIMAS (Cinema of Tears)

Script: Nelson Pereira dos Santos, Sílvia Oroz. Dir: Santos. Players: Raul Cortez. André Barros, Christiane Torloni. Prod: Metavídeo/Riofilme.

CONTERRÃNEOS VELHOS DE GUERRA (Workmen)

Script and Dir: Vladimir Carvalho. Interviews: Oscar Niemeyer, Pompeu de Sousa, Brasília's workers and inhabitants. *Documentary.*

CORISCO E DADA (Corisco and Dada)

Script and Dir: Rosemberg Cariry. Players: Chico Diaz, Dira Paes, Antõnio Leite. Prod: Cariri/Riofilme.

O CORPO (The Body)

Script: José Antõnio Garcia, Alfredo Oroz. Dir: Garcia. Players: Antõnio Fagundes, Marieta Severo, Cláudia Jimenez, Carla Camurati. Prod: Embrafilme.

DEZESSEIS-ZERO-SETENTA (Sixteen-Zero-Seventy)

Script: Vinicius Mainardi, Paulo Giardini, Décio Pinto. Dir: Mainardi. Players: Antõnio Calloni, Maité Proença, Marcélia Cartaxo. Prod: Martes Filme.

ED MORT

Script: Alain Fresnot, José Rubens Chasseraux. Dir: Fresnot. Players: Paulo Betti, Cláudia Abreu, Irene Ravache. Prod: AF Cinema e Vídeo.

ENREDANDO AS PESSOAS (Intriguing the People)

Script: Eder Santos, Fernando Veloso. Dir: Santos. Players:

TOP TEN GROSSING FILMS IN BRAZIL: 1995

	Admissions
Dumb and Dumber	2,788,213
The Mask	2,432,298
Casper	2,378,922
Street Fighter	1,963,152
Batman Forever	1,820,766
The Specialist	1,751,579
Mortal Kombat	1,710,536
Interview with a Vampire	1,635,692
Pocahontas	1,502,424
Legends of the Fall	1,477,376

Compiled from a survey of Jornal do Vídeo, January 1996.

Américo Amarante, Angel de la Guardia, Gemma Belmonte. Prod: Danish Film Institute.

ERA UMA VIZ . . . (One Upon a Time . . .)

Script and Dir: Arturo Uranga. Players: Eduardo Felipe, Rodrigo Penna, Ann Cotrim. Prod: Skylight/Riofilme.

A FELICIDADE É . . . (Happiness Is . . .)

Script and Dir: José Pedro Goulart, José Roberto Rorero, Jorge Furtado, Cecílio Neto. Players: Denise Fraga, Jofre Soares, Deborah Bloch, Paulo Autran. Prod: Super Filmes.

O GUARANY (The Guarani)

Script: José Joffily Filho. Dir: Norma Bengell. Players: Tatiana Issa, Marcio Garcia, Gloria Pires. Prod: Riofilme/Pro Cultura.

FICA COMIGO (Stay With Me)

Script: Jorge Duran. Dir: Tizuka Yamasaki. Players: Antõnio Fagundes, Luciana Rigueira, Vitor Hugo. Prod: Ponto Filmes/Riofilme.

JENIPAPO (The Interview)

Script: Monique Gardenberg, Cyrus Nowrsteh. Dir: Gardenberg. Players: Henry Czerny, Patrick Bauchau, Marília Pera. Prod: Dieto Prods./Riofilme.

O JUDEU (The Jew)

Script and Dir: Tom Azulay. Players: Felipe Pinheiro, Dina Sfat, José Lewgoy. Prod: Portugal/Brasil.

KENOMA

Script: Eliane Caffé, Luis Alberto de Abreu. Dir: Caffé. Players: José Wilker, José Dumont, Leonardo Vilar. Prod: AF Cinema e Vídeo.

O MANDARIM (The Mandarin)

Script and Dir: Júlio Bressane. Players: Fernando Eiras, Giulia Gam, Gal Costa. Prod: Movie Track/Riofilme.

AS MENINAS (The Girls)

Script and Dir: Emiliano Ribeiro. Players: Drica Moraes, Cláudia Liz, Adriana Esteves. Prod: Sofia Carvalhosa Cinematográfica/ Superfilmes.

MENINO MALUQUINHO (The Nutty, Nutty Boy)

Script: Helvécio Ratton, Maria Gessy, Alcione Araujo. Dir: Ratton. Players: Samuel Costa, Patrícia Pillar, Roberto Bomtempo. Prod: Grupo Novo de Cinema/Riofilme.

NO RIO DAS AMAZONAS (On the River of the Amazons)

Script: Ricardo Dias, Júlio Rodrigues. Dir: Dias. With: Paulo Vanzolini. Prod: Cinematográfica Superfilmes/Pro Cultura.

O QU4TRILHO

Script: Leopoldo Serran. Dir: Fábio Barreto. Players: Glória Pires, Patricia Pillar, Alexandre Paternost, Bruno Campos. Prod: Audiovisual/Ministério da Cultura/FINEP.

QUEM MATOU PIXOTE? (Who Killed Pixote?)

Script: José Joffily, Jorge Duran, Paulo Halm. Dir: Joffily. Players: Cassiano Carneiro, Luciana Rigueira, Joanna Fomm. Prod: Coevos Filme/Pro Cultura.

TERRA ESTRANGEIRA (Foreign Land)

Script: Walter Salles Jr, Daniela Thomas, Marcos Bernstein, Millor Fernandes. Dir: Salles, Thomas. Players: Fernanda Torres, Fernando Alves Pint, Tcheky Karyo. Prod: Video Filmes/Riofilme.

TODOS OS CORAÇÕES DO MUNDO (Two Billion Hearts)

Text: Murillo Salles, George

Vecsey, Emanuel Castro. Dir: Salles. Prod: STM/ISL/Worldwide. *Documentary.*

Producers/ Distributors

AF Cinema e Vídeo Ltda
Rua Isabel de Castela
237 - Vila Beatriz
São Paulo
CEP: 05445-010
Tel: (011) 815 6779
Fax: (011) 212 6231

Alvorada
Av. Ipiranga
318 - São Paulo
Tel: (011) 288 8226
Fax: (011) 239 3298

Casa de Promoção do Filme e Vídeo
Rua Padre Antõnio dos Santos
1141 - São Paulo
CEP: 045-63013
Tel: (011) 240 7232
Fax: (115) 349141

Cinematográfica Polifilmes Ltda
Rua do Triunfo
175 - São Paulo
CEP: 012-12010
Tel: (011) 233 8481
Fax: (011) 220 9694

Columbia TriStar Do Brasil
Rua do Triunfo
134/5' - São Paulo
CEP: 012-12903
Tel: (011) 200 4022
Fax: (011) 222 7423

CONSÓRCIO SEVERIANO RIBEIRO E MARCONDES
Marco Aurélio Marcondes
Praça Mahatma Ghandi
2/5' Rio de Janeiro
CEP: 20081 100
Tel: (021) 210 2486
Fax: (021) 220 7499

Espaço Unibanco de Cinema
Rua Augusta
1475 - São Paulo
Tel: (011) 288 6780

The Finishing House
Rua Abolição
165 - São Paulo
CEP: 013-19010
Tel: 5511 605 5699
Fax: 5511 605 7677

Fox Filmes-Warner Bros do Brasil
Calçada dos Cravos
141 - Centro Comercial Alphaville - Barueri - São Paulo
CEP: 06453-000
Tel: (011) 725 599
Fax: (011) 725 0767

Grupo Mundial Filmes
Av. Vereador José Diniz
1548 - Campo Belo - São Paulo
CEP: 04604-002
Tel: 55-11 536 0677
Fax: 55-11 542 6677

Lígia Empresa Cinematográfica Sul
Av. São João
1588 - São Paulo
Tel: (011) 220 6299
Fax: (011) 220 6123

Look Filmes
c/o Denise Jancar
Rua Felix Sousa
71 - Campo Belo
São Paulo
CEP: 046-12080
Tel: (011) 536 9366
Fax: (011) 5561 2121

Lumiere Latin America
Anna Luiza Muller
Rua México
11/11' Rio de Janeiro
CEP: 20006-900
Tel: (55 21) 220 1200
Fax: (55 21) 240 8142

Pandora (C.A.C.AV.)
Rua Nebraska
395 - São Paulo
CEP: 045-60010
Tel: (011) 220 6299
Fax: (011) 530 0839

Paris Filmes
Av. Pacaembu
1702 - São Paulo
Tel: (011) 864 3155
Fax: (011) 872 4498

Playarte Pictures/Playarte Home Video
Av. República do Líbano
215 - São Paulo
CEP: 045-02300
Tel: (011) 575 6996
Fax: (011) 570 0905

PolyGram Film International
Av. Angélica
2318/1' - São Paulo
CEP: 01228-200
Tel: (55 11) 255 9911
Fax: (55 11) 255 3173

São Paulo Production Bureau
Abraham Sochaczewski
Av. Nhandu
754 - São Paulo
CEP: 040-59002
Tel: (558) 32530
Fax: (558) 59271

Sewell Films International
Tel: (212) 053128
Fax: (55 222) 050477

Skylight
Rua Assunçáo
49 - Rio de Janeiro
CEP: 20-000
Fax: (55 21) 552 7048

Top Cinematográfica Gipsy/Top Tape
Fabiana Barrionovo
Av. Grancisco Matarazzo
404 - 6' Água Branca
CEP: 050-01100 - São Paulo
Tel: (011) 826 3066
Fax: (011) 826 6108

United International Pictures
Dora Martins Navarro
Av. Paulista
2444/9=s/91
CEP: (257) 0433 - São Paulo
Tel: (013) 10300
Fax: (214) 8980

Zohar Cinema e Comunicação Ltda
Rua Voluntários da Pátria
455 Botafogo - Rio de Janeiro
CEP: 222-70 000
Tel: (552) 1537 7552
Fax: (552) 1537 768

Useful Addresses

A.N.A.C.
Assocoação Nacional de Cultura Cinematográfica
Aldo Tadeu Macedo de Castro
Rua Pedroso Xavier
238 - São Paulo
CEP: 32020
Tel: (011) 858 4658

Brasil Filmes
Wilson Rodrigues Ferreira
Av. Paulista
2644/12' - São Paulo
CEP: 01310-300
Tel: (011) 258 2094
Fax: (011) 258 2136

Ministério da Cultura
Secretaria Para o Desenvolvimento Audio Visual
Esplanada dos Ministérios
Blobo B/3' - Brasília - DF - 70068
Tel: (5561) 226 6299
Fax: (5561) 321 7738

Post Point
Rua Fiandeiras
962 - São Paulo
CEP: 04545-006
Tel/Fax: (55 11) 822 2983

Pro Cultura
Rua Cardoso de Almeida
1644 - São Paulo
CEP: 050-13 001
Tel: 262 2124
Fax: (011) 872 6846

Cinemateca Brasileira - Ministério da Cultura
Largo Senador Raul Cardoso
207 - São Paulo
CEP: 040-21070
Tel/Fax: (011) 572 4061

Loc. All
Rua França Pinto
1365 - São Paulo
CEP: 040-16035
Tel/Fax: (55 11) 822 2983

Movie Club
Rua do Triunfo
134/5' - São Paulo
CEP: 012-12010
Tel: (011) 200 4022
Fax: (011) 222 7423

BULGARIA

Ivan Stoyanovich

It will not come as news to the informed international public that during 1995 and 1996 so far, Bulgarian economic and social development reached an all-time low. Conspicuously enough, this coincided with the return to power of the former Communist régime. A general impoverishment; widespread criminal activity; feelings of insecurity among the general public; collapse of the banking system – no wonder Western investors have lost interest in Bulgaria, leaving the way open for politically motivated Russian economic pressure. And no wonder Bulgaria has dropped to the bottom in the list of former Communist countries aspiring to join the advanced Western countries.

A slump in artistic and cultural activities was only to be expected in such circumstances, especially in the costly business of film-making. The National Film Centre makes brave efforts to secure additional funds from international sources, such as Eurimages and CNC (Centre National de Cinéma). The Association of Film Producers and individual film directors have followed suit in order to fund their projects. To a certain extent, television has helped film-makers. Yet, the state-owned National Television has been affected by the overall financial crisis, while the existing private TV channels and the advent of nationwide private TV are hindered, not so much by lack of finance as by administrative barriers set up by the present government, suspicious of independent media sources.

In the Realm of the Absurd

So film-makers' efforts have been directed towards entering into co-production with foreign partners on projects likely to ensure a return on investment. And it is hoped that the professional skills and services offered by the technologically well-equipped Boyana Film Centre, at competitive prices, will attract the participation of foreign companies.

Still from ALL UP FROM ZERO, directed by Ivan Pavlov

The more significant feature films already completed include a joint production of Bulgaria, Hungary and France, **The Black Swallow** (*Chernata Lyastovitza*), a study of the emotional world of the gypsies, and the Bulgarian-French production, **The Thundering Stones** (*Tarkalyachty se kamani*), a film-confession by Ivan Cherkelov revealing the author's addiction to Eastern philosophies. The light-hearted comedy **14 Kisses** (*Chetirinadeset tzeluvki*), an all-Bulgarian production by Plamen Maslarov, is already completed, as well as **All Up from Zero** (*Vsichko ot nulata*) by Ivan Pavlov, a film romance with philosophical undertones. A controversial but interesting experiment in the realm of the absurd, made with French financial backing and already shown to the public, is **Tap-Tap** (*Track-track*) by Ilia Kostov.

Talking with Birds (*Razgovor s ptitzi*), a co-production with Russia directed by Rumyana Petkova, and **Late Full Moon** (*Zakasnyala luna*), directed by Eduard Zahariev, are two works combining psychological subtlety with visual richness. The talented young film director Lyudmil Todorov has finished shooting **Emily's Friends** (*Priyatelkite na Emilia*), a Bulgarian-Swiss-French production looking at the life and problems of young people in a complicated world. A co-production of France, Italy, Belgium and Bulgaria, **Mordbureau** (*Mordbyuro*) is a light-hearted crime story concocted by Marko Stoychev.

IVAN STOYANOVICH has been a film critic and publicist since 1966. For some thirty years, he has been Editor-in-Chief of *Bulgarian Film* magazine and then of *Intercine* magazine, as well as Executive Director of Bulgarian National TV (BNT) and Managing Director of the Animation Film Studio, Sofia. He is the author of several books and numerous articles on film and culture.

Still from THE BLACK SWALLOW

TOP TEN GROSSING FILMS IN BULGARIA: 1995

- Desperado
- Braveheart
- Die Hard 3
- Batman Forever
- Legends of the Fall
- Forrest Gump
- The Specialist
- The Mask
- Pulp Fiction
- Dumb and Dumber

Forthcoming Films

ZAKASNYALO PALNOLUNIE (Late Full Moon)

Dir: Eduard Zahariev. Prod: Sinis MM.

PRIYATELKITE NA EMILIA (Emily's Friends)

Dir: Lyudmil Todorov. Prod: Bulgaria, France.

MORDBYURO (Mordbureau)

Executive Prod: Marko Stoychev. Prod: France, Italy, Belgium, Bulgaria.

SULAMIT

Dir: Hristo Hristov. Prod: Slaval and Medius Ltd.

HOLERA PO VREME NA CHUMA (Cholera in the Time of Plague)

Dir: Rangel Valchanov. Prod: Rangel Valchanov.

Useful Addresses

National Film Centre
2a Dondukov Blvd
Sofia 1000
Tel: +(359 2) 883831
Fax: +(359 2) 873626

Bulgarian National Film Library
36 Gurko Street
Sofia 1000
Tel/Fax: +(359 2) 876004

Union of Bulgarian Film-Makers
37 Exarh Josif Street
Tel: +(359 2) 873076, 871519, 882860
Fax: +(359 2) 879530

Bulgarian National Television
29 San Stefano Street
Sofia 1000
Tel: +(359 2) 43481*
International Relations:
Fax: +(359 2) 871871

Boyana Film Company
Kinocentre Boyana
Sofia 1616
Tel: +(359 2) 58131*, 596065, 597159
Fax: +(359 2) 593115

Animation Film Studio, Sofia
Kinocentre Boyana
Sofia 1616
Tel: +(359 2) 595061, 671126
Fax: +(359 2) 597165

Vreme Film Studio
67 Dondukov Blvd
Sofia 1000
Tel: +(359 2) 442823
Fax: +(359 2) 442453

Bulgarsko Video
60 Samokov Blvd
Sofia 1113
Tel: + (359 2) 659272
Fax: +(359 2) 659186

Bulgarian Film Producers Association
67 Dondukov Blvd
Sofia 1000
Tel: + (359 2) 440247, 447226, 442823
Fax: +(359 2) 442453

Bulgarian Private Film Distributors Association
10 Macedonia Blvd
Sofia 1000
Tel: + (359 2) 519288
Fax: +(359 2) 576121

Bulgarian Film & Video Association
127 Rakovska Street
Sofia 1000
Tel: +(359 2) 885028

Video Distribution Association
10 Dunav Street
Sofia 1000
Tel/Fax: +(359 2) 872189

*** telephone exchange operator**

Continued from page 60

out that Neruda was in fact Chilean. Bacalov shrugs off the charge, responding that 'it could hardly have been otherwise, given my origins.' He could also have added that the music features the breathy tones of an Andean flute, an instrument associated rather more with Chile than with Argentina. Other instruments prominently featured include violin, guitar and the archetypally Italian mandolin. But the dominant tone of the score, whose texture remains sunlit and translucent though tinged with melancholy, is set by the use of the bandoneon, an Argentinian cousin of the accordion with a built-in wobble. Radford and Troisi, says Bacalov, 'wanted a delicate film and the music had to follow that line.' I felt that only the bandoneon could convey a sense of great endurance and the precariousness of life.'

Boost for Italian Industry

Three weeks after receiving the Oscar for *Il Postino* Bacalov picked up another award at the BAFTA ceremony in London, the Anthony Asquith Award for Achievement in Film Music. This was on top of two Italian prizes already received: the Nastro d'Argento (Silver Riband) and Globo d'Oro for 1995. While Bacalov confesses himself 'moved and astonished' by the widespread enthusiasm aroused by the film, he's delighted at the boost it's given the film industry of his adopted country. 'It's a success which will also be good for Italy, for Italian cinema, which needs an injection of courage and confidence if it's to continue to fight off the big boys.' Hollywood offers will surely have already arrived, and will continue to do so. But for the time being Bacalov seems intent on remaining in Italy and writing scores for Italian films. It is, he would no doubt observe, what Massimo Troisi would have wanted.

Philip Kemp

Luis Bacalov *photo: CAM s.r.l.*

CANADA

Gerald Pratley

Looking back over the past year in film, there seem to have been more trade forums, seminars, conferences, lectures, speeches, competitions and festivals than there were feature-length films made and shown. Not to forget, of course, the usual additions to government reports on the future of 'our industry' and the many agencies involved in the funding and production of features, documentaries, TV films and programmes.

Breezing through the muddle created by subsidies and co-productions are the American companies who dominate the streets of Toronto and Vancouver, with their massive trailers and equipment taking advantage of the low-value Canadian dollar to film on location. In recent years, our producers, aided and abetted by the media, have joked about being Canada's "Hollywood North". And now it has become a reality. The list of American films and TV programmes made here last year alone would fill this report. Only those moviegoers who stay through the mile-long credits at the end of every film to read the small print would know this, however. The settings are made to appear American because, naturally, the stories for the most part are set in the U.S.

All this work carried out by studios and independents pleases the provincial commissioners no end, and gives them the figures to prove to the politicians that being an appendage of L.A. benefits the Canadian economy. And it probably does; the trade and the governments are coming to believe, quietly of course, that it is much better not to *spend* money making films but rather to *make* money by being Hollywood's North.

Northern Lights

The one bright spot has been the release in specialised cinemas of those domestic films that did manage to find funding from governmental and private sponsorship. Such unlikely box-office contenders as Peter Mettler's **Northern Lights**, Jeremy Podeswa's **The Eclipse,** Holly Dale's **Blood and Donuts**, John Pozer's **The Michelle Apartments** and Bruce MacDonald's **Dance Me Outside** have come and gone, fortunate even to have been considered worthy of the cost of opening a new picture. Robert LePage's **The Confessional** did not do as well in Toronto as in Montréal, even though the reviews were unanimously positive. **Margaret's Museum** was supported with an exhausting cross-country opening tour by Helena Bonham Carter, which dramatically increased the audience for this, at first, problematic picture.

The long-awaited Juneau Report: "Making Our Voices Heard: Canadian Broadcasting and Film for the 21st Century" finally appeared and took up several pages in the daily papers and many hours of special reporting on radio and TV. The committee of three, Pierre Juneau (ex-CBC), Peter Herrndorf (TVO) and Catherine Murray (Simon Fraser University), brought forth some provocative statements and unlikely proposals for fulfilling the Report's subtitle.

On Telefilm, it said the agency spends and loses too much money on commercial pictures rather than on quality films that would encourage "national cinema". On the CBC, it rightly said that the Corporation was preoccupied with commercial and competitive concerns and had drifted away from the true purpose of a public broadcaster. The public already pays $900m for the CBC budget, but the Report suggests more: a 7.5 percent communications tax. The public would have none of it.

On the National Film Board, the Report recommends the selling of its Montréal headquarters and studio, and shutting down its distribution centres in favour of concentrating entirely on television, with its video cassettes being placed in regular libraries. After the announcements were over and the indignation had died down, the national government made sweeping budget cuts to these three agencies and others, and the report itself, costing millions naturally, is shelved and forgotten.

Southern Comfort

Overall, it has become obvious that our feature and animated film companies are now concentrating all their efforts on making motion pictures and TV programmes with American partners for the American market. This means no discernible Canadian identification – even though Canadian film-makers and artists are sometimes involved, they remain mostly unknown. The occasional programme, such as **Due South**, succeeds because of its novelty value – it involves a red-coated Mountie in the U.S. The fact that the RCMP wear their ceremonial uniforms only for tourists and on state occasions, and would not be permitted to operate in the U.S. if they did, is blissfully ignored.

The Alliance company has grown enormous on Telefilm's funds – with Atlantis, Norstar, Astral, Allegro, Cinar and others not far behind. And all dominate the industry with their American-styled and tailored productions. A few feature films, such as **Lives of Girls and Women**, and the long-running TV series, **Anne of Green Gables**, prove to be welcome exceptions. Is this the only way to survive as a result of living next to a giant whose own art and entertainment blankets the country without let-up? How are 100 U.S. TV channels to be resisted? Does anyone want to? Will making audiences more American than we already are be the end result of having spent millions of taxpayers' money in financing Telefilm and the provincial agencies? No one seems to care.

American films are our films, their stars

Still from THE WAR BETWEEN US *photo: Greg Corp/Atlantis Films/Troika Films*

and their television programmes are ours too. The only dents in the surface are Canadian authors and their books and plays, proving perhaps that the word is still as mighty as the sword, if not the picture; British TV programmes on the specialised networks; and Québec's world of film, TV, popular music, concerts and theatre, which remains firmly indigenous and frequently profitable. If this province can make art and entertainment pay on the basis of its subsidies, and create stars and popular performers, why not the rest of the country? The answer may be obvious but the reasons remain less so. And so, American we have become and American we shall remain – on 97% of the country's cinema and TV screens.

GERALD PRATLEY is a distinguished Canadian film historian, teacher and broadcaster. He founded the Ontario Film Institute and has been awarded the Order of Canada.

Recent and Forthcoming Films

BLOOD & DONUTS

Script: Andrew Rai Berzins. Dir: Holly Dale. Players: Gordon Currie, Justin Louis, Helene Clarkson, Fiona Reid, Frank Moore, Hadley Kay, J. Winston Carroll, David Cronenberg. Prod: Dabab Films. 89 mins.

In documentary film-maker Holly Dale's first fiction film, a vampire awakened after a century of sleep by a golf ball finds himself at a loss in the present day. Described as a dark comedy, this limps from one banality to the next.

CURTIS'S CHARM

Script and Dir: John L'Ecuyer, based on the short story by Jim Carroll. Players: Maurice Dean Wint, Callum Keith Rennie, Rachael Crawford, Barbara Barnes-Hopkins, Aaron Tager. Prod: Rapid Dog Films. 80 mins.

The first feature of film student John L'Ecuyer is set in a city slum and concerns two drug addicts, one of whom is possessed by hallucinations and voodoo spells. Endorsed by Atom Egoyan and Patricia Rozema, this low-budget effort shows considerable filmic talent but the events and behaviour it depicts are likely to leave most audiences baffled.

The Leading Worldwide Production Guide

1997 edition published in April.
Separate UK and USA editions also available.

Kemps Film, TV & Video Handbook provides you with complete coverage of the world's major markets, and contains essential information about all stages of the production process.

Invaluable for both International and National information
40,000 entries   53 countries   200 classifications

To order, contact Sara Tyler:
Tel: +44 (0) 171 637 3663 Fax: +44 (0) 171 580 5559

THE DARLING FAMILY

Script: Linda Griffiths, based on her play. Dir: Alan Zweig. Players: Linda Griffiths, Alan Williams. Prod: Darling Family. 86 mins.

An intelligent portrait of a once-loving couple confronted by an unwanted pregnancy who finally face themselves and come to realise how much they have changed. This lively filmed play is thoughtful and perceptive and convincingly played out.

L'ENFANT D'EAU (Water Child)

Script: Claire Wojas. Dir: Robert Menard. Players: David LaHaye, Marie-France Monette. Prod: Max Films. 103 mins.

A mentally retarded man in his 20s and a 12-year-old girl are stranded on a desert island after their tourist plane crashes. The desert island paradise scenario of misunderstandings and the abandonment of society's moral conventions follows – in this instance, depicted with sensitivity and understanding.

HOUSE

Script: Laurie Lynd, Daniel MacIvor. Dir: Lynd. Players: Daniel MacIvor, Patricia Collins, Stephen Ouimette. Prod: Household Entertainment. 85 mins.

Three very good actors attempt courageously but fruitlessly to make something out of this tangled script, divided into ten vignettes, set in a church in which a disturbed young man spews out the violent and paranoid story of his life.

THE LAST SUPPER

Script and Dir: Cynthia Roberts (with Hillar Liitoja, Greg Klymkiw, based on the play by Liitoja). Players: Ken McDougall, Jack Nicholsen, Daniel MacIvor. Prod: Yulyan Motion Pictures. 96 mins.

A brilliant dancer, dying of AIDS and confined to bed, choreographs and performs his ultimate work – his death. This is a filmed play set in a bedroom of shadows, imaginatively treated and brave in its presentation of euthanasia.

LISTE NOIRE (Black List)

Script: Sylvain Guy. Dir: Jean-Marc Vallee. Players: Michel Cote, Genevieve Brouillette, Gilbert Sicotte, Sylvie Bourque, André Champagne. Prod: GPA Films. 90 mins.

A cheap, violent and nasty knock-off of a Hollywood political corruption melodrama involving the plots and prostitutes in the lives of Québec's Supreme Court judges.

LIVE BAIT

Script and Dir: Bruce Sweeney. Players: Tom Scholte, Kevin McNulty, Babz Chula, David Lovgren, Micki Maunsell, Jay Brazeau, Laara Sadiq. Prod: Cypher Films. 84 mins.

A charming and original picture from a young Vancouver film-maker who studied with Mike Leigh; this is a tale of summer life in the well-to-do suburbs, concerning a young man who gets nowhere with the girls of his age, but is taught about love and sex by an older woman. The title, unfortunately, is misleading.

THE MICHELLE APARTMENTS

Script: Ross Weber. Dir: John Pozer. Players: Henry Czerny, Mary Elizabeth Rubens, Daniel Kash, Peter Outerbridge, Nancy Beatty, David Calderisi, Ian D. Clark. Prod: Arto-Pelli MP Inc.

John Pozer *(The Grocer's Wife)* returns four years later with a macabre comedy fantasy about a government auditor (a wasted Henry Czerny) in an imaginary industrial town sent to investigate a corrupt chemical company.

ONCE IN A BLUE MOON

Script and Dir: Philip Spink. Players: Mike MacDonald, Cheryl Wilson, Cody Serpa, Simon Baker, Deanna Milligan. Prod: Blue Moon Films. 93 mins.

A first feature from a director who has specialised in TV films for children, this family story, set in Canada's Centennial Year of 1967, concerns the usual ups and downs between parents and children. Principally, Peter and Sam decide to build a rocket and make it fly. Everyone in the cast works hard to make this domestic world likeable but it lacks charm and depth.

SKIN DEEP

Script: Midi Ondera, Barbara O'Kelly. Dir: Ondera. Players: Natsuko Ohama, Keram Malicki-Sanchez, Dana Brooks, Melanie Nicholls-King, David Crean. Prod: Daruma Pictures. 85 mins.

In this slight and self-indulgent first feature, audiences may experience the pleasure-pain of being tattooed, if they so desire, and join in the pleasure-pain relationships of lesbian love.

THE SUBURBANATORS

Script and Dir: Gary Burns. Players: Joel McNichol, Stephen Spender, Stewart Burdett, Jacob Banigan, Jihad Traya, Ahmad Taha, Rogy Masri. Prod: Burns/Red Devil Films. 87 mins.

Bored youth in Calgary seek out 'something to do' in this largely improvised and uninteresting first feature set in cars, homes and city streets. Only one brief incident, in which a youth describes his efforts to obtain a job, is genuinely funny.

THE WAR BETWEEN US

Script: Sharon Gibbon. Dir: Anne Wheeler. Players: Shannon Lawson, Mieko Ouchi, Robert Wisden, Ian Tracey, Juno Ruddell, Edmond Kata, Robert Ito. Prod: Atlantis Films. 96 mins.

Taking up the controversy over the internment of Japanese residents living on the West Coast in WWII, Anne Wheeler's understanding, humanistic and well-reasoned chronicle of this troubling period is seen through the life of the uprooted Kawashima family. Eventually, it becomes the story of the friendship between two women, the symbol of better times ahead. Wheeler, who is without doubt the most distinguished film-maker at work today outside Québec, has again created a masterpiece of significant social drama – a fitting addition to her two previous and unforgettable wartime films, *A War Story* and *Bye Bye Blues*.

ZIGRAIL

Script: André Turpin, Sophie Leblond, Sylvain Bellmare. Dir. and Photo: Turpin. Players: Andre Charlebois, Dorothee Berryman, Arianne Cordeau, Sonia

Vigneault, Armand Turpin. Prod: Les Productions Jeux d'Ombres. 78 mins.

A 20-ish 'don't know what to do with my life' GenXer decides to travel from Montréal to Istanbul on a motorcycle to meet up with his pregnant girl friend. Not a journey many audiences will find illuminating.

Funding Agencies

Téléfilm Canada
Tour de la Banque Nationale
600 rue de la Gauchetière ouest
14 étage
Montréal, Qué. H3B 4L8
Tel: (514) 283-6363
Fax: (514) 283-8212
Telex: 055-60998
Budget: $M146.4

Ontario Film Development Corporation
175 Bloor St. E.
North Tower, Ste. 300
Toronto, Ont. M4W 3R8
Tel: (416) 314-6858
Fax: (416) 314-6876
Budget: $M15

Société de developpement des entreprises culturelles (SODEC)
1755 boul. René Lévesque est, bur.200
Montréal. Qué. H2K 4P6
Tel: (514) 873-7768
Fax: (514) 873-4388
Budget: $M14.5

British Columbia Film Fund
2225 W. Broadway
Vancouver, B.C. V6K 2E4
Tel: (604) 736-7997
Fax: (604) 736-7920
Budget: $M5

Production, Funding & Distribution

The National Film Board of Canada
Head Office
179 Rideau St.
Ottawa, Ont. K1A 0M9
and
3155 Côte de Liesse Rd.
Ville Saint-Laurent, Qué. H4N 2N4
Postal address:
P.O. Box 6100, Stn. Centre-Ville
Montréal, Qué. H3C 3H5
Tel: (514) 283-9246
Fax: (514) 283-8971
Budget: $M80

Distributors

Allegro Films Distribution Inc.
2187 rue Larivière
Montréal, Qué. H2K 1P5
Tel: (514) 529-0320
Fax: (514) 529-0328

Alliance Releasing
920 Yonge St., Ste. 400
Toronto, Ont. M4W 3C7
Tel: (416) 967-1174
Fax: (416) 967-4358
5 Place Ville Marie, Ste. 1435
Montréal, QC H3B 2G2
Tel: (515) 878-2282
Fax: (514) 878-2419

Alliance International
18 rue Bayard
Place François 1er
75008 Paris, France
Tel: 011 331-53 83 18 00
Fax: 011 331-53 83 18 01
301 North Canon Dr., Ste. 321
Beverly Hills, CA 9-210, U.S.A.
Tel: (310) 275-5501
Fax: (310) 275-5502

Astral Distribution Group
33 Yonge St., Ste. 1020
Toronto, Ont. M5E 1S9
Tel: (416) 956-2000
Fax: (416) 956-2020
Maison Astral
2100 rue Sainte-Catherine ouest, bur. 900
Montréal, Qué. H3H 2T3
Tel: (514) 939-5000
Fax: (514) 939-1515

Atlantis Releasing Inc.
Cinevillage
65 Heward Ave.
Toronto, Ont. M4M 2T5
Tel: (416) 462-0246
Fax: (416) 462-0254

Audio Cine Film/Lapointe Library
8462 Sherbrooke East
Montréal, Qué. H1L 1B2
Tel: (514) 493-8887
Fax: (514) 493-9058

Canadian Film-makers' Distribution Centre
37 Hanna Ave., Ste. 220
Toronto, Ont. M6K 1W8
Tel: (416) 588-0725
Fax: (416) 588-7956

CBC International Sales & Co-productions
250 Front St. West
Toronto, Ont., M5V 3G5
Tel: (416) 205-3500
Fax: (416) 205-3482

CFP Distribution Inc.
2 Bloor St. W., Ste. 1901
Toronto, Ont. M4W 3E2
Tel: (416) 944-0104
Fax: (416) 944-2212
8275 Mayrand
Montréal, Qué. H4P 2C8
Tel: (514) 342-2340
Fax: (514) 342-1922

Cinar Films Inc.
1055 boul. René-Lévesque Est
Montréal, Qué. H2L 4S5
Tel: (514) 843-7070
Fax: (514) 843-7080

Cinéma Esperança International Inc.
96 Spadina Ave., Ste. 301
Toronto, Ont. M5V 2J6
Tel: (416) 703-5000
Fax: (416) 703-5002

Cineplex Odeon Films Canada
1303 Yonge St.
Toronto, Ont. M4T 2Y9
Tel: (416) 323-6600
Fax: (416) 323-6711

Creative Exposure
2236 Queen St. E.
Toronto, Ont. M4E 1G2
Tel: (416) 690-0775
Fax: (416) 690-0755

Ellis Enterprises
1231 Yonge St., Ste. 201
Toronto, Ont. M4T 2T8
Tel: (416) 924-2186
Fax: (416) 924-6115

Films Transit Inc.
402 est rue Notre-Dame
Montréal, Qué. H2Y 1C8
Tel: (514) 844-3358
Fax: (416) 844-7298

Jasmine Tea Films Inc.
83 Rameau Dr., Unit 5
Willowdale, Ont. M2H 1T6
Tel: (416) 493-3584
Fax: (416) 493-9117

Malofilm Distribution Inc.
3575 boul. St-Laurent, bur. 650
Montréal, Qué. H2X 2T7
Tel: (514) 844-4555
Fax: (514) 844-1471
2221 Yonge St., Ste. 400
Toronto, Ont. M4S 2B4
Tel: (416) 480-0453
Fax: (416) 480-0501

Norstar Releasing
86 Bloor St. W., 4th Fl.
Toronto, Ont. M5S 1M5
Tel: (416) 961-6278
Fax: (416) 961-5608

Paragon-International
119 Spadina Ave., Ste. 900
Toronto, Ont. M5V 2L1
Tel: (416) 595-6300
Fax: (416) 977-0489

Prima Film Inc.
1435 Bleury, Ste. 507
Montréal, Qué. H3A 2H7
Tel: (514) 289-0837
Fax: (514) 289-0907

Les Productions la Fête Inc.
225 est rue Roy, Ste. 203
Montréal, Qué. H2W 1M5
Tel: (514) 848-0417
Fax: (514) 848-0064

Société de Distribution Cinéma Libre Inc.
4067 boul. St-Laurent, bur. 403
Montréal, Qué. H2W 1Y7
Tel: (514) 849-7888
Fax: (514) 849-1231

Sullivan Entertainment Inc.
110 Davenport Rd.
Toronto, Ont. M5R 3R3
Tel: (416) 921-7177
Fax: (416) 921-7538

THA Media Distributors
307-1200 West Pender
Vancouver, B.C. V6E 2S9
Tel: (604) 687-4215
Fax: (604) 688-8349
E-mail: thamedia@wimsey.com

Winnipeg Film Group Distribution Office
304-100 Arthur St.
Winnipeg, Man. R3B 1H3
Tel: (204) 942-6795
Fax: (204) 942-6799

CHILE

Hans Ehrmann

There are half a dozen lotteries in Chile benefiting several good causes but, unlike Britain, the arts and cinema don't share in these pennies from heaven. On the other hand, a law supporting local cinema is slowly making its way through a quagmire of commissions and sub-commissions and may eventually find its way to Congress.

National Television took a more concrete step in the direction of co-financing movies, although the results of its initial experience in this field were mixed. **Red Point** *(Punto Rojo)*, a made-for-TV feature, won a satisfactory 16.8 rating, thanks largely to strong promotion and director Alberto Daiber's previous popularity as a host of TV magazine shows. But the reviews were quite the opposite.

The film deals with a saxophone player who is arrested for a minor drugs offence and lands in jail. He talks too much about his well-off girlfriend, who shortly afterwards is kidnapped by one of his cellmates. Apart from a couple of interesting scenes with minor characters, the film suffered from an inconsistent and poorly developed script and inadequate casting of the principals which, added to Daiber's inexperience with actors, led to rather stilted performances.

A Dark World

Tatiana Gaviola's **My Last Man** *(Mi último hombre)*, another first film, also received some seed money from TV but was a quite different experience. Reviews were mixed and the box-office tepid, but Gaviola is a film-maker to watch. The film takes place in an unidentified country in a dark, post-apocalyptic world where Florencia, a television reporter, becomes involved with

Claudia di Girolamo in MY LAST MAN

one of the two lone survivors of a revolutionary terrorist group. The film's strength lies in its atmosphere, but its weakness is a story that lacks sufficient detail both as narrative and as metaphor.

After two years in which film audiences remained even, putting an apparent stop to the decline of previous years, 1995 saw a drop of 6.2%. As usual, about a third of the total audience saw their films on Wednesdays, with a 50% discount on the regular ticket price of US$6.10 (uptown) and US$4.90 (downtown). Conate's monopoly as an exhibitor is still unchallenged but, after considerable procrastination, work has finally begun on the two Santiago multiplexes announced last year by Sumner Redstone's National Amusements. In a country with a total of one hundred screens, twenty more could make a difference. Besides, Conate is transforming the Gran Palace, the largest of Santiago's downtown cinemas, into a four-screen multi, and there are as yet unsubstantiated rumours of more screens at other shopping centres, both in the capital and the provinces.

These new houses don't always increase actual audiences. Last year, the U.S. chain Cinemark, in a joint venture with Conate, inaugurated a seven-screen multiplex in Concepción, a city in the south of Chile, but audiences did not increase as expected. These remained much the same, with people simply shifting their allegiance to the new cinemas. On the other hand, an earlier Cinemark-Conate experience with five screens at a shopping centre in a neighbourhood without cinemas increased Santiago audiences by over 5%.

A Foreign Country

The most unusual event this year – probably due to the cinema centenary celebration – was the publication of three film books. The best was *A Hundred Keys to Cinema's Hundred Years* (Editorial Planeta) by critics Ascanio Cavallo and Antonio Martinez. A well-written and opinionated book, it inevitably led to controversy among film buffs. This was not the case with Julio López Navarro's *The Best Alltime Films* (Editorial Pantalla Grande), which was aimed at general audiences and

TOP TEN GROSSING FILMS IN CHILE: 1995

	Admissions
The Mask	282,000
Pocahontas	226,000
Batman Forever	179,000
Casper	144,000
Die Hard 3	138,000
Pulp Fiction	121,000
Disclosure	116,000
Dumb and Dumber	116,000
101 Dalmatians (reissue)	91,000
Braveheart	86,000

(Based on number of spectators in Santiago. Does not include a further 25,000 for *Braveheart* when same was reissued at Oscar time in 1996.)

covered 151 films in an uncontroversial manner. Although more booklet than book, *El Húsar de la Muerte* (*The Hussar of Death*) deals with a seminal 1925 silent Chilean film starring and also directed by Pedro Sienna. It is the only surviving feature film of that era and took years to restore, a task begun by the University of Chile and finished by the Ministry of Education. The film deals with Manuel Rodriguez, a legendary hero of Chile's 1810 war of independence. His many disguises and the astute tricks he played on the Spanish turned him into a folk hero and the *Hussar*, when it opened in 1925, was a huge popular success. That same year, a total of 16 films were made in Chile. The past is a foreign country. . .

Pedro Sienna, star and director of EL HÚSAR DE LA MUERTE

HANS EHRMANN is a columnist and the film critic on Santiago's daily *La Nación*. Last year, he published a book of interviews with local writers and artists.

Useful Addresses

Arauco Films
(production facility)
Silvina Hurtado 1789
Santiago
Tel: 56 2 209 2091
Fax: 56 2 204 5096

Asociación de Productores de Cine y TV
Huérfanos 878, Depto.918
Santiago
Tel/Fax: 56 2 633 3984

Conate and Chile Films
(studio, lab, distributor and exhibitor)
La Capitania 1200
Santiago
Tel: 56 2 220 3086
Fax: 56 2 211 9826

Filmocentro
(production facility)
Jorge Washington 302
Santiago
Tel: 56 2 341 3100
Fax: 56 2 209 1671

Oficina de Difusión de la Cinematografia Chilena
Villavicencio 352
Santiago
Tel: 56 2 632 6565 or 632 6607
Fax: 56 2 632 6389

Roos Films
(production facility)
Ricardo Matte Pérez 0216
Santiago
Tel: 56 2 341 1188
Fax: 56 2 341 1199

CHINA

Derek Elley

The past 12 months have seen changes that prove once again that nothing can ever be taken for granted in China's film industry. A clear-out of top personnel during the first half of 1966 has seriously dampened the optimism that held sway a year earlier.

A year ago, the distribution business was going through its biggest metamorphosis in 45 years, with a limited number of brand-new "big foreign movies" (code for U.S. and Hong Kong blockbusters) playing in the big cities on a revenue-sharing basis with the producers. Exhibitors were delighted, and wanted more of the same to fill their cinemas; local film-makers had mixed feelings, fearing the annihilation of their own industry; local studios (already allowed to distribute their own productions and foreign co-productions) were also pushing to be allowed to distribute foreign movies, rather than them all going through China

Film. The extra revenue, they argued, could be ploughed back into improving local facilities and productions.

The Bubble Bursts

The Film Bureau (the industry's regulator and chief censor) was maintaining a shaky hold over these conflicting forces, as well as itself being watched by the Ministry of Radio, Film & TV and the Communist Party's propaganda bosses. To outside observers the changes made sense, and it looked as if China was making a (relatively) ordered change to a mixed-market film industry.

Then the bubble burst. First to go in early 1996 was Teng Jinxian, a generally respected figure in a difficult job, to be replaced by Liu Jianzhong. Next to be stripped of power was Tian Congming, in charge of film at the Ministry since January 1992; he was replaced by Zhao Shi, previously head of the Communist Youth League. Also out of the door went China Film head Wu Mengchen, replaced in the summer by Tong Gang, previously deputy director of Xi'an Film Studio. The shuffles in personnel were ascribed to Party propaganda boss Ding Guan'gen.

Essentially, the changes consolidated earlier moves announced in autumn 1995 to break China Film's much-envied monopoly over importing foreign movies and to spread the jam between the studios, beginning with majors like Beijing, Shanghai and Changchun. But with it has also come a new conservatism in censorship.

Still from Zhang Yuan's SONS

In February it was suddenly announced that *GoldenEye* and *Apollo 13* had been rejected by the censors, despite a deal having been made with distributors UIP at the end of the previous year. In May, just prior to its international première at Cannes, *Temptress Moon*, directed by Chen Kaige and funded by Hong Kong-based Tomson Films, was also put on the banned list, effectively robbing the producer of a major slice of revenue. (Chen's next film, a light comedy due to shoot that autumn with actors Ge You and Lü Liping, was also refused permission.)

Also on the shelf are two films executive-produced by Tian Zhuangzhuang from his base at Beijing Film Studio – **How Steel Is Forged,** a film about youth during the 1950s and 1960s, by newcomer Lu Xuechang, and **The Girl from Vietnam** by Wang Xiashuai whose **The Days** played festivals in 1994/95 – and Huang Jianzhong's 1920s revenge drama **Rice,** and Wang Shuo's debut **My Dad.**

LISTEN CHINA!
電影即音樂
聆聽電影
100 YEARS OF CINEMA CAM
C.A.M. ORIGINAL SOUNDTRACKS from the golden years of Italian and French cinema.
Over 170 titles and 75 composers available on compact disc.
Ask for our catalog. Also available on CD-ROM.
CAM Original Soundtracks VIA COLA DI RIENZO, 152 - 00192 ROME (ITALY) - FAX:(+39-6) 687.4046

Back to the Future

The signals being sent out translate into a general note of caution after the runaway atmosphere of 1994/95. Party highups have made it clear that the import of U.S. films will be used to serve the local industry (by generating badly needed revenue) rather than simply filling Hollywood's coffers by opening up the world's largest regulated market to all and sundry.

A sign that business will continue was the February 1996 annoucement that Mike Medavoy's Phoenix Pictures would team with Shanghai Film Studio to open a US$25 million studio making up to ten pictures a year. Phoenix is 20% owned by Sony Pictures Entertainment and 20% by U.K. media group Pearson.

Thanks to U.S. imports box-office revenue almost doubled in 1995. In Peking it rose to 90 million yuan (US$10.8 million), from 50 million in 1994; in Shanghai it hit 230 million yuan (US$27.7 million), up from 140 million yuan.

Many of the past year's notable productions (Chen Kaige's **Temptress Moon**, Zhou Xiaowen's **The Emperor's Shadow** and He Ping's **Sun Valley**), though shot on the Mainland by Mainland-born directors, were in fact funded by Hong Kong-based companies and are discussed in that section of IFG. Reversing the situation, one other film, Yim Ho's **The Sun Has Ears**, was shot by a Hong Kong-based director but financed from the Mainland (by actress Zhang Yu).

The film, which co-won the Best Director Silver Bear at Berlin in 1996, is not quite at the exalted level of Yim's previous *The Day the Sun Turned Cold* but brings a fresh style to familiar material – the story, set in the 1920s, of an affair between a handsome warlord and a poor but ambitious peasant woman. The movie's slightly stylised feel (russety colours, exaggerated sound effects), and Yim's poetic-heroic approach, give the story an almost elemental flavour that's often impressive, plus an irony that's rare in such subject matter. Zhang herself plays the peasant woman.

A Revolutionary Obsession

Other films have been hit-and-miss. Huang Jianxin completed his de facto trilogy on modern Mainland life with **Signal Left, Turn Right**, a comedy set in a driving school that is okay in its own terms but lacks the earlier film's trenchant observation. Zhang Yuan's **Sons** is an interesting but (in Western terms) familiar essay in the "faction" genre, restaging real events in a highly dysfunctional family with the actual people involved.

More marginal production, which in recent years has thrown up fascinating débuts like *The Days* and *Red Beads*, still flourishes, though often with mixed results. Actress Zhang Xiaomin's vanity production, **To the Red Altar**, is a kind of Chinese *The Red Shoes* about a woman who grows up obsessed by the colour red and the effect that the country's "revolutionary" education has had on her psyche.

Not as pretentious, but flawed by stiff dialogue and acting is **Days of Miandi**, the Berlin Film School graduation work of Ma Yingli, shot in Peking. Looking at recent changes in China, and especially its rush to Mammon, the film (which takes its title from the name for Peking's distinctive yellow minicabs) focuses on two women – a musician (Gao Junxia) who returns from Paris and a hippy-ish local photographer (Li Qinqin) who would like to emigrate. Though its working out is often clumsy the theme is pertinent, and Ma could become a name to watch if she graduates to other features.

The 15th Golden Rooster Awards

The awards were made in Peking in October 1995, alongside those for the 16th Hundred Flowers Awards (voted by readers of the large-circulation monthly *Popular Cinema*). Both were for films released in 1994. The main awards were as follows:

Best Film: *Uncle Shan Gang, the Accused.*
Best Directors: Huang Jianxin, Yang Yazhou (*Back to Back, Face to Face*).
Best Script: Fan Yuan (*Uncle Shan Gang, the Accused*).
Best Actor: Li Rentang (*Uncle Shan Gang, the Accused*).
Best Actress: Ailiya (*Ermo*).
Best Supporting Actor: no award.
Best Supporting Actress: Ju Xue (*My Lost Love*).
Best Photography: Bao Xiaoran (*Southern China 1994*).
Best Art Direction: Yang Gang (*The Conqueror*).
Best Editing: Sun Huimin (*Blind Alley*), Nie Weiguo (*Bandit-Killer Desert*).
Best Music: Chang Yuhong (*The Conqueror*).
Best Musical: *The Legend of Mulan.*
Best Sound: no award.
Best First Work by a Director: Fan Yuan (*Uncle Shan Gang, the Accused*), Ning Haiqiang (*Hidden Trajectory*).
Best Documentary: *Ballads of the Past.*
Best Children's Film: no award.
Best Co-production: *Back to Back, Face to Face* (China-Hong Kong).
Special Award: Zhang Jianya, director of *Blind Alley.*

The 18th Hundred Flowers Awards

Best Films: *Uncle Shan Gang, the Accused, Staying in the Village, A Single Woman's Story.*
Best Actor: Li Rentang (*Uncle Shan Gang, the Accused*).
Best Actress: Shen Danping (*Staying in the Village*).
Best Supporting Actor: Xie Yuan (*A Born Coward*).
Best Supporting Actres: Li Yuanyuan (*A Born Coward*).
Best Co-production: *Heaven and Earth* (China-Hong Kong).

Forthcoming Films

YOU HUA HAO HAO SHUO (Breaking Up Is Hard to Do)

Dir. Zhang Yimou. Players: Jiang Wen, Qu Ying, Li Baotian.

MI (Rice)

Dir: Huang Jianzhong. Players: Tao Zeru, Xia Zongyou, Wang Zhensong. Prod: Beijing Film Studio, Beijing Minquan, Yitong.

DONG GONG XI GONG (East Palace, West Palace)

Dir: Zhang Yuan. Players: Hu Jun, Si Han. Prod: Fortissimo, MK2.

YAPIAN ZHANZHENG (The Opium Wars)

Dir: Xie Jin. China-Japan co-production, budgeted at US$3 million.

XIAOCUN WU GUSHI (Village without a Story)

Dir: Yu Xiangyau. Players: Xi Meijuan, Li Wannian. Prod: Tianjin Film Studio.

WODE BABA (My Dad)

Dir: Wang Shuo.

CROATIA

Tomislav Kurelec

After five years of the independent Republic of Croatia, very few people are satisfied with its cinema. The authorities, who partly finance production through the Ministry of Culture, are not satisfied with the way the country is depicted in the movies. And film-makers are not satisfied with the amount of state support, and especially with the lack of a law to clarify the means of subvention and sponsorship of film-making. They are also dissatisfied with the fact that from June 1995 to June 1996 only three feature films – plus a few TV movies – were produced. But the greatest sign of discontent is that shown by the public, which is practically ignoring Croatian cinema.

One reason may be the ticket price – about $4, which is not cheap out of an average monthly salary of $200 – and another the fact that there are nearly 200 American movies, including the biggest current hits, in the theatres. But this situation is not too different from the end of the 80s, when Croatian movies attracted at least ten times more viewers. So it seems that it is the social standing of Croatian cinema which has radically changed.

Still from A JOURNEY ON THE DARK SIDE

Real or Official Truth

Less than ten years ago, the cinema offered the unique possibility of criticising the system. Now most Croatian movies try to explain the whys and wherefores of Serbian aggression, and are all too easily dismissed as propaganda. This was the case with **My Dear Angel**, directed by Tomislav Radić, who made one of the most important modernist movies, **Real Truth** (*Živa istina*, 1971), in the history of Croatian cinema, and who works mostly in the theatre. The war in this new movie is seen through the eyes of a seven-year-old boy, who stopped talking after his village was destroyed and his parents taken into Serbian captivity. He starts talking again when he sees a television programme about an exchange of prisoners and identifies his parents.

Radić is very good at recreating the atmosphere of the beginning of the war in Croatia, but the problem is that the characters are all presented very positively; consequently, most of the critics – especially the younger ones – regarded the movie as a kind of mouthpiece for the official line. Similar criticisms were levelled at **A Journey on the Dark Side** by Davor Žmegač, in which the war is a framework for a kind of road movie about three fugitives from Zagreb: a young man who is a star of children's TV fleeing his creditors, a ten-year-old runaway from a refugee camp, and a girl who can't stand her home full of refugee relatives. When they come to a small town near the occupied area of Croatia, their hardships unite this small group as a family. Žmegač demonstrates his talent in a number of charming and convincing episodes, but the story overall fails to convince because the framework of the war is based mostly on stereotypes.

Ivan Salaj, director of SEE YOU

Still from THE WASHED OUT

Soldier in the Rain

These two films, along with others from previous years, inspired the younger critics to declare the generation gap the main problem of Croatian cinema. The liberation war was mostly fought by twenty-year-olds, and the movies about it will have to be made by them. Proof of their talents has been the prizes won by *Mirna Learns Statistics* (1992) by Goran Dukić, and then by *While Nobody Is Looking* (1993) and *Every Time We Separate* (1995), reviewed in last year's IFG, both by Lukas Nola. In **Wish You Could Hear** by Jelena Rajković (only 43 minutes long), a returned soldier interrupts a late-night classical music programme on radio, threatening to set off an explosion and taking the DJ hostage until he can talk about the mistake made by some journalist which caused the tragedy of his life. The soldier and his hostage gradually draw together against the world outside, forging their own unity against rules made by older people.

These themes are expressed with even more fury in Ivan Salaj's complex and bizarre **See You**. Four friends attempt to hold a funeral for a fifth member of their group killed on the battlefield in 1991. Their plan is to bury him outside the cemetery as a symbol of their alienation and of the frustration, disappointment and desperation of the generation who have also given birth to the New Croatian cinema.

But despite the talent and achievements of this group, they may not represent the only possible future for Croatian cinema. First of all, the financial climate is unfavourable: Goran Dukić is now trying to make a career abroad, and others are not so active any more. And actually the best of these dark movies, the winner of the Croatian Film Festival in 1995 and the Days of Croatian Cinema in 1996, is **The Washed Out**, made by the 38-year-old Zrinko Ogresta. Inspired by the Polish cult writer, Marek Hlasko, and his tales of unassimilated losers in the suburbs of Zagreb, Ogresta's film is about a young student and her soldier boyfriend who cannot find anywhere to make love. In the constant rain which washes out those characters, Ogresta creates a world which is realistic enough in detail, but which also becomes highly metaphoric with complex associations.

Recent and Forthcoming Films

ISPRANI (The Washed Out)

Script and Dir: Zrinko Ogresta. Phot: Davorin Gecl. Players: Katarina Bistrović-Darveš, Filip Šovagović, Josip Kučan. Prod: Jadran Film /Croatian Television.

VIDIMO SE (See You)

Script and Dir: Ivan Salaj. Phot: Vanja Černjul. Players: Nenad Cvetko, Goran Višnjić, Rene Bitorajac, Mislav Vilišić, Nadežda Nola-Perišić. Prod: Jadran Film /Croatian Television/ Academy of Drama Arts.

PUTOVANJE TAMNOM POLUTKOM (A Journey on the Dark Side)

Script: Davor Žmegač, Pavao Pavličić. Dir: Žmegač. Phot:

Slobodan Trninić. Players: Goran Navojec, Edita Majić, Vedran Lulić. Prod: Croatian Television/ Jadran Film.

ANDJELE MOJ DRAGI (My Dear Angel)

Script and Dir: Tomislav Radić. Phot: Tomislav Pinter. Players: Milan Grabovac, Dubravka Ostojić, Matko Raguž, Sunčana Zelenika, Silvia Fink, Vjekoslav Janković, Ivo Gregurević, Iva Marjanović. Prod: Korugva/ Croatian Television.

Producers

Jadran Film
10000 Zagreb
Oporovečka 12
Tel: 2987 222
Fax: 251 394

HRT/Croatian Television
10000 Zagreb
Prisavlje 3
Tel: 616 36 15
Fax: 616 36 21

Zagreb Film
10000 Zagreb
Vlaška 70
Tel: 271 355
Fax: 275 994

Distributors

Adria Film
10000 Zagreb
Ivanićgradska 64
Tel: 23 30 710

Blitz Film
10000 Zagreb
Sv. Mateja 121
Tel: 66 00 968
Fax: 66 01 039

Continental Film
10000 Zagreb
Šoštarićeva 10
Tel: 421 312
Fax: 428 247

Europa Film Video
10000 Zagreb
Šoštarićeva 10
Tel: 278 475
Fax: 276 549

Kinematografi
10000 Zagreb
Tuškanac 1
Tel: 420 466
Fax: 426 531

Promax Film & Video
10000 Zagreb
Unska 2/b
Tel: 61 19 263
Fax: 61 19 301

Oscar Vision
10000 Zagreb
Pierottijeva 3
Tel: 443 938

Poly Bros
10000 Zagreb
Draganička 19
Tel & Fax: 563 236

VEM
Čakovec, Mihovljani
V. Nazora 54
Tel: (385 40) 311 581

CZECH REPUBLIC

Eva Zaoralová

Despite predictions that the boom in the Czech Republic's domestic film industry is over, annual production has not fallen below 18 full-length films. The majority are at least partially produced by Czech TV, if only in the form of so-called technical support for projects which have obtained a grant from the Commission of the State Film Fund. Thus, Czech cinema's main problem is not a lack of money, despite the fact that financial difficulties have delayed the completion of some films, for example, **Passage Through a Deep Forest**, the directorial début of successful cameraman Ivan Vojnár. (Vojnár won the Grand Prix at last year's Karlovy Vary Film Festival for his documentary, *In the Garden*.)

The search for financial support has also hampered production on **Code Name: Ruby**, a sort of modern alchemist fairy-tale written by one of the leading lights of the 1960s 'New Wave', Jan Němec. Financial troubles have resulted in filming being drawn out for over a year. One of Němec's equally famous contemporaries, Juraj Jakubisko, who has now decided to leave Slovakia permanently and settle in Prague, will finish shooting **Unclear Report on the End of the World** this summer. Yet another of that generation is Juraj Herz, who emigrated to Munich many years ago and recently returned on a 'business trip'. He is shooting a film, **Arcade**, from a screenplay by the dissident author, Karel Pecka.

Jiří Menzel is about to start shooting an adaptation of Bohumil Hrabal's novel, *How I Served the English King*, provided he wins a copyright lawsuit against his colleague Karel Kachyna. The latter, an unbelievably productive and hard-working 72-year-old film-maker, shoots an average of two films every three years. His latest, **Fany**, starring the popular Jirina Bohdalová and scripted by leading TV writer, Jirí Hubac, explores the rich subject of mental illness and resembles a female version of the Tom Cruise-Dustin Hoffman film, *Rain Man*. Even though it does not achieve the level of Kachyna's previous film, **Cow**, it remains one of the better offerings in the past season's production.

Still from MASTER OF CEREMONIES

Unto the Next Generation

That said, the average this season was comparatively low. Among the contenders were: Miroslav Balajka's slightly absurd comedy, **. . . Even Death Can Take Nothing**, and the distorted 'modern thriller,' **Best Friends Until We Die**, whose complete lack of visual discipline might or might not be due to the fact that the author is a cameraman by profession.

These films, and Zdeněk Tyc's comic parody, **Seizing the Day**, fall far short of a film like **Kolya**, by the young but very successful director Jan Svěrák (born in 1965). His film possesses many excellent qualities, reflecting professionalism as much as talent, that most contemporary Czech films lack: an excellent screenplay by the director's father, Zdeněk Svěrák, a popular actor and scriptwriter (he also wrote the screenplay of Jiří Menzel's *My Little Village*, nominated for the Oscar in 1987); an outstanding cameraman in Vladimir Smutný; and wonderful acting by Zdeněk Svěrák and Andrei Khalimov as the Russian boy, Kolya. As the first Czech film to be bought by the distribution company Miramax, *Kolya* will also be seen in other European and American cinemas.

Young Men Discovering the World, which won the Grand Prix in the Czech film competition, Finale 96, makes up for a lack of professional technique by its enthusiastic tackling of a topical theme. The director, 23-year-old Radim Spacek, a third-year student at Prague's film school FAMU, shot this feature in the form of a documentary under siege in Sarajevo. By following a neutral witness, the Czech journalist Marek, and his acquaintance from Sarajevo, the film shows how the war in Bosnia affected the lives of young people. Jiří Vercak's satirical comedy, **Master of Ceremonies**, goes back to the years when the Communist régime punished children for the bourgeois background of their fathers.

Films due to be completed this summer include the directorial début of F. A. Brabec with an adaptation of **The King Ubu** by Alfred Jarry. In the fall of 1996, two films based on the successful novels of the writer Viewegh are due for release: an autobiographical chronicle of the 70s, **Wonderful Years for Dog**, a début for Petr Nikolaev; and the post-totalitarian novel, **Education of Girls in Bohemia**, directed by Petr Koliha, an experienced script editor from Czech TV. Vladimir Michalek's second film, **Forgotten Light**, is also much anticipated: a half-real, half-visionary story of a village priest from the 1950s starring the popular comedian Bolek Polivka, this time in a dramatic role. Two débuts are announced for October 1996: **Whisper** by David Ondriček (the son of the world-famous camerman, Miroslav Ondriček) and **Shadow Boundary** by Martin Muller.

Still from BEST FRIENDS UNTIL WE DIE

Reinventing the Golem

The number of cinemas in the Czech Republic keeps falling. In the capital alone, five downtown cinema halls have been closed, and outside the centre it is even worse. Many cinemas have been converted to more profitable uses like game-parlors or skateboard tracks, despite the fact that cinema attendance actually rose slightly in 1995. (In the first months of 1996, it was on the decline again.) American films were very popular with audiences; consequently, the only Czech film we find among the top ten is an adventure comedy, **Once Upon a Time There Was a Cop** (director, Jaroslav Soukup), which unashamedly draws on the proven formula of Hollywood cop stories.

Aside from this, a fairy-tale by Jan Schmidt, **How to Win a Princess**; a 'Czech thriller', **The War of the Colours** (director, Filip Renc); an erotic comedy, **Playgirls** (director, Vit Olmer). And finally, two genuinely valuable films, **Ride** by Jan Sverak and **Thanks for Every New Morning** by Milan Steindler, made it through to the top thirty films distributed in 1995.

In this situation, festivals and different film shows gain in importance. For example, this past spring's Week of French Film organised by the French embassy and Unifrance in Prague was quite successful. Also, The Week of European Film, which was organised for the third time in April 1996, has almost become a tradition. Apart from the active French Institute, the Goethe Institute should be mentioned for their role in bringing to Prague outstanding German film personalities. The great interest in Prague's Febiofest, organised for the fourth time in January 1996, proved that young people are especially interested in getting to know films that have not been available in Czech cinemas for years. Unfortunately, the vast majority of these screenings are accessible only to citizens of the capital, while the countryside is dependent on TV programming. In this respect, channel CT 2's editors have commendably presented several cycles devoted to world-famous film-makers (Carlos Saura, Louis Malle, Jean-Luc Godard, etc.).

The Karlovy Vary International Film Festival is celebrating the 50th anniversary of its founding. It had alternated with the Moscow Film Festival from the end of the 1950s, but since 1994, it has been organised annually again. This is the second year that it will be competing with a newly founded Prague IFF. "The Golden Golem", as the Prague Festival was called in 1995, was 'accidentally' scheduled right before Karlovy Vary. Nevertheless, it is still struggling with a lack of professional organisation at all levels.

EVA ZAORALOVÁ (Hepnerová) is a Czech film critic and editor of the magazine *Film a doba*. She is the author of many essays and books dedicated to Italian and French cinema and she taught film history for ten years at FAMU in Prague. Since 1995, she has been programme director of the Karlovy Vary Festival.

Recent and Forthcoming Films

ZÁHRADA (The Garden)

Script: Martin Šulík, Martin Leščák, Ondrej Šulaj. Dir: Martin Šulík. Phot: Martin Štrba. Players: Roman Luknár, Marián Labuda, Zuzana Šulajová, Jana Švandová, Katarína Vrzalová, Dušan Trančík. Prod: Charlie's Bratislava/ ARTCAM International (Paris)/

STV Bratislava/SFT Koliba/In Film (Prague). A Slovak-Czech co-production.

ARTUŠ, MERLIN A PRCHLÍCI (Arthur, Merlin and Prchlíci)

Script: Kateřina Priščáková. Dir: Věra Šimková-Plívová, Drahomíra Králová. Phot: Antonín Holub. Players: Varerie Kaplanová, Plavel Nový, Veronika Jeníková, Veronika Filipová, Lucie Čechová. Prod: Studio Zlín/Czech Television.

FANY (Fanny)

Script: Jiří Hubač. Dir: Karel Kachyňa. Phot: Jiří Macháně. Players: Jiřina Bohdalová, Jiřina Jirásková, Miroslav Donutil, Martin Huba, Aronšt Goldflam, Oldřich Vlach. Prod: Czech Television/KF a.s./ Cable Plus.

MĚSTEM CHODÍ MIKULAŠ (Santa Claus Is Going Through the City)

Script: Jan Procházka, Karel Kackyňa. Dir: Karel Kachyňa. Phot: Vladimír Smutný. Players: Daniel Douda, Eliška Balzerová, Josef Abrhám, Alena Mihulová, Pavel Nový. Prod: Mirage for Czech Television.

. . . ANI SMRT NEBERE (. . . Even Death Can Take Nothing)

Script: Miroslav Balajka. Dir: Balajka. Phot: Roman Pavlíček. Players: Břetislav Rychlík, Mariana Chmelařová, Jozef Kroner, Ondřej Havelka, Boleslav Polívka, Jaromír Dulava, Lenka Termerová. Prod: In Film Praha/ Charlie's Bratislava/Czech Television.

UŽ (Seizing the Day)

Script: and Dir: Zdeněk Tyc. Phot: Vladimír Holomek. Players: Barbora Hrzánová, Radek Holub, Bohumil Klepl, Vladimír Marek, Magdalena Sidonová, Jorga Kotrbová. Prod: In Film Praha/Czech Television.

HOLČIČKY NA ŽIVOT A NA SMRT (Best Friends Until We Die)

Script, Dir and Phot: Jaroslav Brabec. Players: Veronika Freimanová, Ljuba Krbová, Juraj Šimko, Anna Kolínská, Milena Dvorská. Prod: KF a.s.

JAK CHUTNÁ SMRT

Script: M. Cieslar, Dušan Kukal, Jon Jorlim, based on a story by Ladislav Mňačko. Dir: Milan Cieslar. Phot: Petr Hojda. Players: Juraj Kukura, Miluše Šplechtová, Oto Šrámek, Marek Vašut, Ivana Christová. Prod: Happy Celluloid Ltd.

CEREMONIÁŘ (Master of Ceremonies)

Script: Eva Kantôrková. Dir: Jiří Věrčák. Phot: Josef Špelda. Players: Jan Hrušínský, Jana Paulová, Jana Švandová, Olga Schmidtová, Jiří Krampol, Jiří Klem, Rostislav Kuba. Prod: Czech Television.

KOLJA (Kolya)

Story: Pavel Taussig. Script: Zdeněk Svěrák. Dir: Jan Svěrák. Phot: Vladimír Smutný. Players: Zdeněk Svěrák, Andrei Khalimov, Libuše Šafránková, Ondřej Vetchý, Stella Zázvorková, Ladislav Smoljak, Irina Livanovová, Karel Heřmánek. Prod: Biograf Jan Svěrák Pictures/Portobello Pictures/ Pandora Cinema/Czech Television/ CinemArt/Centre of Czech Video/CNC (Eurimages).

MLADÍ MUŽI POZNÁVAJÍ SVĚT (Young Men Discovering the World)

Script, Dir and Phot: Radim Špaček. Players: Adnan Hasovic, Alexandra Suboticová, Rijad Lutovic, Marek Brodský. Prod: Czech Television.

Producers

AB Barrandov a.s.
Křiženeckého nám. 322
152 53 Praha 5
Tel: 42-2/ 67 07 11 11
Fax: 42-2/ 24 51 06 28

Ateliéry ZLIN a.s.
Filmová 174
761 79 Zlín
Tel: 067/ 527 400
Fax: 067/ 527 510

***Bonton Films a.s.**
Severozápadhí IV/39
141 00 Praha 4
Tel: 42-2/ 748 907
Fax: 42-2/ 765 750

Czech Television
Na Hřebenech 11
140 70 Praha 4
Tel: 42-2/ 2423 02 42
Fax: 42-2/ 2421 42 54

Etamp Film Production s.r.o.
U továren 261
102 00 Praha 10
Tel: 42-2/ 705 257
Fax: 42-2/ 706 077

Febio, Ltd.
Ružová ul. 13
110 00 Praha 1
Tel: 42-2/ 2421 39 33
Fax: 42-2/ 2421 42 54

Heureka Film s.r.o.
Litevská 8
100 05 Praha 10
Tel: 42-2/ 742 558
Fax: 42-2/ 743 413

***Heureka Productions s.r.o.**
Vaníčkova 2
160 17 Praha 6
Tel: 42-2/ 527 418
Fax: 42-2/ 354 772

***KF a.s.**
Jindřisská 34
112 07 Praha 1
Tel: 42-2/ 2421 24 10
Křiženeckého nám. 322
150 00 Praha 5
Tel: 42-2ú/ 6709 11 11
Fax: 42-2/ 6445 111

TOP TEN GROSSING FILMS IN THE CZECH REPUBLIC: 1995

	Admissions
Forrest Gump	611,898
The Specialist	359,018
The Lion King	313,689
Waterworld	222,973
The Mask	207,004
Dumb and Dumber	203,852
Timecop	197,630
Die Hard 3	184,357
Once Upon a Time There Was a Cop (*Czech*)	175,205
Casper	171,059

Mirofilm
Na poříčí 14
110 00 Praha 1
Tel: 42-2/ 2481 09 66
Fax: 42-2/ 2481 06 32

***Space Films s.r.o.**
Karlovo nám. 19
120 00 Praha 2
Tel: 42-2/ 2491 30 43
Fax: 42-2/ 2491 30 45

VaC – Vachler Art Comp.
Na Žertvách 40
180 00 Praha 8
Tel: 42-2/ 68 32 600

**=also distributor*

Distributors

Bonton Film
Národní tř. 28
111 21 Praha 1
Tel: 42-2/ 211 05 248/211 05 236
Fax: 42-2/ 2422 52 63

Filmexport Prague
Na Moráni 5
128 00 Praha 2
Tel: 42-2/ 24 91 52 39
Fax: 42-2/ 29 33 12

Falcon
Stroupežnického 6
150 00 Praha 5
Tel: 42-2/ 538 085, 534 051
Fax: 42-2/ 533 194

Gemini Film s.r.o.
V jámě 1
110 00 Praha 1
Tel: 42-2/ 24 16 24 71
Fax: 42-2/ 24 22 65 62

Intersonic Taunus Prod. Ltd.
Staré Grunty 34
842 24 Bratislava
Tel: 42-7/ 71 10 05
Fax: 42-7/ 72 20 70

Useful Addresses

Film Department of the Ministry of Culture
Valdštejnská 12
110 00 Praha 1
Tel: 42-2/ 513 23 38, 513 24 78
Fax: 42-2/ 53 70 55

Association of Czech Film Artists
Pod Nuselskými schody 3
120 00 Praha 2
Tel: 42-2/ 691 03 10
Fax: 42-2/ 691 13 75

Association of Czech Distributors
Řeznická 3
110 00 Praha
Tel/Fax: 42-2/ 24 91 44 66

Association of Producers in the Audiovisual Industry c/o SPACE Film
Karlovo nám. 19
120 00 Praha
Tel: 42-2/ 20 48 20
Fax: 42-2/ 20 73 23

DENMARK

Ebbe Iversen

Danish film found itself in a very unusual situation in 1996. More talented new films opened than for many years, but they had difficulty finding a domestic audience. This was a major disappointment to the film industry, especially since Danish cinemas otherwise had a good year. In 1995, only nine Danish feature films opened, and the number of tickets sold for domestic films fell 1,543 to only 776,000. But 1996 is seeing a significant rise in attendance. In the first quarter alone, attendance rose by no less than 47 per cent in Copenhagen compared to the same period in 1995.

This, however, is mainly due to a number of popular American films, and the only Danish film to do well commercially in the past year was Peter Schrøder's **Just a Girl** *(Kun en pige)*, based on prominent writer Lise Nørgaard's autobiography about her years as a young girl in provincial Roskilde, dreaming of becoming a journalist. It is a handsome, well-made and quite traditional film about a headstrong young woman breaking out of a suffocating environment. It benefited from the fact that many Danes have read and liked Lise Nørgaard's books.

Division in the House

The most eagerly debated issue of the year in the Danish film world was the new Film House in central Copenhagen. It was due to open in early June – to coincide with the celebration of the 100th anniversary of the first public screening in Denmark – but the official opening was delayed until September, although the Danish Film Workshop, which produces experimental films and videos, moved into the impressive building (formerly headquarters of a publishing company) during the spring.

The building also houses the National Film Board of Denmark (short films and documentaries), the Danish Film Institute (feature films) and the Danish Film Museum (the national film archives), plus three cinemas, a videotheque, library and an exhibition area. One of the ideas behind the Film House is to make the aforementioned institutions more visible to the public; another idea being to make their administration more efficient.

Discussion, however, arose when the consulting company, Performance, hired by the Minister of Culture, Jytte Hilden, to examine the administration, recommended that the hitherto independent film institutions should have one common board of directors and one managing director with two assistant directors dealing with feature films and short films respectively. The National Film Board was in favour of this recommendation, whereas the Danish Film Institute had strong reservations, afraid of losing part of its independence, and it warned of the danger of a politically biased bureaucracy.

Waves Old and New

The most conspicuous new Danish film, of course, is Lars von Trier's **Breaking the Waves** (original title), which was awarded the Grand Prix de Jury at Cannes. The film is a powerful erotic and religious drama, set in a remote Scottish village, about an innocent young woman, Bess – wonderfully played by British newcomer Emily Watson – who sacrifices herself sexually to save her paralysed husband. It is certainly a moving story, whereas opinions differ over its dizzy visual style, marked by the same kind of jumpy hand-held camera that Trier used in his TV series, *The Kingdom (Riget)*. The director, incidentally, spent the summer shooting a number of new

DANISH FILM INSTITUTE

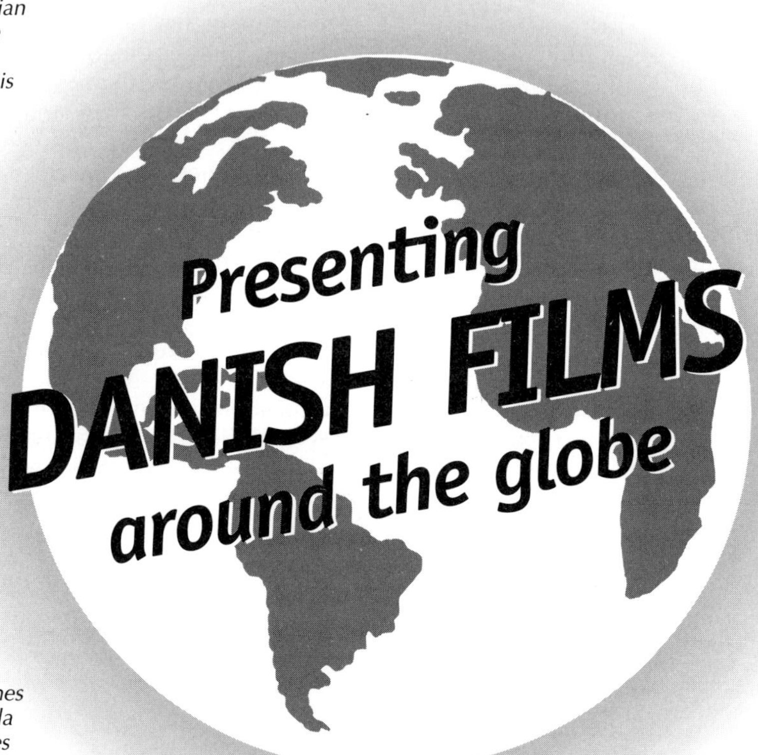

Johannesburg
Santiago de Chile
New York
Malmö
Bruxelles
Buenos Aires
San Sebastian
Melbourne
Sydney
Minneapolis
Göteborg
Porto
Berlin
Portland
Cleveland
Dublin
London
Rouen
Asunción
La Paz
Reykjavik
Havana
Laon
Istanbul
Bonn
Tel Aviv
Riga
Rivertown
Lima
Quito
Seattle
Venice
Bogotá
Cannes
Valenciennes
Barranquilla
Los Angeles
Caracas
Panama
Paris
München
Rome
Moscow
Montevideo
Warszawa
Toronto
Giffoni

Tokyo
Edinburgh
Haugesund
Montréal
Umeå
Rio de Janeiro
Jerusalem
Haifa
Antalya
Vancouver
San Juan
Tampa
Shanghai
Mill Valley
Chicago
San José
Managua
São Paulo
Valladolid
Wien
Singapore
Troia
Lübeck
Puerto Rico
Zlín
Hyderabad
Mannheim
Amsterdam
Oulu
Prague
San Diego
Cairo
Kiel
Gent
Annonay
Stockholm
Mexico City
Belfast
Helsinki
Niger
Lagos
Johannesburg
Capetown
Bangkok
Manilla
Marocco
Sodankyla

Contact Lissy Bellaiche

VOGNMAGERGADE 10 · DK-1120 COPENHAGEN K
TEL +45 3374 3430 · FAX +45 3374 3435

DANISH FILM INSTITUTE

episodes for this internationally popular series.

A couple of venerable practitioners made new films. Octogenarian Astrid Henning-Jensen gave a sympathetic but rather stale account of the troubled relationship between a single mother and her teenage daughter in **Bella, My Bella** *(Bella min Bella)*, and Henning Carlsen went to Norway to shoot his dignified but static romantic drama, **Two Green Feathers** *(Pan)*, based on a novel by the great Norwegian writer, Knut Hamsun.

Knut Hamsun himself – magnificently played by Max von Sydow – is the main character in Swedish director Jan Troell's excellent **Hamsun**, a Danish-Swedish-Norwegian co-production. It deals with the controversial fact that Hamsun, awarded the Nobel Prize for Literature, was an outspoken Nazi sympathiser during the German occupation of Norway. The film tries neither to judge nor to excuse Hamsun, but to understand this proud, complex and politically naive artist, and thanks not least to von Sydow, it succeeds beautifully.

The new young wave in Danish cinema began with Carsten Rudolf's **The Beast Within** *(Menneskedyret)*, about a boy with a troubling ability to see through grown-ups' hypocrisy. This brave and original film by an obviously talented new director was a commercial flop, but it was later awarded the Bodil Prize as the best Danish film of 1995. Other promising new entries include Aage Rais' **The Flyer** *(Anton)*, about a boy who is busy building an aeroplane so that he can fly off to visit his dead father. Carsten Fromberg's **Bad Seed** *(Ondt blod)* is a tense and tough drama about conflicts among a group of young prisoners on a survival trip to an uninhabited Swedish island.

Looking Forward to Snow

Niels Arden's **Portland** (original title) tells an even tougher and more brutal story about two brothers' life in the criminal and drug world of provincial Aalborg. And

Max von Sydow and Ghita Nørby in Troell's masterpiece, HAMSUN

Anders Rønnow Klarlund deals in **The Eighteenth** *(Den Attende)* with a group of people who met on the 18th of May 1993, when police fought (and shot at) stone-throwing demonstrators in the streets of Copenhagen after an EU referendum.

Danish producer Per Holst's film **And All Things Fair** *(Lærerinden)* was nominated for an Academy Award as Best Foreign Language Film. This fine film is directed by the Swede Bo Widerberg and tells in a passionate and non-exploitative way about a teacher's sexual affair with one of her underage pupils. Two feature-length, very interesting documentaries about late, great artists are also worth mentioning: Torben Skjødt Jensen's **Carl Th. Dreyer – My Métier** *(Carl Th. Dreyer – Min metier)* and Christian Braad Thomsen's **Karen Blixen – Storyteller** (original title).

With more than 20 feature films expected to open, 1996 looks to be a remarkable year for Danish films in terms of both quality and quantity. Eagerly anticipated is Palme d'Or and Academy Award winner Bille August's **Miss Smilla's Sense of Snow**

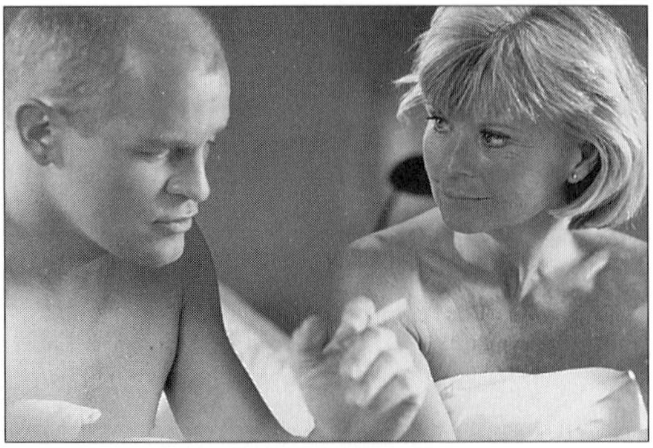

Lars Bom and Lone Hertz in BELLA, MY BELLA

CAMERA FILM

Importer and distributor of quality films from all countries

GRAND 1:2:3:4:5:6

The Leading Danish art cinema in the heart of Copenhagen

Contact:
Annette Trampedach or Kirsten Dalgaard, 8 Mikkel Bryggers Gade, DK-1460 Copenhagen, Denmark. TEL: +45 33 13 61 12 - FAX: +45 33 13 08 82

(Frøken Smillas fornemmelse for sne), based on Peter Høeg's international best-seller about a woman from Greenland and her attempt to solve the mystery of a boy's death. She is played by Julia Ormond; other important parts by Gabriel Byrne and Richard Harris, and the film's main producer is German Bernd Eichinger, who also produced Bille August's *House of the Spirits.*

Much beloved director Søren Kragh-Jacobsen has shot **The Island on Bird Street** *(Huset i Fuglegaden)* in Poland and Germany with Patrick Bergin and Jack Warden in the cast – the story takes place in Warsaw during World War II – while his gifted colleague, Nils Malmros, will shoot his stormy romantic drama, **Barbara** (original title) in the Farö Islands with Norwegian actress Annika von der Lippe.

Jacob Oliver Krarup in THE FLYER

TOP TEN GROSSING FILMS IN DENMARK: 1995

Dumb and Dumber
The Lion King
Die Hard 3
Pocahontas
The Bridges of Madison County
Forrest Gump
101 Dalmatians (reissue)
The Mask
Nine Months
Casper

Last, but not least, it seems that the refreshing and much needed new wave in Danish cinema will continue, as a handful of first feature films by promising young directors is heading for the cinemas – a road movie, **The Biggest Heroes** *(De største helte)* by Thomas Vinterberg, a mediaeval drama, **Eye of the Eagle** *(Ørnens øje)* by Peter Flinth, a Viking story, **The Last Viking** *(Den sidste viking)* by Jesper W Nielsen, and a contemporary crime story, **Pusher** (original title), by Nikolas Winding Refn.

EBBE IVERSEN has been a professional journalist since 1966. He has been film critic of "Berlingske Tidende" since 1973, and is a former co-editor of the magazine "Kosmorama".

National Film Board of Denmark

The Danish contribution to the centenary of cinema was – no surprise – a feature-length documentary on Carl Th. Dreyer, called **My Métier**, by Torben Skjødt Jensen. The film is a respectful portrait of the great Danish film-maker, mingling three elements: clips from his works, rich and humorous anecdotes from actors and members of his crew, and first and foremost Dreyer's own notes on film-making. This story of the shy and modest, and yet so determined and stubborn Dreyer when it came to getting his will on the set, is elegantly told by Skjødt Jensen in *his* way, searching for new expressions as did Dreyer himself.

Documentary portraits seemed to be *in* this year. The Polish director Krzysztof Wierzbicki did the last film before the death of his close friend, for whom he had worked so many times: Krzysztof Kieślowski. Initiated and produced by the Danish company "Kulturmøde film" (Karen Hjort and Marian Hirshorn), **Im So-so** is a well-made television documentary that was widely acclaimed and won the Grand Prix in Marseille at the 1996 "Vue sur les Docs". Kieślowski is in the film, a charming and teasing personality, who is especially preoccupied with his early, critical Polish works that made him leave documentary film-making because it was impossible to say everything in this genre.

Jørgen Leth, so often mentioned as the most prominent Danish documentarist, enjoyed a real come-back after the poor reception for his feature film *Traberg*. Having lived for a decade in Haïti, Leth wanted to portray this political melting pot, using Hi-8 material shot by himself and others, mixed with new 16mm and 35mm footage from previous films shot in Haïti. The film, **Haïti. Untitled**, introduces a dynamic, expressionistic storytelling far removed from the director's language until now. Leth loves the island for its sensibility and rhythm of life, for the small distance between life and death, for its passion. The

SFC

NATIONAL FILM BOARD
OF DENMARK

VOGNMAGERGADE 10
DK-1120 KOBENHAVN K
DENMARK

PHONE: +45 3374 3500
TELEFAX: +45 3374 3565

film is very personal, and yet it also reports on the politics of the country with a fantastic *drive* in the narration, due to the choice of the talented editor, Jakob Thuesen.

Thuesen is no doubt a future star in the Danish documentary firmament. It is so very obvious when you see the Hi-8 shot film, **Under New York**, a brilliantly edited, vital and complex visit to the subway of the Big Apple, catching two people – a police officer and a homeless person – on their way through life, dreaming, hoping.

Two other veterans published portraits this year. The director, Christian Braad Thomsen, also an author, film critic and importer, compiled unseen archive material on Karen Blixen to form the basis of a very charming and clever presentation of the baroness herself. There is much humour in the feature-length documentary **Karen Blixen – Storyteller**. Humour is also very characteristic of another vet in Danish documentaries, Jon Bang Carlsen, who settled down in Ireland for a year to make **It's Now or Never**, which focuses on bachelors on the western coast of the island. Jimmy, the protagonist, is looking for a woman to be with for the rest of his life. She does not have to be pretty as long as she can milk a cow! Bang Carlsen makes his films using a method he himself has called "staged documentarism". He asks real life characters to play themselves in a dialogue, written after a long period of research.

The high quality of Danish cinema for children was sustained with the short fiction film, **The Bogey Man**, directed by Jesper W. Nielsen, a real thriller about two children who imagine that they are threatened by a so-called bogey man who turns out to be a chimney sweep.

Tue Steen Müller

Still from the Statens Filmcentral documentary on Carl Dreyer

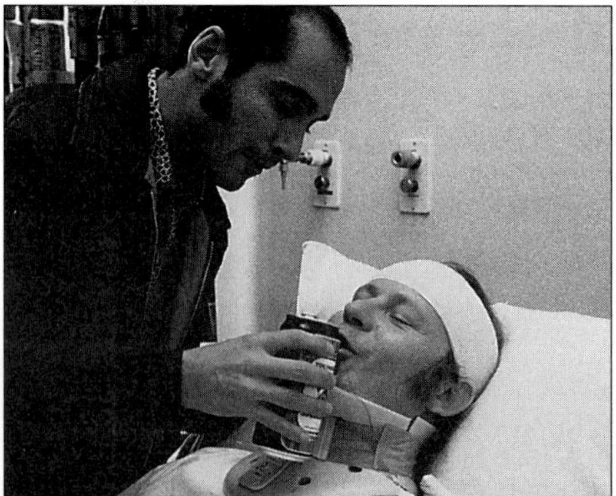

Jean-Marc Barr and Stellan Skarsgård in BREAKING THE WAVES, Denmark's prize-winning film of the year

Producers

ASA Film Production ApS
Mosedalvej
DK-2500 Valby
Tel: 3618 8200
Fax: 3116 8502

Crone Film Produktion A/S
Blomstervænget 52
DK-2800 Lyngby
Tel: 4587 2700
Fax: 4587 2705

Danish Film Studio
Blomstervænget 52
DK-2800 Lyngby
Tel: 4587 2700
Fax: 4587 2705
Telex: 37798 (studio dk)

Domino Film & TV Production
København N
DK-1411
Langebrogade 6 A
Tel: 3296 6644
Fax: 3296 0644

Film & Lyd Produktion A/S
Bredgade 63A
DK-1260 København K
Tel: 3312 1050
Fax: 3312 1093

Grasten Film, Regner
Lykkevej 6
DK-2920 Charlottenlund
Tel: 3163 4424
Fax: 3163 4823

Holst Film A/S, Per
Klampenborgvej 50
2930 Klampenborg
Tel: 45 3963 8866
Fax: 45 3963 5575

Lense-Møller Film ApS, Lise
Fortunvej 56
DK-2920 Charlottenhund
Tel: 3164 2284
Fax: 3164 2269

Locomotion Kofod Schiller Film
Nannasgade 28
DK-2200 København N
Tel: 3183 8900
Fax: 3582 1737

Madsen, Kenneth Filmproduktion A/S
Guldbergsgade 29 F
DK-2200 København N
Tel: 3536 0036
Fax: 3536 0011

Mandart Production
H. P. Ørumsgade 47
2100 Copenhagen

Metronome Productions A/S
Søndermarksvej 16
DK-2500 Valby

Nordisk Film Production A/S
Mosedalvej
DK-2500 Valby
Tel: 3630 1033
Fax: 3116 8502

Obel Film, ApS
A.N. Hansens Allé 23
DK-2900 Hellerup
Tel: 3161 0666
Fax: 3161 0667

Panorama Film International Ltd.
The Old Mill, London Road, Hook, Hants AG27 9EH, England
Tel: (44) 256766-868
Fax: (44) 256768-747

Penta Film
Strandgade 4 B
DK-1401 København K
Tel: 3296 6230
Fax: 3296 0014

Ravn Film og Media Aps
Mosedalvej 11 B
DK-2500 Valby
Tel: 3645 5800
Fax: 3645 0808

Such Such Movies ApS
Blomstervænget 52
DK-2800 Lyngby
Tel: 4587 2700
Fax: 4587 2705

Superfilm Productions
Forbindelssvej 5
DK-2100 København Ø
Tel: 3142 4611
Fax: 3142 4611

Vestergaard Film, Jørgen
Gadekøret 24, Sennels
DK-7700 Thisted
Tel: 9798 50020
Fax: 9798 5020

Victoria Film
Frederiksberggade 16
DK-1459 København K
Tel: 6260 1595
Fax: 6260 1534

Zentropa Entertainments ApS
Ryesgade 106, st.
DK-2100 København Ø
Tel: 3142 4233
Fax: 3142 4299

Distributors

AB Collection
Hirsemarken 3
DK-3520 Farum
Tel: 4499 6200
Fax: 4295 1786

Camera Film
Mikkel Bryggers Gade 8
DK-1460 København K
Tel: 3313 6112
Fax: 3315 0882

Constantin Film ApS
Skelbækgade 1
DK-1717 København V
Tel: 3325 2424
Fax: 3325 0707

Egmont Audio Visual A/S
Skelbækgade 1
DK-1717 København V
Tel: 3325 4000
Fax: 3325 4002

20th Century Fox
Skelbækgade 1, 3
DK-1717 København V
Tel: 3325 4000
Fax: 3325 4002

Gloria Film
Vesterbrogade 149
DK-1620 København V
Tel: 3327 0022
Fax: 3327 0099

Kommunefilm
Baltoppen
DK-2750 Ballerup
Tel: 4265 6262
Fax: 4477 2708

Nordisk Film Distribution A/S
Skelbøkgade 1
DK-1717 København V
Tel: 3123 2488
Fax: 3123 0488

Scala Film
Centrumpladsen
DK-5700 Svendborg
Tel: 6221 8866
Fax: 6221 0821

UIP – United International Pictures
Hauchsvej 13
DK-1825 Frederiksberg C
Tel: 3131 2330
Fax: 3123 3420

Warner & Metronome ApS
Søndermarksvej 16
DK-2500 Valby
Tel: 3146 8822
Fax: 3644 0604

Useful Addresses

Danish Film Institute
Vognmagergade 10
DK-1120 København K
Tel: 45 3374 3430
Fax: 45 3374 3435
Tlx: 31465 dfilm dk

Danish Film Institute Workshop
Vognmagergade 10
DK-1120 København V
Tel: 45 3374 3480
Fax: 45 3374 3490

National Film Board of Denmark
Statens Filmcentral
Film House Denmark
Vognmagergade 10
DK-1120 København K
Tel: 45 3374 3500
Fax: 45 3374 3565

The Danish Film Studio
Blomstervænget 52
DK-2800 Lyngby
Tel: 4587 2700
Fax: 4587 2705

Risby Studios
Ledøjevej 1
DK-2620 Albertslund
Tel: 4262 9646

EGYPT

Fawzi Soliman

In Egypt, the celebration of cinema's centenary was inaugurated with a screening of **Barsoum Searches for a Job**, directed by Mohamed Bayoumy in 1923, and a huge exhibition organised by L'Institut du Monde Arabe. But in the same year, Egyptian cinema was facing a crisis: in 1995, only 24 films were produced and only 31 were released (1985=78 films; 1990=64 films). And most of the films were condemned by critics as shallow and commercial trivia.

Among the exceptions was **Why the Sea Laughs** by M. K. Kaliuby, which won the Egyptian Association of Film Critics' prize as the best film of 1995. But there was a surprise at the Cairo International Film Festival where three new directors appeared with their first films. Two of them are praiseworthy. Magdi Ahmad Ali's **My Life – My Passion** sheds light on feminist issues, dealing with the struggle of three young working women to survive in a difficult social situation. In spite of their setbacks, they manage to keep their dreams. The producer, Raafat El Mihi, himself a scriptwriter and director, is known for his enterprising support of new talent.

The second film, **Kings of the Roads**, directed by Ossama Fawzi, deals with the younger generation. A sensitive subject in an Arab country – sexual relations and adultery – is treated in a courageous manner. Characters are obsessed with the search for a moment of intimacy that can as

Still from MY LIFE – MY PASSION

TOP TEN GROSSING FILMS IN EGYPT: 1995

The Mask
Street Fighter
The Lion King
The Specialist
Forrest Gump
Dumb and Dumber
Braveheart
Time Cop
Nine Months
Waterworld

easily be found while observing a death rite or celebrating a wedding.

To overcome the crisis in Egyptian cinema, a project has been submitted by the Minister of Culture to establish a company drawing on banks, businessmen and film people which could provide the budgets for high-quality films. There were official promises to reduce taxes on imported material, to build new cinema houses and to try to open new markets. In 1995 the "New Egyptian Cinema" lost one of its most important figures. Atef El Tayeb, who died at 47, dealt with exploitation and corruption in films that were distinguished by perceptive historical analysis.

FAWZI SOLIMAN is Vice-President of the Egyptian Film Critics Association, and a member of the higher committee of the Cairo International Film Festival. He has contributed to magazines and newspapers in Egypt and the Arab world.

Still from KINGS OF THE ROADS

YA DONIA – YA GHARAMI (My Life – My Passion)

Script: Mohamed Helmy Helal. Dir: Magdy Ahmed Ali. Phot: Mohsen Nasr. Players: Laila Elwo, Elham Shaheen, Hala Sidqi, Hesham Selim. Prod: Studio 13.

Recent Films

STAKOZA (Lobster)

Script: Abdel Hay Adib. Dir: Isan El Deghedy. Phot: Mohsen Ahmen. Players: Ahmed Zaki, Reaghda, Amina Rizk. Prod: Isan El Deghedy.

EL-NOM FIL – ASSAL (Sound Asleep)

Script: Waheed Hamed. Dir: Sherif Arafa. Phot: Mohsen Ahmed. Players: Adel Imam, Dalal Abdel Aziz. Prod: Waheed Hamed Films.

MEET FOLL (Let's Kill Dad)

Script and Dir: Raafat El-Mihi. Phot: Samir Bahzan. Players: Sherihan Hesham Selim, Hassan Hosni. Prod: Studio 13.

Forthcoming Films

AFAREET EL-ASPHALT (Kings of the Road)

Script: Moustafa Zikri. Dir: Hani Gergis Fawzi. Phot: Tareq El Telmessani. Prod: Gergis Fawzi Films.

ISHARET MEROUR (Traffic Light)

Script: Medhat El Adl. Dir: Khairy Bechara. Phot: Tareq El Telmessani. Prod: Sami El Adl Films.

EL TAHWILA (The Switch)

Script: Youssef Bahnasi. Dir: Amali Bahnasi. Phot: Ghoneim Bahnasi. Players: Farouq El-Fishawi, Nagah El Mogi, Jihan Fadel. Prod: Ahmad Saad Films.

COMA (Al Ghaibouba)

Script and Dir: Hesham Abu El Nasr. Phot: Ibrahim Adel. Players: Ezzat El Alayly, Leila Taher, Sherif Salah el Dine. Prod: Hesham Abu El Nasr Films.

Producers/ Distributors

Sphinx Film
2 Behlar St. (Kasr El Nil St.)
Cairo
Tel: 3920709
Fax: 3920710

Al-Alamia for TV & Cinema
20 Emad El Din St.
Cairo
Tel: 770359/770259
Fax: 770029

Misr International
35 Champolion St.
Cairo
Tel: 5788034/5788124
Fax: 5788032

Egyptian Radio & TV Union
Kornish El Nil
Maspero
Cairo
Tel: 769584/5759313
Fax: 773441

Sobky for Film Prod.
102 Tahrir St.
Dokki
Cairo
Tel: 360662/3499525
Fax: 713384

Misr Film Distribution and Movies Company
85 Ramses Street
Cairo

Al-Ahram for Cinema & Video
1 Abu El Karamat Square
Mohandessin
Cairo
Tel: 3465396
Fax: 3470286

Tamido
95 Mohamed Farid Street
Nozha
Heliopolis
Cairo
Tel: 2470461
Fax: 2471203

Studio 13
2 Soliman El Halaby St.
Cairo
Tel: 5748807
Fax: 5781406

El Sultan Film
102 A Al Haram St.
Giza
Tel: 3855561
Fax: 3860000

Ahmed Saad for Art Prod.
7 Tarek Ibn Ziada St.
Pyramids Avenue
Giza
Tel: 385561
Fax: 384141

Misr Al Arabiya Films
12 Soliman El Halaby St.
Cairo

Shamel Media Prod. & Dist.
6 A Ismail Mohamed St.
Aamelek
Cairo
Tel: 3406580
Fax: 3413367

Useful Addresses

National Film Centre
City of Arts
Al Ahram Avenue
Giza
Tel: 5854807
Fax: 5854701

Cultural Development Fund
Opera Area
Gezira
Cairo
Tel: 3404234/3407001
Fax: 3406759

Academy of Arts
City of Arts
Gamal El Din Al Afaghany St.
Giza
Tel: 5613985
Fax: 5611034

Chamber of Film Industry
33 Oraby St.
Cairo
Tel: 5741677
Fax: 5751583

Festivals

Alexandria Film Festival
9 Oraby St.
Cairo
(Competitive, for Mediterranean countries – and for first films internationally – September)

Cairo International Film Festival
17 Kasr El Nil St.
Cairo
Tel: 3923562
Fax: 3938972
Telex: 21781 CIF FUN
(Competitive, retrospectives and tributes – December)

Cairo International Children's Film Festival
17 Kasr El Nil St.
Cairo
Tel: 3923962
Fax: 3938979
(March)

Ismailia International Film Festival
Cultural Development Fund
Opera House area
El Gezira
Cairo
Tel: 3407001, 3404234
Fax: 3406759
(Shorts, documentaries and cartoons. Competitive. Did not take place 1996)

ESTONIA

Jaan Ruus

The crisis in the domestic film industry, that has been building for some time, came to a peak in 1995. For the first time, feature film production was down to one film. State subsidies weren't so modest for such a little country: $650,000 from the budget and $200,000 through Cultural Endowment, which receives its income from excise taxes on alcohol, tobacco and gambling. But following their old custom, most film-makers still rely totally on the state. The state has not yet joined the international film funds (Eurimage, Media) and there have been no co-production projects. There is neither marketing nor a market itself for Estonian films.

The synopsis of the year's only feature, **Too Tired to Hate** *(Ma olen väsinud vihkamast)*, by former documentary film-makers Renita and Hannes Lintrop, could have been lifted from *Bad Boys*: "An urban melodrama about juvenile prison and a personal vendetta that reaches its peak within prison walls". This film was co-financed by Finnish TV and cost 3 million Estonian crowns (US$260,000).

An active lobby by film-makers of parliament has brought forth $1.2 million from the budget for the whole film industry in 1996, as well as $0.5 million from Cultural Endowment. In May 1996, the Minister of Foreign Affairs announced that Estonia would join Eurimages, which would encourage local producers to participate in international co-productions. Numerous little studios have been born recently, bringing the total to 56, but they mainly make video programmes for TV.

Indiana Jones vs. the EU

The animation tradition has survived thanks to entertaining and educative serials made for Nordic TV channels. Internationally recognised animators Priit Pärn and Janno Põldma completed a cartoon, **1895** for the 100th anniversary of the Lumières' cinema; a witty, tricky animation with absurd humour that seeks adventure in the history of cinema. In Riho Unt's entertaining puppet film, **Back to Europe** *(Tagasi Euroopasse)*, a tenacious and clever Estonian farmer fights for his economic independence against the clerks of European Union in Indiana Jones style. A group of animators named A-film is active in producing cartoons for Danish and other European studios.

There are 158 cinemas in Estonia, 32 of them in urban centres and 126 in the country, all private enterprises that rent buildings from municipalities. Cinemas as places of entertainment don't bring a quick profit and require a huge investment. Therefore, only the two first-night cinemas in the capital, Tallinn, are supplied with Dolby stereo, one of them additionally with digital DTS sound. Admissions dropped to 1.14 million in 1995, 0.8 per capita. 84 new films were screened, 68 of them from the U.S. All the foreign-language films are supplied with subtitles both in Estonian and Russian. A distribution company, MPDE, specialising

Jarl Karjatse and Marek Pavlov in TOO TIRED TO HATE

TOP TEN GROSSING FILMS IN ESTONIA: 1995

	Admissions
Forrest Gump	57,064
Casper	44,506
Batman Forever	38,506
First Knight	33,924
Bad Boys	32,925
Street Fighter	27,977
Richie Rich	27,865
Legends of the Fall	24,416
Junior	24,105
Interview with the Vampire	23,848

in U.S. features, scooped up 80% of the admissions.

The number of video cassette recorder owners has grown from 9% (1993) to 16% (1995). Estonia has three national TV channels (one public and two private). 41% of households own cable TV or a satellite dish and North Estonia is covered by four Finnish channels. The development of cable television has been precipitous, but it provides an enormous black market since there is no effective legislation. The annual "Film of the Year" Aastafilm award, presented by FIPRESCI, was given in 1995 to the cartoon, **1895**.

Still from BACK TO EUROPE, directed by Riho Unt

JAAN RUUS is film critic for the Tallinn-based Estonian weekly *Eesti Ekspress* and Senior Editor of the art monthly, *Teater Muusika Kino*.

Recent and Forthcoming Films

DESINTEGRAATOR (Disintegrator)

Script: Oskar Kurganov, Mati Unt. Dir: Tõnu Virve. Prod: Freyja Film (Estonia)/Fora Film (Russia).

Drama based on the true story of a sensational inventor, Johannes Hint (1914-1985).

MINU LENINID (All My Lenins)

Script and Dir: Hardi Volmer. Prod: Faama Film.

A story about a school to manufacture 'clones' of Vladimir Uljanov-Lenin, organised by a real-life secret service agent, Aleksander Keskküla (1882-1963), who operated in Central Europe at the beginning of the century.

GEORGICA

Script: Madis Kõlv, Sulev Keedus. Dir: Keedus. Phot: Rein Kotov. Players: Evald Aavik, Mair Merekülski. Prod: Baltic Broadcast.

A former African missionary meets a mute boy in Khrushchev-era Estonia.

KARU SÜDA (The Heart of the Bear)

Script: Nikolai Baturin. Dir: Arvo Iho. Prod: Cumulus Projekt.

The wanderings of an Estonian man in Siberia make him a disciple of a shaman of the Evenki tribe.

KEISRI HULL (The Czar's Madman)

Script: Jan Kross. Dir: Roman Baskin, Mikk Mikiver. Prod: FilmiMAX.

Drama about a Baltic-German landowner, Timotheus von Bock, who avoids compromises and refuses to bend to the Russian Czar himself.

PAGULASROMANSS (Romance to Refugee)

Script and Dir: Peeter Urbla. Prod: EXITfilm.

Two Eastern bloc refugees in a totally changed world are unable to find anything to do with their personal freedom.

PUNANE NORMAN (Red Norman)

Script: Olev Remsu, Aare Tilk. Dir: Tilk. Prod: Aristo (Estonia)/ Gamla Stan (Sweden)/Trinity Film (Russia).

An historical drama about the Swedes of the Estonian coast and their fate in Siberia in 1940-1952.

SAATAN JA ARLEKIIN (The Devil and the Harlequin)

Script: Aleksandr Borodjanski. Dir: Mati Põldre. Prod: Lege Artis Film.

An opera singer doomed by a fatal disease at the height of his success stages Mozart's *Don Giovanni*. Based on the life of popular Estonian singer Georg Ots (1920-1975).

Producers

Aristo
Uus 3
EE 0001 Tallinn
Tel: +372 (2) 44 53 37
Fax: +372 (2) 60 14 23

Baltic Broadcast
Narva mnt 11 A
EE 0001 Tallinn
Tel: +372 640 83 93
Fax: +372 640 83 94

Cumulus Projekt
Uus 3
EE 0001 Tallinn
Tel: +372 (2) 42 66 45
Fax: +372 (2) 640 91 18

Eesti Joonisfilm
Harju 9
EE 0001 Tallinn
Tel: +372 (2) 44 49 94
Fax: +372 (2) 43 41 56

Eesti Kroonikafilm
Harju 9
EE 0001 Tallinn
Tel: +372 (2) 44 50 29
Fax: +372 (2) 44 37 61

Eesti Telefilm
Faehlmanni 12
EE 0100 Tallinn
Tel: +372 (2) 43 45 40
Fax: +372 (2) 43 41 56

EXITfilm
Kaupmehe 6
EE 0001 Tallinn
Tel: +372 631 79 95
Fax: +372 (2) 44 84 16

Faama Film
Harju 9
EE 0001 Tallinn
Tel: +372 (2) 44 37, 72,
+372 5 237 579
Fax: +372 (2) 44 37 72

FilmiMAX
Uus 3
EE 0001 Tallinn
Tel: +372 (2) 44 34 36
Fax: +372 (2) 60 14 23

Freyja Film
Regati 8
EE 0019 Tallinn
Tel: +372 (2) 23 86 82
Fax: +372 (2) 23 86 82

Gavia Film
Uus 3
EE 0001 Tallinn
Tel: +372 (2) 43 45 39

Lege Artis Film
Uus 3
EE 0001 Tallinn
Tel: +372 (2) 60 27 95
Fax: +372 (2) 60 14 23

Monofilm
Tammsaare tee 110-35
EE 0029 Tallinn
Tel: +372 (2) 53 14 02

Nukufilm
Kaupmehe 6
EE 0001 Tallinn
Tel: +372 (2) 44 27 70
Fax: +372 (2) 44 27 70

Olav Neuland FPR
Sihi 22
EE 0016 Tallinn
Tel: +372 (2) 51 03 45

OMAfilm
Tatari 21B-12
EE 0001 Tallinn
Tel: +372 (2) 44 82 22

Polarfilm
Gonsiori 29
EE 0001 Tallinn
Tel: +372 (2) 42 18 20
Fax: +372 (2) 42 49 62

Rao Heidmets Filmstudio
Tartu mnt. 47-48
EE 0001 Tallinn
Tel: +372 (2) 42 67 48

SEE
Uus 3
EE 0001 Tallinn
Tel: +372 (2) 44 66 44
Fax: +372 (2) 44 66 44

Tallinnfilm
Harju 9
EE 0001 Tallinn
Tel: +372 (2) 44 20 88
Fax: +372 (2) 44 37 61

Weiko Saawa Film
Nikolai 15-4
EE 3600 Pärnu
Tel: +372 44 43 869

Distributors

BDG
Vana-Posti 8
EE 0001 Tallinn
Tel: +372 631 43 94
Fax: +372 631 30 23

FilmiMAX
Uus 3
EE 0001 Tallinn
Tel: +372 (2) 44 34 36
Fax: +372 (2) 60 14 23

Meedium
Narva mnt. 63
EE 0106 Tallinn
Tel: +372 (2) 42 57 10,
+372 (2) 42 59 30
Fax: +372 (2) 42 72 51

MPDE
Pärnu mnt. 45
EE 0001 Tallinn
Tel: +372 631 45 46
Fax: +372 631 30 23

THE FINNISH FILM FOUNDATION

★ *The dominant force in Finnish film financing.*

★ *International promotion of all Finnish films.*

★ *Extensive post-production facilities including a state-of-the-art sound studio.*

K 13, Kanavakatu 12, 00160 Helsinki
Tel: + 358 (9) 0 6220 300
Fax: + 358 (9) 0 6220 3060

FINLAND

Matti Apunen

In June 1996, a special train brought cinema to the railway station in Helsinki, just as it did 100 years ago when the first movie reels arrived from St. Petersburg on June 28, 1896. Unfortunately, the centennial frenzy isn't reflected at the box-office. If the 1994-95 season was bedecked with hopeful signs, then the autumn of 1995 saw many of those hopes going down the drain. Admissions decreased from 5.6 million (1994) to 5.3 million. This was especially marked in big cities like Helsinki, where theatres sold 200,000 less tickets than in 1994.

The worst of signs and losses, though, was the sudden death of Matti Pellonpää in July 1995. Pellonpää was a permanent member of Aki Kaurismäki's ensemble, and the spirit and mood of Kaurismäki's films was often embodied in the melancholic, earnest characters Pellonpää played so brilliantly. He won the European film prize for best actor four years ago.

Where's the New Blood?

Cinema attendance in Finland is usually heavily affected by sports events, and 1996 is certainly full of major sports festivities. But what many may find surprising is that in Finnish theatres European films are doing better than in other European countries. Every fifth movie shown in Finland in 1994 was of European origin. The market share of Hollywood films (66%) is less than that of most Americanised market areas. The bad news is that Finns are the second laziest cinema-going nation in Europe, after Luxembourg. Denmark, very comparable to Finland in terms of population, sells almost twice as many cinema tickets.

Markku Pölönen's **The Last Wedding** helped to brighten the season, but Pölönen's 'magic realism' can't by itself lift the gloom of the film community, a mood that might best be described as "What now?" Where's the new blood? It is emblematic that this year many of the national Jussi film awards were left on the shelf, including the prize for best actor. *The Last Wedding* came home with three Jussis, including that for best direction. Pölönen's film was the engine that pulled the market share of domestic films up to 10.5% after the disastrous 4% of 1994, the lowest ever.

But even the Finns turned a cold shoulder to their Golden Boy in Hollywood, Renny Harlin. *Cutthroat Island* was a huge disappointment at the box office, after the negative word-of-mouth reached Harlin's homeland. Instead, middle-aged audiences queued to see Jane Austen on the big screen. *Sense and Sensibility* was the sleeper hit of early 1996 (total admissions, 166,000).

Kati Outinen and Markku Peltola in Aki Kaurismäki's DRIFTING CLOUDS

FINNKINO

EXHIBITION

DISTRIBUTION

VIDEODISTRIBUTION

FINNKINO OY, Koivuvaarankuja 2, SF-01640 Vantaa
Phone +358-0-131 191, Telefax +358-0-1311 9300

Quiet After the Storm

The controversial MD of the Finnish Film Foundation, Marianne Möller, was replaced in late 1995 by Jouni Mykkänen, 57, an experienced television manager, who was expected to bring a steadying authority after years of constant turmoil. The message from Finnish Minister of Culture, Claes Anderson, was short but clear: "Bury the disputes and start working". Mykkänen's second-in-command is Erkki Astala, the former PR and international relations officer of Aki Kaurismäki's Villealfa production company. Astala was appointed the head of production, responsible for allocating the support money of FIM 34.2 ($US 7.4m). The new policy of the FFF seems to be to concentrate on fewer projects.

A committee on film financing was appointed in January 1996, its task being to outline measures that will increase public support and introduce tax breaks for film investment. Public financial support for the cinema has dropped about 30% in the 1990s.

Jarmo Mäkinen in THE LAST WEDDING, directed by Markku Pölönen

MATTI APUNEN is film critic and editor of the Sunday section for the Tampere-based morning newspaper *Aamulehti*.

Recent and Forthcoming Films

CONDITION RED

Script: Andrea Degas, Mika Kaurismäki. Dir: Kaurismäki. Players: James Russo, Cynda Williams, Paul Calderon. Prod: Marianna Films.

KAUAS PILVET KARKAAVAT (Drifting Clouds)

Script and Dir: Aki Kaurismäki. Phot: Timo Salminen. Players: Kari Väänänen, Kati Outinen. Prod: Villealfa.

KIVENPYÖRITTÄJÄN KYLÄ (The Last Wedding)

Script and Dir: Markku Pölönen. Phot: Kari Sohlberg. Players: Martti Suosalo, Henrika Andersson, Matti Varjo. Prod: Dada Filmi.

SEASICK

Script: Iiro Küttner. Dir: Veikko Aaltonen. Players: Bob Peck, Katrin Cartlidge, John Castle. Prod: Villealfa.

ISÄLTÄ POJALLE (From Father to Son)

Dir: Peter Lindholm. Players:

TOP TEN GROSSING FILMS IN FINLAND: 1995

	Admissions
The Last Wedding *(Finnish)*	278,495
Forrest Gump	255,716 (prem. 1994: total attendance 588,464)
The Lion King	248,363 (prem. 1994: total attendance 458,401)
Die Hard 3	211,728
The Bridges of Madison County	202,661
Apollo 13	196,021
Batman Forever	186,622
Waterworld	153,097
GoldenEye	150,157
Kummeli Stories *(Finnish)*	147,890

Tommi Korpela, Marika Parkkomäki.

TOMAS

Dir: Raimo O. Niemi. Players: Arttu Kapulainen, Janika Jokela.

GOING TO KANSAS CITY

Dir: Pekka Mandart. Prod: Mandart Productions.

THE VILLAGE

Dir: Kari Väänänen. Prod: Aki and Mika Kaurismäki for Villealfa.

Producers

Dada-Filmi
Kolmas linja 5
SF-00530 Helsinki
Tel: (0) 73 77 88
Fax: (0) 73 07 34

Filminor
Lemuntie 7 C
SF-00510 Helsinki
Tel: (0) 75 05 00
Fax: (0) 75 09 00

Harlin/Selin Productions
Mikonkatu 9
SF-00100 Helsinki
Tel: (0) 17 41 91
Fax: (0) 622 34 03

Jörn Donner Productions/Giron Filmi
Pohjoisranta 12
SF-17000 Helsinki
Tel: (0) 135 60 60
Fax: (0) 135 75 68

Kinofinlandia
Maneesikatu 1-3 J
SF-00170 Helsinki
Tel: (0) 278 17 83
Fax: (0) 278 17 63

Kinotar/Filmzolfo
Meritullinkatu 33
00170 Helsinki
Tel: (0) 135 18 64
Fax: (0) 135 78 64

Kanotuotanto
Katajanokankatu 6
SF-00160 Helsinki
Tel: (0) 66 32 17
Fax: (0) 66 20 48

Marko Röhr Productions
Kiilantie 22
SF-10320 Karjaa
Tel: (11) 362 36
Fax: (11) 36 286

Mondo Furioso Film Productions
Nilsiänkatu 15
00510 Helsinki
Tel: (0) 701 21 64
Fax: (0) 70 12 16 81

Reppufilmi Oy
Pohjoinen rautatienkatu 17 A
SF-00100 Helsinki
Tel: (0) 49 82 84
Fax: (0) 44 18 43

Villealfa Filmproductions Oy/Sputnik Films/Marianna Films
Pursimiehenkatu 25
SF-00150 Helsinki
Tel: (0) 622 18 11
Fax: (0) 622 38 55

Distributors

Cinema Mondo
Unioninkatu 10 A 23
SF-090130
Tel: (0) 62 95 28
Fax: (0) 63 14 50

Finnkino
Koivuvaaranjuja 2
SF-01640 Vantaa
Tel: (0) 13 11 91
Fax: (0) 13 11 93 00

Kinoscreen
Katajanokankatu 6
SF-00100 Helsinki
Tel: (0) 66 37 17
Fax: (0) 62 20 48

Miofilm Oy/Urania Film Oy
Hiidetie I A 7
SF-90230 Oulu
Tel: (81) 314 17 32
Fax: (81) 314 17 30

United International Pictures
Kaisaniemenkatu I C 98
SF-00100 Helsinki
Tel: (0) 66 21 66
Fax: (0) 66 50 05

Warner Bros Finland
Kaisaniemenkatu I B a
SF-00100 Helsinki
Tel: (0) 63 82 88
Fax: (0) 63 81 61

Useful Addresses

Central Organisation of Finnish Film Producers
Kaisaniemenkatu 3 B 29
SF-00160 Helsinki
Tel: (0) 63 63 05

Finnish Film Foundation
Kanavakatu 12
SF-00160 Helsinki
Tel: +358-0-6220 300
Fax: +358-0-6220 3060, 6220 3050
Internet: lumo@kaapeli.fi

Finnish Cinema Association
Finnish Film Chamber
Kaisaniemenkatu 3 B
SF-00100 Helsinki
Tel: (0) 63 63 05

Finnish Broadcasting Company (YLE)
TV Centre
SF-00024 Helsinki
Tel: (0) 148 01

FRANCE

Michel Ciment

The good news this year was enough to give another confidence boost to the French film industry. There were 129.7 million admissions in 1995 (as against 124.4 the year before), a result unequalled elsewhere in Europe or in Japan. Furthermore, French films accounted for 35.42% of tickets sold (as against 28.33% in 1994), and American films had to settle for 54.4%, their lowest share of the market in any European country. There were 2.29 seats sold per head of population as against less than two in neighbouring countries.

Ninety-seven French films were produced (85 in 1994), to which could be added 32 co-productions with a French minority share. Of those, 33 were first features and 16 second features: one half of the output thus came from beginners or young directors, a healthy sign of the renewal of talent. The strong attendances of recent years were also good news for producers, and for the government's *"fonds de soutien"* (fed by the tax levied on tickets at the box-office), permitting investment in future production.

TV channels also helped to boost production. Of the 2,722 million francs invested in French films, 35% came from the TV channels (with an increase of 165 MF from the Canal Plus cable channel and of 95 MF from the other channels), 25% from French producers, 10% from foreign producers (with an increase of 45 MF), 10% from the *fonds de soutien,* and 10% from Sofica. M6, another TV channel, and Arte, the French-German cultural network, increased their participation: three films being produced by the former and five by the latter. But it is Canal Plus which is playing the key role, pre-buying three quarters of its production (all its films having a budget over 13 MF and investing altogether 668.5 MF).

The High and the Low

The average budget for a film rose from 22.5 MF in 1993 to 26.1 in 1994 and 28 in 1995. 24 films in 1995 had a budget between 40 and 90 MF, as against only 14 in 1994. However, only two projects rose above 90 MF in 1995 as against four the year before, perhaps because only one of them, **Les Anges gardiens** (135 MF) was a huge success, the other three (**Le Hussard sur le toit**, 176 MF; **Les Misérables**, 120 MF; and **La Cité des enfants perdus**, 90 MF) being a disappointment at the box-office. The tendency of recent years was confirmed with a sharp decline in medium budget films (25 MF) and a wide gulf

FRANCE!
LE CINEMA EST AUSSI MUSIQUE.
ECOUTEZ LE CINEMA.

100 YEARS OF CINEMA CAM

C.A.M. ORIGINAL SOUNDTRACKS from the golden years of Italian and French cinema.
Over 170 titles and 75 composers available on compact disc.
Ask for our catalog. Also available on CD-ROM.

CAM Original Soundtracks VIA COLA DI RIENZO, 152 - 00192 ROME (ITALY) - FAX:(+39-6) 687.4046

between big commercial films (above 40 MF) and art-house features (under 20 MF and often 10 MF).

One film out of two was an international co-production (only 30% at the end of the 1980s), and the role of funding bodies - such as Eurimages, ECO (for central and eastern European films), and Fonds Sud (for North African and African films) to grow. But it is reassuring that foreign films with a large French investment do not look like tasteless Europuddings but strongly reflect their cultural origins. Mike Leigh's **Secrets and Lies**, though mostly produced by Ciby 2000, was no less a Mike Leigh film - as, in the same way, **Underground**, with Ciby financial backing (and another Palme d'or, for that matter) was a pure Kusturica movie.

Among the foreign co-producers, Italy made a comeback as France's leading partner (21 films), followed by Great Britain (11), Germany and Spain (eight), Portugal (seven), Belgium and Switzerland (six). European cinema (France included) had a 44% share of the market. Conversely, France invested 35% more money into foreign productions. This international dynamism saw the Algerian Merzak Allouache, the Georgian Nana Djordjadze, the Italian Marco Ferreri, the Norwegian Nils Gaup, the Polish Agnieszka Holland, the Russian Pavel Lounguine, the Chilean Raoul Ruiz, the Anglo-Indian-American Ismail Merchant and Flora Gomez, from Guinea-Bissau, make their new films as French productions.

While 40 companies produced one film this year, the bulk of production came from a few big companies which invested from 150 MF to 350 MF. The results did not always meet expectations. The need to have attractive projects led to more and more financially ambitious productions, but ten out of fifteen big-budget films did not achieve their aims in terms of audiences. **Les Ange gardiens** and **Gazon maudit**, for instance proved extremely popular. But Maurice Pialat's **Le Garçu** and Alain Corneau's **Le Nouveau Monde** - to name two leading film-makers - had poor returns at the box-office.

A Double Threat

The distribution system again saw the domination of French and American films, 136 and 134 respectively, out of a total of 371 (75%). This leaves a weak proportion of European films, though 19 British features were distributed in 1995 as against 13 the year before. However, the fate of national films and of American films was as usual quite different, the Hollywood product being much more exposed: 47% of the American films were released in more than 100 theatres, but only 16% of the French films. The summer, which has long been considered a doomed season by distributors, now belongs entirely to the Hollywood companies, who managed to have four of the 20 biggest successes of the year released in July and August: **Die Hard with a Vengeance**, **Batman Forever**, **Bad Boys** and **First Knight**.

While 164 distribution companies were active (413 are registered), ten of them dominate the market, with 89% of the box office. Gaumont Buena Vista lead the way (21.7%), followed by AMLF (15.8%), UIP (11.7%), Columbia (8.6%), Warners (8.2%), and UGC Fox (8%). This concentration creates problems for the many independent producers who have difficulty finding a slot to release their films and in the meantime have to pay high interest rates. But France remains a unique country to see films, and not only because of the number of new releases. 4,185 different films were shown during the year, including revivals, recent films still on release, and the new offerings. This multiplicity of choice is made possible by the number of theatres: 4,367 with a capacity of 529,938 seats.

The opening of six new multiplexes (added to four that opened in 1993 and 1994) represent a new phenomenon in France and a double threat: they tend to favour blockbusters at the expense of more original films, and they endanger the small theatres in the centre of cities. In Paris, UGC has opened a complex of 15 screens in Les Halles, the heart of the city, with a resulting decrease in attendance in the

Fanny Ardant in Patrice Leconte's RIDICULE, which opened the 1996 Cannes Festival with great distinction
photo: Catherine Cabrol

Latin Quarter theatres. But there are still 803 art-house cinemas, and those in the provinces are helped by ADRC (Agency for the Regional Development of Cinema).

A Society Made in the Salon

French cinema proved its continuing creative vitality at the latest Cannes Film Festival. Five native films were in competition (**Ridicule**, **Un Héros très discret**, **Comment je me suis disputé**, **Trois vies et une seule mort**, **Les Voleurs**) and were, on the whole, critically well-received (**Un Héros très discret** winning the best screenplay award). A sixth, **Conte d'été** by Eric Rohmer, might have competed with a fair chance of success instead of being screened on the closing night of "Un Certain Regard". Furthermore, at least a dozen French features — including some first films — were programmed in the various sections and provoked real interest.

The opening night film, Patrice Leconte's **Ridicule**, and Jacques Audiard's **Un Héros très discret**, both period films, broke with the usually academic style of historical reconstruction. Leconte has recreated the court of Versailles a few years before the Revolution with great visual flair, his usual sense of comedy, and a freedom in evoking the past. He wittily comments on the French love for social life and what it entails: the competition to show oneself as more clever and biting tham the next courtier, with all the possible dramatic consequences. French civilisation is partly a product of *salon* society (beginning in the 17th century) and the film — brilliantly played by Fanny Ardant, Jean Rochefort and particularly Charles Berlin — might be extended as a comment on the Cannes Film Festival!

A few months earlier Leconte had offered a wonderful farce, **Les Grands Ducs**, about second-rate theatre actors touring the provinces in some inane boulevard comedy. The film is also about role-playing and appearances with tragic undertones. It was savagely attacked by the press, who in the past would have accepted the comic extravagance of an Italian film but refused to accept that a Frenchman could be as extreme in his verbal and visual humour as well as in his bad taste. An exceptional trio – Philippe Noiret, Jean-Pierre Marielle and Jean Rochefort – played the 'hams' with obvious relish.

Like Leconte's *Ridicule,* Jacques Audiard's second feature, **Un Héros très discret,** reasserts the quality of writing and the importance of imagination all too often sacrificed in a cinema more devoted to the protrayal of daily life. The protagonist admirably embodied by Mathieu Kassovitz is a young man without personality who, at the end of World War II, as the opportunity presents itself, decides to play the role of a resistant and manages to convince everyone that he was indeed part of the Gaullist underground movement. The story of course serves as a metaphor for recent French history, since both Gaullists and Communists managed, in the late 1940s and 1950s to reconstruct a fake glorious past that eclipsed the collaboration of the Vichy regime. Not until 1970 and *The Sorrow and the Pity* did a more complete picture of France during the Occupation start to appear. Audiard's troubling, funny, intelligent film never allows the audience to feel comfortable, the charm of the leading actor working against the villainy of his character.

By comparison, other period films fared less well. **Les Caprices du fleuve** by actor-director Bernard Giraudeau, is a verbose account of slavery in Africa during the Ancien Regime, full of pretty pictures and good intentions; **Madame Butterfly** a stilted rendering by Frédéric Mitterand of the Puccini opera; **Beaumarchais l'insolent** by Edouard Molinaro, inspired by a little-known Sacha Guitry play, lacked the lightness of the writer's own films but offered at least a brilliant performance by Fabrice Luchini. The only film of some real value in the classical mould was Jean-Paul Rappeneau's **Le Hussard sur le toit,** because of its meticulous sense of detail, its rejection of cheap emotion through an aristocratic style of distancing master shots, and its subtle sense of rhythm. Set in the luscious landscapes of the South of France, the film nicely captures Jean Giono's original novel while not fully convincing us that it was such good material for the screen. If Rappeneau's film was the most expensive in the history of French cinema, Philippe Colin's **Les Derniers Jours d'Emmanuel Kant** may have been one of the cheapest - and no less interesting for that. In a minimalist style, it recounts the old philosopher's daily life garden, his conversation, his idiosyncracies, his moments of bad temper. An elegant cameo with a tongue-in-cheek detachment.

When Comedy Took Over

As the list of the top grossing films shows, only comedies (with the brilliant exception of *Nelly and M. Arnaud*) have been able to challenge the Hollywood blockbusters. **Les Anges gardiens** reunites the team of *Les Visiteurs* with the addition of Gérard Depardieu. **Les Trois Frères** uses the absurdist talent of Les Inconnus, a group of TV stand-up comedians, but the best of them all — not such a feat — was, probably **Le Bonheur est dans le pré**, by Etienne Chattiliez. This revolves around a TV programme about the search for a missing person in which Michel Serrault (superb as usual) takes advantage of his resemblance to another man to leave his current wife and find a new home.

Chantal Akerman did not really manage to capture the spirit of classical Hollywood screwball comedy in her **A Couch in New York** (shot in English), nor Didier Lepêcheur to recall the anarchist and surrealist spirit of Jacques Prévert in **Des Nouvelles du bon dieu**. But Pierre Salvadori confirmed the talent revealed in his first film with his new feature, **Les Apprentis**, about two clumsy burglars (delightfully played by Guillaume Depardieu and François Cluzet). No less successful was Cedric Klapisch with **Chacun cherche son chat**, an exploration, à la René Clair, of a popular district of Paris discovered through the search for her cat by its charming owner.

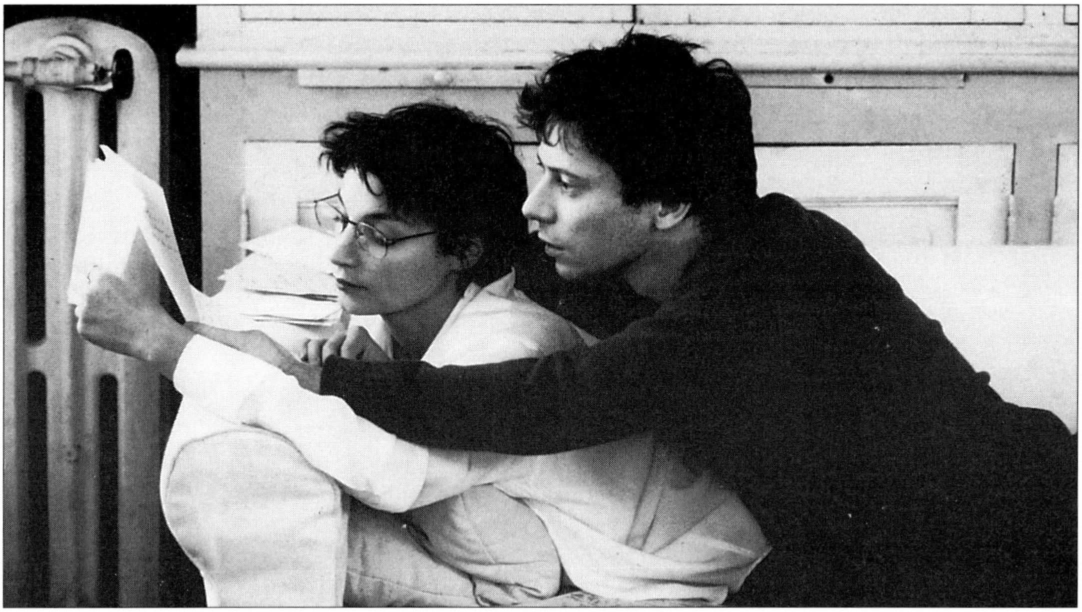

Jeanne Balibar and Mathieu Amahic in COMMENT JE ME SUIS DISPUTE... *photo: Jean-Claude Lother*

For the younger generation of film-makers, the observation of love and friendship between men and women is decidedly the predominant theme. In his three hour **Comment je me suis disputé... (ma vie sexuelle)**, Arnaud Desplechin tried to sum up these preoccupations. Brilliantly acted and directed, ambitious in its polyphonic structure, the film suffers at times from a complacent script but nevertheless confirms Desplechin as a very promising talent.

Some of these new directors come from the FEMIS, the national film school, and have found supportive young producers (Pascal Caucheteux, Philippe Rossignon, Alain Rocca) who share their artistic ambition. The themes of their films are close to those of the New Wave, with an interest in existential problems (states of unease, lonely women in search of love, private violence) and in oblique portrayals of the French social scene.

Film-makers in the Landscape

The exceptional number of talented women directors was confirmed this year by four newcomers who proved their audacity in their choice of fresh material. Diane Bertrand's **Un samedi sur la terre** constructs a puzzle about a killing on a sunny country road and the various characters involved. Sandrine Veysset's **Y aura-t-il de la neige à Noel ?** depicts the life of a mother brutalised by her often absent lover but who finds comfort in her seven children while running her farm in the south of France. Lucile Hadzihalilovic's stark **La Bouche de Jean Pierre** deals powerfully with child abuse in the outskirts of Paris, while Judith Cohen's **La Croisade d'Anne Buridan** playfully investigates, à la early Godard, the political aspirations of young people today.

This interest in reality is of course reflected in a number of remarkable documentaries, such as **Afriques: comment ça va avec la douleur**, Raymond Depardon's long cinema essay on his relationship to the African continent, on its political turmoil and the nature of cinéma vérité, as he travels from Johannesburg to Cairo. Also notable were Jean Michel Carre's **Visiblement je vous aime**, with its mixture of documentary and fiction, about a re-education centre for delinquents, Claire Simon's **Coute qui coute**, about the economic and human problems of a small enterprise which prepares ready-made meals, and **Microcosmos**, a dazzling investigation of the world of insects by Claude Nuridsany and Marie Perennou.

Contributions from well-known figures in the cinematographic landscape included André Téchiné's **Les Voleurs**, which confirmed his taste for psychological portraits in the classical French tradition, and Maurice Pialat's **Le Garçu**, which pushed to the extreme his concern with the naked truth of raw reality. This consists of moments in the life of a father in his relationship with his wife, his mistress, his young son and his dying father: no plot, no spectacular scenes, only a hypersensitive approach which has disconcerted the fans of Gérard Depardieu.

Catherine Breillat's **Parfait amour!** is less an enquiry about a murder than a portrayal of the destructive power of passion. An older woman develops an affair with a young man and, when he leaves her, sets out to provoke him into killing her. Bertrand Blier in **Mon homme** also deals in his characteristic style (provocative vulgarity, characters talking to camera) with a couple, this time a pimp and his girl. Anouk Grinberg gives a stunning performance for which she received the best actress award at the Berlin Film Festival. Eric Rohmer's **Conte d'été** found the 76-year-old director in top shape with his new ironical and witty tale about a young man on holiday in Brittany hesitating between three girls, and finally escaping abruptly from this impossible dilemma.

Raoul Ruiz's **Trois vies et une seule mort** is one of the best films of this prolific director, a humorous, surrealistic charade with Marcello Mastroianni living a quadruple life in which fiction has the logic of dreams, in a Paris lovingly explored by this South American artist who has made the French capital his second home.

Finally, the surprise of the year was probably **A la vie, à la mort!** by Robert Guédiguian, a director who has worked in the margin of the industry, shooting in Marseille with the same group of actors. His sixth film recalls the warmth and humanity of French films of the 1930s, with its group of unemployed characters made up of a striptease girl, café owner, charwoman, prostitute, old anarchist, who help each other to survive in a difficult world.

When Claude Sautet received for the second time the coveted Delluc Prize for his masterpiece *Nelly and M. Arnaud,* he regretted that Guédiguian did not win it in his stead. A fitting homage to a director who, against all the odds, has proven by his sheer capacity to make personal films in hard conditons the truth of his morality tale about solidarity and the necessity of fighting against adversity.

TOP GROSSING FILMS IN PARIS: 1995

	Admissions
Seven	1,107,605
Le Bonheur est dans le pré	1,085,325
Les Trois Frères	1,035,821
Pocahontas	886,680
Les Anges gardiens	877,584
GoldenEye	756,602
Pédale Douce	723,207
Twelve Monkeys	531,500
Casino	515,500
Beaumarchais	505,637
Nelly et M. Arnaud	501,942

Producers

Alexandre Films
14 rue de Marignan
75008 Paris
Tel: 44 95 89 89
Fax: 42 89 26 89

Caméra One
38 rue du Bac
75007 Paris
Tel: 45 49 09 79
Fax: 45 49 93 69

CIBY 2000
90 avenue des Champs
Elysées,
75008 Paris
Tel: 44 21 64 00
Fax: 40 76 02 75

Cinéa
87 rue Taitbout
75009 Paris
Tel: 44 91 94 14
Fax: 40 16 19 11

Films Alain Sarde
17 rue Dumont d'Urville
75116 Paris
Tel: 44 43 43 70
Fax: 47 20 61 50

Film Par Film
10 avenue George 5
75008 Paris
Tel: 40 73 84 20
Fax: 47 23 95 68

Flach Films
47 rue de la Colonie
75013 Paris
Tel: 44 16 40 00
Fax: 45 80 40 01

Gaumont
30 avenue Charles de Gaulle,
92200 Neuilly
Tel: 46 43 20 00
Fax: 46 43 21 68

Hachette Première
10 rue de Marignan,
75008 Paris
Tel: 42 25 19 70
Fax: 42 56 00 81

IMA Productions
3 rue de Liège
75009 Paris
Tel: 40 23 48 10
Fax: 40 82 97 01

MK2 Productions
55 rue Traversière,
75012 Paris
Tel: 43 07 92 74
Fax: 43 41 32 30

Les Productions Lazennec
5 rue Darcet,
75017 Paris
Tel: 43 87 71 71
Fax: 43 87 17 74

Pandora Cinéma
7 rue Keppler,
75116 Paris
Tel: 40 70 90 90
Fax: 40 70 90 91

Renn Productions
10 rue Lincoln,
75008 Paris
Tel: 40 76 91 00
Fax: 42 25 12 89

Le Studio Canal +
6 Boulevard de la République
92514 Boulogne
Tel: 46 10 12 00
Fax: 46 10 12 40

Téléma
26 rue Danton
92300 Levallois Perret
Tel: 47 58 67 30
Fax: 47 58 81 16

UGC Images
24 avenue Charles de Gaulle,
92200 Neuilly
Tel: 46 40 44 00
Fax: 46 24 37 28

Distributors

AFMD
18 rue Troyon
75017 Paris
Tel: 44 09 08 08
Fax: 47 64 14 27

A.M.L.F.
10 rue Lincoln,
75008 Paris
Tel: 40 76 91 00
Fax: 42 25 12 89

B.A.C.
5 rue Pelouze,
75008 Paris
Tel: 44 70 92 80
Fax: 44 70 90 70

Ciby Distribution
90 avenue des Champs Elysées
75008 Paris
Tel: 44 21 64 00
Fax: 44 21 64 35

Diaphana Distribution
50 rue de Paradis
75010 Paris
Tel: 44 79 92 92
Fax: 42 46 54 48

Gaumont/BVI
5 rue du Colisée
75008 Paris
Tel: 46 43 24 53
Fax: 46 43 20 47

Mercure Distribution
48 rue de la Colonie
75013 Paris
Tel: 45 89 80 00
Fax: 45 65 07 47

Metropolitan Filmexport
116 bis avenue des
Champs Elysées
75008 Paris
Tel: 45 63 45 60
Fax: 45 63 77 31

Polygram Distribution (ex Pan Européene)
107 Boulevard Péreire
75017 Paris
Tel: 44 15 66 66
Fax: 47 64 36 38

Pyramide Film
5 rue Richepanse,
75008 Paris
Tel: 42 96 01 01
Fax: 40 20 02 21

TF1 International
305 avenue le Jour se Lève
92656 Boulogne Cedex
Tel: 41 41 25 70
Fax: 41 41 21 33

UFD
2 avenue Montaigne
75008 Paris
Tel: 53 67 17 17
Fax: 53 67 17 00

Sales Agents

Gaumont
30 avenue Charles de Gaulle,
92200 Neuilly
Tel: 46 43 20 00
Fax: 46 43 21 68

Président Films
2 rue Lord Byron
75008 Paris
Tel: 45 62 82 22
Fax: 45 63 40 56

Roissy Films
10 avenue George V
75008 Paris
Tel: 53 67 31 00
Fax: 47 23 79 88

Seawell Films
45 rue Pierre Charron
75008 Paris
Tel: 47 20 18 73
Fax: 47 20 15 43

UGC
24 avenue Charles de Gaulle,
92200 Neuilly
Tel: 46 40 44 00
Fax: 46 24 37 28

World Marketing Film
8 rue Lincoln
75008 Paris
Tel: 42 25 84 20
Fax: 42 25 67 52

Useful Addresses

Centre National de la Cinématographie (CNC)
12 rue de Lubeck
75116 Paris
Tel: 44 34 34 40
Fax: 47 55 04 91

Unifrance Film International
4 Villa Bosquet,
75007 Paris
Tel: 47 53 95 80
Fax: 47 05 96 55

The largest entertainment news-gathering staff...

...in the world

More than 50 correspondents in more than 40 locations worldwide.

VARIETY

Objective. Respected. Preferred.

GERMANY

Jack Kindred

Pragmatism is the philosophy of the young generation of German film-makers, and it's paying off at the box- office. Just as the New German film-makers turned their backs on "Grandpa's Cinema", in the so-called 1962 Oberhausen Manifesto, newcomers like farmer-turned-film-maker Detlev Buck, Sönke Wortmann and Rainer Kaufmann have rebelled in their turn and replaced a cinema of auteurs with one of commercial journeymen. Their aim is to recapture the home crowd from Hollywood and, with limited budgets and other constraints, they are succeeding by giving the moviegoing public what it is supposed to want, entertainment.

Kings of the Box-office

By the end of 1995, the year when the industry marked the 100th anniversary of film, producer Bernd Eichinger's *Der Bewegte Mann*, released in Britain as **The Most Desired Man** and in the U.S. as **Maybe, Maybe Not**, had clocked-up 6.5 million admissions since its release in October, 1994. And Wortmann's gay-scene comedy was still going strong into 1996. Other big home-grown hits included Kaufmann's hilarious **Talk of the Town** (*Stadtgespräch*), which attracted 1.6 million patrons, and Doris Dörrie's bitter-sweet **Nobody Loves Me** (*Keiner liebt mich*), which had 1.3 million. Going into 1996, the trend continued with Buck's latest comedy, **Jailbirds** (*Männerpension*), whose admissions soon totalled a phenomenal 3.1 million.

Not far behind was Wortmann's latest opus, **The Superwife**, (*Das Superweib*), which had taken 2.1 million admissions in the few weeks since its March launch. A pop music comedy directed by Roland Willaert, **Bathsalts** (*Abbuzzel*), billed as the Hessian answer to Monty Python and the Marx Brothers, attracted more than 700,000 admissions over a twelve-week period. Joseph Vilsmaier's **Brother of Sleep** (*Schlafes Bruder*), a Golden Globe nominee, also fared well with 908,383 visitors since its October, 1995, release. However, more serious works such as the love triangle drama **Silent Night** (*Stille Nacht*), from director Dani Levy, and Michael Verhoeven's **My Mother's Courage** (*Mutters Courage*), a film in which Germans confront their past, failed to make a showing in the charts (500,000 admissions is considered the mark of success).

Although the American majors have had limited success in the past distributing locally produced movies, they've taken another look at the growing popularity of the new wave of German films. Munich-based Buena Vista's distribution expertise helped *Talk of the Town* (1.5 million admissions) and *Nobody Loves Me* (1.3 million) to become the top German titles in 1995. In Hamburg, Warner Bros picked up Romuald Karmaker's **The Deathmaker** (*Der Totmacher*) after the film's success in Venice, with star Götz George being named best actor. Based on the true story of a serial killer in the 1920's, the movie still recorded 400,000 admissions despite its

Maria Schrader and Pierre Sanoussi-Bliss in KEINER LIEBT MICH, directed by Doris Dörrie

Götz George in DER TOTMACHER

grisly theme. Warners carried on with two further releases of German movies in the spring of 1996, the action thriller **Dangerous Dowry** (*Nur aus Liebe*), and **Peanuts**, a spoof based loosely on a financial scandal. Both, however, disappointed at the box office. Notwithstanding, Warners clinched a five-year output deal with Bio-skop Film, the producer of *Peanuts.*

Other American majors also found the going hard with certain German films, Buena Vista failing badly with *Silent Night*. But the majority of made-in-Germany movies found independent distribution. The Americans failed to grab the Tobis release, **The Ogre** (*Der Unhold*), which Volker Schlöndorff took time out from managing the revamped Babelsberg studios to direct. Constantin Film in Munich releases all of Bernd Eichinger's movies, including his latest, *The Super Wife*, and Pandora-Film has Hark Bohm's **For Ever and Ever**. Of the 120 feature films produced in Germany in 1995, 63 were released and quite a few others found distributors for later launch.

Land of Darkness and Multiplexes

Although the German film failed to improve its market share in 1995, overshadowed by U.S. productions, most German exhibitors were satisfied, even though attendance dropped by nearly eight million to 124.5 million admissions. Germany's 1,999 theatres, furnishing 3,901 screens, took in DM 1,183 billion (US$825.5 million) in 1995, compared with DM 1.228 billion ($857 million) the previous year. Tickets saw a slight increase to an average of DM 9.54 (US$6.65). The Film Promotion Board, which compiled the statistics, said the increase had little effect on attendance.

A mild cause for optimism, however, was the increase in the number of multiplexes, which totalled 17 at the end of 1995. And at least three more of these multi-screen, luxury complexes were in the planning stage, reflecting the industry's *sangfroid* in the face of the digital TV threat. Multiplexes in both the eastern and western areas of the reunited nation drew an encouraging 13.7 million patrons, about 11% of the total number of moviegoers.

The upswing in German films in the face of competition from the U.S. majors could in part be due to a rethinking of film support programmes, which in 1995 saw the state and federal governments earmarking DM 200 million (US$140 million) in subsidies. The four largest regional subsidy boards – the North-Rhine Westphalia Film Foundation, Hamburg's Film Promotion Board, the Berlin/Brandenburg Film Board, and the Film and Television Fund in Bavaria, as well as the Federal Film Board (FFA) in Berlin – no longer mete out production financial support, unless the package appears to have genuine commercial possibilities. Selection committees seldom approve of a film project without a prior agreement with a distributor and a comprehensive marketing concept. The FFA allocated DM 13.7 million (US$12 million) for 17 projects in 1995.

Upcoming films in production in 1996 include the tragi-comedy **Knocking on**

TOP TEN GROSSING FILMS IN GERMANY: 1995

	Admissions
While You Were Sleeping	3,971,646
The Lion King	3,754,462
Casper	3,405,876
Die Hard 3	3,202,391
Stargate	3,001,465
Waterworld	2,989,907
Disclosure	2,899,188
Apollo 13	2,762,194
Pocahontas	2,532,769
The Most Desired Man (*German*)	2,531,855

Heaven's Door, a Mr Brown Entertainment/Buena Vista co-production directed by and starring Til Schweiger. Helmut Dietl's social comedy **Rossini** features Mario Adorf, Heiner Lauterbach, Götz George and Gudrun Landgrebe, and director Peter Sehr's feature film drama **Obsession** (*Sucht*) delves into the loss of Jewish culture in Germany. Volker Schlöndorff's *The Ogre*, his first film in five years, was slated for the Cannes festival but was held up in post-production.

And finally, one of the most interesting projects in the pipeline is versatile producer Eberhard Junkersdorf's $15 million animation film, **The Fearless Four**, a modern version of the Grimm brothers' fairy tale, "The Bremen Town Musicians". Junkersdorf founded the studio, Munich Animation, especially for the project.

JACK KINDRED, ex university professor, musicologist, classical pianist and wire service editor, reports on the German media scene from Munich.

Recent and Forthcoming Films

ALLES NUR TARNUNG (Life Is a Bluff)

Script and Dir: Peter Zingler. Phot: Jorg Seidl. Players: Marlo Adorf, Elke Sommer. Prod: ZZ-Film.

DIEBIN EN (Lady Thieves)

Script: John Salvati, Jan Dreyer. Dir: Peter Weck. Phot: Wolfgang Treu. Players: Christiane Hörbinger, Lena Stolze, Jennifer Nitsch, Francis Fulton-Smith. Prod: Roxy Film.

ECHTE KERLE (Real Guys)

Script and Dir: Rolf Silber. Phot: Jürgen Herrmann. Players: Christoph Ohrt, Tim Bergmann, Carin Tietze. Prod: Cobra Film.

THE FEARLESS FOUR

Script: Bert Henry, Georg Reishelt, Dagmar Kekulee. Dir: Michael Coldewey, Jürgen Richter. Prod: Bioskop Film. *Animation.*

FüR IMMER UND IMMER (For Ever and Ever)

Script and Dir: Hark Bohm. Phot: Arthur Reinhart. Players: Johanna ter Steege, Jeanette Arndt, Liliana Bohm. Prod: Hamburger Kino Kompanie.

HARALD

Script and Dir: Jürgen Egger. Phot: Seamus McGarvey. Players: Heinrich Schafmeister, Martina Gedeck, Ingo Naujoks. Prod: Kinowelt.

HAPPY WEEKEND

Script and Dir: Eddi Herzog. Phot: George Fick. Players: Erik Goertz, Anton Rattinger, Isabel Trimborn. Prod: Senator Film.

IRREN IST MÄNNLICH (To Err Is Masculine)

Script: Kit Hopkins. Dir: Sherry Hormann. Phot: Gerard de Battista. Players: Herbert Knaup, Corinna Harfouch, Dominik Graf. Prod: Hager Moss Film.

KNOCKING ON HEAVEN'S DOOR

Script: Thomas Jahn. Dir: Til Schweiger. Players: Schweiger, Jan-Josef Liefers. Prod: Mr Brown Entertainment.

Katja Riemann and Hannes Jaenicke in DANGEROUS DOWRY

KING OF EVERGREEN

Script and Dir: Dietmar Klein. Phot: Ciro Cappellari. Players: Diether Krebs, Tilo Prückner, Eva Ebner. Prod: Schramm Film.

DAS LEBEN IST EINE BAUSTELLE (Life Is a Construction Site)

Script: Wolfgang Becker, Tom Tykwer. Dir: Becker. Phot: Martin Kukula. Players: Jürgen Vogel, Christiane Paul. Prod: X-Filme Creative Pool.

MÄNNERPENSION (Jailbirds)

Script and Dir: Detlev Buck. Phot: Slawomir Idziak. Players: Detlev Buck, Til Schweiger, Heike Makatsch, Marie Bäumer. Prod: Boje Buck.

NUR AUS LIEBE (Dangerous Dowry)

Script and Dir: Dennis Satin. Phot: Jörg Widmer. Players: Katja Riemann, Hannes Jaenicke, Heinz Hoenig, Daniela Lunkewitz. Prod: Eine ena Film/Warner Bros./Film Deutschland Produktion.

PEANUTS

Script: Peter Zingler, Eberhard Junkersdorf. Dir: Carlo Rola. Phot: Peter Ziesche. Players: Ulrich Müne, Iris Berben, Sonja Kirchberger, Marita Marschall. Prod: Bioskop Film.

ROHE OSTERN (No Panic!)

Script: Matthias Dinter. Dir: Michael Gutmann. Phot: Johannes Geyer. Players: Anian Zollner, Julia Jager. Prod: Tele-München.

STADTGESPRÄCH (Talk of the Town)

Script: Ben Taylor. Dir: Rainer Kaufmann. Phot: Klaus Eichhammer. Players: Katja Riemann, August Zirner, Martina Gedeck, Kai Wiesinger. Prod: Studio Hamburg Produktion.

STILLE NACHT (Silent Night)

Script: Klaus Chatten. Dir: Dani Levy. Phot: Charly Koschnick. Players: Maria Schrader, Jürgen Vogle, Marc Schlichter, Ingrid Caven. Prod: X-Filme.

STILL MOVIN'

Script: Jack Engelken. Dir: Niki Stein von Kamienski. Phot: Wolfgang Aichholzer. Players: Kai Wiesinger, Leonard Lansink, Jochen Nickel, Sandra Speichert. Prod: F & B Entertainment.

DAS SUPERWEIB (The Super Wife)

Script and Dir: Sonke Wortmann. Phot: Tom Fahrmann. Players: Veronica Ferres, Joachim Krol, Liselotte Pulver, Til Schweiger. Prod: Constantin Film.

DER UNHOLD (The Ogre)

Script: Jean-Claude Carrière, Volker Schlöndorff. Dir: Schlöndorff. Phot: Bruno de Keyzer. Players: John Malkovich, Marianne Sägebrecht, Armin Mueller-Stahl. Prod: Studio Babelsberg/Renn Production (Paris).

DER TOTMACHER (The Deathmaker)

Script and Dir: Romuald Karmakar. Phot: Fred Schuler. Players: Götz George, Jürgen Hentsch, Pierre Franckh. Prod: Pantera Film.

THE TRIP

Script and Dir: Wolfgang Büld. Phot: Tomas Erhart. Players: Esther Schweins, Dieter Thomas Kuhn, Herbert Feuerstein. Prod: Vision Film.

UND KEINER WEINT MIR NACH (And Nobody Weeps For Me)

Script: Willy Purucker. Dir. and Phot: Joseph Vilsmaier. Players: Peter Ketnath, Nino Hoss. Prod: Lunaris Film/Neue Constantin.

WORKAHOLIC

Script and Dir: Sharon von Wietersheim. Phot: Gerard Vandenberg. Players: Christiane Paul, Tobias Moretti, Ralf Bauer, Nadeshda Brennicke. Prod: Tele-München.

Producers

Allianz Filmproduktion GmbH
Leibnitzstr. 60
10625 Berlin
Tel: (30) 323 9011
Fax: (30) 323 1693

Anthea Film GmbH
Widenmayerstr. 4
80538 Munich
Tel: (89) 226 194
Fax: (89) 221 251

Bavaria Film GmbH
Bavariafilmplatz 7
80336 Geiselgasteig/Munich
Tel: (89) 6499 2389
Fax: (89) 649 2507

BioSkop-Film GmbH
Türkenstr. 91/111
80799 Munich
Tel: (89) 394 987
Fax: (89) 396 820

Capitol Film + TV International GmbH & Co. Vertriebs KG
Harvestehuder Weg 43
20149 Hamburg 13
Tel: (40) 411 79-0
Fax: (40) 411 70-199

Connexion-Film Vertriebs & Produktions GmbH & Co.
Harvestehuder Weg 45
20149 Hamburg
Tel: (40) 411 79 300
Fax: (40) 411 79 399

Franz Seitz Produktions GmbH
Beichstr. 8
80802 Munich
Tel: (89) 391 1123
Fax: (89) 340 1291

Willy Bogner Film GmbH
Sankt Veitstr. 4
81673 Munich
Tel: (89) 436 06-0
Fax: (89) 436 06 429

CCC Filmkunst GmbH
Verlangerie Daumstr. 16
13599 Berlin
Tel: (30) 334 200-1
Fax: (30) 334 0418

CineVox Film GmbH
Bavaria Filmplatz 7
80336 Geiselgasteig
Tel: (89) 649 541
Fax: (89) 791 2164

Manfred Durniok Produktion
Hausotterstr. 36
13409 Berlin
Tel: (30) 491 8045
Fax: (30) 491 4065

Impuls Film
Grazestr. 20
30519 Hanover
Tel: (511) 835 001
Fax: (511) 838 6253

Hermes Film GmbH
Kaiserplatz 7
47441 Munich
Tel: (89) 394 368
Fax: (89) 344 363

Lisa Film GmbH
Widenmayerstr. 48
80538 Munich
Tel: (89) 227 195
Fax: (89) 291 156

Mondada Film
Klausenerstr. 19
8154 Munich
Tel: (89) 692 5884
Fax: (89) 691 6709

Neue Constantin Film GmbH
Kaiserstr. 39
47441 Munich
Tel: (89) 3860 9221/2
Fax: (89) 3860 9242

Oko-Film GmbH
Mauerkircherstr. 3
81679 Munich
Tel: (89) 987 666
Fax: (89) 987 602

Olga Film GmbH
Tengstr. 16
80798 Munich
Tel: (89) 271 2635
Fax: (89) 272 5768

Studio Hamburg
Tonndorfer Hauptstr. 90
22045 Hamburg
Tel: (40) 6688-0
Fax: (40) 665 601
(40) 6688 4370

Rialto Film GmbH
Bismarckstr. 108
13469 Berlin
Tel: (30) 310-000-0
Fax: (30) 310 00 559

Roxy-Film GmbH
Schützenstr. 1
80335 Munich 2
Tel: (89) 555 341
Fax: (89) 594 510

Tele-München GmbH
Kaufingerstr. 25
80331 Munich
Tel: (89) 296 661
Fax: (89) 227 875

Vision Film GmbH
Kurfürstenplatz 4
80796 Munich
Tel: (89) 390 025
Fax: (89) 395 569

Von Vietinghoff Filmproduktion
Potsdamerstr. 199
10783 Berlin
Tel: (30) 216 8931
Fax: (30) 215 8219

Regina Ziegler Filmproduktion
Budapesterstr. 35
10789 Berlin
Tel: (30) 261 8071
Fax: (30) 262 8213

Distributors

Ascot Filmverleih GmbH
St. Annastr. 16
80538 Munich
Tel: (89) 29 69 95
Fax: (89) 33 18 39

Columbia TriStar Filmgesellschaft GmbH
Ickstattstr. 1
80469 Munich
Tel: (89) 23 69-0
Fax: (89) 26 43 80

Concorde Filmverleih GmbH
Widenmayerstr. 5/6
80538 Munich
Tel: (89) 22 07 44
Fax: (89) 29 64 50

Futura/Filmverlag GmbH
Rambergstr. 5
80799 Munich

Tel: (89) 38 170-1
Fax: (89) 38 17 00 20

Helkon Media Filmvertrieb
Widenmayerstr. 36 GmbH
80538 Munich
Tel: (89) 291 60 490
Fax: (89) 291 37 20

Highlight Film Verleih GmbH
Herkomerplatz 2
81679 Munich
Tel: (89) 92 69 66 02
Fax: (89) 98 15 43

Impuls Film
Grazerstr. 10
30519 Hanover
Tel: (0511) 83 50 01
Fax: (0511) 838 6253

Jugend Film Verleih GmbH
Reichsstrasse 15
14052 Berlin
Tel: (30) 300 6970
Fax: (30) 300 697 11

Kinowelt Filmverleih GmbH
Pfisterstr. 11
80331 Berlin
Tel: (89) 219 937-0
Fax: (89) 219 93 744

Metropol Filmverleih GmbH
Viktoriastr. 34
80803 Munich
Tel: (89) 39 30 96
Fax: (89) 39 63 03

NEF 2 Filmverleih GmbH
Erhardstr. 8
80469 Munich
Tel: (89) 201 1747
Fax: (89) 201 1634

ScotiaFilm GmbH
Possartstr. 14
81679 Munich
Tel: (89) 413 090-0
Fax: (89) 470 6320

SenatorFilm GmbH
Kurfürstendamm 65
10707 Berlin
Tel: (30) 880 91 700
Fax: (30) 880 91 790

20th Century Fox of Germany GmbH
Postfach 70 11 22
60561 Frankfurt am Main
Tel: (69) 60 90 20
Fax: (69) 62 77 16

United International Pictures GmbH
Hahnstr. 31-35
60528 Frankfurt am Main
Tel: (69) 66 98 19-0
Fax: (69) 666 6509

Warner Bros Film GmbH
Hans-Henny-Jahn-Weg 35
22085 Hamburg
Tel: (40) 22 650-0
Fax: (40) 22 650 259

Useful Addresses

Verband der Filmverleiher e.V (VDI)
(Assn. of Distributors)
Kreuzberger Ring 56
65205 Wiesbaden
Tel: (611) 77892-0
Fax: (611) 7789212

Export Union
Türkenstr. 93
80799 Munich
Tel: (89) 39 00 95
Fax: (89) 39 52 23

Production team behind HAPPY WEEKEND: producer Hanno Huth, Erik Goertz, director Eddie Herzog, and Ralf Richter

GREECE

Yannis Bacoyannopoulos

Greeks are beginning to feel they have reached saturation point as far as television is concerned. In actual fact, although they are avid viewers of current affairs and talk shows, they are much less interested in fiction programmes. This is reflected in a marked return of audiences to movie theatres. An increase of around 10% in admissions and box-office receipts has been observed. Improvements continued in existing movie theatres (those that were renovated reported a spectacular increase in box-office receipts), while new theatres were opened, especially in the residential suburbs of Athens where none had existed. The possibility of creating the first two multiplex theatres, one in the northern and the other in the southern suburbs, may also radically change the capital's film map.

A new feature this year has been the extension of the period of first-run movies into the summer months, when they have been shown in open air theatres with singular success. The result has been an increase in the total number of new films from about 180 in 1994-95 to at least 220. But the breakdown of films has also changed in a promising manner. Of course, American blockbusters still prevail, but there has been a significant increase in the number of European films as well as films from the rest of the world.

The amazing success of Kusturica's *Underground* (140,000 admissions) was followed by that of *Il Postino* (85,000 admissions) and *La Haine* (55,000 admissions). Other art films were limited to 10,000-30,000 admissions. At any rate, American films are not expected to exceed 80-82% of the box-office, which would mean a drop of at least 5%.

Unfortunately, the reaction of local audiences to Greek films has been negative. Even Theo Angelopoulos' **Ulysses' Gaze**, winner of the Grand Jury Prize at Cannes, was unable to exceed the 60,000 admissions mark. Others fell below 15,000-20,000 admissions. The fact that theatres were tied up by the fiercely competitive distributors of foreign films only partly accounts for this apathy.

In addition to the question of inadequate distribution, there are also production problems. The Greek Film Centre remains the major financial backer and independent producers shy away from the prospect of poor financial returns. The Ministry of Culture subsidised the GFC with 5 million ECUs in 1996 which in turn made 4.5 million ECUs available for film production, 70% greater than the figure for 1994. The GFC is seeking to work out a new policy which will make it the development and regulatory agency of a financially healthier and broader production mechanism.

A Happy Odyssey

Greek films fared much better internationally. The major retrospective of 100

Still from Voulgaris's ACROPOLE

The G.F.C.
brings you
close
to Greek
Movies
GREEK
FILM
CENTRE
10, PANEPISTIMIOU AVENUE • 106 71 ATHENS GREECE
TEL.: (01) 3634.586 - 3631.733 • FAX: 3614.336 • TELEX: 222614 GFC

Still from LIKE A PRAIRIE COCK IN WYOMING

films at the Centre Pompidou in Paris attracted tens of thousands of viewers and provided the nucleus for other important events that were organised in Geneva and Lausanne, in Madrid and Barcelona, and in Toronto and Montréal. The Minister of Culture, Stavros Benos, has created a constantly expanding network of municipal movie theatres that will showcase European and Greek productions, and is pushing for a total revision of film policy and of the relative legislative framework.

Among the new films, Pantelis Voulgaris' **Acropole** brings back to life the mythical world of the musical theatre of the 50s and 60s, with the traditional romantic conflict backstage. Vassiliki Iliopoulou confirmed the promise she

TOP TEN GROSSING FILMS IN GREECE: 1995-1996

	Admissions
Pocahontas	175,000
Seven	175,000
Heat	175,000
Underground	140,000
GoldenEye	140,000
Dangerous Minds	135,000
Waterworld	135,000
Braveheart	125,000
Casino	120,000
First Knight	120,000

Note: These figures are for the Greater Athens area only. Statistics are unconfirmed officially and based on information from distribution offices.

Still from DREAM AGAINST A WHITE BACKGROUND

Still from THREE SEASONS

showed in her first film with her second, **Desire**. Two siblings abandoned and separated since childhood, in different institutions, find each other again in the wilderness of a modern megacity.

Three young directors distinguished themselves with their first films: Dimitris Indares' **Like a Prairie Cock in Wyoming**, about an irresolute, good-hearted young man in a world that is falling apart; Fotini Siskopoulou's **Life on Sale**, in which a writer weaves imaginary stories about the people around him; and Eleni Alexandraki's **A Drop in the Ocean**, in which an actress is caught between her passion for the stage and her love for a social misfit. Stavros Tsiolis continued to spin his modern fairy-tales, bright voyages into the Peloponnese, with **The Lost Treasure of Hursit Pasha**.

Other noteworthy films included Giorgos Karypidis' **Bewitched**, Isavella Mavraki's **Transito**, Thanassis Scroubelos' **Hawaii**, Giorgos Zervoulakos' **Orpheus Descending**, Cristos Shopachas' **The Wing of the Fly**, George Katakouzinos' **Zoe** and Nikos Triandafyllidis' **Radio Moscow**. Antoinetta Angelidi (**The Hours**) and Costas Sfikas (**Paul Klee's Prophetic Bird of Sorrows**) continued on the lonely creative road of experimental cinema. Finally, Thomas Moschopoulos' **Meri Amen**, Fotos Lambrinos' **Birthday Party – A Silent Balkan Story** and Panos Bournias' **Tanah Lot, at the End of the World**, were three full-length documentaries that stood out.

YANNIS BACOYANNOPOULOS has worked for many Greek newspapers and magazines, beginning in 1960. For the past twenty years, he has been the film critic of the Athens daily *Kathimerini* and Greek State Television ET-1.

See page 265 for list of Greek Recent and Forthcoming Films

HONG KONG

Derek Elley

As the territory hurtles towards its July 1997 deadline for the handover to China, the local Cassandras have been busier than ever predicting the imminent collapse of Hong Kong's film industry. Continuing migration to Hollywood by some of the leading lights and still falling revenues for local pictures seem to support many of their arguments, but it is still premature to begin the last rites for an industry which remains the powerhouse of the region and managed to release 140 titles during 1995, the same number as the previous year.

Box-office receipts for Hong Kong movies fell to some HK$750 million (US$99 million), from HK$940 million the previous year. Total admissions (for all films) were 14.2 million, against 20.2 million in 1994 and 33.6 million in 1993. Though the public still turned out in record numbers for Jackie Chan's **Rumble in the Bronx** (HK$56.9 million), there was a huge gap between those highs and the more standard fare. A few star vehicles managed to plug the gap: popular comedian Stephen Chow had a couple of hits (the two-part **A Chinese Odyssey**; and **Sixty Million Dollar Man**). The message has been clear for some time: audiences will support "event" films which offer them something they can't get in other media, but will no longer pay relatively stiff admissions prices for substandard quickies.

It is not even as if (despite the relentless propaganda of U.S. distributors) that audiences are deserting local films for American imports: only two Hollywood pictures got into the 1995 top ten (*Die Hard with a Vengeance* and *Batman Forever*). In Taiwan, where local film-makers have lost touch with their audience, the market long since fell to U.S. movies. The irony is that Hong Kong, seemingly the most "international" Chinese-speaking territory, is the fiercest adherent to films in its own dialect – when they are good.

Signal Failures

The basic facts are still that after the U.S. and India, Hong Kong is the largest producing territory in the world; and after the U.S. it is the second largest exporter of its movies – reportedly HK$1 billion (US$130 million) a year. But with other sources of entertainment growing every year Hong Kong clearly has to spread its limited amount of capital over fewer pictures to retain audiences. One sobering statistic is that over 70% of film companies in the territory made a loss in 1995.

Stars' skyrocketing fees are taking no account of the industry's condition, leading at least one prominent member of the community, actress-director Sylvia Chang, openly to criticise this trend of the past few years. Forced to demand higher prices from overseas markets, producers have already met resistance from distributors in Taiwan and elsewhere. There's also the added problem of the continuing brain drain to the U.S.

Gong Li in Chen Kaige's TEMPTRESS MOON

John Woo has since been joined in Hollywood by actor Chow Yun-fat (*Replacement Killers*) and directors Ringo Lam (*The Exchange*, a.k.a. *Bloodline*), Tsui Hark (*The Colony*), Ronnie Yu, Kirk Wong and, at time of writing, probably Stanley Tong (Jackie Chan's regular). Chan himself, since the success of *Rumble in the Bronx*, is enjoying unprecedented popularity in the U.S., after three previous attempts to crack the market in the past 15 years. With *Rumble* shot in Vancouver, *Thunderbolt* half-shot in Japan, and *Police Story 4 – First Strike* and *A Nice Guy* made in Australia, Chan looks increasingly like an émigré film-maker.

What nobody knows – as the signals are still mixed, and no firm guidelines established – is how the Hong Kong industry will fare after July 1997. Technically, Hong Kong films could be in for a bonanza, getting unrestricted entry into the China of which they are part, but it looks likely that Peking will still limit them to protect its home-grown industry. Following changes of personnel in Peking in early 1996, the climate on the mainland has turned more conservative after two years of relative openness; one of the first decrees by the new film apparatchiks was further to limit Hong Kong product.

Leave-taking

The prolific Tsui Hark has had an up-and-down past year in his box-office fortunes but all four films have something to offer, virtually forming a panorama of his styles before moving to Hollywood. Tsui hit box-office gold with the wonderfully accomplished food comedy **The Chinese Feast** (about competing chefs, one from Hong Kong, the other from the mainland), flopping miserably with the period romantic comedy **Love in the Time of Twilight**, taking a completely different stylistic direction with the bloody, hand-held swordplay drama **The Blade**, and then having his name taken off Hong Kong prints of his 1996 New Year comedy **Tri-Star**, a crazed but often enjoyable teaming of stars Leslie Cheung, Anita Yuen and Lau Ching-wan.

Jackie Chan's three movies during the past year have also swung back and forth stylistically. **Rumble in the Bronx** is a kind of modern, sanitised version of Bruce Lee's xenophobic *The Way of the Dragon*, with Chan battling American street trash while trying to help Anita Mui make a go of it with her supermarket. Surprisingly light on action scenes, it gets by on Mui's wonderfully scatty performance, but is let down by a ragged ending featuring a hovercraft in the streets of "New York". **First Strike** features an equally perfunctory ending to its tale of Chan caught up in nuclear smuggling; best, and most traditional of all, is **Thunderbolt,** a racing car drama featuring some breath-taking set-pieces and Chan in uncommonly serious mode.

Peace Hotel, actor Chow Yun-fat's final film before moving to Hollywood, is an unsteady attempt at a Chinese Western, merging the Chinese "deserted inn" tradition with cowboy images closer to Sergio Leone. Director Ringo Lam's farewell movie, **The Adventurers**, is more successful; an ambitious character study of a Cambodian Chinese avenging his parents' massacre that would have been even better with someone other than Andy Lau in the lead.

The best straightforward action-adventure of the past year was **Dr. Wai in the Scripture with No Words**, a bouncy Indiana Jones-like period romp with Jet Li, Rosamund Kwan, Takeshi Kaneshiro, and Charlie Young, directed by the experienced Ching Siu-tung. Equally cinematic, though in a more studied way, is Ronnie Yu's **The Phantom Lover**, the latest Chinese remake of the *Phantom of the Opera* story, shot on huge sets built in Peking and teaming Leslie Cheung and Taiwanese actress Wu Ch'ien-lien.

Hong Kong Dreaming

Four other Hong Kong-financed productions began their round of international festivals during the first half of 1996 – all shot on the mainland by mainland-born directors, but often including off-shore

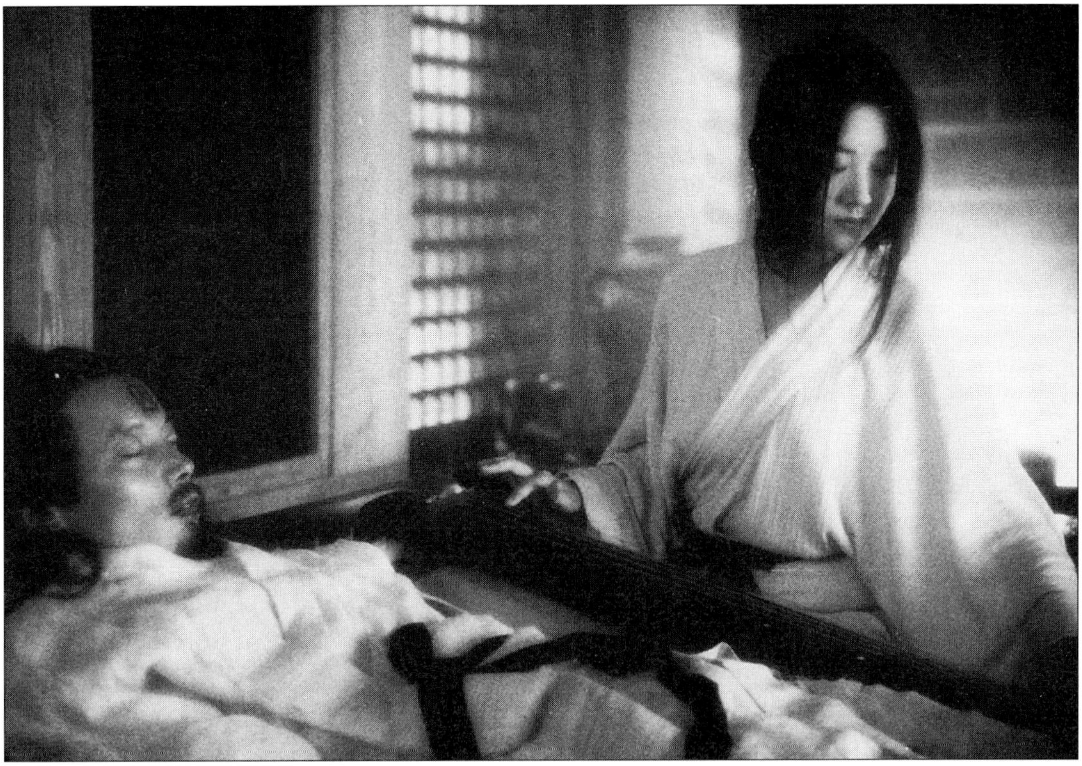

Ge You and Xu Qing in THE EMPEROR'S SHADOW

Chinese actors and totally relying on Hong Kong financing. Making the biggest splash was Chen Kaige's **Temptress Moon** which, after a tortuous production history that included firing the lead actress halfway through and shutting down for five months before casting Gong Li in the part, finally emerged at Cannes in 1996 to a decidedly mixed reception.

The 1930s romantic drama, set in a decaying household, is a thorough visual treat, with Chris Doyle's camerawork paralleling a woozy opium dream. But Gong is miscast and far too wooden for the devilish lead role and, despite a terrific opening that recalls Zhang Yimou's *Shanghai Triad* in its heady boldness, the script doesn't know how to develop the characters in its second act.

More successful overall, if a tad long for its measured pace, is He Ping's **Sun Valley**, a melancholic swordplay "Western" set in a snowy valley in Western China. As the mysterious avenger and the lonely innkeeper, Zhang Fengyi and Taiwanese actress Yang Kuei-mei meld beautifully, and the film has He's characteristic gift for landscape. Much smaller but wonderfully engaging is the return by Fifth Generation figurehead (and former boss of Xi'an Film Studio) Wu Tianming to film-making after some six years of self-exile in the U.S. **The King of Masks** is a project that was handed to him by Shaw Bros., but on

Zhang Fengyi as the swordsman in He Ping's SUN VALLEY

TOP TEN GROSSING FILMS IN HONG KONG: 1995

	(HK$ million)
Rumble in the Bronx*	56.9
Thunderbolt*	45.6
Sixty Million Dollar Man*	35.2
Die Hard 3	32.6
The Chinese Feast*	31.1
Full Throttle*	30.5
A Chinese Odyssey Part Two: Cinderella*	26.8
Batman Forever	26.1
A Chinese Odyssey Part One: Pandora's Box*	25.2
Peace Hotel*	24.8

* Hong Kong production.

which he has put his own fingerprint of meticulous character observation allied to a traditional, unflashy shooting style.

On a level of its own is **The Emperor's Shadow**, a leap into big-budget costume drama by Zhou Xiaowen. In one stroke the film redefines a genre that has long been saddled with stiff dialogue and acting, over-complex story-lines, and hordes of characters. Here Zhou focuses on the chamber story of a psychological game between the first emperor of a united China (played by Jiang Wen with both presence and subtlety) and his boyhood friend-turned-foe, a wily court musician (the wry Ge You). Technically smooth and full of unfamiliar details in the art direction, this is a drama that grips through the power of its performances rather than the spectacle of its mounting.

Josephine Siao in HU-DU-MEN

On a sadder note, one should note the deaths in 1996 of three major figures: director Lo Wei in January; veteran Cantonese actor Kwan Tak-hing (famous for playing Wong Fei-hung) in June; and Mandarin heart-throb of the 1950s and 1960s, Chao Lei, also in June.

DEREK ELLEY has been associated with IFG for more than 20 years, during which time he has written extensively on East Asian cinema. An associate editor of Variety, he is also editor of the annual Variety Movie Guide. He is currently completing A Handbook of Chinese Cinema.

15th Hong Kong Film Awards

The following awards were announced on April 28, 1996:

Best Film: *Summer Snow.*
Best Director: Ann Hui (*Summer Snow*).
Best Script: Chan Man-keung (*Summer Snow*).
Best Actor: Roy Chiao (*Summer Snow*).
Best Actress: Josephine Siao (*Summer Snow*).
Best Supporting Actor: Law Kar-ying (*Summer Snow*).
Best Supporting Actress: Karen Mok (*Fallen Angels*).
Best Newcomer: Mou Kai-yin (*Those Were the Days*).
Best Photography: Christopher Doyle (*Fallen Angels*).
Best Action Direction: Stanley Tong, Jackie Chan (*Rumble in the Bronx*).
Best Editing: Kong Chi-leung (*Full Throttle*).
Best Art Direction: Eddie Ma (*The Phantom Lover*).
Best Original Song: "Always Because of You" (from *Peace Hotel*).
Best Costume Design: William Chang, Yeung Sin-ling (*The Phantom Lover*).
Best Original Music: Frankie Chan (*Fallen Angels*).

Forthcoming Films

A NICE GUY

Dir: Sammo Hung. Players: Jackie Chan, Li Ting-yü. Prod: Golden Harvest/New Line. Shot in English.

WHO'S THE WOMAN, WHO'S THE MAN

Dir: Peter Chan. Players: Leslie Cheung, Anita Yuen, Anita Mui.

THE BUENOS AIRES AFFAIR

Dir: Wong Kar-wai. Players: Leslie Cheung, Tony Leung Chiu-wai, Maggie Cheung.

KITCHEN

Dir: Yim Ho, from Banana Yoshimoto's book. Players: Nobuko Tomita, Chan Siu-cheun, Lo Kar-ying. Prod: Golden Harvest (HK)/Amuse (Japan).

HALF A LIFETIME'S ROMANCE

Dir: Ann Hui, from the novel by Eileen Chang. Players: Leon Lai, Wu Ch'ien-lien. Prod: Mandarin Films (Hong Kong)/CMPC (Taiwan).

HUNGARY

Derek Elley

Though there have been occasional signs during the past year of a move towards more audience-accessible works, of the three major Central European film industries, Hungarian cinema still remains the most rooted in its auteurist heritage forged during the years of total state subsidies. Both Poland and the Czech Republic have developed more broad-based industries which have come up with sizeable local hits that audiences have supported in large numbers. But despite occasional triumphs like Róbert Koltai's comedy *We Never Die* (1993), Hungary has yet to produce a flow of box-office hits, and no director has tapped into the public imagination like the Czech Republic's Jan Šveřák or Poland's Wladyslaw Pasikowski.

Of the two most avowedly popular films during the past year, Róbert Koltai's *Szamba* (largely funded by HBO Hungary, in its first venture into film production) failed to duplicate the success of *We Never Die*, both artistically and commercially. And both that and András Kern's romantic comedy-drama *Stracciatella* were completely ignored in the prizes handed out at the 27th Hungarian Film Week Awards in Budapest in February 1996.

In a sign of the still unresolved tensions between the auteurist and market-led camps, the movie that swept the awards was Péter Gothár's *Letgohang Vaska*, an

Enikö Eszényi, Marianne Szalay, and Dorottya Udvaros in BITCHES

allegorical, symbol-laden fantasy solidly in the country's distinguished arthouse tradition. And in a further sign of how foreign programmers still categorise Hungarian production, it was this film, more than any of the others, that went on to tour festivals (including the Quinzaine at Cannes 1996).

With funding from the Hungarian Motion Picture Foundation showing no increase to take account of ever-rising inflation, film-makers are still being driven to international co-productions to raise finance, with none of the major support from local TV that typifies production in Poland (where Telewizja Polska has a hand in almost every movie). Despite this fact, however, the majority of Hungarian films are still strongly auteurist led – art with a capital A.

Changes on the exhibition side, with the arrival of the first multiplexes in Budapest in autumn 1996, means that Hungarian films may find it easier to get showings if exhibitors are prepared to gamble one screen out of several (rather than their sole screen) on local fare. The concept has worked in other territories, though at the end of the day the onus is still on film-makers to come up with accessible movies.

Koltai's **Szamba,** one of the most eagerly awaited productions, turned out to be a likeable if rather sprawling, unfocused work. It centres on a small-town ham actor (played by the director) whose son initially rebels against his father's wishes to follow him on to the boards but finally ends up becoming an actor in his own way. Set in rural Hungary during the 1970s and 1980s, it is more a multi-character study than a cohesive father-son drama, and uncharacteristically lapses into pretension during its latter stages.

Far better is popular actor András Kern's directorial début, **Stracciatella** (*Sztracsatella*), a comedy-drama about a famous conductor who goes through a mid-life crisis and ends up having an affair with the young psychiatrist (Enikö Eszényi) at the mental hospital he's consigned to. For Hungarian viewers, the film has an extra level of meaning as Kern dubs Woody Allen's voice locally: there is a little of the American comedian's self-irony here, but the movie still stands on its own feet as an enjoyable, smoothly shot, romantic comedy-drama.

One of the year's major disappointments was **Bitches** (*Csajok*), the first film by Ildikó Szabó since her moody drama *Child Murders* (1993). Where the previous film was tightly structured, highly atmospheric and in black-and-white, *Bitches* is self-indulgent, loosely scripted and in bright poster colours. Though the film drew some local acclaim for its accurate portrait of relations between the sexes, to foreign eyes this is an outdated attempt at the female bonding movie.

Similarly madcap but at least possessed of an overall guiding spirit is Péter Gothár's **Letgohang Vaska: Tales from the Lager** (*Hagyjállógva Vászka: Lágermese*), a fable about two crooks, one from the city and one from the country, who are able to fly above the roofs of St. Petersburg and break into the State Bank with impunity. Totally Russian in its sensibility (and soundtrack), and full of imagery that is largely incomprehensible to non-Central Europeans, the movie works as a kind of allegory about modern Russia (though the setting is Soviet) and the split between urban and rural existence.

In a year thin on veteran directors, three big names got together on the portmanteau **Let's Love Each Other . . .** (*Szeressük egymást gyerekek . . .*), uniting Pál Sándor, Károly Makk and Miklós Jancsó in very different takes on contemporary Hungary. Sándor's black-and-white episode (*Fire, Fire . . .*), set among a group of homeless, is the most fantastical, a bleak comedy buoyed by circus-like playing by Enikö Eszényi and veterans Hédi Temessy and Dezsö Garas. Makk's episode (*Hungarian Pizza*) is basically a black shaggy dog tale centred on a tramp who holds up a family that's just ordered a pizza. Jancsó's segment (*The Great Brain Death*) is characteristically the most *outré* of the lot, a

Helen Baxendale and Caroline Loncq as the English and American women in BOLSHE VITA

whirligig of tracking cameras, powerplays and TV screens that show the maestro's old techniques alive and well but ever more puzzling as to their precise meaning.

The only veteran with a full-scale feature on show was Márta Mészáros, whose **The Seventh Room** (*A hetedik szoba*) was a solid if rarefied return to form. The film shows a side of the director that surfaces only occasionally in beautifully turned period tales. Here the subject is German-Jewish philosopher Edith Stein (1891-1942) who became a Carmelite nun and perished in World War 2. Stunningly shot in burnished colours by Polish cameraman Piotr Sobociński, and beautifully acted by Maja Morgenstern, the film is more a portrait of the woman's interior journey than a fully worked out drama about Stein herself, of whom we learn little. But it is good to see Mészáros still capable of making a controlled, almost ascetic piece of cinema on this level after the messy histrionics of *Foetus* (1994).

Similarly controlled, but disappointingly flat after his previous *Red Funfair* (1992) and *Anna's Film* (1994) is György Molnár's early twentieth-century household drama **The Bad Doctor** (*A rossz orvos*), about a divorced, middle-class couple haunted by their child's misdiagnosed death. Traditionally Hungarian in its setting and style, János Erdélyi and Dezsö Zsigmond's **The Woman** (*Az asszony*) is a very solid drama that revisits a real-life story the directors previously examined in a documentary. Set after the failure of the 1956 counter-revolution, and entirely based on a small country farm, the film spins a convincingly claustrophobic drama around the tale of a man (Károly Eperjes), sentenced to death, who is hidden by his family in a hole in the ground to escape the authorities.

Amid the twenty or so movies of the 1995-96 season – back to the 1994 level, though still lower than pre-1989 days – one of the best of the year was the first feature by Ibolya Fekete, previously a scriptwriter with György Szomjas before going independent. Based on an idea spun off her

LET'S LOVE EACH OTHER (the segment directed by Károly Makk)

two-part video documentary *Children of Apocalypse* (1992), **Bolshe Vita** (*Bolse vita*) is one of the finest portraits of the social changes that have taken place in Hungary over the past six years.

Through the interweaving stories of a group of Russians who meet up with two young western women (British and American) in the summer of 1989, the movie accurately paints the mood and euphoria of the time as the traditional borders relaxed and Budapest became a centre for east-west migration. *Bolshe Vita* is an often funny and ultimately moving testimony to a period when everything briefly seemed possible in Central Europe. Though occasionally rough at the edges, Fekete's movie was the most impressive début of the year.

DEREK ELLEY has been associated with IFG for more than 20 years, during which time he has written extensively on East Asian cinema. An associate editor of Variety, he is also editor of the annual Variety Movie Guide. He is currently completing A Handbook of Chinese Cinema.

27th Hungarian Film Week Awards

The following were the main awards at the Week on February 13, 1996:

Best Film: *Letgohang Vaska.*
Best Director: Péter Gothár (*Letgohang Vaska*).
Best Cinematography: Francisco Gozón (*Letgohang Vaska*).
Best First Film: Ibolya Fekete (*Bolshe Vita*).
Gene Moskowitz Prize (foreign critics): *Bolshe Vita.*
People's Choice Award (readers of PM magazine): *Stracciatella* and *Szamba.*

Thomas Borbás - Zebra Film Hungary
Film and Television Production, Coproduction,
Distribution, Facilities, Information, Agency,
Representation, Contacts, Database
all over the World
Ph: (36-1) 302 22 69 Fax: (36-1) 132 40 67
E-Mail: zebra@hungary.net
H-1063 Budapest Munkácsy M. 21.

TOP TEN GROSSING FILMS IN HUNGARY: 1995

	(million forints)
Die Hard 3	92.5
Dumb and Dumber	73.1
The Specialist	66.2
The Mask	65.9
Outbreak	64.5
Junior	59.2
Casper	56.2
Waterworld	53.2
Apollo 13	49.7
Street Fighter	48.6

Recent and Forthcoming Films

JANCSI ÉS JULISKA (Hansel and Gretel)

Dir: Péter Gothár. Prod: Magic Media (Hungary)/47ème Parallèle (France)/Dor Film (Austria). Casting as of summer 1996.

MINDENÁRON (At Any Means)

Dir. György Szomjas. Players: Ildikó Bánsági, Sándor Gáspár, György Dörner. Prod: Hunnia Film Studio.

FRANCISKA VASÁRNAPJA (The Sundays of Frances)

Dir: Sándor Simó. Players: Jiří Menzel, Éva Kerekes, Dénes Ujlaki. Prod: Neuropa.

MAGYAR DEKAMERON (Hungarian Decameron)

Dir: Ildikó Enyedi. Players: Dávid Jánosi, Márta Angyal. Prod: MTV-FMS (Hungary)/Haut et Court (France)/Eurofilm Studio.

HOSSZÚ ALKONY (Long Twilight)

Dir: Attila Janisch. Players: Mari Töröcsik, András Fekete, Dénes Ujlaki. Prod: MTV-FMS, Budapest Film Studio (Hungary)/Eurofilm Studio.

A WITMAN FIÚK (The Witman Boys)

Dir: János Szász. Players: Maja Morgenstern, Alpár Fogarasi, Szabolcs Gergely, Dominika Ostalowska, Péter Andorai. Prod: Budapest Film Studio, MTM (Hungary)/47ème Parallèle (France)/Zebrafilm.

EGY TÉL AZ ISTEN HÁTA MÖGÖTT (A Winter behind God's Back)

Dir: Can Togay. Prod: Magic Media (Hungary)/47ème Parallèle (France)/Magellan Film (Belgium). Casting as of summer 1996.

SZÖKÉS (Escape)

Dir: Livia Gyarmathy. Players: Daniel Olbrychski, Artur Zmijewski, Krzysztof Kolberger. Prod: BGB, MTM (Hungary)/OKO Film (Poland).

SIMON MÁGUS (Simon, the Magician)

Dir: Ildikó Enyedi. Prod: Budapest Film Studio, Három Nyul, Artcam Intl. Casting as of summer 1996.

A SZERENCSE LÁNYAI (Daughters of Luck)

Dir: Márta Mészáros. Players: H. Starodub, Jan Nowicki, Marek Kondrat. Prod: Budapest Film Studio (Hungary)/Studio Filmowe Perspektywa (Poland).

SZENVEDÉLY (Passion)

Dir: György Fehér. Players: Ildikó Bánsági, János Derzi, Dzsoko Roszich. Prod: MTV Drama Studio/Budapest Film Studio.

A VILÁG LEGKISEBB ALAPITVÁNYA (The Smallest Foundation of the World)

Dir: Ferenc Kardos. Players: Hédi Temessy, Dorottya Udvaros, Dzsoko Roszich. Prod: Budapest Film Studio.

A JÁTÉKOS (The Gambler)

Dir: Károly Makk. Players: Michael Gambon, Jodhi May, Polly Walker. Prod: Obtektiv Film Studio/Marc Vlessing.

KINAI VÉDELEM (Chinese Defence)

Dir: Elemér Ragályi (assisted by Tamás Ascher). Players: Andor Lukáts. Prod: Objektiv Film Studio.

GLÓRIA (Gloria)

Dir: Péter Gárdos. Prod: Objektiv Film Studio. Casting as of summer 1996.

A VÁD (The Charge)

Dir: Sándor Sára. Players: Sándor Szakácsi, Kati Lázár, Zsolt Anger, Kitty Kéri, Zoltan Varga. Prod: Objektiv Film Studio.

TÖKÉLETES KÖR (Perfect Circle)

Dir: Ademir Kenovic. Prod: Objektiv Film Studio, and others.

TORONYÓRA (The Clock Tower)

Dir: Ömer Kavur. Prod: Objektiv Film Studio, and others.

SZÜRKE GALAMB (Grey Pigeon)

Dir: Gergely Z. Horváth. Prod: Hunnia Film Studio. Casting as of summer 1996.

FÜRÉSZPOROS MESÉK (Sawdust Tales)

Dir: Baris Pirhasan. Players: Hugh O'Connor, Károly Eperjes, Julia Brendler, David Harries, Hürdem Gürel. Prod: Focus Film (Budapest)/Medias Res (Berlin)/ Medy Apim (Istanbul).

Producers

InterPannonia
(animation, also distribution)
Gyarmat utca 36
1145 Budapest
Tel: 267-6514, 267-6515
Fax: 267-6516

Béla Balázs Studio
Bajcsy-Zsilinszky ut 36-38
1054 Budapest
Tel/Fax: 111-2809, 131-8129

Budapest Film Studio
Róna utca 174
1045 Budapest
Tel: 251-8985
Fax: 251-8985

Focus Film
Pasaréti út 122
1026 Budapest
Tel: 176-7484
Fax: 176-7493

Forum Film
Könyves Kálmán Körút 13-15
1057 Budapest
Tel/Fax: 215-3745

Hunnia Studio
Róna utca 174
1145 Budapest
Tel: 252-3170
Fax: 251-6269

Magic Media
Róna utca 174
1145 Budapest
Tel: 163-3479
Fax: 263-3479

Movie Innovation Partnership (MIP)
Kinizsi utca 28
1092 Budapest
Tel: 218-3600, 218-0983
Fax: 216-3601

Novofilm
(also services)
Városmajor utca 20
1121 Budapest
Tel: 155-5440, 155-2621
Fax: 155-9177

Objektiv Film Studio
Róna utca 174
1145 Budapest
Tel: 252-5359
Fax: 251-7269

Pannonia Film
(animation)
Hüvösvölgyi út 64
1021 Budapest
Tel: 176-3333
Fax: 176-3409

Transatlantic Media Associates (TMA)
(also services)
Táltos utca 4
1123 Budapest
Tel: 155-3200
Fax: 175-2444

Satellit-Film/Europe 2000
(also services)
Finkenstrasse 48
8130 Stamberg
Germany
Tel: 8151-3551
Fax: 8151-28544
ALSO
Róna utca 174
1145 Budapest
Tel/Fax: 183-5930

Varga Studio
(animation, F/X)
Raktár utca 25-31
1035 Budapest
Tel: 168-8296
Fax: 168-6418

Distributors

Budapest Film
Báthori utca 10
1054 Budapest
Tel: 132-8198, 111-2494
Fax: 111-2687, 131-5946
(festivals, foreign promo)
Városligeti fasor 38
1068 Budapest
Tel: 351-7760, 351-7761
Fax: 268-0070, 176-1322

Flamex
Labanc utca 22B
1021 Budapest
Tel: 176-1534
Fax: 176-0596

Hungarofilm
(also production services)
Báthori utca 10
1054 Budapest
Tel: 111-0020, 131-4746
Fax: 153-1850

InterCom
Karolina út 65
1113 Budapest
Tel: 209-0933
Fax: 209-0930

UIP-Dunafilm
Tarogato út 2-4
1021 Budapest
Tel: 176-2333
Fax: 176-7291

Useful Addresses

Cinemagyar
(foreign sales)
Báthori utca 10
1054 Budapest
Tel: 111-4614, 132-8729
Fax: 153-1317

Filmunio Hungary
(festivals, foreign promo)
Városligeti fasor 38
1068 Budapest
Tel: 351-7760, 351-7761
Fax: 268-0070, 351-7766

S-media 2000
Szemlöhegy 28-30
1022 Budapest
Tel/Fax: 326-0698

Hungarian Film Institute
Budakeszi út 51 B
1012 Budapest
Tel: 176-1018, 176-1322
Fax: 176-7106

Assoc. of Hungarian Film & TV Artists
Városligeti fasor 38
1068 Budapest
Tel/Fax: 342-4760

Assoc. of Hungarian Film Distributors
Karolina út 65
1135 Budapest
Tel/Fax: 295-5001

Hungarian Film Institute
Budakeszi út 51B
1012 Budapest
Tel: 176-1018, 176-1322
Fax: 176-7106

Motion Picture Foundation of Hungary (MMA)
Városligeti fasor 38
1068 Budapest
Tel: 351-7696
Fax: 268-0070

Mafilm Corp.
(studio complex)
Róna utca 174
1145 Budapest
Tel: 252-2870
Fax: 251-1080

ICELAND

Thorfinnur Ómarsson

The year when the seventh art celebrated its first centenary, seven Icelandic features – more than ever – were premièred in this country of only 270,000 inhabitants. Ironically, 1995 was also the year when the box office for domestic productions declined more than ever since continuous film-making started with the creation of the Icelandic Film Fund in 1979. For the first time in years, none of the seven features reached the top ten-grossing list. Even worse, for the first time no Icelandic feature had more than 20,000 admissions.

The reasons for this are not simple, especially since most of the films received wonderful reviews. Obviously, the era when Icelanders – Europe's most frequent movie goers – went to see a domestic film just because it was Icelandic, is over. Therefore, it's no surprise that the box-office share of domestic productions in the five Nordic countries is the smallest in Iceland. Only 5% of the tickets sold in Iceland are for Icelandic features, while in Sweden the figure is 15-20%. Yet the total admissions in Iceland are the highest in Europe – in a capital city of 140,000, 1.3 million tickets are sold every year, and the variety of films (excluding festivals) is greater in Iceland than in other Nordic countries, with more than 200 films distributed annually.

But if competition in local film-making is tough, this barely begins to describe the TV battlefield. After the creation of Channel 3 and the recreation of Sýn, four channels are competing for the country's audience. Iceland could eventually become practically the only country in the world which supports three pay-TV channels. The battle is, indeed, bloody, especially since some of the owners are also competing as leading film distributors and cinema exhibitors.

Fragility and Diversity

Icelandic production is in quite a fragile state. In a report published by the Association of Icelandic Artists, film production is considered to have reached its lowest level ever. As usual, the local box office says hardly anything about the chances of a wider audience. The best example is Friðrik Thór Friðriksson's **Cold Fever**, which after a frosty reception at home went on to earn the best ever world-wide box-office for an Icelandic feature. After collecting a prize at the Edinburgh Festival, it received marvellous reviews in

Your source of information on Icelandic films.
The Icelandic Film Fund
Laugavegur 24, 101 Reykjavík, Iceland, tel. +354 562 3580, fax +354 562 7171
Email: filmfund@centrum.is

Hanna María Karlsdóttir and Egill Ólafsson in AGNES

practically all the British press, making a U.S. mission indeed possible.

Even though the situation may look precarious in terms of financing, this thriving production community has produced a diversity of work. In late 1995, three of Iceland's best films to date met the public: Hilmar Oddsson's **Tears of Stone**, Gísli Snær Erlingsson's **Benjamin Dove** and Egill Eðvarðsson's **Agnes**.

Originally, director and co-writer Hilmar Oddsson was to make a TV documentary about the life and music of Jón Leifs, who only achieved in the late 1980s the reputation he deserved as probably the most gifted Icelandic composer, but the story turned out to be ideal for a dramatic feature. The result is a taut fiction, rather loosely derived from actual events. Beautifully photographed by Icelandic veteran Sigurður Sverrir Pálsson and Polish master Slawomir Idziak, the film is a visual gem, expressing the complex and dramatic life of Leifs, mostly in Nazi Germany.

Gudbjörg Thoroddsen in BENJAMIN DOVE

With *Benjamin Dove*, Gísli Snær Erlingsson established himself as one of the country's most talented directors. The film was selected for the Berlin Children's Film Festival, but was probably too mature to play purely to an audience of children. Egill Eðvarðsson's *Agnes* is a dramatic, carnal love story, based on events that led to the last public execution in Finland, around 1830. Selected for Berlin's Panorama, this beautiful film was the second successful feature collaboration of Eðvarðsson and DP Snorri Thórisson, whose Pegasus Films has become one of the industry's largest.

Running On

After the record year of 1995, only two films were scheduled for release in 1996. In spring, Ásdís Thoroddsen premiered her second feature, **Dreamhunters**, an off-beat urban comedy about two 20-year-olds and their search for the dream boy. In spite of fair reviews, it fell flat at the box office, but one recalls that Thoroddsen's first film, *Ingaló*, also failed domestically but ended up with a best-film prize at Rouen and was selected for the Critics' Week in Cannes.

The second feature, Friðrik Thór Friðriksson's **Devil's Island**, is planned for Christmas. Based on a best-selling trilogy by scriptwriter Einar Kárason, the story has already been transformed into a hit stage play and hopefully will do the same in cinemas. Set in the 1950s, this wonderful story of unique characters living in barracks made by the British and American armies during World War II should find international distribution in early 1997.

Although few films are opening, there are several interesting projects in production. Three years after the local hit *Wallpaper*, Júlíus Kemp has gone on to shoot a stylish, low-budget road-movie, which takes place somewhere in Europe in the year 2000, and tells of young people running away from the city on a stolen credit card. The second feature shot this summer was Einar Heimisson's directorial début, **Maria**, with German actress Barbara Auer. It tells the story of a young woman

Still from Asdís Thoroddsen's DREAMHUNTERS

Still from NO IS NO ANSWER, directed by Jón Tryggvason

fleeing from Lübeck to Iceland at the end of World War II, and becoming one of 200 German women who actually settled down on Icelandic farms. The film is an Icelandic-German co-production of Friðriksson's Icelandic Film Corporation and the Munich-based Blue Screen Productions.

A Once and Future Land

Friðriksson's company is currently producing every other feature in the country. Other productions in preparation include Oskar Jónasson's second feature, *Pearls and Pigs,* a comedy set in a bakery and described by the writer-director as a "bakerythriller". Jónasson's début, *Remote Control,* was a huge box-office success in Iceland four years ago, and was selected for "Un Certain Regard" in Cannes in 1993.

The best news is that the two directors who started the so-called Spring in Icelandic film-making back in 1979, Ágúst Guðmundsson and Hrafn Gunnlaugsson, are back on track. Guðmundsson will base his first feature since 1984 on a short story by Nobel prize-winner William Heinesen. Gunnlaugsson, who came to international attention with his Viking trilogy in the 1980s, is preparing his long-awaited drama of a mediaeval witch hunt. A pet project for many years, this could put him back on the map as the country's leading director.

Iceland's unspoilt scenery seems increasingly attractive as a location, especially for science-fiction projects. George Lucas' resumption of the *Star Wars* series may include scenes shot in the moon-like landscape. Other directors drawn to Icelandic locations include Luc Besson, who wanted the unique icebergs of Europe's largest glacier for the final scene in **The Fifth Element**. Meanwhile, Einar Thór Gunnlaugsson, a London-based Icelandic director, plans to shoot his British-Icelandic **Sweet Bananas** in rural Iceland, with a cast of established British actors and an Icelandic crew.

THORFINNUR ÓMARSSON has been a journalist and film critic for more than a decade. Since 1993, he has been the editor of Iceland's highest rating TV-magazine programme. He has recently been appointed Head of the Icelandic Film Fund.

Useful Addresses

Icelandic Film Fund
P.O. Box 320
121 Reykjavík
Tel: 354-562 3580
Fax: 354-562 7171

Association of Icelandic Film Producers
Pósthússtraeti 13
P.O. Box 476
121 Reykjavík
Tel: 354-562 8188
Fax: 354-562 3424

Ministry of Culture and Education
Sölvhólsgötu 4
101 Reykjavík
Tel: 354-560 9500
Fax: 354-562 3068

TOP TEN GROSSING FILMS IN ICELAND: 1995

	Admissions
Forrest Gump	68,000
The Lion King	57,000
Dumb and Dumber	51,500
Die Hard 3	44,000
Batman Forever	30,000
GoldenEye	30,000*
Casper	29,000
French Kiss	27,000
Apollo 13	24,000
Outbreak/	23,000
Waterworld	23,000

*GoldenEye opened just before Christmas 1995 and went on to a total of 65,000.

Association of Film Distributors in Iceland
Laugarásbíó
Laugarási
104 Reykjavík
Tel: 354-553 8150
Fax: 354-568 0910

Háskólabíó
Hagatorg
107 Reykjavík
Tel: 354-561 1212
Fax: 354-562 7135

Regnboginn – Skífan
Hverfisgötu 54
Tel: 354-525 5000
Fax: 354-525 5001

Laugarásbíó
Laugarási
104 Reykjavík
Tel: 354-553 8150
Fax: 354-568 0910

Sam-Film
Álfabakka 8
109 Reykjavík
Tel: 354-587 8904
Fax: 354-587 8910

Bergvík Film Distribution
Ármúli 44
P.O. Box 8534
108 Reykjavík
Tel: 354-588 7966
Fax: 354-588 0288

INDIA

Uma da Cunha

What goes up must come down. The fortunes of the Bombay film industry proved this in the space of a few months as a euphoric start gave way to an increasingly despondent 1996. Towards the end of 1995, around Diwali, the festival of prosperity, a series of unexpected successes hit the country's movie houses. Audiences have returned, rejoiced the film wallahs. Then came the downside. The first half of 1996 brought a string of resounding flops, most of them huge, multi-star spectaculars.

The film industry found itself imperilled on many fronts: an extortionist star system that yielded precious few returns; exorbitant production costs; theatre rentals spiralling. And, to cap it all, films bombing one after the other. The reason should have been apparent even to the blinkered film trade. The 1995 year-end hits such as **Rangeela**, which made a star of upcoming actress Urmila Matondkar, and which is still running in its eighth month, or the family drama **Dilwale Dulhaniya Le Jayenge**, the music of which has kept it going even longer, or **The Bandit Queen** with its nudity and strong language — each had a dash and a flair that magnetised

Beauty queen Aishwaria Rai

audiences. The flashy, much-touted 1996 offerings, such as **Trimurti** and **Rajkumar**, among a dozen others, were routine, slap-dash affairs and so were ignored.

But scriptwriters are used to easy, imitative ways, working with the same mixture of ingredients or blandly making hybrid copies of recent American hits. Mahesh Bhatt's **Criminal** was a poor man's *Fugitive. Sleeping with the Enemy* inspired three simultaneous rehashes: **Yarana** (bombed), **Darrar** (yet to be released), and **Agni Sakshi**, the lone mid-year success scoring mainly thanks to macho star Nana Patekar.

The box-office débâcle had another message. Family films based on young love and filial values were losing out. The primary ingredient now had to be violence and action because audience patterns were changing. These have also brought about innovations in distribution. *Bandit Queen* had a strangely rollercoaster run in India. It was censored, put on hold, cleared, nominated for the Oscars and then withdrawn, banned, unbanned, became a huge box-office success, was banned again and unbanned, and finally went on to win the coveted government-sponsored National Film Award for the Best Hindi Film and Best Actress (Seema Biawas). Its Bombay distributors, Shringhar Films, noting the film's all-male audiences, deduced that women were too embarrassed by its explicitness to be comfortable viewing it with their menfolk and families. So they instituted "Ladies Only" matinees, and women flocked to them.

Past Glory, Today's Bottom Line

1996, of course, is the year to remember past glory, this being the centenary year of cinema's arrival in India. It was on July 7, 1896, that Marius Sester, assistant to the Lumière brothers, stopped in Bombay en route to Australia to give the "first cinematographic show". India went wild over the new sensation, forcing the organisers to extend screenings from the "Europeans only" Watson's Hotel to the more accessible Novelty Cinema (showing films to this day). But in fact, the centenary year was almost passed over without acknowledgement in India. The best tribute came as a magnificent book called *So Many Cinemas: The Motion Picture in India*, by veteran short film-maker B.D. Garga. Yet to be seen is Mrinal Sen's NFDC/BBC-produced contribution to the world centenary of cinema. In this series, Sen is one of eighteen international directors giving a personal account of their country's film history.

The 1995 figures revealed India still to be the world's largest film producer. 795 films

Still from KATHA DON GANPATRAONCHI

Still from THE SQUARE CIRCLE

were made, as against 754 the previous year, reversing the steady downward trend of recent years. Telugu led the list as usual with 168 films (174 in 1994), Tamil 165 (155), Hindi 157 (155), Kannada 89 (73), Malayalam 83 (71), Bengali 26 (44), Marathi 22 (22), English (4), Oriya 13 (14), Punjabi 12 (11), Nepali 11 (10), Gujurati 9 (6), Bhojpuri 6 (4), Assamese 4 (6), Rajhasthai 3, Manipuri 2 (on a par with 1994), Harayanvi, Tulu, Nagpuri, Bodo, Urdu, Sindhi (one each, as in 1994). One film was made with music only (no dialogue).

Significantly, the import of foreign films went up from 175 to 220. The Star Movie and TNT channels, along with the foreign movies shown on India's national network Doordarshan, seem to stimulate an appetite for foreign movies. Hollywood and British films came in swiftly, and some imported films, boosted by the fantastic success of *Jurassic Park*, were cautiously released in dubbed Indian languages, outstanding among them being *Baby's Day Out* and *Speed*.

Still from Sudhir Mishra's IS RAAT KI SUBAH NAHIN

More for Art

For the neglected art film, 1996 promised a step forward. Plus Channel, under the leadership of Amit Khanna, introduced a scheme for financing around fifteen films a year and guaranteeing them distribution through the established Rajshri Pictures, a company with a solid base in India and abroad. Under Plus Channel's sponsorship, a whole new crop of films are emerging, made by India's most notable directors, such as Shyam Benegal, Mrinal Sen, Gautam Ghose, Sudhir Mishra, Sai Paranjpye and Aruna Raje. That these films will be seen soon after completion is a whole new experience for Indian audiences.

In the U.S., nine prints of Satyajit Ray's films, restored to pristine condition by Sony Pictures Classics, have launched a revival of the master's work. Filmopolis Pictures, distributors of *Target*, based on Ray's last script and directed by his son Sandip, released the film at New York's Film Forum and thereafter in fifty U.S. cities. At home, mid-1996 looked hopeful with leading film-makers hard at work. Shyam Benegal's **Making of the Mahatma** was premièred in Durban, South Africa, on April 14, with Nelson Mandela urging people to see it. Benegal's next feature, **Sardari Begum**, was ready by June. Ketan Mehta is starting a trilogy, **Kartoos**, about the 1897 Sepoy Mutiny, the harbinger of India's independence.

More Indians living abroad are making films on Indian themes. At the forefront are two formidable women film-makers. Mira Nair, who has a dual home in India-Uganda, premièred her latest work, **Kamasutra**, and Deepa Mehta, living in Canada, was ready with her first film set in India, **Fire**. Both are daring and unconventional films based on original scripts. Others on the international scene are the Canadian-based Srinivas Krishna, with his second film, **Lulu** (Cannes, 1996), and U.K.-domiciled Udyan Prasad with his first feature, **Brothers in Trouble** (London Film Festival, 1995), about early illegal immigrants hiding out in London.

India's excitement was short-lived when Martin Scorsese arrived to film **Kundan**, followed by the French director Jean-Jacques Annaud making **Seven Years in Tibet** (with Bombay action-actor Danny Dengonzpa in a lead role). Diplomatic considerations led the government to withdraw permission to shoot these films. Swiss film-maker Markus Imhoof (*The Boat Is Full*) stuck it out over two years to direct **Fire in Paradise** in Cochin (introducing Bombay actress Gita Nair), and L.A.-based Ashok Amritraj produced his latest feature, **Jungle Boy**, shooting the family adventure story of talking animals in Bangalore, with Bombay newcomer Asif Mohamad playing the lead. Indian director Waris Hussein, whose base is London, is expected back as well, to make his first feature film in India, based on Firdaus Kanga's book *Trying to Grow*, produced by the BBC.

Kiron Kher in Shyam Benegal's SARDARI BEGUM

UMA DA CUNHA heads Medius-India Services Pvt Ltd, a company that provides promotional and executive services for films shooting in India. She is *Variety's* correspondent in India and a consultant on film programming for festivals in India and abroad.

Recent and Forthcoming Films

INDIAN

Lang: Tamil/Hindi versions. Dir: Shankar. Phot: Jeeva. Players: Kamal Haasen, Manisha Koirala, Urmila Matondkar, Sukanya. Prod: M. Ratnam.

An elderly patriot who refers to himself as "Indian", living on his memories of his years with the underground Indian National Army, sees his daughter die as a result of his ideology. He uses his prowess at an ancient Indian martial art to annihilate those responsible.

SARDARI BEGUM

Lang: Hindi. Story/Script: Khalid Mohamad. Dir: Shyam Benegal. Phot: Sanjay Dharamkar. Players: Amrish Puriu, Kiran Kher, Rajit Kapur, Smriti Mishra, Salim Ghouse, Rajeshwari Sachdev. Prod: Plus Channel.

In old walled Delhi, a famous classical singer, Sardari Begum, now in semi-retirement, is training her daughter Sakini to carry on her tradition. Her death by accident in a communal flare-up becomes a media event and leads to a series of extraordinary revelations.

SAAZ (The Melody)

Lang: Hindi. Script and Dir: Sai Paranjpye. Players: Shabana

TOP FIVE GROSSING FILMS IN INDIA: MID 1995 TO MID 1996

Dilwale Dulhania Leh Jayenge (Dir: Aditya Chopra)
Rangeela (Dir: Ramgopal Verma)
Agni Sakshi (Dir: Parto Ghosh)
Bandit Queen (Dir: Shekhar Kapoor)
Sajan Chale Sasural (Dir: David Dhawan)

Azmi, Zakir Hussain, Aruna Irani, Parikshat Sahni, Ayesha Dharker, Raghubir Yadav. Prod: Plus Channel.

Tracing the life of a playback singer in Bombay's film industry, this musical extravaganza will have 11 songs composed by four eminent music directors (Hazarika, Zakir Hussain, Rajkamal, Yashwant Dev) with lyrics by Javed Akhtar.

DAYRA (The Square Circle)

Lang: Hindi. Script: Tim Murari. Dir: Amol Palekar. Phot: Debu Deodhar. Players: Nirmal Pandey, Sonali Kulkarni. Prod: Pravesh Sippy/Gateway Entertainment.

Traditionally, Indian men working in theatre, dance or film played women's roles because it was considered improper for women to display themselves. Some of these men chose to remain women in their daily lives. In this film, such a man finds himself caught up in a world that is brutal to defenceless women.

CHAR ADHYAY (Four Paths)

Lang: Hindi. Script and Dir: Kumar Shahani, from a story by Rabindranath Tagore. Phot: K.K. Mahajan. Players: Sumanto Chattopadhyay, Nandini Ghosal, Ramchandra Pratihari, Kaushik Gopal, Shruti Yusuf. Prod: NFDC.

A tale of love and violence played out against the backdrop of the terrorist phase of the Indian freedom struggle. Set in the 30s, the film sets up disturbing resonances with present times.

IS RAAT KI SUBAH NAHIN (On This One Night)

Lang: Hindi. Script and Dir: Sudhir Mishra. Phot: Sukumar Jatania. Players: Asish Vidhyarthi, Nirmal Pandey, Tara Deshpande, Smriti Mishra, Murad Ali. Prod: Plus Channel.

The tale of a hard day's night, when an advertising man caught between an adoring wife and a resentful mistress unwittingly insults an underworld don, whose gang then set out for revenge.

KATHA DOAN GANPATRAONCHI (The Tale of Two Ganpatraos)

Lang: Marathi. Script: Shanta Gokhale. Dir: Arun Khopkar. Phot: Rafey Mehmood. Players: Mohan Agashe, Dilip Prabhavalkar, Uttara Baokar, Prashant Subedar, Renuka Shahane. Prod: NFDC/Doordarshan.

A free adaptation of Nikolai Gogol's "The Story of How Ivan Ivanovich Quarrelled with Ivan Nikiforovich", which tells how two close friends quarrel over something which is of no use to either of them and destroy each other in the process.

PRICE OF FREEDOM

Lang: Assamese. Script and Dir: Jahnu Barua. Phot. P. Rajan. Lead Player: Sanjay Saba. Prod: Dolphin Communication.

1943: the true story of a non-violent freedom fighter, Kushal Pandit, who at the height of India's struggle for independence, was wrongly arrested by the British for a terrorist offence and subsequently hanged.

GUDIA (The Doll)

Lang: Hindi. Script, Dir and Phot: Gautam Ghose. Lead player; Mithun Chakrabarti. Prod: Plus Channel.

The star attraction in the small-town troupe of ventriloquist Hameed is their talking doll Urvashi, who epitomises every male sexual fantasy, from child-woman and coquette to seductress. In Bombay, the troupe's marginal existence assumes many other dimensions.

KARTOOS (A War Epic)

Lang: Hindi/English versions. Script: Dusty Hughes (English)/Javed Akhtar (Hindi). Dir: Ketan Mehta. Players: Sanjay Dutt, Manisha Koirala. Prod: Ketan Mehta/Channel 4.

An account of the so-called Sepoy Mutiny of 1857 against the powerful East India Company which that year introduced bullets coated with cow and pig fat. Cows are sacred to Hindus; pigs are forbidden for Muslims. The sepoys refused to use the bullets. The impasse led to a major war, the closure of the East India Company and the Crown taking over rule of India. Director Mehta intends to release Part I on April 8, 1997, to commemorate the 140th anniversary of the mutiny; Part II on India's Independence Day, August 15; and Part III at the end of the year.

ANANDAM (The Ecstasy)

Lang: Tamil. Dir: Mani Ratnam. Phot: Santosh Sivam. Players: Mithun Chakraborty, Mohanlal, Aishwaria Rai. Prod: Madras Talkies.

A film with two parallel narratives, one about a love triangle and the other about unrequited love. Each of the protagonists is an amalgam of real-life personalities who are linked to politics.

TARA RUM PUM PUM

Lang: Hindi. Story and Dir: Shekhar Kapoor. Phot: Ashok Mehta. Players: Preity Zinta, Piyush Soni. Prod: Quasar Films.

A small-town youth gets a scholarship to an urban college and is confronted with very different standards of behaviour. The film sees the impact of Western television on the way middle-class teenagers in India behave.

FIRE

Lang: English/Hindi. Script and Dir: Deepa Mehta. Phot: Charles Newttgens. Players: Shabana Azmi, Khulbushan Kharbanda, Nandita Sen, Javed Jaffrey, Ranjit Chowdhury, Kushal Rekhi. Prod: Trial by Fire Films.

A new bride joins an extended family living in a present-day Delhi typified by fast-food meals, video rentals and guru worship. Her presence triggers tensions as her independent ideas clash with the values of her elders.

FIRE IN PARADISE

Lang: French/German/English/ Malayalam. Story: Markus Imhoof, Shaji Karun. Dir: Imhoof. Phot: Lukas Strebel. Players: Gita Nair, Georgette Zellweger, Gustav Walser, Helga Oppliger. Prod: Paradies Filmproduction, Zurich.

Two European women meet on a ship bound for Cochin, South India. One is going to marry a missionary whom she has never seen. She sees the strained life he leads with the locals and the European community and the resentment towards her of his attractive Malayal female worker. Internal and external pressures lead to a change of heart.

JUNGLE BOY

Language: English. Script: Damian Lee. Dir: Allan Goldstein. Phot: Ashok Amritraj. Players: Jeremy Roberts, David Fox, Lee Roberts, Asif Mohomed. Prod: Amritraj International, Los Angeles.

An adaptation of the Kipling stories in which an Indian teenager, abandoned in the jungle as a child, is raised among animals and is able to converse with them.

Still from Sai Paranjpye's SAAZ

Useful Addresses

All India Film Producers Council
Rajkamal Studios
Parel
Mumbai - 400 012
Tel: (022) 412 1787/413 7063/
413 7069

Film Makers Combine/Indian Motion Pictures Producers Association
Imppa House
Dr. Ambedkar Road
Bandra (W)
Mumbai - 400 050
Tel: (022) 648 6344/648 6345/648 0757/648 5097/648 1760
Fax: (022) 648 0757

Film Producers Guild of India Ltd
Rajkamal Studio
Near M.G. Hospital
Parel
Mumbai - 400 012
Tel: (022) 413 3042/413 6571
Fax: (022) 413 5640

Indian Film Directors Association
501 Navin Asha
Dadasaheb Phalke Road
Dadar
Mumbai - 400 014
Tel: (022) 411 1106

Indian Film Exporters Assocation
5-C Everest Building
Tardeo
Mumbai - 400 034
Tel: (022) 495 1688/495 1808/
494 9480
Fax: (022) 495 2062

Indian Motion Pictures Distributors Association
33 Vijay Chamber
Tribhuvan Road
Mumbai - 400 004
Tel: (022) 388 4422/388 4489
Fax: (022) 388 4448

Andhra Pradesh Film Chamber of Commerce
Flat No. 1, 5-9-22/42
Adarsh Nagar
Hyderabad - 83
Tel: (040) 22 1010

Eastern India Motion Pictures Association
98-E Chowringhee Square
Calcutta - 700 072
Tel: (033) 27 4040/27 4041/27 4042

Kanataka Film Chamber of Commerce
28 First Main Crescent Road
High Grounds
Bangalore - 1
Tel: (080) 27819/75371

South India Film Chamber of Commerce (SIFCC)
Film Chambers Building
T.R. Sundaran Avenue
605 Anna Salai
Cathedral P.O.
Madras - 600 006
Tel: (044) 827 9175/827 5642
Fax: (044) 827 5870

Film Federation of India
Everest Building
Tardeo
Mumbai - 400 034
Tel: (022) 495 2062
Fax: (022) 495 2062

Indian Documentary Producers Association
223 Famous Building
Dr. E. Moses Road
Mahalakshmi
Mumbai - 400 011
Tel: (022) 492 0757
Fax: (022) 492 0757
Grams: Docuprod

Films Division (FD)
Film Bhavan
24 Dr. Gopalrao Deshmukh Road
Mumbai - 400 026
Tel: (022) 386 4233
Fax: (022) 386 0308

National Film Development Corporation (NFDC)
Discovery of India Building
Nehru Centre
Dr. Annie Besant Road
Worli
Mumbai - 400 018
Tel: (022) 494 9753
Fax: (022) 494 9751

Doordarshan Kendra/Doordarshan Bhavan
Mandi House
Copernicus Marg
New Delhi - 110 001
Tel: (011) 387786/382021/382488
Fax: (011) 386507

Directorate of Film Festivals
Lok Nayak Bhavan
Khan Market
New Delhi - 110 011
Tel: (011) 615953
Fax: (011) 694920

Film and Television Institute of India (FTII)
Law College Road
Pune - 410 004
Tel: (0212) 331559/331010

National Film Archives of India
Law College Road
Pune - 410 004
Tel: (0212) 359 487
Fax: (0212) 370 027

INDONESIA

Marselli Sumarno

The domination of American films in Indonesia seems to be strengthening. One indication is that it used to be the case that every year the top ten box-office films included two or three Mandarin titles, but in 1995 only one Mandarin film triumphed at the box-office – the soft-porn **Erotic Black Magic**.

Local production in 1995 was still down – about ten titles – and of this small number, most were exploitation movies. But when even titles like **Nocturnal Desire 2** (*Gairah Malam 2*) fail at the box-office, one begins to wonder. Five years ago the number of movie houses stood at over 3,000, but now less than half that number remain. Those still doing good business are the cineplex chain of the 21 Group, with over 600 cinemas presenting first-run Hollywood films.

A Tale of Two Tastes

Imported films may be damaging Indonesia's film industry, but another factor is the growth of the TV industry, which now comprises one state-owned and five commercial channels. In the last few years, the national film industry has also been divided into two extremes: films appealing to low-brow taste and those appealing to high-brow taste. What is lacking are films pitched somewhere in between.

Films at the lower end of the scale can be profitable provided they are produced for not more than US$150,000. Meanwhile, films appealing to high-brow taste – the production of which in the last few years has been spearheaded by young director Garin Nugroho – still find it difficult to enter the market. His second film, **Letter to an Angel** (*Surat Untuk Bidadari*, 1994) and his latest, **And the Moon Dances** (*Bulan Tertusuk Ilalang*, 1995), have yet to be released.

In Search of New Forms

Nevertheless, Garin is a new phenomenon in the Indonesian film world in the 1990s.

MARSELLI SUMARNO is a film critic and Head of the Filmology Department, Faculty of Film and Television, IKJ.

He persistently seeks new forms of expression; an adventurousness which won him the international critics' award at the 1996 Berlin Film Festival for *And the Moon Dances*, and the best director award at the Nantes Film Festival in 1995. The challenge, of course, is to create a market for his alternative cinema and to continue to find producers.

Following in his footsteps are four young directors (Mira Lesmana, Nan Triveni, Mohamad Rivai, Rizal Mantovani), who have previously made commercials and documentaries. They will each contribute an episode to an omnibus film, **Dead End** (*Kuldesak*). Gotot Prakosa, who has previously made short films, will make his first feature film, experimental in nature, under the title **Sleep Walker** (*Berjalan di Atas Awan*). "In the present condition, the films we make must be either utterly crazy or utterly commercial", Gotot has said.

To Dub or Not to Dub

To help revive the film industry, the National Film Advisory Board is to encourage the setting up of a Film Finance Corporation, which will facilitate producers in finding loans. TV channels will also be invited to participate in film production. To spur this revival, the board plans to produce an epic, **Fatahillah**, with a thirteenth-century historical background. This film is designed for theatrical distribution and also to be aired as a mini-series (in 13 episodes) on TV. But with a projected production cost of US$1 - $1.5 million, many parties doubt whether the project can be profitable.

There was heated controversy recently when the Minister of Information and the Minister of Education and Culture appealed for all foreign films to be dubbed into Indonesian. This was strongly resisted by many parties in the film business, including theatre owners, and it was finally decided that it should be a matter of individual discretion.

The noted director, Wim Umboh, died at the age of 63, after a career that included many successful melodramas in the 1970s and 80s: **Young Bride and Bridegroom** (*Pengantin Remaja*), **Marriage** (*Perkawinan*) and **Love** (*Cinta*).

Recent and Forthcoming Films

BERJALAN DI ATAS AWAN (Sleep Walker)

Script, Dir and Phot: Gotot Prakosa. Players: Christine Hakim. Prod: PT Eka Praya.

FATAHILLAH

Script: Misbach Yusa Biran. Dir: Chaerul Umam, Imam Tantowi. Prod: PT Bangun Citra Nusantara.

GAIRAH MALAM III (Noctural Desire III)

Script and Dir: Prawoto S. Rahardjo. Phot: Heru Susanto. Players: Dias Astuti, Malvin Sheana, Eddy Chaniago. Prod: Elang Perkasa Film.

KULDESAK (Dead End)

Script and Dir: Mira Lesmana, Nan Triveni, Mohamad Rivai, Rizal Mantovani. Phot: Yadi Sugandi, Yudhi Datau, Roy Lolang, Nur Hidayat. Prod: Day for Night.

MISTIK EROTIK (Erotic Mystic)

Script: Armantono. Dir: Emil G. Hampp. Phot: Tantra Suryadi. Players: Febby Lawrence, Malfin Shayna, Ibra Ashari. Prod: PT Rapi Film.

Producers

PT Eka Praya Film
Jalan Bakti no. 20
Blok S
Kebayoran Baru
Jakarta
Tel: 7206127, 7396918

PT Rapi Film
Jalan Cikini II/7
Jakarta Pusat
Tel: 357135, 332860

PT Parkit Film
Roxi Mas
Blok C-2 no. 31-34
Jakarta
Tel: 3867315, 3867316

PT Elang Perkasa Film
Jalan Kayu Putih 4/48
Jakarta Timur
Tel: 4700801

PT Prasidi Teta Film
Jalan Dr. Sahardjo 149 J
Jakarta Selatan
Tel: 8282740, 8281324

TOP TEN GROSSING FILMS IN INDONESIA: 1995

Goldeneye
Die Hard 3
Under Siege 2
Casper
Forrest Gump
Batman Forever
The Assassin
Disclosure
Waterworld
Erotic Black Magic (*Mandarin*)

PT Kanta Film
Jalan Kayu VI B/28
Jakarta Timur
Tel: 4896434

PT Bola Dunia Film
Jalan Pintu Air 51 C
Jakarta Pusat
Tel: 3843983, 3848721

PT Sepakat Bahagia Film
Jalan Mangga Besar Raya 107
Blok D-7
Jakarta Pusat
Tel: 6496657

PT Virgo Putra Film
Jalan KH Hasim Ashari Dalam III
Jakarta Pusat
Tel: 363308

PT Cipta Permai Indah Film
Jalan Raya Gunung Sahari no. 1
Blok B-16
Jakarta
Tel: 6296363, 6299694

Note: PT is a short form for Limited Company.

Distributors

PT Satrya Perkasa Estetika
(European/American importer)
Subentra Building
Jalan Gatot Subroto Kav. 21
7th floor
Tel: 5220022

PT Suptan Film
(Mandarin importer)
Subentra Building
Jalan Gatot Subroto Kav. 21
7th floor
Tel: 5220022

PT Buana Indah Film
(Asia non-Mandarin)
Jalan Pintu Air 51 C
Jakarta
Tel: 3843983, 3848721

Useful Addresses

Directorate for Film and Video Development
Ministry of Information
Jalan Merdeka Barat 9
Jakarta
Tel: 377408

Perum Produksi Film Negara
(State Production Film Centre)
Jalan Otto Iskandardinata 125-127
Jakarta Timur
Tel: 8192508

Fakultas Film dan Televisi
(Faculty of Film and Television - The Jakarta Institute of the Arts)
Jalan Cikini Raya 73
Jakarta Pusat
Tel: 323603, 3156176

Badan Pertimbangan Perfilman Nasional
(National Film Advisory Board)
Jalan Menteng Raya 62
Jakarta Pusat
Tel: 320773, 336106

Persatuan Produser Film Indonesia
(Indonesian Film Producers Association)
Pusat Perfilman H. Usmar Ismail
Jalan Rasuna Said
Jakarta 12940
Tel: 5254076, 5250558

Karyawan Film dan Televisi
(Association of Film and TV Technicians)
Pusat Perfilman H. Usmar Ismail
Jalan Rasuna Said
Jakarta 12940
Tel: 525091, 5251992

Sinematek Indonesia
Pusat Perfilman H. Usmar Ismail
Jalan Rasuna Said
Jakarta 12940
Tel: 5256891

Televisi Republik Indonesia
(TVRI, state-owned TV network)
Jalan Gerbang Pemuda
Senayan
Jakarta
Tel: 5704732

PT Indosiar Visual Mandiri
(Indosiar)
Jalan Damai no. 11
Jakarta Barat
Tel: 5655752

PT Rajawali Citra Televisi Indonesia
(RCTI)
Jalan Raya Perjuangan
Kebon Jeruk
Jakarta 11530
Tel: 5303540-50

PT Surya Citra Televisi
(SCTV)
Wisma AKR 2nd floor
Jalan Panjang no. 3
Jakarta 11530
Tel: 5311155, 5493135

PT Cakrawala Andalas Televisi
(ANTeve)
Mulia Centre Building
7th floor Suite 711
Jalan HR Rasuna Said
Jakarta 12940
Tel: 52222086

Still from NOCTURNAL DESIRE III

IRAN

Jamal Omid

Iranian cinema in the past year had two different aspects. Outwardly – that is, on the international scene – the successful trend of the previous years continued. Iranian films were presented at competitive and non-competitive events around the world, often to great acclaim. During the past year, the Iranian cinema was represented in over 150 film events, and over 200 sales transactions involving 147 pictures were concluded with buyers in more than 30 countries. This was a remarkable achievement for the Iranian cinema which, in spite of its long history of film-making, has been able to achieve such success only in recent years.

On the other hand, the Iranian film industry has rarely faced a crisis similar to the one with which it has had to grapple during the past year. A period of intense inflation, and loss of capital by film-makers, resulted in the resignation, after only a 15-month tenure, of the deputy minister of cinematographic affairs, Mehdi Faridzadeh. He was succeeded by Ezzatollah Entezami, who did not hesitate to make known his preferred policies, involving all phases of film-making, film distribution and exhibition, as well as the participation of Iranian films at foreign film festivals.

But producers who had been expecting

FARABI
CINEMA
FOUNDATION
PRODUCTION
EXPORT
PROMOTION
CO.PRODUCTION
DISTRIBUTION
IMPORT
PROMOTING IRANIAN CINEMA
ALL OVER THE WORLD
55, SIE-TIR Street, TEHRAN 11358 / I.R.IRAN
TEL: (98 21) 671010 / 678156
FAX: 678155
R. ABEDINI

to start production in the autumn as in previous years, and were counting on reducing production costs through careful economic planning, lost considerable time as they waited to see how the changes in the bureaucratic system would affect their projects. This in itself only intensified the crisis. The new deputy minister put into effect comprehensive supporting measures aimed at encouraging investment in film projects. By the time of the Fajr International Film Festival in February 1996, the annual showcase for Iranian cinema, nearly 70 films could be presented.

Parvis Parastui and Naser Hosseini in LEILI IS WITH ME

Qualitatively, however, output falls into two broad categories. First, there was the commercial cinema produced mostly by those private investors who have been advocating a non-subsidised film industry run totally by the private sector with limited government control. Secondly, there were the productions of serious artists who are anxious to preserve their traditional culture, values and national identity. The conflict between these two groups deepened the crisis in the Iranian cinema in spite of its international successes. It exhausted a great deal of the managerial abilities of the previous deputy minister for cinematographic affairs, making it impossible for him to create a common ground of understanding between the two groups.

The new deputy minister's encouragement of the serious artists included financial as well as moral support, and he secured a considerable amount of credit – about five times the amount of the previous year – for the promotion of Iranian cinema. (One third of the credit has been allocated to low-interest loans for the renovation of movie theatres, to be repaid on long-term instalments).

By the end of July 1996, over 40 film projects were in various stages of production, and although this is about the same number as 1995, it is quite contrary to the expectations of some experts who believed that the new policies and production practices, together with insufficient box-office receipts, would reduce film-making to a record low level. As the majority of film projects in Iran get underway in late September and early October, there should be no concern about the volume of film production in the current year.

TOP GROSSING FILMS IN IRAN: 1995

Iranian Films	
I Want to Live (Iraj Qaderi)	$292,000
The Blue-Veiled (Rakhshan Bani-etemad)	$212,000
Salaam Cinema (Mohsen Makhmalbaf)	$129,000
Pari (Dariush Mehrjui)	$117,000
Flight from the Camp	$116,000
Foreign Films	
The Thunder Kid	$22,000
The Castle	$18,000
Giant Thunders	$14,000

Recent Films

LEILY BA MAN AST (Leili Is with Me)

Script: Reza Maqsudi, Kamal Tabrizi. Dir: K. Tabrizi. Phot: Mojtaba Rahimi. Players: Parviz Parastui, Mahmud Azizi, Shohreh Lorestani. Prod: Sobhan Cinema Company/Farabi Cinema Foundation.

Leili Is with Me is the first war comedy of the post-revolutionary era and may turn out to be the top box-office success of the year. The fourth full-length feature of the 37-year-old director, Kamal Tabrizi, it is about a television cameraman who fearfully travels to a combat zone, and in spite of his efforts to get out of the area under enemy fire, is unwittingly put in the position of being a hero.

DAKAL (The Derrick)

Script and Dir: Abdolhassan Barzideh. Phot: Haj Mohammad Davudi. Players: Mohammed Reza Iran-Manesh, Mehdi Qolipoor, Nilufar Mahmudi. Prod: Centre for Promotion of Documentary and Experimental Cinema/Cultural Centre of Islamic Revolutionary Guards.

This début by Hassan Barzideh is an uncommon war movie in which the director attempts to evaluate his characters, and focuses on their awakening to social values.

GABBE/BREAD AND THE VASE

Script and Dir: Mohsen Makhmalbaf. Phot: Mahmud Klari. Players: Abbas Siahi, Shaqayeq Judat, Hossein Moharrami. Prod: Khalil Doruchi, Khalil Mahmudi.

Mohsen Makhmalbaf is the best-known Iranian film-maker of the post-revolutionary era. In his latest two films, *Gabbe* and *Bread and the Vase*, he presents two different sets of values and approaches to film-making. *Bread and the Vase* is an autobiographical account of the film-maker's youthful period as a political activist, and *Gabbe* is an account of the production of a certain type of carpet, but quite unlike the usual yawn-inducing documentaries of its kind. A picture of poetic beauty, *Gabbe* is imbued with a love of life and cinema, as well as being a tribute to these anonymous artisans.

BAZMANDE (The Survivor)

Script and Dir: Seifollah Dad. Phot: Alireza Zarrindast. Players: Salmi Almesri, Basam Kusa, Jamal Soleiman. Prod: Sina Film Cultural Institute.

Dad's third feature recounts the story of a Palestinian family in Haifa in 1948, presenting the wrongs they suffered through a meticulous cinematic language.

BOOY-E PIRAHAN-E YUSEF (Scent of Joseph's Shirt/The Minoo Tower)

Script and Dir: Ebrahim Hatamikia. Phot: Aziz Sa'at. Players: Ali Nasirian, Niki Karimi, Jafar Dehghan. Prod: Majid Modarresi.

In his latest two films, Ebrahim Hatamikia has experimented with two distinct modes of expression. In *Scent of Joseph's Shirt*, a father holds to his belief that his missing son has not been killed in action and will someday return with other released PoW's. In *The Minoo Tower*, a young man, the only survivor from a group that built a watch-tower on the Minoo Island, is asked at the end of the war to go back to the island and dismantle the tower. The former employs a conventional, classical cinematic language, while the latter is a bold experiment at intertwining impressions of the war with the imagery of religious mysticism.

CROSSING THE RED LINE

Script: Seyed Ali Reza Sajadpour. Dir: Jamal Shorje. Phot: Reza Banki. Players: Jafar Dehqan, Atila Pesyani. Prod: Sima Film/Zeitoun Cultural Organisation.

CHILDREN OF THE SKY

Script and Dir: Majid Majidi. Phot: Parviz Malakzadeh. Players: Mohammad Amirjani, Fereshte Sarabandi. Prod: Institute for the Intellectual Development of Children and Young Adults.

SACK OF RICE

Script: Houshang Moradi Kermani, Mohammad Ali Talebi. Dir: M. A. Talebi. Phot: Farhad Saba. Players: Masoume Eskandar, Jeiran Abadzadeh, Hossein Kalantari, Shirin Bina. Prod: M. A. Talebi.

JOURNEY TO MORNING

Script and Dir: Abbas Kiarostami. Phot: Homayoun Paivar. Players: Homayoun Ershadi, Abdolhossein Baqeri, Elham Imani. Prod: Abbas Kiarostami.

THE PARTY

Script and Dir: Masud Kimia'ie. Phot: Alireza Zarrindast. Players: Fariborz Arabnia, Behzad Khodareisi, Shahrzad Abdolmajid. Prod: Amir Hossein Sharifi (Afaq Film).

FROM THE SOUTH TO THE NORTH

Script and Dir: Touraj Mansouri. Phot: Reza Mohajer. Players: Daryoush Arjomand, Mohammad Sadeqi, Fariborz Arabnia. Prod: Touraj Mansouri.

LAND OF THE SUN

Script and Dir: Ahmad Reza Darvish. Phot: Mohammad Aladpoush. Players: Khosrow Shakibail, Golchehre Sajadieh, Saiid Poursamimi. Prod: Nouredin Hejazi/A.R. Darvish/ Farabi Cinema Foundation.

LOVE SQUADRON

Script: Ebrahim Hatamikia, Saied Hajimiri. Dir: S. Hajimiri. Phot: Saied Sadeqi. Players: Faramarz Sediqi, Moharam Zeinalzadeh, Esmaiil Slotanian. Prod: Sobhan Film.

Still from GABBE, directed by Mohsen Makhmalbaf

A MAN LIKE THE RAIN

Script and Dir: Saied Soheili. Phot: Parviz Malekzadeh. Players: Hossein Ansari, Fateme Sameti. Prod: Centre for Documentary and Experimental Film-making.

GREAT, VERY GREAT

Script and Dir: Farzin Mehdipour. Phot: Bahram Badakhshani. Players: Davoud Rashidi, Hadi Mohammad Doust. Prod: Gholgon Film.

SHADOW TO SHADOW

Script and Dir: Ali Zhakan. Phot: Parviz Malakzadeh. Players: Niki Karimi, Khosro Shakibai, Firooz Behjat Mohammadi. Prod: Sima Films, M.A. Soltanzadeh.

SUN DUSTS

Script: Mohammad Ali Hossein-Nezhad, Mohammad Hossein Haghighi. Dir: M.H. Haghighi. Phot: Mohammad Taghi Paksima. Players: Manuchehr Azar, Mahdi Gholi Poor, Rambod Javan, Hossein Mahjub, Shahnin Alizadeh, Ali Dehkordy, Jamileh Sheikhi. Prod: Channel Two (I.R.I.B.)/Manuchehr Shahsavari.

SEVEN STONES

Script: Mehdi Sajadechi. Dir: Seyed Abdol Reza Navabesafavi. Phot: Reza Razi. Players: Daryoush Arjomand, Amin Tarokh, Atila Pesyani, Bijan Emkanian. Prod: Sima Film.

THE AMBUSH

Script and Dir: Hamid Kheiredin. Phot: Mohammad Dormanesh. Players: Mohammad Kasebi, Reza Iranmanesh, Gholamreza Ali Akbari, Habi-o-lah Hadad. Prod: Institute for the Intellectual Development of Children and Young Adults.

SON OF THE CLOCK

Script and Dir: Abolfazi Jalili. Phot: Abolfazi Jalili. Player: Samad Khani. Prod: Channel Two (I.R.I.B).

THE TURTLE

Script and Dir: Ali Shah Hatami. Phot: Hossein Maleki.

THE FRONTIER

Script and Dir: Akbar Sadeqi. Phot: Majid Majidi. Players: Garsha Raufi, Davud Asadi, Hossein Molla Qasemi, Morteza Ahmadi, Gorji, Sorush Khalili. Prod: Sima Film/Film Iran.

THE GALLANT

Script: Mahdi Ahmadi. Dir: Jamshid Ahangran. Phot: Daryoush Ayari. Players: Jamshid Hashem Poor, Farimah Farjami, Hossein Maleki, Mohammad Poor Gholami, Amir Saied Nia, Houshang Dibaiyan. Prod: Filmsazan Co-operative.

CHARIOT OF DEATH

Script and Dir: Reza Qahremani. Phot: Reza Mohajer. Players: Faramarz Qaribiyan, Reza Kiyaniyan, Reza Fayazi, Reza Iranmanesh. Prod: Jozan Film.

THE EVENTFUL JOURNEY

Script and Dir: Siyamak Atlasi. Phot: Mazyar Parto. Players: Ferdos Kaviani, Mehrane Mahin Torabi, Siamak Atlasi, Nikoo Kheradmand, Azita Lachini. Prod: Siyamak Atlasi.

MINA AND THE BUD

Script and Dir: Mohammad Hossein Poor, Jahan Khadem-Al-Meleh. Phot: Iraj Safavi . Players: Nazanin Saghari, Sara Hosseiniyan, Alireza Khamse, Farokh Lagha Hushmand, Morteza Ahmadi, Soraya Soltani, Fatemeh Abassi. Prod: Barnameh Tasvir-e Khorasan Co.

THE PROFESSIONAL

Script: Fereydoun Zhourak. Dir: Esmaeil Falah Poor. Phot: Esfandiyar Shahidi. Players: Parviz Poor Hosseiny, Changiz Vosughi, Sahar Khiz. Prod: Lofti/Zhourak/Chehre Azad Co-operative.

THE STORM

Script and Dir: Mohammad Bozorgnia. Phot: Hassan Gholizadeh. Players: Ezatolah Entezami, Majid Mozafari, Jamshid Jahanzadeh, Danial Hakimi. Prod: Ministry of Petroleum.

THE UGLY AND THE BEAUTIFUL

Script and Dir: Ahmad Reza Motamedi. Phot: Mohammad Alad Poosh. Players: Mahdi Hashemi, Saied Poorsamimi, Parviz Poor Hosseini. Prod: Chashm-e Sevom Co.

THE UNFORGIVEN

Script: Mohammad Hossein Latifi. Dir: Iraj Qaderi. Phot: Ali Reza Zarindast. Players: Behzad Javanbakhsh, Mahaya Petrosian, Afsane Baygan, Bijan Emkanian. Prod: Morteza Shayeste (Hedayat Film).

THE MIRACLE OF LAUGHTER

Script: Ali Reza Khamse, Ferydoun Hassanpoor, Davoud Mirbbagheri, Yadolah Samadi. Dir: Y. Samadi. Phot: Nemat Haqiqi. Players: Mahdi Hashemi, Keihan Maleki, Faghihi Soltani. Prod: Y. Samadi and the Art Bureau of the Islamic Propagation Organisation.

SANDSTORM

Script: Javad Shamaghdari, Saied Soheili. Dir: J. Shamaghdari. Phot: Mohammad Taghi Paksima. Players: Ahmad Najafi, Bahman Dan, Mahshid Afsharzadeh. Prod: Shahed Television Group.

WAITING FOR THE MORNING

Script: Mohsen Damadi, Zia-e-Din Naderi. Dir: Majid Javanmard. Phot: Mahdi Majd Vaziri Nasab. Players: Faramarz Qaribian, Farhad Jam, Jamshid Jahanzadeh. Prod: Ramin Abbas Zadeh/I.R.I.B.

THE SOUTH IS WAITING

Script and Dir: Parviz Shahbazi. Phot: Farzad Jodat. Players: Reza Moqadam, Nasiri Jozani, Elyas Salani. Prod: Channel Two. (I.R.I.B).

TEARS AND SMILES

Script and Dir: Shapoor Qarib. Phot: Hassan Pooya. Players: Jamshid Mashayekhi, Faramarz Qaribiyan, Mahnaz Afzali. Prod: Abd-Al-Reza Saatchi Fard.

LEADEN STARS

Script and Dir: Mahdi Vedady. Phot: Farhad Saba. Players: Fariborz Arabnia, Danial Hakimi, Malihe Nazari.

Producers/ Distributors

Hedayat Film Organisation
2nd Floor
No. 15, 7th St,
Khaled Eslamboli Ave.
Tehran
Tel: (0098-21) 8727188-9

Jozan Film
No. 20 Razmandegan Alley
Ghafari St., Jam St.
Motahari Ave
Tehran
Tel: (0098-21) 8837271/832704

Novin Film Organisation
No. 15, Passage 48
Jomhuri Ave (Serah Jomhuri)
Tehran
Tel: (0098-21) 6403697

Sina Film
Varavini, Soleiman Khater
(Amir Atabak) St
Motahari Ave
Tehran
Tel: (0098-21) 837732/8837471

Pakhshiran Cinema Organisation
Somayeh St
Bahar St
Tehran
Tel: (0098-21) 8825052/8824057

Children's Literature Mansion
No. 135 Kashef (Noor) St
Hedayat Ave
Tehran
Tel: (0098-21) 7532181

Co-operatives

Filmsazan Cinema Organisation
No. 7 Ghaffari Alley
Bahar Mastan St
Haft Tir Sq.
Tehran
Tel: (0098-21) 830676

Hamrah Film Production Co-operative
No. 64 Aljavad Mosque Alley
Haft Tir Sq.
Tehran
Tel: (0098-21) 8846140

Sobhan Film
No. 45 Noori Alley
Vali-e Asr Ave
Tehran
Tel: (0098-21) 6401807

Laleh Cinema Organisation
Lalezarno St
Tehran
Tel: (0098-21) 6452954

Purlka Film
No. 119 Forsat St
Taleghani Ave
Tehran
Tel: (0098-21) 8828442

Shiraz Film Organisation
No. 1/56 Neaufle le Chateau St
Tehran
Tel: (0098-21) 672985/677952

Sepahan Cinema Organisation
No 126 Razi St
Jomhuri Ave. Tehran
Tel: (0098-21) 673047/676268

Resane Ama
No. 138, Shahid Beheshti Ave
15779
Tehran
Tel: (0098-21) 8744694/8746275-6

Yaran Film
No. 80, Haeri 1 Alley
Shahid Gholamreza Adibi St.
Zendan Junction, Dr. Shariati Ave.
Tehran
Tel: (0098-21) 8702552

Didar Film
3rd Floor, No. 24
Behrouzi Alley, Amir Abad Ave.
Tehran
Tel: (0098-21) 929057/928034

Noor Film
No. 9, Aza Shahr St.,
Iran Shahr Ave.
Tehran
Tel: (0098-21) 834889

Emrooz Film
21rd Floor, No. 27,
Shahid Ghandi Sq.,
Sohrevardi Ave.
Tehran
Tel: (0098-21) 862621/862583

Afagh Film
No. 23 Shahid Amini Alley
Saie Park
Vali-e Asr Ave,
Tehran
Tel: (0098-21) 8884541/8798588

Shekufa Film
Cultural Artistic Institute
2nd Floor, No. 18,
Amir Parvis Alley
Abu Reyhan St. Enqelab Ave.
Tehran
Tel: (0098-21) 6416939

Useful Addresses

Institute for Cinematic and Television Affairs of the Janbazan Foundation
Abbasabad Ave (corner of Vali-e Asr)
Tehran
Tel: (0098-21) 8713303

Shahed Television Group
No. 89, Sarv Alley
Vali-e Asr Ave
Tehran
Tel: (0098-21) 8781810/8786497

Centre for Documentary and Experimental Film Making
No. 17, Shahid Ghandi Sq.
Sohrevardi Ave.
Tehran
Tel: (0098-21) 8601241-2/8601275

Sima Film
No 35 Kuhyar St
Shahid Fayasi
(Fereshte) Ave 19658
Tehran
Tel: (0098-21) 2219531/2237695

Farabi Cinema Foundation
No. 55, Sie-e Tir Ave
Tehran 11358
Tel: (0098-21) 678156

Channel Two (I.R.I.B.)
Alvand St
Argentina Sq.
15875 Tehran
Tel: 8776081-9

Art Bureau of the Islamic Propagation Organisation
Sotudeh Alley
Rasht St
Hafez Ave
Tehran

Institute for the Intellectual Development of Children and Young Adults
No. 24 Khaled Slamboli St.
Shahid Beheshti Ave
Tehran
Tel: (0098-21) 8710661/8715545-7

Saba Cultural Artistic Company
No. 73,
Yakhchal St.,
Dr. Shariati Ave
Tehran
Tel: (0098-21) 2000596/2000594

Niki Karimi in SCENT OF JOSEPH'S SHIRT, directed by Ebrahim Hatamikia

IRELAND

Michael Dwyer

Film production in Ireland enjoyed a remarkable year in 1995 with 17 feature films and several international television series going before the cameras. Most remarkably – and most emphatically endorsing the policies of the country's Arts and Culture minister, Michael D. Higgins – as many as ten of those 17 features were made by Irish directors, six of them making their feature film débuts.

It was not entirely plain sailing. There was dismay in the summer of 1995 when the high-profile *Divine Rapture* collapsed in the early stages of production because of financial problems; Marlon Brando, Johnny Depp and Debra Winger were working on the film in the south of Ireland when the production ran out of money.

The Irish company, Hell's Kitchen, which produced *In the Name of the Father* and *Some Mother's Son*, suffered a setback in the spring of 1996 when its production, *The Bells of Hell*, based on the life of Irish writer Brendan Behan, had to close down when Sean Penn, who was to play the central role of Behan, withdrew from the project "for personal reasons". The producers hope to get the film off the ground in the near future.

The spring of 1996 also witnessed important changes in the Irish government's Section 35 tax relief scheme, when restrictions were imposed by the Department of Finance. The changes essentially will benefit small-to-medium budget productions, but one producer, Kieran Corrigan of Merlin Films, said the capping of the amount that could be raised for films costing over £15 million meant that bigger films probably would not come to Ireland.

Lonely at Home

The upsurge in cinema attendances continued steadily throughout 1995 and the number of screens increased, with Virgin opening a nine-screen complex in Dublin city centre and UCI beginning construction on its third multiplex in Dublin's suburbs. The figures for 1996 are even more promising: rolling admissions for the year from May 1995 to April 1996 amounted to 10.8 million, and the April 1996 figure of 850,000 admissions represents an increase of 20.9% on admissions for April 1995.

The biggest box-office hits in the first half of 1996 included *Babe, Seven, Toy Story, Trainspotting, Heat, Jumanji* and *The Birdcage*. However, despite all the media coverage given to the upswing in film production in Ireland, very few Irish or Irish-made films made any impact at the Irish box office. Mel Gibson's *Braveheart*, which was filmed substantially in Ireland, and Irish director Pat O'Connor's **Circle of Friends**, set and shot entirely in Ireland, were very successful, taking over £1 million each. But Irish audiences mostly stayed away from the indigenous productions, many of which were released with minimal publicity and some restricted to art-house release.

Following the 1995 controversy over the censor's banning of Oliver Stone's *Natural Born Killers*, there was a more subdued reaction when two more films were banned during the subsequent 12 months – Paul Verhoeven's *Showgirls* and Robert Rodriguez's *From Dusk Till Dawn*.

Turning 11 years old this year, the Dublin Festival had a very successful run, with attendances for afternoon shows rising most significantly. Scottish director Gilles

MacKinnon and American independent film-maker Todd Haynes were the subject of tribute programmes in Dublin and both visited the festival. The event's international guests also included director Michael Verhoeven, joined by Pauline Collins, the leading actress of his new film, *My Mother's Courage*; and Luce Vigo, who introduced a complete programme of films directed by her father, Jean Vigo.

The Cork Film Festival celebrated its 40th birthday in October 1995 and featured a lively and informative public interview with veteran producer Roger Corman, who has opened a studio in the west of Ireland. A few weeks later, the much-expanded French Film Festival in Dublin delivered its most ambitious programme to date, with a guest list headed by the iconic Jean-Pierre Léaud. Arthur Penn was the special guest of the Galway Film Fleadh in July 1995, but the event was overshadowed by the death of one of its most active regular participants, Irish producer and director, Tiernan MacBride.

MICHAEL DWYER is Film Correspondent of *The Irish Times*. He also contributes to *The New York Times*. He is President of the Federation of Irish Film Societies.

GUILTRIP

Script and Direction: Gerry Stembridge. Photography: Eugene O'Connor. Editing: Mary Finlay. Production Design: David Wilson. Music: Brendan Power. Players: Andrew Connolly, Jasmine Russell, Michelle Houlden, Peter Hanly. Produced by Temple Films. 89 mins.

An auspicious début for its writer-director, Gerry Stembridge, *Guiltrip* deals with shocking psychological violence in the marriage of an army corporal and his wife. The film takes place over the course of one crucial, tempestuous night, cutting rhythmically and in a non-chronological order to parallel events in each of the characters' lives on the previous day.

Full of bottled-up rage, Liam (Andrew Connolly) strictly applies the discipline of army life within his own home – interrogating his quiet, patient wife, Tina (Jasmine Russell), about her every move when he is at the barracks, and even forcing her to enter and read out his instructions to her from a standing orders book. Stembridge's intricately structured script consistently rings true in this disturbing psychological horror movie, relieved only by some sharp humour.

Eamon Hunt and Michelle Houlden in GUILTRIP
photo: Pat Redmond

Michael Dwyer

KOREA

Script: Joe O'Byrne, John D'Alton and Cathal Black, adapted from the short story by John McGahern. Direction: Cathal Black. Photography: Nic Morris. Editing: Emer Reynolds. Production Design: Ned McLoughlin. Music: Stephen McKeon. Players: Donal Donnelly, Andrew Scott, Fiona Molony, Vass Anderson. Produced by Cathal Black Films/Black Star Films. 75 mins.

Eleven years after the release of the gritty contemporary Dublin drama, *Pigs*, Cathal Black makes a welcome return to the screen with this accomplished rural period drama. *Korea* is set in a lakeside Co. Cavan village in 1952, at the time of the rural electrification scheme. While many people are celebrating this progress, others remain rooted in the past and the village lies in the shadow of two wars – the Korean war, which had claimed the life of a local lad, and the Irish Civil War, which had left a legacy of deep-rooted bitterness and resentment.

Donal Donnelly and Vass Anderson in KOREA

Andrew Scott, an impressive young newcomer, plays Eamon Doyle, a quiet-natured 17-year-old, whose father, John (Donal Donnelly), a lonely widower and Civil War veteran, combines an uneasy mix of stubborn pride and repressed feeling. The film tenderly catches Eamon's tentative relationship with Una (Fiona Molony), the daughter of John's longtime enemy (Vass Anderson). Thoughtful and intimate, *Korea* is richly expressive cinema in which looks and glances speak volumes. Visually, it is consistently striking with lighting cameraman Nic Morris assembling a succession of haunting compositions.

Michael Dwyer

NOTHING PERSONAL

Script: Daniel Mornin, adapted from his novel *All Our Fault*. Direction: Thaddeus O'Sullivan. Photography: Dick Pope. Editing: Michael Parker. Production Design: Mark Geraghty. Music: Philip Appleby. Players: Ian Hart, John Lynch, James Frain, Michael Gambon, Gary Lydon, Maria Doyle Kennedy. Produced by Little Bird for Channel 4 Films. 85 mins.

Set during an uneasy ceasefire in Belfast in 1975, Thaddeus O'Sullivan's film opens with an explosion – the senseless bombing of a pub by the IRA. In another part of the city, the loyalist and nationalist paramilitaries are discussing a truce. Liam Kelly (John Lynch), a Catholic single father in his thirties, is captured and tortured by cold-blooded loyalist thugs – Kenny and the psychotic Ginger – despite his protestations that he is "not involved".

Set over the course of an edgy 24 hours,

TOP TEN GROSSING FILMS IN IRELAND: 1995

Batman Forever
Casper
Braveheart
GoldenEye
Interview with the Vampire
Circle of Friends
Die Hard 3
The Santa Clause
Apollo 13
While You Were Sleeping

(compiled from a survey of Irish film distributors and exhibitors).

John Lynch and James Frain in NOTHING PERSONAL

the film captures the fear and desperation of the endemic violence as impressionable youngsters from both sides of the divide are drawn in. Edited down to a lean 85 minutes, *Nothing Personal* clearly suffers from several elements having ended up on the cutting-room floor. Daniel Mornin's screenplay also relies too heavily on narrative contrivances and is most unconvincing in its awkwardly melodramatic resolution. That said, O'Sullivan elicits vivid performances from his three central actors, and the film's anti-violence stance is firm and uncompromising throughout.

Michael Dwyer

Recent and Forthcoming Films

THE BOY FROM MERCURY

Script and Dir: Martin Duffy. Phot: Seamus Deasy. Players: Rita Tushingham, Hugh O'Conor, James Hickey, Tom Courtenay. Prod: Mercurian Productions.

THE BUTCHER BOY

Script: Neil Jordan, Patrick McCabe. Dir: Jordan. Phot: Adrian Biddle. Players: Eamon Owens, Alan Boyle, Stephen Rea, Ian Hart, Fiona Shaw. Prod: Warner Bros.

THE DISAPPEARANCE OF FINBAR

Script: Dermot Bolger, Sue Clayton. Dir: Clayton. Phot: Eduardo Serra. Players: Jonathan Ryhs-Myers, Luke Griffin, Lorraine Pilkington, Sean McGinley. Prod: Film Four/ Pandora/ First City/ Samson/Victoria Films.

DRIFTWOOD

Script and Dir: Ronan O'Leary. Phot: Billy Williams. Players: James Spader, Anne Brochet, Barry McGovern. Prod: Mary Breen-Farrelly Productions.

FRANKIE STARLIGHT

Script: Chet Raymo, Ronan O'Leary. Dir: Michael Lindsay-Hogg. Phot: Paul Laufer. Players: Anne Parillaud, Matt Dillon, Gabriel Byrne, Corbin Walker. Prod: Ferndale Films.

A FURTHER GESTURE

Script: Ronan Bennett. Dir: Robert Dornhelm. Phot: Andrzej Sekula. Players: Stephen Rea, Marie Doyle Kennedy, Brendan Gleeson, Rosanna Pastor, Jorge Sanz. Prod: Samson Films.

GOLD IN THE STREETS

Script: Elizabeth Gill, Noel Pearson. Dir: Gill. Phot: Jack Conroy. Players: Ian Hart, Jared Harris, James Belushi. Prod: Ferndale Films.

LAST OF THE HIGH KINGS

Script: David Keating, Gabriel Byrne. Dir: Keating. Players: Byrne, Catherine O'Hara, Jared Leto, Christina Ricci. Prod: Parallel Film Productions.

MICHAEL COLLINS

Script and Dir: Neil Jordan. Phot: Chris Menges. Players: Liam Neeson, Julia Roberts, Aidan Quinn, Stephen Rea, Alan Rickman. Prod: Neil Jordan Productions.

MOLL FLANDERS

Script and Dir: Pen Densham. Phot: David Tattersall. Players: Robin Wright, Morgan Freeman, Stockard Channing, Brenda Fricker. Prod: Moll Flanders Productions.

THE RUN OF THE COUNTRY

Script: Shane Connaughton. Dir: Peter Yates. Phot: Mike Southon. Players: Albert Finney, Matt Keeslar, Victoria Smurfit. Prod: Country Productions.

SNAKES AND LADDERS

Script: Trish McAdam, Gina Moxley. Dir: McAdam. Phot: Dietrich Lohmann. Players: Moxley, Pom Boyd, Sean Hughes, Rosaleen Linehan. Prod: Livia Films.

SOME MOTHER'S SON

Script: Terry George, Jim Sheridan. Dir: George. Players: Helen Mirren, Fionnuala Flanagan, Aidan Gillen, David O'Hara. Prod: Hell's Kitchen Productions.

SPAGHETTI SLOW

Script: Valerio Jalongo, Barry Devlin. Dir: Jalongo. Phot: Cian De Buitlear. Player: Brendan Gleeson. Prod: The Good Film Company.

THE SUN, THE MOON AND THE STARS

Script and Dir: Geraldine Creed. Phot: Ciaran Tanham. Players: Angie Dickinson, Jason Donovan. Prod: Blue Light Productions.

THIS IS THE SEA

Script and Dir: Mary McGuckian. Phot: Des Whelan. Players: Samantha Morton, Ross McDade, Richard Harris, Gabriel Byrne, John Lynch. Prod: Pembridge Productions.

TROJAN EDDIE

Script: Billy Roche. Dir: Gilles MacKinnon. Phot: John de Borman. Players: Richard Harris, Stephen Rea, Angeline Ball, Brendan Gleeson, Sean McGinley. Prod: Stratford Productions.

THE VAN

Script: Roddy Doyle, based on his novel. Dir: Stephen Frears. Phot: Oliver Stapleton. Players: Colm Meaney, Donal O'Kelly, Ger Ryan. Prod: Deadly Films.

Producers

Ferndale Films
4 Harcourt Terrace
Dublin 2
Tel: 676 8890
Fax: 676 8874

The Good Film Company
15 Vesey Place
Monkstown
Co Dublin
Tel: 284 4881
Fax: 284 4882

Hell's Kitchen Productions
All Hallows College
Grace Park Road
Dublin 9
Tel: 836 8052
Fax: 836 8441

Little Bird Productions
122 Lower Baggot Street
Dublin 2
Tel: 661 4245
Fax: 660 0351

Merlin Films International
41 Fitzwilliam Place
Dublin 2
Tel: 676 4460
Fax: 676 4368

Temple Films
4 Windmill Lane
Dublin 2
Tel: 671 9313
Fax: 671 9323

Distributors

Abbey Films
35 Upper Abbey Street
Dublin 1
Tel: 872 3422
Fax: 872 3687

Clarence Pictures
13 Merrion Square
Dublin 2
Tel: 661 4022
Fax: 661 4186

Columbia TriStar Films
Merchant's Court
24 Merchant's Quay
Dublin 8
Tel: 679 8234
Fax: 679 8237

Light House Cinema
12 Anglesea Street
Dublin 2
Tel: 679 9585
Fax: 679 9586

PolyGram Filmed Entertainment
Whitefriars
Aungier Street
Dublin 2
Tel: 475 7700
Fax: 475 7860

Warner Bros
Russell House
Stokes Place
St Stephen's Green
Dublin 2
Tel: 478 4000
Fax: 478 4572

United International Pictures
D'Olier Chambers
D'Olier Street
Dublin 2
Tel: 679 2433
Fax: 679 8801

Useful Addresses

Ardmore Studios
Herbert Road
Bray
Co Wicklow
Tel: 286 2971
Fax: 286 1894

The Arts Council
70 Merrion Square
Dublin 2
Tel: 661 1840
Fax: 676 0436

Espace Video Europeen (EVE)
6 Eustace Street
Dublin 2
Tel: 679 5744
Fax: 679 9657

Film Institute of Ireland
6 Eustace Street
Dublin 2
Tel: 679 5744
Fax: 679 9657

Film Makers Ireland
19 Duke Street
Dublin 2
Tel: 671 3525
Fax: 671 3505

Irish Film Board
Rockfort House
St Augustine Street
Galway
Co Galway
Tel: 091 561398
Fax: 091 561405

Irish Film Centre
6 Eustace Street
Dublin 2
Tel: 679 5744
Fax: 679 9657

Irish Trade Board
Merrion Hall
Strand Road
Dublin 4
Tel: 269 5011
Fax: 269 5820

Radio Telefis Eireann (RTE)
Donnybrook
Dublin 4
Tel: 208 3111
Fax: 208 3080

ISRAEL

Dan Fainaru

The good news this year is that 14 feature films are about to be completed; not bad for a country with a population of five million. The bad news is that this is about all the good news there is. One disappointment followed another during the last twelve months, and the exasperated industry is wondering whether it has any future at all.

A massive $50 million co-production fund – pledged, delayed, postponed and pledged again over the last couple of years by the Ministry of Industry and Trade – was supposed to be the venture that would help Israeli films graduate to the big time. But after the 1996 elections, with Labour out and the Likkud in, the new minister in charge, Anatol Sharanski, decided he had better things to do with his budget and threw the project out the window. International productions are less eager than ever to use Israeli locations and crews, possibly because of security problems, but also because of local prices and low government incentives.

Audiences for Israeli films continue to decline, and producers would be the first to tell you that even the grosses of 'hits' like **Lovesick, Passover** or **Under the Domim Tree** fall far behind their cost. Distribution abroad has remained a hopelessly disorganised affair, since individual producers, who do not pull sufficient weight on their own, seem unable to join forces in order to obtain better exposure on international markets. Meanwhile, the state agencies that should be concerned obviously aren't.

The last straw, one that could easily break many backs, came in June, when United Studios shut down the only film laboratory in the country. This means that any feature production will in future have to ship its dailies abroad, rearrange its production schedule accordingly, and reshuffle the budget to accommodate delays, additional shooting, transport costs and lab expenses abroad. When the average working cost of an Israeli film is still around $7-8,000,000, such adjustments are both meaningful and painful.

And That Was the Good News

No wonder the 1996 edition of the Jerusalem Film Festival turned into a long litany of complaint, with actors, directors, producers and every other interested party bemoaning the fate of the Israeli cinema, blaming the new régime for its insensitivity to the needs of the industry, and warning that it stands on its last legs.

I F C
information
international
ventures
insurance
incentives
facilities
features
facts
figures
financing
contacts
coordination
co-productions
crews
paving the way for smooth production work in Israel
Israel Film Centre
Ministry of Industry and Trade, P.O. Box 299, Jerusalem, Israel
Tel: +972-2-6220608. Fax: +972-2-6236303, 6245110

The Fund for the Promotion of Israeli Quality Films (budget: $4.5 million) may offer up to $400,000 per film, but its only available partners right now are the television channels, free and cable, whose contributions are far too modest when the rising costs of production are taken into account. Not to mention that, in order to get the television channels in, producers have to divest themselves of most TV rights which, in many cases, are the only real sources of income for Israeli films once they manage to cross international borders.

A second, much smaller fund ($1.2 million), dedicated to documentaries, has been busily backing projects in the course of the last year. But since most of its output, shot on video and co-produced by the TV channels, consists of extended TV reports or interviews on topical subjects, rather than fully-fledged films, they may grab media attention and find slots in specialised international festivals, but hardly qualify as film production. Recently, a third but even smaller fund ($300,000) has been set up, its purpose (social themes) vague at best and its resources sufficient to cover its overheads but not much more.

Given these conditions, it is hardly surprising that graduating classes of talented film students from Tel Aviv University and the Jerusalem Film School, after showing much promise and often winning international awards, opt for commercials, TV shows and soap operas. And once there, it is very difficult for them to be recuperated for any other purpose.

Slim Chances to Travel

Of the films made last year, some were signed by seasoned veterans making their first feature in a long time. No less than ten years separate Rafi Bukaee's remarkable début, *Avanti Popolo*, from **Marco Polo**, a previously untold adventure of the Venetian traveller in the Holy Land; 18 years after Igal Bursztyn's first feature (*Belfer*), he finally has a new one, **Everlasting Joy**, a philosophical tale placing Baruch Spinoza in a contemporary popular Tel Aviv suburb; Moshe Mizrahi returned from a long silence, and an even longer absence from Israeli cinema, with **Women**, a 19th-century tale of love, devotion and sacrifice taking place in an exceedingly orthodox Jewish community.

A different case is Amos Gitai, by far the most prolific and probably also the most controversial Israeli film-maker in recent years. His main body of work has been made outside the country. **Devarim** (screened in one of the Venice 1995 sidebars) is his first Israeli feature; a static, intellectual, calculated version of an intensely emotional novel, considered one of the best ever written in the Hebrew language. Audiences at the Jerusalem Film Festival, so far the only ones in Israel exposed to these pictures, did not display much enthusiasm for any of them, and in most cases the critics did not respond any better. Also, with the exception of Mizrahi, none of them as yet has a local distribution deal.

The newcomers aren't having a much better time of it. Arnon Zadok, one of the best screen actors in the country, directed his first film, **White Night** (Young Audience Award in the Cannes Directors' Fortnight), the true story of a convict who beats drug addiction in jail. But the picture was in and out of the local cinemas before anyone noticed it. **Birds in Neutral**, a clumsy adolescent romp by Eyal Shirai and Galit Eshkol, seems to have done better, while **Dogs are Colour Blind**, a rather contrived attempt at screwball comedy, may score even more, if only because it features several local TV stars. But its chances to travel are slim at best.

Far more interesting are two other firsts, Avi Folman and Ori Sivan's **Saint Clara** (Special Jury Prize in Karlovy Vary) and Joseph Pitchhadze's **Under Western Eyes** (see separate reviews). But how soon and to what effect they are going to be released here is still not clear. For, like everywhere else, local distribution is ruled more than ever by the American studios through the two leading theatre circuits, Globus Group and Israeli Theatres. Together these two now cover almost 80% of the country's screens and both are closely associated with one or other of the majors. Art distributors, fewer than ever now, have to rely on special venues such as the Tel Aviv Museum (managed by one of them, Semadar Azriely) or the Tel Aviv Cinemathèque, whose second theatre is used for repertory programmes.

DAN FAINARU is an Israeli film critic and journalist who is Editor in Chief of the European Film Review, and has been correspondent for I.F.G. for several years. A former director of the Israeli Film Institute, he is a familiar face at the world's major and minor festivals alike.

KLARA HAKEDOSHA (Saint Clara)

Script: Ari Folman, Ori Sivan, based on a novel by Jelena Kohoutova and Pavel Kohout. Direction: Folman, Sivan. Photography: Valentin Belanogov. Editing: Dov Steiner. Music: Barry Saharov. Players: Lucy Dubinchek, Halil Elohev, Maya Maron, Joahnie Peterson, Yigal Naor. Produced by Marek Rozenbaum, Uri Sabag, for Transfax Films. 84 mins.

Avi Folman and Ori Sivan, whose only previous film-making experience was an ironic, half-hour documentary on the hallucinating reactions of various Israelis to the Gulf War, have confidently graduated to features with this fresh adaptation of a Czech novel written while Soviet tanks were still patrolling the streets of Prague. The picture, first unveiled in the Berlinale Panorama, was awarded a Special Jury Prize at Karlovy Vary.

Lucy Dubinchek (right) in SAINT CLARA

It is about an adolescent girl with a gift for clairvoyance and some of her classmates, who rebel against authority and set out to make up a world of their own. Devoid of the political intentions the story might have originally had, it is now clearly a coming-of-age tale showing kids who brave their despotic teachers and overcome the negligence of their parents in a world doomed for destruction, as the grotesque reports seen on the ever-present TV sets keep reminding us.

Set in an unidentifiable industrial shantytown (this must be the least Israeli-looking film shot in this country), bathed in an ominous red glow, the allegorical plot slips into outright parody every time grown-ups are involved but stays remarkably close to reality when dealing with the kids. As the luminous, soulful Clara who can see the future as long as she does not fall in love, Lucy Dubinchek is a real asset.

Given the limitations of their budget, Folman and Sivan have managed to come up with a remarkable visual concept and maintain it throughout the picture. The only hint that the film was shot in Israel are the use of various accents and modes of behaviour among the adults, indicating the multiplicity of origins in a country where everyone is an immigrant, and emphasising the presence of Russian newcomers (Clara's family) not yet integrated in their new country.

Dan Fainaru

Still from AS TEARS GO BY

ZOLGOT HAD'MAOTH ME'ATZMAN (As Tears Go By)

Script and Direction: Eitan Green. Photography: Amnon Salomon. Editing: Era Lapid. Production Design: Boaz Katzenelson. Music: Adi Renert. Players: Arie Moscona, Av Grainik, Yael Stern-O'Dwyer, Meital Trabelsi. Produced by Regev-Dvash Productions. 85 mins.

Eitan Green's predilection for understatement is taken to new extremes here, in this an intimate drama about a shy, introvert youth who can't pass his driving test because under stress his eyes water, his view is impaired, and he loses control. Whether this small, unprepossessing story will capture the fancy of large audiences will depend, to a great extent, on their willingness to identify with the diffident main character and his troubles.

Itzhak is definitely a late bloomer. An only son, his military service behind him, he still lives at home with his parents and shares with his father the responsibility for a modest public address business catering to weddings and bar mitzvahs. The father, a gregarious, lively character, would like to expand, but for that he would need a second car; hence his eagerness to see his son get hold of his licence. But Itzhak keeps failing, not only at driving, but at all other adulthood tests, until his father's heart condition and a girl's outright rejection of his timid advances pushes him to take some drastic measures.

A keen observer of human nature, Green has lovingly fashioned this low-key plot. But by defusing every possible emotional outburst and insistently under-directing his actors, he may well find himself with only a limited number of dedicated spectators willing to dig down for those things not said or shown in the open.

Dan Fainaru

LEN'EGED EYNAIM MA'ARAVIOTH (Under Western Eyes)

Script and Direction: Joseph Pitchhadze. Photography: Shai Goldman. Editing: Dov Steuer. Art Direction: Shahar Katzav, Giora Asaulov. Music: Berry Sakharof. Players: Eyal Schechter, Liat Glick, Ezra Kafri, Carmel Betto, Yohanan Harrison, Gideon Shemer, Picho Ben Zur. Produced by Dubi Baruch and Joseph Pitchhadze for November Films. 95 mins.

This début by a Georgian-born graduate of the Tel Aviv University, awarded top honours at the 1996 Jerusalem Film Festival, owes much of its style and approach to Wim Wenders and Michelangelo Antonioni. As unconcerned as his two spiritual mentors with proper storytelling, Joseph Pitchhadze's main concern is atmosphere, mood and message. A tragi-comic road movie, his film traces the journey of an architect, living in Berlin, who returns to Israel to attend his father's funeral, only to discover that he has been brought back under false pretences. His father, a former Russian spy, has broken out of jail and the secret service hopes the son will lead them to him.

The plot proceeds at a leisurely pace as the architect, accompanied by a girl he picks up at the airport, meets some of his and his father's former friends, listens to cassettes sent to him through the mail, and reluctantly follows the obvious tracks that will lead him to the fatal encounter with his parent. The secret agents (the film's comic relief) maintain constant surveillance, once in a while intervening and goading him on. But the journey itself soon becomes secondary to the young director's speculations on the everlasting conflict between fathers and sons and their love-hate relationship. That and many other subjects – such as the nostalgia of Russian immigrants for their native land, the relics of Bauhaus architecture surviving in Tel Aviv, objective reality in black-and-white versus subjective reality in colour, or the majestic scenery of the Negev where fate finally works itself out.

Still from UNDER WESTERN EYES

Never less than exciting visually, and making magnificent use of rarely seen locations, Pitchhadze's film marks the arrival of an exciting new talent on the Israeli scene. His narrative may leave something to be desired, and he is often lured into indulging pretty pictures at the expense of his actors, but this is a commendable and promising effort.

Dan Fainaru

Distributors

Globus Group
(UIP, MGM Pathé, Cannon, Warner)
10 Glinkson St.
Tel Aviv
Tel: 972-3-200221
Fax: 972-3-283187

A.D. Matalon & Co.
(Columbia TriStar, Twentieth Century Fox, Orion)
15 Hess St.
Tel Aviv
Tel: 972-3-29625, 296251
Fax: 972-3-292977

Forum/Israeli Theatres
91 Medinath Hayehudim St.
P.O. Box 12598
Herzlyia Pituakh 46766
Tel: (09) 562111
Fax: (09) 561581

Shapira Films
34 Allenby St.
Tel Aviv
Tel: 972-3-5102539
Fax: 972-3-5101370

Gelfand Films
34 Allenby St.
Tel Aviv
Tel: 972-3-657010
Fax: 972-3-657994

Shani Films
Dizengoff Centre
Tel Aviv
Tel: 972-3-5288282
Fax: 972-3-204749

Erez Films
32 Allenby St.
Tel Aviv
Tel: 972-3-658654
Fax: 972-3-659874

Nachshon Films
22 Harakevet St.
Tel Aviv
Tel: 972-3-5660015
Fax: 972-3-615112

Shoval Films
32 Allenby St.
Tel Aviv
Tel: 972-3-659288
Fax: 972-3-659289

Tamuz Films
5 Pinsker St.
Tel Aviv
Tel: 972-3-201512

Useful Addresses

Israel Film Centre
Ministry of Industry & Trade
P.O. Box 299
94190 Jerusalem
Tel: 972-2-750433, 750297
Fax: 972-2-245110

Israeli Film Institute
5 Yelin Mor St.
Tel Aviv 67058
Tel: 972-3-5616098
Fax: 972-3-5611658

Israel Film & TV Producers Association
Attn. Katriel Schory
26 Ruppin St.
Tel Aviv 63457
Tel: 972-3-226116
Fax: 972-3-235821

Jerusalem Cinematheque & Israeli Film Archive
11 Hebron Rd.
Jerusalem
Tel: 972-2-724131
Fax: 972-2-713044

Tel Aviv Cinematheque
2 Shprintzak St.
P.O. Box 20370
Tel Aviv 61203
Tel: 972-3-6917181
Fax: 972-3-6962841

ITALY

Lorenzo Codelli

For the first time in many years, the 60 national releases in Italy doubled their percentage of the gross to 18.9% (from 9.9%). American imports meanwhile rose to 62.4%. Over two dozen Italian movies – especially those made by newcomers, with unknown names – failed to attract more than a few customers in sparse towns, but the overall outcome means a welcome shift in audience tastes. The new centre-left government – which includes the influential Culture and Show Business Minister, Walter Veltroni, an avowed film buff – could help by introducing efficient tax shelters, among other legislative measures. But the real problem remains how to encourage distributors and exhibitors to shed their traditional mistrust of Italian movies.

Grassroots Cinema

What they will gamble on are the kind of surefire comic vehicles that were wheeled out for Christmas 1995. Carlo Verdone's **Viaggi di nozze** clocked up two-and-a-half million admissions, thanks to the unbeatable alliance between producer/

distributor Vittorio Cecchi Gori and Warner Bros Italia, but also thanks to the popular Roman clown's satirical malice. As savage as the best *commedie all 'italiana* of the golden age, his three episodes about three miscast couples enduring honeymoons, all starring the quick-change Verdone, mock the meanness of proletarian as well as bourgeois Catholics.

The second Christmas hit, **Vacanze di Natale 95**, concocted by smart tycoon Aurelio de Laurentiis and left-handedly assembled by Neri Parenti, has sex-hungry buffoons Massimo Boldi and Christian De Sica holidaying this time at Aspen, Colorado, instead of Cortina or Sardinia. A younger face, Leonardo Pieraccioni, stars in his own first farce, **I laureati**, about the rivalries between a bunch of students in ever-so-pleasant Tuscany.

This is the region beloved of established *metteurs en scène* Bernardo Bertolucci and Paolo & Vittorio Taviani. Bertolucci has chosen a lovely villa with a scenic vineyard near Siena for **Stealing Beauty**, a film which allows him to become a virgin artist again by sharing the sense of wonder of his American protagonist, Liv Tyler. She becomes enchanted by the countryside while looking for her real father and a passionate lover. It's too bad that in Cannes and abroad this harmonious little symphony – Bertolucci's most personal statement in decades – has not had the welcome it received at home.

The Tavianis' adaptation of Goethe's *Elective Affinities* (**Le affinità elettive)** is a romance imbued with a tragic vision of

Liv Tyler in Bertolucci's STEALING BEAUTY
photo: Peter Mountain

paradise lost. Idiosyncratic Florentine comedian-director Alessandro Benvenuti knows how to make the most of his own lyrical countryside in **Ivo il tardivo**, in which he plays a retarded savage in love.

Cinema from the Page

Literary adaptations are not exactly a new trend, but this year seemed to turn up a larger crop than usual. **Va' dove ti porta il cuore**, by Cristina Comencini, made a rather cheap, cold melodrama of the rather moving grandmother-granddaughter relationship in Susanna Tamaro's bestseller. Teenage audiences were rightly disappointed by Enza Negroni's simplistic **Jack Frusciante è uscito dal gruppo**, based on

ASCOLTACI ITALIA!
IL CINEMA È ANCHE MUSICA.
ASCOLTA IL CINEMA.

C.A.M. ORIGINAL SOUNDTRACKS from the golden years of Italian and French cinema.
Over 170 titles and 75 composers available on compact disc.
Ask for our catalog. Also available on CD-ROM.

CAM Original Soundtracks **VIA COLA DI RIENZO, 152 - 00192 ROME (ITALY) - FAX:(+39-6) 687.4046**

VISUAL

ANICA

The italian cinema industry
presents the new production at
MIFED 1996
and welcomes all the operators
participating at the Market

Anica office in Milan: 137 A1

ANICA
promotes Italian Cinema worldwide
at Festivals and Markets

Head office
00198 Roma - viale Regina Margherita, 286
tel.: 39-6-44231480 fax: 39-6-4404128

Chiava Caselli and Peter Weller in Antonioni's AL DI LA DELLE NUVOLE

the cult original by Enrico Brizzi about a student's first loves and rock inclinations.

Even 82-year-old Michelangelo Antonioni, for his long-awaited comeback after an illness, chose to retell some of the short stories he published in *Quel bowling sul Tevere* (1983). His own role as a wandering director – played by a puzzled John Malkovich in connecting segments arranged by Wim Wenders – is the main focus of **Al di là delle nuvole**. He spies on casual, loveless encounters from Portofino to Ferrara, from Paris to Aix en Provence, which look highly Antonioni-esque, empty mirrors professionally polished by Alfio Contini's imagery but not much enhanced by Tonino Guerra's script. Maurizio Nichetti vainly tried to appeal to families with **Palla di neve**, adapted from Emilio Nessi's too gentle Save-the-Dolphin fable. And Lina Wertmüller's **Ninfa plebea** killed any erotic current in Domenico Rea's wartime nymphet's saga.

There's a whole catalogue of perversions in **Fermo posta Tinto Brass**, in which the director exposes plenty of buxom bums, his *idée fixe*. Pupi Avati exorcises atavistic ghosts in **L'arcano incantatore**, in which he returns to his horror *métier* with an 18th century legend of a young unfrocked priest who discovers an evil bishop's secret gifts amidst dismantled castles, dark lakes and Umbrian valleys.

Cinema from the Past

Veterans Mario Monicelli and Carlo Lizzani have tried to recreate past milestones. Monicelli's **Facciamo paradiso** parodies late 60s political upheavals, while **Celluloide** by Lizzani and scriptwriter/novelist Ugo Pirro analyses the efforts by Roberto Rossellini, Sergio Amidei, Anna Magnani and their colleagues to shoot *Roma città aperta* after the Liberation. The budgets of both pictures seem unfortunately inadequate for their historical ambitions. Also marred by poor means, Dino Risi's **Giovani e belli** is an amusing cavalcade of collapsing ideals, which only had a clandestine release in spite of TV star Anna Falchi's popularity.

Alberto Sordi in ROMANZO DI UN GIOVANE POVERO

Tributes to Neo-realist masters also feature in Giuseppe Tornatore's **L'uomo delle stelle**, in which Sergio Castellitto plays a mendacious travelling cameraman in post-war Sicily. Ex-superstar Alberto Sordi, playing one of his meannest characters, a would-be uxoricide manipulating an unemployed hired assassin, could not save Ettore Scola's thriller **Romanzo di un giovane povero** at the box-office. The same must be said of Asia Argento's sour performance in his father Dario's **La sindrome di Stendhal**, another boring 'mystery' from an impoverished shlockmeister.

Asia performs more convincingly in Peter Del Monte's intimist road movie, **Compagna di viaggio**. An adaptation of a very successful stage comedy, **Uomini senza donne** by playwright Angelo Longoni, launches a couple of film kids: Gianmarco Tognazzi and Alessandro Gassman, playing misogynistic, egocentric Casanovas as their illustrious fathers Ugo and Vittorio frequently did. Ricky Tognazzi, the late Ugo's other son, prefers to stay behind the camera. His well-intentioned, expressionistic **Vite strozzate** attacks usury, a spreading scourge, casting gorgeous Sabrina Ferrilli among the victims of rather one-dimensional villains.

Newcomers Spit in Your Face

The most discussed débutants, Sicilian ex-videomakers Daniele Ciprì and Franco Maresco, refused to screen their black-and-white opus, **Lo zio di Brooklyn**, at the Venice Festival since Gillo Pontecorvo did not allow them to compete for the Golden Lion. Hated by many, hailed by a few, their rough pot-pourri of early Pasolini and Buñuel provocations, starring crazy vagrants copulating with donkeys, belching and swearing around a starkly noir Sicily, threatens to bury its own quite original visual style and some biting jokes.

Less aggressive than *Libera*, his first movie, Pappi Corsicato's **I buchi neri** features a liaison between a gay truck driver and a whore – blonde mini-Venus Iaia Forte. Corsicato's fondness for grotesque symbols and ravaged Neapolitan landscapes often suggests a kind of high-brow science fiction. Ex-documentary maker Mimmo Calopresti was lucky enough to get support from Nanni Moretti for **La seconda volta**, a sincere portrayal of the post-terrorist era in subdued half-tones.

Moretti, now occupied as manager of his trendy Nuovo Sacher film theatre in Trastevere, Rome, directed an extremely funny short about his daily worries, **Il**

Nanni Moretti and Valeria Bruni-Tedeschi in LA SECONDA VOLTA

SACIS
66, VIA TEULADA
00195 ROME - ITALY
TEL. (6) 374981
FAX (6) 3723492

STUDIO VITALE

TOP TEN GROSSING FILMS IN ITALY: 1995/96

	Gross (lire)
Viaggi di nozze (*Italy*)	24,300,689,000
Pocahontas	20,773,233,000
Vacanze di Natale 95 (*Italy*)	19,956,477,000
Seven	18,686,694,000
Braveheart	14,769,102,000
Casper	14,325,002,000
Heat	13,195,886,000
Dumb and Dumber	11,525,545,000
Apollo 13	11,393,977,000
First Knight	11,141,080,000

(Source: *Giornale dello Spettacolo*)

giorno della prima di *Close Up*. An army of famous actors and film-makers appear briefly in a curious portmanteau film by Daniele Cesarano, **Il cielo è sempre più blu**, a generous canvas, à la Robert Altman, of Rome's disconnected people.

Sergio Castellitto in Tornatore's L'UOMO DELLE STELLE

Bibliomania

Ace screenwriter Suso Cecchi d'Amico remembers her career and friends in *Storie di cinema (e d'altro)* (Garzanti). Tullio Kezich reissues a diary on a legendary shoot, *Su La dolce vita con Federico Fellini* (Marsilio). A useful critical yearbook is *Cinema italiano, Annuario 1995,* by Paolo D'Agostini (Il Castoro). Paolo Mereghetti's giant *Dizionario dei film 1996* (Baldini & Castoldi) assembles 13,500 film reviews. Centro Sperimentale di Cinematografia is carrying on with their detailed filmographies – *1911* plus *1912* – while restarting their house magazine, *Bianco e nero*. Gremese Editore gives us another instalment of the essential *Dizionario del cinema italiano,* about the 70s. Twelve restored shorts by twelve Italian masters are studied by Lino Micciché in *Studi su dodici sguardi d'autore in cortometraggio* (Associazione Philip Morris). Two Neo-realist masterpieces are analysed in two oversized albums: *Umberto D* (Mediaset), and *Il cappotto* (Lindau Editore).

LORENZO CODELLI has written for many books and periodicals, including *Positif*. He is a member of the board of the Cineteca del Friuli, and of the Pordenone Silent Film Festival.

IN DARK BLUE THE COUNTRIES WHERE SACIS HAS DISTRIBUTED THE ITALIAN SOCCER CHAMPIONSHIP 1996/97

THE ITALIAN LEAGUE WORLDWIDE, SINCE 1975

INTERNATIONAL DISTRIBUTION

SACIS SCORES WITH SOCCER RIGHTS

SOCCER=SUCCESS:
ITALIAN CHAMPIONSHIP BROADCAST
TO 105 COUNTRIES

Rome 00195 • 66, Via Teulada - Ph. 6/374981 Fax 6/3723492 SACIS INTERNATIONAL

Recent Films

LE AFFINITA' ELETTIVE (Elective Affinities)

Script and Dir: Paolo and Vittorio Taviani. Phot: Giuseppe Lanci. Players: Jean-Hughes Anglade, Isabelle Huppert, Fabrizio Bentivoglio. Prod: Filmtre/Gierre Film/Rai (Rome)/Florida Movies/ F3 Cinéma/Canal + (Paris).

AL DI LA' DELLE NUVOLE (Beyond the Clouds)

Script: Michelangelo Antonioni, Tonino Guerra, Wim Wenders. Dir: Antonioni, Wenders. Phot: Alfio Contini. Players: John Malkovich, Chiara Caselli, Fanny Ardant. Prod: Sunshine/Cinéa (Paris)/Road Movies (Berlin)/ Cecchi Gori Group/Rai (Rome).

L'ARCANO INCANTATORE (The Arcane Enchanter)

Script and Dir: Pupi Avati. Phot: Cesare Bastelli. Players: Carlo Cecchi, Stefano Dionisi. Prod: DueA/Filmauro.

I BUCHI NERI (Black Holes)

Script and Dir: Pappi Corsicato. Phot: Italo Daniele Petriccione. Players: Iaia Forte, Vincenzo Peluso. Prod: Filmauro.

CELLULOIDE (Celluloid)

Script: Ugo Pirro, Furio Scarpelli, Carlo Lizzani, from Ugo Pirro's novel. Dir: Lizzani. Phot: Giorgio Di Battista. Players: Massimo Ghini, Giancarlo Giannini, Anna Falchi. Prod: Dean Film/Istituto Luce/Production Group/Telepiù.

IL CIELO E' SEMPRE PIU' BLU (The Sky Is So Blue)

Script: Daniele Cesarano, Paolo Marchesini. Dir: Antonello Grimaldi. Phot: Alessandro Pesci. Players: Enrico Lo Verso, Sergio Rubini, Gianmarco Tognazzi. Prod: Fandango/Colorado Film/ Bim Distribuzione.

COMPAGNA DI VIAGGIO (Travelling Companion)

Script: Peter Del Monte, Gloria Malatesta, Claudia Sbarigia. Dir: Del Monte. Phot: Giuseppe Lanci. Players: Michel Piccoli, Asia Argento. Prod: Alia Film/Istituto Luce/Rai.

FACCIAMO PARADISO (Let's Make Paradise)

Script: Leo Benvenuti, Piero De Bernardi, Suso Cecchi d'Amico, Mario Monicelli, from the novel by Giuseppe Pontiggia. Dir: Monicelli. Phot: Tonino Delli Colli. Players: Margherita Buy, Philippe Noiret, Lello Arena. Prod: Clemi Cinematografica.

FERIE D'AGOSTO (August Holidays)

Script: Paolo Virzì, Francesco Bruni. Dir: Virzì. Phot: Paolo Carnera. Players: Silvio Orlando, Ennio Fantastichini, Sabrina Ferrilli. Prod: Cecchi Gori Group Tiger Cinematografica.

FERMO POSTA TINTO BRASS (Poste Restante Tinto Brass)

Script: Tinto Brass, Aurelio Grimaldi, Claudio Lizza. Dir: Brass. Phot: Dante Della Torre. Players: Tinto Brass, Cinzia Roccaforte, Laura Gualtieri. Prod: California Film/Produttori Associati.

GIOVANI E BELLI (Young and Beautiful)

Script: Bernardino Zapponi, Dino Risi. Dir: Risi. Phot: Maurizio Calvesi. Players: Anna Falchi, Luca Venantini. Prod: Produttori Associati/California Film.

IO BALLO DA SOLA (Stealing Beauty)

Script: Bernardo Bertolucci, Susan Minot. Dir: Bertolucci. Phot: Darius Khondji. Players: Liv Tyler, Jeremy Irons, Jean Marais. Prod: Recorded Picture Company (London)/UGC Images/Canal +/ France 2 Cinema (Paris)/Fiction (Rome).

IO E IL RE (Me and the King)

Script: Lucio Gaudino, Ivan Orano, Claver Salizzato. Dir: Gaudino. Phot: (b&w): Cesare Bastelli. Players: Carlo delle Piane, Franco Nero, Laura Morante. Prod: DueA Film/Rai.

IO NO SPIK INGLISH

Script: Enrico and Carlo Vanzina. Dir: Carlo Vanzina. Phot: Gianlorenzo Battaglia. Players: Paolo Villaggio, Ian Price. Prod: Italian International Film.

IVO IL TARDIVO (Retarded Ivo)

Script: Ugo Chiti, Nicola Zavagli, Alessandro Benvenuti. Dir: Benvenuti. Phot: Blasco Giurato. Players: Alessandro Benvenuti, Francesca Neri. Prod: Union P.N.

JACK FRUSCIANTE E' USCITO DAL GRUPPO (Jack Frusciante Has Left the Band)

Script: Enrico Brizzi, Enza Negroni, from the novel by Enrico Brizzi. Dir: Negroni. Phot: Alessio Torresi Gelsini. Players: Stefano Accorsi, Violante Placido. Prod: Brosfilm/Medusa Film.

I LAUREATI (The Graduates)

Script: Giovanni Veronesi, Leonardo Pieraccioni. Dir: Pieraccioni. Phot: Alessandro Pesci. Players: Leonardo Pieraccioni, Gianmarco Tognazzi, Maria Grazia Cucinotta. Prod: Cecchi Gori Group.

MARCIANDO NEL BUIO (Marching in the Dark)

Script: Claudio Lizza, Massimo Spano. Dir: Spano. Phot: Bruno Cascio. Players: Massimo

Iaia Forte in I BUCHI NERI

Dapporto, Jean Marc Barr. Prod: Zeudi e Franco Cristaldi Film.

NINFA PLEBEA (Plebeian Nymph)

Script: Lina Wertmüller, Ugo Pirro from the novel by Domenico Rea. Dir: Wertmüller. Phot: Ennio Guarnieri. Players: Lucia Cara, Raoul Bova, Stefania Sandrelli. Prod: Italian International Film/ Eurolux Produzione.

PALLA DI NEVE (Snowball)

Script: Gianni Romoli, Stefano Sudriè, Maurizio Nichetti, Ciro Ippolito, from the novel by Emilio Nessi. Dir: Nichetti. Phot: Cristiano Pogany. Players: Paolo Villaggio, Alessandro Haber. Prod: Italian International Film/Eurolux Produzione.

PASOLINI, UN DELITTO ITALIANO (Pasolini – An Italian Crime)

Script: Marco Tullio Giordana, Stefano Rulli, Sandro Petraglia. Dir: Giordana. Phot: Franco Lecca. Players: Giulio Scarpati, Claudio Amendola, Ivano Marescotti. Prod: Numero 5/Cecchi Gori Group Leopard/ Cecchi Gori Group Tiger.

ROMANZO DI UN GIOVANE POVERO (The Novel of a Poor Young Man)

Script: Ettore Scola, Silvia Scola, Giacomo Scarpelli. Dir: Ettore Scola. Phot: Franco Di Giacomo. Players: Alberto Sordi, Rolando Ravello, André Dussolier. Prod: Mass Film/Matopigia/Studio E.L./ Istituto Luce (Rome)/Les Films Alain Sarde (Paris).

LA SECONDA VOLTA (The Second Time)

Script: Mimmo Calopresti, Francesco Bruni, Haidrun Schleef. Dir: Calopresti. Phot: Alessandro Pesci. Players: Nanni Moretti, Valeria Bruni Tedeschi. Prod: Sacher Film/Rai (Rome)/ Banfilm/La Sept Cinéma/Canal + (Paris).

SELVAGGI (Savage People)

Script: Enrico and Carlo Vanzina. Dir: Carlo Vanzina. Phot: Gian Lorenzo Battaglia. Players: Ezio Greggio, Leo Gullotta, Antonello Fassari. Prod: Video 80.

LA SINDROME DI STENDHAL (The Stendhal Syndrome)

Script: Dario Argento, Franco Ferrini, from the novel by Graziella Magherini. Dir: Argento. Phot: Giuseppe Rotunno. Players: Asia Argento, Thomas Kretschmann. Prod: Medusa Film.

UOMINI SENZA DONNE (Men Without Women)

Script: Angelo Longoni from his own play. Dir: Longoni. Phot: Alfio Contini, Nino Celeste. Players: Alessandro Gassman,

Gianmarco Tognazzi. Prod: Thunder Film/Cecchi Gori Group Tiger Cinematografica.

L'UOMO DELLE STELLE (The Star Man)

Script: Fabio Rinaudo, Giuseppe Tornatore. Dir: Tornatore. Phot: Dante Spinotti. Players: Sergio Castellitto, Tiziana Lodato, Leopoldo Trieste. Prod: Cecchi Gori Group Tiger Cinematografica/Rai.

VACANZE DI NATALE 95 (Christmas Holidays 95)

Script: Neri Parenti from the story by Carlo and Enrico Vanzina's. Dir: Parenti. Phot: Gianlorenzo Battaglia. Players: Christian De Sica, Massimo Boldi, Luke Perry. Prod: Filmauro.

VA' DOVE TI PORTA IL CUORE (Follow Your Heart)

Script: Roberta Mazzoni, Cristina Comencini, from the novel by Susanna Tamaro. Dir: Comencini. Phot: Roberto Forza. Players: Virna Lisi, Margherita Buy. Prod: Videa.

IL VERIFICATORE (The Surveyor)

Script: Stefano Incerti, Gianni Molino. Dir: Incerti. Phot: Pasquale Mari. Players: Antonio Iuorio, Roberto De Francesco. Prod: Nutrimenti Terrestri/Teatri Uniti.

VIAGGI DI NOZZE (Honeymoons)

Script: Carlo Verdone, Leo Benvenuti, Piero De Bernardi. Dir: Verdone. Phot: Danilo Desideri. Players: Carlo Verdone, Claudia Gerini, Veronica Pivetti. Prod: Cecchi Gori Group Tiger Cinematografica.

VITE STROZZATE (Strangled Lives)

Script: Simona Izzo, Giuseppe Manfredi, Graziano Diana, Ricky Tognazzi. Dir: Tognazzi. Phot: Alessio Torresi Gelsini. Players: Sabrina Ferrilli, Vincent Lindon. Prod: Cecchi Gori Group.

LO ZIO DI BROOKLYN (The Uncle from Brooklyn)

Script and Dir: Daniele Ciprì, Franco Maresco. Phot (b&w): Luca Bigazzi. Players: Pippo Augusta, Francesco Arnao. Prod: Filmauro.

Useful Addresses

Agis
Via di Villa Patrizi, 10
00161 Roma
Tel: 884731
Fax: 8848079

Anica
Viale Regina Margherita, 286
00198 Roma
Tel: 8841272
Fax: 44231838

Banca Nazionale del Lavoro
Piazza San Bernardo, 101
00100 Roma
Tel: 47021
Fax: 47025179

CAM
Via Cola di Rienzo 152
000192 Roma
Tel: 687 4220
Fax: 687 4046

Carol Levi Company
Via G. Carducci, 10
00100 Roma
Tel: 486961
Fax: 4871150

Cinecittà
Via Tuscolana, 1055
00173 Roma
Tel: 74641, 722931
Fax: 7222155

Cecchi Gori Group
Via Valadier 42
00100 Roma
Tel: 324721
Fax: 32472302

Direzione Generale dello Spettacolo
Via della Ferratella in Laterano, 45-51
00184 Roma
Tel: 7732

Ente Cinema
Via Tuscolana, 1055
00173 Roma
Tel: 722221/722861
Fax: 7221863

Film Export Group
Via Polonia, 9
00198 Roma
Tel: 8554266, 8444187
Fax: 8550248

Fininvest
Largo del Nazareno, 3
00197 Roma
Tel: 67381
Fax: 67386050

Filmauro
Via della Vasca Navale, 58
00146 Roma
Tel: 5576207
Fax: 5590670

International Recording
Via Urbana, 172
00184 Roma
Tel: 4821066, 4819006, 4827970
Fax: 4745246

Istituto Luce
Via Tuscolana, 1055
00173 Roma
Tel: 722931
Fax: 7222090

Kinepolis SpA
Via Pontina KM23
00128 Roma
Tel: 5050545
Fax: 5050119

Loeb and Loeb
Piazza Digione, 1
00197 Roma
Tel: 874557

Penta Film
Via Aurelia Antica, 422
00165 Roma
Tel: 663901
Fax: 66390450

Still from LO ZIO DI BROOKLYN

MYSTFEST XVIII, 1997
International Mystery Film Festival
MYSTFEST
Cattolica, Italy 22 - 28 giugno 1997
Centro Culturale Polivalente
Tel. +39 541/967802 Fax +39 541/967803

Rai – Radiotelevisione Italiana
Viale Mazzini, 14
00195 Roma
Tel: 3878

RCS
Via Mecente 91
20138 Milano
Tel: 580811
Fax: 58011890

Sacis
Via Teulada 66
00195 Roma
Tel: 374981
Fax: 3723492

JAPAN

Frank Segers

The dark days in Japan appear to be over. The nation's stubborn recession is ebbing. The double trauma of 1995's Kobe earthquake and the Tokyo subway gassings, which prompted national self-doubt of ontological proportions, are safely in the past. Ever the mirror to larger social events, Japan's film industry is staging at least a mini-comeback.

1995 ended an embarrassing slide in national film attendance. The number of moviegoers increased 3.3% over 1994's dismal total of 123 million, the lowest level in history. Box-office revenues rose 2.8% while the average admission price – the highest in the world – actually dipped slightly to Y1,243 (nearly US$12). Total film rentals from domestic and foreign film distribution rose 6.7% to Y68,473 million (US$646 million). The number of titles released in 1995 rose in both foreign and domestic categories, and exports of Japanese films, thanks to perennially popular animation, exceeded US$30 million for the first time – a huge 58% increase from 1994.

Perhaps most significant, Japan's decaying theatre infrastructure is being overhauled as perhaps never before, thanks to fresh competition from a familiar source, the U.S. The nation's number of theatres rose slightly to 1,776, the second consecutive yearly boost. Local independent importers-distributors, who have had their share of woes recently, seem to be bouncing back, adapting to an ever-more competitive international market. Although Matsushita took its lumps with its aborted acquisition of Hollywood's MCA – and Sony is still toughing it out with its Columbia TriStar unit – Japanese film companies are launching a number of foreign initiatives, although on a much more modest scale.

SHIBATA ORGANISATION INC.

Distributes in Japan

André Techiné (LES ROSEAUX SAUVAGES)
Wim Wenders (LISBON STORY)
Mitsuo Yanagimachi (PAO-JINAG-HU)
Jim Jarmusch (DEAD MAN)
Théo Angelopoulos (LE REGARD D'ULYSSE)
Michelangelo Antonioni (BEYOND THE CLOUDS)
Cédric Klapisch (CHACUN CHERCHE SON CHAT)
Bo Widerberg (ALL THINGS FAIR)
Mike Leigh (SECRETS AND LIES)
Jane Campion (THE PORTRAIT OF A LADY)

2-10-8, Ginza, Chuo-ku, Tokyo
Tel: (3) 3545-3411 Fax: (3) 3545-3519

Masatoshi Nagase, Toshiyuki Nishida, and Hidetaka Yoshioka in A CLASS TO REMEMBER 2
photo: Shochiku

American Godzilla Shakes the Status Quo

It's not yet time to break out the champagne, however. While distributor earnings from foreign (read largely U.S.) films in 1995 jumped 12.2% to Y43,130 million (US$407 million), rentals from Japanese film releases dipped 1.4% to Y25,343 million (US$239 million). That meant that the Japanese share of the national market dropped to 37% from 1994's 40.1%. The foreign film share, on the other hand, increased to 63% from 1994's 59.9%. Revenues from sales-rentals of videocassettes decreased by 3.6% during 1995, and the key TV stations – public NHK plus five commercial networks – proved to be ever pickier buyers of feature film product. And, if it wasn't for the astonishingly successful results logged by Gaga Communications in 1995 – with its release of *The Mask* with Jim Carrey – revenues of the indie importer-distributor group would have been flat.

In his speech at December's 40th Film Day ceremonies in Tokyo, Shigeru Okada, the powerful behind-the-scenes figure who is chairman of Toei Co., said he feared the Japanese film share of the market might further decrease to the 30% level. Okada was upbeat about the presence of high-powered American-based theatre exhibitors in Japan, presumably on the assumption that increased attendance would lift all boats, including those of Japanese studios. For his part, Shochiku Co president, Toru Okuyama, told the press at the end of 1995 that perhaps it's best to return to the old "studio system" – he cited former Hollywood moguls Darryl Zanuck and Samuel Goldwyn – and stress individual creativity within such a system. Despite all the talk of multimedia and software product, he said, it is the "talent, passion and sensibility" of individuals that is key.

One market reality is inescapable. The influx of American exhibition into Japan in 1995 and this year is shaking up the theatrical status quo in ways that the Japanese studios might find uncomfortable. The majors – Toho, Shochiku and Toei –

have long regarded their exhibition holdings as lynchpins of their operations. Shochiku and Toei distribute imported product on a jointly owned foreign circuit while Toho runs its own foreign circuit. These holdings have given the majors effective control of the highly lucrative distribution of imported films, particularly U.S. blockbusters. Perhaps for the first time, that hold is being challenged by American companies – Kansas City-based American Multi Cinema, Time-Warner, Paramount and Universal.

AMC recently opened a £5-million, 13-screen multiplex – the largest in Japan – in the southern city of Fukuoka, going head to head with Toho, which controls the majority of the city's 13 general audience cinemas. The site was chosen because real estate is cheaper than in Tokyo or Osaka – the decline in prices throughout the country has favoured U.S. exhibitor entry – and because the multiplex is part of a popular entertainment complex. Paramount and Universal studios have formed a joint venture to open their first two theatres this year, with plans for 20 more by the end of the decade. Time-Warner in partnership with Japanese retailer Nichii Co. began early, opening the first multiplex in 1993, and by the end of the decade hopes to have 180 screens in Japan.

Japanese Animation Strikes Back

All this has spurred Toho and Shochiku to spruce up existing facilities and to build new ones. The latter plans no less than 100 multiplex situations on 15 sites over the next three years. By one estimate, Japanese and foreign exhibitors will add 1,000 screens by the year 2,000. That would effectively increase existing theatrical stock by about a third. Getting a supply of quality Japanese films of broad international appeal to play those screens may be a trickier matter. The roster of top Japanese films in 1995 covers the usual territory of melodrama, animation, Tora-san and Godzilla. That's not to derogate animation. Daiei, which has re-entered the production fray with a bang, came up with a charming **Mimi O Sumaseba**, from director Yoshibumi Kondo, the top-grossing Japanese film of 1995.

Misa Shimizu and Kouji Bessho in Shohei Imamura's THE EEL *photo: Shochiku*

The film won plaudits from critics as well, and may be one reason why Daiei and sister animation company, Studio Ghibli – both units of Tokuma Publishing – recently signed a deal with Walt Disney calling for the former to supply Disney with eight animated features for distribution on home video. In addition, the arrangement calls for Disney to handle several live action features for video distribution, including Daiei's **Shall We Dance?** from director Masayuki Suo. This extraordinarily appealing film, about the adventures of a Japanese salaryman who takes ballroom dancing lessons on the sly, gracefully combines comedy and social commentary in a single, well-made package.

As for Tora-san, news broke on August 7 that Kiyoshi Atsumi had died of lung cancer at age 68. A former burlesque comic, Atsumi was to a generation of filmgoers Mr. Torajiro, or Tora-san, the star of Shochiku's enormously successful **Otoko**

wa tsurai yo (*It's Tough Being a Man*) series. Begun in 1969, the series produced 48 instalments – the last will be distributed later this year as part of Shochiku's traditional New Year programme – making it the longest-running film series in history. It was also a goldmine for Shochiku, grossing more than 41 billion yen (US$387 million).

Although Atsumi was a versatile comedian and serious actor in other roles, he was so closely identified by the Japanese public as Tora-san that his roundish, heavily jowled face was said to be more widely recognised than the Emperor's. The Tora-san character, moulded by director-writer Yoji Yamada, was a poor, uneducated travelling pedlar who pursued slapstick humour and unrequited romance in equal measure. The series, set in old Tokyo amidst Tora-san's loving but baffled family, was largely propelled by neighbourly spats that sent Tora-san packing all over Japan seeking fresh romance. Inevitably, Tora-san returned home, re-embraced by his family, taking his legions of film fans back to a warmer, more traditional time of old-world values.

Not to Win a Prize in Tokyo

The Tokyo International Film Festival, headed by Yasoyoshi Tokuma (who also heads Daiei), did not fare well in 1995. For the first time in three years, the event was held with no market, a big handicap in terms of attracting high-powered foreign visitors. Several interesting new Japanese titles played the festival. Film criic Makoto Shinozaki made his impressive début with **Okaieri**, about a marriage troubled by schizophrenia. Ataru Oikawa's **The Boy Made in Japan** pairs a lonely boy, who once tried to kill his father, with a young woman who uses a pacemaker; Go Riju's **Berlin** is a tricky film-within-a-film puzzler about a disappearing prostitute; and Yasuo Furuhata's **Kura** is a period-piece based on Miyao Tomiko's novel about a blind girl who becomes Japan's first sake brewer. The festival ended on a downbeat note when the main competition jury failed to award a top prize for either best film or best actor. "Such a situation could have been avoided if there were any worthwhile Japanese films", snapped Tokuma.

Two of Japan's most established directors, Yoji Yamada and Nagisa Oshima, are working on new projects. Yamada, who directed the 'Tora-san' series, is making **Gakko II**, the sequel to his earlier work about a school for the disabled in northern Japan. Oshima, whose last film was *Max, Mon Amour* for French producer Serge Silberman ten years ago, is set to make **Gohatto**, a period adaptation of Ryotaro Shiba's samurai drama, *Shinsengumi Keppuroku*. The producer is Kazuyoshi Okuyama – the son of Shochiku's president – who is the studio's driving production force these days. It was the younger Okuyama who met Robert De Niro in 1994 to discuss a 50-50 co-production deal with the actor's Tribeca Productions. Decision on a property is expected in 1997.

On the importer-distributor front, Nippon Herald Films shed control of its 15-year-old Herald Ace subsidiary to Japanese publisher Kadokawa. The family is perhaps best recalled, unfortunately, for the drug-related arrest and conviction of film producer-director Haruki Kadokawa. The former Nippon Herald subsidiary is now known as Ace Pictures, and has just acquired the film rights to Junichi Waranabe's novel, *Shitsurakuen*, with the film version to be directed by Yoshimitsu Morita. Toho-Towa, which did not have a banner year in 1995, has joined with the Marubeni Trading company in a consortium (that includes the BBC and Tele-München) acquiring distribution rights to product from Hollywood's Cloud Nine independent. First title from the deal is Paramount's s-f outing, *The Relic*, from director Peter Hyams.

FRANK SEGERS writes for *Variety* and specialises in Far Eastern entertainment issues.

TOP TEN GROSSING FILMS IN JAPAN: 1995

	Gross in dollars
Die Hard 3	$45.3 million
Speed	$42.5 million
Forrest Gump	$36.5 million
The Bridges of Madison County	$21.7 million
Waterworld	$19.8 million
Apollo 13	$18.9 million
Mimi O Sumaseba	$17.5 million
The Mask	$16.9 million
Godzilla vs. Space Godzilla	$15.6 million
Tora-San (Otokowa Tsuraiyo)	$14.6 million

Statistics

Figures for the period January-December 1995, with previous year's figures in brackets.

Number of cinemas		
total	1,776	(1,758)
for domestic films only	483	(521)
for foreign films	643	(673)
for both categories	650	(564)

Number of films distributed	610	(553)
domestic films	289	(251)
foreign films	321	(302)

Box office

annual		
admissions	127,040,000	(122,990,000)
gross theatre receipts (million yen)	157,865	(153,590)
average admission fee (yen without tax)	1,243	(1,249)

Film rentals (millions of yen)

Japanese films	25,343 (37% of total)	(25,711)(40.1% of total)
Foreign films	43,130 (63% of total)	(38,441) (59.9% of total)
Total film rentals	68,473	(64,152)

Useful Addresses

Assn. for the Diffusion of Japanese Films Abroad
(UniJapan Film)
Ginza 5-9-13
Tokyo

Cine Saison
Asako Kyobashi Bldg. 2F
6-13 Kyobashi, 1-Chome
Chuo-ku
Tokyo

Daiei Co., Ltd.
1-18-21 Shimbashi
Minato-ku
Tokyo

Dela Corp.
Razan Bldg. 813
7-15-13 Roppongi
Minato-ku
Tokyo

Gaga Communications
East Roppongi Bldg.
3-16-35 Roppongi
Minato-ku
Tokyo

Kuzui Enterprises
Jingumae-Otowa Heights 201
5-50-3 Jingumae
Shibuya-ku
Tokyo

Nippon Herald Films
11-1, 5-Chome
Ginza
Chuo-ku
Tokyo 104 Japan

Shibata Organisation
(France Eigasha)
2-10-8 Ginza
Chuo-ku
Tokyo

Shochiku Co.
13-5 Tsukiji 1-chome
Chuo-ku
Tokyo

Toei Co.
2-17. 3-chome
Ginza
Chuo-ku
Tokyo

Toho International Co.
Hibiya Park Bldg.
8-1 Yurakucho, 1-chome
Chiyoda-ku
Tokyo

Toho-Towa Co.
6-4 Ginza
2-chome
Chuo-ku
Tokyo

Tohokushinsha Film Co.
17-7 Akasake, 4-chome
Minato-ku
Tokyo

SOUTH KOREA

Frank Segers

The Korean cinema world remains a tantalising if frustrating environment for both domestic and foreign film-makers and distributors. Tantalising because it is so big, the largest in Asia outside Japan with a US$241 million annual gross in 1995. Frustrating because, in several serious respects, it appears to be going nowhere in a hurry.

Despite a wealth of new talent whose films broadly reflect social concerns and pop culture fads – one new film, **Corset**, about the romantic travails of an overweight designer, addresses the current consumer preference for designer undergarments – the Korean market is largely flat and directionless. Cable TV was introduced in 1995 and video rentals were brisk but, according to critic and academic Cho, Hee-Moon, who has charged the Korean film industry with being stagnant, "On the surface it appears that the motion picture industry was stimulated by these media, but in reality it was not. Co-operation between the industry and the new media was not successfully accomplished in 1995".

A Home for Spielberg?

Cho may have to reassess this in the light of recent developments. A number of foreign partnerships have developed between the major Korean conglomerates, the *chaebols*, and overseas production entities. Daewoo Corporation recently formed a three-film co-production deal with Los Angeles-based InterLight Pictures. Samsung Group, Korea's largest *chaebols*, had paid US$60 million for a 7.4% slice of Hollywood independent, New Regency Productions. Hyundai Group's Diamond Ad Ltd. formed a film production alliance with France's Canal Plus. Kolon Industries is negotiating with the Walt Disney company in the areas of animation and character licensing.

More significantly, Mie Kyung (known overseas as Miky Lee) – the granddaughter of Lee, Byung Chull, who assembled the Samsung Group – is involving herself in films internationally, and at home in interesting ways. Her base in Korea is the Cheil Foods and Chemicals company, last year a US$1.8 billion giant which Lee runs with her 36-year-old younger brother, Lee, Jai Hyun (Americans call him "Jay"). Cheil has invested US$300 million for an 11% stake in Hollywood's Dreamworks SKG, and is working with an Australian-based company to build multiplexes in Korea.

On the domestic front, Cheil is trying to work with Dreamworks, the company formed by Steven Spielberg, Jeffrey Katzenberg and David Geffen, to make films at home with the likes of director Kim, Jong-Hak and screenwriter Song Ji Na, collaborators on a tough TV drama about the 1980 massacre of pro-democracy demonstrators in Kwangju. One of the hurdles is the huge gap in the state of movie-making technique between Seoul and Hollywood. Jay Lee reportedly shocked Spielberg by bluntly underscoring the frustrations of trying to get movies made at home. "If you had been born in Korea you would have ended up in a mental hospital", Lee is reported to have said.

None the less, dozens of local film-makers contributed titles of note in 1995, and escaped institutionalisation. The number of domestic releases in 1995, 64, was identical to 1994's output. The total of foreign imports released during the year fell nearly 20%, however, which may have had something to do with the 6% drop from 1994 in overall film attendance. The total box-office rose 2%, which means theatre exhibitors jacked up admission prices a bit.

But it's still very much the case that when Hollywood sneezes, Seoul catches a cold. Hollywood dominates the screens in this market, especially since the major studios began opening directly controlled distribution offices in Seoul in 1988. The top-grossing Korean film in 1995, Lee, Kwang-Hoon's **Doctor Bong**, a romantic comedy about a lusty widower who runs a dental clinic, did roughly a third of the business generated by 1995's top foreign hit, *Die Hard 3*. The number 10 top-grossing foreign title, Warner's *Terminal Speed*, very nearly outpulled the good dentist.

Feminism and Fun

As is common with Korea's resolutely populist cinema, big-grossing titles were often the most acclaimed by critics. This was particularly true of Lee, Min-Yong's **A Hot Roof**, which finished number four on the top ten chart while winning the 38-year-old a Best Young Director citation at the annual Grand Bell Awards (Korea's equivalent of the Oscars) and finishing number four on the top ten list of films most favoured by critics. Why all the fuss? Largely because the film, disguised as social comedy, presents a strongly feminist statement. It touches a sensitive chord – the role of women in still traditional Korean society. It also helps, of course, that many of the nation's filmgoers are women.

A Hot Roof was shot in the hot, humid summer of 1995 at an apartment complex torn down shortly after filming finished. It's about ten women who take refuge on the roof of the complex after pummelling a wife-beater to death. Director Lee perhaps ingenuously contends that the film is really about the problems of all underprivileged groups. Audiences at the 20th Hong Kong Festival earlier this year weren't buying – the film was a hit because of its blend of social comedy and feminism.

The Hong Kong Festival devoted a considerable amount of screen and printed programme time to Korean cinema this year, to excellent result. The programme offered a retrospective of 12 classic Korean titles, two contemporary titles and a documentary, as well as a seminar discussion of post-war Korean films. Screened was Park, Kwang-su's **A Single Spark**, which was the top choice of critics in 1995 as well as a commercial hit (number five on the top ten list). Remarkable, since *Spark* is a tough-minded recollection based on the suicide by self-immolation of a labourer and sweatshop protester in the 70s. "I found myself wondering how a young person today might react if faced with what Jeon Tae-il faced in the 60s", said Park.

Probably the year's most controversial film was not a feature but a documentary: director Byun-Young-joo's **Murmuring**. It's about a subject that is still a sensitive issue in Japan and Korea – the tragedy of Korean "comfort women", abducted by the Japanese military as teenagers and shipped off to the front to service typically as many as 30 troops a day. Byun, 30, shot the film in 16mm, and was a bit surprised to see her film become not only a commercial success in her homeland but a hit in the Hong Kong Festival. It focuses on six Korean women forced into prostitution and what became of their lives after World War II. Its strongly feminist statement is unmistakeable, as is the director's courage in tackling an explosive political and social subject.

Another far slicker outing, **Terrorist**, also won commercial success and plaudits from the reviewers. An unapologetically action-oriented film from director Kim, Young-bin, it tells of two orphaned brothers who become policemen and then fall out when one gets involved in an organised crime plot. Not for the cinematically faint-hearted, *Terrorist* is replete with violence and gunplay tempered, John Woo-style, by the close bonding of the brothers. Superbly made, the film won a best actor Grand Bell citation for Choi, Min-Soo and best photography and editing nods as well.

What would a year without a costume drama be in Korean cinema? No telling, since 1995's sampling of the genre was director Park, Chong-won's well-received **Eternal Empire**, about political struggles in the 18th-century Chosun Dynasty. King Chung-jo overreaches; his ministers apply the brakes; the battles rage; and there's a mystery about a missing diary. Intrigue oozes from the screen. Modified mayhem and sultriness are given off by **Deep Scratch**, director Kim, Sung-Hong's popular tale of a nasty woman driven by envy to disrupt the tranquil domestic life of an old acquaintance.

In **301, 302**, director Park, Cheol-Soo focuses on two women in neighbouring apartments who suffer from opposite eating disorders, binge-eating and anorexia. In a distinctly lighter vein, director Kang, Woo-Suk's **How to Top My Wife** tells the story of a film company executive who tries in vain to dump his spouse for a younger, more pliant woman. Audiences took to the film, making it Korea's second most popular domestic title in 1995.

Shaking up a Snoozy Market

For its part, the Korean Motion Picture Promotion Corporation was kept busy with presentations of selected domestic titles at 23 festivals, notably including Berlin (traditionally receptive ground). A film week in Holland was also presented, not to mention this spring's successful representation at the 20th Hong Kong Festival. The KMPPC's new studio complex just outside Seoul is expected to be fully constructed by the end of 1996. The facility has been opening in stages since 1993, and a total of 63 productions have made use of it since its inception.

As far as the *chaebols* are concerned, the KMPPC says their involvement in the film industry has been increasing "every year". The conglomerates, spurred by the coming of cable and satellite TV, have been "indirectly involved" in the production of 14 films in 1995, and seven more titles in the first half of 1996. "The success or failure of smaller producers depends upon their relationships with the conglomerates as investors", says the KMPPC. *Chaebols* and technology – perhaps the formula for shaking up this still snoozy film market.

Grand Bell Awards

Best Film: *Henequen* directed by Kim, Ho-Son, produced by Hap Dong Film Co. and Young Hwa Seisang Co.
Best Director: Kim, Ho-Son for *Henequen*.
Special Jury Prize: *A Petal* directed by Chang, Sun-Woo, produced by Mirashin Korea Film Co.
Best Actor: Choi, Min-Soo for *Terrorist*.
Best Actress: Shim, Hye-Jin for *The Ginko Bed*.
Best Supporting Actor: Kim, Il-Woo, for *Hak-Saeng Bu-goon Shin-Wi*.
Best Supporting Actress: Kim, Chung for *Henequen*.
Best Screenplay: Shared by Kim, Sang-Soo and Ji, Sang-Hak for *Hak-Saeng Bu-Goon Shin-Wi*.
Best Photography: Shin, Ok-Hyun for *Terrorist*.
Best Editing: Park, Soon-Duk for *Terrorist*.

TOP TEN GROSSING DOMESTIC FILMS IN SOUTH KOREA: 1995

	Admissions
Doctor Bong	376,443
How to Top My Wife	344,900
Terrorist	320,919
A Hot Roof	274,568
A Single Spark	235,935
Deep Scratch	131,969
Run Away with Money	117,894
Gun and Gut	110,743
The Hair Dresser	105,863
Who Makes Me Crazy?	103,763

Best Music: Won, Il for *A Petal.*
Best New Director: Shared by Lee, Min-Yong for *A Hot Roof* and Kang, Chai-Kyu for *The Ginko Bed.*

FRANK SEGERS is a *Variety* staffer who has long specialised in Asian cinema.

Useful Addresses

Da Moa Films Co. Ltd.
164-7, Nonhyun-dong
Kangnam-gu
Seoul

Dong-A-Exports Co. Ltd
120-1, 1-ga, Changchung-dong
Chung-gu
Seoul

Dong Bo Film Corp.
Bong Wo Bldg., 2nd Floor F
203, 31-7, Changchung-dong
1-ga, Chung-gu
Seoul

Han Jin Enterprises Co. Ltd.
62-15, 3-ga. Pil-dong, Chung-gu
Seoul

Jimi Films Co. Ltd.
151-11, Ssanglim-dong
Chung-gu
Seoul

Motion Picture Promotion Corporation of Korea
206-46 Chongnyangni-dong
Tongdaemun-gu
Seoul
Tel: +82 2 958 7600
Fax: +82 2 958 7530

Tae Hung Production Co. Ltd.
16-6, 2-ga, Pildong
Chung-gu
Seoul

Hap Dong Film Co. Ltd.
59-7, Kwansoo-dong, Chongno-gu
Seoul

Hwajin Film Co.
52-111, Chongun-dong
Chongno-gu
Seoul

Hyunjin Film
5th Floor, Chiam Bldg.
73-1, 5-ga, Chungmuro
Chung-gu
Seoul

LATVIA

Andris Rozenbergs

With allocations to the film industry approximating zero, it is a wonder where people still get the energy to create. Even more astonishing is that these very humble, black-and-white productions succeed in captivating the interest of international film festivals and audiences.

Flower beds and Marshes

Laila Pakalnina is a name to conjure with in recent Latvian cinema. Laila lives in a very peculiar and picturesque suburb of Riga. Near a highway leading to the airport, an area of little houses is laid out, girdled by not very thoroughly cultivated rows of vegetables and flower beds. There are blocks of rental houses dating from the first industrial revolution when Riga burst out of the city walls, expanding over sandy plains and marshy meadows, covering them with plants and encircling them with cheap lodgings for the working classes.

The third and fourth generations of those people, the genuine inhabitants of Riga, still live there. Historical cataclysms, wars and revolutions, have changed their lives very little. Now they are old and cannot leave their flats. Their only link with the outside world is the mail, which every morning can bring a new miracle – a new Christ is born or the pensions are raised . . .

So one could summarise Laila Pakalnina's most recent film, **The Mail**. She and cinematographer Gints Bërzinš know exactly how to capture a face behind a dim window at the very moment it is touched by an oblique sunbeam in spring, or an almost indiscernible figure in the dark of a half-closed doorway. This somehow impressionistic flow of images is accompanied by a very inventive sound-track, without dialogue or commentary.

The Mail and the earlier *The Ferry* earned their author a FIPRESCI diploma in Cannes, where they were selected for the section, "Un Certain Regard". It was the first time a Latvian film took part in such a prestigious event. But this style of objective observation has a long and honourable history in Latvian cinema. In the early 60s director Aivars Freimanis and cameraman Ivars Seleckis made a short documentary, *The Coast*, employing the same technique as Laila Pakalnina thirty years later.

Before Crocodile Dundee

Aivars Freimanis directed the only Latvian feature film produced in the last two and a half years – **The Nest**, a documentary-like account of the everyday life of a young forester's family in a nature reserve. The film has screened in a dozen international festivals and won the FIPRESCI diploma in Stockholm and the Bronze Rose in Bergamo.

Ivars Seleckis chose a very exotic character for his full-length documentary, **The Crocodile's Move** — a Latvian legionnaire who, after the war, settled in Australia where he earns his living hunting crocodiles TV reporters nicknamed him "Crocodile Harry" (he is a prototype for the Paul Hogan hero, 'Crocodile Dundee'). In Latvia, three elderly women, who perhaps all loved Harry when they were all at school together, transport a huge sculpture of crocodile to set up as a monument on the ruins of his house.

They meet different people on the road, talk about their beloved, invoke historical events, and discuss the future, how to survive. The makers of this provocative, sometimes not very coherent 'road movie', try to dig down through the anecdote, through the banality, to capture the great movements of History in which the Latvian nation has been involved so deeply that it almost perished.

ANDRIS ROZENBERGS has made seven fiction films and a dozen documentaries. He is also responsible for the foreign relations of the Latvian National Film Centre.

Recent and Forthcoming Films

LIGZDA (The Nest).

Script and Dir: Aivars Freimanis. Phot: Viktors Gribermanis. Prod: Film Studio "TRĪS".

GĀJIENS AR KROKODĪLU (The Crocodile's Move)

Script: Imants Ziedonis. Dir. and Phot: Ivars Seleckis. Prod: Norberts Klaucēns.

PRĀMIS (The Ferry).

Dir: Laila Pakalnina, Phot: Gints Bërzinš. Prod: Film Studio "Kaupo".

PASTS (The Mail).

Dir: Laila Pakalnina, Phot: Gints Bërzinš. Prod: Film Studio "Zalktis".

A look at habitual things, habitual movements, habitual life.

KOMĒTA "LATAVIO" VAI DZĪVE Nr.2 (Cometh "Latavio" or the Life No.2)

10 diploma works from 10 graduates of the Culture Academy of Latvia, Department of Film Directing.

EDUARDS TISSE (Eduard Tisse)

Script: Agris Redovičs. Dir: Dzintra Geka. Prod: Juris Podnieks Studio.

A documentary to celebrate the 100th anniversary of Sergei Eisenstein's director of photography, Eduard Tisse.

Useful Addresses

National Film Centre.
Smerla Str. 3, Riga, LV-1006, Latvia.
Tel: +371-2-520411
Tel/Fax: +371-7242031
Fax: +371-782 84 08

Riga Motion Picture Studio.
Smerla Str. 3, Riga, LV-1006, Latvia.
Tel: +371-755 17 06
Fax: +371-782 84 08

Latvian Film Producers' Association
Meistaru Str. 10, Riga, LV-1050, Latvia
Tel: +371-721 69 57
Fax: +371-721 09 08

Latvian Filmmakers' Union
Elizabetes Str. 22, Riga,
LV-1050, Latvia.
Tel/Fax: +371-728 85 36

LITHUANIA

Grazina Arlickaite

Lithuanian films hardly ever achieve a place in the country's top ten list. Moreover they have been almost excluded from Lithuanian movie screens: the screening of native films in a non-commercial film centre, "Skalvija", is considered to be a benevolent cultural deed. The purpose of the film centre is mainly to screen European films.

The top ten list reveals one positive pan-European aspect: the leader on Lithuanian screens was the French film, *Les Visiteurs.* But it seems that Lithuanian society, as a whole, has become very passive about going to the movies lately. At present, film is one of the cheapest forms of entertainment in Lithuania. The ticket price ranges from US$1.00 to $1.50 However, the movie theatres themselves are in a dishevelled state. Unheated halls, uncomfortable seats and bad projection equipment discourage even the aficionado from going to the movies.

At present, there are two film distribution companies in Lithuania. One is a state-run company called Lietuvos Kinas (the Lithuanian Film), and the other is a private concern called Cinemark. The latter distributes Hollywood movies and co-operates with corresponding American film distribution companies in Latvia and Estonia. But fifty percent of the purchases of the state film distribution company are also American movies (of the remainder, thirty percent are French and the final twenty percent from various countries). The likelihood of the Lithuanian screen becoming more American is obvious. Cinemark is also considered the only company in Lithuania that has legalised its activity and strictly dissociated itself from video and film pirates.

Cosmic Spaces

The real problem is that the present Lithuanian government does not have a national cultural strategy that embraces film finance, production and distribution. Lithuanian feature films have stagnated as a result of the decline in film production, poor technical facilities and the allowance the government has allotted to film development.

No Lithuanian feature film has been fully financed by the government in the past few years. However, Sarunas Bartas, a young Lithuanian director, has made a film, **Musu nedaug** (*Few of Us*, 1996), that was screened at the Cannes Film Festival this year (the first Lithuanian film to be shown there for fifteen years). This was a co-production of three countries (France, Portugal, Lithuania), made in a small independent Lithuanian studio, Kinema.

It is about a nomadic Siberian tribe called the Tafolar, who today number less than 400. The majority are hopeless alcoholics with no conception of their past or their origins and with little future but self- destruction. The cosmic expanses of the Siberian Altaj are a mute witness to the tragedy of the Tafolar people. This is the only information given by the film before the story starts, although it is worth mentioning a documentary about the same tribe made by Sarunas Bartas with the director Valdas Navasaitis ten years ago which serves as a kind of prelude to *Few of Us*.

A fireman's helicopter lands at a small village in the Eastern Sajanai mountains near the Baikal lake where a girl alights. She meets a descendant of the *tafolarai* tribe. They start arguing and this escalates to the point where the girl kills the man with a knife. Later, for no reason, another man is killed. The girl stays in the village. At the symbolic level, the film expresses the balance between individuals and the universe, between eternity and the past, the loneliness that can overwhelm people whether they live at the foot of a mountain or in a skyscraper.

Universal Language

Few of Us shares with two of Bartas' previous films — *Trys dienos* (*Three Days*, 1991) and *Kordirius* (*A Corridor*, 1995) — the same conception of silence, a rejection of action narrative, an atmospheric suggestiveness and a strong harmony of sound and image. Out of a synthesis of several arts, the director finds a universal film language comprehensible to people in many parts of the world.

The appearance of two professional actors, Jekaterina Golubeva and Minoru Hideshima, among the locals does not affect the film's reality. It is not the story itself that makes the film meaningful, but the faces the camera studies. In this endless, subtly filmed space, the only conventional language, is the song of a well-known Russian poet, Sergei Jesenin, sung by the drunk *tafolars*.

DR. GRAZINA ARLICKAITE lectures in the Film and Theatre Department of the Lithuanian Music Academy. He heads the Department of International Relations and Sales in the Lithuanian Film Studio.

TOP TEN GROSSING FILMS IN LITHUANIA: 1995

Les Visiteurs (France)
Basic Instinct
Four Weddings and a Funeral
Dinosaurs Return (Japan)
Cliffhanger
Pulp Fiction
The Piano
Lock Up (U.S.)
Un Indien dans la ville (France)
Strasti po Anzelike (Russia)

Studios

Litnek
Nemencines pl.4
2016 Vilnius
Lithuania
Arunas Stoskus
Producer
Tel: (370 2) 768 381
Fax (370 2) 727 702

Kinema
Grybautoju 30
2000 Vilnius
Lithuania
Daiva Vaitickunaitc
Producer
Tel: (370 2) 770 148/769 594
Fax: (370 2) 619 507

Studija 2000
Nemencines pl.4
2016 Vilnius
Lithuania
Kestutis Petrulis,
Vytautas Zalakevicius
Producers
Tel: (370 2) 768 909
Fax: (370 2) 483 690

Lithuanian Film Studio
(State-run)
Nemencines pl.4
2016 Vilnius
Lithuania
Robertas Urbonas
Director
Tel: (370 2) 763 444
Fax: (370 2) 764 254

Distributors

Cinemark
Birutes 18
2004 Vilnius
Lithuania
Algis SemeskeviCius
President
Tel: (370 2) 220 730
Fax: (370 2) 223 716

Lietuva
Pylimo 17
2001 Vilnius
Lithuania
Vida Ramaskiene
Director
Tel: (370 2) 623 484
Fax: (370 2) 623 484

LUXEMBOURG

Jean-Pierre Thilges

Between the government rethinking and restructuring its tax-incentive programmes, local studios struggling to attract international productions to the tiny Grand Duchy, producers farming out more and more as pan-European co-productions, at least four animation companies setting up or consolidating their trade, and the Utopia Group finally obtaining a building permit for its long-gestating Utopolis Tenplex, Luxembourg has seen some strange goings-on over the last twelve months.

Production of indigenous feature films has been pretty dormant recently. Pol Cruchten's sophomore effort, **Black Dju**, opened to rather mixed reviews and – though the film stars French actor Philippe Léotard in good form – it has failed to work up much interest in the international market place. Cruchten and author Frank Feitler switched direction during production and turned what was to be a slapstick comedy on everyday racism into a brooding melodrama, with most of the laughs being of the unintentional variety.

Stalled Breakthrough

Although, on the technical side, the film is Luxembourg's most achieved effort to date, its mixed-up dramatics and pretentiousness undermined what could have been the country's best bet for a breakthrough in the international market-place. Reception of director Claude Waringo's stunning documentary on Edward Steichen, was a lot better, with the film briskly selling to broadcasters around the world. At press-time, Samsa Film were going into production on Luis Galvao Teles' upcoming feature, **Three Wishes**, starring a roster of well-known European actresses.

If production of feature films has been stagnant at best, Samsa's ongoing ventures into international co-productions resulted in the company's name appearing on two features in the Directors' Fortnight at the 1996 Cannes Film Festival, where Jean-Pierre and Luc Dardenne's **La Promesse** and Merzak Allouache's **Salut Cousin**! attracted huge crowds and did good business. Also seen in one of the Cannes sidebars was Peter Greenaway's **The Pillow Book**, a film that was largely shot on the sound stages of Delux Productions. Finally, Samsa continued to turn out a variety of excellent short films, of which Sophie Langevin and Frank Raybaut's beautiful **Biouel** (18 mins.), Geneviève Mersch's iconoclastic and celebrated **Roger** (30 mins.), and Bady Minck's experimental **Mecanomagie** (15 mins.) were the best.

Other interesting shorts produced in Luxembourg were the animated **Crucy Fiction** by Daniel Wiroth (6 mins.), **A Walk in the Park** by Paola Piozzi (Monipoly Productions, 5 mins.), **Melludram** by Roger Leiner (Animafo, 9 mins.), and finally, two mini-features: Pol Cruchten's ill-advised **Sniper** (Samsa, 7 mins.) and Andy Bausch's beautifully produced **Letters Unsent** (Lynx Productions, 21 mins.,

Still from LETTERS UNSENT

b&w.), starring German actors Otto Sander and Karin Baal together with a variety of local talent.

Other activities in Luxembourg included the shooting of major scenes of Anthony Waller's upcoming **An American Werewolf in Paris** at the Delux Studios; Andy Bausch preparing a sequel to his much-loved **Troublemaker**, as well as a rockumentary on the music of Native Americans called **Rock Around the Teepee**; and Paul Thiltges (no kin) of Monipoly putting the finishing touches to the Italian-Swiss-Luxembourg production of Enzo d'Alo's **La freccia azzurra**, a much-touted and heavily pre-sold animated feature which was anticipated to open the 1996 Venice Film Festival.

Utopian Dreams

Exhibition business continued briskly in 1995, but, due to a lack of attractive product (apart from the ongoing success of Disney's *The Lion King*, with an all-time record of 62,847 tickets, no film managed blockbuster status) attendance figures failed to surpass previous high levels. While the seven screens operated by the local Utopia Group consolidated their market share and sold over 480,000 tickets in 12 months, the competing Ciné Cité S.A. (5 screens) saw their attendance figures drop further to an estimated 240,000, mostly due to the fact that their theatres have not been refurbished to meet current technical standards.

After a five year-gestating period, Utopia's long-overdue multiplex project, the 10 THX-screen, 2,700 seat, state-of-the-art theatre, conceived in co-operation with the Belgian exhibition giant, Kinepolis Group (who acquired 10% of Utopia), was finally given the go-ahead by local authorities. This exciting development in a totally underscreened region (in cinema's heyday, Luxembourg operated 58 screens, the current count being 17), coupled with the ever-increasing taste of local audiences for American popcorn movies, as well as high-brow art-house fare, is expected to boost attendance figures from the current 720,000 tickets to well beyond the million mark in the next few years.

The next couple of years will be crucial for the survival of film production in the Grand Duchy. If the audiovisual authorities can get their act together, and if the local directors and producers start to make movies which people want to see, Luxembourg should be able to create a market niche for some of its quirky product. Without this common effort by everybody concerned, before the end of the decade, the Luxembourg film mouse that roared will raise no more than a squeak.

JEAN-PIERRE THILGES is an ex-money broker, still a film critic and a Western buff, and currently involved in bringing the multiplex boom to Luxembourg. An obsessive collector of laserdiscs, he would appreciate a release of Douglas Sirk's movies on disc.

Useful Addresses

Centre National de l'Audiovisuel
5, route de Zoufftgen
L-3598 Dudelange
Tel: (352) 51 91 83
Fax: (352) 52 06 55

Delux Productions
Studio Luxembourg
2, rue Nicolas Bové
L-1253 Luxembourg
Tel: (352) 25 42 83
Fax: (352) 44 06 40

Lynx Productions
34, avenue Victor Hugo
L-1750 Luxembourg
Tel: (352) 22 06 36
Fax: (352) 22 10 38

Mediaport Luxembourg
Maison de Cassal
5, rue Large
L-1917 Luxembourg
Fax: (352) 47 56 62

Samsa Film
1, rue de Nassau
L-2212 Luxembourg
Tel: (352) 45 19 60 1
Fax: (352) 44 24 29

Utopia Cinemas & Video S.A.
16, avenue de la Faïencerie
L-1510 Luxembourg
Tel: (352) 46 49 02
Fax: (352) 22 46 12

TOP TEN GROSSING FILMS IN LUXEMBOURG: 1995

	Admissions
The Lion King	29,793*
While You Were Sleeping	18,893
Pocahontas	17,261+
The Mask	16,793
Die Hard 3	15,787
Apollo 13	15,113+
Disclosure	14,600
Nell	14,379
Casper	13,803+
Waterworld	12,781+

* 29.793 tickets sold in 1995. Total tickets sold (1994/1995) 62.847
+ Tickets sold in 1995; exclusive run continued into 1996

MALAYSIA

Baharudin A. Latif

When *The First and Last Lover* (1993) struck a chord with the cinemagoing public, it touched off a flood of effervescent teenage soap opera-type melodramas that has continued unabated. Those after entertainment with any semblance of intelligence have had to seek alternative options; one which many have found is the internet.

Thanks to this state of affairs, actor-producer-director Yusof Haslam rules. His first try at the youth market, *Love's Grief*, took in $1.7 million, and its sequel did an astounding $2.5 million. His third, **Maria Mariana**, returned $1.9 million in 33 days and is still counting at press time. Clones have inevitably dotted local screens, but they have been a sorry lot – **Amelia, White Silk, The Fate of Love** and **Love in the Dust**. Even the presence of lower echelon pop singers could not redeem them.

Yusof's Midas touch seems to be fail-proof as all five films produced by his company have been profitable, an enviable record by any standard. Only Jackie Chan has been able to surpass him, with the latter's latest stunts extravaganza, **Police Story 4: First Strike**, earning $3.72 million, the highest take so far of any film.

The cineplex sector has expanded tremendously, with the Tanjung Golden Village conglomerate leading the way and revitalising the cinemagoing habit via its multiplexes in the Klang Valley, the country's fastest growing region and site of the federal capital. A joint venture between Tanjung Public Co. of Malaysia, Golden

T.S. Jeffrey in VALLEY OF VENGEANCE

Mohd. Zafrie in THE THING

Sharifah Norzaleenda in HURRICANE

Harvest of Hong Kong and Village Roadshow of Australia, the company's plans will culminate in a 13-cinema flagship at the Kuala Lumpur City Centre (KLCC), scheduled for completion in 1997-98. By this time, about 40 new ultra-modern cineplexes will be ready, with other major players being Cathay Cinemas and Golden Communications. A new era of cinema-going is about to overtake the country.

Studies have shown that Malaysia has a screen density of only 12.6 screens per million population, compared to 20 or 30 for Thailand, Singapore and Hong Kong. Unfortunately, imported films like *Jumanji*, *Seven*, *Toy Story* and others are shown in these plush cinemas while local films are still dumped into old and uncomfortable movie houses. Worse yet, many local first-runs, because of their restricted appeal, are shown in dingy video arcades.

By early August 1996, Measat-1 (Malaysia East Asia Satellite), launched on January 13, will have some 20 around-the-clock satellite channels in commercial operation to supplement the existing four terrestrial stations and one cable network. Paul Edwards, the Chief Executive Officer of the Measat Broadcast Network, has said four of the channels will run local programmes in the national language, Bahasa Melayu, for up to 10 hours a day. The station has set up two units to acquire and commission programmes, spawning a number of hastily formed consortiums undertaking rush jobs to complete hour-long and multi-episode dramas.

But with so many companies zealously opting for Measat-sponsored programmes — as the return on their investment is faster and more certain — feature film production is seriously threatened. When the Indonesian government went on a privatisation spree with its television industry some years ago, production companies abandoned feature production to chase television contracts and produce something like 500-700 titles a year. As a result, the Indonesian film industry collapsed and is today a mere shadow of its former glory. The Malaysian film industry seems destined to repeat the experience. It is up to the National Film Development Corporation of Malaysia (FINAS) to avert the approaching disaster – that is, if it is even aware of it.

BAHARUDIN A. LATIF has written on Malaysian cinema since the 60s, for *Variety, Movie/TV Marketing, Asia Magazine, Asiaweek*, etc.

Recent Films

BADAI MENTERA (Hurricane)

Script and Dir: Zulkifli M. Osman. Phot: Zainal Othman. Players: Khairil Anwar, Vanidah Amran, Sharifah Norzaleenda, Dol Baser, M. Rajoli, Ahmad Marbawi. Prod: Grand Brilliance.

LURAH DENDAM (Valley of Vengeance)

Script: Grand Brilliance Script Panel. Dir: Raja Ahmad Alauddin. Phot: Jeffrey Yusof, Indra Che Muda. Players: Ridzuan Hashim, Eizlan Yusof, Chef Wan Ismail, Raja Azura, Oneie Hartina Ahmad, Janet Khoo, T.S. Jeffrey. Prod: Grand Brilliance.

Producers/ Distributors

Grand Brilliance Sdn. Bhd.
99L, Jalan Tandok
off Jalan Bangsar
59100 Bangsar
Kuala Lumpur
Tel: (603) 284-6900
Fax: (603) 284-6864

Berjaya Films Production Sdn. Bhd.
194A, Jalan Tun Sambanthan
50470 Kuala Lumpur
Tel: (603) 274-1093/274-7815
Fax: (603) 274-2720

RJ Film Production Sdn. Bhd.
Building Information Centre (BICMA)
Jalan 243/51A
46100 Petaling Jaya
Selangor DE

Pesona Productions Sdn. Bhd.
159A, Jalan Aminuddin Baki
Taman Tun Dr. Ismail
60000 Kuala Lumpur
Tel: (603) 719-1603
Fax: (603) 719-1588

Sunny Lim Corporation Sdn. Bhd.
60B, Faber Plaza
Jalan Desa Bakti
58100 Kuala Lumpur
Tel: (603) 781-3881/783-9018
Fax: (603) 781-4724

Useful Addresses

FINAS
(The National Film Development Corporation of Malaysia)
Studio Merdeka Complex
Lot 1662, Hulu Kelang
68000 Selangor DE
Tel: (603) 408-5722
Fax: (603) 407-5216

PFM
(Association of Malaysian Film Producers)
Studio Merdeka Complex
Lot 1662, Hulu Kelang
68000 Selangor DE
Tel: (603) 408-4660
Fax: (603) 407-2271

MEXICO

Tomás Pérez Turrent and Gillian Turner

Film production in Mexico has been almost crippled by the current economic crisis. In 1994, only 34 films were produced, and in 1995 the number toppled to 12; the least, that is, since 1932, which was the year after sound movies began to be made in Mexico. IMCINE, the state production company, participated only in the co-production of one film with a private producer, and intervened in the production of **Edipus, the Mayor** *(Edipo, el Alcalde)* by Jorge Ali Triana with a script by Gabriel García Márquez, this being a co-production with Spain.

Televicine, a subsidiary of the giant television corporation Televisa, in previous years the most important production company, only produced or co-produced six films. The rest were made by private companies, four being neophytes with no previous experience in film production. One film was initiated by a co-operative, but has not been finished because of financial problems. The prospect for 1996 looks slightly better, at least with regard to quality. In March 1996, Arturo Ripstein started filming his latest movie, **Rojo Carmesi**, which will probably be ready for the Venice Film Festival.

This is the plight of an industry which at one time produced an average of 110 films a year, and dominated the Spanish-speaking markets. Nowadays, the market for Mexican films shrinks ever more, with no possibility of incorporating the new techniques and distribution possibilities created by laser disc. Some American companies specialising in 'classic' cinema have reissued a few films by Luis Buñuel and Indio Fernandez, and a few more recent films can also be found, such as **Como Agua para Chocolate, Danzon, El Callejon de los Milagros**, but these are really the exception to the rule.

In distribution and exhibition, 1995 was characterised as usual by the almost total dominance of Hollywood films (60% of the total). Mexican films accounted for only 15%, the remaining 25% being shared by films of 17 different nationalities. Just as in 1994, the ten most successful box-office

Still from EL ANZUELO

films were from Hollywood, the first non-American film (*Nostradamus*: England/Germany/Romania) appearing in 20th place. The first Mexican film is no. 37 on the list (**El Callejon de los Milagros**), preceded by 34 U.S. films, the above-mentioned *Nostradamus* and one Australian film, *Babe*. The business outlook is the same as usual, although this year also saw a decline in attendance — logical enough, taking into account the alarming decrease in the buying power of most people's salaries.

TOMÁS PÉREZ TURRENT is a film critic for various newspapers and magazines in Mexico and abroad. He also teaches the History of Film and Scriptwriting. He has written the screenplays for 16 films and in 1994, he received a three-year scholarship from Mexico's National System for Creators.

TOP TEN GROSSING FILMS IN MEXICO: 1995*

	Admissions
Casper	1,423,776
Batman Forever	1,148,215
Disclosure	801,029
Waterworld	797,253
Frankenstein	705,165
Pocahontas	686,089
Congo	662,353
Die Hard 3	550,302
Apollo 13	531,950
A Walk in the Clouds	493,728

*Mexico City and the metropolitan area: population 22 million

Recent and Forthcoming Films

EL AMOR DE TU VIDA, S.A. (The Love of Your Life, Inc.)

Script: Malu Huacuja del Toro. Dir: Leticia Venzor. Phot: Cludio Rocha. Players: Cinthy Klitbo, Jaime Garza, Dario T. Pie, Regina Orozco, Lisa Owen, Arleta Jerzioska. Prod: Christiane Bach, Humberto Zurita for Televicine.

UN HILITO DE SANGRE (A Trace of Blood)

Script: Alejandro Lubezki, based on the novel by Eusebio Ruvalcaba. Dir: Erwin Newmayer. Phot: Guillermo Granillo. Players: Diego Luna, Jorge Martinez de Hoyos, Aba Castro, Claudette Maille, Antonio Serrano, Naoto Matsumoto. Prod: Gustavo Montiel, Erwin Newmayer for CCC.

JUEGO LIMPIO (Fair Play)

Script: Ana Elena Cruz. Dir: Marco Julio Linares. Phot: Henner Hofmann. Players: Claudia Ramírez, Dario T. Pie, Leticia Perdigón, Wolf Ruvinskis, Carlos Bracho, Juan Carlos Colombo. Prod: Jorge Santoyo, Manuel Cristino for Producciones Dinamo/Unic, S.A. de C.V.

UN PEDAZO DE NOCHE (A Sliver of Night)

Script: Roberto Rochín, Tomás Pérez Turrent, Elias Nahmías, based on a short story by Juan Rulfo. Dir: Roberto Rochín. Phot: Arturo de la Rosa. Players: Dolores Heredia, Eduardo Von, Armando García. Prod: Roberto Rochín for Imcine, DPC.

RECLUSORIO I (Penitentiary I)

Script: Carlos Enrique Taboada, Ismael Rodríguez. Dir: Ismael Rodríguez. Phot: Guillermo Granillo. Players: Beatriz Aguirre, Pedro Armendáriz, Fernando Casanova, Roberto Ballesteros, Joaquín Cordero, Kate del Castillo, Ignacio López Tarso. Prod: Ismael Rodríguez Jr. for Películas Rodríguez S.A. de CV./ Televicine.

SALON MEXICO

Script: Eliseo Alberto, José Luis García Agraz, Fernando Cámara, based on the short story by Rafael Ramírez Heredia and the film *Salón México* by Emilio Fernández. Dir. José Luis García Agraz. Phot: Carlos Marcovich. Players: María Rojo, Blanca Guerra, Manuel Ojeda, Edith González, Demián Bichir, Alberto Estrella, Tiaré Scanda, Gina Moret, Steve Brown, Luis de Icaza. Prod: Ignacio Sada for Televicine.

SOBRENATURAL (Supernatural)

Script: Daniel Gruener, Gabriel González Meléndez, based on the novel by Gabriel González Meléndez. Dir: Daniel Gruener. Phot: Rodrigo Prieto. Players: Susana Zabaleta, Alejandro Tomassi, Delia Casanova, Ricardo Blume, Francis Laboriel, Zaide Silvia Gutiérrez, Roberto Cobo. Prod: Ivan Lipkies, Dulce Kuri for Televicine.

ENTRE PANCHO VILLA Y UNA MUJER DESNUDA (Between Pancho Villa and a Naked Woman)

Script: Sabina Berman, based on her play. Dir: Berman, Isabelle Tardan. Phot: Claudio Rocha. Players: Diana Bracho, Arturo Rios, Jesus Ochoa, Pilar Mata, Gabriel Porras, Marta Aura, Delia Casanova, Zaide Silvia Gutierrez. Prod: Televicine (Hugo Green, Maika Bernard).

An adaptation of a successful stage play by Sabina Berman, who is co-director and also adapted her own play for this, her first full-length film (she had previously co-directed a very attractive short). The film concerns the relationship of a mature woman of good social status with a writer. Neither wishes to commit to a lasting relationship and this eventually drives them apart. Between the two of them is Pancho Villa, the subject of the writer's present book and something of an alter ego, giving him advice on how to treat women. The film is an amusing and intelligent account of the obsession with 'machismo' represented by Pancho Villa, but the material has not been fully adapted for the screen and tends to fall into repetition.

EL ANZUELO (The Come-on)

Script: Ernesto Rimoch, Eva Saraga. Dir: Rimoch. Phot: Jorge Medina. Players: Mariana Lecuona, Bruno Bichir, Alvaro Guerrero, Ana Ofelia Murguia, Damian Alcazar, Jorge Galvan,

Still from SALON MEXICO

Martha Navarro. Prod: Francisco Athie, Carolina Amador for Artifice Producciones-Imcine.

The first full-length fiction film by Ernest Rimoch, a graduate of the London International Film School (1980-82), and the director of a full-length documentary, *The Line (La linea)*, about the border between Mexico and the United States. During a wedding and the party afterwards, a large amount of money is stolen, which leads to revelations about the key characters and an abrupt turnaround in their destinies. The film's observation of human behaviour is sharp, with an acid and often cruel tone, playing on such themes as family, duty, lies, pretensions and deceptions.

Producers

Alameda Films
Av. Division del Norte 2462-501
03300, Mexico D.F.
Tel: 525 688 0330/5085/7318
Fax: 525 605 8911

Amaranta Films
Eje 10 Sur,
Henriquez Urena 395
Col. Santo Domingo
Coyoacan
04369, Mexico D.F.
Tel: 525 610 1037/1772/1171
Fax: 525 610 1725

Direccion de Cortometraje (formerly Didecine)
Av. Division del Norte 2462, 3 piso
03300, Mexico D.F.
Tel: 525 688 7614/7079
Fax: 525 688 7611

Producciones Rosas Priego
Av. Division del Norte 2462, 4 piso
03300, Mexico D.F.
Tel: 525 688 7022/7223
Fax: 525 688 7044

Rio Mixcoac, S.C.L.
Morelos 33-4
Col. Torriello Guerra
Tlalpan
14060, Mexico D.F.
Tel: 525 665 6417/8998
Fax: 525 665/9123

Tabasco Films
Cuernavaca 17
Col. Condesa
06140, Mexico D.F.
Tel: 525 286 1860/1890
Fax: 525 286 2063

Televicine
Benito Juarez 7
Col. del Carmen
Coyoacan
04100, Mexico D.F.
Tel: 525 659 2961/7168
Fax: 525 554 3698

Distributors

Cine Alternativo
Pereferico Sur 4121
Col. Fuentes de Pedregal
14141, Mexico D.F.
Tel: 525 420 1309, 645 4080
Fax: 525 645 5704

Columbia TriStar/Buena Vista
Edif. Plaza Reforma
Prol. Paseo de la Reforma 600, PH-331
Col. Santa Fe Pena Blanca
01210, Mexico D.F.
Tel: 525 258 2700/2702
Fax: 525 570 1012/0957

Gussi (Artecinema/Videomax)
Gob. Ignacio Esteva 70
Col. San Miguel Chapultepec
Mexico D.F.
Tel: 525 277 8999, 271 0955
Fax: 525 516 5729

Latina, S.A.
Estudios Churubusco
Atletas 2
Col. Country Club
04220, Mexico D.F.
Tel: 525 544 7805
Fax: 525 549 1820

Twentieth Century Fox
Queretaro 65B, 2 piso
Col. Roma
06700, Mexico D.F.
Tel: 525 574 2869/7068
Fax: 525 574 6150; 564 8111

United International Pictures
Ejercito Nacional 343, 2 piso
Col. Granada
11520, Mexico D.F.
Tel: 525 255 2102/2203/5476
Fax: 525 255 5657; 203 2881

VideoCine (incl. Warner)
America 173
Col. Parque San Andres
04040, Mexico D.F.
Tel: 525 544 4405; 5493100
Fax: 525 549 2911

VideoVisa
Av. Acoxpa 444
Col. Vergel del Sur
14340, Mexico D.F.
Tel: 525 229 3100/3110
Fax: 525 230 3332

Useful Addresses

Asociacion de Productores y Distribuidores de Peliculas Mexicanas
Av. Division del Norte 2462, 8 piso
03300, Mexico D.F.
Tel: 525 688 7251/8705
Fax: 525 688 7378

Camara Nacional de Cine (CANACINE)
Gen. Anaya 198
Col. San Diego Churubusco
04120, Mexico D.F.
Tel: 525 688 0442/3258
Fax: 525 8810

Cinemex
Montes Urales no 723
Col. Lomas de Chapultepec
México D.F. C.P. 11000
Tel: 540 6954; 520 51 84

Compañia Operadora de Teatros
Insurgentes Sur 453
C.P. 06170
Tel: 264 0678; 264 1358; 264 1340; 264 5104
Fax: 264 7701; 164 5104

Direccion General de Actividades Cinematograficas, UNAM
San Ildefonso 43
Col. Centro
06020, Mexico D.F.
Tel: 704 3700; 702 4454
Fax: 702 4503

MOROCCO

Roy Armes

The Fourth Moroccan National Film Festival, held in Tangiers, offered an invaluable overview of Moroccan film production in the mid-1990s. Following similar festivals held in Rabat (1982), Casablanca (1984) and Meknes (1991), this Fourth Festival presented 11 features (all of which had received assistance from the government Aid Scheme of up to £150,000) and 22 shorts, made over a three-year period. The Aid Scheme (Fonds d'aide à la production cinématographique nationale), which was reformed in 1987, has allowed the production, since 1988, of some 30 feature films and over 20 shorts, representing a government investment in the film industry of over 40m dirams (some three million pounds).

The Festival opened with a feature-length work made to celebrate the centenary of cinema, **Five Films for a Hundred Years**, comprising 20-minute pieces by four established directors (Farida Belyazid, Jillali Ferhati, Albdelkader Lagtaa and Hakim Noury) and a newcomer, Omar Chraibi. The result is uneven, the more interesting pieces being those which directly reflect the directors' own childhood memories of the discovery of cinema: Belyazid's **On the Terrace**, Ferhati's **The Blue Handkerchief** and Noury's **Imperial Cinema**.

One of the other features presented was Mohamed Abderrahmane Tazi's **In Search of My Wife's Husband**, noted in last year's IFG and one of the few recent Moroccan features to get any sort of international release. Tazi has since completed a 13-minute short, **Stolen Images**, and is now working on a sequel to his 1993 comedy, **Still in Search of My Wife's Husband**. Two film-makers were able to achieve the remarkable feat of presenting two feature films, in a context where four or five years between features is the norm. Hakim Noury, who made his first feature, *The Postman*, in 1980 and had to wait a decade to complete his second, *The Hammer and the Anvil*, in 1990, showed **Stolen Childhood**, the story of a ten-year-old maid working for a rich family in Casablanca who gets pregnant but is abandoned by her lover, and **The Dream Thief**, the story of a man who emerges from five years in prison with a dream of going to Canada and who meets a young man with whom he can exchange his fears and ambitions. Another director to make two features in the early 1990s is Mustapha Derkaoui, who presented **Game (I) in the Past** and **The Seven Gates of the Night**, as well as a 35mm short, **The Big Allegory**.

Out of Reach

Jillali Ferhati, who won the grand prix at the national festival at Meknes in 1991, with *The Beach of Lost Children*, also presented a new work. **Make-believe Horses** focuses on an ill-matched group of individuals all of whom dream of going abroad: Mohamed to see a horse race, Ali to have an operation to restore his sight, Fatima to join her mother. Mohamed (played by Ferhati himself) enters a fantasy world by pretending to his wife that he has actually reached Paris, and embarks on a

Still from MAKE-BELIEVE HORSES

life of crime to finance his longed-for escape. This is a suffocating world, reminiscent in some ways of French 30s poetic realism: the enigmatic blind man, a setting of bleak, rain-swept streets, characters whose dreams are blocked, escape which is always just beyond reach.

Other established film-makers represented at the festival were the dramatist and actor Nabyl Lahlou with his sixth film, **The Night of the Crime**, and Hassan Benjelloun with his second, **Yarit**. Ahmed Yachfine's second feature, **Khafaya**, was made a decade after his first, but the most remarkable return was that of Hamid Benani. His pioneering first feature, **Traces** (*Wechma*), which helped to establish the intellectual and experimental trend which has continued to run through Moroccan cinema, was made as early as 1970. Twenty-five years separate it, therefore, from his second feature, an adaptation of Tahar Benjelloun's novel, **Prayer for the Absent One**.

Documentary work in Morocco remains strong. The prolific Izza Genini, having completed her eleven-part series on Moroccan popular music, *Morocco: Body and Soul*, has made **Moussem**, about the annual festival in Moulay Abdellah, and a fifty-minute video set in her birthplace, **Seeking Ouled Moumen**. Among younger documentarists coming to prominence are Hassan Alaoui, with his fourth short, **Aïdi**, and Daoud Aoulad Syad, whose mid-1990s output includes *Ochre Memory, Between Absence and Forgetfulness*, and, more recently, **The River**.

ROY ARMES has written several books on film history, and specialises in African Cinema. He also teaches film in London.

Recent Films

CINQ FILMS POUR CENT ANS (Five Films for a Hundred Years)

Script and Dir: Jillali Ferhati *(The Blue Handkerchief)*, Farida Benlyazid *(On the Terrace)*, Hakim Noury *(Imperial Cinema)*, Omar Chraïbi *(Lumière)*, Abdelkader Lagtâa *(Happy End)*. Phot: Abdelkrim Derkaoui, Kamal Derkaoui. Players: Amina Rachid, Mouna Fettou, Fatima Kheir, Nezha Zakaria, Aid Mouhoub, Omar Chanbout, Salah Eddine Benmoussa, Rachid El Wali, Abdellah Lamrani, Hassan El Fad, Maria Kachani. Prod: Moroccan Productions.

L'ENFANCE VOLÉE (Stolen Childhood)

Script and Dir: Hakim Noury. Phot: Girolamo Larosa. Players: Fadila Masrour, Touria Alaoui, Mustapha Zaari, Fairzouz Kairouani. Prod: MPS (Sarim Fassi Fihri).

VOLEUR DE RÊVES (The Dream Thief)

Script and Dir: Hakim Noury. Phot: Girolamo Larosa. Players: Rachid Fekkak, Rachid El Wali, Fatima Khair. Prod: MPS (Sarim Fassi Fihri).

JEU (I) AU PASSÉ (Game (I) in the Past)

Script and Dir: Mustapha Derkaoui. Phot: Mohamed Kamal Drerkaoui. Players: Mustapha Derkaoui, Natalia Jasina, Yelena Kosenkova, Luc Guedouchi, Abdellali Douahi, Omar Chraibi. Prod: Art 7.

LES SEPT PORTES DE LA NUIT (The Seven Gates of Night)

Script and Dir: Mustapha Derkaoui. Phot: Abdelkrim Derkaoui. Players: Abdellah Addich, Hamid Zoughui, Naima Ilyass, Leila Moutbaa. Prod: Art 7.

CHEVAUX DE FORTUNE (Make-believe Horses)

Script and Dir: Jillali Ferhati. Phot: Gilberto Azevedo. Players: Nezha Rahil, Jillali Ferhati, Hamid Zoughi, Brigitte Rouan, Jean Louis Richard, Driss Karimi, Larbi Yacoubi, Hicham Ibrahimi. Prod: Heracles Productions.

LA NUIT DU CRIME (The Night of the Crime)

Script and Dir: Nabyl Lahlou. Phot: Ahmed Zine Bessa. Players: Nabyl Lahlou, Sophia Hadi, Safy Boutella, Salim Berrada, Mohamed Ghaghat, Khadija Marrakchi. Prod: Loukkouss Films.

YARIT

Script: Abdou Laraki, Hassan Benjelloun. Dir: Benjelloun. Phot: Thierry Lebigre. Players: Abdellah Chakiry, Saïda Baadi, Hassan El Fad, Fatima Ouachay, Mustapha Mounir. Prod: Bentagerla.

KHAFAYA

Script: Ahmed Yachfine, Fatima Chebchoub. Dir: Yachfine. Phot: Abdelkrim Derkaouli. Players: Abdelwahab Doukkali, Saïda

Baadi, Larbi Batma, Mohamed Miftah, Souad Sabir. Prod: Mirror Production.

LA PRIÈRE DE L'ABSENT (Prayer for the Absent One)

Script: Hamid Benani, Mohamed Tozey, from the novel by Tahar Benjelloun. Dialogue: Hamid Benani, Mohamed Kharat. Dir: Benani. Phot: Tonino Maccopi, Girolamo Larosa. Players: Hamid Baskit, Saâdia Azagoun, Abdelkebir Reguegna, Khadija Ferhi. Prod: Lumière de la Ville/Atlantis Film International.

Useful Addresses

Centre Cinématographique Marocain
(Moroccan Film Centre)
Quarter industriel
avenue Al-Majd, BP 421
Rabat, Morocco
Tel: 79 81 10/79 81 11.
Fax: 79 81 08

Chamber of Film Distributors
36 boulevard d'Anfa
Casablanca, Morocco
Tel: 27 20 81

Rencontres du Cinéma Africain de Khouribga
(Film Festival)
Municipalité de la ville
de Khouribga
Khouribga, Morocco
Tel: 2123 493 404
Fax: 2123 492 623

NETHERLANDS

Pieter van Lierop

It must have been a good year for a small film nation like Holland when it wins the Oscar for the best foreign language film. Marleen Gorris achieved this with her feminist dream film, **Antonia's Line**, reported on in last year's edition. But this is not the only event to cheer the Dutch film world. The jury of the Dutch Film Festival in Utrecht (held every September) thought there was an even better feature, and gave the Golden Calf to **Little Sister** by Robert Jan Westdijk. *Antonia's Line* did receive prizes for best director and the best female lead, Willeke van Ammelrooy. That *Little Sister* ran off with the top award could be regarded as a sensation, because until Westdijk's film was premièred at the festival, very few had even heard of him. But everyone was delighted by his directing début by Westdijk and his producer, Clea de Koning, financed entirely with private contributions.

Little Sister is an example of the functional use of the subjective camera in a story about a power struggle between brother and sister. One gets the impression they haven't met for years when Martin turns up on Danny's doorstep, with a film camera already rolling. He wants to make a film about her and reveals himself to be an impressario at intrigue, able to prise Danny away from her lover and her best friend. The girl appears to accept the situation reluctantly, but she isn't completely helpless. She sometimes seems to ignore her brother-become-camera, but then falls for the attention before catching him unawares and grabbing the camera to reverse the roles.

There's a sizzling finale in which the truth comes out about a mystery from the

Willeke van Ammelrooy and Marleen Gorris clutching their Golden Calves for ANTONIA'S LINE at Utrecht in 1995 *photo: Marnix Schmidt*

Kim van Kooten in LITTLE SISTER

past that reeks of incest. The main theme of the film is that reality is relative and that a camera confers power. The greatest charm of *Little Sister* is in its refreshing energy, the humour and spontaneity with which the narrative reveals the world of Amsterdam youth. The young actors are strikingly natural and the 21-year-old leading lady is a winner.

In early 1996, *Little Sister* enjoyed a very satisfying release in Holland and Westdijk was also very successful internationally. *Little Sister* won the Silver Alexander at the Festival of Thessaloniki, the Special Jury Prize and the Audience Award at Turin, and the main prize, the Golden Tulip, at Istanbul. There are also high hopes for **The Dress** internationally. Director Alex van Warmerdam won two European film awards (Felixes) with his last film, *The Northerners*, and his latest work is even stronger. It is a serial narrative with a black humour reminiscent of Buñuel's *Cet Obscur Objet du désir* or Iosseliani's *Les Favoris de la lune*. Van Warmerdam links together several tragi-comic incidents about the life of a dress. Eventually, a dead urban nomad is cremated in it. In *Abel* and *The Northerners*, the director employed an extreme theatrical stylisation. This time, he moves to the Dutch landscape with no less charming results.

Of Queens and Chess

Au Revoir is a wonderful new film by Heddy Honigmann. It won the audience prize at the Locarno Festival in 1995 and the best actress award for Johanna ter Steege. She has a passionate affair with Guy van Sande who is already married to Els Dottermans. It's a very simple plot but the sensitive realism employed by Honigmann and her actors is very moving. **Marie Antoinette Is Not Dead** is a feminist morality play directed by Irma Achten. Without a great deal of respect for the true course of history, and with plenty of funny anachronisms, it uses the wife of France's King Louis XVI to demonstrate that, as soon as women get too close to power, they promptly become the target of mud-slinging by the media. And preferably with insinuations about disorderly sexual conduct, because the men who control the mass media are still afraid of the mystery of female sexuality. Achten light-heartedly packs her morality play with images that are rather static, at times looking like *tableaux vivants*.

Female directors seem to be doing especially well at present. In early 1995, Maria Peters released an excellent film for youth, **The Purse Snatcher**, which drew large audiences in Holland and won a series of international awards. In late 1995, it was the turn of Esmé Lammers with **Long Live the Queen**. This was able to interest ten-year-olds in the noble game of

Johanna ter Steege and Nelleke Zitman in AU REVOIR (TOT ZIENS)

chess, explaining the rules *en passant* in a fairy-tale adventure.

Alongside these films there have also been purely commercial successes. **Flodder 3**, by Dick Maas drew an audience of 400,000. **Filmpy** was first screened in mid-December and had been seen by nearly 600,000 by New Year, before hitting a million in January. The critics hated it, but it earned an estimated eight million dollars. Surprisingly, the director was Paul Ruven, who has made a name for himself with sophisticated art films made on a minimal budget. Six weeks after the première of *Filmpy*, Ruven had already shot, cut and premièred a new film (**Sur Place** with Katerina Golubeva as an East European refugee in Amsterdam) at the Rotterdam International Film Festival. It was greeted by good reviews but a tiny audience.

Holland is almost euphoric about admissions in general, which seem to herald an about-turn in the decline of recent years. With 17,182,377 tickets sold in 1995, the cinemas had their best year since 1984, and the first few months of 1996 were nine percent up on the same period in 1995.

Up in Smoke

Documentary makers have displayed a striking interest in Indonesia recently, to mark the 50th anniversary of the unilateral declaration of independence from its Dutch colonial rulers. After **Mother Dao** by Vincent Monnikendam and **Tabé Tuan** by Tom Verheul, came Niek Koppen's **Battle of the Java Sea**, Jan van den Berg's **Prisoner of Java** and Bernie Ijdis' **The Great Post Road** (*Jalan Rava Pos*). The most impressive documentary of the year, however, was Jaap van Hoewijk's **Procedure 769, Witnesses to an Execution**. Eye-witness accounts and 'logbook' notes from the prison are used to reconstruct the execution of serial killer Robert Alton Harris in April 1992 in California.

Holland fixes its government grants to cultural institutions for a four-year

Ariane Schluter and Alex van Warmerdam in THE DRESS

Monique van de Ven and Tiba Tossijn in LONG LIVE THE QUEEN

period; the coming period is from 1997 to 2000. The Dutch Film Fund at present has a budget of more than 17 million guilders (just over 10 million dollars). 15.5 million guilders are in the form of ministerial grants. The Cultural Council has advised the minister responsible to increase the grant to the Film Fund by a million a year for three years in a row. This is a lot less than what the Fund itself thinks it needs to prevent Dutch film fading away. Optimists talk of a budget rising from over 24 million in 1997 to almost 38 million in 2000.

Fund director Rieclef Rienstra regards an industry infrastructure for film as vital, and has unveiled plans for extra support involving the Ministries of Economic Affairs and Finance as well as Culture. One idea is for a "matching fund" to provide additional finance for "commercially conceived feature films with audience potential". Rienstra is also very interested in encouraging Dutch film talent to gain experience in international co-productions. The demand, once strict, that film productions should be in Dutch has been abandoned. The fund wants to reserve a separate entry for international co-productions, rising from 2.7 million in 1997 to 6 million in 2000.

This shift of priorities was strikingly evident at the last Cannes Film Festival, where no less than four films made with support from the Dutch Film Fund were screened in the competition and in "Un Certain Regard": **Breaking the Waves** by Lars von Trier, **The Pillow Book** by Peter Greenaway, **Haifa** by Rashid Masharawai and **Buenos Aires Vice Versa** by Alejandro Agresti. None of these films had a Dutch director or was partly shot in Holland or was even in Dutch. Cannes didn't want to programme a 'real' Dutch film in any section, but 100,000 dollars of Dutch tax money went up in smoke at a gigantic firework display. We're a generous people.

PIETER VAN LIEROP is film editor of the *Utrechts Nieuwsblad* since 1974, also serving the 18 daily papers syndicated in the Netherlands Press Association (GPD). He has been a correspondent for the International Film Guide since 1981.

Pierre Bokma in PUNK LAWYER

Producers

AFI/Added Films International
Lange Muiderweg 616
1398 PB Muiden
Tel: +31 2942 63277
Fax: +31 2942 64868

Argus Film Productions
P.O. Box 58188
1040 HD Amsterdam
Tel: +31 20 6931379
Fax: +31 20 5974412

Ariel Film Produkties
Prinsengracht 770
1017 LE Amsterdam
Tel: +31 20 6388199
Fax: +31 20 6380149

Belbo Film Productions BV
Sarphatikade 11
1071 WV Amsterdam
Tel: +31 20 6387999
Fax: +31 20 6388209

Bergen
Haarlemmerstraat 124 a
1013 EX Amsterdam
Tel: +31 20 6269991
Fax: +31 20 6262070

Bert Haanstra Films BV
Verlengde Engweg 5
1251 M Laren
Tel: +31 2153 82428
Fax: +31 2153 82428

Cilia van Dijk
Ged. Voldersgracht 20
2011 WD Haarlem
Tel: +31 23 5314273
Fax: +31 23 5421097

CinéTé Film Prods.
Elisabeth Wolffstraat 45
1053 TR Amsterdam
Tel: +31 20 6855339
Fax: +31 20 6891954

Cine Ventura
Hudsonstraat 52
1057 SN Amsterdam
Tel: +31 20 6837439
Fax: +31 20 6160500

DNU Film BV
Rolf Orthel/Evelyn Voortman
Zoutkeetsgracht 116-1
1013 LC Amsterdam
Tel: +31 20 6220255
Fax: +31 20 6261885

Ecco Films
Orlow Seunke
P.O. Box 53223
1007 RE Amsterdam
Tel: +31 20 6239457
Fax: +31 20 6237900

First Floor Features
P.O. Box 30086
1303 AB Almere
Tel: +31 36 5327003
Fax: +31 36 5327940

Graniet Film
Marc van Warmerdam/
Ton Schippers
Anjeliersstraat 470
1015 NL Amsterdam
Tel: +31 20 4212820
Fax: +31 20 6251024

Grote Broer Filmwerken
Clea de Koning/
Robert Jan Westdijk
P.O. Box 58141
1040 HC Amsterdam
Tel: +31 20 6161879/6224705
Fax: +31 20 6161879

Linden Film BV
Chopinstraat 25
1077 GM Amsterdam
Tel: +31 20 6793128
Fax: +31 20 6641046

Lowland Productions
Duivendrechtsekade 82
1096 AJ Amsterdam
Tel: +31 20 6680492
Fax: +31 20 6941018

Lucid Eye Productions
Oude Schans 69 A
1011 KW Amsterdam
Tel: +31 20 6230354
Fax: +31 20 6382968

MGS Film Amsterdam BV
Golden Egg Film
Singel 64
1015 AC Amsterdam
Tel: +31 20 6231593/6629960
Fax: +31 20 6243181

Molenwick Film Productions
Tuinstraat 64-66
1015 PG Amsterdam
Tel: +31 20 6248805
Fax: +31 20 6386384
ext. 0005/6252296

Moskito Film
Oostelijke Handelskade 12
1019 BM Amsterdam
Tel: +31 20 6381924
Fax: +31 20 6381855

Movies Film Productions BV
Postbus 432
1200 AK Hilversum
Tel: +31 35 261500
Fax: +31 35 248418

Nico Crama Films
Nico Crama
Stevinstraat 261
2587 EJ The Hague
Tel: +31 70 3544964

Odusseia Films
Eddy Wijngaarde
Stadhouderskade 6
1054 E5 Amsterdam
Tel: +31 20 6071199
Fax: +31 20 6071198

Praxino Pictures BV
Onstein 190
1082 KN Amsterdam
Tel: +31 20 6466121
Fax: +31 20 6613411

Rolf Orthel Film Prods.
Zoutkeetsgracht 1161
1013 LC Amsterdam
Tel: +31 20 6220255
Fax: +31 20 6261885

Fons Rademakers Prods. BV
Prinsengracht 685
1017 JT Amsterdam
Tel: +31 20 6221298

Red Dog Productions
Valeriusstraat 111
1075 ER Amsterdam
Tel: +31 20 6625747
Fax: +31 20 6756901

Roeland Kerbosch Film Prods. BV
Keizersgracht 678
1017 ET Amsterdam
Tel: +31 20 6230390
Fax: +31 20 6279879

Scorpio Verstappen Films BV
P.O. Box 245
1000 AE Amsterdam
Tel: +31 20 6225552
Fax: +31 20 6208660

Shooting Star Filmcompany BV
Prinsengracht 546
1017 KK Amsterdam
Tel: +31 20 6247272
Fax: +31 20 6268533

Sigma Film Productions BV
Bolensteinseweg 3
3603 CP Maarssen
Tel: +31 3465 70430/70431
Fax: +31 3465 69764

Van der Staak Film Prods.
Jacob Oliepad 2
1013 DP Amsterdam
Tel: +31 20 6260634

Jos Stelling Film Prods. BV
Springweg 50-52
3511 VS Utrecht
Tel: +31 30 313789
Fax: +31 30 310968

Studio Nieuwe Gronden
Van Hallstraat 52
1051 HH Amsterdam
Tel: +31 20 6867837
Fax: +31 20 6824367
Telex: 12682 sngfp

Distributors

Argus Film BV
P.O. Box 18269
1001 ZD Amsterdam
Tel: +31 20 6254585
Fax: +31 20 6268978

Cinemien
Entrepotdok 66
1018 AD Amsterdam
Tel: +31 20
6279501/6238152/6258357
Fax: +31 20 6209857

Columbia TriStar Films (Holland) BV
P.O. Box 533
1000 AM Amsterdam
Tel: +31 20 5737655
Fax: +31 20 5737656

Concorde Film
Lange Voorhout 35
2514 EC The Hague
Tel: +31 70 3605810/3924571
Fax: +31 70 3604925
Telex: 34568 cofil nl

Contact Film Conematheek
P.O Box 3100
6802 DC Arnhem
Tel: +31 85 434949
Fax: +31 85 511316

Express Film
Heemraadschapslaan 13
1181 TZ Amstelveen
Tel: +31 20 6412331

Filmtrust BV
Molenkade 57A
1115 AC Duivendrecht
Tel: +31 20 6957719/6955503
Fax: +31 20 6956625

Holland Film Releasing BV
De Lairessestraat 111-115
1075 HH Amsterdam
Tel: +31 20 5751751
Fax: +31 20 6622085

Arjan Edereen and Paul de Leeuw in FILMPY, seen by over a million people in Holland

Hungry Eye Pictures BV
Duivendrechtsekade 82
1096 AJ Amsterdam
Tel: +31 20 6686126
Fax: +31 20 6683452

International Art Film
Vondelpark 3
1071 AA Amsterdam
Tel: +31 20 5891418/5891426
Fax: +31 20 6833401

Melior Films BV
Steynlaan 8
1217 JS Hilversum
Tel: +31 35 245542
Fax: +31 35 235906

Meteor Film BV
Postbus 432
1200 AK Hilversum
Tel: +31 35 261500
Fax: +31 35 248418

The Movies BV
Postbus 432
1200 AK Hilversum
Tel: +31 35 261500
Fax: +31 35 248418

Shooting Star Film Distributors
Prinsengracht 546
1017 KK Amsterdam
Tel: +31 20 6247272
Fax: +31 20 6268533

Useful Addresses

Ministry of Education, Culture and Science
Department of Film
P.O. Box 3009
2280 ML Rijswijk
Tel: +31 70 3406148
Fax: +31 70 3405742

COBO Fund
Jeanine Hagen
Postbus 26444 (NOS TV)
1202 JJ Hilversum
Tel: +31 35 775348

Dutch Film and Television Academy
(Nederlandse Film en Televisie Academie)
Ite Boeremastraat 1
1054 PP Amsterdam
Tel: +31 20 6830206
Fax: +31 20 6126266

Dutch Film Fund
(Stichting Nederlands Fonds voor de Film)
Jan Luykenstraat 2
1071 CM Amsterdam
Tel: +31 20 6643368
Fax: +31 20 6750398

Holland Film Promotion
Jan Luykenstraat 2
1071 CM Amsterdam
Tel: +31 20 6644649
Fax: +31 20 6649171

MEDIA Desk/AV Platvorm
P.O. Box 256
1200 AG Hilversum
Tel: +31 35 238641
Fax: +31 35 218541

Netherlands Institute for Animation Film
Bachlaan 640
5011 BN Tilburg
Tel: +31 13 562925
Fax: +31 13 562428

Sources
(Stimulating Outstanding Resources for Creative European Screenwriting)
Jan Luykenstraat 92
1071 CT Amsterdam
Tel: +31 20 6720801
Fax: +31 20 6720399

Association of Dutch Film Theatres. (Associated with the Netherlands Cinematographic Assn.)
(Associate van Nederlandse Film Theatres)
Prinsengracht 770
1017 LE Amsterdam
Tel: +31 20 6267602
Fax: +31 20 6275923

Europe Cinema Nederland
P.O. Box 75242
1070 AE Amsterdam

GNS
(The Filmmakers Society of the Netherlands)
P.O. Box 581
1000 AN Amsterdam
Tel: +31 20 6765088
Fax: +31 20 6765837

KNF
(Circle of Dutch Film Critics)
Snelliuslaan 78
1222 TG Hilversum
Tel: +31 35 856115

The Netherlands Cinematographic Foundation
(Nederlandse Federatie van Cinematografie)
Jan Luykenstraat 2
1071 CM Amsterdam
Tel: +31 20 6799261
Fax: +31 20 6750398

NBF
(The Association of Film and TV Directors)
Jan Luykenstraat 2
1071 CM Amsterdam
Tel: +31 20 6646588
Fax: +31 20 6643707

NEW ZEALAND

Peter Calder

The New Zealand film industry continues to exude more promise than product and the last year could most charitably be described as one of consolidation. The New Zealand Film Commission, funded by a combination of state and lottery money, has long been the principal start-up backer of film projects. But it has had to cut its coat to suit an effectively shrinking allocation of cloth in recent years.

The government grant was cut in 1992 from $US3 million to barely $US600,000, and although the Commission's slice of lottery profits was increased commensurately, that is contestable, not guaranteed, funding. The Commission's budget this year is barely $US7 million, half of what it needs and much less than it deserves given the high international profile of the industry in recent years, according to its chief executive. There are signs that the Commission will reassume the sales role that it sought to shed last year; the loss of income has been sorely felt.

In the meantime, though, it has concentrated its resources on script development, particularly by making small grants to new writers to develop treatments and then assigning them to producers if matters proceed. Thus, though little has reached the screen locally or internationally, there are many projects in the wings: Commission literature lists almost three dozen films in development and the industry is in good heart.

Toby Fisher in THE WHOLE OF THE MOON

Invisible Life

Production has also slowed because the Commission has insisted that producers gain some of their production finance from, or against, presales rather than fully funding films itself. An exception is **The Ugly**, a horror movie which is the feature début of Scott Reynolds, who made the stylish noir short, *A Game with No Rules.* **But You're My Venus**, for example, which was to have starred *Once Were Warriors* sensation Rena Owen and been directed by Stewart Main *(Desperate Remedies)*, languishes in limbo for want of completion finance.

Despite record successes recently, local investors remain wary about committing venture capital, not least because some questionable tax practices by film investors in the early 80s are currently the subject of highly publicised official scrutiny at a government enquiry. Up to half of local films' budgets are now coming from foreign sources (notably Germany and Canada), which has raised concern among some local film-makers about the cultural integrity of the product and the industry.

But there are plenty of signs of life (see forthcoming films). The Auckland production company Isambard has signed a co-production deal with a Canal Plus subsidiary to make 12 "family feature films", and United Artists have guaranteed large-scale American distribution. Shooting on the first began in August. *The Climb,*

Still from TOPLESS WOMEN TALK ABOUT THEIR LIVES

starring John Hurt, is directed by Bob Swain, the Paris-based American who made the French thriller, *La Balance*. Meanwhile, American television has shot dozens of episodes of the cult TV hits *Hercules: The Legendary Journeys* and *Xena: Warrior Princess* on locations here.

Of several films loudly proclaimed when they were in production, local audiences have seen nothing, although they were in the market at Cannes: **Jack Brown, Genius**, about a modern-day inventor whose head is invaded by a mediaeval monk; the teen cancer drama, **The Whole of the Moon**, a co-production with Canada; and **The Flight of the Albatross**, a cross-cultural love story starring *Warriors'* Taungaroa Emile (this last was scheduled for July release at the time of writing).

Comfort Investment

If New Zealanders' production of movies stuttered somewhat in the last year, our moviegoing did not. The '90s have seen a surge in attendances as the tired and tatty stand-alones of a complacent duopoly have been replaced with multiplexes funded by massive investment by local entrepreneurs and the Australian giants, Village and Hoyts. Smaller independent distributors have proliferated in an active market (the range of product, particularly art-house, has exploded). The bigger distributors have encouraged the cinema development by offering both good product supply and terms to exhibitors prepared to invest in audience comfort.

NEW ZEALAND'S
NEW FEATURES

HARRY SINCLAIR'S
TOPLESS WOMEN
TALK ABOUT THEIR LIVES
Starring Daniele Cormack

SCOTT REYNOLDS'
THE UGLY
An interview with a serial killer
with Paolo Rotondo, Rebecca Hobbs
and Jennifer Ward-Lealand

GREGOR NICHOLAS'
BROKEN ENGLISH
A cross-cultural love story starring
Aleksandra Vujcic and Rade Serbedzija

IAN MUNE'S
THE WHOLE
OF THE MOON
Introducing Toby Fisher
and Nikki Si'ulepa

ALL PRODUCED WITH MAJOR INVESTMENT FROM THE
NEW ZEALAND FILM COMMISSION
NEW ZEALAND MOVIES ARE OUR BUSINESS
PO Box 11-546, Wellington, New Zealand. Fax 64-4-384 9719

TOP TEN GROSSING FILMS IN NEW ZEALAND: 1995

	Admissions (Thousands)
Forrest Gump	622
Babe	534
Braveheart	457
Muriel's Wedding	444
Dumb and Dumber	437
Priscilla, Queen of the Desert	426
Batman Forever	411
GoldenEye	399
Casper	375
Toy Story	339

The figures haven't matched the dazzling results of the early 90s (New Zealand's increase in admissions in 1993 led the world), but we remain the world's fourth most enthusiastic moviegoers outside the U.S. (after Singapore, Hong Kong and Iceland). The number of screens has risen by 80% (from 140 to 288) since 1991, and admissions have increased more than commensurately, climbing from six million to 14 million.

Still from BROKEN ENGLISH

The industry was saddened by the deaths (of cancer) in 1996 of Bruno Lawrence, the rough-hewn star of many of the films in the country's cinematic renaissance, and of Jim Booth, the producer who spotted and nurtured the brilliance of Peter Jackson.

PETER CALDER, who has been the film writer and critic for the *New Zealand Herald* since 1985, is a freelance script editor and consultant in Auckland.

Recent Films

BONJOUR TIMOTHY

Script: David Preston, from a story by David Parry. Dir: Wayne Tourell. Phot: Matt Bowkett. Players: Dean O'Gorman, Sabine Karsenti, Milan Borich. Prod: Tucker Films/Cinar of Montréal. Charming and romantic comedy in which exchange student Michel turns out to be Michelle with exciting results for her teenage host. Performed poorly at local box office despite energetic if hammy performance by teenage TV heartthrob Dean O'Gorman. First feature for TV veteran Tourell.

CHICKEN

Script and Dir: Grant Lahood. Phot: Allen Guilford. Players: Bryan Marshall, Ellie Smith, Cliff Curtis. Prod: Keirfilm. Feature début for Lahood whose short, *Lemming Aid*, was a Palme d'Or winner. Messy and muddled blackish comedy about a 60s rock legend who fakes his own death to revive his career - then finds himself the target of a death threat.

FLIGHT OF THE ALBATROSS

Script: Riwia Brown. Phot: Martin Gressman. Dir: Werner Meyer. Players: Taungaroa Emile, Julia Brendler, Jack Thompson. Prod: Top Shelf Productions/Fritz Wagner Filmproduktion. Teenage cross-cultural love story swamped by overwrought mumbo-jumbo about Maori curse. Good-looking island setting and first outing since *Once Were Warriors* for Emile.

JACK BROWN GENIUS

Script: Tony Hiles, Peter Jackson, Frances Walsh. Dir: Hiles. Phot: Allen Guilford. Players: Timothy Balmes, Nicola Murphy, Edward Campbell. Prod: Wingnut Films.

THE WHOLE OF THE MOON

Script: Richard Lymposs, Ian

Mune. Dir: Mune. Phot: Warrick Attewell. Players: Toby Fisher, Nikki Si'ulepa. Prod: Tucker Films/Cinar of Montréal.

BROKEN ENGLISH

Script: Gregor Nicholas, Johanna Piggott, Jim Salter. Dir: Nicholas. Phot: John Toon. Players: Rade Serbezija, Madeline McNamara, Aleksandra Vujcic. Prod: Communicado.

TOPLESS WOMEN TALK ABOUT THEIR LIVES

Dir: Harry Sinclair. Script: Sinclair. Phot: Dale McCready. Players: Danielle Cormack, Willa O'Neill, Joel Tobeck. Prod: John Swimmer Ltd. Feature début for Sinclair who was half of the excellent fringe music theatre duo, The Front Lawn. A development of the world's first mini-soap (which was produced for television in 55 four-minute episodes).

THE UGLY

Script and Dir: Scott Reynolds. Phot: Simon Raby. Players: Paolo Rotondo, Rebecca Hobbs, Jennifer Ward-Lealand. Interview with a serial killer. Prod: Essential Productions.

Producers

Communicado Communications
P.O. Box 5779
Auckland
Tel: (09) 379 3734
Fax: (09) 8885

Essential Productions
P.O. Box 90 056
Auckland Mailing Centre
Auckland
Tel: (09) 378 0529
Fax: (09) 378 1662

Fiona Copland
P.O. Box
106028 Auckland
Tel: (09) 377 5573
Fax: (09) 377 5574

The Gibson Group
119 Taranaki Street
Wellington
Tel: (04) 384 7789
Fax: (04) 384 4727

Isambard Productions
P.O. Box 41066
St Lukes
Auckland
Tel: (09) 849 7772
Fax: (09) 849 7755

Keirfilm
P.O. Box 9121
Wellington
Tel: (04) 382 8877
Fax: (04) 385 9790

Kiwi Film Productions
P.O. Box 6698
Wellington
Tel: (04) 384 4060
Fax: (04) 384 3774

Pacific Films
P.O. Box 6249
Wellington
Tel: (04) 382 9539
Fax: (04) 382 9916

Pinflicks Productions
P.O. Box 9438
Wellington
Tel: (04) 387 8741
Fax: (04) 387 8794

Plumb Productions
P.O. Box 2070
Wellington
Tel: (04) 385 1283
Fax: (04) 382 8787

Preston-Laing Productions
P.O. Box 9175
Wellington
Tel: (04) 384 6405
Fax: (04) 384 7406

South Pacific Pictures
P.O. Box 35656
Auckland
Tel: (09) 444 3000
Fax: (09) 443 5900

Top Shelf Productions
P.O. Box 9101
Wellington
Tel: (04) 382 8364
Fax: (04) 801 6920

Tucker Films
P.O. Box 90405
Auckland Mall Centre
Auckland
Tel: (09) 360 1312
Fax: (09) 376 2295

James Wallace Productions
P.O. Box 67057
Auckland
Tel: (09) 302 5271
Fax: (09) 302 5272

Wingnut Films
P.O. Box 9101
Wellington
Tel: (04) 382 8364
Fax: (04) 801 6920

Distributors

Blue Angel Films
P.O. Box 56 444
Dominiom Road
Auckland
Tel: (09) 630 0838
Fax: (09) 638 7474

Colombia TriStar
P.O. Box 68 041
Newton
Auckland
Tel: (09) 302 2223
Fax: (09) 302 2887

Essential Films
P.O. Box 90 056
Auckland Mailing Centre
Auckland
Tel: (09) 378 0529
Fax: (09) 378 1662

Everard Films
P.O. Box 3664
Auckland
Tel: (09) 302 1193
Fax: (09) 302 1192

Footprint Films
P.O. Box 1852
Auckland
Tel: (09) 309 8388

Hoyts Entertainment (NZ)
P.O. Box 6923
Auckland
Tel: (09) 309 0955

REP Distribution
P.O. Box 90 171
Auckland
Tel: (09) 360 2360
Fax: (09) 360 2920

Roadshow Film Distributors
P.O. Box 68246
Auckland
Tel: (09) 377 9669
Fax: (09) 377 9449

Twentieth Century Fox
P.O. Box 6923
Wellesley Street
Auckland
Tel: (09) 309 0955
Fax: (09) 309 0967

United International Pictures (NZ)
P.O. Box 105263
Auckland
Tel: (09) 379 6269
Fax: (09) 379 6271

Useful Addresses

Avalon Studios
P.O. Box 31-444
Lower Hutt
Tel: (04) 619 0600
Fax: (04) 619 0464

Independent Producers and Directors Guild
P.O. Box 3969
Wellington
Tel/Fax: (04) 385 8055

N.Z. Film Archive
Cnr Jervois Quay/Cable St
Wellington
Tel/Fax: (04) 385 8055

N.Z. Film Commission
P.O. Box 11546
Wellington
Tel: (04) 385 9754
Fax: (04) 384 9719

N.Z. on Air
P.O. Box 9744
Wellington
Tel: (04) 382 9524
Fax: (04) 382 9546

Project Blue Sky
P.O. Box 6619
Auckland
Tel: (09) 358 7104
Fax: (09) 483 3528

NORWAY

Trond Olav Svendsen

In the winter of 1996, the Norwegian Film Institute, a body with wide-ranging responsibilities in funding and marketing Norwegian films as well as film preservation, moved into its new headquarters in downtown Oslo. *Filmens hus* (the House of Film), as it was officially baptised, with its six spacious floors, is a great improvement on the old military hospital where the Institute was formerly housed. Its absorption of the National Film Board of Norway in 1993, and the subsequent reorganisation, has greatly enlarged the Institute, and a new setting had to be found. Other institutions are also moving in, including the Audiovisual Production Fund, the Norwegian Cinema and Film Foundation, and the Federation of Film Societies. The building has two excellent cinemas available to the Cinematek, for critics' previews and other functions.

Filmens hus, in other words, will represent a stronghold of Norwegian government-supported film activities. The time chosen for this is not accidental. Norwegian film production at the moment seems to be developing into something much more diversified than ever before. The number of productions has for two or three years been increasing, and in the 1995/96 season reached 16 features including four documentaries. No masterpiece may have emerged from this yet, and there is no discernible Norwegian 'New Wave'. But the growth of Norwegian cinema is evident.

Made Great by Adversity

It must be said that the effort to relaunch the documentary as a cinematic staple has been quite unsuccessful. The documentaries presented have been too close to TV

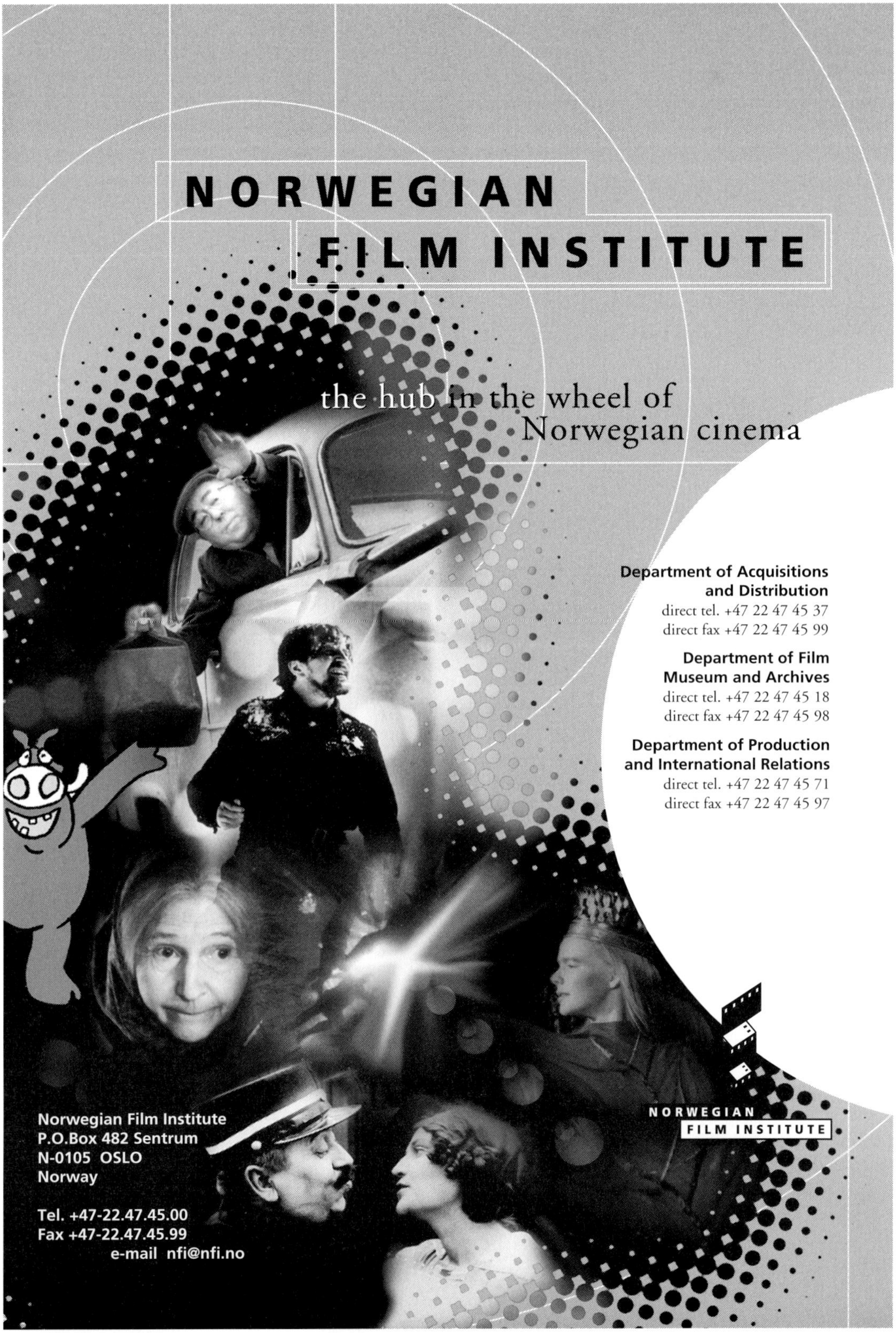
NORWEGIAN
FILM INSTITUTE
the hub in the wheel of
Norwegian cinema
Department of Acquisitions
and Distribution
direct tel. +47 22 47 45 37
direct fax +47 22 47 45 99
Department of Film
Museum and Archives
direct tel. +47 22 47 45 18
direct fax +47 22 47 45 98
Department of Production
and International Relations
direct tel. +47 22 47 45 71
direct fax +47 22 47 45 97
Norwegian Film Institute
P.O.Box 482 Sentrum
N-0105 OSLO
Norway
Tel. +47-22.47.45.00
Fax +47-22.47.45.99
e-mail nfi@nfi.no
NORWEGIAN
FILM INSTITUTE

TOP TEN GROSSING FILMS IN NORWAY: 1995

	Admissions
Kristin Lavransdatter *(Norwegian)*	385,606
The Lion King	323,877
Die Hard 3	320,120
Dumb and Dumber	268,530
The Bridges of Madison County	233,719
Forrest Gump	220,172
Pocahontas	159,010
The River Wild	125,468
While You Were Sleeping	118,620
Disclosure	114,188

Maria Theisen in Berit Nesheim's THE OTHER SIDE OF SUNDAY *photo: Barbara Halden*

aesthetics for comfort, and their various muckraking efforts – with subjects like secret intelligence networks within government and police corruption – have been largely ignored by audiences. An exception was **Meeting Halldis** by René Bjerke, a fairly well-received portrait of the poet Halldis Moren Vesaas, who died not long after the film was made.

At the box-office, the most evident recent Norwegian success has been **Kristin Lavransdatter**, Liv Ullmann's second film as director. It is based on a novel by Sigrid Undset that won her the Nobel Prize for Literature in 1928 and has always been popular in Norway. It has been translated into a number of languages, being perhaps best known to Catholics since Undset was a convert and her themes often reflect her faith. It helped the film that it seemed to be one of those projects that finally triumphs after much adversity.

Voices were raised against it when it was still being financed, since it would tie up a large amount of the money allocated to film in Norway. Later its cost overruns caused the studio head at Norsk Film A/S, Esben Høilund Carlsen, to leave office. Its critical reception could be characterised as somewhere between good and mixed. But the box-office figures spoke clearly: *Kristin Lavransdatter* left both die-hard Bruce Willis and dumb Jim Carrey far behind and became one of the major box-office successes in Norwegian cinema history.

In a Dreary Place

No other Norwegian film came close to that performance, but there were several interesting features that struggled to get a grip on contemporary issues. One was **Shut Up and Listen!**, directed by the reliable (and ambitious) Erik Gustavson. It was better than its English title suggests, a decidedly unromantic look at a couple working a Norwegian show-biz circuit, he as a stand-up comedian and she as a singer. The film boasts good performances from Kjersti Holmen and Bjørn Floberg, but the otherwise inventive script by novelist Lars Saabye Christensen contained too few laughs.

Parts of Emil Stang Lund's **The Virgins of Riga**, a comedy about Norwegian businessmen in the Baltic, were successful, but the whole was less than those parts. Sirin Eide made quite a successful début with **Goodbye 13!**, a coming-of-age-story

Still from Emil Stang Lund's THE VIRGINS OF RIGA

with fair performances. And last but not least, Berit Nesheim made **The Other Side of Sunday**, another spirited film about being young and wanting to grow up, this time set in the 1950s. Young Maria's fate is to be the daughter of a puritanical parson at the dawn of rock 'n' roll. One understands her fear of growing up to be one of the unsmiling and sexless women of the parish.

Hans Petter Moland made the striking **Zero Kelvin**, a group portrait of three men isolated from the world in Greenland in the 1930s. One of them is a seasoned polar traveller and misogynist (Stellan Skarsgård), the second a scientist (Bjørn Sundquist). The last is a failed poet who has left his sweetheart in Oslo to put his manhood to the test in the Arctic winter. The film successfully evokes the dreary landscape of both Greenland and the men's minds, but the true nature of the poet somehow remains in the shadows.

TROND OLAV SVENDSEN has a history degree from the University of Oslo, and works as a critic and film historian. He has published a Theatre and Film Encyclopedia, and is currently at work on a new edition of the large Norwegian Encyclopedia.

KRISTIN LAVRANSDATTER

Script: Liv Ullmann, based on the novel by Sigrid Undset. Direction: Ullmann. Photography: Sven Nykvist. Players: Elisabeth Matheson, Bjørn Skagestad, Sverre Anker Ousdal, Rut Tellefsen. Produced by Norsk Film. 188 mins. (Norwegian version).

The early 14th century. Young Kristin, daughter of a landowner, is to be married to the son of another wealthy man. But during a stay at a convent, she falls in love with the knight Erlend, a charming and independent man with a reputation as a womaniser. Their feelings for each other are mutual, however, and the story ends with their marriage.

Liv Ullmann's film reveals a strong interest in the classics of Nordic literature, evident in many Scandinavian films of the 1980s and 1990s. Many will find the film's pulse a bit on the slow side and the editing sluggish. Sverre Anker Ousdal and Ruth Tellefsen give warm performances as Kristin's parents, but Elisabeth Matheson as Kristin leaves something to be desired. The fault perhaps lies with the script, which does not seem to give her much more to do than fall in love. The film is shot by Sven Nykvist in the subdued colours and simple compositions of mediaeval tapestries.

Trond Olav Svendsen

Recent and Forthcoming Films

EGGS

Script and Dir: Bent Hamer. Phot: Erik Poppe. Players: Sverre Hansen, Kjell Stormoen, Leif Andrée. Prod: BulBul Films.

FARLIG FARVANN
(Dangerous Waters)

Script: Axel Hellstenius. Dir: Lars Berg. Phot: Kjell Vassdal. Players: Petronella Barker, Nils Ole Oftebro, Morten Faldaas. Prod: Wildhagen Produksjon.

PAKTEN
(Waiting for Sunset)

Script: Leidulv Risan, Arthur Johansen, Arthur Oberholzer. Dir: Risan. Players: Robert Mitchum, Cliff Robertson, Erland Josephson, Espen Skjønberg. Prod: Norsk Film/Yellow Cottage.

HØRER DU IKKE HVA JEG SIER!
(Shut Up and Listen!)

Script: Lars Saabye Christensen, Eirk Gustavson. Dir: Gustavson. Phot: Philip Øgaard. Players: Bjørn Floberg, Kjersti Holmen, Keve Hjelm, Ingerid Vardun. Prod: Nordic Screen Development.

KJÆLIGHETENS KJØTERE
(Zero Kelvin)

Script: Lars Bill Lundholm. Dir: Hans Petter Moland. Phot: Philip Øgaard. Players: Stellan Skarsgård, Gard B. Eidsvold, Bjørn Sundquist. Prod: Norsk Film.

BOOMERANG

Script: Trond Kvist, Gunnar Vikene. Dir: Kvist. Phot: Kjell Vassdal, Sjur Aarthun. Prod: Montage Film & Videoproduksjon. *Documentary.*

SEBASTIAN

Script and Dir: Svend Wam. Phot: Per Kållberg. Players: Hampus Björch, Nicolai Cleve Broch, Ewa Fröling, Helge Jordal. Prod: Mefistofilm.

BAK DIN RYGG
(Behind Your Back)

Script: Gerhard Helskog. Dir: Aslaug Holm, Helskog. Prod: Rubicon TV. *Documentary.*

MØTE MED HALLDIS
(Meeting Halldis)

Script: René Bjerke, Halldis Moren Vesaas. Dir: Bjerke. Phot: Kjell Vassdal. Prod: Elysium. *Documentary.*

JOMFRUENE I RIGA
(The Virgins of Riga)

Script: Morten Barth. Dir: Emil Stang Lund. Phot: Paul René Roestad. Players: Helge Jordal, Aurelia Kalnina, Jon Eikemo, Philip Zandén. Prod: Nordic Screen Development.

MYGGEN
(The Mosquito)

Script and Dir: Thomas Robsahm. Phot: Gaute Gunnari. Prod: Speranza Film.

ALDRI MER TRETTEN!
(Goodbye 13!)

Script: Sirin Eide, Maureen Thomas. Dir: Eide. Phot: Kjell Vassdal. Players: Sofie Cappelen, Martine Karlsen, Anne Krigsvoll, Svein Roger Karlsen. Prod: Moviemakers.

SØNDAGSENGLER
(The Other Side of Sunday)

Script and Dir: Berit Nesheim. Phot: Arne Borsheim. Players: Maria Theisen, Bjørn Sundquist, Hildegunn Riise, Sylvia Salvesen, Martin Garfalk. Prod: Norwegian Broadcasting Corporation.

MARKUS OG DIANA

Script: Klaus Hagerup. Dir: Svein Scharffenberg. Phot: Svein Krøvel. Players: Robert Reierskog, Laila E. Goody, Klaus Hagerup. Prod: Northern Lights Film & TV.

HUSTRUER III
(Wives III)

Script and Dir: Anja Breien. Phot: Halvor Næss. Players: Frøydis Armand, Katja Medbøe, Anne Marie Ottersen. Prod: Norsk Film/Magdalenafilm.

HAMSUN

Script: P. O. Enquist. Dir: Jan Troell. Phot: Jan Troell, Mischa Gavrushov. Players: Max von Sydow, Ghita Nørby, Annette Hoff, Sverre Anker Ousdal. Prod: Nordisk Film Produksjon/Svensk Filmindustri/Norsk Film.

JAKTEN PÅ NYRESTEINEN
(Hunting the Kidneystone)

Script and Dir: Vibeke Idsøe. Phot: Erik Poppe. Players: Torbjørn Jensen, Benjamin Helstad, Jenny Skavlan, Terje Strømdahl, Morten Faldaas, Kjersti Holmen. Prod: Filmkameratene.

TASHUNGA

Script: Sergio Donati, Paul Ohl. Dir: Nils Gaup. Players: Christopher Lambert, James Caan. Prod: Nordic Screen Development.

THE ENIGMA KNUT HAMSUN

Script: Robert Ferguson, Jonathan Rumbold. Dir: Bentein Baardson. Phot: Erling Thurmann-Andersen. Players: Lars Øyno, Per Sunderland, Kjersti Holmen, Astrid Folstad, Erik Hivju. Prod: Norwegian Broadcasting Corporation/Northern Lights Film & TV.

STOL PÅ MINISTEREN
(The Minister of State)

Script and Dir: Paul-Anders Simma. Phot: Hans Welin. Prod: Moviemakers.

MAJA STEINANSIKT
(Maja Stoneface)

Script: Elsa Kvamme. Dir: Lars Berg. Prod: Magdalenafilm/ Norsk Film.

BLIND GUDINNE
(Blind Goddess)

Script: Morten Barth. Dir: Carl Jørgen Kiønig. Prod: Nordic Screen Development.

BRENT AV FROST
(Burnt by the Frost)

Script: Knut Erik Jensen, Alf R. Jacobsen. Dir: Jensen. Phot: Svein Krøvel. Prod: Barentsfilm/ Norsk Film.

BUDBRINGEREN
(Junk Mail)

Script: Pål Sletaune, Jonny Berg. Dir: Pål Sletaune. Phot: Kjell Vassdal. Prod: Moviemakers.

ETTERFØLGEREN
(The Successor)

Script: Henning Mankell. Dir: Tor M. Tørstad. Prod: Studio Regin/Norwegian Broadcasting Corporation.

GURIN MED REVEROMPA
(Gurin with the Foxtail)

Script: Vibeke Idsøe. Dir: John M. Jacobsen. Prod: Filmkameratene.

Robert Reierskog and Laila E Goody in MARKUS AND DIANA
photo: Bård Løvvig

HVALENS ØYE
(The Eye of the Whale)

Script and Dir: Bent Hamer. Phot: Erik Poppe. Prod: BulBul Film.

INSOMNIA

Script: Nikolaj Frobenius. Dir: Erik Skjoldbærg. Prod: Nordic Screen Development.

MENDEL

Script and Dir: Alexander Røsler. Phot: Helge Semb. Prod: Northern Lights Film & TV.

ONKEL OSCAR
(Uncle Oscar)

Script and Dir: Evald Otterstad. Phot: John Christian Rosenlund. Prod: Wildhagen Produksjon.

SALIGE ER DE SOM TØRSTER
(Blessed Be Those Who Thirst)

Script: Axel Hellstenius. Dir: Carl Jørgen Kiønig. Prod: Nordic Screen Development.

Producers

Barentsfilm AS
P.O. Box 4383 Torshov
N-0402 Oslo
Tel: 22 02 35 18
Fax: 22 02 35 10
Contact: Jan Gammleng

BulBul Film A/S
Collets gt. 12 A
N-0169 Oslo
Tel: 22 46 97 94
Fax: 22 46 97 94
Contact: Bent Hamer

Caprino Filmcenter A/S
Mario Caprinos vei 3
N-1335 Snarøya
Tel: 67 53 31 95
Fax: 67 58 14 70
Contact: Ivo Caprino

Dis Film A/S
Parkvn. 47B
N-0256 Oslo
Tel: 22 44 26 88
Fax: 22 55 78 45
Contact: Mona Hoel

Elysium AS
Waldemar Thranes gt. 75
N-0175 Oslo
Tel: 22 20 47 60
Fax: 22 20 47 46
Contact: Bent Rognlien

Filmhuset A/S
President Harbitz gt. 22 A
N-0259 Oslo
Tel: 22 56 21 00
Fax: 22 55 15 40
Contact: Egil Ødegård

Filmkameratene A/S
P.O. Box 6868 St. Olavs plass
N-0130 Oslo
Tel: 22 33 47 50
Fax: 22 33 27 97
Contact: John M. Jacobsen

Magdalena Film A/S
President Harbitz gt. 21
N-0259 Oslo
Tel: 22 56 22 78
Fax: 22 56 22 79
Contact: Bente Erichsen

Mefistofilm A/S
Gyldenløves gt. 41
N-0260 Oslo
Tel: 22 43 82 60
Fax: 22 55 77 77
Contact: Petter Vennerød

Merkurfilm A/S
Astrids vei 10
N-0275 Oslo
Tel: 22 43 11 17
Fax: 22 44 00 40
Contact: Petter Vennerød

Motlys A/S
Islandsgt. 6
N-0658 Oslo
Tel: 22 68 60 63
Fax: 22 68 21 91
Contact: Sigve Endresen

MovieMakers A/S
P.O. Box 6858 St. Olavs plass
N-0130 Oslo
Tel: 22 36 09 90
Fax: 22 36 41 28
Contact: Petter Bøe, Dag Nordahl

Nordic Screen Development AS
Wedel Jarlsbergs vei 36
N-1342 Jar
Tel: 67 52 54 60
Fax: 67 12 37 73
Contact: Petter Borgli, Sissel Hansen

Norsk Film A/S
P.O. Box 4
N-1342 Jar
Tel: 67 52 53 00
Fax: 67 12 51 08
Contact: Tom Remlov

Northern Lights Film & TV Produksjon A/S
P.O. Box 104
N-1342 Jar
Tel: 67 52 53 30
Fax: 67 52 53 40
Contact: Axel Helgeland

National Broadcasting Corporation
Drama
Gullhaug torg 2
N-0483 Oslo
Tel: 22 45 89 21
Fax: 22 45 74 35
Contact: Oddvar Bull Tuhus

Regional Film A/S
Nydalsvn. 33E
N-0483 Oslo
Tel: 22 95 20 69
Fax: 22 95 20 49
Contact: Trond G. Lockertsen, Inge Tenvik

Rubicon TV A.S
Gullhaug torg 3
P.O. Box 44 Grefsen
N-0409 Oslo
Tel: 22 02 35 50
Fax: 22 02 35 53
Contact: Svein Trælvik

Speranza Film A/S
Eugenies gt. 15
N-0168 Oslo
Tel: 66 91 40 87
Fax: 66 91 40 97
Contact: Thomas Robsahm

Studio Regin A/S
Lofotgt. 2
N-0458 Oslo
Tel: 22 38 22 23
Fax: 22 38 13 18
Contact: Sverre Pedersen

Unni Straume Filmproduksjon A/S
Corso Anita Garibaldi 45
I-040 19 Terracina
Italy
Tel: +39 773 7001 83
Fax: +39 773 7001 83

ViPro A/S
Hamna 20
P.O. Box 238
N-6101 Volda
Tel: 70 07 81 94
Fax: 70 07 88 19
Contact: Jørn Brente

Wildhagen Produksjon A/S
Kragsvei 9B
N-0391 Oslo
Tel: 22 14 83 66
Fax: 22 14 83 44
Contact: Christian Wildhagen

Yellow Cottage AS
Wedel Jarlsbergs vei 36
N-1342 Jar
Tel: 67 52 53 45
Fax: 67 52 53 49
Contact: Aage Aaberge

Distributors

Action Film A/S
Box 9343 Vålerenga
N-0610 Oslo
Tel: 22 67 31 31
Fax: 22 67 30 05
Contact: Tore Erlandsen

Arthaus
Dronningens gt. 16
N-0152 Oslo
Tel: 22 47 46 85
Fax: 22 47 46 92
Contact: Svend B. Jensen

BV Film A/S
P.O. Box 17
N-4262 Avaldsnes
Tel: 52 84 35 44
Fax: 52 84 35 75
Contact: Bjørg Veland

Europafilm A/S
Stortingsgt. 30
N-0161 Oslo
Tel: 22 83 42 90
Fax: 22 83 41 51
Contact: Åge Hoffart, Erik Sælen

AS Fidalgo
P.O. Box 2054 Posebyen
N-4602 Kristiansand
Tel: 38 02 40 04
Fax: 38 02 23 54
Contact: Frank L. Stavik

Kommunenes Filmcentral AS
P.O. Box 411 Sentrum
N-0103 Oslo
Tel: 22 41 43 25
Fax: 22 42 14 69
Contact: Knut Bohwim

Norsk FilmDistribusjon A/S
P.O. Box 1178 Sentrum
N-0107 Oslo
Tel: 22 82 78 00
Fax: 22 82 78 10
Contact: Frida Ohrvik

SF Norge A/S
Box 6868 St. Olavs pl.
N-0130 Oslo
Tel: 22 33 47 50
Fax: 22 42 72 93
Contact: Bjørn Hoenvoll

Tour de Force AS
Georgernes V. 3
N-5011 Bergen
Tel: 55 32 25 90
Fax: 55 32 37 40
Contact: Tor Fosse

United International Pictures
P.O. Box 7134 Majorstua
N-0307 Oslo
Tel: 22 56 61 15
Fax: 22 56 71 81
Contact: Liv Jacobsen

Warner Bros. (Norway) A/S
P.O. Box 7053 Homansbyen
N-0306 Oslo
Tel: 22 43 18 00
Fax: 22 04 91 55
Contact: Jon Narvestad

Useful Addresses

The Audiovisual Production Fund
Dronningens gt. 16
N-0152 Oslo
Tel: 22 47 46 50
Fax: 22 47 46 91
Contact: Kirsten Bryhni

The National Association of Municipal Cinemas
Kongens gt. 23
N-0153 Oslo
Tel: 22 33 05 30
Fax: 22 42 89 49
Contact: Lene Løken

Still from SEBASTIAN, directed by Svend Wam.
photo: Erik Aavatsmark

National Centre for Screen Studies
Storengveien 8B
N-1342 Jar
Tel: 67 53 00 33
Fax: 67 12 48 65
Contact: Toril Wien

The Norwegian Federation of Film Societies
Dronningens gt. 16
N-0152 Oslo
Tel: 22 47 46 80
Fax: 22 47 46 92
Contact: Jan H. Kortner

Norwegian Film and Video Producers' Association
Dronningens gt. 16
N-0152 Oslo
Tel: 22 47 46 78
Fax: 22 47 46 88
Contact: Tom G. Eilertsen

Norwegian Film Critics' Association
P.O. Box 352 Sentrum
N-0101 Oslo
Tel: 22 41 94 09
Fax: 22 42 03 56
Contact: Lisa Kristin Strindberg/Kristin Oldeide

Norwegian Film Distributors' Association
Nedre Vollgt. 9
N-0158 Oslo
Tel: 22 42 48 44
Fax: 22 42 30 93
Contact: Kristin Hoenvoll

Norwegian Film Festival
P.O. Box 145
N-5501 Haugesund
Norway

The Norwegian Film Institute
P.O. Box 482 Sentrum
N-0105 Oslo
Tel: 22 47 45 00
Fax: 22 45 47 97
Contact: Jan Erik Holst

Norwegian Film Workers' Association
Storengvn. 8 B
N-1342 Jar
Tel: 67 59 10 00
Fax: 67 12 48 65
Contact: Rolv Håan

PAKISTAN

Aijaz Gul

The resurgence of Urdu cinema, which began in 1985 with almost half-a-dozen hits, is continuing in 1986. The official PTV (Pakistan Television Corporation) and private NTM (Network Television Marketing) can be partly credited for the upswing. Apart from giving films wide publicity, television broadcasts half-a-dozen regular weekly programmes featuring songs from films, interviews and studio round-ups, lead by *Lollywood Top Ten* (a movie songs hit parade named after Lahore, the main film centre).

Actress-producer-director Shamim Ara again hit the jackpot with **Love '95**, filmed in Turkey with Reema and Babar. Her second film, **In-Laws** (*Hum to Chalay Susral*) was filmed in Sri Lanka with the same cast. And her third film, **Miss Istanbul**, again featured the same cast with the same picture-postcard Turkey. Shamim Ara is now a factory manufacturing films on a quarterly basis. These quickies are scripted by her husband, Dabirul Hassan, and consistently lack originality or interest. Her material revolves around rich boys, dancing girls, smugglers, patriots and a transvestite or two. Her films are also full of sexual innuendo and erotic heaving, but scarcely come to terms with the problems women face in Pakistan today.

Actor Javed Sheikh made his directorial début last year with **Hardship** (*Mushkil*), about bonded child labour. In 1996, Sheikh turned out **Chief Sahib**, a smash-hit musical comedy about slum dwellers in Instanbul being forced out by a rich entrepreneur. Director Iqbal Kashmiri's comedy **Jumble** (*Mamla Garbar Hai*), filmed in Sri Lanka, also played well. Last year, Iqbal Kashmiri's **Scared** (*Jo Darr Gaya Woh Marr Gaya*), filmed in the Philippines with Nadeem, Javed Sheikh and Atiqa, was another success.

Perhaps the only creative director working in the commercial cinema is Syed Noor. He has scripted over 200 features, and in 1995-96 directed half-a-dozen films, including **Lifesaver** (*Jeeva*) and **Melody** (*Sargam*). *Melody* was a delightful musical in which Zeba Adnan played the double role of mother and daughter. Adnan's score was a highlight of the film. Syed Noor's other achievements in 1996 included a comedy **Thief** (*Chor Machay Shor*), a family drama, **Veil** (*Ghunghat*), and a heavy drama, **Winds** (*Hawain*).

Looking back at 1995, a total of 64 features were produced (Pushto: 23; Punjabi: 17; Urdu: 16; Punjabi-Urdu: 8). In January 1996, the all-time superstar of Punjabi films, Sultan Rahi, was shot dead

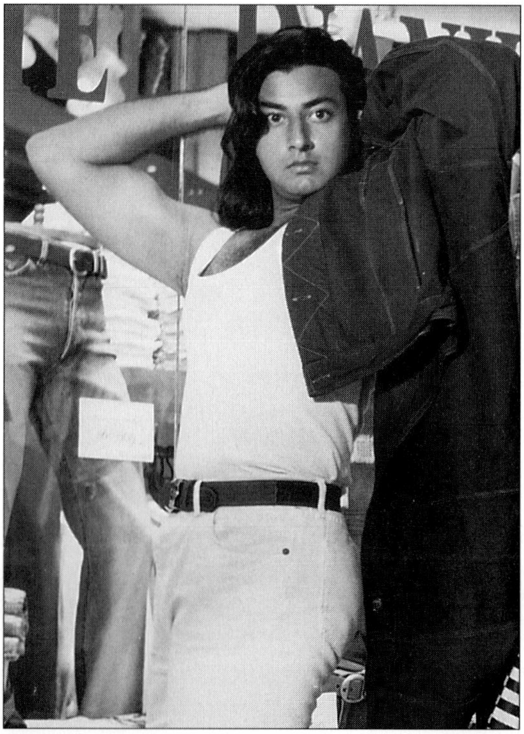

Babar Ali in LOVE '95

during a stopover on the Rawalpindi-Lahore highway. He began his career as an extra and appeared as the lead in over 700 features, a feat worthy of the Guinness Book of Records. He was loud both in dialogue and action; vengeance and bloodbaths were his forte. Punjabi cinema flourished due to him, and without him it may face a severe slump. Other losses in 1996 were scriptwriter-producer-director-poet Masroor Anwar and cameraman Babar Bilal, who died on location in Singapore.

Foreign films received a jolt in 1995-96 when the CBR (Central Board of Revenue) increased import duty tenfold. Many importers boycotted the unilateral increase and refused to pick up the prints dumped at Karachi and Lahore. Even prestigious English cinemas like Nishat, Capri, and Prince (Karachi) and Alfalah, and Gulistan (Lahore) were forced to programme low-brow local titles. Apart from cheap titles from Hong Kong, the only notable releases were *Speed*, *The Last of the Mohicans* and *Desperado*. Big importers still hope to bring in *GoldenEye*, *Die Hard with a Vengeance* and *Sleepless in Seattle* in the latter part of 1996.

AIJAZ GUL earned his MA in Cinema from USC, Los Angeles. He has written three books on Pakistani and French films. He has written numerous articles on film and presently works for the National Film Development Corporation.

Superstar Sultan Rahi, shot dead in 1996.

Recent and Forthcoming Films

GHUNGHAT (Veil)

Script and Dir: Syed Noor. Players: Resham, Arbaz, Shan, Mohsin

A family drama of love and sacrifice.

MUMMY

Script: Mohiuddin Nawab. Dir: Iqbal Kashmiri. Players: Atiqa, Nadeem, Reema, Faisal.

A story of love and affection between a mother and son.

TOP TEN GROSSING FILMS IN PAKISTAN: 1995

Munda Bigra Jai (The Brat)
Jo Darr Gaya Woh Marr Gaya (Scared)
Jeeva (Lifesaver)
Sarak (Street)
Madam Rani
Chaudhry Badshah (Feudal Lord)
Wehshi Aurat (Woman Hunt)
Mushkil (Hardship)
Sargam (Melody)
Jungle Ka Qanoon (Jungle Law)

HAWAIN (Winds)

Script and Dir: Syed Noor. Players: Nadeem, Saud, Reema, Resham.

An action film with of an old father's sentiments.

SANGAM (Acquaintance)

Script and Dir: Syed Noor. Players: Resham, Shan, Afzal, Saleem Sheikh.

A love triangle with good music.

Useful Addresses

NAFDEC
National Film Development Corporation Limited
56-F Jinnah Avenue (Blue Area)
Islamabad
Pakistan
Tel: 0092-51-920 3853,
0092-51-920 3548
Fax: 0092-51-210 108

Central Board of Film Censors
Street No. 55
Sector F-6/4
Islamabad
Pakistan
Tel: 0092-51-920 4387
Fax: 0092-51-210 108

Ministry of Culture
Block-D, Pak Secretariat
Islamabad
Pakistan
Tel: 0092-51-920 2893,
0092-51-920 1301
Fax: 0092-51-210 108

PFPA
Pakistan Film Producers Association
Regal Cinema Building
Shahrah-e-Quaid-e-Azam
Lahore
Pakistan
Tel: 0092-42-732 2904
Fax: 0092-42-724 1264

D. J. FILMS
4 Royal Park
Lahore
Pakistan
Tel: 0092-42-636 3349
Fax: 0092-42-586-2265

Eveready Pictures
4th Floor
Eveready Chambers
I.I. Chundrigar Road
P.O. Box No. 139
Karachi
Pakistan
Tel: 0092-21-263 4817
0092-21-263 4818
Fax: 0092-21-732 3435

Evernew Pictures
2 Abbot Road
Lahore
Pakistan
Tel: 0092-42-631 6929
Fax: 0092-42-571 2734

Mandviwalla Entertainment
Nishat Cinema Building
M.A. Jinnah Road
Karachi
Pakistan
Tel: 0092-21-722 3535
Fax: 0092-21-772 7259

Shera Films
2 Abbot Road
Lahore
Pakistan
Tel: 0092-42-636 2486

PERU

Isaac León Frias

1992 ended with a package of government regulations that brought to an end 20 years of active promotion of short film making, a period which had also seen the volume and quality of feature films increase. In 1993, the short film virtually vanished from all theatres in which they had been shown under the "mandatory exhibition" stipulation. Production was halted and dozens of short films were left with no expectation of release.

In May 1993, the 6th Short Film National Festival, organised by the Asociación de Cineastas del Perú (ACDP), took place for the last time to date in Lima. The quality of work shown had been remarkable. Feature films have also suffered from these measures. In 1993 three Peruvian films were released: *Reportaje a la muerte*, directed by Danny Gavidia; *Todos somos estrellas*, directed by Felipe Degregori; and *La vida es una sola*, directed by Marianne Eyde. In 1994 only one film was released, *Sin compasión*, directed by Francisco

Lombardi, based on Dostoievski's *Crime and Punishment*.

In 1995 again, only one film was released: **Anda corre vuela**, filmed three years before, directed by Augusto Tamayo. The film's exhibition was a complete fiasco. In the first half of 1996, another feature film, shot four years ago, was released: **Asia, el culó del mundo**, directed by Juan Carlos Torrico. Francisco Lombardi finished shooting *Bajo la piel*, a Peruvian-Spanish co-production which will be released in the second half of the year. Also awaiting release are **La lengua de los zorros** and **Pachacutec**, directed by Federico García, and **Creación heroica**, about the life of José Carlos Mariátegui.

1993 and 1994 were years of intense activity for Peruvian film-makers, not in shooting films but in conducting meetings and negotiations that were to lead to a new film law. Early in 1993, the ACDP suffered an internal division. A small but influential group, including Federico García, Juan Carlos Torrico, Fernando Espinoza and Marianne Eyde, founded the Sociedad Peruana de Directores y Productores Cinematográficos (SOCINE). Veteran film-maker Armando Robles Godoy joined them in negotiating new legislation on behalf of the film industry.

SOCINE accused ACDP of excessive weakness vis-à-vis the exhibitors who demanded a bigger share of the profits. The new situation, however, compelled film-makers to negotiate directly with the exhibitors. ACDP and SOCINE each sent their own movie bills to the Congreso Constituyente Democrático (CCD), the name given to the new parliamentary organisation that replaced the chambers after the coup of President Alberto Fujimori on April 5, 1992. Over a year, the bills were integrated into one and, after various negotiations, approved by CCD. However, Fujimori's government objected to the law because they considered it a protectionist regulation.

Under a new law finally approved in May 1995, the production of feature and short films is encouraged with a kind of prize-giving system. Twice a year, a jury will chose three feature film projects to receive an award that will cover a significant portion of the budget. There will be awards for 48 short films in four annual contests. A new organisation, Consejo Nacional de Cinematografia (CONACINE), was established in late 1995 to administer the law. So far this outfit doesn't have the necessary funds, fixed by law, for initiating the contests.

Recent and Forthcoming Films

REPORTAJE A LA MUERTE (Newscast to Death)

Script: José Watanabe. Dir: Danny Gavidia. Phot: Eduardo Dávila. Players: Diego Bertie, Marisol Palacios. Prod: Casablanca (Perú)/Bolivar Films (Venezuela)/ICAIC (Cuba), with the Foreign Affairs Ministry of France.

TODOS SOMOS ESTRELLAS (We Are All Stars)

Script: Ronny Temoche. Dir: Felipe Degregori. Phot: Eduardo Dávila. Players: Mariela Balbi, María Elena Alva, Hernán Romero, Ricardo Fernández. Prod: Torre de Babel Producciones Cinematográficas.

LA VIDA ES UNA SOLA (You Only Live Once)

Script and Dir: Marianne Eyde. Phot: César Pérez. Players: Milagros del Carpio, Aristóteles Picho, Rosa María Olórtegui. Prod: Diana Cabrera for Kusi Films.

SIN COMPASION (No Mercy)

Script: Augusto Cabada. Dir: Francisco J. Lombardi. Phot: Pili Flores Guerra. Players: Diego Bertie, Adriana Dávila, Jorge Chiarella. Prod: Inca Films/Amaranta (México)/Ciby 2000 (Paris).

LA LENGUA DE LOS ZORROS (The Language of Foxes)

Script: Federico García, Rafael Villalba. Dir: García. Phot: Danny Gavidia. Players: Baldomero Cáceres, Lucía Melgar, Zully Azorin, Ciro Umeres. Prod: Cinematográfica Kuntur/Grupo Chaski/Percy Velit/Instituto Cinematográfico del Arte y la Industria Cinematográficos (ICAIC).

TOP TEN GROSSING FILMS IN PERU: 1995

	Admissions
The Mask	281,550
Casper	221,313
Batman Forever	151,933
Street Fighter	94,850
The Page Master	93,956
Pocahontas	93,387
Die Hard 3	83,797
Dumb and Dumber	76,731
Junior	72,720
Congo	63,653

PACHAKUTEQ

Script: Federico García, César Musitani. Dir: García. Phot: José Riera. Prod: Cinematográfica Kuntur.

ANTUCA

Script and Dir: Maria Barea. Phot: César Pérez. Players: Graciela Huayhua, Maria E. Sandoval, Eduardo Cesti. Prod: Producciones Warmi Cine y Video.

ANDA CORRE VUELA . . . (Go Run Fly)

Script: José Watanabe. Dir: Augusto Tamayo. Phot: Danny Gavidia. Players: Marino León, Rosa Isabel Morffino. Prod: Stefan Kaspar for Casablanca Films.

ASIA, EL CULO DEL MUNDO (Asia, the Asshole of the World)

Script: Gianfranco Annichini, Juan Carlos Torrico. Dir: Torrico. Phot: Juan Durán. Players: Javier Valdez, María Angélica Vega, Enrique Victoria. Prod: Películas del Pacífico.

Useful Addresses

CONACINE
Museo de la Nación
Av. Javier Prado 2465
8' Piso
Lima
Tel: (51-14) 4377607 - 4769892

SOCINE
(Sociedad Peruana de Directores y Productores Cinematográficos)
Tel/Fax: (51-14) 791722

Asociación de Cineastas del Perú
Calle Manco Capac 236
Miraflores
Lima
Tel: (51-14) 4461829

Filmoteca de Lima
Paseo Colón 125
Lima
Tel: (51-14) 234732 - 235149
Fax: (51-14) 236332

Producciones Inca Films
La Florida 180
San Isidro
Lima
Tel: (51-14) 221427
Fax: (51-14) 406390

PHILIPPINES

Agustin Sotto

Ishmael Bernal's untimely death on June 2, 1996, from a heart attack, robbed the country of one of its most provocative film directors and brought to a close an era of film-making that peaked during the Marcos years. Both Bernal and his artistic rival, the late Lino Brocka, directed their best films in the shadow of the dictatorship; quite ironically, their careers waned with the return of democracy.

Bernal's best films, *Manila by Night, Street Smart (Wating); Pleasure (Aliw),* and *Wrenched from Heaven (Hinugot sa Langit),* drew on the habitual sins and tawdry pleasures of overpopulated Manila. Bernal's people have a huge capacity for life, but their spirit is compromised by the intrinsic duplicity of human nature and by the hypocritical ways of an unforgiving city.

The demise of Bernal and Brocka also highlights the real lack of serious contenders among the younger directors. Much of the standard fare of recent Philippine cinema is tolerable because the actresses have imbued their roles with some emotional insight and the authentic ring of real experience. Their male counterparts are just as proficient but suffer from a lack of challenging roles.

Leading the pack is Nora Aunor, who recently won the best actress award at the Cairo International Film Festival for **The Flor Contemplacion Story**, the account of a Filipino domestic convicted of murder in Singapore. Also in the forefront is Jaclyn José, to whom the Amiens International Film Festival paid a deserving tribute in 1994. José's performances have rare emotional nuance, and her anguished characters in her best films, *Macho Dancer, Private Show* and *The Flor Contemplacion Story,* possess an effortless radiance.

Lea Salonga won the Olivier and the Tony Awards for the role of Kim in the West End and Broadway productions of *Miss Saigon*. She returned to her home country to appear in **If It Could Be Repeated** (*Sana Maulit Muli*), a drama of American immigration in which a local boy runs after his girlfriend who is starting to take on disturbingly foreign manners. Other gifted actresses include Lolita Rodriguez, Helen Gamboa, Gina Alajar, Vilma Santos and Lorna Tolentino.

Say It with Roses

With regard to film production, the Philippines' output has remained steady at around 130 films a year. This is phenomenal as the national cinemas of its neighbours have practically collapsed. To help regain lost ground in the international arena, the Philippine Film Development Foundation has set up the International Film Festival Committee (IFFCOM), whose brief is to give financial support to films selected for international film festivals. In this way, the government is awakening to the need to promote Filipino talent abroad.

Albert Martinez and MichelleAldana in SEGURISTA

Among the new films of interest is **Escape** (*Escapo*), directed by Chito Ronö, which underscores the dearth of films that depict the Marcos period. Indeed, it is an embarrassment that Philippine cinema has shown no interest in those traumatic years. *Escape* tells of a daring breakout from an army detention cell by two opponents of the Marcos régime. The film, however, glorifies the deliverance of its protagonists in rather messianic terms, and is largely inadequate in detailing the intricacies of power. Except for one scene in which Imelda Marcos sashays around, strewing her former adversary's coffin with rose petals, the film never really catches the country's political madness.

Michelle Aldana and Ruby Moreno in THE INSURANCE AGENT

Deep in Paradise (*Mulanay*) looks into the plight of committed physicians who practise in rural areas. One such doctor (Jaclyn José), fresh from her oath-taking, enlists in a government programme, "Doctors to the Barrios", and is given a distant posting. She struggles to improve the health and sanitation conditions, but soon realises the powerlessness of individual effort and tries to coax the community into mass action. While the film is clearly government-financed, director Gil Portes and screenwriter Clodualdo del Mundo have, at least, succeeded in keeping its developmental aims unobtrusive.

Redeem Her Honour (*Ipaglaban Mo*) is taken from a popular television serial and features two sensational rape cases. One looks into an uncle's seduction of his naive niece; the other tackles a rich kid's obsession with a married woman. Director Marilou Diaz Abaya transcends the prurient with the help of her actors who give the timeworn material emotional depth. Ricky Davao, Sharmaine Arnaiz and Elizabeth Oropesa are particularly impressive.

The Insurance Agent (*Segurista*) explores a Filipino karaoke bar, closely patterned after its Japanese model, where guest relations officers (GROs) work like geishas and offer a titillating evening along with the drinks. One GRO has to rescue her family from the misfortunes brought about by a volcanic disaster and supplements her income by working as an insurance agent in the daytime. As a come-on, she offers a night on the town to her clients. Director Tikoy Aquiluz weaves into the narrative a meditation on chance and the large part it plays in our lives, particularly when it's as spectacular as the eruption of Mt. Pinatubo, probably the most powerful of the century. All the more reason to take out an insurance policy.

Recent Films

ESCAPO (Escape)

Script: José F. Lacaba, Roy Iglesias. Dir: Chito Roño. Players: Christopher de Leon, Richard Gomez, Dina Bonnevie.

MULANAY (Deep in Paradise)

Script: Clodualdo del Mundo. Dir: Gil Portes. Players: Jaclyn José, Gina Alajar, John Arcilla, Noni Buencamino.

SEGURISTA (The Insurance Agent)

Script: José F. Lacaba, Amado Lacuesta. Dir: Tikoy Aquiluz. Players: Michelle Aldana, Ruby Moreno.

SA NGALAN NG PAG-IBIG (In the Name of Love)

Script: George Kabrisante. Dir: Maryo de los Reyes. Players: Lorna Tolentino, Christopher de Leon.

DAHAS (Violence)

Script: Roy Iglesias. Dir: Chito Roño. Players: Maricel Soriano, Richard Gomez, Ton-Ton Gutierrez.

Useful Addresses

Film Development Foundation
CCP Complex
Roxas Boulevard
Manila

Film Division
Cultural Center of the Philippines
Roxas Boulevard
Manila

Society of Film Archivists
C63A Gueventville II
Libertad
Mandaluyong

Film Department
College of Mass Communication
University of the Philippines
Diliman
Quezon City

Film Committee
National Commission for Culture and the Arts
Intramuros
Manila

POLAND

Wanda Wertenstein

An old Polish saying could be applied to the present condition of our cinema: "The situation is good but not hopeless". The scale of production is more or less stationary – about thirty feature films a year. We are reaping the benefits of the system of state support for film production introduced in 1991: the Script Agency and the Film Production Agency, together with large-scale funding of feature film production by Polish Television and developing international co-productions (particularly after Poland joined Eurimages). There is enough money for film-making, and through the Film Distribution Agency, backing for events such as the Gdynia Festival of Polish Feature Films, the Festival of Central European Cinema, the Warsaw International Film Festival and the International Festival of the Art of Cinematography, "Camerimage". And with its 34-year-old tradition there is the Kraków International Short Film Festival.

Production companies, like Zanussi's TOR, or Morgenstern's Perspektywa, or the Przykowski Studio for Young Film, Makers, are only partially financed from state funds and generate most of their own income. Independent film producers are today responsible for about 50% of feature film production; about 80% of theatrical films are backed by the State Film Production Agency and/or Polish Television. Owing to the various forms of national financing plus international co-productions, a good script and a promising or experienced director can fairly easily find the necessary finance. What may be less satisfying are the films themselves. . .

The good news is the success of Maciej Slesicki's first feature, **Dad** (*Tato*), based on his own script, the story of a father's struggle for the custody of his daughter against his mentally deranged wife. The film placed sixth – and the only Polish production – in the list of top ten grossing films for the first three months of 1996. Slesicki is a "movie brat"; his mother, Barbara Slesicka, was a producer for many years and a production manager for Andrzej Wajda. **Virus**, from another Slesicki script, is being directed by Janusz Kidawa-Bioński. Also in production is an adaptation of Dostoievsky's *A Gentle Woman*, previously made by Robert Bresson.

Among non-fiction films worth particular attention is the work of documentary film-maker Irena Kaminska. Her new film, **The Church on Mount Zion**, is a fascinating account of a congregation of Messianic Jews in Jerusalem (mostly immigrants from the U.S.) who, while remaining Orthodox

Still from Juliusz Machulski's GIRL GUIDE

Jews, believe that Jesus really was the Messiah promised by the Bible.

While the Polish cinema manages to cope pretty well with the organisational and financial problems of the transformation to a free-market economy, the artistic results are less satisfactory. There are too many facile imitations of American models, though with the occasional happy outcome such as Juliusz Machulski's absurd comedy, **Girl Guide**, the Grand Prix winner of the Polish Feature Film Festival of 1995.

Krzysztof Kieślowski (1941-96)

The pride of Polish cinema, Krzysztof Kieślowski passed away on March 13, 1996, after unsuccessful heart surgery. Born in Warsaw in 1941, he attended the School of Theatrical Techniques (1957-62), then entered the famous Łódź Film School (1962-68), and after graduation joined the Warsaw Documentary Films Studio.

His documentaries won festival awards in Krakow, Mannheim, Gdanśk, Moscow, Lyon, Chicago, Nyon, São Paulo. He lectured on directing and scriptwriting in Katowice (1979-82), in West Berlin (1984), Helsinki (1988), and Switzerland (1985, 1988). Between 1968 and 1975 he made 13 documentaries and, in 1975, his first feature film, *The Staff;* more documentaries and short features followed, and in 1979 Kieślowski made one of his most important films, *Camera Buff*. This was followed by *Railway Station* and *Talking Heads* (1980); *Chance* and *Short Working Day* (1981); *No End* (1984); *A Short Film about Killing* and *A Short Film about Love* (1988); the remaining parts of the *Decalogue* (1989); *The Double Life of Véronique* (1991); *Three Colours – Blue* (1993); *Three Colours – White* (1993); *Three Colours – Red* (1994). For *Blue,* Kieślowski received the Golden Lion of the Venice Film Festival in 1993.

CWAŁ (At Full Gallop)

Script and Direction: Krzysztof Zanussi. Photography: Jarosław Żamojda. Music: Wojciech Kilar. Players: Maja Komorowska, Bartosz Obuchowicz, Karolina Wajda, Piotr Szwedes, Andrzej Szenajch, Piotr Adamczyk. Prod: Film Studio TOR/TVP S.A.

The horse is a totemic figure in Polish national mythology; a kind of mystic link unites the rider and the horse. If, in Poland today, very few have the chance and the means to ride horseback, many cultivate the memory of family equestrian traditions. Andrzej Wajda's father was a cavalry officer (and my own uncles fought as volunteers in a cavalry regiment in the Polish-Bolshevik war of 1920). Not an anti-Bolshevik war but an anti-Stalinist one is remembered by Krzysztof Zanussi in *At Full Gallop*.

A small boy, the son of a Polish officer who remained in England after the war, lives in the care of an 'aunt', probably once well off but now working as a clerk in a post office. In the oppressive atmosphere of Stalinism in full bloom, she manages to organise a sort of private equestrian club. The group has a few good horses, keeps them secretly in the stables of a Warsaw racetrack, and regularly goes riding.

The story is told with a sardonic sense of humour, and the images of the young riders and their horses galloping through forests and fields are a treat for every horse-and-film-loving viewer. Maja Komorowska, in the role of the 'aunt' creates a brave and irresistibly funny character who owes her safety (in those grim years of arbitrary arrests and invented charges) to creation of the artful double identity she has two passports and two jobs, appearing once as herself, the instigator of the riding group, and at another time as her sister, the modest post-office employee.

The riding scenes in the woods and fields around Warsaw are delightful, the meeting of the horses and a tank frightening and funny, and many of the equestrian scenes irresistibly lively.

Karolina Wajda (Andrzej Wajda's daughter) in Krzysztof Zanussi's AT FULL GALLOP *photo: Piotr Bujnowicz*

The controversial ending of the film, where Zanussi himself appears and tells the true story of this private (and in those years illegal) horse-riding club, is maybe not the best idea, but one can forgive the director this very private comment on the film's authentic background.

Wanda Wertenstein

WANDA WERTENSTEIN is a veteran film critic who also worked with Jerzy Bossak in Warsaw Documentary Films' Studio; made some documentaries herself; and has translated film books from English and Italian. She has published a book on Wajda and a study of his famous Film Unit "X".

TELEWIZJA KRAKÓW

Great location for award winning productions.

The largest and the most modern studio available in Poland for film and TV production (1000 sq.m, height 13m). Professional equipment, skilled technicians and internationally competitive rates. Location famed for Renaissance castle and unique Old Town.

The best for film making in Poland. Spielberg was more than satisfied, you will be too.

Phone 48 12 / 61 50 00, Fax 48 12 / 23 65 12
Telewizja Polska S.A. Oddział w Krakowie
Ul.Krzemionki 30, 30-955 Kraków, Poland

TOP TEN GROSSING FILMS IN POLAND: 1995

	Admissions
Casper	1,301,836
The Lion King	1,245,029
Pocahontas	823,444
The Mask	752,143
Dumb and Dumber	706,417
Forrest Gump	656,544
Baby's Day Out	638,414
Waterworld	577,568
Stargate	577,153
Priest	432,038

By courtesy of Info Box Office, Kraków.

Recent and Forthcoming Films

ARGONAUCI (Argonauts)

Script: Andrzej Kondratiuk. Dir: Janusz Kondratiuk. Phot: Tomasz Michałowski. Players: Zbigniew Buczkowski, Zbigniew Mazurek, Eugeniusz Privieziencew, Stanisława Celińska. Prod: Iga-Film/WFDIF/APF/Polish Television S.A.

BANDYTA (Bandit)

Script: Cezary Harasimowicz. Dir: Maciej Dejczer. Phot: Andrzej Prokop. Music: Michał Lorenc. Players: Til Schweiger, Polly Walker, John Hurt, Pete Postlethwaite. Prod: Heritage Films (Warsaw)/Douek Prod./ Boje Buck Prod. (Berlin).

NOWY WŁADCA (The New Master)

Script: Wojciech Marczewski, based on a story by Witold Zalewski. Dir: Marczewski. Phot: Krzysztof Ptak. Music: Zbigniew Preisner. Players: Janusz Gajos, Jerzy Radziwiłowicz, Krzysztof Wakuliński. Prod: Maciej Strzembosz/APF/Studio A.

DESZCZOWY ŻOŁNIERZ (Rain Soldier)

Script: Wiesław Saniewski, Tomek Tryzna. Phot: Przemysław Skwierczyński. Players: Antonina Choroszy, Mariusz Bonaszewski, Jan Nowicki, Artur Żmijewski, Łukasz Nowicki, Maciej Kozłowski, Edwin Petrykat. Prod: Saco Films/TVP S.A./WFF-Wroclaw/Vacek Film.

DUBLET (Doublet)

Script: Maciej Dutkiewicz, Robert Bruttner. Dir: Dutkiewicz. Phot: Krzysztof Ptak. Players: Kasia Kowalska, Marek Kondrat, Katarzyna Skrzynecka, Robert Janowski, Jan Frycz, Jan Peszek, Stanisława Celinska, Cezary Pazura, Radek Pazura, Zdzisław Wardejn. Prod: Skorpion Art/ APF/TVP S.A.

DEBORAH

Script and Dir: Ryszard Brylski. Phot: Przemysław Skwierczyński. Players: Olgierd Łukaszewicz, Renata Dancewicz, Maria Pakulnis, Jerzy Zelnik, Władysław Kowalski. Prod: Karol Irzykowski Studio/APF/TVP S.A./Studio Indeks/WFF Wrocław/ Odra-Film.

DZIECI I RYBY (Kids and Fishes)

Script and Dir: Jacek Bromski. Phot: Witold Adamek. Players: Anna Romantowska, Gabriela Kownacka, Jan Frycz. Prod: Film Studio Zebra.

FOTOAMATOR (Amateur Photographer)

Script: Arnold Mostowicz, Krzysztof Krauze, Dariusz Jabłoński. Dir: Krauze. Phot: Łukasz Kuźmicki. Prod: Apple Film/TVP S.A. (Poland)/MDR Arte (Germany)/Canal Plus (France).

GIRL GUIDE

Script and Dir: Juliusz Machulski. Based on a story by Michał Szczepański. Phot: Witold Adamek. Players: Renata Gabrielska, Paweł Kukiz, Tomasz Tomaszewski, Stanisław Radwan, Jean Cerbajal. Prod: Close-Up Productions for TVP S.A.

JUBILEUSZ (Jubilee)

Script and Dir: Zbigniew Kamiński. Based on the novel *Germans* by Leon Kruczkowski. Phot: Zbigniew Wichlacz. Players: Beata Tyszkiewicz, Katarzyna Figura, Edward Żentara. Prod: Rubikon (U.S.A.)/ Figaro (Poland)/APF/TVP S.A.

KRATKA (Grate)

Script: Paweł Łoziński, Piotr Czekanowski. Dir: Łoziński. Phot: Jacek Bławut. Players: Jerzy Kamas, Michał Michalak. Prod: Film Studio TOR/TVP S.A.

KROL OLCH (The Ogre)

Script: Volker Schlöndorff, Jean Claude Carrière. Dir: Schlöndorff. Phot: Bruno De Keyzer. Players: John Malkovich, Armin Müller-Stahl, William Cochrna, Gottfried John, Seino Ferch, Marianne Sägebrecht, Agnes Sorel. Prod: Studio Babelsberg GmbH/ Recorded Picture Company (London)/Heritage Films (Warsaw)/ Renn Productions.

KSIEGA WIELKICH ŻYCZEN (The Book of Great Wishes)

Script and Dir: Sławomir Kryński. Phot: Tomasz Wert. Players: Gustaw Holoubek, Aleksander Machalica, Danuta Szaflarska. Prod: SF Indeks/APF/Canal Plus/ Polsat/WFF Łódz.

MATKA SWOJEJ MATKI (One Mother Only)

Script: Joanna Żółkowska, Robert Gliński. Dir: Gliński. Phot: Jarek Szoda. Players: Maria Seweryn, Krystyna Janda, Joanna Żółkowska, Wanda Wiłkomirska, Jerzy Stuhr, Jerzy Karaszkiewicz, Stanisława Celińska, Emilian Kamiński. Prod: Heritage Films/APF/Filmcontract/ Canal Plus/TVP S.A.

ODWIEDZ MNIE WE SNIE (Visit Me in My Dream)

Script: Renata Frydrych. Dir: Teresa Kotlarczyk. Phot: Krzysztof Pakulski. Players: Danuta Stenka, Ewa Gawryluk, Joanna Jeżewska, Zbigniew Zamachowski, Emilia Szcześniak, Sławomir Orzechowski, Krystyna Tkacz. Prod: Fokus Film/APF/TVP S.A.

OPOWIESCI WEEKENDOWE (Week-End Stories)

Script and Dir: Krzysztof Zanussi. Phot: Edward Kłosiński. Prod: Film Studio TOR/TVP S.A.

1. DAMSKI INTERES (FEMININE BUSINESS)
Players: Joanna Szczepkowska, Anna Nehrebecka, Magdalena Zawadska, Magdalena Warzecha.

2. SŁABA WIARA (WEAK FAITH)
Players: Dorota Segda, Maciej Orłoś, Marek Kondrat, Stanisława Celińska, Małgorzata Pritulak.

3. UROK WSZETECZNY (LECHEROUS CHARM)
Players: Zbigniew Zapasiewicz, Maciej Robakiewicz, Katarzyna Herman.

POZNAN '56

Script: Filip Bajon, Andrzej Górny. Dir: Bajon. Phot: Łukasz Kośmicki. Players: Michał Żebrowski, Agata Kulesza, Tadeusz Szymkow, Olaf Lubaszenko, Bronisław Pawlik, Zdzisław Wardejn. Prod: Film Studio Dom/TVP S.A./Foundation Poznan '56/TVP S.A.

PANNA NIKT (Miss Nobody)

Script: Radosław Piwowarski, from a novel by Tomek Tryzna. Dir: Andrzej Wajda. Phot: Krzysztof Ptak. Players: Anna Wielgucka, Anna Mucha, Anna Powierza, Stanisława Celińska, Jan Tomaszewski. Prod: Film Studio Perspektywa/TVP S.A./WFDiF.

PO LATACH (After Years)

Script and Dir: Andrzej Barański. Phot: Krzysztof Ptak. Players: Jan Peszek, Jan Wieczorkowski, Joanna Brodzik, Marek Walczewski, Beata Tyszkiewicz, Artur Barciś, Jan Frycz, Roman Klosowski, Wladyslaw Kowalski. Prod: Skorpion Film for TVP S.A.

PUŁKOWNIK BUNKIER (Colonel Bunkier)

Script and Dir: Kujtim Cashku. Phot: Jerzy Rudziński, Albanian Cameraman. Players: Anna Nehrebecka, Albanian players. Prod: Film Studio DOM/APF (Poland) ORA Film (Albania)/3B Productions (France).

SZABLA OD KOMENDANTA (Sword from the Commander)

Script and Dir: Jan Jakub Kolski. Phot: Piotr Lenar. Players: Bronisław Pawlik, Franciszek Pieczka, Witold Pyrkosz, Wiesław Golas, Wojciech Malajkat, Grażyna Błęka-Kolska, Anna Majcher. Prod: Figaro Sp./APF/TVP S.A./Canal Plus/ Odra-Film/Film-Art.

SIODMY POKOJ (Seventh Room)

Script: Marta Mészaros, Eva Pataki, Roberta Mazzoni. Dir: Mészaros. Phot: Piotr Sobociński. Players: Maja Morgenstern, Jan Nawrocki, Adriana Asti, Anna Polony, Jerzy Radziwiłowicz. Prod: Film Studio TOR/Morgan Film/Budapest Film/ TVP S.A.

SŁODKO-GORSKI (Bitter-Sweet)

Script and Dir: Władysław Pasikowski. Phot: Paweł Edelman. Players: Anita Werner, Rafał Mohr, Rafał Olbrychski, Bogusław Linda, Cezary Pazura, Magda Stużyńska. Prod: Visa Film/Canal Plus/Łódz Film Centrum/Syrena Group/Viktonex/ Foto Relax.

SŁONECZNY ZEGAR (Sundial)

Script and Dir: Andrzej Kondratiuk. Phot: Andrzej Kijowski. Players: Katarzyna Figura, Iga Cembrzyńska, Andrzej Kondratiuk. Prod:Iga Film.

SZAMANKA (Shamanist)

Script: Manuel Gretkowska. Dir: Andrzej Żuławski. Phot: Andrzej Jaroszewicz. Players: Iwona Petrykowska, Bogusław Linda, Piotr Wawrzyńczak, Paweł Delag, Zdzisław Wardejn, Alicja Jachiewicz, Jolanta Grusznic, Piotr Machalica, Artur Krajewski, Piotr Zelt, Agnieszka Wagner, Jacek Sobieszczański. Prod: Visa Film/Canal Plus.

WEZWANIE (Emergency Call)

Script: Maciej Karpiński. Dir: Mirosław Dembiński. Phot: Witold Adamek. Player: Jadwiga Jankowska-Cieślak. Prod: Film Studio Perspektywa for Polish Television S.A.

ŻARNOWIEC

Script and Dir: Radosław Piwowarski. Phot: Piotr Wojtowicz. Players: Katarzyna Figura, Katarzyna Gajdarska, Waldemar Błaszczyk, Jerzy Trela, Zuzia Zjawińska. Prod: Studio DT Film for TVP S.A.

ŻOŁTA ROŻA (Yellow Rose)

Script and Dir: Antonio Mitricevski. Phot: Bartłomiej Maj. Players: Agnieszka Wagner, Nicola Rostanowski. Prod: SF Logos/TVP S.A./APF/Vardar Film (Macedonia)

Producers

Film Studio Dom
Puławska 61
02595 Warsaw
Tel: 48.22.455065

Film Studio Kadr
Puławska 61
02595 Warsaw
Tel: 48.22.454923

Film Studio Oko
Puławska 61
02595 Warsaw
Tel: 48.22.454041, ext. 222

Film Studio Perspektywa
Puławska 61
02595 Warsaw
Tel/Fax: 48.22.455494

Film Studio Tor
Puławska 61
02595 Warsaw
Tel/Fax: 48.22.455303

Film Studio Zebra
Puławska 61
02595 Warsaw
Tel/Fax: 48.22.455484

Film Studio Zodiak
Puławska 61
02595 Warsaw
Tel: 48.22.452047

Karol Irzykowski Film Studio
Mazowiecka 11
00052 Warsaw
Tel: 48.22.276653, 276656

Film Studio Kronika
Chełska 21
00724 Warsaw
Tel/Fax: 48.22.416221

S.F. Semafor
Pabianicka 34
93513 Łódź
Tel/Fax: 48.42.814120

Studio Indeks
Targowa 61/63
90323 Łódź
Tel: 48.42.205126

Łódź Film Centre
Łąkowa 29
90554 Łódź
Tel: 48.42.367500
Fax: 48.42. 360487

WFDiF (Wytwórnia Filmów Dokumentalnych i Fabularnych)
Chełmska 21
00724 Warsaw
Tel: 48.22.411211
Fax: 48.22.415891

Independent Producers

Apple Film Production Ltd.
Pl. Konstytucji 3/10
00647 Warsaw
Tel/Fax: 48.22.290754

Ekran Bis
Łąkowa 29
90554 Łódź
Tel: 48.42.372577
Fax: 48.42.362046

Feniks Film
Chełmska 21
00724 Warsaw
Tel/Fax: 48.22.413821

Figaro
Chełmska 21
00724 Warsaw
Tel/Fax: 48.2.6356130

Focus Producers Ltd.
Ryżowa 42
02495 Warsaw
Tel: 48.2.6627586
Fax: 48.2.6627083

Fokus Film Ltd.
Okrąg 4/45
Tel: 48.42.297003

Gambit Productions
Przemysłowa 7
02496 Warsaw
Tel/Fax: 48.2.6674596

Heritage Films
Marszałkowska 2/6
00581 Warsaw
Tel: 48.2.6252601
Fax: 48.2.6252693

Marek Nowowiejski Film Productions
Chełmska 21
00740 Warsaw
Tel/Fax: 48.2.6443400

MS Film
Chełmska 21
00724 Warsaw
Tel: 48.22.405056
Fax: 48.22.405935

N (Independent Studio "Niezależni")
Lajkonika 5
04110 Łódź
Tel: 48.42.861394

Pleograf Ltd.
pl. Mirowski 18
00138 Warsaw
Tel/Fax: 48.22.208342

MM Potocka Productions
Puzonistów 4
02876 Warsaw
Tel: 48.2.6439556
Fax: 48.2.6439553

Skorpion Film
Chełmska 21
00724 Warsaw
Tel/Fax: 48.22.416171

Distributors

Film Agency Silesia-Film
Kościuszki 88
40519 Katowice
Tel/Fax: 48.832.512284
and
al. Ujazdowskie 20/10
00478 Warsaw
Tel/Fax: 48.2.6284518

Gentrum Filmowe Graffiti Ltd.
Sw. Gertrudy 5
31046
Tel: 48.12.211628
Fax: 48.12.211402

Fundacja Sztuki Filmowej
Andersa 1
00174 Warsaw
Tel: 48.22.311636
Fax: 48.2.6352001

MAF – Młodzieżowa Akademia Filmowa
Marszałkowska 28
00639 Warsaw
Tel/Fax: 48.2.6289698

Black Cat
Magnoliowa 2
20208 Lublin
Tel/Fax: 48.81.774654

Iti Cinema
Marszałkowska 138
00004 Warsaw
Tel: 48.22.269862
Fax: 48.22.268552

Solopan Film Centrum
Krakówskie Przedmieście 21/23
00071 Warsaw
Tel/Fax: 48.2.6350044

Syrena Entertainment Group
Marszałkowska 115
00102 Warsaw
Tel: 48.22.273503
Fax: 48.22.275648

Vision
Rydygiera 7
01793 Warsaw
Tel: 48.22.390753
Fax: 48.22.391367

Imp Poland
Hoża 66/68
00950 Warsaw
Tel/Fax: 48.2.6287691

Imperial Entertainment
Kolska 12
01045 Warsaw
Tel: 48.22.472052
Fax: 48.22.430585

Artvision
Jerolimskie 125/127
01017 Warsaw
Tel: 48.2.6289315
Fax: 48.22.467239

Useful Addresses

Committee for Cinema
Krakowskie Przedmieście 21/23
00071 Warsaw
Tel: 48.22.267489
Fax: 48.22.276233

Telewizja Kraków
Ul. Krzemionki 30
30-955 Kraków
Tel: 48.12.61 50 00
Fax: 48.12.23 65 12

Script Agency
Chełmska 21
00724 Warsaw

Film Distribution Agency
Trębacka 3
00074 Warsaw
Tel: 48.2.6352038
Fax: 48.2.6351543

Film Polski
Mazowiecka 6/8
00048 Warsaw
Tel: 48.22.268455
Fax: 48.22.262370

Polish Television
Woronicza 17
00950 Warsaw
Tel: 6478000

Association of Polish Film-makers
Krakowskie Przedmieście 41
00071 Warsaw
Tel: 48.22.276785

Association of Independent Film Producers
Ryżowa 42
02495 Warsaw
Tel: 48.2.6627083

PORTUGAL

John Hopewell

Early in 1996, a youngish Portuguese director, Joaquim Leitao, achieved the unthinkable. His fourth feature, **Adam and Eve** (*Adao e Eva*), grossed a little under $1 million in Portugal, an all-time record for a domestic film. In doing so, it flew in the face of modern industry wisdom, which says that Portugal lacks a large home market, so film directors can't appeal to large audiences. Ergo, they don't have to try. For better or worse, the glory of Portuguese cineastes has also been their bane: their radical singularity and unfettered creative freedom.

Adam and Eve, moreover, impinges on the central economic and cultural debate in Portugal: its scramble to modernise. Most Portuguese films still hark back – some would say anachronistically – to auteurist attitudes of the 1960s. The accessible *Adam and Eve*, in contrast, is as modern as Portuguese films have yet come. It toplines Portugal's only homegrown Hollywood assets: Maria de Madeiros (*Pulp Fiction*) and Joaquim de Almeida (*Desperado*). It is set against the glitzy *Hola*-land of Portugal's new private TV networks. And it rings several, more outré, sexual changes.

Madeiros plays Catarina, Portugal's top TV host. She has a feisty female lover, Té, and she also takes up, but is never totally taken in by, Francisco (Almeida), a macho

Still from INÊS OF PORTUGAL

steeped in charm and whisky. And she seeks out another man, Spanish social militant Rafael, for the sole purpose of procreation. *Adam and Eve*'s farcical subplot grates at times, but this is a significant picture, setting new standards in modernity, in its focus, style, production and marketing.

Not So New Generation

Leitao's highly contemporary comedy may not herald a broader revolution in Portuguese film-making, however. True, a new generation of film-makers is now beginning to emerge – directors such as Joaquim Sapinho, Abi Feijó, Pedro Sarrazina, Teresa Villaverde and Bruno de Almeida. Yet, as with their forebears, a radical eclecticism is still the hallmark of their work.

Showcased at Locarno in 1995, and more of a calling card than a fully rounded feature, Sapinho's feature-film début, **Haircut** (*Corte de cabelo*), practises a laid-back neo-realism, laced with ciné-vérité home-video sequences. A bride, Rita (Carla Bolito), cuts her gorgeous tresses on the morning of her wedding. She and her camera-toting boyfriend marry; tiff; break-up; Rita (and the film) drifts around Lisbon; the couple finally make up.

Backed by the up-market production outfit Imagen Real, another newcomer, José Carlos de Almeida, spent much of 1996 shooting an epic, **Ines of Portugal** (*Ines de Portugal*), a visceral mediaeval mix, if rushes are anything to go by, of love, lust, betrayal, murder and torture. Treading typically disparate ground, first-timer Carlos da Silva has teamed up with the admired George Sluizer (*Utz, The Vanishing*) on **Dying to Go Home** (*Mortinho por Chegar a Casa*), an odd-ball contemporary black comedy, set for release in the autumn of 1996. And Leao Lopes had his début, the social drama **Contenda Island** (*Ilhéu de Contenda*), selected for the new directors section at the Montréal Film Festival in 1996. The most eagerly awaited film début of the year, however, is probably Bruno de Almeida's **On the Run**, a $2.0-2.5 million New York drama in the U.S. indie tradition from an English-language script by Joseph Minion, writer of Scorsese's *After Hours*.

Golden Oldies

But older generations of Portuguese directors and producers show no sign of giving up the ghost. The 88-year-old Manoel de Oliveira's new film, **Party**, starring Michel Piccoli and Irene Papas, went into post-production in mid-1996. Having made the impressive rights-of-passage film, **Signs of Fire** (*Sinais de Fogo*), about adolescents growing up in the long shadow of the Spanish Civil War, Luis Filipe Rocha is preparing **Goodbye, Father** (*Adeus Pai*), which looks like a tearjerker aimed squarely at the commercial market. Meanwhile, Oliveira's producer, the prolific, globetrotting Paulo Branco, has spread his net even wider, making films with the Paris-based Chilean, Raoul Ruíz, **Three Lives and Only One Death** (*Trois vies et une seule mort*), and the Lithuanian Sarunas Bartas, **Few of Us**, both of which played at Cannes in 1996.

Few of Us, which screened in "Un Certain Regard", takes Antonioni's non-communication to a literal, if demanding conclusion. A girl arrives in a village, becalmed in the mountains and in monotony. Some 80 film minutes later, she is suddenly attacked by two vodka-soused youths. Stunningly shot, bereft of dialogue and camera movement, *Few of Us* is a daunting exercise in aesthetic discipline which can only be taken on its own terms.

A Threat to Identity

In competition, the four-part **Three Lives and Only One Death** proved a delightful turn-up for the books with a surprisingly jocose and accessible Ruíz casting a vintage Marcello Mastroianni in four roles: an ex-husband, an ex-professor of anthropology, an ex-château owner and an industrial magnate. Ruíz finally lets on that Mastroianni's four roles are in fact different personae of the same individual, who suffers from a multi-personality disorder. One of Ruíz's running gags is that people in the film lose their identities on Rue

Still from DYING TO GO HOME, by Carlos Silva and George Sluizer

Maastricht, victims of Europeanisation. António Guterres' Socialist Party, which won Portugal's October 1995 general elections, shares something of the same fear. Through the Portuguese Film and Audiovisual Institute (IPACA), it almost doubled support for the film industry in 1996 to Esc (1,400$9.1) million. IPACA now allows directors to present their projects for funding.

It's a measure that seeks to preserve the great tradition of modern Portuguese cinema: its great disparity, bolstered by a vast, often exotic range of co-production structures, such as the Brazilian-Portuguese drama, **The Jew** (*O Judeu*), Jom Tob Azulay's harrowing tale of anti-Semitism in 18th-century Brazil. The government's new measures may ease newcomers into subsidy awards. The simple fact remains, however, that in 1996 there aren't enough of them.

Two new hothouses for talent have emerged in Lisbon. Producer Rosi Burguete aims to find funding for "Wide Shot", a portfolio of 20 fiction shorts by young film-makers. Two had been completed by May 1996.

And in Oporto, Filmografo, founded and run by the magnificent film director Abi Feijó, continues to produce some exciting animated shorts: the latest is Pedro Serrazina's **The Tale of the Cat and the Moon** (*Estória do Gato e da Lua*), an ingratiating black-and-white tale of a cat who falls in love with the moon, which drew applause during its competition screening in Cannes in 1996.

JOHN HOPEWELL represents *Variety* in Spain and Portugal and has written numerous articles and two books on Spanish cinema.

UNIPORTUGAL

PORTUGUESE FILMS
LIBRARY
FROM 1923 TO 1996

Av. Duque Loulé, 79 r/c-1050 Lisboa
Tel: 3149326/3140339 Fax: 3533075

TOP TEN GROSSING FILMS IN PORTUGAL: 1995

	Admissions
Waterworld	273,360
Pocahontas	272,100
Nell	247,346
Die Hard 3	241,828
Batman Forever	218,263
Outbreak	217,877
Disclosure	216,257
GoldenEye	215,238
First Knight	211,336
Apollo 13	201,405

Recent and Forthcoming Films

ADAO E EVA (Adam and Eve)

Script and Dir: Joaquim Leitao. Phot: Juan Molina. Players: Maria de Madeiros, Joaquim de Almeida, Karra Elejaide, Ana Bustorff. Prod: MGN Filmes/SIC (Portugal)/CPA (Spain)/Artcam (France).

ADEUS PAI (Goodbye, Father)

Script and Dir: Luis Filipe Rocha.

CINCO DIAS, CINCO NOITES (Five Days, Five Nights)

Script: José Fonseca e Costa, Jennifer Field, from the novel by Manuel Tiago. Phot: Affonso Beato. Players: Vitor Norte, Paulo Pires, Ana Padrao, Canto e Castro. Prod: Madragoa Filmes.

CORTE DE CABELO (Haircut)

Script and Dir: Joaquim Sapinho. Phot: Luis Correia. Players: Carla Bolito, Marco Delgado, Francisco Nascimento, Manuela Viegas. Prod: Rosa Filmes.

DYING TO GO HOME (aka The Crows of Saint Vincent).

Script: Carlos da Silva, Jennifer Field. Dir: da Silva, George Sluizer. Phot: Theo Bierkens. Players: Diogo Infante, Maria d'Aires, Huub Stapel, Jack Wouterse, Phoa Yan Tiong, Cecilia Guimaraes. Prod: Europa 7 Filme (Portugal)/Taiga Filmes (Netherlands)/The Spice Factory (U.K.)/Tiger Films.

FEW OF US

Script, Dir and Phot: Sarunas Bartas. Players: Katerina Golubeva, Sergei Tulayev, Minoru Hodeshima, Piotr Kishteev. Prod: Madragoa Filmes (Portugal)/Gemini Films (France)/ Studio Kinema (Lithuania).

INES DE PORTUGAL (Ines of Portugal)

Script: José Carlos de Almeida, Joao Aguiar. Dir and Phot: de Almeida. Players: Ruy de Carvalho, Cristina Homem de Mello, Heitor Lourenço. Prod: Imagem Real/Edecine (Portugal)/ C. Producciones/TVG (Spain)/ Odessa (France).

ILHÉU DE CONTENDA (Contenda Island)

Script: José Fanha, Leao Lopes. Dir: Lopes. Phot: Joao Abel Aboím. Players: Joao Lourenço, Camacho Costa, Isabel de Castro, Filipe Ferrer. Prod: Vermedia/Sociedade de Produçao de Projectos/Saga Film.

O JUDEU (The Jew)

Script: Geraldo Carneiro, Millor Fernandes, Gilvan Pereira. Dir: Jom Tob Azulay. Phot: Eduardo Serra. Players: Felipe Pinheiro, Dina Sfat, Mário Viegas, José Lewgoy. Prod: Animatógrafo/ Produçao de Filmes/Metrofilme (Portugal)/Tatu Filmes/A & B Produçoes (Brazil).

ON THE RUN

Script: Joseph Minion. Dir: Bruno de Almeida. Prod: MGN Filmes.

OS OLHOS DA ASIA (The Eyes of Asia)

Script: Joao Mário Grilo, Paulo Filipe. Dir: Grilo. Phot: Joao Paulo Costa. Players: Joao Perry, Geraldine Chaplin, Yoshi Oida. Prod: Madragoa Filmes (Portugal)/Gemini Films (France).

PARTY

Script and Dir: Manoel de Oliveira. Phot: Renato Berta. Players: Irene Papas, Leonor Silveira, Michel Piccoli, Rogério Samora. Prod: Madragoa Filmes/Gemini Films (France).

PO DI SANGUI

Script: Flora Gomes, Anita Fernandez. Dir: Gomes. Phot:

Vincenzo Marano. Players: Edna das Neves, Ramiro Naka, Jorge Quintino Biague, Iapatia Karina de Sá Silva. Prod: S.P. Filmes/ Les Matins Film (France)/SP Filmes/Arco Iris.

TROIS VIES ET UNE SEULE MORT (Three Lives and Only One Death)

Script: Raoul Ruíz, Pascal Bonitzer. Dir: Ruíz. Phot: Laurent Machuel. Players: Marcello Mastroianni, Anna Galiena, Marisa Paredes. Prod: Gemini Films.

Producers

Animatógrafo/Companhia de Filmes do Principe Real
Rua de Rosa, 252, 2º
1200 Lisbon
Tel: (351) 1 3475372
Fax: (351) 1 3473252

Europa 7
Rua dos Caetanos, 16 - 1º
1200 Lisbon
Tel: (351) 1 3430488
Fax: (351) 1 3429677

Filmógrafo
Rua Nova da Alfandega, 108, 1º
4000 Oporto
Tel: (351) 2 2088152
Fax: (351) 2 2088153

Francisco Manso Produçao-Realizagao Cinema e TV
Avenida Almirante Reis, 1, 1º, DTº
1150 Lisbon
Tel: (351) 1 8851758
Fax: (351) 1 8852678

G.E.R. (Grupo de Estudos e Relizaçoes)
Av. Estados Unidos América 51, 5ºD
1700 Lisbon
Tel: (351) 1 804677
Fax: (351) 1 8489801

Madragoa Filmes/Gemini Films
Av. D. Manuel 1, nº 3
2890 Alcochete
Lisbon
Tel: (351) 1 2342185/2225/2233
Fax: (351) 1 2342202

MGN Filmes
Rua de S. Bento, 644, 4º Esq.
1200 Lisbon
Tel: (351) 1 3887276
Fax: (351) 1 3887281

Rosa Filmes
Campo de Cebolas, 17, 2º, Esqº
1100 Lisbon
Tel: (351) 1 8880325
Fax: (351) 1 8870827

S.P. Filmes
Rúa Das Pracas, 60, 1º DTº
Lisbon
Tel: (351) 3964222/3960225
Fax: (351) 3971352

Distributors

Filmes Castelo Lopes
Rua de Sto Amaro à Estrêla, 17A
1200 Lisbon
Tel: (351) 1 3955951/2/6
Fax: (351) 1 3955924

Filmes Lusomundo
Praça de Alegría, 22
1294 Lisbon
Tel: (351) 1 3474561
Fax: (351) 1 3465349

Atalanta Filmes
Av. Joao Crisóstomo, 38 C, 1º, Esc.3
1000 Lisbon
Tel: (351) 1 3531585/9
Fax: (351) 1 3531636

Useful Addresses

Instituto Português da Arte Cinematográfica e Audiovisual (IPACA)
Rua S. Pedro de Alcántara 45, -1º
1200 Lisbon
Tel: (351) 1 3466634/3468445
Fax: (351) 1 3472777

Media Desk, Portugal
Rua S. Pedro de Alcántara, 45, 1º
1200 Lisbon
Tel: (351) 1 3478644
Fax: (351) 1 3478643

Radiotelevisao Comercial (RTC)
Av. Fontes Pereira de Melo, 17-19, 2º-3º
1000 Lisbon
Tel: (351) 1 3528835
Fax: (351) 1 3557076

Radiotelevisao Portuguesa (RTP)
Av. 5 de Outubro, 197
1094 Lisbon Codex
Tel: (351) 1 7575070/7931774
Fax: (351) 1 7933054

Tobis Portuguesa
Praça Bernardino Machado
1700 Lisbon
Tel: (351) 1 7595425
Fax: (351) 1 7589622

Sociedade Independente de Comunicaçao (SIC)
Estrada da Outurela, 119
Linda-A-Velha
2795 Carnaxide
Tel: (351) 1 4173138/71
Fax: (351) 1 4173119/20

Televisao Independente (TVI)
Edificio Al Tejo, Rua 3, 6' piso, Sala 609
Urbaniçao de Matunha
1900 Lisbon
Tel: (351) 1 8687970
Fax: (351) 1 7941241

Tobis Portuguesa
Praça Bernardino Machado
1700 Lisbon
Tel: (351) 1 7595425
Fax: (351) 1 7589622

UniPortugal
Av. Duque de Loulé, 79 - r/c
1000 Lisbon
Tel: (351) 1 3140339/9326
Fax: (351) 1 3533075

(continued from page 154)

Recent and Forthcoming Films

OI APONTES (The Absent Ones)

Script: Nikos Panayotopoulos, Nikos Grammatikos. Dir: N. Grammatikos. Players: Nikos Georgakis, Georgios Evyenikos, Vangelis Mourikis, Tassos Noussias, Constantinos Staridas, Emilios Hilakis, Antonis Antoniou. Prod: Hyperion Productions/ Greek Film Centre.

OLA TA DILINA (All the Twilights)

Script and Dir: Mathios Yamalakis. Prod: Greek Film Centre/Swedish Television/ Mathios Yamalakis.

PARALAVETE DIORISMON (The Appointment)

Script: Michalis Ahouriotis, Christos Papadimoulis, Spyros Grintzos. Dir: M. Ahouriotis. Players: Antonis Theodorakopoulos, Vassilis Eftaxopoulos, Manolis Destouinis, Katy Ibrohori, Dinos Makris, Telemachus Papageorgiou, Yannis Emmanouil. Prod: Greek Film Centre/Olympus Films E.E./ Cinerama Ltd.

O ERYENIS (The Bachelor)

Script: Nikos Panayotopoulos, Vangelis Raptopoulos. Dir: N. Panayotopoulos. Players: Stratos Tzortzoglou, Kariofilia Karabeti, Akis Sakellariou, Lida Matsangou, Stathis Livathinos, Natalia Dragoumi. Prod: Greek Film Centre/Mariana Films.

VALKANIZATER (The Balkan Connection)

Script and Dir: Sotiris Goritsas. Players: Gerassimos Skiadaressis, Yota Festa, Stelios Mainas. Prod: Greek Film Centre/Mythos/Sotiris Goritsas/Tchapline Film (Bulgaria)/ Thelma Film (Switzerland).

O VARONOS (The Baron)

Script: Babis Tsikliropoulos. Dir: Nikos Zervos. Players: Costas Kakkavas, Vana Pefani, Alkis Panagiotides, Georgia Zoi, Alina Fotetsou. Prod: Greek Film Centre/Forum/Dionysis Maniatis.

PRIN TO TELOS TOU KOSMOU (Before the End of the World)

Script and Dir: Panayotis Maroulis. Players: Aris Lembessoploulos, Olia Lazaridou, Christos Kalavrouzos, Giorgos Kentros, Giorgos Moroyannis, Costas Flokatoulas. Prod: Hyperion Productions/Greek Film Centre.

BLACK-OUT

Script and Dir: Menelaos Karamangiolis. Players: Hanna Schygulla, Myrto Alikaki, Cleon Grigoriadis, Alkis Kourkoulos, Kariofilia Karabeti, Dimitris Papaioannou, Nikos Georgakis, Elena Nathanail, Freddy Vianellis. Prod: Greek Film Centre/ Pausilypon Films Ltd/MACT Production (France)/ Animatografo Producao de Filmes (Portugal).

BUSINESS STA VALKANIA (Business in the Balkans)

Script and Dir: Vassilis Boudouris. Players: Alexandros Logothetis, Costas Evripiotis, Vassilis Diamantopoulos, Natalia Dragoumi, Daniela Nane. Prod: Vassilis Alatas.

CAVAFY

Script and Dir: Ianis Smaragdis. Players: Vassilis Diamantopoulos, Dimitris Katalifos, Dimitris Papadimitriou. Prod: Greek Film Centre/ETI/Lumiere LTT Cyprus/ Alexandros Film.

O ORGASMOS TIS AGELADAS (Cow's Orgasm)

Script: Olga Mallea, Apostolos Alexopoulos, (in collaboration with) Yannis Botsis. Dir. O. Mallea. Players: Natalia Stylianou, Irini Balta, Eleni Yerassimidou, Iro Mane, Costas Koklas, Vladimiros Kyriakidis. Prod: Hyperion Productions, Attica.

ONEIRO SE ASPRO FONDO (Dream Against a White Background)

Script and Dir: Dimitris Spyrou. Players: Vassilis Langos, Katia Gerou, Vassilis Kolovos, Adamantios Lemos. Prod: Greek Film Centre/Dimitris Spyrou.

ELEATIS XENOS

Script and Dir: Dimos Theos. Players: Regina Remencius, Telemachos Krevaikas, Yannis Nezis, Costas Yantzos, Iphigenia Makatouni. Prod: Greek Film Centre/Dimos Theos Productions/ Asia Film (Turkey)/ Focus Film (Hungary).

O KATO KOSMOS (Hades)

Script: Stelios Haralambopoulos, Thanos Lambropoulos, (in collaboration with Vangelis Papadakis). Dir: S. Haralambopoulos. Players: Giorgos Moroyannis, Nadia Deliglanni, Marianthe, Sontaki, Evri Sofroniadi, Dimitris Tzoumakis, Pericles Moustakis, Manos Vacoussis, Panos Cranidiotis. Prod: Thanos Lambropoulos/Greek Film Centre.

IDAII MYTHI (Idaean Myths)

Script and Dir: L. Haronitis. Prod: Greek Film Centre/L. Haronitis. *Documentary.*

MARIA-ELECTRA

Script and Dir: Stella Belessi. Players: Alexandra Batsalia, Giorgos Zachariadis, Vana Xylouri, Stelios Kalathas. Prod: Selini Films/Greek Film Centre/ Orphee Productions (France)/ Katerina Pavla Rakovska (Bulgaria).

SFAGI TOU KOKORA (Slaughter of the Cock)

Script: Dimitris Nollas, Andreas Pantzis. Dir. A. Pantzis. Players: Valeria Golino, Seymour Cassel, George Choraface, Mathias Habisch, Imma Piro. Prod: Greek Film Centre/Kourian Film/ Stephania Film Production (Cyprus)/Nutrimenti Terrestri (Italy)/Mallam for Cinema and TV (Syria)/Ishkov Film (Bulgaria).

TRIS EPOCHES (Three Seasons)

Script: Maria Iliou, Giorgos Bramos. Dir: M. Iliou. Players: Yota Festa, Giorgos Constas, Grigoris Patrikareas, Fenya Papadodima, T. Apostolou, George Moutsios. Prod: Greek Film Centre/Poli-Plio Films/Ognon Pictures (France).

MI MOU APTOU (Touch Me Not)

Script and Dir: Dimitris Yiatzusakis. Players: Giorgos Ninios, Eleni Gasouka, Rania Schiza, Costas Sfikas, Paschalis Tsarouchas, Sotiris Catsenos, Maria Kyriaki, Costas Kafassis, Costas Tzouvaras, Taygeti. Prod: Greek Film Centre/ Cinegram S.A./Anosi S.A./ Dimitris Yiatzusakis.

PROS TIN ELEFTHERIA (Towards Freedom)

Script: Haris Papadopoulos, M. Faeinos. Dir. H. Papadopoulos. Players: Mary Chronopoulou, Nikos Kourkoulos, Dimitris Papamichail, Giorgos Kimoulis, Stratos Tzortoglou. Prod: Greek Film Centre/Dourios Ippos.

ANEMOS PANO APO TIN POLI (Wind Over the City)

Script: Petros Sevastikoglou, Olga Mikhailova, (in collaboration with) Alexandros Kakavas. Dir: P. Sevastikoglou. Players: Marina Vlady, Zinoviev Gert, Sergei Desnitski, Genadi Nazarof, Anna Yanofskaia, Taras Koliadof. Prod: Stefi Film/Greek Film Centre.

The Ultimate Entertainment
Resource Guide On CD-ROM

- 10 years of box office data
- 200 entertainment industry events
- 800 theatrical reviews
- 1,500 production & distribution company phone numbers
- 1,000 L.A. restaurant listings
- on-location production information and more

COMPACT
VARIETY

For information, call (213) 549-4180 or e-mail compact@variety.cahners.com

ROMANIA

Cristina Corciovescu

Romanian cinema, unfortunately, has yet to find its feet after the 1989 'earthquake'. This was beneficial in terms of opening up freedom of speech, but a real disaster for the financial state of the film industry. Yearly production is still five to six films, and audiences in the cinema halls are in constant decline. Consequently, the future of the national cinema is in the hands of those managers able to find the best financial facilities. In this respect, film production in Romania is governed by two patterns: the old one, made up of the "misfits", is still captive to the old models, still dependent on state subvention (enough for four films a year at the most); the "flexibles", on the other hand, are eager to fight for private investment both from Romania and abroad.

The Independents

It is best to start with them, as their efficiency has been obvious for the last few years. The most ambitious Romanian film producer is Titi Popescu, one of the most skilled former executives at the National Film Studio, Bucharest, currently the head of the FILMEX Studio. He aims to produce high-quality work which will not only interest the domestic audience but also the international film festivals. The projects will capitalise on well-known talents and also promote gifted new ones. Last but not least, FILMEX will hopefully find its own place among international film producers. These goals were realised (with the help of MK2, Canal Plus, etc.) in a number of works which represented Romania in several international competitions.

Among them were: **The Oak** (1992), **An Unforgettable Summer** (1994), **Too Late** (1996) – all directed by Lucian Pintilie, certainly the most prominent contemporary film-maker; and some débuts: **Where the Sun Is Cold** (1990) by Bogdan Dumitrescu, **Trahir** (1992) by Radu Mihaileanu and **E pericoloso sporgersi** (1992) by Nae Caranfil. FILMEX also served as executive producer in some international productions located in Romania: **Nostradamus** (1993) by Roger Christian, and Bertrand Tavernier's recent **Captain Conan**. These were complicated productions, involving period sets for the first and thousands of extras for the second, which takes place during WW1.

Domino Film, a younger studio, was exclusively involved in 1995 on producing (alongside Les Films du Rivage, France) the second film of Nae Caranfil, **Asphalt Tango**, an ambiguous road movie starring Charlotte Rampling. Two other independent studios are Atlantis Film, which has recently turned to producing films for television in conjunction with producers from abroad (TF1, France 2, M6), and Castel Film, which has co-produced American movies such as **Oblivion** and seems to have already created its own audience.

Hidden Things

The most interesting of all the 1995 premières is **State of Things**, directed by Stere Gulea (main prize at the 1st edition of the San Marino Film Festival). The story takes place during *those* days of December '89: a young nurse is involved in the upheavals and discovers, first in amazement then in terror, the hidden nature of the political system. Finally, she becomes one of the victims of the security system, which still has everything under control. A film directed with an outstanding control of dramatic tension, this is an impressive drama of the individual crushed by the machinery of power, a film which displays both the director's skill and political commitment.

Still from STATE OF THINGS

The same events – seen from a different political point of view, and at a different level of artistry – are at the core of **Point Zero**, the most recent work of the veteran Sergiu Nicolaescu. This is an action movie whose pretext – during December '89, two American secret agents come to Romania to get the Ceausescu jewellery – immediately consigns it to the cheap exploitation category. Two other well-known film-makers who seem recently to have tired are Andrei Blaier, whose **Terente** – inspired by a real character – disguises its emptiness with vulgar commercialism, and Mircea Veroiu, whose **At the Orient's Gates** does not achieve the beauty and subtlety of the original, a classic Romanian novel.

1995 was also the year of Marius Sopterean's début with **Confession**, a strange love story unfortunately damaged by an overly obvious – even if sincere and well-intended – religious message.

CRISTINA CORCIOVESCU is a film critic, film producer and author of several books on cinema.

TOP TEN GROSSING FILMS IN ROMANIA: 1995

	Admissions
The Specialist	673,600
Paradise Live (Romanian)	564,538
Time Cop	563,545
Street Fighter	497,058
Baby's Day Out	447,004
Forrest Gump	423,440
Bad Boys	327,784
Junior	315,312
Interview with the Vampire	292,606
Batman Forever	282,992

Producers

Atlantis Film
Str. Gral. Berthelot nr. 52
Bucharest
Tel: (401) 312 48 50
Fax: (401) 312 40 25

Castel Film
Str. Lucaci nr. 44
Bucharest
Tel: (401) 621 50 65
Fax: (401) 322 38 79

Cinerom
Bd. M. Kogalniceanu nr. 11, sector 5
Bucharest
Tel: (401) 311 27 10
Fax: (401) 311 30 80

Domino Film
Str. Dr. Felix nr. 59, et. 1
Bucharest
Tel: (401) 210 37 13/223 46 69
Fax: (401) 312 96 09

Filmex
Str. Pictor Verona nr. 2, sector 1
Bucharest
Tel: (401) 615 89 13/615 90 38
Fax: (401) 312 13 88

Distributors

Guild Film Romania
Bd. Republicii nr. 51, et. 1, ap. 7
Bucharest
Tel: (401) 614 88 46
Fax: (401) 312 50 95

Media Pictures International
Str. Armeneasca nr. 8
Bucharest
Tel: (401) 614 01 56
Fax: (401) 312 41 40

Q.C.B.
Str. Piscului nr. 16, sector 4
Bucharest
Tel/Fax: (401) 675 44 01

Romania Film
Str. Thomas Massaryk nr. 25
70231 Bucharest
Tel: (401) 210 73 98/210 78 35
Fax: (401) 611 76 60

Useful Addresses

Centrul National al Cinematografiei
Str. Thomas Massaryk, nr. 25
70231 Bucharest
Tel: (401) 211 25 16
Fax: (401) 211 36 88

Uniunea Cineastilor
Str. Mendeleev nr. 28-30, sector 1
70169 Bucharest
Tel: (401) 650 42 65
Fax: (401) 311 12 46

Film School
Romania
Academia de Teatru si Film
Str. Matei Voievod nr. 75-77, sector 2
73226 Bucharest
Dean: Elisabeta Bostan

Film Archive
Romania
Arhiva Nationala de filme
Str. Thomas Massaryk nr. 25
70231 Bucharest
Tel/Fax: (401) 211 22 60
Director: Savel Stiopul

Magazine
ProCinema
Str. Luterana nr. 11, et. 2, sector 1
Bucharest
Tel: (401) 323 58 56
Fax: (401) 323 59 92
Monthly with reviews, profiles, articles and interviews

RUSSIA

Andrew Horton & Michael Brashinsky

One of the biggest hits in Russia last season was **All Will Be Well** *(Vsyo budet khorosho)*, a comic melodrama directed by Dmitry Astrakhan. A cynical crowd-pleaser, it proved how desperate Russian audiences have grown and how much they are willing to forgive just for the promise of the title. "All will be well" – nothing could be more welcome in a country stuck at a political and economic crossroads, exhausted by the unending Chechen war and frightened by the newly materialised Communist threat.

By some peculiar logic, the year of cinema's centenary turned out to be one of the weakest in recent memory, almost everywhere in the world. In Russia, it was worsened by economic instability, resulting in an almost complete withdrawal of private capital from the industry, which made this the most difficult of the post-Soviet film seasons.

On a spring day in 1996, 119 films were playing in and around Moscow; of them, only 17 were Russian. "In order for the St. Petersburg industry to survive", wrote Alexander Golutva, the Director General of Lenfilm Concern, "it must produce at least

Sergei Bodrov, Jr., in PRISONER OF THE MOUNTAINS

ten features a year". Only eight were made this past season by Lenfilm, while Mosfilm, the country's main major, completed 17. In May 1996, 11 features were in pre-production at Mosfilm; four were in production and four in post-production. Four productions were stalled.

Of the 35 features made in 1995 with the participation of Roskomkino, the State Ministry of Film, 15 were fully and the rest partially financed by the state. This was six titles more than in 1994, the ministry's statistics said; but what it didn't say was that, a year ago, the state was investing in less than half of the country's output, while this year the figure 35 represents three-quarters of Russia's output. (Curious to note the 'generic' breakdown of the season's films: of the 35, Roskomkino states, ten were "films on contemporary themes"; seven were adaptations of Russian literary classics; eight were historical pictures; six were comedies and four were films for children and young adults.)

Russian film-makers would like to believe that this was the most crucial year of chaos and crisis. "The worst is over", they cite a popular joke. "Now let's see if the patient is alive". It has become clear that the only way for the national cinema to survive is through state support. The system has finally come full circle and become centralised, but the state still has no funds to invest in moving images.

Lumière, Balalaika and Co.

Loud fanfares at the St. Petersburg "Aquarium" theatre marked the occasion, on May 4, 1896, of the first public screening in Russia. Nearby, a small crowd of unemployed documentary film-makers had gathered, holding placards that read, "One day of your festivities costs one year in the work of our studio!" (Production of non-fiction cinema has practically ceased this season.) On screen, the centenary was marked by **Arrival of the Train** *(Pribytie poezda)*. The American *Four Rooms* meets the French *Lumière & Co.* in this self-conscious compilation of four unrelated shorts by Russia's leading young directors.

The omnibus takes off with Alexander Khvan's "The Wedding March" *(Svadebnyi marsh)*, a piece of film-school Antonioni-ism, in which lovers lie in bed with their backs to each other and say painful things like, "How could you?", instead of participating in Russia's growing capitalist economy. Formally trim, "Exercise #5" (the director, Dmitry Meskhiev, must have meant us to think of *8½*) takes place on an idle movie set and is shot from the 'point of view' of an inactive camera. It says nothing, but does so nicely. Vladimir Khotinenko, maker of the 1993 hit *Makarov*, called his entry "The Road" (*Doroga*); it's a trip into the contemporary Russian landscape, starting off from Fellini's *La Strada*, although the result is rather forced and mechanical. The most successful of the four is Alexei Balabanov's stylish and poignant "Trofim", set in 1904. A Russian peasant, who has killed his younger brother, flees to St. Petersburg and is accidentally filmed by a Lumière cinematographer, making a picture called *L'Arrivée d'un train russe.* In 1995, he is cut out of the footage by the film-makers, interested only in the images of the railway station.

Cinema Year Zero

Incidentally, that start of a new century in film meant more than just a historical celebration for the country's film-makers. Having so vigorously deconstructed the old Soviet culture in the years after *glasnost*, they now find themselves without a foundation, and no national cinema is possible in such a state. True, the Soviet culture was undemocratic, heavily censored, isolationist and artificially bred. But it also provided a high standard of quality and a tradition that went beyond the dogma of "socialist realism". Many contemporary Russian films look and sound amateur, as though made by professionals who have set about unlearning every skill they had because it was taught them by an unjust teacher. Some, unconsciously, look back to the past.

Oleg Menshikov in PRISONER OF THE MOUNTAINS

Moscow Holiday (*Moskovskiye kanikuly*) is an inane screwball comedy which tries to recreate the charm of the Soviet romantic comedy of the 1970s (it was written by Alexander Braginsky, the co-creator of the most successful of those, Eldar Ryazanov's *The Irony of Fate* and *The Office Romance*). Some, like Karen Shakhnazarov's **American Daughter** *(Amerikanskaya doch)*, look hopefully to the West. A father-and-child road movie, this could be retitled *Moscow, Texas*, complete with Ry Cooderesque guitar score and even a husband-and-wife telephone conversation through thick plexiglass.

The more inspired works in this grim film season were comedies. Russia's response to Robert Altman (and the highest-grossing film of the year) was **Hodge-Podge** *(Shirli-Myrli)*, by Vladimir Menshov, the director of the Oscar-winning *Moscow Does Not Believe in Tears.* This featured just about every Russian-speaking movie star in a madcap, low-comedy adventure. From St. Petersburg came Alexander Rogozhkin's **The Peculiarities of the National Hunt** *(Osobennosti natsionalnoi okhoty)*, a droll, absurdist farce in the vein of *The Discreet*

Charm of the Bourgeoisie, about a group of six men, five Russians and a Finn who is writing a book on Russian hunting. In Buñuel's film, the characters never got to eat; in Rogozhkin's film, they never get to hunt. Instead, they drink heavily and go through a series of 'tall tales'. The film makes fun of several Russian peculiarities, including the inability to match the word to the deed and a passionate urge to lie to foreigners about their country.

By far the best Russian film of the year was Sergei Bodrov's **Prisoner of the Mountains** *(Kavkazsky plennik),* based on a Tolstoy novella that is set – a century and a quarter ago – in war-torn Chechnya. The film follows two modern-day Russian PoWs – one a wide-eyed recruit (the director's son, Sergei Bodrov Jnr., in an impressive acting début), another a burnt-out romantic (Oleg Menshikov, from *Burnt by the Sun*). A natural-born storyteller, Bodrov comes of directorial age in this picture: one can tell by how the screen gleams and pulsates *outside* the story. The film plays like a military march on a gramophone whose speed is slightly off; its air is at once dense and transparent. The tension comes from a subtle juxtaposition of the characters – whose development is psychologically spare – with the landscape, whose breathtaking richness seems inappropriate, even mocking. In its unsentimental tone, in its distrust of close-ups and faith in gesture, Bodrov's style resembles Bresson's.

Bodrov is one of the few Russian film-makers who remained unaffected by the debilitating turmoil of the post-*glasnost* years (in part, because he divided his time between Moscow and Los Angeles). This may be what the Russian cinema has to do to survive the chaos: shake off the immediate past and realise itself as part of the world.

MICHAEL BRASHINSKY writes a film column for *The Westsider* in New York City and teaches film studies at the School of Visual Arts. He is co-author of *The Zero Hour: Glasnost and Soviet Cinema in Transition* and co-editor of *Russian Critics on the Cinema of Glasnost* (both with Andrew Horton).

Recent and Forthcoming Films

AMERIKANSKAYA DOCH (American Daughter)

Script: Alexander Borodyansky, Karen Shakhnazarov. Dir: Shakhnazarov. Phot: Vladimir Shevtsik. Players: Alison Whitbeck, Vladimir Mashkov, Mariya Shukshina, Armen Dzhigarkhanian. Prod: Karavan Ltd./Boris Giller.

BARYSHNYA-KRESTYANKA (The Lady Peasant)

Script: Alexander Zhitinsky, Alexei Sakharov, based on a novella by Alexander Pushkin. Dir: Sakharov. Phot: Nikolai Nemolyaev. Players: Yelena Korikova, Leonid Kuravlyov, Vassily Lanovoi. Prod: Ritm Studio (Mosfilm) /Roskomkino.

DELEGATSIYA (The Delegation)

Script and Dir: Alexander Galin. Phot: Mikhail Agranovich. Players: Inna Churikova, Luca Barbareschi, Ekaterina Grabbe, Yelena Mayorova, Tamara Kotikova, Tatyana Galchenko, Andrei Smirnov. Prod: Casanova Entertainment (Russian/Italian).

DEREVYANNAYA KOMNATA (The Wooden Room)

Script and Dir: Yevgeny Yufit, Vladimir Maslov. Phot: Roman Lugovskoi. Players: Tatyana Verkhovskaya, Vladimir Maslov, Igor Bezrukov, Sergei Tsvetkov. Prod: Mzhalala-Film.

KAKAYA CHUDNAYA IGRA (What a Wonderful Game)

Script and Dir: Pyotr Todorovsky. Phot: Yury Raisky. Players: Andrei Ilyin, Gennady Nazarov, Denis Konstantinov, Gennady Mitnik. Prod: TPF Mirabel/Krug (Mosfilm)/Roskomkino/TV6/ Russian Film Company.

KAVKAZSKY PLENNIK (Prisoner of the Mountains)

Script: Arif Aliev, Sergei Bodrov, Boris Giller. Dir: Bodrov. Phot: Pavel Lebeshev. Players: Oleg Menshikov, Sergei Bodrov Jnr., Susanna Mekhralieva, Jemal Sikharulidze, Alexander Bureyev, Valentina Fedotova, Alexei Zharkov. Prod: AO Karavan/BG Productions/Roskomkino.

KONTSERT DLYA KRYSY (Concert for a Rat)

Script: Timur Vaulin, Oleg Kovalov, Vladimir Maslow. Dir: Kovalov. Phot: Evgeny Shermergor. Players: Yelena Savina, Pyotr Zaitchenko, Fedor Konovalov. Prod: Lenfilm/ Hermitage Bridge/ Roskomkino.

LETNIYE LYUDI (Summer People)

Script: Sergei Ursulyak, based on

a play *The Vacationers* by Maxim Gorky. Dir: Ursulyak. Phot: Sergei Yurizditsky. Players: Sergei Makovetsky, Irina Kupchenko, Svetlana Ryabova. Prod: Roskomkino/East-European Film Company.

MANIYA ZHIZELI (Giselle's Mania)

Script: Dunya Smirnova, Alexei Uchitel. Dir: Uchitel. Phot: Sergei Lando. Players: Galina Tyunina, Mikhail Kazakov, Yevgeny Sidikhin, Sergei Vinogradov, Ivan Okhlobystin, Andrei Smirnov. Prod: Roskomkino/Lenfilm/Rock Studios.

MOSKOVSKIYE KANIKULY (Moscow Holiday)

Script: Emil Braginsky. Dir: Alla Surikova. Players: Leonid Yarmolnik, Irina Selezneva, Natalya Gundareva. Prod: MAVR/ Roskomkino.

MUZYKA DLYA DEKABRYA (Music for December)

Script: Ivan Dykhovichny, Marina Sheptunova. Dir: Dykhovichny. Phot: Sergei Kozlov. Players: Yelena Safonova, Dmitry Dykhovichny, Grigory Gladyi, Natalia Zhukova. Prod: Tzekh.

OSOBENNOSTI NATSIONALNOI OKHOTY (Peculiarities of the National Hunt)

Script and Dir: Alexander Rogozhkin. Phot: Andrei Zhegalov. Players: Ville Haapassalo, Alexei Buldakov, Viktor Bychkov, Semen Strugachev, Sergei Kupriyanov, Sergei Russkin. Prod: Lenfilm/ Roskomkino.

PERVAYA LYUBOV (First Love)

Script and Dir: Roman Balaian, based on a short novel by Ivan Turgenev. Phot: Pavel Lebeshev. Players: Anna Mikhalkova, Oleg Yankovsky, Andrei Ishchenko, Marina Neyolova, Alexander Abdulov. Prod: Ostrov/Roskomkino/ Innova-Film.

PRIBYTIE POEZDA (Arrival of the Train)

The Wedding March. Script: Alexander Detkov. Dir: Alexander Khvan. Phot: Anatoly Susekov. Players: Anna Syomkina, Alexander Kaidanovsky, Alexei Zhirov.

Exercise #5. Script: A. Tigai. Dir: Dmitry Meskhiev. Phot: S. Machilsky. Players: A. Krasko, Nina Usatova, Irina Metlitskaya.

Trofim. Script: Alexei Balavanov, Sergei Selyanov. Dir: Balabanov. Phot: Sergei Astakhov. Players: Sergei Makovetsky, Igor Shibanov, Zoya Bouriak.

The Road. Script: Valery Zolotukha. Dir: Vladimir Khotinenko. Phot: Georgy Rerberg. Players: Yevgeniya Smolyaninova, Garik Sukachevm, Vladimir Ilyin. Prod: Roskomkino/Kinoforum/Association of Young Film-makers/NTV.

SHIRLI-MYRLI (Hodge-Podge/ What a Mess . . .)

Script: Vladimir Menshov, Vitaly Moskalenko, Andrei Samsonov. Dir: Menshov. Phot: Vadim Alisov. Players: Valery Garkalin, Vera Alentova, Inna Churikova, Armen Dzhigarkhanian, Oleg Tabakov. Prod: Mosfilm/Genre Studios/Roskomkino/Tepcobank.

VREMYA PECHALI ESHCHYO NE PRISHLO (The Time for Sorrow Hasn't Come Yet)

Script: Mikhail Konovalchiuk and Sergei Selyanov. Dir: Selyanov. Phot: Denis Shchiglovsky. Players: Valery Priemykhov, Pyotr Mamonov, Marina Levtova, Mikhail Svetin. Prod: Lenfilm Studio.

VSYO BUDET KHOROSHO (All Will Be Well)

Script: Oleg Danilov. Dir: Dmitry Astrakhan. Phot: Yuri Vorontsov. Players: Olga Ponezova, Anatoly Guravlyov, Alexander Zbruyev, Mark Garanok. Prod: Nicola Film/Fora Film/Roskomkino/Lenfilm Studios.

ZONA LYUBE (Zone of Lyube)

Script and Dir: Dmitry Zolotukhin. Phot: Oleg Martynov. Players: Marina Leftova. Prod: Belyi Veter Concern/Matvienko Centre.

Useful Addresses

Double D Agency
(sociological research, publishing)
7 Maly Gnezdnikovsky per.
Suite 604
103877 Moscow
Tel: (095) 229-7921
Fax: (095) 369-1815

Gorky Film Studios
8 Eisenstein St.
129226 Moscow
Fax: (095) 188-9871
Telex: 411941

Intercinema Agency
(distribution, production)
Contact: Raissa Fomina at Kinocentre (see below)

Kinocentre
(programmes, publishing, museum, information, production)
15 Druzhinnikovskaya St.
123242 Moscow
Tel: (095) 255-9489 or 255-9087
Fax: (095) 973-2029
Telex: 411070 CENTRE

Lenfilm Concern
10 Kemennoostrovsky Ave.
197101 St. Petersburg
Tel: (812) 232-8374
Fax: (812) 232-8881 or 233-2174
Telex: 121534 FILM SU

Mosfilm Concern
1 Mosfilmovskaya St.
119858 Moscow
Tel: (095) 147-7042
Fax: (095) 938-2083
Telex: 411293 MSFILM SU

Tri Te Studios
11 Maly Kozikhinsky Lane
103009 Moscow

TTL Studio
8 Eisenstein St.
129226 Moscow
Tel: (095) 181-6052
Fax: (095) 188-9287

SERBIA & MONTENEGRO

Goran Gŏcić

Amid the misfortune of the UN sanctions imposed on Serbia and Montenegro, there was some good fortune, too: industrial inactivity helped to clear up the air and rivers, and the absence of U.S. majors made room for the distribution of European – notably French – movies. Actually, only the U.S. majors strictly restrained from selling their goods here, while nobody else – including indies such as Miramax and New Line – gave a hoot about the UN blockade, which was supposed to be both economic and cultural.

Since the sanctions were lifted in early 1996, the majors have found their place in the Serbian film market again, signing mostly with privately owned distribution companies. After four long years, Warner and Columbia were the first to team up with Tuck Vision; Fox and UIP followed, choosing Bandur Film and Vans respectively, while Buena Vista is still indecisive, pondering several offers. The audience is also back in the cinemas, to create (or greet) the success of domestic films such as **Premeditated Murder** *(Ubistvo sa predumišljajem)* or foreign co-productions such as *Underground*. Admissions in Belgrade's largest cinema network, Beograd film, rose by 55% in 1995; new cinemas have been opened, and some of the old ones reopened.

Landscape after Battle

Since the war in the former Yugoslavia is over, perhaps it's a good time to make films about it. The subject may even be about to become a hit – Steven Spielberg is reportedly producing a movie about the break-up of Yugoslavia. The civil war has been the subject of some Serbian films, but this season's plots – as in *Premeditated Murder* or **Dark Is the Night** *(Tamna je noć)* – concentrate on post-war traumas. *Premeditated Murder* is probably the best that the Serbian film industry can offer at this moment. It has the most plausible and precise characterisation recently seen in domestic cinema.

The secret is, partly, its literary basis, a novel by the highly regarded Serbian writer, Slobodan Selenić. Despite its absurdist tone, this is a story which makes a lot of sense. *Premeditated Murder* is Gorčin Stojanović's film début although, like Fassbinder, whose work he has staged, he previously had a long and rich experience in the theatre. This is most noticeable in his impeccable handling of actors. The most striking in the impressive cast was probably Branka Katić, who has developed into the leading young actress in Serbia, adding a touch of pathos to her typecasting in several films as a neurotic teenager.

Among comedies – probably the most difficult of all cinema genres – **Third Time Lucky** *(Treća sreća)* proved quite successful at the box office, but **A Boy from Junkovac** *(Dečak iz Junkovca)* was absolutely hilarious. Shot on a shoestring budget *in vérité*-style video, it was another impressive entry by a newcomer, Dejan Zečević. He also directed one episode in **Package Tour** *(Paket aranžman)* – A *jeune cinema* omnibus film. Mladen Matičević and Ivan Markov, two more members of the Serbian "video guerrilla" group shot **Ghetto** *(Geto)*, featuring the denizens of Belgrade's rock'n'roll and avant-garde *demi-monde*. Radomir Belačević, the real-life hero of *A Boy from Junkovac*, follows in a comic tradition in Serbian cinema, exemplified by the strongman in Dušan Makavejev's *Innocence Unprotected*.

Someone Else's Dream

Like Emir Kusturica's 1995 Golden Palm

Still from THIRD TIME LUCKY

winner, *Underground*, **Tragedy Burlesque**, directed by Goran Marković, took its tone from screenwriter Dušan Kovačević: sad, satirical, over-the-top comedy, parodying not only history but the genre itself. But while *Tragedy Burlesque* was the biggest domestic flop of 1995, *Underground* was Serbia's biggest box-office hit.

The prolific screenwriter Gordan Mihić, who has had more than thirty scripts filmed, was represented by two films this season: **Someone Else's America** *(Tudja Amerika)* and **Terrace on the Roof** *(Terasa na krovu)*. On the latter, which stars his daughter Ivana Mihić, he also served (for the third time in his long career) as director. Both films are fairly routine, small family dramas, but *Someone Else's America*, directed by Goran Paskaljević, was more generously budgeted ($5m), better shot (Giorgos Arvanitis, who works with Theo Angelopoulos), and better acted (above all, by Tom Conti) than the rule. It is about Serbian immigrants living on the fringes of the American dream in New York.

Last – and perhaps the least – is **Whirlpool of Passion**, a work with rich 'ethnic' content, loosely based on the work of the 19th-century Serbian writer Borislav Stanković. Its exotic (Turkish) look may find an audience in art houses abroad, but it is almost certain to flop at home. However, the budget (around $2m) is exceptionally large by Serbian movie industry standards. Films like *Underground*, or the omnibus *Love + Hate – European Stories*, didn't have any Serbian funding. However, they at least belong to some extent to Serbian culture, successfully combining the language and quantities of local talent (actors, directors, writers, crews, producers and production facilities) with foreign (French, German, Danish) financing.

GORAN GOČIĆ is a freelance film and art critic. He has written for numerous magazines and daily papers. His monograph *Andy Warhol and Strategies of Pop* is in print. He is preparing another book on contemporary cinema.

TOP TEN GROSSING FILMS IN BELGRADE: 1995

	Admissions
Underground	176,620
Stargate	63,043
Die Hard 3	60,243
Premeditated Murder (*Serbian*)	49,273
Third Time Lucky (*Serbian*)	43,507
Malice	41,601
The Shawshank Redemption	41,555
Judge Dredd	36,464
Three Colours: Blue	31,953
Four Weddings and a Funeral	29,790

Source: Satelit magazine.

Recent and Forthcoming Films

BALKANSKA PRAVILA (Balkan Rules)

Script: Radoslav Pavlović. Dir: Darko Bajić. Phot: Radan Popović. Players: Branislav Lečić, Ana Sofrenović. Prod: Magic Line/RTV Serbia.

BILA JEDNOM JEDNA ZEMLJA/ PODZEMLJE (Underground)

Script: Dušan Kovačević, Emir Kusturica. Dir: Kusturica. Phot: Vinko Filač. Players: Miki Manojlović, Mirjana Joković. Prod: CiBy 2000 (France)/ Pandora (Germany).

DEČAK IZ JUNKOVCA (A Boy from Junkovac)

Script and Dir: Dejan Zečević. Phot: Miloš Stefan Kresoja. Players: Radomir Belačević, Marko Debović. Prod: MP Agencija–Zoja Todorić/RTV Serbia.

DO KOSYE (To the Bone)

Script: Srdjan Andjelić, Slobodan-Boban Skerlić. Dir: Skerlić. Phot: Dušan Joksimović. Players: Lazar Ristovski, Nikola Djuričko. Prod: Monte Royal Pictures, Beograd.

DOVIDJENJA U ČIKAGU (See You In Chicago)

Script: Zoran and Dragan Čalić. Dir: Zoran Čalić. Phot: Aleksandar Petković. Players: Velimir-Bata Živojinović, Nikola Simić. Prod: Viktorija film/RTV.

LOVE + HATE – EUROPEAN STORIES (omnibus) Serbian story: SVINJE I BISERI (Pigs and Pearls)

Script and Dir: Dragan Nikolić. Phot: Radoslav Vladić. Players: Vladica Milosavljević, Dragan Bjelogrlić. Prod: Such Much Movies (Denmark).

PAKET ARANŽMAN (Package Tour) (omnibus)

Script: Djordje Milosavljević. Dir: Ivan Stefanović/Dejan Zečević/ Srdan Golubović. Phot: Miloš Stefan Kresoja. Players: Rastko Lupulović, Milica Mihajlović, Bojan Zirović, Milena Pavlović, Boris Milivojević, Zoran Cvijanović. Prod: MP Agencija–Zoja Todorić/Avala Film International/Fakultet Dramskih umetnosti/RTV Serbia.

NEČISTA KRV (Whirlpool of Passion)

Script: Stojan Stojčić, Slaven Radovanović, based on the works of Borislav Stanković. Dir: Stojčić. Phot: Mišo Samoilovski, Andrej Čertov, Milan Spasić. Players: Rade Šerbedžija, Maja Stojanović. Prod: DD "Nečista krv", Beograd.

TUDJA AMERIKA (Someone Else's America)

Script: Gordan Mihić. Dir: Goran Paskaljević. Phot: Giorgos Arvanitis. Players: Miki Manojlović, Tom Conti. Prod: Macht Productions/Pandora Cinema/ Canal Plus /Guisiana Ltd (France)/Intrinsica Films/Light-works Edition Systems (U.K.)/ Lichtblick Filmproduktion (Germany)/ Stefi 2 (Greece)/Singidunum Film Production (Ireland/Serbia)/RTV Serbia.

URNEBESNA TRAGEDIJA (Tragedy Burlesque)

Script: Dušan Kovačević, based on his own play. Dir: Goran Marković. Phot: Radoslav Vladić. Players: Vojislav Brajović, Sonja Savić. Prod: Dari films/ Compagnie des films/La Sept Cinema (France)/Multumex Films (Bulgaria)/Monte Royal Pictures, Beograd.

Useful Addresses

Monte Royal Pictures
(Independent Producer)
Skerlićeva 30
11000 Beograd
Tel: (38111) 43 17 26
Fax: (38111) 44 41 951

MP Agencija
(Independent Producer)
Teodora Drajzera 19
11000 Beograd
Tel: (38111) 66 68 66
Fax: (38111) 66 00 84

Institut za film
(Yugoslav Film Institute)
Čika Ljubina 15
11000 Beograd
Tel: (38111) 62 51 31
Fax: (38111) 63 42 53

Avala Film International DD
(Production Company & Studio Facilities)
Kneza Višeslava 88
11030 Beograd
Tel: (38111) 55 73 31
Fax: (38111) 55 94 74

Vans
(Independent Producer & Distributor)
Njegoševa 84
11000 Beograd
Tel: (38111) 43 24 92
Fax: (38111) 43 42 26

Beograd Film
(Chain of Theatres)
Terazije 40
11000 Beograd
Tel: (38111) 68 89 40
Fax: (38111) 68 79 52

First Production
(Independent Distributor)
Kumodraška 176/6
11040 Beograd
Tel: (38111) 47 14 03
Fax: (38111) 47 32 07

Tuck
(Independent Distributor)
Velikomoravska 11-15
11000 Beograd
Tel: (38111) 42 46 66
Fax: (38111) 41 31 77

M Export-Import
(Independent Distributor)
Dragačevska 6
11000 Beograd
Tel: (38111) 41 24 17
Fax: (38111) 40 92 67

Sinema Dizajn
(Independent Producer)
Ustanička 125/1
11000 Beograd
Tel: (38111) 48 82 377
Fax: (38111) 48 88 011

SLOVAKIA

Hana Cielová

Slovakia is one of the small European countries (five million inhabitants) which can produce only a few films a year. A significant recent success has been Martin Šulík's **The Garden** *(Záhrada)*, a co-production with Czech TV and France, which received five of the annual Czech Lion awards and did very well at many international festivals. An award supporting the distribution of the film in Germany (Mannheim FilmFest, 1995) was given to the German distributor, Arsenal Film. Following positive audience responses, not only in Mannheim (Audience Prize, 1995), *The Garden* was also bought for theatrical distribution in Holland, France and some other European territories – a considerable success for a small Slovak film.

After a relatively prolific year in 1995, with six new feature films, 1996 is looking rather poor: only two new films have been finished and entered distribution. **Jašek's Dream** *(Jaškov sen)*, the comeback of veteran director Eduard Grečner, who was unable to work for many years under Communism is, unfortunately, a disappointment: too conventional and old-fashioned, it failed to strike a chord with either critics or audiences. The second film, the documentary feature, **Paper Heads** *(Papierové hlavy)*, was the most eagerly awaited event of the year. A project of the renowned Slovak director, Dušan Hanák, it was produced by Marián Urban from ALEF Bratislava, along with many others: Les Films de l'Observatoire, EOS Films, ZDF-ARTE, Slovak TV, KF Praha, and with the financial support of Pro Slovakia, SFÚ-NKC, Eurimages, CNC, MAP-TV, and some other institutions.

Monumental Mosaic

Dušan Hanák was born in 1938 in

TOP TEN GROSSING FILMS IN SLOVAKIA: 1995

	Admissions
The Lion King	441,086
Dumb and Dumber	224,426
The Mask	182,122
The Specialist	162,007
Stargate	123,040
Interview with the Vampire	109,714
Casper	106,633
Die Hard 3	104,208
Colour of Night	103,338
Forrest Gump	99,669

Bratislava; from 1960-1965, he studied at Prague's Film Academy, FAMU. He directed several documentary films, and in 1969 he made his first feature, **322**. He became one of the most important personalities of the new Slovak cinema. His films (many of them prohibited during the Communist era) received numerous international awards, and some of them, notably **Pictures of the Old World** *(Obrazy starého sveta)*, **Rose Dreams** *(Ružové sny)* and **I Love, You Love** *(Ja milujem, ty miluješ)*, are milestones in Slovak film history.

After the 'Velvet Revolution' in 1989, Hanák put all his energy into the highly ambitious *Paper Heads*, which he said would deal with freedom and its limitations, the relationship between a citizen and power, as well as the various violations of human rights in modern history. One guiding motive was the feeling that we still cannot cope with our own past. This is both an emotional picture about a human being living in a totalitarian society and a monumental mosaic, mapping out the double history of Czechoslovakia during the years of Communism.

The confrontation between official history, represented by old propaganda films and the authentic statements of witnesses and victims, the people who survived the Communist concentration camps and prisons, shows the typical schizophrenia in which millions of people lived. for many years. The obvious discrepancy of these two completely different versions of history is shown with a dry humour; no commentary is needed.

Hanák has said he wanted to use film archive materials in a contrapuntal and even humorous way. The symbols of Communist power, the paper portraits of the leaders, were always brought out on May 1st, the most important Communist holiday. After 1989, these "paper heads" lost their magic power and became harmless and ridiculous. Nevertheless, there is still a possibility that the old days are not gone forever and that some paper heads might return, even if with new faces and new slogans.

In the last few months, democracy in Slovakia has been considerably threatened by new laws whose express purpose is to "protect the republic", but which could be used as a weapon against some journalists or artists. In Slovak TV, people who were active in the 'Velvet Revolution' are being forced to leave, and television is gradually becoming the weapon of the new official propaganda. This danger, of course, exists not only in Slovakia but in all post-Communist countries. That's why Hanák's film is so important right now. We can forgive but we should not forget: the one who forgets his past too quickly can all too soon lose his future.

HANA CIELOVÁ is a freelance film critic and scriptwriter as well as programme adviser to various international film festivals.

Recent and Forthcoming Films

JAŠKOV SEN (Jašek's Dream)

Script and Dir: Eduard Grečner. Phot: Laco Kraus. Prod: Slovak TV.

PAPIEROVÉ HLAVY (Paper Heads)

Script and Dir: Dušan Hanák. Phot: Alojz Hanúsek. Prod: ALEF.

RIVERS OF BABYLON

Script: Peter Pištánek, Marián Urban, Vlado Balco. Dir: Balco. Phot: Martin Štrba. Players: Andy Hryc, Vlado Hajdu, Diana Mórová. Prod: ALEF.

JESEŇ (Autumn)

Script: Jana Skořepová. Dir: Eva Borušovičová. Prod: Charlie's.

Still from PAPER HEADS, directed by Dušan Hanák

Producers

ALEF
Uršulínska 9
811 01 Bratislava
Tel: (42 7) 533 4812
Fax: (42 7) 531 9406

Ars Media
Brečtanová 1
833 14 Bratislava
Tel/Fax: (42 7) 373 758

Barok Film
Konventná 8
811 03 Bratislava
Tel: (42 7) 531 9372
Fax: (42 7) 371 426

HQ Agency
Nevädzová 2
821 08 Bratislava
Tel/Fax: (42 7) 236 606

JMB Film and TV Production
Koreničova 12
811 03 Bratislava
Tel/Fax: (42 7) 315 778

ARTTEP
Hlavná 30
900 31 Stupava
Tel: (42 7) 935 349
Fax: (42 7) 935 452

Atan Studio
Mliekárenská 10
824 95 Bratislava
Tel/Fax: (42 7) 212 803

B.M.A.
Drieňová 3
821 02 Bratislava
Tel/Fax: (42 7) 230 408

Charlie's
Špitálska 4
811 09 Bratislava
Tel: (42 7) 36 34 30/36 33 96
Fax: (42 7) 32 36 78

Partnerfilm
Brečtanová 1
833 14 Bratislava
Tel: (42 7) 371 966
Fax: (42 7) 371 126

SFT-Koliba Film Studios
Brečtanová 1
833 14 Bratislava
Tel: (42 7) 377 303/371 921
Fax: (42 7) 372 224

TF Art Production
Pribinova 25
810 11 Bratislava
Tel: (42 7) 210 4738/210 4740
Fax: (42 7) 210 4741

Distributors

Gemini Film
Štefanikova 47
811 04 Bratislava
Tel: (42 7) 491 127, 491 084
Fax: (42 7) 496 361

Intersonic Taunus Productions
Staré Grunty 36
842 25 Bratislava
Tel/Fax: (42 7) 722 070

Tatra Film
Priemyselná 1
821 09 Bratislava
Tel: (42 7) 526 33 11, 526 76 81
Fax: (42 7) 215 685

Bioscop
Hviezdoslavovo nám. 17
811 02 Bratislava
Tel: (42 7) 335 049
Fax: (42 7) 335 815

Saturn Entertainment
Viedenská cesta 10
851 01 Bratislava
Tel: (42 7) 845 954, 850 016
Fax: (42 7) 845 969

Butterfly Entertainment Group
Martanovičova 23
800 00 Bratislava
Tel: (42 7) 310 369
Fax: (42 7) 310 371

SLOVENIA

Milan Ljubić

After several years which might take their theme from the title of a film made by Franci Slak fifteen years ago – *Crisis Period* – we can welcome changes for the better in 1996. In Ljubljana, Celje, Maribor, Kranj, and other towns throughout Slovenia, cinemas have been modernised. After the crisis in the second half of the 80s and the beginning of the 90s, cinema admissions have begun to rise, which has permitted more intensive investment in improvements.

The future has already arrived in the form of auditorium seating by the renowned Italian manufacturer Lino Solegi; Dolby surround-sound equipment; crystal screens from Great Britain; the creation of a network of sales outlets that will make it possible to purchase tickets in advance for all cinemas at any other cinema; the introduction of automatic ticket dispensers with paycards and computer links to sales outlets beyond the cinemas themselves, e.g. in department stores, stations, etc.

Television may be the competitor of cinema, but one thing is clear: television is not the competitor of film itself. At the end of 1995 and the beginning of 1996, two new commercial TV stations commenced operation in Slovenia – POP TV and TV3. Along with the national station, TV Slovenija, now celebrating its 35th anniversary, and the first commercial TV station, Kanal A, they filled the airways with a variety of films, which are the most popular television programmes in Slovenia. The selection of new films in the cinemas and the full-day scheduling on TV have had a powerful effect on video activities: the number of video rental outlets has almost halved. From a high of over 200 videothèques, only around 120 were still operating by the middle of 1996.

Local Heroes

Slovene films generally receive more criticism than praise in Slovenia. But two new films have received a really favourable response from audiences and critics alike. They are **Carmen**, written and directed by Metod Pevec, based on his novel of the same name (or rather, the novel was based on the script), and **Halgato**, directed by Andrej Mlakar, based on a novel by Feri Lainsček.

The independence of Slovenia and its secession from Yugoslavia is a theme treated by director Božo Šprajc in his film **Felix**, which survived several pitfalls in its co-production agreements between Slovenia, France, Croatia and Macedonia. As often happens in a small film industry, Šprajc had to bear most of the burden and production costs himself.

Express is a first feature film, still unfinished, by Igor Sterk. And although this is a début, Sterk himself has been close to film-making since early childhood. His father, a famous Slovene stunt-man, and his mother, an actress in several TV serials, met while filming; his uncle was the production manager and executive producer of several Slovene films, and his grandfather and grandmother were well-known bit-part players for many years.

Damjan Kozole has shot his third feature film, **Inscription Above a City**, which he describes as a "black comedy on the lives of artists". Like his first two, *Fateful Telephone* and *Remington*, this takes place in the present and deals with the younger generation. Another newcomer, Mitjo Novljana, shot his first feature film, **Melita**, while the veteran Karpo Godina is planning his next production, **Snakeskin**. Among the veterans, one can also count

Still from INSCRIPTION ABOVE A CITY

Boris Jurjaševič, whose next project is entitled **Everything Is Just Jazz**.

For small countries and small film industries, it is a fact that the largest producer of films is television. Slovenia is no exception. Using its own production facilities, TV Slovenija shot the film **Radio Doc**, directed by Miran Zupanić. It was the co-producer of **Striptih,** written, directed and produced by Filip Robar Dorin; and **Prophecy of Fire,** written and directed by Michael Benson. These films were also financially supported by the Slovene Film Fund.

After years of crisis, when Slovene film-making has not been very dynamic, it has been encouraging in 1996 to see doors opening outside Slovenia as well. Slovene cinéastes have made guest appearances in Denmark and in Russia, with a screening of Slovene productions there accompanied by an exhibition of film posters.

MILAN LJUBIĆ, director, columnist and producer, was born in Tuzla in 1938 and graduated from the Film Department of the Ljubljana Academy of Theatre, Radio, Film and Television Arts. He is the director of numerous films and the author of many books on film.

TOP TEN GROSSING FILMS IN SLOVENIA: 1995

	Admissions
Casper	134,380
The Mask	121,986
Dumb and Dumber	118,292
Legends of the Fall	84,677
The Specialist	80,989
Waterworld	74,175
Interview with the Vampire	64,636
Die Hard 3	64,331
GoldenEye	64,234
While You Were Sleeping	60,100

Producers

Arkadena
1234 Mengeš
Brodišče 23
Ind. cona Trzin
Tel/Fax: (+386-61) 714-889

Bindweed Soundvision
1000 Ljubljana
Cankarjeva 4/1
Tel/Fax: (+386-61) 22 11 94

E-motion Film d.o.o.
1000 Ljubljana
Kersnikova 4
Tel: (+386-61) 132-91-12
Fax: (+386-61) 329-185

Infomedia 3 Filming d.o.o.
(Film production, distribution and other film services)
1001 Ljubljana
P.O. Box 2053
Tel: (+386-61) 17-10-689, 17-10-679, 17-10-680
Fax: (+386-61) 13-13-261

Pegaz Film d.o.o.
(Film and video production)
1000 Ljubljana
Rozmanova 15
Tel/Fax: (+386-61) 131-33-45

Studio MI
1000 Ljubljana
Linhartova 8
Tel: (+386-61) 302-322, 132-70-85
Fax: (+386-61) 314-564

Vertigo d.o.o.
1001 Ljubljana
Zelena pot 17
Tel: (+386-61) 132-91-12

Distributors

Carnium Trade
4000 Kranj
Hrastje 106
Tel: (+386-64) 326-288

Continental Film
1000 Ljubljana
Kersnikova 1
Tel: (+386-61) 131-91-67, 131-91-79
Fax: (+386-61) 131-90-64

Franci Slak, director and producer

Film Plus
1000 Ljubljana
Kvedrova 9
Tel: (+386-61) 444-352
Fax: (+386-61) 444-880

Infomedia 3 Filming d.o.o.
1001 Ljubljana
P.O. Box 2053
Tel: (+386-61) 17-10-689, 17-10-679, 17-10-680
Fax: (+386-61) 13-13-261

Ljubljanski Kinematografi - Warner Bros
1000 Ljubljana
Miklošičeva 38
Tel: (+386-61) 131-62-01. 310-270
Fax: (+386-61) 316-242

Starec Distribution
6000 Koper
Garibaldijeva 11
Tel/Fax: (+386-66) 23-788

Trias
1000 Ljubljana
Beethovnova 6
Tel: (+386-61) 216-343
Fax: (+386-61) 210-107

Useful Addresses

AGRFT – Film Academy
1000 Ljubljana
Nazorjeva 3
Tel: (+386-61) 210-412
Fax: (+386-61) 210-450

The Association of Film Creators of Slovenia – DSFD
1000 Ljubljana
Zrinjskega 9
Tel: (+386-61) 325-971

Slovene Cinemateque
1000 Ljubljana
Miklošičeva 26
Tel: (+386-61) 311-391
Fax: (+386-61) 311-391

Slovene Film Museum
1000 Ljubljana
Mestni trg 17
Tel: (+386-61) 212-728
Fax: (+386-61) 210-142

Slovene State Archives
1000 Ljubljana
Zvezdarska 1
Tel: (+386-61) 125-12-22, 125-12-66

Slovenia Television
1550 Ljubljana
Kolodvorska 2-4
Tel: (+386-61) 13-11-333
Fax: (+386-61) 317-479

Subtitling Laboratory Film Plus d.o.o.
1000 Ljubljana
Kvedrova 9
Tel: (+386-61) 444-352
Fax: (+386-61) 444-880

SOUTH AFRICA

Martin Botha

In March 1995, the old South African film subsidy system ceased to exist, and since then the film industry has waited to hear what incentives the government would put in place to encourage film-making in this rapidly changing country. A White Paper will hopefully articulate the policy which will determine the development of the local industry and the establishment of a statutory body for channelling financial and administrative aid to this industry.

An interim fund was announced by the Department of Arts, Culture, Sciences and Technology during May 1996 to address the needs of the industry until a film statutory body is established. The department has allocated 10 million rand in the financial year 1996/1997 towards the development of the industry. Twenty percent of the budget has been allocated to the development of film scripts; thirty percent will be spent on film education and training in mainly disadvantaged communities; and the rest will be used to assist film projects.

Born Again

Despite the current lack of a comprehensive film subsidy scheme, a few co-productions were completed in South Africa and some are still in progress. Two major productions were **Cry, the Beloved Country** and **The Making of the Mahatma**. Darrell Roodt's finest film to date, *Cry, the Beloved Country* was launched in four countries and two continents towards the end of 1994 and received critical acclaim in the U.S.

Scriptwriter Ronald Harwood (*The Dresser*) has adapted Alan Paton's novel in one of the best films to come out of South Africa. Set in the 1940s, it follows the journey of a Zulu pastor, Stephen Kumalo (brilliantly portrayed by James Earl Jones), from rural Zululand to Johannesburg, to look for his son. Kumalo's journey brings him into direct conflict with a white man, James Jarvis (movingly portrayed by Richard Harris), who has lost his son in a violent crime. Through various tragic events, both men are forced to learn the lesson of forgiveness with dignity, a theme which is so relevant to all South Africans at the moment.

Also very moving is Shyam Benegal's **The Making of the Mahatma**, which deals with Gandhi's encounters with racism in South Africa and how it shaped his philosophy of passive resistance. It is an austere filmic portrait with a strong emphasis, like *Cry, the Beloved Country*, on humanism and forgiveness.

Babel, a British/South African co-production, was shot in six weeks in Soweto, Hillbrow, Yeoville and other parts of Johannesburg at the beginning of 1996. The director, Les Blair, sets out to explore contemporary South African society by focusing on six working-class South Africans from very different backgrounds who were formerly separated by apartheid. **Fools** is a co-production between France and South Africa and gives the young Ramadan Suleman a chance to direct his first feature film. Even **Born Free** has been remade as a co-production between South Africa and the U.S.A. Hopefully, it will be more of a success than another remake during the past year: producer Duncan MacNeillie's **Jock** was a remake of a Gray Hofmeyr film of the 1980s, **Jock of the Bushveld**, which was very successful with both local audiences and reviewers. The new version was neither.

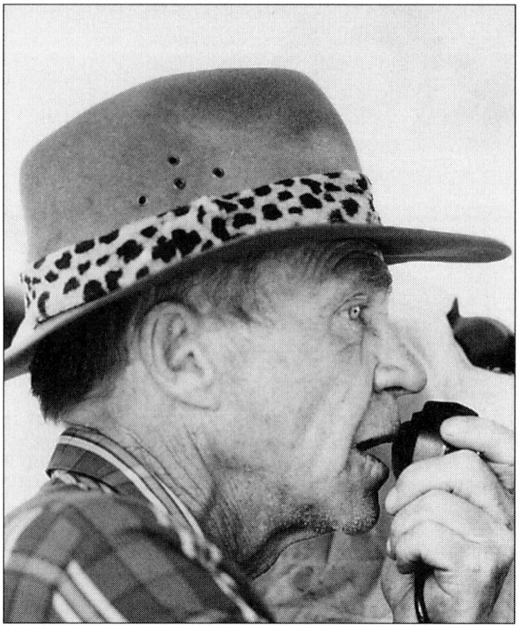

Veteran director Jamie Uys, who died during 1996

Inside & Outsiders

A handful of new local features were also completed but not yet released. Darrell Roodt's latest film, **The Spear**, features Ice Cube as a young South African exile returning after twelve years to look for his younger brother. He is confronted with the growing drug sub-culture in the country. Arthur Penn shot his latest film in South Africa: **Inside** deals with apartheid and was screened at Cannes in 1996.

It was also a sad year for the local film industry with the passing of veteran film-maker Jamie Uys. Uys will be remembered for his magnificent images of the Namib and Kalahari deserts in films such as **Dirkie** and his brilliant 'personal' documentary, **Beautiful People**. After his huge box-office success with the comedy, **The Gods Must Be Crazy**, Uys came in for criticism over the racial aspects of the film.

Under apartheid, many voices were silenced and marginalised in the film and television industries: blacks, women, gays and lesbians. It is therefore important that first-time directors such as Ramadan Suleman should get a chance to make a feature film. But the new South African constitution also prohibits discrimination against gays and lesbians, and it is noteworthy that a small gay cinema is beginning to emerge.

In 1989, Melanie Chait's **Out in Africa** became the first South African film to deal with the gay liberation struggle. This short film is a moving tribute to two gay South African men, Simon Nkoli and Dr Ivan Toms. Dr Toms was the first white South African to refuse to serve in the South African defence force; Simon Nkoli was one of the Delmas trialists.

An important new voice in the creation of a South African gay and lesbian cinema is Luiz Barros. Barros was a third-year BA student at the University of the Witwatersrand when he made **Pretty Boys**, a film about two male prostitutes discussing their lives. The film attempts to explore the possibility of prostitution as a positive experience. **Clubbing** revolves around six twentysomething friends who meet one evening before they go out clubbing. With this film, Barros captured the decline of the white ruling class in a society in which the rules are changing, in which they are no longer assured of a future of privilege.

Barros' latest short film, **Hot Legs**, is a revenge fantasy in which a young gay doctor seeks revenge on a man he once loved by holding him captive in a motel. Together, the two characters relive their past and look at how they became the people they are. Barros is in the process of directing two feature-length films, **Homo Sapiens** and **A Family Affair**. South Africa's Gay and Lesbian Film Festival has become one of the most popular annual events.

DR MARTIN BOTHA is a senior lecturer in communication studies at the University of South Africa. He is responsible for three books on South African cinema, and was involved in the drafting of a White Paper for future film policy in South Africa. He is currently working on a book about the portrayal of gays and lesbians in African, Asian and Latin American cinema.

TOP TEN GROSSING FILMS IN SOUTH AFRICA: 1995

- The Mask
- Dumb and Dumber
- GoldenEye
- Die Hard 3
- Casper
- Bad Boys
- Disclosure
- Legends of the Fall
- Braveheart
- Time Cop

Recent and Forthcoming Films

A FAMILY AFFAIR

Script and Dir: Luiz Barros. Prod: Marc Schwingens, Underdog Pictures.

BABEL

Dir: Les Blair. Phot: Sean McGarvey. Players: Baby Cele, Michele Burgers, Danny Keogh, Nomsa Nene, Sam Mofokeng, Joe Nina, Grace Mahlaba, Vanessa Cook, Marcel van Heerden, Lional Newton, Rapulana Seiphemo, Thulani Nyembe. Prod: Parallax Pictures/ Xencat Pictures (Indra de Lanerolle and Jeremy Nathan)/ Channel Four Films.

BORN FREE

Dir: Tommy Lee Wallace. Prod: Moviworld (South Africa)/Lourin Salob (U.S.A.).

BRIDGE OF TIME

Dir: Jorge Montesi. Players: Susan Day, Cecily Tyson. Prod: Helena Spring, Scy Productions.

CRY, THE BELOVED COUNTRY

Script: Ronald Harwood, based on the novel by Alan Paton. Dir: Darrell James Roodt. Phot: Paul Gilpin. Players: James Earl Jones, Vusi Kunene, Richard Harris, Leleti Khumalo, Ian Roberts, Charles S. Dutton, Eric Miyeni. Prod: Anant Singh, Distant Horizon Productions. In association with Videovision Entertainment/Investec Bank Limited/Alpine Films.

DANGER ZONE

Script: Jeff Albert. Dir: Alan Eastman. Players: Robert Downey Jnr, Billy Zane, Lisa Collins, Ron Silver, Carrie Tagawa, Patrick Shai, Chris Buchanan. Prod: Nu World.

FOOLS

Script: Bhekisiswe Peterson, Ramadan Suleman. Dir: Suleman. Prod: JBA Prods (Paris), Jacques Bidou.

HOMO SAPIENS

Script and Dir: Luiz Barros. Prod: Marc Schwinges, Underdog.

HOT LEGS

Script and Dir: Luiz Barros. Players: David Dukas, Gerrie Barnard. Prod: Marc Schwinges, Underdog.

INSIDE

Script: Bima Stagg. Dir: Arthur Penn. Players: Lou Gossett Jnr, Eric Stoltz, Nigel Hawthorne, Louis Van Niekerk, Ian Roberts, Patrick Shai. Prod: Hilliard Elkins, David Dwight, Michael Games, Film Afrika Worldwide.

JOCK

Script: Duncan MacNeillie. Dir: Danie Joubert. Players: Sean Gallagher, Ron Smerczak, Wilson Dunster, Russel Savadier, Robert Urich. Prod: Duncan MacNeillie.

THE MAKING OF THE MAHATMA

Script: Fatima Meer, Shyam Benegal, Shama Zaidi. Dir: Benegal. Phot: Ashok Mehta. Players: Rajit Kapur, Pallavi Joshi, Keith Stevenson, Paul Slabolepszy, Himal Devnarain. Prod: Ravi Gupta (India) and Anant Singh (South Africa)/ National Film Development Corporation (India)/South African Broadcasting Corporation. In association with the Gandhi Memorial Committee (South Africa)/Department of Arts, Culture, Science and Technology (South Africa)/Institute for Black Research (University of Natal, South Africa).

SHINE

Script and Dir: Vusi Twala. Players: Zandile Nhlapho, Billy Smith. Prod: Vusi Twala Entertainment.

THE SPEAR

Script: Greg Latter, Darrell James Roodt. Dir: Roodt. Players: Ice Cube, Elizabeth Hurley, Ving Rhames. Prod: Helena Spring (Scy Productions)/Gillian Shorten (New Line Cinema).

WAR HEAD

Script: Jeff Albert. Dir: Mark Roper. Players: Frank Zagarino, Joe Lara, Elizabeth Giordano. Prod: Danny Lerner, Nu Image.

Producers

Free Film Makers
Loli Repanis
24 Rocky Street
Bellevue
Johannesburg 2128
Tel: (27-11) 4873477
Fax: (27-11) 4871533

Independent Film Centre
Carl Fischer
P.O. Box 89271
Lyndhurst 2106
Johannesburg
Tel: (27-11) 7862360
Fax: (27-11) 4405132

Videovision Enterprises
Anant Singh
134 Essenwood Road
Berea
Durban 4001
Tel: (27-31) 224000
Fax: (27-31) 222444

Toron International
Edgar Bold
2 Johannesburg Road
Gresswold
Johannesburg 2106
Tel: (27-11) 7862360
Fax: (27-11) 4405132

Scy Productions
Helena Spring
P.O. Box 2980
Randburg 2125
Tel: (27-11) 7891353
Fax: (27-11) 7891376

Sonneblom Films
Katinka Heyns
P.O. Box 3940
Honeydew 2010
Tel: (27-11) 7942100
Fax: (27-11) 7942061

Nu World Services
Danny Lerner
P.O. Box 3903
Booysens
Johannesburg 2000
Tel: (27-11) 4944311
Fax: (27-11) 4941236

Underdog Productions
Marc Schwinges
P.O. Box78965
Sandton 2146
Tel: (27-11) 8868279
Fax: (27-11) 8861926

Distributors

Nu Metro
P.O. Box 392026
Bramley
Johannesburg 2018
Tel: (27-11) 8807040
Fax: (27-11) 4427030

Ster-Kinekor
Mandy Prosser
P.O. Box 76461
Wendywood 2144
Tel: (27-11) 4557700
Fax: (27-11) 4440659

UIP Warner
7 Junction Avenue
Castrol House
Parktown
Johannesburg 2000
Tel: (27-11) 4844215
Fax: (27-11) 4843339

Useful Addresses

The Cape Film and Video Foundation
P.O. Box 16597
Vlaeberg 8018
Cape Town
Tel: (27-21) 4346606
Fax: (27-21) 4344730

Department of Arts, Culture, Science and Technology
Neville Singh
Private Bag x894
Pretoria 0001
Tel: (27-12) 3146389
Fax: (27-12) 3232720

The Film and Television Federation
P.O. Box 25003
Ferreirasdorp 2048
Tel: (27-11) 7261850
Fax: (27-11) 4823381

Film Resource Unit
Training, Distribution
and Resource Centre
Gate 2
Newtown Cultural Precinct
1 President Street
Newtown
Johannesburg 2001
Tel: (27-11) 8384280/1/2
Fax: (27-11) 8384451
email: fru@wn.apc.org

The French Institute of South Africa
Alexandre de Clermont-Tonnerre
P.O. Box 542
Newtown 2113
Tel: (27-11) 8360561/3
Fax: (27-11) 8360564

Screen Africa
Angela van Schalkwyk
29 Linden Road
Strathavon
Sandton 2031
Tel: (27-11) 8843162
Fax: (27-11) 8839281

Showdata
Johan Blignaut
P.O. Box 15756
Vlaeberg
Cape Town 8018
Tel: (27-21) 245483
Fax: (27-21) 245483
e-mail: admin@showdata.org.za
http://www.showdata.org.za

Southern African International Film & Television Market
Dezi Rorich
Tel: (27-11) 7143229
Fax: (27-11) 7143275
email: saftvm@sabc.co.za
http://www.showdata.org.za/market

Women in Film
Merrilee Kick
P.O. Box 130982
Bryanston 2021
Tel: (011) 7065784

SPAIN

Peter Besas

Spanish cinema is in a ferment of activity. Films in production or already in the offing include high-budgeted productions, such as those from the powerful Sogetel media group – Fernando Trueba's **Two Much** or Vicente Aranda's **Libertarias** – or, at the other extreme, sober and hard-hitting dramas such as Enrique Gabriel's **In the Stinking Gutter** (*En la puta calle*).

Production in Spain last year rocketed to 56 features. But more important than how many films are being shot is the volume of money and creative talent being channelled into major new productions, and the increasing links between local and international producers which enable Spanish films, as well as their actors and directors, to break into wider markets. Almodóvar, Aranda, Bigas Luna and others have long since made names for themselves. But a new wave of film-makers in their 30s and 40s is now coming to the fore.

They include Julio Medem, (**Earth** [*Tierra*], this year's official Cannes entry), Mariano Barroso (**Ecstasy** and **My Soul Brother** [*Extasis* and *Mi Hermano del Alma*]), Juanma Bajo Ulloa (**The Dead Mother** [*La Madre Muerta*]), Daniel Calparsoro (**Leap into the Void** [*Salto al Vacío*]), Alex de la Iglesia (**The Day of the Beast** [*El día de la bestia*]), and Manuel Gómez Pereira (**Mouth to Mouth** [*Boca a Boca*]). Moreover, in contrast to the 'auteurs' of the past, who were at once producers, directors and scriptwriters, much of the new wave of Spanish cinema is being produced by financially solid companies, sometimes with links to powerful foreign groups.

Multi-partners

Thus Spain's biggest producer, Sogetel, is allied to the Prisa publishing group, as well as to Polygram and Canal Plus. ESICMA, controlled by Elías Querejeta, is partly owned by France's UGC. The Almodóvar brothers' El Deseo outfit, partnered with the French CiBy 2000, is producing various films each year not directed by Pedro. Other producers such as Fernando Colomo, Eduardo Campoy, José Luis Cuerda, Gerardo Herrero and Manuel Pereira, some of whom also double as directors, are preparing slates of new films using dynamic young talent as well as established directors such as Emilio Martinez-Lázaro and Alfonso Ungría.

Bigas Luna is responsible for one of the most ambitious projects, in conjunction with French producer Daniel Toscan du Plantier, UGC, Italy's Rodeo Drive and Spain's Star Line Productions. This will be

ESCUCHANOS ESPAÑA!
EL CINEMA ES TAMBIEN MUSICA.
ESCHUCHA EL CINEMA.
100 YEARS OF CINEMA CAM
C.A.M. ORIGINAL SOUNDTRACKS from the golden years of Italian and French cinema.
Over 170 titles and 75 composers available on compact disc.
Ask for our catalog. Also available on CD-ROM.
CAM Original Soundtracks VIA COLA DI RIENZO, 152 - 00192 ROME (ITALY) - FAX:(+39-6) 687.4046

Sogepaq International

1996 - 1997 LINE-UP

PERDITA DURANGO
Directed by Alex de la Iglesia. (English Language)
Starring Rosie Perez and Javier Bardem

EL AMOR PERJUDICA SERIAMENTE LA SALUD
(Love can Seriously Damage your Health)
Directed by Manuel Gómez Pereira

EN BRAZOS DE LA MUJER MADURA
(In Praise of Older Women)
Directed by Manuel Lombardero
Stars including Faye Dunaway, Joanna Pacula

KILLER TONGUE
Directed by Alberto Sciamma. (English Language)
Starring Robert Englund, Melinda Clarke & Jason Durr

TRANVIA A LA MALVARROSA
(The Tramway to Malvarrosa Beach)
Directed by Jose Luis García Sánchez

PERDONA BONITA PERO LUCAS ME QUERIA A MI
(Excuse me deary but Lucas loved me)
Directed by Felix Sabroso & Dunia Ayuso

LA CELESTINA
Directed by Gerardo Vera.

TU NOMBRE ENVENENA MIS SUEÑOS
(Your name is poison to my dreams)
Directed by Pilar Miró

MAS ALLA DEL JARDIN
(Beyond the Garden)
Directed by Pedro Olea

SOLO SE MUERE DOS VECES
(You only die twice)
Directed by Esteban Ibarretxe

World Sales: Sogepaq International

Gran Via 32, 1º, 28013, Madrid, Spain Tel: (34-1) 524 7220 Fax: (34-1) 521 0875 a modern-day **Carmen** trilogy, budgeted at around $20 million. The first part "Bambola", went into production last May; the second, "Titanic Chambermaid", is due to be completed by the end of the year.

Many of the current screenplays reflect the tensions and changes of modern Spain, largely concentrating on areas such as crime, violence and sex rather than politics or aesthetics. None the less, 40% of films shot in 1995 were comedies, still the most popular genre and the one that is most likely to compete effectively with American films.

But historical cinema can also be a big draw, as was proved by Aranda's *Libertarias*, set in the Civil War. Or it can be an oddball picture such as Alex de la Iglesias' **Day of the Beast** (*El día de la bestia*). Period pieces in the vein of Juan Piquer's **Devil's Island**, Juan Miñón's **The Legend of Balthazar, the Castrate**, Juan Pinzas' **The Legend of a Maid**, and Rafael Monleón's **The Invisible Boy** are also popular.

The trend towards more international and commercial Spanish films is expected to be given a further boost under the conservative Partido Popular government, which replaced the Socialists in March of 1996. But efforts are expected to be bi-partisan after the appointment in May of José María Otero as Director General of Cinematography. Otero, in fact, had been spokesman for the FAPAE, the producers' association, during the last few years of Socialist rule, and before that worked with the Media Programme, Spanish Television and the Barcelona Film Festival.

Cosy Tent-fellows

After years of internal warring, the diverse sectors of the Spanish audiovisual industry seem to have found a satisfactory way of cohabiting, as was seen at the 1996 Cannes Film Festival when the Film Institute, Spanish Television, Catalan Films, the FAPAE and the San Sebastian Film Festival all cosily shared the same tent.

Meanwhile, pre-production subsidies, other than for novice producer/directors, have been curtailed, and the emphasis is on making films that will interest local audiences and obtain adequate commercial results. Helping in this respect are new commitments to feature film financing and foreign sales from leading television networks, such as Spanish Television (RTVE), Antena 3 TV, Canal Plus and even Telecinco, all of whom are making a considerable investment in cinema.

Still from EN LA PUTA CALLE

The average budget of a Spanish film in 1995 rose to 247 million pesetas (about $2 million), and 13% of features topped the 400 million pesetas ($3.5 million) mark. In part thanks to this emphasis on more commercial product, Spanish films cornered 11.88% of their local market (up from 8.31% the previous year). The downside was that films sold didn't fare well abroad. *Two Much*, the comedy with Antonio Banderas and Melanie Griffith, was a flop in the U.S., and Almodóvar's **The Flower of My Secret** (*La flor de mi secreto*) had poorer box-office returns than most of his earlier films.

PETER BESAS has lived in Madrid since the mid-1960s and is chief of Variety's Latin American bureau. He has written various books, including a history of Spanish cinema.

EL DESEO, S.A. PRESENTA:
un film de
MONICA LAGUNA
TENGO UNA CASA
NANCHO NOVO
PEDRO ALONSO
SILKE
ERNESTO ALTERIO
con la participación de:
tve
Televisión Española,S.A.
CANAL+
una película de daniel calparsoro
najwa nimri alfredo villa ion gabella
colaboración de charo lópez
pasajes
tve
con la participación de: Televisión Española,S.A.
CANAL+
mi nombre es
SOMBRA
UN FILM DE
Gonzalo Suárez
UNA PRODUCCIÓN
DITIRAMBO FILMS
ROCABRUNO S.A.
PRODUCTORES ASOCIADOS
EL DESEO S.A.
AGUSTIN Y PEDRO ALMODÓVAR
CON LA COLABORACIÓN DE:
tve
Televisión Española,S.A.
CANAL+
EURIMAGES
FRANÇOIS-ERIC GENDRON
AMPARO LARRAÑAGA
JEAN-CLAUDE ADELIN
ELENA FERNÁNDEZ
EL DESEO S.A.
C/RUIZ PERELLO, 15 - 28028 MADRID - SPAIN - TEL: (34 - 1) 725 - 0107 FAX: (34 - 1) 355 - 7467

TOP TEN GROSSING FILMS IN SPAIN: 1995

Casper	$9,126,000
Pulp Fiction	8,938,000
Pocahontas	8,429,000
First Knight	7,165,000
Die Hard 3	7,140,000
Waterworld	7,015,000
Disclosure	6,712,000
Legends of the Fall	6,694,000
A Walk in the Clouds	6,494,000
The Lion King	6,192,000

Note: *The Lion King* opened on October 28, 1994 and grossed an additional $15,762,000 in 1994.
Figure for *Pulp Fiction* does not include 10 days of grosses in December 1994.

Recent and Forthcoming Films

EL DIA DE LA BESTIA (The Day of the Beast)

Script: Alex de la Iglesia, Jorge Guerricaechevarría. Dir: A. de la Iglesia. Phot: Flavio Martinez Labiano. Players: Alex Angulo, Armando de Razza, Santiago Segura, Terele Pávez. Prod: Iberoamericana Films/Sogetel/ M.G. SRL.

Way-out drama about frenzied theologian waiting for the Antichrist, who is aided by a TV guru and a heavy metal hoodlum.

FLAMENCO

Script and Dir: Carlos Saura. Phot: Vittorio Storaro. Players: Paco de Lucia, Manolo Sanlúcar, Lole y Manuel, Joaquin Cortés. Prod: Juan Lebrón Producciones.

Feature-length, sweeping film taking in the best of flamenco music and dancing.

EXTASIS (Ecstasy)

Script: Mariano Barroso, Joaquín Oristrell. Dir: M. Barroso. Phot: Flavio Martinez Labiano. Players: Javier Bardem, Federico Luppi, Silvia Munt. Prod: Tornasol Films.

Three young men decide to rob their families and live by their wits. But when one is arrested, the plan goes awry.

SHAMPOO HORNS

Script and Dir: Miguel Toledano. Phot: Alfredo Mayo. Players: James St. James, "Brie" and other non-professionals from club scene. Prod: ESICMA.

Gay scene and drag queens in and around New York's Limelight and The Tunnel clubs.

BAMBOLA

Script: Bigas Luna, Cesare Frugoni. Dir: Luna. Players: Valeria Marini, Jorge Perugorría. Prod: Star Line/Medusa Rodeo/Drive.

Erotic drama, part of *Carmen* trilogy.

EL PASAJERO CLANDESTINO (The Clandestine Passenger)

Script: Agusti Villaronga, Isona Passola, Pierre Javaux. Dir: Villaronga. Phot: Carles Gusi. Players: Simon Callow, Bruno Todeschini, Merce Pons, Alexandre Slotto, Rosa Novell. Prod: Massa D'Or Produccions/ Tornasol Films.

Exotic intrigue set in Tahiti suggested by a Simenon story.

EN BRAZOS DE LA MUJER MADURA (In Praise of Older Women)

Script: Manuel Lombardero, Rafael Azcona, based on the novel by Stephen Vizinczey. Dir. Lombardero. Phot: José Luis Alcaine. Players: Joanna Pacula, Faye Dunaway, Juan Diego Botto. Prod: Sogetel/ Lolafilms.

Generational love and sex, shot in Barcelona.

MAS ALLA DEL JARDIN (Beyond the Garden)

Script: Mario Camus, based on a novel by Antonio Gala. Dir: Pedro Olea. Phot: José Luis Alcaine. Players: Giancarlo Giannini, Concha Velasco, Fernando Guillén. Prod: Iberoamericana Films.

An unfulfilled aristocratic married woman from Seville seeks love and adventure in exotic Africa with a former lover.

Producers

Iberoamericana Films
Velázquez 12
Madrid 28001
Tel: 4314246
Fax: 4355994

El Deseo S.A.
Ruiz Perelió 15
Madrid 28028
Tel: 7250285
Fax: 3557467

Elias Querejeta
Maestro Lasalle 21
Madrid 28016
Tel: 345 7139
Fax: 345 2811

Aurum Films
Calle Gomera 12
San Sebastián de las Reyes
Madrid 28700
Tel: 651-0900

Cartel
Poligono Ind. "Los Alamillos"
c/Lanzarote 4
San Sebastián de los Reyes
Madrid 28700
Tel: 654-2857
Fax: 654-3455

Avanti Films
Ronda de San Pedro 46
Barcelona 08010
Tel: 268-1233
Fax: 268-1617

Sogetel
Gran Via 32
Madrid 28013
Tel: 521-7405
Fax: 523-2366

ESICMA
Maestro Lasalle 24-26
Madrid 28016
Tel: 345-8708
Fax: 359-6683

Atrium Films
Fernán González 28
Madrid 28009
Tel: 431-4790
Fax: 431-7555

Lola Films
Pintor Gimeno 12
Barcelona 08022
Tel: 418-4044
Fax: 418-4748

Distributors

Disney/Buenavista
José Bardasano
Baos 9, Madrid 28016
Tel: 383-0312
Fax: 766-9241

United International Pictures
Plaza del Callao 4
Madrid 28013
Tel: 5227261
Fax: 532-2384

Warner Bros
Manuel Montilla 1
Madrid 28016
Tel: 3506200
Fax: 3451948

Lauren Films
Balmes 87
Barcelona 08008
(In Madrid: Tetuán 29
Madrid 28013
Tel: 3235400 (Barcelona)
5218285 (Madrid)
Fax: 323-6155 (Barcelona)

Araba Films
San Prudencio 13
Vitoria 01005
Tel: 140126
Fax: 143156

Musidora Films
Princesa 17
Madrid 28008
Tel: 541-6869
Fax: 541-5482

Twentieth Century Fox
Avda de Burgos 8A
Madrid 28036
Tel: 302-4481
Fax: 383-8081

Prime Films
Clara del Rey 17
Madrid 28002
Tel: 5190181
Fax: 413-0772

Alta Films
Martin de los Heros 12
Madrid 28008
Tel: 5422702
Fax: 542-8777

Columbia Pictures
Hernandez de Tejada, 3
Madrid 28027
Tel: 377-7100
Fax: 377-7128

Wanda Films
Avda. Europe 9
Pozuelo 28224
Tel: 352-8376
Fax: 352-8371

Golem Distribution S.A.
Avda. de Bayona 52
Pamplona 31008
Tel: 260243
Fax: 171058

Cine Company
Zurbano 74
Madrid 28010
Tel: 4422944
Fax: 441-0098

Ivex Films
Paseo San Gervasio 16
Barcelona 08022
Tel: 418-4858
Fax: 418-5070

Sogepaq
Gran Via 32
Madrid 28013
Tel: 522-0529
Fax: 521-0875

Useful Addresses

Federación de Productores de Cine (FAPAE), Producers' Assoc.
Caidos de la División
Azul 1
Madrid 28016
Tel: 350-4030
Fax: 350-4677

Spanish Culture Ministry (Film Institute)
San Marcos 40
Madrid 28004
Tel: 532-5089
Fax: 531-9212

Fedicine (Distributors' Association)
Velázquez 10
Madrid 28001
Tel: 576-9511
Fax: 578-0028

Federación de Exhibidores (Exhibitors' Association)
Velázquez 10
Madrid 28001
Tel: 576-9913

Catalan Film & TV
Diputació 279
Barcelona 08007
Tel: 4881038
Fax: 4874192

Academia de las Artes y las Ciencas Cinematograficas de España
Sagasta 20
Madrid 28004
Tel: 593-4648
Fax: 593-1492

SRI LANKA

Amarnath Jayatilaka

In 1997, Sri Lanka will celebrate the 50th anniversary of Sinhala cinema. (The first Sinhala film was exhibited on January 21, 1947.) It will also be a crucial year for the growth of the national cinema as the "New Deal" under the new administration of the National Film Corporation will be launched to coincide with the anniversary. A committee appointed in September 1995 to examine the situation of the film industry handed in its interim report to the President on April 9, 1996.

The report dealt with such matters as the 'backlog' in distribution, the revision of the ticket structure, support for domestic film production, the improvement of cinemas, the reactivation and enhancement of the National Film Development Fund (NFDF), the establishment of a National Film Institute and National Film Archive, support for the participation of Sri Lankan films in international festivals, and the liberalisation of film imports.

Reducing the Queues

The most immediate and critical issue facing domestic film production is the long queue of films awaiting release. Among the measures the committee recommends is the introduction of a 'sixth circuit', the removal of a 14-day compulsory exhibition period, and a revised holdover level. Films may also be categorised so that: (a) films of high artistic quality (fifth circuit films); (b) films thought to be commercially viable; and (c) films thought to be commercially non-viable, are released in an alternating sequence.

It has also been recommended that once the backlog is cleared, 'fifth circuit' films should be released in all circuits. The interim report envisages a situation where, after clearing the backlog, the NFC is no longer committed to the distribution of each and every film produced in the country.

The Committee places major emphasis on the revitalisation of the NFDF. Measures have been suggested to create an increased flow of funds to this institution. The NFDF is expected to play a major role in supporting national film production, encouraging and supporting young talent, and assisting in the improvement of cinema exhibition.

To Encourage Art and Commerce

The private sector should be left relatively

Mahinda Perera in VEILS OF MAYA, directed by Vishvanath B. Keerthisena

free to import films, so long as an average level of 68% screen time for nationally produced films is not adversely affected, and the additional earnings from a liberalised film import policy are taxed in order to encourage and support national film production.

One of the important recommendations of the Committee is the immediate establishment of a National Film Institute. It would be funded by the NFDF and is expected to play a vital role in developing film culture, film education and also in training and research. National Film Archives would be established as a special arm of the institute, which would also incorporate a library and a conservation laboratory.

In 1995, 24 Sinhala films, 32 English-language movies and 25 Tamil films imported from India were released. The soft-porn film **Agevairaya**, in black-and-white, became the most popular movie and had a release run of 22 prints. The average release of a Sinhala film is normally limited to less than 14 prints. Among the American films, only *Speed* and *Home Alone 2* became major hits.

AMARNATH JAYATILAKA is a filmologist and one of the leading personalities in the Sinhala cinema. He lives periodically in Hollywood where he is the Vice-President of AmeriLanka Entertainment Inc.

SIHINA DESHAYEN (The Veils of Maya)

Script: George Kaperonis. Direction: Vishvanath Buddhika Keerthisena. Photography: Suminda Weerasinghe. Editing: Elmo Halliday. Music: Earny Pieris, V.B. Keerthisena. Produced by Buddhi Keerthisena. 100 mins.

In the context of Sri Lanka's cinematic history, *The Veils of Maya* represents a new genre – the experimental film. The fact that it has been released within the mainstream distribution system is a tribute to that system. In Sri Lanka, under the Film Corporation Act, all films, unless they are shot upside-down, must legally be shown.

Being the first truly experimental film in our 50-year history is both its strength and its weakness. To the average filmgoer, brainwashed by the idiocies of our commercial films, *The Veils of Maya* may be some sort of aberration; incomprehensible, eccentric, a cinematic oddity. The work of a young film-maker trained in a prestigious film school in America, who has been exposed to the best of Asian and world cinema, it has inevitably been shaped by a variety of influences, some healthy, some positively harmful.

But Vishvanath has, if not in his style then in his structure, tried to build on a Sri Lankan historical theme. The film centres on a theatre group, rehearsing the betrayal and capture of the last king of Kandy. It becomes a meditation on treachery, violence and death, interlinking them not only through the main text of the play but radiating out to the personal relationships of the actors and actresses.

Death, magnificently mimed by Mahinda Perera, is the eponymous figure haunting the players; emerging from the sea, riding in a bus blown up by terrorists. Reality and fantasy, dreams and visions, humour and sexuality are woven into the fabric – pretentious maybe, but an adventure in movie-making.

Lester James Peries

Useful Addresses

EAP Films and Theatres Ltd.
122 Ward Place
Colombo 7
Tel: 694517/694608
Fax: 694845
(Producer/Importer/Exhibitor)

Ceylon Entertainments Ltd.
35 Dharmapala Mawatha
Colombo 7
Tel: 325264
(Importer/Exhibitor)

Ceylon Theatres Ltd.
8 Sir C. Gardiner Mawatha
Colombo 2
Tel: 431243
(Producer/Importer/Exhibitor)

National Film Corporation
224 Bauddhaloka Mawatha
Colombo 8
Tel/Fax: 580247
(State sector corporation)

SWEDEN

Git Scheynius

Swedish cinema has always been very popular in Sweden. Next to France, Sweden is considered the European country whose national cinema maintains the strongest position in competition with American movies. During the first months of 1996, Swedish movies reached a record-breaking level. Their box-office share reached 32%, the highest level since the early '60s. Sweden has thus surpassed France for the popularity of its domestic cinema.

Three movies, above all, contributed to this success: the blockbuster **The Hunters** *(Jägarna)*, a highly acclaimed thriller set in Northern Sweden, by Kjell Sundvall; Bo Widerberg's impressive comeback, **All Things Fair** *(Lust och fägring stor)*, and Harald Hamrell's directorial début, **Winter Bay** *(Vinterviken)*. After the first six months of 1996, *The Hunters* is the number one movie in Sweden, with more than 600,000 admissions. Also in the top ten are *All Things Fair* and the comedy, **Bert – The Last Virgin** *(Bert – den sista oskulden)*, directed by Tomas Alfredsson.

Summer at the Box-Office

All Things Fair, which had its Swedish première in 1995, gave director Bo Widerberg well-deserved international recognition. He received the jury's special prize at the Berlin Film Festival, and from

Still from Bille August's JERUSALEM
photo: Bengt Wanselius

Hollywood came an Oscar nomination for Best Foreign Film. At home, the movie received three Golden Bugs (the Swedish Academy Awards), for best film, best director and best supporting actor.

Two Golden Bugs went to Susanne Bier's **Like It Never Was Before** *(Pensionat Oskar):* to Loa Falkman for best actor, and Jonas Gardell, one of Sweden's leading authors, for the script. The Golden Bug for best leading actress went to Gunilla Röör for her work in Kristian Petri's beautiful début, **Between Summers** *(Sommaren).* This was Sweden's only contribution to Cannes 1995, where it had its world première in La Quinzaine des Réalisateurs. Petri was also involved in another prize-winning movie, the outstanding documentary, **The Atlantic** *(Atlanten),* for which Jan Röed received a Golden Bug for best photography.

The Swedish box office for 1995 was topped by Colin Nutley's **House of Angels – The Second Summer** *(Änglagård – andra sommaren),* a follow-up to one of the biggest Swedish box-office successes of the '90s, *House of Angels (Änglagård,* 1992). After *The Lion King* came the Swedish thriller **Vendetta**, by first-time director Mikael Håfström and based on the journalist and author Jan Guillou's best-selling novel. Another of last year's box-office hits was **One in a Million** *(En på miljonen),* a comedy written and directed by the energetic duo Hannes Holm and Måns Herngren, who have worked mostly in television.

Cinema in Sweden today attracts large audiences, and the number of productions has increased as a result of an agreement between the film industry and the Swedish government. The 1995-96 slate of films includes several first-time directors, although the lack of good scripts is still a problem despite an education programme for scriptwriters set up by the Dramatic Institute a few years ago.

Mother Land

Three major movies of interest are currently in production, all of them based on literature: **Jerusalem,** the breakthrough novel of Selma Lagerlöf (1858-1940), Swedish literature's mother and Nobel Prize winner, is currently being adapted for the screen by Bille August, director of *The Best Intentions (Den Goda Viljan), Pelle the Conqueror (Pelle Erövraren)* and *The House of the Spirits. Jerusalem* is an epic novel of religious revival and love, based on the true story of the Swedish family Ingemarsson, who in 1896 were among the 40 adults and children from Dalarna in Sweden to emigrate to the holy city of Jerusalem. They were poor farmers, touched by the ecstatic visions of the charismatic revivalist, Hellgum. *Jerusalem* is an international production featuring such leading Swedish actors as Pernilla August, Reine Brynolfsson and Max von Sydow.

Another production to look forward to is Kjell Åke Andersson's adaptation of Göran Tunström's critically acclaimed **The**

Johan Widerberg and Tomas von Brömssen in Bo Widerberg's ALL THINGS FAIR *photo: Per Holst Film*

Christmas Oratorio *(Juloratoriet),* also based on a family story and set in the county of Värmland. *Juloratoriet* is a novel in the spirit of Selma Lagerlöf and includes the same strong themes of religious and existential need. Anders Grönros' **The Children Of the Glassblowers** *(Glasbläsarns barn),* a Scandinavian co-production based on Maria Gripe's best-selling novel set in 19th-century Sweden, will hopefully follow in the spirit of Grönros' previous movie, the critically acclaimed and tenderly realised youth film, *Agnes Cecilia.*

Other films in production include Colin Nutley's **That's Life** *(Sånt är livet),* Måns Herngrens and Hannes Holm's love comedy, **Adam & Eva,** and the TV satire **Monopoly** *(Monopol)* by Claes Eriksson. Daniel Bergman is preparing his next movie, **Swedish Heroes** *(Svenska Hjältar),* and directors such as Bo Widerberg, Jan Troell and Stefan Jarl are all in pre-production on new features.

GIT SCHEYNIUS is director of the Stockholm International Film Festival and the publisher of Sweden's biggest film magazine, Cinema.

Recent and Forthcoming Films

ADAM & EVA (Adam & Eva)

Script and Dir: Hannes Holm, Måns Herngren. Phot: Mats Olofsson. Players: Björn Kjellman, Josefin Nilsson, Tintin Anderzon. Prod: Svensk Film industri/SVT Drama/Swedish Film Institute.

ATT STJÄLA EN TJUV (To Steal a Thief)

Script and Dir: Clas Lindberg. Phot: Peter Kruse. Players: Robert Gustavsson, Tova Magnusson-Norling, Vanna Rosenberg. Prod: Cinetofon/ Sandrew Film/Blackstone Pictures.

TOP TEN GROSSING FILMS IN SWEDEN: 1995

	Admissions
House of Angels – The Second Summer *(Swedish)*	755,438
The Lion King	747,863
Vendetta *(Swedish)*	584,281
Forrest Gump	535,607
Die Hard 3	459,136
GoldenEye	392,874
Pocahontas	390,240
101 Dalmatians	385,198
Léon	355,154
One in a Million *(Swedish)*	354,411

BENGBULAN (Bent Bengt)

Script: Nils Gredeby. Dir: Suzanne Osten. Phot: Göran Hallberg. Players: Emelie Ekenborn, Lena Klingwall, Erik Gustavsson. Prod: Migma Film/Rock Film/Swedish Film Institute.

DEN VITA LEJONINNAN (The White Lioness)

Script: Lars Björkman. Dir: Pelle Berglund. Phot: Tony Forsberg. Players: Rolf Lassgård, Charlotte Sieling, Rino Brezina. Prod: Sandrew Film/SVT 2 Malmö/ Swedish Film Institute.

DRÖMPRINSEN - FILMEN OM EM (About Em)

Script and Dir: Ella Lemhagen. Phot: Anders Bohman. Players: Jenny Lindroth, Niclas Olund, Tomas Norström. Prod: Studio Lagnö/Svensk Filmindustri/SVT Drama.

ELLINORS BRÖLLOP (Ellinor's Wedding)

Script and Dir: Henry Meyer. Phot: Sten Holmberg. Players: Fanny Risberg, Jonas Malmsjö, Ivan M. Peterson. Prod: Omega Film & Television/Sandrew Film/ Tonservice/TV 1000.

GLASBLÄSARNS BARN (The Glassblower's Children)

Script and Dir: Anders Grönros. Phot: Philip Øgaard. Players: Stellan Skarsgård, Pernilla August, Oliver Peldius. Prod: Nordisk Screen Production/ Zentropa Production/ Mutter Media/TV 1000.

HAMSUN (Hamsun)

Script: Per Olov Enquist. Dir: Jan Troell. Phot: Troell, Micha Gavrjusjov. Players: Max von Sydow, Ghita Nørby, Annette Hoff. Prod: Nordisk Film/Merkur Film/Svensk Filmindustri.

HARRY & SONJA (Harry and Sonja)

Script and Dir: Björn Runge. Phot: Ulf Brantås. Players: Stellan Skarsgård, Viveca Seldahl, Sten Ljunggren. Prod: Memfis Film/ Sveriges Television TV2/ Zentropa Entertainments.

JAG ÄR DIN KRIGARE (Nature's Warrior)

Script and Dir: Stefan Jarl. Phot: Per Källberg. Players: Robin Milldoff, Viggo Lundberg, Micke Persbrandt. Prod: Svensk Filmindustri/SVT Drama/Per Holst Film.

JERUSALEM (Jerusalem)

Script and Dir: Bille August. Phot: Jörgen Persson. Players: Ulf Friberg, Maria Bonnevie, Pernilla August. Prod: SVT Drama/ Metronome Productions/ Danish Film Institute.

JULORATORIET (The Christmas Oratorio)

Script: Kjell-Åke Andersson, Kjell Sundstedt. Dir: Andersson. Phot: Harald Paalgard. Players: Peter Haber, Lena Endre, Henrik Linnros. Prod: Sveriges Television SVT2, Göteborg/ Sandrew Film/ Nordic Film & TV Fund.

JÄGARNA (The Hunters)

Script: Kjell Sundvall, Björn Carlström. Dir: Kjell Sundvall. Phot: Kjell Lagerroos. Players: Rolf Lassgård, Lennart Jähkel, Helena Bergström. Prod: Spice Filmproduktion/Sandrew Film/ TV 1000.

LILLA JÖNSSONLIGAN (The Jönsson Gang)

Script: Mikael Hylin, Christjan Wegner. Dir: Christjan Wegner. Phot: Per Källberg. Players: Kalle Eriksson, Jonathan Fulmée, Fredrik Glimskär. Prod: Spice Produktion/TV4/TV 1000.

MONOPOL (Monopoly)

Script and Dir: Claes Eriksson. Phot: Dan Myhrman. Players: Knut Agnred, Kerstin Granlund, Peter Rangmar. Prod: Svensk Filmindustri/Kulturtuben/Claes Eriksson Produktion.

9 MILLIMETER (9 Millimetre)

Script: Abou-Bakre Aalam, Peter Lindmark, Frank Ågren. Dir: Lindmark. Phot: Crille Forsberg. Players: Paolo Roberto, Astrid Assefa, Ivan Mathias Petersson. Prod: Spice Produktion/CCP/ TV 1000.

PASSAGERAREN (The Passenger)

Script and Dir: Michael Druker. Phot: Harald Paalgard. Players: Amanda Ooms, Peter Andersson, Mathias Eckhoff. Prod: Omega Film & Television/Svensk Film industri/Tonservice Löthner & Löthner.

RUSAR I HANS FAMN (Rushing into His Arms)

Script and Dir: Lennart Hjulström. Phot: Roland Lundin. Players: Gunilla Nyroos, Reine Brynolfsson, Anna Björk. Prod: GötaFilm/Svensk Filmindustri/ Sveriges Television TV2.

SVENSKA HJÄLTAR (Swedish Heroes)

Script: Reidar Jönsson. Dir: Daniel Bergman. Phot: Esa Vuorinen. Players: Niclas Olund, Cajsa Lisa Ejemyr, Kent Arne Dahlgren. Prod: Svensk Filmindustri/TV4/Swedish Film Institute.

SÅNT ÄR LIVET (That's Life)

Script and Dir: Colin Nutley. Phot: Peter Mokrosinski. Players: Helena Bergström, Lena Nyman, Sven-Bertil Taube. Prod: Sweetwater/Svensk Filmindustri/ SVT Göteborg.

Thomas Hedengran and Rolf Lassgård in Kjell Sundvall's THE HUNTERS
photo: Per Pettersson

VACKERT VÄDER (Summertime)

Script and Dir: David Flamholc. Phot: Mårten Nilsson. Players: Mischa Moszkowicz, Stina Beck, Fredrik Dolk. Prod: Caravan Film/Swedish Film Institute.

VINTERVIKEN (Winter Bay)

Script: Harald Hamrell, Sara Keldt, Mats Wahl. Dir: Hamrell. Phot: Roland Sterner. Players: David Tainton, Lina Englund, Martin Lindqvist. Prod: FilmLance International/TV4/TV 1000.

Producers

Cinema Art Productions
Box 20105
S-161 02 Bromma
Tel: +46-8 799 69 00
Fax: +46-8 98 10 05

FilmLance International
Box 27156
S-102 52 Stockholm
Tel: +46-8 665 11 00
Fax: +46-8 662 04 44

Götafilm
Haraldsgatan 6
S-413 14 Göteborg
Tel: +46-31 82 55 70
Fax: +46-31 82 08 60

Mekano Film & Television
Box 27837
S-115 93 Stockholm
Tel: +46-8 663 10 55
Fax: +46-8 667 26 54

Memfis Film & Television
Upplandsgatan 35
S-113 28 Stockholm
Tel: +46-8 33 55 76
Fax: +46-8 30 99 34

MovieMakers Sweden
Råsundavägen 150
S-171 30 Solna
Tel: +46-8 730 28 50
Fax: +46-8 730 28 53

Moviola Film
Box 20102
S-161 02 Bromma
Tel: +46-8 799 69 00
Fax: +46-8 29 13 86

Omega Film & Television
Box 27888
S-115 93 Stockholm
Tel: +46-8 20 05 55
Fax: +46-8 20 05 95

Pictures in Motion
Box 16371
S-103 26 Stockholm
Tel: +46-8 762 77 00
Fax: +46-8 762 77 60

Reaction Pictures
Drakens gränd 6
S-111 30 Stockholm
Tel: +46-8 20 34 50
Fax: +46-8 20 34 23

Sandrew Film
Box 5612
S-114 86 Stockholm
Tel: +46-8 23 47 00
Fax: +46-8 10 38 50

Spice Produktion
Box 20105
S-161 02 Bromma
Tel: +46-8 799 69 00
Fax: +46-8 98 68 63

Svensk Filmindustri
S-127 83 Stockholm
Tel: +46-8 680 35 00
Fax: +46-8 710 44 60

Sveriges Television/Drama
S-105 10 Stockholm
Tel: +46-8 784 00 00
Fax: +46-8 664 54 18

Sweetwater
Grev Turegatan 21
S-114 38 Stockholm
Tel: +46-8 662 14 70
Fax: +46-8 662 14 71

Viking Film
Sturegatan 8
S-114 35 Stockholm
Tel: +46-8 679 91 15
Fax: +46-8 679 91 20

Distributors

Atlantic Film
Box 21112
S-100 31 Stockholm
Tel: +46-8 30 52 30
Fax: +46-8 30 52 80

Buena Vista International
Box 5631
S-113 86 Stockholm
Tel: +46-8 440 52 00
Fax: +46-8 678 07 28

Columbia TriStar Films
Box 9501
S-102 74 Stockholm
Tel: +46-8 658 11 40
Fax: +46-8 84 12 04

Egmont Film
Box 507
S-183 25 Taby
Tel: +46-8 510 100 50
Fax: +46-8 510 120 46

Folkets Bio
Box 2068
S-103 12 Stockholm
Tel: +46-8 402 08 20
Fax: +46-8 402 08 27

Fox Film
S-127 83 Stockholm
Tel: +46-8 680 35 00
Fax: +46-8 710 44 60

Novemberfilm
Nidarosgatan 4, 2tr.
S-164 34 Kista
Tel: +46-8 751 51 44
Fax: +46-8 632 01 85

Polfilm
Östra Rönneholmsvägen 4
S-211 47 Malmö
Tel: +46-8 12 40 44
Fax: +46-8 12 40 44

Sandrew Film
Box 5612
S-114 86 Stockholm
Tel: +46-8 23 47 00
Fax: +46-8 10 38 50

Scanbox Sweden
Box 111 28
S-161 11 Bromma
Tel: +46-8 28 51 11
Fax: +46-8 28 41 11

Sonet Film
Box 20105
S-161 02 Bromma
Tel: +46-8 799 69 00
Fax: +46-8 28 58 34

Svensk Filmindustri
S-127 83 Stockholm
Tel: +46-8 680 35 00
Fax: +46-8 710 44 60

Triangel film
Box 285
S-201 22 Malmö
Tel: +46-40 12 55 47
Fax: +46-40 12 90 99

United International Pictures
Box 9502
S-102 74 Stockholm
Tel: +46-8 616 74 00
Fax: +46-8 84 38 70

Warner Bros
Box 9503
S-102 74 Stockholm
Tel: +46-8 658 10 50
Fax: +46-8 658 64 82

Willmar Andersson Film
Box 5612
S-114 86 Stockholm
Tel: +46-8 23 47 00
Fax: +46-8 10 38 50

Useful Addresses

The National Archive of Recorded Sound and Moving Image
Box 27890
S-115 93 Stockholm
Tel: +46-8 783 37 00
Fax: +46-8 663 18 11

The Swedish Film Distributors' Association
Box 49084
S-100 28 Stockholm
Tel: +46-8 785 04 00
Fax: +46-8 653 24 25

Swedish Film Institute
Box 27126
S-102 52 Stockholm
Tel: +46-8 665 11 00
Fax: +46-8 661 18 20

Swedish Film Producers' Association
Box 1008
S-171 21 Solna
Tel: +46-8 730 57 80
Fax: +46-8 27 37 45

The Swedish Institute
Cultural Film Events
Box 7434
S-103 91 Stockholm
Tel: +46-8 789 20 00
Fax: +46-8 20 72 48

The Swedish National Board of Film Censors
Box 7728
S-103 95 Stockholm
Tel: +46-8 24 34 25
Fax: +46-8 21 02 78

SWITZERLAND

Christoph Egger

If box-office figures were the measure of Swiss films, they would come out rather poorly. That is, if they were shown theatrically at all. The best films, however, have been doing quite well. **Adultère (mode d'emploi)** by Christine Pascal is as intelligent, funny and well-acted a story as audiences and critics could ask for. In her third feature as a director, the late French actress (married to Swiss producer Robert Boner) made a skilled comedy of errors, one that has been called a "manual for adultery".

Making Up the Numbers

Karin Viard plays a young Paris architect who (rightly) suspects she is being cheated on by her architect husband, and so starts her own love affair. The lack of outstanding actors is clearly a problem for small countries and Switzerland has always been forced to find reinforcements from abroad. Karin Viard also plays the main role in **Fourbi**, Alain Tanner's 'remake' of his 1971 *La Salamandre*. Her Rosemonde is more down-to-earth than the one played by Bulle Ogier, and certainly less enigmatic. The film itself blends a deliberately old-fashioned *mise en scène* and the director's familiar left-wing sentimentalities with a fresh look at his young characters trying to make their way in the general chaos that the title implies.

Viard's liaison in *Adultère* is played by Richard Berry, who also takes the main role in another Swiss film, Marcel Schüpbach's **Les agneaux**. As in *Happy End* (1987), Schüpbach chooses a bloody ending, but here it comes as no surprise but rather as a relief, perhaps signifying some kind of redemption. From the beginning, a somewhat over-intense Berry plays a husband and father of two children – the "lambs" of the title – with a streak of madness that is arresting enough but does not leave much room for development.

Two other films have found clever ways of coping with the problem of native resources. For **Broken Silence**, his first movie for theatrical release, the German TV director Wolfgang Panzer (who has been working in Switzerland for many years) persuaded Michael Moriarty to take an essential role in the framing story. This account of a monk who leaves his remote convent in Switzerland to travel all the way through India to Indonesia, where he cannot help but break his vow of silence, is a remarkable example of a low-low-budget production that still meets high demands.

Another pleasant surprise of the past

SWISS FILMS

The Swiss Film Center is a non-profit making organization which supports all aspects of professional independent film-making by means of specific promotions and by providing information in Switzerland and abroad.

Swiss Film Center

Neugasse 6, P.O. Box, CH-8031 Zürich
Tel: ++41/1/272 53 30, Fax: ++41/1/272 53 50

TOP TEN GROSSING FILMS IN SWITZERLAND: 1995

	Admissions
GoldenEye	466,115
The Lion King	369,610
Nell	356,470
Pocahontas	327,307
Apollo 13	325,129
Disclosure	309,549
French Kiss	305,580
While You Were Sleeping	295,070
Casper	287,935
Die Hard 3	287,372

year was **Liebe Lügen** – the title can be read as "Dear Lies" as well as "Love Lies" – by Christof Schertenleib. The Berne film-maker, who trained in Vienna, exhibits an unusual freshness and sense of humour in his first full-length feature. The film concerns a group of men and women who may – or may not – be having intimate relationships, and who also live in different places in Switzerland and Austria, travelling all the time from one place to another, which prompts a very creative use of the language problem. This Swiss version of *sex, lies and videotape* (without the latter) probes perceptively, if not too deeply, into contemporary relationships.

The Truth, 24 times...

Forthcoming are new films by Jean-Luc Godard (**For Ever Mozart**), Anne-Marie Miéville (**Nous sommes tous encore ici**), Markus Imhof's story of a young Swiss woman arriving in India before World War I to become a missionary's wife (**Flammen im Paradis**), and Richard Dindo's portrait of Breyten Breytenbach (**Une saison au paradis**). Fredi M. Murer will start his promising double-feature project, **Twice the Whole Truth**, in summer 1997.

Not only is the documentary itself alive and well in Switzerland, but it also has a festival dedicated to it, the Cinéma du réel, as Jean Perret, the new director, now calls the Festival International du film documentaire de Nyon. Swiss films now have a new forum, though it remains to be seen whether established directors will choose Nyon for the world première of their films.

Daniel Schmid still chose Locarno for **The Written Face**, a beautiful reflection – in a metaphorical as well as a literal sense – on the art of Kabuki and some of its greatest interpreters. **Signers Koffer** by Peter Liechti is also the portrait of an artist: the artist as fire-worker. Action-artist Roman Signer explodes objects in front of erupting volcanoes and geysers, sets off rockets or makes chairs fly – a funny, sometimes noisy business in what is at times an almost philosophical visual essay on the principles governing mechanics *and* man's pleasure.

Devils Don't Dream by Andreas Hoessli is an interesting report on the fate of Jacobo Arbenz, the 50s Guatamelan president of Swiss ancestry who was overthrown by the CIA and disappeared from history. **Magic Matterhorn** by Anka Schmid is a not too successful but often funny attempt to investigate *the* symbol of 'Swissness'. **Besser und besser**, the first film by the former director of the Swiss Film Centre, Alfredo Knuchel (co-author Norbert Wiedmer), is an intense portrait of a 'typical' Swiss family confronted with not quite so typical problems, from unemployment to drugs to affiliation with a religious sect.

CHRISTOPH EGGER covers cinema in the media section of the *Neue Zürcher Zeitung* for which he has written since 1978. He is also a member of the Swiss Jury for quality awards and has taught film criticism at the University of Zürich.

Julia Maraval and Alexis Tomassian in Marcel Schüpbach's LES AGNEAUX

Recent and Forthcoming Films

LE ACROBATE

Script: Silvio Soldini, Doriana Leondeff, Laura Bosio. Dir: Soldini. Phot: Luca Bigazzi. Players: Anna Galiena, Valeria Golino. Prod: Aran Film/Vega Film.

LES AGNEAUX

Script: Pascal Bonitzer, Marcel Schüpbach. Dir: Schüpbach. Phot: Denis Jutzeler. Players: Richard Berry, Brigitte Roüan, Julia Maraval, Alexis Tomassian. Prod: Les Productions JMH/ Galatée Films.

BESSER UND BESSER

Script: Alfredo Knuchel. Dir: Knuchel, Norbert Wiedmer. Phot: Wiedmer, Peter Guyer. Prod: Biograph Film/Alfredo Knuchel. *Documentary.*

DEVILS DON'T DREAM! – NACHFORSCHUNGEN ÜBER JACOBO ARBENZ GUZMÁN

Script and Dir: Andreas Hoessli. Phot: Matthias Kälin. Prod: Espaces film. *Documentary.*

FARINET, HÉROS ET HORS-LA-LOI

Script: Denis Rabaglia. Dir: Yvan Bütler. Phot: Jacky Mahrer. Players: Stéphane Freiss, Jean-

The Film Department of PRO HELVETIA
Arts Council of Switzerland

promotes Swiss cinema. We arrange and coordinate seasons, retrospectives and other special film events around the world. We specialize in bilateral exchange with film archives, universities, arthouses, ministries of cultural, etc.

Hirschengraben 22, P.O. Box, CH-8024 Zurich
Phone: ++41 (1) 267 71 71, Fax: ++41 (1) 267 71 08, Telex: 817599

Marc Bory, Florence Darel. Prod: Les Productions Crittin & Thiébaud/ Septembre Productions/ Magma Film.

FLAMMEN IM PARADIES

Script: Markus Imhoof, Judith Kennel. Dir: Imhoof. Phot: Lukas Strebel. Players: Elodie Bouchez, Laurent Grévill, Bruno Todeschini. Prod: Thelma Film/ Zero Film/Ciné Manufacture.

FOR EVER MOZART

Script and Dir: Jean-Luc Godard. Phot: Jean-Marc Fabre. Players: Jean-Louis Richard, Harry Cleven, Lou Castel, Keith Jarret. Prod: Vega Film/Avventura Films.

GATE, GATE, PARAGATE

Script: Nguy Ngu, Hô Quang Minh. Dir: Hô Quang Minh. Phot: Le Dinh An. Players: Phuong Dung, Le Tuan Anh, Hoang Phuc. Prod: Hô Quang Minh/Giai Phong Films.

KATZENDIEBE

Script: Walter Bretscher, Patrick Frey, Beat Schlatter. Dir: Markus Imboden. Phot: Rainer Klausmann. Players: Patrick Frey, Beat Schlatter, Babett Arens, Andrea Guyer. Prod: Vega Film.

KRÄUTER UND KRÄFTE

Script: Jürg Neuenschwander, Alex Sutter. Dir: Neuenschwander. Phot: Patrick Lindenmaier. Prod: Carac Film/ Container TV. *Documentary.*

MAGIC MATTERHORN

Script and Dir: Anka Schmid. Phot: Ciro Cappellari. Players: Geschwister Pfister. Prod: Mano Film/Insert Film. *Documentary.*

MOTOR NASCH

Script and Dir: Sabine Gisiger, Marcel Zwingli. Phot: Helena Vagnières. Prod: Videoladen. *Documentary.*

NOEL FIELD – THE FICTITIOUS SPY

Script and Dir: Werner Schweizer. Phot: Helena Vagnières, Thomas Hartmann. Prod: Dschoint Ventschr. *Documentary.*

PESSOA

Script: Heinz Bütler, Jean Odermatt. Dir: Bütler. Phot: Beat Kuert. Players: Odo Samel, Jessica Früh, Werner Lüdi, Burhan Oeçal. Prod: Xanadu Film.

REIZENDES GIFT

Script and Dir: Priska Forter, Martin Forter. Phot: Priska Forter, Christian Schläpfer. Prod: Fama Film. *Documentary.*

UNE SAISON AU PARADIS

Script and Dir: Richard Dindo. Phot: Pio Corradi, Jürg Hassler. Prod: Lea Produktion/Les Films d'ici. *Documentary.*

SIGNERS KOFFER

Script and Dir: Peter Liechti. Phot: Liechti, Peter Guyer. Prod: Peter Liechti Filmproduktion/ Recycled TV. *Documentary.*

A TICKLE IN THE HEART

Script: Joel Rubin, Rita Ottens, Stefan Schwietert. Dir: Schwietert. Phot: Robert Richman. Players: The Epstein Brothers. Prod: Neapel Film/Oe-Film/Zero Film. *Documentary.*

Producers

Ascot/Elite
(production and distribution)
see address under Distributors

Balzli & Cie Filmproduktion
Hauptstrasse 33
CH-2560 Nidau
Tel: +41 32 51 75 10
Fax: +41 32 51 28 10

Boa Filmproduktion AG
Neugasse 6
CH-8005 Zürich
Tel: +41 1 271 04 64
Fax: +41 1 271 05 18

CAB Productions SA
17, rue du Port-Franc
CH-1003 Lausanne
Tel: +41 21 312 80 56
Fax: +41 21 312 80 64

Carac Film AG
Zinggstrasse 16
CH-3007 Berne
Tel: +41 31 372 00 40
Fax: +41 31 372 04 81

Catpics Coproductions AG
Steinstrasse 21
CH-8003 Zürich
Tel: +41 1 451 23 58
Fax: +41 1 462 01 12

Still from Christof Schertenleib's LIEBE LÜGEN

Ciné Manufacture SA
8, Côtes-de-Montbenon
CH-1003 Lausanne
Tel: +41 21 311 58 58
Fax: +41 21 312 93 43

Arthur Cohn
Gellerstrasse 18
CH-4052 Basel
Tel: +41 61 312 12 42
Fax: +41 61 312 07 17

Condor Films AG
Restelbergstrasse 107
CH-8044 Zürich
Tel: +41 1 361 96 12
Fax: +41 1 361 95 75

Dschoint Ventschr Filmproduktion AG
Zentralstrasse 150
CH-8003 Zürich
Tel: +41 1 456 30 20
Fax: +41 1 456 30 25

Fama Film AG
(production and distribution)
Balthasarstrasse 11
CH-3027 Berne
Tel: +41 31 992 92 80
Fax: +41 31 992 64 04

J.M.H. Productions SA
P.O. Box 58
CH-2005 Neuchâtel
Tel: +41 38 29 00 20
Fax: +41 38 29 00 29

Bernard Lang AG
(production and distribution)
Dorfstrasse 14d
CH-8427 Rorbas
Tel: +41 1 865 66 27
Fax: +41 1 865 66 29

Les Productions Crittin & Thiébaud SA
12, rue Grenus
CH-1201 Geneva
Tel: +41 22 731 69 64
Fax: +41 22 738 27 25

T & C Film AG
Seestrasse 41a
CH-8002 Zürich
Tel: +41 1 202 36 22
Fax: +41 1 202 30 05

Thelma Film AG
Josefstrasse 106
CH-8031 Zürich
Tel: +41 1 271 81 24
Fax: +41 1 271 33 50

Triluna Film AG
Neugasse 6
CH-8005 Zürich
Tel: +41 1 273 00 53
Fax: +41 1 273 01 06

Vega Film AG
Sophienstrasse 2, P.O. Box
CH-8030 Zürich
Tel: +41 1 252 60 00
Fax: +41 1 252 66 35

Distributors

Alexander Film
Lägernstrasse 6, P.O. Box 590
CH-8037 Zürich
Tel: +41 1 362 84 43
Fax: +41 1 361 16 03

Alpha Films SA
P.O. Box 176
CH-1211 Geneva 12
Tel: +41 22 789 45 45
Fax: +41 22 789 35 55

Buena Vista Int. Ltd
Am Schanzengraben 27
CH-8002 Zürich
Tel: +41 1 201 66 55
Fax: +41 1 201 77 70

Columbus Film AG
Steinstrasse 21
CH-8036 Zürich
Tel: +41 1 462 73 66
Fax: +41 1 462 01 12

Elite Film AG
Molkenstrasse 21
CH-8026 Zürich
Tel: +41 1 298 81 81
Fax: +41 1 298 81 70

Fama Film AG
(production and distribution)
see address under Producers

Filmcooperative
Fabrikstrasse 21, P.O. Box 172
CH-8031 Zürich
Tel: +41 1 271 88 00
Fax: +41 1 271 80 38

Focus Film AG
Zollikerstrasse 20
CH-8032 Zürich
Tel: +41 1 382 33 88
Fax: +41 1 382 33 89

Frenetic Film AG
Bachstrasse 9, P.O. Box
CH-8038 Zürich
Tel: +41 1 483 06 60
Fax: +41 1 483 06 61

Bernard Lang AG
(production and distribution)
see address under Producers

Look now!
Staffelstrasse 10
CH-8045 Zürich
Tel: +41 1 201 24 40
Fax: +41 1 201 24 42

Monopole Pathé Films SA
Neugasse 6, P.O. Box 299
CH-8031 Zürich
Tel: +41 1 271 10 03
Fax: +41 1 271 56 43

Praesens Film AG
Münchhaldenstr. 10, P.O. Box 3223
CH-8034 Zürich
Tel: +41 1 422 38 32
Fax: +41 1 422 37 93

Rialto Film AG
Neugasse 6, P.O. Box 299
CH-8021 Zürich
Tel: +41 1 271 42 00
Fax: +41 1 271 42 03

Sadfi SA
8, rue de Hesse, P.O. Box
CH-1211 Geneva 11
Tel: +41 22 311 77 67
Fax: +41 22 781 31 19

Stamm Film AG
Löwenstrasse 20, P.O. Box
CH-8023 Zürich
Tel: +41 1 211 66 15
Fax: +41 1 212 03 69

Trigon-Film, Filmverleih Dritte Welt
Rösmattstrasse 6
CH-4118 Rodersdorf
Tel: +41 61 731 15 15
Fax: +41 61 731 32 88

Twentieth Century Fox
P.O. Box 1049
CH-1211 Geneva 26
Tel: +41 22 343 33 15
Fax: +41 22 343 92 55

UIP (Schweiz) GmbH
Signaustrasse 6, P.O. Box 295
CH-8032 Zürich
Tel: +41 1 383 85 50
Fax: +41 1 383 61 12

Warner Bros.
Studerweg 3, P.O. Box
CH-8802 Kilchberg
Tel: +41 1 715 50 11
Fax: +41 1 715 34 51

Useful Addresses

Swiss Film Centre
Neugasse 6, P.O. Box
CH-8031 Zürich
Tel: +41 1 272 53 30
Fax: +41 1 272 53 50
Lausanne Office (for French-speaking countries):
33, rue St-Laurent
CH-1003 Lausanne
Tel: +41 21 311 03 23
Fax: +41 21 311 03 25

Federal Office of Culture Film Department
Hallwylstrasse 15
CH-3003 Berne
Tel: +41 31 322 92 71
Fax: +41 31 322 92 73

Pro Helvetia Arts Council of Switzerland
Film Department
Hirschengraben 22, P.O. Box
CH-8024 Zürich
Tel: +41 1 267 71 71
Fax: +41 1 267 71 08

Swiss Film Producers' Association SFP
Zinggstrasse 16
CH-3007 Berne
Tel: +41 31 372 40 01
Fax: +41 31 372 40 53

Swiss Film and Video Producers
Weinbergstrasse 31
CH-8001 Zürich
Tel: +41 1 266 64 46
Fax: +41 1 262 29 96

Procinéma
Swiss Association of Exhibitors and Motion Picture Distributors
Effingerstrasse 11, P.O. Box 8175
CH-3011 Berne
Tel: +41 31 381 50 77
Fax: +41 31 382 03 73

SYRIA

Rafik Atassi

1995 was not a fruitful year for the Syrian cinema either in production or distribution. Only one feature was completed, **Ascent of Rain**, by Abdullalif Abdulhamid, whose previous two films – *Nights of the Jackal* and *Verbal Messages* – were the biggest box-office successes in Syrian history. But while these two films dealt with his own minority group, the "Alawailes", in the north-western villages of the country, his new film proved to be a surprise.

It takes place in the city, and it centres on an ageing writer, now bereft of his wits and left alone by his family with little to sustain

Hanan Shkeir in AL-LAJAT

him but his dreams and fantasies. *Ascent of Rain* was shown in competition at the 9th Damascus Film Festival, along with **Al-Lajat**, written and directed by Riad Shaya, which deals with another minority group, the "Druz" in the south. Both films have yet to be shown commercially, although they have been seen at film festivals around the world. It's a fate they share with Osama Mohammad's **Stars of Midday** and Mohammad Malas' **The Night**, which were produced years ago.

A Plan for All Seasons

The Syrian National Film Organisation is the only film producer left in the country after the private producers deserted for the more lucrative fields of TV and video production. Its head, film-maker Marwan Haddad, is fond of announcing ambitious future plans, and the latest version is a proposal to make seven feature films and many short documentaries.

At the top of the list we find two veteran directors: Nabil Maleh (*The Leopard, Fragments, Extras*) is now preparing a new film, **Hasiba**, based on a novel by Khairi Dahabi; and Samir Zekra is preparing a film, **The Dust of Strangers**, about a Syrian historical figure, Abdulrahman Al-Kawakbi, who rebelled against Turkish occupation in the last century. Raymon Butrus (*Al-Tahaleb*) began shooting his second film, **On the Move**, in his hometown of Hama, and Ghassan Shmeit will join him soon on his next film, **Zahr Al-Rumman** (although his first feature, *Something Is Burning*), was not well received.

Under the plan, two new film-makers will have a chance to make their débuts. Munner Fanary's **Hananou** is about another Syrian national hero who participated in the revolt against French occupation in the 30s, and the actress Waha Raheb will venture behind the cameras for **Dreams**. Her short, *Our Grandmothers*, was well received five years ago.

Haddad himself is currently writing a script on the Syrian hero Youssef Azma, who was Minister for War when the French invaded Syrian territory in 1921, and who preferred to die on the battlefield than surrender to the colonial power. Seven films, most of them having to do with historical figures, is an ambitious programme. How far into the future it will take us remains to be seen.

RAFIK ATASSI is a Syrian film critic who has written many books on Arabic cinema, and contributes to numerous journals in the Arabic world and abroad. He has prepared several scripts for cinema and TV and has a weekly cinema programme on Syrian TV. He is currently director of programmes for the Syrian satellite channel.

TOP TEN GROSSING FILMS IN SYRIA: 1995

Bekhil and Adila (Adel Imam – Egypt)*
The Terrorist (Adel Imam – Egypt)*
Cliffhanger
Under Siege
The Last Action Hero
Baby's Night Out
Universal Soldier
Home Alone 2
Forrest Gump
The Bandit Queen (India)

*The Egyptian comedian Adel Imam is a box-office phenomenon throughout the Arab world; for the third year in a row, two of his films have grossed far more than any other film, foreign or local, in Syria.

Producers

National Film Organisation
Rawda
Damascus
Tel: 3334200

Nader Atassi
Fardous str
Damascus
Tel: 2216009

Tahseen Kawadri
Tigheez str
Damascus
Tel: 2230767

Ghanem Films
Malki
Damascus
Tel: 3336279

Igraa Films
Khateeb str
Damascus
Tel: 4441446

Raja Group
Salhia
Damascus
Tel: 3324533
Fax: 3324539

Cham Al-Dawlia
Mezza
Damascus
Tel: 6133382

Distributors

Tiba and Abboud
Fardous str
Damascus
Tel: 2221096

Mamoun Serri
Fardous str
Damascus
Tel: 2211888

Shamra
Mezza
Damascus
Tel: 6662812

Ibrahim Nejma
Ayyar str
Damascus
Tel: 4427008

Useful Addresses

Cham Cinema
Maysaloun str
Damascus
Tel: 2232300

Boraq
Mazraa
Damascus
Tel: 4449306

Haysam Hatahet
Salheia
Damascus
Tel: 2222212

Saad
Baghdad str
Damascus
Tel: 4427153

Daoud Sheikhani
Rawda
Damascus
Tel: 3333491

Damascene Rose
Abdul Masih Atia
Tijara
Damascus
Tel: 4457532

Syndicate of Artists
Baghdad str
Damascus
Tel: 4445809

Syrian TV
Omayad Square
Damascus
Tel: 2212000

Bahjat Khouri
Kowatli str
Homs
Tel: 224357

Al-Dawlia
Ahmad Shehabi
Aleppo

Still from THE ASCENT OF RAIN

Still from AL-LAJAT, a study of marital life in the Druz area

TAIWAN

Derek Elley

Taiwanese cinema is at its lowest ebb since the late 1970s, with local production at an all-time nadir, the market swamped by U.S. product, and even Hong Kong films struggling to find an audience. In a year when the island's two leading lights, Edward Yang and Hou Hsiao-hsien, both came up with disappointing works, the future for local production looks bleaker than ever before.

The figures for 1994 give some idea of the problem: 18 Taiwanese productions were released, against 138 from Hong Kong. Since then the situation has worsened: in 1995 not one Hong Kong film made the box-office top ten, which was totally dominated by U.S. movies. The highest Hong Kong grossers (see table) were the Jackie Chan films *Rumble in the Bronx* and *Thunderbolt*, followed by *God of Gamblers' Return*.

However, the box-office figures for Taiwanese films put the whole problem into sharp perspective. The top-grosser, the big-budget, mainland-shot war drama *Don't Cry, Nanking*, managed only NT$6.5 million ($240,000), followed by *Tropical Fish* (NT$4.2 million) and Steve Wang's *The Daughter-in-Law* (NT$3.3 million; see IFG 1996). Hou Hsiao-hsien's *Good Men, Good Women* grossed NT$960,000 ($35,500).

Still from Edward Yang's MAHJONG

Aside from the indefinable factor of changing tastes, the relative demise of Hong Kong fare in a market it traditionally dominated has been ascribed to producers asking unreasonably high prices (forced on them by Hong Kong actors' rocketing demands). After being badly burned by some flops in 1994, Taiwanese distributors are now much more cautious in their buying.

Auteurism Run Amok

But the screen space given to Hong Kong movies is still ample compared with that for local productions: exhibitors just don't want to show them. Edward Yang has reportedly decided not even to open his latest film, **Mahjong**, on the basis that the expense would never be recouped. However, most film-makers have nobody but themselves to blame. The Taiwanese public's loss of faith in its own movies is the ultimate price of auteurism run amok, a (largely government-supported) policy that has everything to do with winning prizes at foreign film festivals and indulging artistic pretensions while ignoring the entertainment needs of audiences.

One solution proposed from within the industry is to invest in movies shot on the mainland and concentrate on distribution there. The production company Long Shong, which largely financed *Don't Cry, Nanking (Nanjing 1937)* has already announced it is to pull out of production, following losses on several pictures by "name" directors. Taiwan's industry desperately needs more directors of the calibre of Ang Lee, who can make quality movies that still find audiences. Lee is still promising to return home again (this time for a costume swordplay project), when he can find time between U.S. pictures.

Edward Yang's long-awaited **Mahjong** (*Majiang*) turned out to be not as wilfully obscure as his previous *A Confucian Confusion*, but very mixed in its achievement. A complex web of overlapping stories centred on a collection of Chinese and foreigners in contemporary Taipei, the film is much more successful in its Chinese-language segments than in its forced (and often unnatural) sections in English.

Starting with the kidnap of a young French woman (Virginie Ledoyen) by a group of teenage wannabe gangsters, the movie fans out to embrace a cross-section of the various constituents of modern Taiwanese society to show the loss of values following the breakdown of traditional Confucian beliefs. The theme (a favourite of Yang's) is valid, but the film is too sprawling and unfocused for its own good.

It is, however, far more engaging than Hou Hsiao-hsien's **Goodbye South, Goodbye** (*Nanguo zaijian, nanguo*), the second film in his current contract with Japan's Shochiku. Where his previous *Good Men, Good Women* at least had some historical resonances, this latest (widely trumpeted as a major change in style) is almost a parody of his alienating style, following a group of losers led by a small-time gangster (Jack Kao) on an odyssey to the south of the island. The minimalist, ennui-laden content is made more obscure by huge lacunae: Hou's original cut of the two-hour film reportedly ran six hours.

Familiar Territory

The past year's best film came not from Yang or Hou but from Wan Jen, whose steady career has not had such a high festival profile. Though it could do with some tightening, **Super Citizen Ko** (*Chaoji da guomin*) is a quiet but often horrifying look at Taiwan's White Terror of the 1950s, through the memories of an old man (the superb Lin Yang) searching for a dead friend's grave. The film started life as an update on his 1985 social panorama *Super Citizen*, but developed into Wan's most deeply felt and serious work to date – the first explicitly political movie (in the Western sense) to come out of Taiwan.

More familiar in its territory, but drawing good reviews from its Critics' Week slot in the 1996 Cannes Festival, is **A Drifting Life** (*Chunhua menglu*), the first feature by former documentary maker Lin

Lin Yang in SUPER CITIZEN KO

Cheng-sheng. Set in the countryside during the 1950s and 1960s, and centred on a young man who is faced with fulfilling family duties just when he has found happiness with his second wife, the film is unremarkable stylistically and recalls a host of other period Taiwanese movies, but has a genuine feels for its characters and an unforced warmth.

Livelier, and full of quirky visual touches and offbeat characters, is TV director Ch'en Yü-hsün's **Tropical Fish** (*Redai yü*), a film centred on youngsters that plays equally

TOP TEN GROSSING FILMS IN TAIPEI: 1995

	(NT$ million)
Die Hard 3	137.3
Apollo 13	74.0
Waterworld	72.2
Under Siege 2	70.7
Stargate	68.3
Outbreak	64.5
Congo	60.6
While You Were Sleeping	60.6
Disclosure	59.3
The Shawshank Redemption	58.4

Of other notable films, Jackie Chan's *Rumble in the Bronx* grossed NT$54.0m, his subsequent *Thunderbolt* NT$37.5m, *Clear and Present Danger* NT$58.3m, *Judge Dredd* NT$55.5m, the Hongkong production *God of Gamblers' Return* NT$47.7m, and *Showgirls* NT$44.5m. US$1=NT$27.

*Began release in late Dec. '94.

well to children and adults. Revolving around a kid who should be studying for a key exam but instead ends up involved in a kidnapping, the film takes a good-natured look at adolescent growing-pains as well as the crazed local media. It's an entertaining, likeable movie that bodes well for the young director.

DEREK ELLEY has been associated with IFG for more than 20 years, during which time he has written extensively on East Asian cinema. An associate editor of Variety, he is also editor of the annual Variety Movie Guide. He is currently completing A Handbook of Chinese Cinema.

32nd Golden Horse Awards

The following were the main awards announced on December 9, 1995:

Best Film: *Summer Snow.**
Best Director: Hou Hsiao-hsien *(Good Men, Good Women).*
Best Original Script: Ch'en Yu-hsün *(Tropical Fish).*
Best Adapted Script: Chu T'ien-wen *(Good Men, Good Women).*
Best Actor: Lin Yang *(Super Citizen Ko).*
Best Actress: Josephine Siao *(Summer Snow).**
Best Supporting Actor: Law Kar-ying *(Summer Snow).**
Best Supporting Actress: Wen Ying *(Tropical Fish).*
Best Photography: Lee Ping-bing *(Summer Snow).**
Best Editing: William Chang, Wong Ming-lam *(Fallen Angels).**
Best Production Design: William Chang *(Fallen Angels).**
Best Costume Design: Ting Yuen-tai *(Evening Liaison).**
Best Action Direction: Cory Yuen, Cory Yuen Stunt Team, Sammo Hung Stunt Team *(Thunderbolt).**
Best Music: Lee Shou-ch'üan, Fan Tsung-p'ei *(Super Citizen Ko).*
Best Song: Ch'en Sheng *(The Peony Pavilion).*
Best Sound: Tu Tu-chih *(Good Men, Good Women).*
Life Achievement Award: Lee Hsing.
Special Award for a Mainlander: Jet Lee.

*Hong Kong production.

Recent and Forthcoming Films

TAIPING, TIANGUO (Buddha Bless America)

Dir: Wu Nien-jen. Player: Lin Cheng-sheng.

FEI TIAN (Accidental Legend)

Dir: Wang Hsiao-ti. Players: Niu Cheng-tse, Renee Liu, Miao T'ien, K'o Hsiao-pao, Lei Ming. Prod: CMPC.

HELIU (The River)

Dir: Ts'ai Ming-liang. Players: Li K'ang-sheng, Ch'en Chao-jung. Prod: CMPC. In production summer 1996.

MEILI ZAI CHANGGE (Beautiful When Singing)

Dir: Li Cheng-sheng. Players: Renee Liu Tseng Ching, Miao T'ien. Prod: CMPC. In production summer 1996.

HONG SHIZI (Red Persimmon)

Dir: Wang T'ung. Players: T'ao Shu, Shih Chün, Wang Chüan, Lu Chih. Prod: CMPC.

JINTIAN BU HUIJIA (Tonight Nobody Goes Home)

Dir: Sylvia Chang. Players: Sihung Lung, Kuei Ya-lei, Yang Kuei-mei, Winston Chao, Renee Liu. Prod: CMPC.

AH CHUNG

Dir: Chang Tso-chi. Players: Lieh Sheng-chung, Chou Shou-min, Lu Ying, Ho Huang-chi. Prod: Hong Rong Films.

MODENG GONGHEGUO (Modern Republic)

Dir: Mark Lee. Players: Jeff Huang, Stanley Huang, Steven Lin, Yang Kuei-mei, Li T'ien-lu. Prod: Unique Entertainment.

WANREN QINGFU (Everyone's Lover)

Dir: T'ao Shu-hua, from the novel by Yüan Ch'iung-ch'iung. Players: Joan Chen, Sihung Lung, Tony Leung Kar-wai, Yang Kuei-mei.

Useful Addresses

Central Motion Picture Corp. (CMPC)
8/F, 116 Hanchung St.
Taipei
Tel: (886-2) 371-5191
Fax: (886-2) 331-0681

Chang-Hong Channel Film & Video Co.
3/F, No. 9, Alley 6, Lane 166
Section 3, Hsinyi Rd.
Taipei
Tel: (886-2) 705-2603
Fax: (886-2) 709-0334

Long Shong Pictures
2nd floor, 113 Hankou St., Section 2
Taipei
Tel: (886-2) 311-0249
Fax: (886-2) 314-5157

Scholar Films Co.
10th floor, 88 Omei St.
Taipei
Tel: (886-2) 361-5850
Fax: (886-2) 311-9692

3-H Films
3rd floor, No. 19, Lane 2
Wanli St.
Taipei
Tel: (886-2) 230-0136

Taiwan Film Centre
4th floor, No. 19, Lane 2
Wanli St.
Taipei
Tel: (886-2) 239-6026
Fax: (886-2) 239-6501

THAILAND

Anchalee Chaiworaporn

Ironically, the box-office in Thailand has been booming, due to a multiplexing blitzkrieg, while the number of features produced has continued to drop. In 1995, only 41 films were made, compared with 57 in 1994 and 64 the year before.

The first multiplex theatres were opened in 1994 by Entertain Golden Village (EGV). They proved so popular that EGV could open 62 multiplexes in Bangkok in less than two years. The new technology on offer might be a delight to audiences, but their real attraction is the menu of movies available in one place. Traffic in Bangkok is a major problem, and multiplexes eliminate the need to travel between theatres.

EGV was the creation of three companies: the Thai-based movie mogul family of Poolvoraruk, the Singapore-based Golden Harvest Company, and the Australian Village Roadshow Company. After EGV's success, a number of businessmen rushed to share in the bonanza, and in two years about 180 multiplex theatres were built in Bangkok alone. By 1998, two hundred more will open.

Foreign films have mainly reaped the rewards. In 1995, 300 foreign films were released, nearly eight times the number of domestic films (41). Foreign films in Thailand come mainly from two places: Hollywood and Hong Kong. But it is the American majors that have profited from the multiplex boom. Once upon a time, more Hong Kong movies were screened in Thailand, but their numbers have been declining in recent years due to their repetitious action and comedy formulas. From 144 films in 1993, they have dropped to 117 in 1995, while American releases in 1995 doubled to 183 from 98 two years earlier.

Compared to Thai films, however, Hong Kong films are still fortunate. They have retained their popularity up-country, though here audiences may not have much choice. Local distributors prefer booking cheap Hong Kong movies or Thai B-graders to their theatres. And independent or art films have the least luck of all. In Bangkok, some art films will have a brief run. One hears of filmgoers in remote villages travelling for many hours to Bangkok to see films at the weekend.

Though still lagging behind in numbers, the Thai industry did exhibit some signs of both box-office success and a development in quality. Three Thai films managed to gross more than Bt50 million (US$2 million), breaking the record of Bt45 million set in 1993 by the Thai blockbuster *Kawao Thee Bangphleng*. These films were mostly pitched at the teenage audience,

Teen-drama SIA DAI broke the Thai box-office record

particularly the number one hit, **Romantic Blues** (*Lok Thang Bai Hai Nai Khon Diao*), about two brothers falling in love with the same girl. Both the lead actor and actress are pop stars in their own right, and their soundtrack album was released with the film.

But the film was also welcomed by the critics, and received eight National Film Awards, including best picture and best director. Two Thai films, **Once Upon a Time...** (*Kallakhrung Nueng Muea Chao Nee*) and *Ruen Mayura*, were often shown in the international markets. And those in the industry began talking about Thai films going abroad.

The veteran director Prince Chatreechalerm Yukol struck it rich at the box office for the first time in his career with another teenage entry, **To Deplore** (*Sia Dai*). This is a social drama about four teenage girls who run away from home and become involved in child prostitution. The third biggest hit was **The Destined Couple** (*Khoo Kam*), about a love affair between a Japanese naval officer and a Thai woman during the Second World War. This is the eighth remake of a popular novel.

Nine other films grossed more than Bt13 million (US$520,000) in 1995. These would have been bank-busting figures by Thai standards a few years ago, but not any more. Production and promotion costs have risen precipitously, to Bt10 million (US$400,000) and more. *The Destined Couple* was only a marginal financial success, since Grammy Film shelled out Bt40 million (US$1,600,000) for production and approximately another Bt20 million (US$800,000) for promotion. The question also arises whether the declared gross is a true barometer of a film's success. The true gross of some films is hidden because many film companies want to avoid paying higher taxes.

The highest hopes for the Thai movie industry in 1995-96 were pinned on the intervention of the country's top two record companies, RS Film and Grammy Film. RS Film had never dabbled in this area of show business before, but employed veteran director Adirek Wattaleela to manage its film department. Grammy Film already had its own TV production house under the name Exact

TOP TEN GROSSING FILMS IN THAILAND: 1995

	*Baht million**
Die Hard 3	60
Lok Thang Bai Hai Nai Khon Diao (Thai)	60
Sia Dai (Thai)	52
Khoo Kam (Thai)	50
Waterworld	48
Batman Forever	47.2
Casper	46.6
Congo	45.5
Kerd Eek Thee Tong Mee Ther (Thai)	40
Forrest Gump	36

*Baht, average exchange rate, 25 baht per U.S. Dollar

Top singer Thongchai McIntyre in KHOO KAM

Co., and is thus more equipped with its own professional directors.

After their success, other film companies began to go the multi-media route. Saha Mongkol Film, which previously distributed foreign films and produced Thai movies, announced their intention of creating a record company. Some new film companies were also born: the well-known director Bandit Ritthakol formed Star Pictures, which will give both old and new names the opportunity to direct.

Producers

Five Star Productions Co., Ltd.
157/9 Soi Areesamphan 2
Bangkok 10310
Fax: 2462105, 2457931

Star Pictures International
61/1 Soi Thaweemitr 2
Rama 9 Rd., Huaykwang
Phyathai, Bangkok 10400
Fax: 2781486

R.S. Film
419/1 Chetchotisak Building
Ladphrao 15 (Soi Chomphon)
Jatujark, Bangkok 10900
Fax: 5112324

Grammy Film
209/1 CMIC Tower B,
Sukhumvit 21, Klong Toey
Bangkok 10110
Fax: 6640246

Saha Mongkol Film Co., Ltd.
Mongkol Film Bldg.
1081/5 Phaholyothin Rd.,
Phyathai, Bangkok 10400
Fax: 2710620

Tai Entertainment
79/23 Srinakarin Rd.,
Nongbon, Pravej
Bangkok 10260
Fax: 3660377

N.K. Entertainment
261/107 Charansanitwong Rd.,
Bangkok Noi
Bangkok 10700
Fax: 4128102

Kantana Motion Picture Co., Ltd.
333 Soi Ratchadanivej 19
Pracha-u-tit Rd., Huay Kwang
Bangkok 10310
Fax: 2754530

UMA 1991 Co., Ltd.
34 Soi Santisevee
Pradipat Rd. 12
Phyathai, Bangkok 10400
Fax: 2794003

Foreign Film Distributors

United International Pictures
SEI Bldg., Room 605
315 Silom Road
Bangkok 10500
Fax: 2367597

Nondhanan Entertainment Co., Ltd.
113/10 Soi Surawong Center
Surawong Rd., Bangkok 10500
Fax: 2385290

Mongkol Cinema Co., Ltd.
Mongkol Film Bldg.
1081/5 Phyathai
Samsen-nai Bangkok 10400
Fax: 2710620

Useful Addresses

Department of Motion Picture and Still Photography
Faculty of Communication Arts
Chulalongkorn University
Phaya Thai Rd., Bangkok 10330

Film Department
Faculty of Journalism and Mass Communication
Thammasat University
2 Phrachan Rd.,
Bangkok 10200

National Film Archive
4 Chao Fah Road
Bangkok 10200

TUNISIA

Roy Armes

Tunisian cinema continues to have plenty of films either on release or in production. After three short films, Mohamed Zran has finally got a feature film project, **Essaïda**, in production. Taieb Louhichi – still best known, perhaps, for his first feature, *Shadow of the Earth* – has a project called **Moon Wedding**, and Ali Labidi is still working on his long-planned historical piece, **Redeyef 1954**. Best news of all, Nouri Bouzid is at work on a new feature – his first since *Bezness* in 1992 – **Girl from a Good Family** *(Bint familia)*.

Of the films on release, one of the most striking is **The Fire Dance**, directed by one of the Arab world's rare female feature film directors, Selma Baccar, who made her only previous feature, *Fatma 75*, back in 1978. *The Fire Dance* tells of the life of Habiba M'Sika, a singer and dancer who created her own band of devoted admirers but also scandalised Tunisian audiences in the 1920s. She was a woman caught up in a period of turmoil: a nationalist but someone influenced by European ideas; a woman passionate about traditional Arab poetry, but influenced by the life style of some of the more outrageous European performers of the period: Sarah Bernhardt, Isadora Duncan and Loie Fuller. Almost as important as the personal trajectory of the singer herself are the mutations of Tunisian society in a period of huge foreign influence, yet marked, at the same time, by a growing awareness of a distinct cultural identity. The 1920s emerge as a period of tolerance and interaction, before the rigidities of today became fixed.

In Search of Lost Liberty

Ferid Boughedir's **One Summer at La Goulette** also looks back to the past, in this case to the Tunisian port-resort of La Goulette in the 1960s. But in fact this is very much the timeless narrative world of Boughedir's earlier and more accomplished 1990s feature, *Halfaouine*. The attempt to set the new film's action specifically in July 1967 (the eve of the Six Day War) is clumsy, and the film lacks the clear narrative line that helped make *Halfaouine* such a success. Here the storyline would better sustain a soap opera than a 90-minute narrative: three girls who are close friends (the Christian Tina, the Jewish Gigi and the Muslim Meriem) play a game of swapping their (equally religiously variegated) boyfriends and are caught by their parents. Can the close lifelong friendships of their fathers survive? *One Summer at La Goulette* is an uneven and untidily constructed film, complete with touches of nudity which will doubtless ensure its success with Tunisian audiences. Its plea for the tolerance which marked Boughedir's own childhood in Tunis is admirably stated.

The same nostalgia for a liberal past – though more soberly expressed – is to be found in the work of Mahmoud Ben Mahmoud, who has made several video documentaries as well as two features, *Crossings* and the co-directed *Chichkhan*. His latest 30-minute documentary, **Albert Samama-Chikli**, traces the life of the pioneer Tunisian film-maker (1872-1934) who, in the early 1920s, made both the first Tunisian fictional short and the first silent Tunisian feature. The latter film, *The Girl from Carthage (Aïn al-ghazal*, 1924), which was shot by the Jewish Chikli, starred his Christian daughter Haydée and a Muslim co-star, and was produced under the benevolent eye of the Bey of Tunis, who even came to watch the shooting. A bygone age, but also a remarkable achievement by Chikli, who emerges as one of the Third World's great film pioneers.

Nothing could be further in tone or texture from the nostalgia and pleas for tolerance of these Tunisian-made works than **Bye Bye**, shot in Marseilles by the principal Tunisian-born director living in exile, Karim Dridi, who two years ago made an impressive début with *Pigalle*. Two brothers – an adolescent (Ismaël) and a 14-year-old (Mouloud) – arrive in Marseilles to stay for a fortnight with their aunt and uncle, en route (perhaps) to North Africa, where their parents have returned. The film paints a vivid picture of émigré life in the slums around the port: the overcrowding at home paralleled by the close intermingling in the nearby streets, where sex, violence, vandalism and racism are all turned inwards. The action has its racial aspects, bringing the emigrants into conflict with the local whites, but the key does not lie in this racial distinction: any friend or neighbour is a likely victim of vandalism, treachery and crime. Dridi's view of urban life is harsh and uncompromising, and he keeps his (often hand-held) camera close into the action to powerful, dramatic effect.

Recent Films

BYE BYE

Script: Karim Dridi, Marie Léotard. Dir: Dridi. Phot: John Mathieson. Players: Sami Bouajila, Nozha Kouadra, Philippe Ambrosini, Ouassini Embarek, Jamila Darwich-Farah, Frédéric Andrau, Sofiane Mammeri, Marie Borowski. Prod: ADR (France)/La Sept Cinéma/ Thelma Filmd AS (Zurich)/ SNC/CMC/TSR/Canal Plus.

LA DANSE DU FEU (The Fire Dance)

Script and Dir: Selma Baccar. Phot: Allal Yahioui. Players: Souad Amidou, Feodine Atkine, Nejib Belkadhi, Noureddine Ben Aziza. Prod: Intermédia Productions/Phenicea Films/ ERTT (Tunisia)/CAAIC (Algeria)/Canal Horizons/Auraman (France).

UN ÉTÉ À LA GOULETTE (One Summer at La Goulette)

Script and Dir: Ferid Boughedir. Phot: Robert Alazraki. Players: Gamil Ratib, Mustapha Adouani, Guy Nataf, Yvo Salerno, Mohamed Driss, Amel Hedhili. Prod: Marsa Films (France)/ Cinarès (Tunisia)/Lamy Films/ RTBF/La Sept Cinéma.

ESSAÏDA

Script and Dir: Mohamed Zran. Phot: Jean-Claude Couty. Players: Hichem Rostom, Chadly Bouzayen, Myriam Amarouchene, Faozia Badre, Abdallah Maymoun, Tayeb Oueslati. Prod: Sangho Films.

ALBERT SAMAMA-CHIKLI

Script and Dir: Mahmoud ben Mahmoud. Phot: Youssef Ben Youssef. Prod: Alif Productions (France).

Useful Addresses

Carthage Image
(Formerly SATPEC: Film Laboratory)
20 avenue Taeib Mehri
Gammarth 2003
Tunisia
Tel: 2161 740 944

ERRT (Establissement de la Radiodiffusion Télévision Tunisienne)
(National Television Company)
71 rue de la Liberté
Tunia 1004
Tunisia
Tel: 2161 287 300
Fax: 2161 785 146

Canal Horizons Tunisie
(Television Company)
rue de la Monnaie
Tunia 1000
Tunisia
Tel: 2161 333 100
Fax: 2161 333 104

Journées Cinématographiques de Carthage
(Biennial Film Festival)
5 rue Ali Belhouane
2070 La Marsa
Tunisia
Tel: 2161 745 355
Fax: 2161 745 564

SeptièmArt
(Film journal)
B.P. 992
1045 R.P. Tunisia
Tel: 256 904

Festival International du Film Amateur de Kelibia (FIFAK)
(Film Festival)
B.P. 116
1015 Tunis
Tel: 2161 280 298

TURKEY

Atilla Dorsay

For the first time in a decade, Turkey did not have a stand at the 1996 Cannes Film Festival due to the indecision of the Ministry of Culture. This was because there was no ministry, nor a prime minister, nor a government, after an ongoing political crisis left Turkey in a political void. The creation of a coalition did not really help matters because of the lack of agreement between the two partners involved. Nevertheless, the state film subsidy, which stopped a year ago because of severe economic problems, was resumed. Combined with private TV sponsors and the European Eurimages fund, it could give serious backing to production.

About 20 films were made last year but only half of them had a theatrical release. Turkish cinema veterans – directors, actors and technicians – united to create a Foundation for the Turkish Cinema. They financed two films made up of five sketches each: **Loves with Gravity** (*Yerçekimli Aşklar*) and **Everything Untold About Love** (*Aşk Üzerine Söylenmemiş Herşey*). Some of those episodes were among the best films ever made in the Turkish cinema, especially those by Zeki Ökten, Atif Yilmaz, Erden Kiral, Ali Özgentürk and Bariş Pirhasan. The latter film was chosen to open the big Turkish cinema retrospective at the Beaubourg in Paris (105 films, from the beginning to the present, to be shown between April and October 1996). But public response in Turkey was worse than poor, so this cinema-saving initiative proved a flop.

Down These Mean Streets

The middle generation has produced some interesting films. **The Cockroach** (*Böcek*) deciphered the character of an authoritarian police commissar in the post-coup days of the early 80s. The energetic Yavuz Özkan began a trilogy of films depicting male-female relations within the present-day Turkish bourgeoisie. The first of them, **Anatomy of a Woman** (*Bir Kadinin Anatomisi*), was a psychologically acute portrait of a contemporary woman and a box-office success. Canan Gerede, in her second film, **Love Is Colder than Death** (*Aşk Ölümden Soğuktur*), explored the harsh realities of love and passion. Drawing her inspiration as well as her title from Fassbinder, she turned the artificial İstanbul of the film's background into a personal and persuasive world of her own.

Two newcomers surprised us. Biket İlhan, another woman director, based her first film on a well-known novel of her ex-husband, Attila İlhan. **The Man in the Street** (*Sokaktaki Adam*) was a revamped *film noir* and a period piece of 1950s İstanbul. Kutluğ Ataman, an ambitious young director who has studied in the U.S. and made some successful shorts, finally presented the Turkish-American co-production he made some time ago: **The Serpent's Tale** (*Karanhk Sular*). A dazzling visual experience and a rather surealistic tale, this tells of the strange link between an old Ottoman family and their last descendant. Making remarkable use of an unknown and mysterious İstanbul, the young director makes the town a major ingredient of his stunning mystical story.

Taking Off

Some other interesting films financed mainly by state television, TRT, were broadcast without a theatrical release and therefore received little critical attention. But the biggest event of 1995 and the early months of '96 has been **Istanbul Beneath My Wings** (*İstanbul Kanatlarimin Altinda*) by a young director, Mustafa Altioklar,

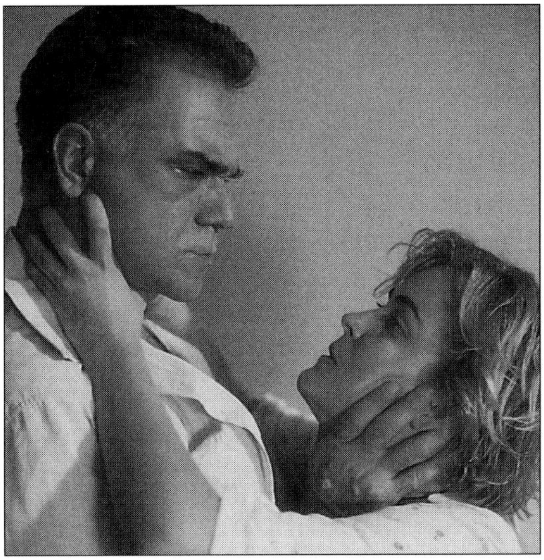

Still from Ümit Elçi's THE COCKROACH

who has made some short films and, four years ago, a first feature, **The Balcony** (*Denize Hançer Düştü*). His new film deals with an interesting and controversial personality of Ottoman history, Hezarifen Ahmet Çelebi, who supposedly lived in the 17th century and dreamt of being the first man to fly. He seems, according more to legend than authenticated history, to have succeeded. Launching himself from the top of the Galata tower, with two wings manufactured by himself and others, he is said to have landed safely on the other side of the Bosphorus.

This historical film, a super-production between Turkey and Spain, is the first Turkish film to attract large audiences for many years: almost 400,000 admissions within the first few months. But it has also rekindled old arguments about censorship and free speech. Not that it was censored: for some time, film censorship has only existed in theory and no major Turkish or foreign film has been censored for many years. But the new coalition's Minister of Culture condemned the film as "an insult to our ancestors", because Sultan Murat 4 is shown as a bisexual and a drunk.

The fact that this is not the major concern of the film, and that anyway the sultan was no real saint, did not stop the minister from starting a campaign against Altioklar's film and turning it, of course, into a bigger hit than it would have been. But the main thing remains the hope and optimism that this film has brought into the darkness of Turkish cinema. After this huge commercial success, people have started to believe again in the possibility of success and many new projects are about to begin.

Oranges, Clockwork and Golden

More than 200 foreign films, mostly from the U.S., entered distribution last year. The majors as usual dominated the market, but American independents and films from all over the world were also shown. The top-ten list does not include any surprises compared to the rest of the world. Twenty-four national critics meanwhile made their traditional yearly choices, and their five best were as follows: Angelopoulos/*Ulysses' Gaze*, Bryan Singer/*Usual Suspects*, Mel Gibson/*Braveheart*, Peter Greenaway/*The Cook, the Thief, His Wife and Her Lover*, Stanley Kubrick/*A Clockwork Orange* (shown in Turkey for the very first time!).

Theatres continued to multiply, mainly in the big towns. About 20 new screens opened in İstanbul alone, and more than 30 are under construction, all as modern multiplexes. Admission prices for first-run films rose to 400,000 Turkish liras, which is around five dollars. In Antalya, the 32nd national festival awarded the Golden Orange to Ümit Elçi's *Cockroach*. The 15th İstanbul Film Festival, with a jury headed by Robert Wise, gave its Golden Tulip prize to the Dutch film, *Little Sister*, by Robert Jan Westdjik. The FIPRESCI prizes in Istanbul went to *The Confessional* by Robert Lepage and, among the Turkish films, to **80. Step** (*Sekseninci Adim*) by Tomris Giritlioğlu, one of the TV productions already mentioned.

ATILLA DORSAY was born in 1939 in Izmir and has been a film critic since 1966. He is the author of 15 books on the cinema, is president of SIYAD, the Turkish film critics' association, and a member of the organising committee of the Istanbul Film Festival.

TOP TEN GROSSING FILMS IN TURKEY: 1995

	Admissions
The Lion King	885,000
Braveheart	750,000
Ace Ventura: When Nature Calls	560,000
Richie Rich	558,000
Seven	385,000
Casper	375,000
Disclosure	358,000
İstanbul Beneath My Wings (*Turkish*)	330,000
101 Dalmatians	327,000
Waterworld	290,000

Recent Films

İSTANBUL KANATLARIMIN ALTINDA (Istanbul Beneath My Wings)

Script and Dir: Mustafa Altioklar. Phot: Uğur İçbak. Players: Ege Aydan, Beatriz Rico, Okan Bayülgen, Savaş Ay. Prod: Umut Sanat Ürünleri.

AŞK ÖLÜMDEN SOĞUKTUR (Love Is Colder than Death)

Script and Dir: Canan Gerede. Phot: Jürgen Jürges. Players: Bennu Gerede, Kadir İnanir. Prod: Scarabee Films (Paris)/Sinegroup (Turkey).

SEKSENİNCİ ADIM (80. Step)

Script: Mehmet Eroğlu. Dir: Tomris Giritlioğlu. Phot: Yavuz Türker. Players: Zühal Olcay, Levent Ülgen, Haluk Bilginer. Prod: TRT-Turkish State TV.

BİR KADININ ANATOMİSİ (Anatomy of a Woman)

Script and Dir: Yavuz Özkan. Phot: Ertunç Sęnkay. Players: Hülya Avşar, Mehmet Aslantuğ, Uğur Polat. Prod: Z Film.

SOĞUK GECELER (Cold Nights)

Script and Dir: Kadir Sözen. Phot: Ertunç Şenkay. Players: Menderes Samancilar, Rahim Çakmak. Prod: Par Productions.

AŞK ÜZERİNE SÖYLENMEMİŞ HERŞEY (Everything Untold About Love)

Dir: Ömer Kavur, İrfan Tözüm, Yusuf Kurçenli, Erden Kiral, Zeki Ökten. Players: Zühal Olcay, Lale Mansur, Hale Soygazi, Fikret Kuşkan, Tarik Akan, Serap Aksoy. Prod: Sinema Vakfi.

YERÇEKİMLİ AŞKLAR (Loves with Gravity)

Dir: Orhan Oğuz, Ali Özgentürk, Bariş Pirhasan, Memduh Ün, Atif Yilmaz. Prod: Sinema Vakfi.

Useful Addresses

Çağdaş Sinema Oyunculari Derneği (ASOD)
(The Association of Actors)
Istiklal Caddesi, Atlas sineması pasajı, C Blok 53/3
Beyoğlu
Istanbul
Tel: (212) 251 97 75
Fax: (212) 251 97 79

Çizgi Filmciler Derneği
(The Association of Animated Film-makers)
P.K. 420 Galatasaray
Istanbul
Tel: (212) 244 34 99

Dünya Kitle İletişim Vakfi
(World Mass Communication Foundation)
Özveren Sokak No 3/8 Demirtepe
06570 Ankara
Tel: (312) 229 99 33-34
Fax: (312) 231 00 88

Film Yönetmenieri Derneği (FİLM-YÖN)
(The Association of Film Directors)
Ayhan Işik Sokak
28/1 Beyoğlu
80060 Beyoğlu, Istanbul
Tel: (212) 244 01 38
Fax (212) 245 71 94

Film Yapimcilari Derneği (FİYAP)
(The Association of Film Producers)
Gazeteci Erol Dernek Sokak No 8, Beyoğlu, Istanbul
Tel: (212) 266 13 87
Fax (212) 266 63 51

İstanbul Kültür ve Sanat Vakfi
(The Istanbul Culture and Arts Foundation)
İstiklal Caddeşi No 146
Luvr Apt. Beyoğlu
800070 İstanbul
Tel: (212) 251 22 34
Fax (212) 249 77 71

Sinema Yazarlari Derneği (SİYAD)
(The Association of Film Critics)
Gazateci Erol Dernek Sokak, No 11/3 Beyoğlu, İstanbul
Tel: (212) 251 70 73
Fax (212) 243 25 30

Türkiye Sinema ve Audiovisuel Kültür Vakfi (TÜRSAK)
(The Turkish Cinema and Audiovisual Culture Foundation)
Gazeteci Erol Dernek Sokak No 11/2
Hanif Han,
Beyoğlu, Istanbul
Tel: (212) 244 52 51
Fax (212) 251 67 70

Standart Film
Erol Dernek Sokak, Erman Hat
Kan 2,
Beyoğlu, Istanbul
Tel: (212) 243 33 97
Fax (212) 252 98 50

UIP – Filmcivik ve Ticaret Ltd.
Eytam Cad. 16/16 80200 Maçka,
Istanbul
Tel: (212) 225 92 22
Fax (212) 225 91 92

Umut Samut Ürünleri
Halaskargazi Cad. Gazi Ethem Paşa
Sitesi,
No 214/7 8022o Şişli,
Istanbul
Tel: (212) 230 40 41
Fax (212) 232 35 83

İstanbul Film Ajansi – İFA
Gazeteci erol Dernek Sokak,
Hanif Han, 11/5
Beyoğlu, Istanbul
Tel: (212) 245 56 02
Fax (212) 245 54 17

Z Film
Valikonağı Caddesi, Akkirmanlı
Sokak,
Nayır Sitesi
D Blok No. 55 Nişantaşi, Istanbul
Tel: (212) 247 67 25
Fax (212) 247 67 25

Alfa-Film
İstiklal Caddesi No 140
Beyoğlu, Istanbul
Tel: (212) 243 63 40
Fax (212) 243 31 08

Asya Film
Gazeteci Erol Dernek Sokak Erman
Han,
Kat I Beyoğlu, Istanbul
Tel: (212) 251 41 71
Fax (212) 293 34 98

Erler Film
Kodaman Sokak No 106-108,
80220 Nişantaş,
Istanbul
Tel: (212) 224 06 09
Fax (212) 224 06 05

Magnum Film
P trak Sokak 7/4
34800 Yeşilyurt,
Istanbul
Tel: (212) 573 28 79
Fax (212) 573 73 43

Mine Film
Ayhan Işık Sokak, Girik Han,
28/3, Beyoğlu, Istanbul
Tel: (212) 243 02 00
Fax (212) 245 67 74

Özen Film
Sakızağacı Cad.
No 21 Beyoğlu,
Istanbul
Tel: (212) 245 58 54
Fax (212) 244 58 51

UNITED KINGDOM

George Perry

On so many occasions, the British film industry has experienced a surge of optimism only for it to be cruelly dashed by yet another of its perennial crises. Surprisingly, the upturn noted last year has continued and sceptics are beginning to wonder just how much longer it can last. The approaching General

HEAR THIS, ENGLAND!
CINEMA IS ALSO MUSIC.
LISTEN TO CINEMA.
100 YEARS OF CINEMA
C.A.M. ORIGINAL SOUNDTRACKS from the golden years of Italian and French cinema.
Over 170 titles and 75 composers available on compact disc.
Ask for our catalog. Also available on CD-ROM.
CAM Original Soundtracks VIA COLA DI RIENZO, 152 - 00192 ROME (ITALY) - FAX:(+39-6) 687.4046

The most underrated performance (and film) of the year: Ian McKellen in RICHARD III *photo: Mayfair/Guild*

Election suggests that the government – after showing signs at last of recognising film's importance to the economic infrastructure – will subordinate the concerns of the industry to what are regarded as more important issues for voters.

For the second year running, more than 80 British features were made (in 1989, by comparison, only 30 were completed). Studios have consistently been busy. Among the larger international productions at Shepperton have been **Evita**, directed by Alan Parker for the Robert Stigwood Organisation, Richard Attenborough's **In Love and War** for New Line, Miramax's **Wings of the Dove**, directed by Iain Softley, and Charles Sturridge's **One Golden Afternoon** for Working Title. At Pinewood, Phillip Noyce has directed **The Saint** for Paramount; **The Fifth Element**, starring Bruce Willis, was made by Luc Besson for Sony; and Elstree, closed in 1993 by its previous owner, Brent Walker, prepared to reopen under the aegis of the local authority, Hertsmere, with a new film by Stanley Kubrick, **Eyes Wide Shut**, starring Tom Cruise and Nicole Kidman.

Upgrading a Poor Relation

British studios are once again attractive to American producers. Brian De Palma's *Mission: Impossible*, one of the year's U.S. box-office hits, was based at Pinewood, and George Lucas is proposing to shoot his new *Star Wars* films at Leavesden, the studio that came into existence for *GoldenEye*, the last Bond film to be made in Albert R. Broccoli's lifetime.

While the American presence is good news for the studios and the industry's craftsmen, it is perceived in some quarters as a threat to indigenous film-making, which is seen to exist only as a poor relation. Positive encouragement came when Mike Leigh's **Secrets and Lies** scored a triumph at Cannes, winning the Palme d'Or, the Critics' prize, the Ecumenical Jury prize and the Best Actress award for Brenda Blethyn. Andrew Macdonald and

Danny Boyle's **Trainspotting** also became one of Britain's biggest successes, although the heavy Edinburgh brogue called for subtitling in the United States, and even Sassenach prints had on-screen translation for one sequence.

In July, a group of the larger contractors in the ITV network – Carlton, Granada, United News and Media, Yorkshire-Tyne-Tees, HTV and Scottish TV – announced a five-year investment of £100 million in up to ten films a year. Coupled with the government's pledge of £80 million from National Lottery funds, it helped to boost investment in British film in the first half of 1996 to £323 million, almost double the previous year's £172 million. The Rank Organisation also returned to fully financing production, through its distribution arm, RFD.

The independent Film Finance Advisory Committee, chaired by Sir Peter Middleton, recommended that lottery money be used to finance three mini-studios, eventually to be merged into one, to operate on the Hollywood pattern, so that investment could be made on a slate of productions rather than on the much riskier one-off basis. The report also recommended the abolition of the withholding tax on the salaries of non-resident stars, a 100 percent write-off for production costs in the year they are incurred – both of which have been unsuccessfully lobbied for in past years – and for Britain to rejoin the Council of Europe's Eurimages programme.

Restoration

Exhibition continued its upward progress, and 1996 admissions are projected to reach 135 million. As well as the appeal of films on offer, there is a distinct correlation between the availability and quality of cinemas with box-office returns. With the opening of further multiplexes, the number of screens topped 2,000, and over 60 new sites are due to open in the next two years. Virgin Cinemas, which acquired 119 MGM cinemas, sold 90 of them on to a management team headed by Barry Jenkins. The name chosen for the spin-off circuit was ABC, reviving both a name and a logo that had been phased out many years earlier when EMI sold the group to Cannon.

The resurgent ABC announced that they would improve and extend existing cinemas, and also construct 17 entirely new multiplexes. Virgin, meanwhile, planned to use the proceeds from the sale to increase their multiplex sites to 37, making it the U.K.'s largest operator. Virgin's new multiplex at Rochester, Kent, experimented with a facility called The Silver Screen, a superior theatre with extra legroom and a bar dispensing food and drinks during shows.

A new entrant to the exhibition sector was a wholly British company, Cine-UK, started by Steve Weiner, formerly managing director of Warner Bros Theatres (U.K.). The first of its dozen multiplexes, some with 14 screens, opened at Stevenage in the summer.

This year, Britain celebrated the first century of cinema, taking as its starting point the arrival of the Lumière brothers and their projector at the Empire, Leicester Square, in March 1896 where, sandwiched between variety turns, it became a sensation. Among the many Cinema 100 events were exhibitions and special film shows around the country, the première of **Restoration**, the world première in Cardiff of the 76-year-old silent epic, **The Life Story of David Lloyd George**, a film which had been mysteriously withdrawn and thought lost, and the appearance on walls of plaques commemorating notable British film personalities. In June for one day, every cinema in Britain charged £1 for admission, an experiment that brought out the crowds in many places, and could well be repeated.

GEORGE PERRY is film editor of the *Sunday Times*, co-editor of *1,000 Makers of the Cinema*, and author of several books on film. From 1991 until 1994, he was chairman of the Critics' Circle.

Marianne Jean-Baptiste and Brenda Blethyn in Mike Leigh's SECRETS AND LIES, released through Film Four Distributors

SECRETS AND LIES

Script and Direction: Mike Leigh. Photography: Dick Pope. Editing: Jon Gregory. Music: Andrew Dickson. Players: Timothy Spall, Phyllis Logan, Brenda Blethyn, Claire Rushbrook, Marianne Jean-Baptiste, Michele Austin, Lee Ross. Produced by CiBy 2000/ Thin Man Films/Channel Four Films. 141 mins.

Mike Leigh's darkly humorous vision of humankind has hitherto bordered on the misanthropic, his victims ending up emotionally stripped and all too aware of their state of unhappiness. A Leigh situation that would suggest such an outcome is constructed here. Hortense (Marianne Jean-Baptiste) is a young, middle-class black woman, an optometrist who lives alone. Her foster-mother has died, and a social worker helps her to locate her real mother who gave her away as a baby.

She is Cynthia (Brenda Blethyn), middle-aged and unmarried, living in a south-east London terrace house with her daughter Roxanne (Claire Rushbrook), who has found a job sweeping the streets. Cynthia's brother Maurice (Timothy Spall) is a suburban photographer whose wife Monica (Phyllis Logan) is a social climber and disapproves of her sister-in-law. The eruption of Hortense into their lives is an extraordinary catalyst which, after the initial shock, has the effect of easing and strengthening the strained family links, rather than forcing them further apart.

The acting is of a high order, and Spall, a Leigh regular, is particularly touching in a role that calls for him to be tender and supportive, while Blethyn manages to invest Cynthia with good humour and vulgarity without tipping the role into caricature. For a Leigh film to end on a feel-good note is a welcome treat.

George Perry

SENSE AND SENSIBILITY

Script: Emma Thompson, from the novel by Jane Austen. Direction: Ang Lee. Photography: Michael Coulter. Editing: Tim Squyres. Music: Patrick Doyle. Players: Emma Thompson, Tom Wilkinson, Harriet Walter, Gemma Jones, Hugh Grant, Kate Winslet, Alan Rickman, Greg Wise. Producer: Lindsay Doran for Columbia TriStar.

Emma Thompson's Cambridge degree in English clearly was not in vain. Her screenplay from Jane Austen's first novel is an admirable adaptation, giving it a coherent, manageable structure while delightfully conveying the author's ironic humour. Ang Lee, the Taiwanese director of *The Wedding Banquet*, seems completely at home with the intricacies of the social order in late 18th-century England, and understands the declining status of the Dashwood women after the death of the familial head.

Elinor (Thompson) is pragmatic and therefore sensible, but unable to express her emotions, while Marianne (Kate Winslet) is incapable of reining-in her sensibility, to the extent that she has what today would be seen as a nervous breakdown when her romance with the rakish Willoughby (Greg Wise) goes awry. Alan Rickman is obliged to play a boring character, the steadfast Colonel Brandon, but gives him wit and dignity, and Hugh Grant as the tongue-tied Edward Ferrers once again proffers his blushing, embarrassed, timid Englishman, when it is actually an appropriate interpretation.

George Perry

Begbie, Spud, Renton and Sick Boy in PolyGram's TRAINSPOTTING

Emma Thompson, star and screenwriter of SENSE AND SENSIBILITY

TRAINSPOTTING

Script: John Hodge, based on the novel by Irvine Welsh. Direction: Danny Boyle. Photography: Brian Tufano. Editing: Masahiro Hirakubo. Players: Ewan McGregor, Ewen Bremner, Jonny Lee Miller, Kevin McKidd, Susan Vidler, Kelly Macdonald, Robert Carlyle. Produced by Andrew Macdonald, a Figment film in association with Noel Gay Motion Picture Company for Channel Four.

The controversy created by Andrew Macdonald and Danny Boyle's exhilarating follow-up to *Shallow Grave* hung on its perceived approval of drug usage, in that the central character, Renton (Ewan McGregor) is a heroin addict living in an Edinburgh den of other junkies. There is a sense of the addictive charge that ignites the habitual user, but the film also endeavours to express the anti-social negativity that goes with it.

Renton's first attempt to cold-turkey is humorous and eloquent; the second, an enforced bid after an overdose, is surreal, and a sequence in which he attempts to retrieve two opium suppositories from a foul lavatory bowl is outright fantasy. The most shocking incident is the cot death of Alison's baby. The druggies are incapable of finding an appropriate response until one of them announces that he is preparing a new shot. *Trainspotting* is also endowed with much dark humour and energy. A new, vigorous, Scottish impetus is now being felt in British cinema.

George Perry

TOP TEN GROSSING FILMS IN THE UK: 1995

	Admissions
Batman Forever	£20.2m
Casper	£16.0m
Braveheart	£11.2m
Apollo 13	£10.5m
Interview with the Vampire	£10.5m
Die Hard 3	£10.2m
Stargate	£9.8m
Pocahontas	£9.7m
Dumb and Dumber	£9.5m
Waterworld	£8.4m

Recent and Forthcoming Films

AN AMERICAN WEREWOLF IN PARIS

Script and Dir: Anthony Waller. Phot: Egon Werdin. Players: Tom Everett Scott, Julie Delpy, Vince Vieluf, Julie Bowen. Prod: J&M Entertainment.

BENT

Script: Martin Sherman. Dir: Sean Mathias. Phot: Yorgas Arvanitis. Players: Clive Owen, Lothaire Bluteau, Brian Webber, Ian McKellen. Prod: Bent Prods./ Channel Four Films/Nippon Development and Finance/Arts Council of England.

BLOOD AND WINE

Script: Nick Villiers, Alison Cross. Dir: Bob Rafelson. Players: Jack Nicholson, Jennifer Lopez, Stephen Dorff, Michael Caine, Judy Davis. Prod: Recorded Picture Company.

B. MONKEY

Script: Michael Thomas, Andrew Davies. Dir: Michael Radford. Prod: Scala Prods./Miramax.

THE BUTCHER BOY

Script: Neil Jordan, Pat McCabe. Dir: Jordan. Phot: Adrian Biddle. Players: Tom Wilkinson, Helen Baxendale, Clive Russell, James Fleet. Prod: Butcher Boy Films/Warner Bros.

CARLA'S SONG

Script: Paul Laverty. Dir: Ken Loach. Players: Scott Glenn, Robert Carlyle, Oyanka Cabezas. Prod: Parallax Pictures/Channel Four Films.

EXTREME MEASURES

Script: Tony Gilroy. Dir: Michael Apted. Players: Hugh Grant, Gene Hackman, Sarah Jessica Parker, David Morse, Bill Nunn. Prod: Simian Films.

FIERCE CREATURES

Script: John Cleese, Iain Johnstone. Dir: Robert Young. Players: John Cleese, Kevin Kline, Jamie Lee Curtis, Michael Palin. Prod: Jersey Film.

HAMLET

Dir: Kenneth Branagh. Players: Kenneth Branagh, Julie Christie, Billy Crystal, Gérard Depardieu, Charlton Heston, Derek Jacobi, Jack Lemmon, Robin Williams, Kate Winslet. Prod: Castle Rock.

IN LOVE AND WAR

Script: Anna Hamilton Phelan. Dir: Richard Attenborough. Players: Sandra Bullock, Chris O'Donnell, Mackenzie Astin, Ingrid Lacey. Prod: Love and War Prods./New Line.

MIKE LEIGH UNTITLED '96

Script and Dir: Mike Leigh. Players: Mark Benton, Kate Byers, Katrin Cartlidge, Andy Serkis. Prod: Thin Man Films/Channel Four Films.

MRS. DALLOWAY

Dir: Marleen Gorris. Players: Vanessa Redgrave. Prod: Bill Shepherd.

THE REVENGERS' COMEDIES

Script: Malcolm Mowbray. Players: Helena Bonham Carter, Steve Coogan, Sam Neill, Richard E. Grant. Prod: Artisan Films/BBC Films.

ROSEANNA'S GRAVE

Script: Ian La Frenais, Saul Turteltaub, Dick Clement. Dir: Paul Weiland. Players: Jean

Reno, Mercedes Ruehl, Polly Walker. Prod: Hungry Eye Trijbits & Worrell.

SARAJEVO

Script: Frank Cottrell Boyce. Dir: Michael Winterbottom. Players: Stephen Dillane, Woody Harrelson, Marisa Tomei, Kerry Fox, Emily Lloyd. Prod: Channel Four Films/Miramax Films.

THE SERPENT'S KISS

Script: Tim Rose Price. Dir: Philippe Rousselot. Phot: Jean Francois Robin. Players: Ewan MacGregor, Greta Scacchi, Pete Postlethwaite, Richard E. Grant. Prod: J&M Entertainment/ NEF/Red Parrot/Berryer/RPB Prods.

THE SLAB BOYS

Script and Dir: John Byrne. Phot: Seamus McGarvey. Players: Robin Laing, Russell Barr, Bill Gardiner, Louise Berry. Prod: Skreba Film/Wanderlust/Channel Four Films/Arts Council of England and Scotland/Glasgow Film Fund.

STIFF UPPER LIPS

Script and Dir: Gary Sinyor. Players: Peter Ustinov, Prunella Scales, Georgina Cates, Samuel West, Brian Glover. Prod: Chrysalis Films.

SURVIVING PICASSO

Script: Ruth Prawer, Jhabvala. Dir: James Ivory. Players: Anthony Hopkins. Prod: Merchant Ivory Productions/ David L. Wolper Productions.

VICIOUS CIRCLES

Script: Sandy Whitelaw, Stephen O'Shea. Dir: Whitelaw. Phot: Romain Winding. Players: Carolyn Lowery, Paul Mipp, Jerome Davis, Camilla Overbye-Roos. Prod: Scala Prods.

WINGS OF THE DOVE

Script: Hossein Amini. Dir: Iain Softley. Phot: Eduardo Serra. Players: Helena Bonham Carter, Linus Roache, Alison Elliot, Elizabeth McGovern, Michael Gambon. Prod: Renaissance Films.

THE WOODLANDERS

Script: David Rudkin. Dir: Phil Agland. Players: Jodhi May, Rufus Sewell, Polly Walker, Emily Woof. Prod: River Films.

Producers

Allied Entertainment
3-4 Ashland Place,
London W1M 3JH
Tel: (171) 224 1992
Fax: (171) 224 0111

British Film Institute Production
29 Rathbone Street,
London W1P 1AG
Tel: (171) 636 5587
Fax: (171) 580 9456

British Lion
Pinewood Studios,
Iver Heath, Bucks. SL0 0NH
Tel: (1753) 651 700
Fax: (1753) 656 391

Chrysalis Films
8-10 Great Titchfield Street,
London W1P 7AA
Tel: (171) 462 6000
Fax: (171) 436 3738

Dakota Films
6 Meard Street,
London W1V 3HR
Tel: (171) 287 4329
Fax: (171) 287 2303

Enigma Productions
13-15 Queens Gate Place
Mews, London SW7 5BG
Tel: (171) 581 0238
Fax: (171) 584 1799

Euston Films
Pinewood Studios,
Iver Heath,
Bucks. SL0 0NH
Tel: (1753) 650 222
Fax: (1753) 654 321

Mark Forstater Productions
Suite 66, Pall Mall Deposit,
124-128 Barbley Road,
London W10 6BL
Tel: (181) 964 1888
Fax: (181) 960 9819

Goldcrest Films and Television
65-66 Dean Street,
London W1R 3HP
Tel: (171) 437 8696
Fax: (171) 437 4448

Greenpoint Films
5A Noel Street,
London W1V 3RB
Tel: (171) 437 6492
Fax: (171) 437 0644

Jim Henson Productions
30 Oval Road
London NW1 7DE
Tel: (171) 428 4000
Fax: (171) 428 4001

J&M Entertainment
2 Dorset Square,
London NW1 6PU
Tel: (171) 723 6544
Fax: (171) 724 7541

Little Bird
7 Lower James Street,
London W1R 3PL
Tel: (171) 434 1131
Fax: (171) 434 1803

Mayfair Entertainment International
110 St. Martin's Lane,
London WC2N 4AD
Tel: (171) 304 7911
Fax: (171) 867 1184

Merchant Ivory Productions
46 Lexington Street,
London W1P 3LH
Tel: (171) 437 1200
Fax: (171) 734 1579

Metrodome Films
40 Crawford Street,
London W1H 2BB
Tel: (171) 723 3494
Fax: (171) 724 6411

NFH
37 Ovington Square,
London SW3 2LJ
Tel: (171) 584 7561
Fax: (171) 589 1863

Parallax Pictures
7 Denmark Street,
London WC2H 8LS
Tel: (171) 836 1478
Fax: (171) 497 8062

Portobello Productions Ltd.
42 Tavistock Road,
London W11 1AW
Tel: (171) 379 5566
Fax: (171) 379 5599

Prominent Features
68A Delancey Street,
London NW1 7RY
Tel: (171) 284 0242
Fax: (171) 284 1004

Recorded Picture Company
24-26 Hanway Street,
London W1P 9DD
Tel: (171) 636 2251
Fax: (171) 636 2261

Red Rooster Films
29 Floral Street,
London WC2E 9DP
Tel: (171) 379 7727
Fax: (171) 379 5756

Sands Films
119 Rotherhithe Street,
London SE16 4NF
Tel: (171) 231 2209
Fax: (171) 379 5756

Scala Productions
39-43 Brewer Street,
London W1R 3PD
Tel: (171) 734 7060
Fax: (171) 437 3248

Skreba Films
5A Noel Street,
London W1V 3RB
Tel: (171) 437 6492
Fax: (171) 437 0644

Michael White Productions
48 Dean Street,
London W1V 5HL
Tel: (171) 734 7707
Fax: (171) 734 7727

Distributors

Buena Vista International
Beaumont House,
Kensington Village,
Avonmore Road,
London W14 8TS
Tel: (171) 605 2890
Fax: (171) 605 2827

Columbia TriStar Film Distributors
Sony Pictures Europe House
25 Golden Square
London W1R 6LU
Tel: (171) 533 1111
Fax: (171) 533 1105

Twentieth Century Fox
20th Century House,
31-32 Soho Square,
London W1V 6AP
Tel: (171) 437 7766
Fax: (171) 434 2170

U.I.P.
Mortimer House,
37-41 Mortimer Street,
London W1A 2JL
Tel: (171) 636 1655
Fax: (171) 636 4118

Warner Bros.
135 Wardour Street,
London W1V 4AP
Tel: (171) 734 8400
Fax: (171) 437 9544

INDEPENDENTS

Artificial Eye
13 Soho Square,
London W1V 5FB
Tel: (171) 437 2552
Fax: (171) 437 2992

Blue Dolphin Films
40 Langham Street,
London W1N 5RG
Tel: (171) 255 2494
Fax: (171) 580 7670

British Film Institute
21 Stephen Street,
London W1P 1PL
Tel: (171) 255 1444
Fax: (171) 436 7950

Electric Pictures
15 Percy Street,
London W1P 8FD
Tel: (171) 636 1231
Fax: (171) 636 1675

Entertainment Film Distributors
27 Soho Square,
London W1V 5FL
Tel: (171) 439 1606
Fax: (171) 734 2483

Film Four Distribution
Castle House,
75-76 Wells Street,
London W1P 3RE
Tel: (171) 436 9944
Fax: (171) 436 9955

First Independent Films
69 New Oxford Street,
London WC1A 1DG
Tel: (171) 528 7767
Fax: (171) 528 7771

Gala Films
26 Danbury Street,
London N1 8JU
Tel: (171) 226 5085
Fax: (171) 226 5897

Guild Film Distribution
Kent House,
14-17 Market Place,
Great Titchfield Street,
London W1N 8AR
Tel: (171) 323 5151
Fax: (171) 631 3568

ICA Projects
12 Carlton House Terrace,
London SW1Y 5AH
Tel: (171) 930 0493
Fax: (171) 873 0051

J&M Entertainment
2 Dorset Square,
London NW1 6PU
Tel: (171) 723 6544
Fax: (171) 724 7541

Mainline Pictures
37 Museum Street,
London WC1A 1LP
Tel: (171) 242 5523
Fax: (171) 430 0170

Metro Tartan
79 Wardour Street,
London W1V 3TH

Tel: (171) 734 8508
Fax: (171) 287 2112

Rank Film Distributors
127-133 Wardour Street,
London W1V 4AD
Tel: (171) 437 9020
Fax: (171) 434 3689

SALES AGENTS

Jane Balfour Films
Burghley House,
35 Fortess Road,
London NW5 1AD
Tel: (171) 267 5392
Fax: (171) 267 4241

Capitol Films
23 Queensdale Place,
London W11 4SQ
Tel: (171) 471 6000
Fax: (171) 471 6012

Castle Rock International
8 Queen Street,
London W1X 7PH
Tel: (171) 409 3532
Fax: (171) 499 9885

CiBy Sales
10 Stephen Mews,
London W1P 1PP
Tel: (171) 333 8877
Fax: (171) 333 8876

Cine Electra
National House,
60-66 Wardour Street,
London W1V 3HP
Tel: (171) 287 1123
Fax: (171) 722 4251

Chrysalis Films International
8-10 Great Titchfield Street,
London W1P 7AA
Tel: (171) 462 6000
Fax: (171) 436 3738

Film Four International
124 Horseferry Road,
London SW1P 2TX
Tel: (171) 306 8602
Fax: (171) 306 8361

Goldcrest Film & Television
65-66 Dean Street,
London W1R 3HP
Tel: (171) 437 8696
Fax: (171) 437 4448

J&M Film Sales
2 Dorset Square,
London NW1 6PU
Tel: (171) 723 6544
Fax: (171) 724 7541

Majestic Films International
Gloucester Mansions,
Cambridge Circus,
London WC2H 8HD
Tel: (171) 836 8630
Fax: (171) 836 5819

Polygram Film International
4th Floor, Oxford House,
Oxford Street,
London W1N 0HQ
Tel: (171) 307 1300
Fax: (171) 307 1301

Rank Film Distributors
127-133 Wardour Street,
London W1V 4AD
Tel: (171) 437 9020
Fax: (171) 434 3689

The Sales Company
62 Shaftesbury Avenue,
London W1V 7AA
Tel: (171) 434 9061
Fax: (171) 494 3293

Smart Egg Pictures
11-12 Barnard Mews,
London SW11 1QU
Tel: (171) 924 6284
Fax: (171) 924 5650

Victor Films
28 Chandos Street,
London W1M 0EH
Tel: (171) 636 6620
Fax: (171) 636 6511

Vine International Pictures
3rd Floor, Astoria House,
62 Shaftesbury Avenue,
London W1V 7DE
Tel: (171) 437 1181
Fax: (171) 494 0634

Useful Addresses

British Academy of Film and Television Arts (BAFTA)
195 Piccadilly,
London W1V 9LG
Tel: (171) 734 0022
Fax: (171) 734 1792

British Board of Film Classification (BBFC)
3 Soho Square,
London W1V 5DE
Tel: (171) 439 7961
Fax: (171) 287 0141

British Actors Equity
Guild House,
Upper St. Martins Lane,
London WC2H 9EG
Tel: (171) 379 6000
Fax: (171) 379 7001

The British Council
11 Portland Place,
London W1N 4EJ
Tel: (171) 389 3068
Fax: (171) 389 3041

British Film Commission
70 Baker Street,
London W1M 1DJ
Tel: (171) 224 5000
Fax: (171) 224 1013

British Screen Finance
14-17 Wells Mews,
London W1P 3FL
Tel: (171) 323 9080
Fax: (171) 323 0092

Cinema Exhibitors' Association (CEA)
22 Golden Square,
London W1R 3PA
Tel: (171) 734 9551
Fax: (171) 734 6147

Directors' Guild of Great Britain
Suffolk House,
Whitfield Place,
London W1P 5SF
Tel: (171) 383 3858
Fax: (171) 383 5173

PACT
Gordon House,
Greencoat Place,
London SW1P 1PH
Tel: (171) 233 6000
Fax: (171) 233 8935

Scottish Screen Locations
74 Victoria Crescent Road,
Glasgow G12 9JN
Tel: (141) 339 1500
Fax: (141) 339 7744

U.S.A.

William Wolf

To rake in the megabucks recently we've had Jan De Bont's special effects-laden, tornado-blown but silly **Twister,** Brian De Palma's action-slick but improbable **Mission: Impossible,** and Roland Emmerich's apocalyptic block-buster **Independence Day,** as well as the family-oriented, computer-animated **Toy Story.** But the best choices for the more serious filmgoer once again could be found in the independent sector. Particularly sophisticated and amusingly quirky was the crime film **Fargo**, the lastest effort of brothers Joel and Ethan Coen. This won widespread approval, although it angered some Minnesota residents who felt their state unjustly satirised.

Lone Stars

Despite traditional obstacles, films not typical of the mainstream were plentiful and often well appreciated. They included **Welcome to the Dollhouse**, Todd Solondz's poignant look at the struggles of a teenager; **Walking and Talking**, Nicole Holofcener's entertaining, sensitive account of a long-time friendship between two women; **Flirting with Disaster**, David O. Russell's frequently uproarious comedy about a man who was adopted as a child and his obsession with finding his biological parents; **I Shot Andy Warhol**, Mary Harron's colourful reprise of the Warhol cultural era; and **Lone Star**, John Sayles' atmospheric mystery tale reflecting ethnic conflicts along the Texas-Mexico border (see reviews).

Many more varied achievements come to mind. James Mangold's **Heavy**, popular at the Toronto International Film Festival and the Sundance Festival, featured a touching performance from Pruitt Taylor Vince as an overweight restaurant worker who is desperately lonely and needs to change his life. Bruno Barreto's **Carried Away** boldly and maturely dealt with love between an ageing teacher (Dennis Hopper) and his longtime companion (Amy Irving), and his fling that threatens their relationship. Henry Jaglom's **Last Summer in the Hamptons**, mixed the artistic pretensions and aspirations of theatre folk with their turbulent personal lives, and also presented the last, shimmering performance of the late Viveca Lindfors.

At the Sundance Festival, Castle Rock was so impressed with Lee David Zlotoff's mature, involving drama, **The Spitfire Grill**, about a woman ex-con tragically trying to make good, that it paid $10 million for it, a record for acquisitions at

LISTEN UP, AMERICA!
CINEMA IS ALSO MUSIC.
LISTEN TO CINEMA.
100 YEARS OF CINEMA CAM
C.A.M. ORIGINAL SOUNDTRACKS from the golden years of Italian and French cinema.
Over 170 titles and 75 composers available on compact disc.
Ask for our catalog. Also available on CD-ROM.
CAM Original Soundtracks VIA COLA DI RIENZO, 152 - 00192 ROME (ITALY) - FAX:(+39-6) 687.4046

Sundance. Another hit there was Jim McKay's **Girls Town**, dealing with a group of high-school girls.

Jonathan Demme and Barbet Schroeder teamed to present the work of a newcomer, director Tim McCann, whose **Desolation Angels,** showcased at the Toronto and Telluride festivals, dramatised the consequences of a man's macho attempt to deal with the rape of a woman friend by an acquaintance. Robert M. Young's **Caught** starred Edward James Olmos, Maria Conchita Alonso and impressive newcomer Arie Verveen as an ill-fated threesome in a steamy but predictable drama reminiscent of *The Postman Always Rings Twice* minus the murder plot. Richard Pearce's **A Family Thing** was a moving story of a Southerner who learns he has a black half-brother, providing a strong vehicle for Robert Duvall and James Earl Jones, as well as for Irma P. Hall as a feisty and wise elderly woman.

The Players Are the Thing

Susan Sarandon won an Oscar for her powerful performance as a nun trying to bring moral redemption of a kind to a condemned killer in Tim Robbins' **Dead Man Walking**, and Sean Penn won the best actor Silver Bear at the Berlin Festival for his memorable portrayal of the condemned. That film's success unfortunately overshadowed the commendable but underrated **Last Dance**, directed by Bruce Beresford and enhanced by the superb acting of Sharon Stone as a woman sentenced to death. Nicolas Cage took the best actor Oscar for his performance as the alcoholic in Mike Figgis' haunting downer

Sharon Stone in LAST DANCE
photo: Touchstone/Zade Rosenthal

Susan Sarandon and Sean Penn in DEAD MAN WALKING *photo: PolyGram/Demmie Todd*

Will Smith and Harry Connick Jr. in the all-conquering INDEPENDENCE DAY *photo: Fox/Claudette Barius*

Leaving Las Vegas, as did Cage's co-star Elisabeth Shue as a hooker on the skids.

One of the year's great acting coups was the performance by Mira Sorvino as the delightfully candid prostitute in Woody Allen's spirited, often very funny **Mighty Aphrodite**. Sorvino, a real find, walked off with the best supporting actress Oscar. Kevin Spacey, a best supporting actor Oscar winner for **The Usual Suspects**, received well-earned recognition for his prolific work. Richard Gere was in top form as the overly ambitious lawyer in **Primal Fear**, and Demi Moore turned on the heat in the drama **Striptease**.

Anthony Hopkins demonstrated that he didn't have to look like Richard Nixon to capture effectively the disgraced President in Oliver Stone's **Nixon**, which drew a mixed response. Al Pacino and Robert De Niro gave off sparks in Michael Mann's cops and robbers tale, **Heat**, and De Niro was impressive again in Martin Scorsese's flashy Las Vegas saga, **Casino**. John Travolta brightened Barry Sonnenfeld's spoof on gangsters and movie-making as a smart, brazen enforcer in the satirical **Get Shorty**. Michael Douglas was entertaining as a Clinton-like President in Rob Reiner's frothy, romantic **The American President**. Richard Dreyfuss was popular for his heart-felt performance as the teacher in **Mr. Holland's Opus**. Talented Nathan Lane, playing a night-club drag queen, became a fully fledged movie star in **The Birdcage**, Mike Nichols' recycling of *La Cage aux folles* into a gay romp set in Florida. Robin Williams was also on target as the lover and father.

Al Pacino demonstrated that he had talent behind the camera as well as in front of it with his film **Looking for Richard**, an off-beat exploration of Shakespeare's *Richard III* that Pacino unveiled at Cannes. Robert Altman was back at Cannes with his **Kansas City**, an ode to the city's musical history, and he received a lifetime achievement award. Although not his best, Bernardo Bertolucci's sensual, beautifully

Billy Zane as THE PHANTOM
photo: Paramount/Andrew Cooper

Emmanuelle Béart and Tom Cruise in MISSION: IMPOSSIBLE *photo: Paramount/Murray Close*

filmed co-production, **Stealing Beauty**, highlighting the much-publicised Liv Tyler, still demonstrated the director's consummate ability. Vastly under-appreciated was Terry Gilliam's **12 Monkeys**, a complex, gripping drama about saving the world from lethal disease, with a gritty performance by Bruce Willis.

The Documentary Closet

Documentaries are as difficult as ever to market. But fine work is being done by many practitioners, and ways are found to reach a public, often in a combination of televised and theatrical release. One of the year's best – entertaining as well as informative – was **The Celluloid Closet**, a witty look at the treatment of gays throughout the history of cinema, based on a book by the late Vito Russo. Directed by Rob Epstein and Jeffrey Friedman, it was a hit at the New York and Toronto festivals before its release.

Joe Berlinger and Bruce Sinofsky made the penetrating and unsettling **Paradise Lost: The Child Murders at Robin Hood Hills**, a study of a crime in Arkansas and, beyond that, a revealing look at the locality and its inhabitants. Despite the many works concerning Holocaust victim Anne Frank, a new documentary, **Anne Frank Remembered**, directed by Jon Blair, dug deeply into her story and constituted a fresh look.

Nick Broomfield chose as his most recent subject **Heidi Fleiss: Hollywood Madam**, which looked at the life and times of the woman whose arrest titillated Hollywood and threatened embarrassing revelations. Mark Rappaport's **From the Journals of Jean Seberg**, an entry in both the Toronto and New York festivals, was problematic in that it gave the impression of being a documentary about the star's tragic life but was really Rappaport's riff on the Seberg story with purely fictional journals.

The Downside

There was the inevitable slew of entries that failed with critics and didn't excite the public. The Sydney Pollack remake of **Sabrina**, teaming Harrison Ford and Julia Ormond, turned out to be a bad idea. Another ill-advised remake was Jeremiah Chechik's **Diabolique**, which obliterated the mystique inherent in Henri-Georges Clouzot's chilly 1955 forerunner. Geena Davis as a pirate may have seemed like a good concept, but Renny Harlin's **Cutthroat Island** was an expensive flop. Pen Densham's **Moll Flanders**, based on the character from Daniel Defoe's novel and starring Robin Wright, opened to a yawn. Jim Jarmusch's **Dead Man**, starring Johnny Depp in a somewhat satirical Western saga, was pretentious, dull and lacking the wit of other Jarmusch films.

Lee Tamahori's **Mullholland Falls** muddled along as a far-fetched police and military yarn despite the presence of Nick Nolte, Melanie Griffith and John Malkovich. Much was made when Jim Carrey was paid $20 million to star in **The Cable Guy**. The film that resulted was trounced by critics,

Steve Buscemi and Ingmar Bergman discovery Peter Stormare in FARGO *photo: James Bridges*

and depending on its ultimate box-office take, could heighten concern about the runaway deals actors have been getting as the costs of Hollywood budgets continued to escalate.

Changing Partners, Tightening Belts

Even as many independent films were getting made, it became harder for small distribution companies to land the ones that could bring the best grosses. That's because Miramax, Sony Classics and Fine Line have the money and clout to grab the most promising films at prices that less affluent companies can't match.

Ever since Michael Ovitz left his company, the Creative Artists Agency (CAA), to take the number two spot at Disney, eyes were on the agency scene to see what the outcome would be. The result: Ovitz's much-publicised move made the agency business a looser field, minus the overwhelming clout that CAA wielded under his power.

TOP TEN GROSSING FILMS IN THE U.S. & CANADA: 1995

	Gross in dollars
Batman Forever	$184.0 million
Apollo 13	$172.1 million
Toy Story	$146.2 million
Pocahontas	$141.5 million
Ace Ventura: When Nature Calls	$104.2 million
Casper	$100.3 million
Die Hard 3	$100.0 million
GoldenEye	$92.4 million
Crimson Tide	$91.4 million
Waterworld	$88.2 million

Disney itself made news announcing a belt-tightening 50% cutback in the number of films it would produce, but was busy promoting its merchandising business and playing a major role in the redevelopment of the Times Square area in New York. Meanwhile, it released yet another animated film, **The Hunchback of Notre Dame**, with the hope of a new box-office bonanza and merchandising tie-in profits.

WILLIAM WOLF is an American film critic and journalist whose work has appeared in *Cue, New York Magazine,* Gannett publications, and a variety of leading newspapers, magazines and journals. He teaches at New York University and is the author of *Landmark Films: The Cinema and Our Century.*

WELCOME TO THE DOLLHOUSE

Script and Direction: Todd Solondz. Photography: Randy Drummond. Editing: Alan Oxman. Music: Jill Wisoff. Players: Heather Matarazzo, Eric Mabius, Brendan Sexton Jnr, Daria Kalinina, Angela Pietropinto, Matthew Faber. Produced by Ted Skillman, Todd Solondz. 87 mins.

The insecurities involved in growing up at the junior high school age are captured with entertaining poignancy in the compelling tale of Dawn, a youngster played with natural candor and innocence by novice Heather Matarazzo. Suffering through miserable school days in a New Jersey town, Dawn is painfully plain, the kind of insignificant girl who is ridiculed as a kook or absurdly branded as a lesbian. She is ignorant about sex but longs for an experience. When a boy, who also has problems, threatens to rape her after school, she is at once scared but curious.

Writer-director Todd Solondz, who tried Hollywood but found the deals that he could make unfulfilling, opted for this quirky film that, while ultimately melodramatic and rough around the edges, has an emotional base of truthfulness. It took the Grand Prize at the Sundance Festival and was a hit in New York's Museum of Modern Art and Film Society of Lincoln Center New Directors/New Films Series. Surely *Welcome to the Dollhouse* will remind many of the rejections they endured in school, no matter where they grew up. This is the kind of truthful film you don't find coming out of Hollywood.

Heather Matarazzo in Sony Pictures Classics' WELCOME TO THE DOLLHOUSE photo: Jennifer Carchman

William Wolf

WALKING AND TALKING

Script and Direction: Nicole Holofcener. Photography: Michael Spiller. Editing: Alisa Lepselter. Music: Billy Bragg. Players: Anne Heche, Catherine Keener, Todd Field, Kevin Corrigan, Liev Schreiber. Produced by Ted Hope, James Shamus. A Good Machine/Zenith production. 90 mins.

A first feature by writer-director Nicole Holofcener that's fresh, entertaining and sensitive in its treatment of a female friendship that begins in childhood and blossoms into adult give-and-take. Holofcener, whose film was chosen for the New Directors/New Films showcase in New York, has the gift of seeing life's problems through a prism of humour, and her woman's viewpoint uncovers comedy

Catherine Keener and Anne Heche in WALKING AND TALKING

in situations a male film-maker would overlook or see from a different perspective.

Holofcener is fortunate to have the services of two excellent actresses. Anne Heche and Catherine Keener, playing the respective roles of Laura, uncertain about her impending marriage, and Amelia, who has trouble establishing a relationship. Both women emerge as likeable, and they are easy to connect with, thanks to the film's jaunty pace, funny takes on various frustrations and good supporting performances.

William Wolf

FLIRTING WITH DISASTER

Script and Direction: David O. Russell. Photography: Eric Alan Edwards. Editing: Christopher Tellefsen. Music: Stephen Endelman. Players: Ben Stiller, Patricia Arquette, Tea Leoni, Alan Alda, Mary Tyler Moore, George Segal, Lily Tomlin. Produced by Dean Silvers. 87 mins.

The quest of an adopted son to find his biological parents provides the basis for frequent hilarity in a pleasurable, off-beat comedy spiced with welcome talent in the writing and directing, as well as in the performances. Ben Stiller, who has been enjoying a growing reputation as an actor and gaining recognition as a director (*The Cable Guy*), makes an appealing leading man as Mel, the son obsessively committed to his search despite the obstacles strewn along his cross-country path.

Tea Leoni is delightful as the psychologist who goes along to videotape the hunt as her research project. She comes on strong to susceptible Mel, whose wife (Patricia Arquette) and new baby son tug on his conscience. George Segal and Mary Tyler Moore ham it up amusingly as Mel's hurt, over-protective adoptive parents, and there are some extremely funny scenes involving Lily Tomlin and Alan Alda when the trail leads to them. The odyssey is probably dragged out too far and too incredibly, but that's easy to forgive in a comedy that shows so much brightness and provokes so many laughs. *Flirting with Disaster* marks a promising step for writer-director Russell, who gained attention with his earlier *Spanking the Monkey*.

William Wolf

Patricia Arquette, Ben Stiller and Tea Leoni in FLIRTING WITH DISASTER, from Miramax *photo: Jon Ragel*

Kris Kristofferson in John Sayles's LONE STAR, from Castle Rock Entertainment *photo: Alan Papper*

Lili Taylor in Mary Harron's I SHOT ANDY WARHOL, produced by Samuel Goldwyn and released through Orion
photo: Bill Foley

I SHOT ANDY WARHOL

Script: Mary Harron, Daniel Minahan. Direction: Mary Harron. Photography: Ellen Kuras. Editing: Keith Reamer. Music: John Cale. Players: Lili Taylor, Jared Harris, Stephen Dorff, Martha Plimpton, Lothaire Bluteau. Produced by Tom Kalin, Christine Vachon. A Samuel Goldwyn presentation. 100 mins.

The still fascinating Andy Warhol era, complete with his bizarre following in a New York sub-culture, is vividly brought to life in director Mary Harron's oddity. It definitely has international appeal as a strange slice of 60s Americana. At the centre is the true story of how, in 1968, Valerie Solanas, a disgruntled feminist author and fringe character, vindictively shot Warhol, seriously but not fatally.

The drama, showcased in the New Directors/New Films annual New York event, also serves as a vehicle for actress Lili Taylor, who gives a terrific, energetic performance as the volatile Solanas. Taylor imbues Solanas with a mix of earthiness and desperation. Consumed by the passion of her ideas and scrounging for a living by any means available, Solanas writes a feminist manifesto. Her fear of being exploited, part justified, part paranoid, combined with being first accepted then rejected by Warhol and his cronies, sets off her outburst. Director Harron recalls some of Warhol's own film work as she recreates the atmosphere of the artist's loft and the ambience that attracted and reflected an assortment of oddballs. Jared Harris is believable in the part of Warhol, and Stephen Dorff does a worthy job as the tragic transvestite Candy Darling.

William Wolf

LONE STAR

Script, Direction and Editing: John Sayles. Photography: Stuart Dryburgh. Music: Mason Daring. Players: Chris Cooper, Elizabeth Pena, Kris Kristofferson, Matthew McConaughey, Ron Canada, Clifton James, Joe Morton, Miriam Colon. Produced by Maggie Renzi, Paul Miller. 138 mins.

John Sayles has fashioned in *Lone Star* an especially accomplished tale that says much about America and its racial and cultural divisions. In a sense, the entire film is a metaphor for a nation coming to terms with its troubled past and still conflicted present, yet the story is framed as an intensely personal one with a mystery to boot.

The setting is a town along the border between Texas and Mexico. The action is triggered by the discovery of human remains in a stretch of desert. The town sheriff, effectively played by Chris Cooper, starts to investigate and is soon caught up in a mess dating back to the 1950s. It involves the sheriff's father (Matthew McConaughey), also once a sheriff and a legend in whose shadow his son has grown up. Out of the past is another lawman (Kris Kristofferson), with a mean and trigger-happy reputation. Beneath it all is a tense atmosphere of small-town corruption.

The drama flits between the 1950s and the present with well-integrated flash-backs. The story is deepened through a strained love affair between the young sheriff and a pretty Mexican-American woman (Elizabeth Pena), the daughter of a widow (Miriam Colon) who has trouble coming to terms with her own past. Joe Morton plays another key character, an African American army officer.

Sayles weaves all these elements into a colourful Western tapestry and provides an unusual glimpse into contemporary border life. The film tends to ramble and the resolution is melodramatic, but there is considerable satisfaction in watching the various lives and problems unfold in the hands of a superior film-maker.

William Wolf

Recent and Forthcoming Films

ABSOLUTE POWER

Dir: Clint Eastwood. Players: Clint Eastwood, Gene Hackman, Ed Harris, Judy Davis, Laura Linney, Scott Glenn, Dennis Haysbert, E.G. Marshall. Prod: Malpaso/Castle Rock.

ANNA KARENINA

Script and Dir: Bernard Rose. Players: Sophie Marceau, Sean Bean, Mia Kirschner, Alfred Molina, Fiona Shaw, James Fox. Prod: Icon Prods.

APT PUPIL

Script: Brandon Boyce. Dir: Bryan Singer. Players: Ian McKellen, Brad Renfro, Joe Morton, Kevin Pollack. Prod: Apt Pupil Prods.

BATMAN AND ROBIN

Script: Akiva Goldsman. Dir: Joel Schumacher. Players: George Clooney, Chris O'Donnell, Alicia Silverstone, Arnold Schwarzenegger. Prod: Warner Bros.

CHAIN REACTION

Script: Jonathan Lemkin, Michael Bortman. Dir: Andrew Davis. Phot: Frank Tidy. Players: Keanu Reeves, Morgan Freeman, Rachel Weisz, Fred Ward. Prod: Fox.

THE CHAMBER

Script: William Goldman. Dir: James Foley. Phot: Ian Baker. Players: Chris O'Donnell, Gene Hackman, Faye Dunaway, Bo Jackson, Millie Perkins. Prod: Imagine Entertainment.

CITY OF INDUSTRY

Script: Kenneth Solarz. Dir: John Irvin. Players: Harvey Keitel, Stephen Dorff, Famke Janssen, Timothy Hutton, Wade Dominguez. Prod: Kolar Prods/Largo Entertainment.

COPLAND

Script and Dir: James Mangold. Players: Robert De Niro, Sylvester Stallone, Ray Liotta, Michael Rapaport, Janeane Garafalo. Prod: Miramax.

DANTE'S PEAK

Script: Les Bohem. Dir: Roger Donaldson. Players: Pierce Brosnan, Linda Hamilton. Prod: Universal.

DEAR GOD

Script: Warren Leight. Dir: Garry Marshall. Phot: Chuck Minsky. Players: Greg Kinnear, Laurie Metcalf, Maria Pitillo. Prod: Paramount.

DESPERATE MEASURES

Script: David Klass, Neal Jimenez. Dir: Barbet Schroeder. Players: Michael Keaton, Andy Garcia. Prod: Mandalay Entertainment.

THE DEVIL'S OWN

Script: Kevin Jarre. Dir: Alan J. Pakula. Phot: Gordon Willis. Players: Harrison Ford, Brad Pitt, Margaret Colin, Ruben Blades, Treat Williams. Prod: Columbia.

DONNIE BRASCO

Script: Paul Attansio, Joseph Pistone. Dir: Mike Newell. Players: Al Pacino, Johnny Depp. Prod: Undercover Pictures.

THE EIGHTH DAY

Script and Dir: Andrew Niccol. Players: Uma Thurman, Ethan Hawke, Jude Law, Alan Arkin. Prod: Columbia.

EVITA

Script and Dir: Alan Parker. Players: Madonna, Antonio Banderas, Jonathan Pryce, Jimmy Nail. Prod: Cinergi.

FRIGID & IMPOTENT

Script: Carter Blanchard, Joshua Stern. Dir: Gregg Araki. Players: Drew Barrymore. Prod: Single Cell Prods.

GHOSTS OF MISSISSIPPI

Script: Lewis Colick. Dir: Rob Reiner. Players: Alec Baldwin, Whoopi Goldberg, James Woods, Craig T. Nelson. Prod: Castle Rock.

G.I. JANE

Script: Danielle Alexandra, David Twohy. Dir: Ridley Scott. Players: Demi Moore, Viggo Mortensen, Anne Bancroft, Jason Beghe. Prod: Scott Free Prods.

THE HONEST COURTESAN

Script: Jeannine Dominy. Dir: Marshall Herskovitz. Players: Catherine McCormack. Prod: Warner Bros.

ICE STORM

Script: James Schamus. Dir: Ang Lee. Players: Kevin Kline, Sigourney Weaver, Joan Allen, Elijah Wood, Christina Ricci. Prod: Icy Films.

INCOGNITO

Script: Jordan Katz. Dir: Peter Weller. Players: Jason Patric, Irene Jacob. Prod: Warner Bros.

JERRY MAGUIRE

Script and Dir: Cameron Crowe. Players: Tom Cruise, Cuba Gooding Jr., Renee Zellweger, Kelly Preston. Prod: Gracie Films.

THE JETSONS

Script: Scott Alexander, Larry Karaszewski. Dir: Joe Dante. Prod: Turner Pictures.

JINGLE ALL THE WAY

Script: Randy Kornfield, Deborah Kaplan, Harry Elfont, Chris Columbus. Dir: Brian Levant. Players: Arnold Schwarzenegger, Sinbad, Phil Hartman, Rita Wilson, Jim Belushi. Prod: Fox.

JUNGLE2JUNGLE

Script: Bruce A. Evans, Raynold Gideon, Charlie Peters. Dir: John Pasquin. Players: Tim Allen, Martin Short, Lolita Davidovich, JoBeth Williams. Prod: Baboon Prods.

L.A. CONFIDENTIAL

Dir: Curtis Hanson. Players: Kevin Spacey, Russell Crowe, Guy Pearce, Kim Basinger, Danny DeVito, James Cromwell. Prod: New Regency.

THE LONG KISS GOODNIGHT

Script: Shane Black. Dir: Renny Harlin. Players: Geena Davis, Samuel L. Jackson. Prod: Juno Pix.

MEN IN BLACK

Script: Ed Solomon. Dir: Barry Sonnenfeld. Players: Tommy Lee Jones, Will Smith, Linda Fiorentino. Prod: Amblin Entertainment.

MICHAEL

Script: Nora Ephron, Delia Ephron, Pete Dexter, James Quinlan. Dir: Nora Ephron. Players: John Travolta, Andie MacDowell, William Hurt. Prod: Alphaville Prods.

MY BEST FRIEND'S WEDDING

Script: Ron Bass. Dir: P.J. Hogan. Players: Julia Roberts, Dermot Mulroney. Prod: TriStar.

MY FAVOURITE MARTIAN

Script: Paul Weitz, Chris Weitz. Dir: Joe Dante. Prod: Warner Bros.

MY FELLOW AMERICANS

Script: Jack Kaplan, Richard Chapman, Peter Tolan. Dir: Peter Segal. Players: Jack Lemmon, James Garner, Dan Aykroyd, Lauren Bacall. Prod: Peters Entertainment.

NIGHTWATCH

Script: Steven Soderbergh. Dir: Ole Bornedal. Players: Nick Nolte, Ewan MacGregor. Prod: Dimension Films.

NOTHING TO LOSE

Script and Dir: Steve Oedekerk. Players: Tim Robbins, Martin Lawrence. Prod: Touchstone Pictures.

ONE NIGHT STAND

Script: Joe Eszterhas. Dir: Mike Figgis. Players: Wesley Snipes, Robert Downey Jr., Nastassja Kinski, Ming-Na Wen, Kyle MacLachlan. Prod: New Line.

OUT TO SEA

Script: Robert Jacobs. Dir: Herbert Ross. Players: Jack Lemmon, Walter Matthau. Prod: Davis Entertainment.

THE PEACEMAKER

Dir: Mimi Leder. Players: George Clooney, Nicole Kidman, Gary Werntz, Holt McCallany, Joan Copeland. Prod: Dreamworks SKG.

THE QUEST FOR CAMELOT

Script: Elizabeth Chandler, Jacqueline Feather, David Seidler. Dir: Bill Kroyer, Frederick DuChau. Voices: Christopher Reeve, Eric Idle. Prod: Warner Bros.

RANSOM

Dir: Ron Howard. Players: Mel Gibson, Rene Russo, Gary Sinise. Prod: Segue Prods./Imagine Entertainment/Touchstone Pictures.

THE SAINT

Script: Wesley Strick, Jonathan Hensleigh. Dir: Phillip Noyce. Players: Val Kilmer, Elisabeth Shue, Henry Goodman. Prod: Paramount British Pictures.

SEVEN YEARS IN TIBET

Script: Becky Johnston. Dir: Jean-Jacques Annaud. Players: Brad Pitt, David Thewlis. Prod: Mandalay Entertainment/TriStar.

STARSHIP TROOPERS

Script: Ed Neumeier. Dir: Paul Verhoeven. Phot: Jost Vacano. Players: Casper Van Dien, Dina Meyer, Denise Richards, Jake

Busey, Neil Patrick Harris, Michael Ironside. Prod: TriStar.

SUBURBIA

Script: Richard Linklater, Eric Bogosian. Dir: Linklater. Players: Parker Posey, Giovanni Ribsi, Nicky Katt, Dina Spydey. Prod: Castle Rock.

THAT OLD FEELING

Script: Leslie Dixon. Dir: Carl Reiner. Players: Bette Midler, Dennis Farina, Danny Nucci. Prod: Dixon, Bonnie Bruckheimer.

TITANIC

Script and Dir: James Cameron. Players: Kate Winslet, Leonardo DiCaprio. Prod: Fox.

WASHINGTON SQUARE

Dir: Agnieszka Holland. Players: Jennifer Jason Leigh, Ben Chaplin, Albert Finney. Prod: Caravan Pictures.

Producers/ Distributors

Alliance Communications Corp.
920 Yonge Street
Toronto
Ontario M4W 3C7, Canada
Tel: (416) 967 1174

Alliance Productions
301 N. Canon Drive #321
Beverly Hills
CA 90210
Tel: (310) 275 5501
Fax: (310) 275 5502

Amblin Entertainment
(see DreamWorks)

American Zoetrope
916 Kearny Street
San Francisco
CA 94133
Tel: (415) 788 7500
Fax: (415) 989 7910

Beacon Communications Inc.
1041 N. Formosa Ave.
Santa Monica Bldg., #200
Los Angeles
CA 90046
Tel: (213) 850 2651
Fax: (213) 850 2613

Brillstein-Grey Entertainment
9150 Wilshire Blvd., #350
Beverly Hills
CA 90212
Tel: (310) 275 6135
Fax: (310) 275 6180

Cappa Productions
(Martin Scorsese)
445 Park Ave., 7th Floor
New York
NY 10022
Tel: (212) 906 8800
Fax: (212) 906 8891

Caravan Pictures
3000 West Olympic Blvd., Bldg. 5
Santa Monica
CA 90404
Tel: (310) 264 4400
Fax: (310) 264 4404

Castle Rock Entertainment
335 N. Maple Drive, #135
Beverly Hills
CA 90210
Tel: (310) 385 2300
Fax: (310) 285 2345

Cinergi Productions Inc.
2308 Broadway
Santa Monica
CA 90404
Tel: (310) 315 6000
Fax: (310) 828 0443

Columbia Television
(TV production)
10202 West Washington Blvd.
Culver City
CA 90232
Tel: (310) 280 8000
Fax: (310) 204 1300

Disney
(Distributor)
500 South Buena Vista St.
Burbank
CA 91521
Tel: (818) 560 1000

Donner/Shuler Donner Productions
Lauren Shuler Donner
4000 Warner Blvd., Bldg. 103, Room 4
Burbank
CA 91522
Tel: (818) 954 3611
Fax: (818) 954 3475

Richard Donner
4000 Warner Blvd., Bldg. 102
Burbank
CA 91522
Tel: (818) 954 3961
Fax: (818) 954 4908

Douglas Reuther Productions
The Lewis Bldg.
5555 Melrose Ave.
Hollywood
CA 90038
Tel: (213) 956 5700
Fax: (213) 862 1177

DreamWorks
100 Universal City Plaza
Bungalow 477, Universal City
CA 91608
Tel: (818) 777 4600
Fax: (818) 509 1433

The Robert Evans Company
The Lubitsch Bldg., #117
5555 Melrose Ave.
Hollywood
CA 90038
Tel: (213) 862 8800
Fax: (213) 862 0070

Finerman Productions, Wendy
10202 West Washington Blvd.,
Tristar 224
Culver City
CA 90232
Tel: (310) 280 4650
Fax: (310) 280 1495

40 Acres & a Mule Filmworks
(Spike Lee)
124 Dekalb Ave.
Brooklyn
NY 11217
Tel: (718) 624 3703

Fox Searchlight Pictures
10201 W. Pico Blvd., Bldg. 38, 1st Floor
Los Angeles
CA 90035

Tel: (310) 369 4402
Fax: (310) 369 2359

Hanna-Barbera Productions Inc.
3400 Cahuenga Blvd.
Hollywood
CA 90068
Tel: (213) 851 5000

Hollywood Pictures
(Distributed through Buena Vista)
500 South Buena Vista St.
Burbank
CA 91521
Tel: (818) 560 1000

Imagine Films Entertainment Inc.
1925 Century Park East #2300
Los Angeles
CA 90067
Tel: (310) 277 1665
Fax: (310) 785 0107

Ixtlan Productions
201 Santa Monica Blvd. #610
Santa Monica
CA 90401
Tel: (310) 359 0525

King World Entertainment
12400 Wilshire Blvd. #1200
Los Angeles
CA 90025
Tel: (310) 826 1108
Fax: (310) 207 2179

Kopelson Prods., Arnold
6100 Wilshire Blvd. #1500
Los Angeles
CA 90048
Tel: (213) 932 0500
Fax: (213) 932 0238

Kushner-Locke Co.
11601 Wilshire Blvd., 21st Floor
Los Angeles
CA 90025
Tel: (310) 445 1111
Fax: (310) 445 1191

The Ladd Company
Chevalier 117
5555 Melrose Ave.
Hollywood
CA 90038
Tel: (213) 956 8055
Fax: (213) 862 1115

TWISTER dominated U.S. screens in the early part of the summer

Malpaso Productions
4000 Warner Blvd.
Burbank
CA 91522
Tel: (818) 954 1228

Maverick Productions
8000 Beverly Blvd.
Los Angeles
CA 90048
Tel: (213) 852 1177
Fax: (213) 852 1505

Metro-Goldwyn-Mayer Inc.
(Distributor)
2500 Broadway St
Santa Monica
CA 90404
Tel: (310) 449 3000

Miramax Films
(Distributor/Producer)
375 Greenwich Street
New York
NY 10013
Tel: (212) 941 3800
+
7920 Sunset Blvd., #230
Los Angeles
CA 90046-3353
Tel: (213) 845 4200
Fax: (213) 845 4214

Morgan Creek Productions
4000 Warner Blvd., Bldg. 76
Burbank
CA 91522
Tel: (818) 954 4800
Fax: (818) 954 4811

MTV
10 Universal City Plaza
30th Floor, Universal City
CA 91608
Tel: (818) 505 7800
Fax: (818) 505 7817

New Line Cinema
(Distibutor/Producer)
116 North Robertson Blvd. #200
Los Angeles
CA 90048
Tel: (310) 854 5811
Fax: (310) 854 1824

New Regency Productions Inc.
4000 Warner Blvd., Bldg. 66
Burbank
CA 91522
Tel: (818) 954 5948
Fax: (818) 954 3295

Northern Lights Productions
(see Ivan Reitman)

Paramount Pictures
(Distributor)
5555 Melrose Ave.
Hollywood
CA 90038
Tel: (213) 956 5000

Paramount TV
5555 Melrose Ave.
Hollywood
CA 90038
Tel: (213) 956 5000

Peters Entertainment
4000 Warner Blvd.
Burbank
CA 91522
Tel: (818) 954 4960
Fax: (818) 954 4983

PolyGram Filmed Ent.
9348 Civic Centre Drive, #300
Beverly Hills
CA 90210
Tel: (310) 777 7700
Fax: (310) 777 7709

Red Wagon Productions
TriStar Bldg. 212
10202 W. Washington Blvd.
Culver City
CA 90232
Tel: (310) 280 4466
Fax: (310) 280 1480

Reitman Productions, Ivan
100 Universal City Plaza, Bldg. 489
Universal City
CA 91608
Tel: (818) 777 8080
Fax: (818) 733 0689

Rudin Productions, Scott
5555 Melrose Ave.
Hollywood
CA 90038
Tel: (213) 862 4600
Fax: (213) 862 1045

Rysher Entertainment
2401 Colorado Blvd., Bldg. A, 2nd Floor
Santa Monica
CA 90404

Saban Entertainment
10960 Wilshire Blvd.
Los Angeles
CA 90024
Tel: (310) 235 5100
Fax: (310) 235 5102/3

Silver Pictures
4000 Warner Bi #90
Burbank
CA 91522
Tel: (818) 954 4490
Fax: (818) 954 3237

Sony Pictures Inc.
(Distributor)
10202 West Washington Blvd.
Culver City
CA 90232
Tel: (310) 280 8000
Fax: (310) 204 1300

South Side Amusements
(Robert Zemeckis)
100 Universal City Plaza
Bungalow 127, Universal City
CA 91608
Tel: (818) 777 8313
Fax: (818) 733 1447

Spelling Television, Aaron
5700 Wilshire Blvd., #575
Los Angeles
CA 90036
Tel: (213) 965 5700
Fax: (213) 965 5895

Tisch Company, Steve
3815 Hughes Ave.
Culver City
CA 90232
Tel: (310) 838 2500
Fax: (310) 204 2713

Trimark Pictures
(Distributor/Producer)
2644 30th St.
Santa Monica
CA 90405
Tel: (310) 399 8877
Fax: (310) 392 0252

TriStar
(Distributor)
10202 West Washington Blvd.
Culver City
CA 90232
Tel: (310) 280 7700

Turner Pictures
1888 Century Park East, #1400
Los Angeles
CA 90067
Tel: (310) 551 6300
Fax: (310) 788 4254

Twentieth Century Fox
10201 West Pico Blvd.
Los Angeles
CA 90035
Tel: (310) 369 1000
Fax: (310) 369 2735

Universal City Studios Inc.
(Distriutor)
100 Universal Plaza
Universal City
CA 91068
Tel: (818) 777 1000

Universal Television
100 Universal City Plaza
Universal City
CA 91608
Tel: (818) 777 1000

Warner Bros. Inc.
(Distributor)
4000 Warner Blvd.
Burbank
CA 91522
Tel: (818) 954 6000

Wildwood Enterprises Inc.
(Robert Redford)
1101 Montana Ave., #E
Santa Monica
CA 90403
Tel: (310) 395 5155
Fax: (310) 395 3975

Wind Dancer Films
500 South Buena Vista St.
Burbank
CA 91521
Tel: (818) 560 1151
Fax: (818) 953 7401

Winkler Films Inc.
211 S. Beverly Drive, #200
Beverly Hills
CA 90212
Tel: (310) 858 5780
Fax: (310) 858 5799

Useful Addresses

Academy of Motion Picture Arts and Sciences
8949 Wilshire Blvd.
Beverly Hills
CA 90211
Tel: (310) 247 3000

American Film Institute
John F. Kennedy Centre for the Performing Arts
Washington
D.C. 20566
Tel: (202) 828 4000
Fax: (202) 659 1970

The Directors Guild of America Bldg.
7920 Sunset Blvd. #230
Los Angeles
CA 90046
Tel: (213) 845 4200
Fax: (213) 845 4218

Mira Sorvino, Academy Award-winner for Woody Allen's MIGHTY APHRODITE

Independent Feature Film Project
104 W. 29th Street. 12th Floor
New York
NY 10001
Tel: (212) 465 8200
Fax: (212) 465 8525
+
5550 Wilshire Blvd., #204
Los Angeles
CA 90036
Tel: (213) 937 4379
Fax: (213) 937 4038

Motion Picture Association of America (MPPA)
15503 Ventura Blvd.
Encino
CA 91436
Tel: (818) 995 6600
Fax: (818) 382 1799

NATO/ShoWest
116 North Robertson Blvd., #708
Los Angeles
CA 90048
Tel: (310) 657 7724
Fax: (310) 657 4758

VENEZUELA

Luis Sedgwick Báez

Considering the bleakness of the current economic climate, it is encouraging to see sunny days being forecast for the Venezuelan film industry. Financial gaps are being patched up with joint ventures and co-productions. **Celestial Clockwork** (*Mecánicas celestes*), the new film by Fina Torres, which received financial backing from France and Spain, was released this year after doing a tour of world festivals (Berlin, Chicago Latino, Cartagena and La Habana). Luis Armando Roche's **Out in the Open** (*Aire libre*) received its première at the Cinemateca Nacional and was supported by Canadian aid. **The Crystal Mountain** (*La montaña de cristal*) by Joaquin Cortés was co-produced with Spain. **Nude with**

Av. Diego Cisneros, Edificio Centro Colgate, Ala Sur,
Piso 2, Los Ruices. Apartado Postal 70102. Caracas Venezuela
Phone numbers: (58-2)238-1622 / 238-1050 / 238-1775
Fax: (58-2) 239-4786 / 238-5230. E-mail:dahbarcnac@true. net

Centro Nacional **Autónomo** de Cinematografía

VENEZUELA 1996-1997

CHRISTIAN VADIM, ROY DUPUIS, CARLOS CRUZ
AIRE LIBRE
THREE EXPLORERS FIND FRIENDSHIP IN THE WILDERNESS.
DIRECTED BY LUIS ARMANDO ROCHE

CORAZONES NEGROS
THEIR LOVE WAS PERFECT. IT WAS A SHAME SHE WAS DEAD.
DIRECTED BY GABRIELA RANGEL

CARLOS MATA, LOURDES VALERA, DANIEL ALVARADO
DESNUDO CON NARANJAS
A FIGHT FOR LOVE IN A TIME OF DEATH.
DIRECTED BY LUIS ALBERTO LAMATA

DESPEDIDA DE SOLTERA
THIRTEEN WOMEN AND ONE UNFORGETABLE BRIDAL SHOWER.
DIRECTED BY ANTONIO LLERANDI

ARIADNA GIL AND ARIELLE DOMBASLE
MECÁNICAS CELESTES
A CINDERELLA STORY FOR THE 90'S. DIRECTED BY FINA TORRES

LA NAVE DE LOS SUEÑOS
A JOURNEY OF HOPE AND DISAPPOINTMENTS. DIRECTED BY CIRO DURÁN

JOSÉ SANCHO
LA MONTAÑA DE CRISTAL
A JUNGLE OF DANGERS AND DIAMONDS. DIRECTED BY JOAQUÍN CORTÉS

TOKYO-PARAGUAIPOA
TWO WORLDS FIGHTING FOR LOVE AND HONOR. DIRECTED BY LEONARDO HENRÍQUEZ

TRAMPA PARA UN GATO
IN TIME OF WAR, RADIO CAN KEEP YOU ALIVE. DIRECTED BY MANUEL DE PEDRO

LAURA DEL SOL
SANTERA
LOGIC AND SUPERSTITION FIGHT IN HER HEART. DIRECTED BY SOLVEIG HOOGESTEIJN

Daniel Alvarado and Lourdes Valera in Luis Alberto Lamata's NUDE WITH ORANGES

Ariadna Gil and Evelyne Didi in Fina Torres's CELESTIAL CLOCKWORK

Oranges (*Desnudo con naranjas*) by the acclaimed Luis Alberto Lamata (*Jericó*) was, however, a thoroughly Venezuelan enterprise.

1994 was a landmark year for the local industry. The Centro Nacional Auntónomo de Cinematográfia, CNAC (National Film Center), was created, replacing the old FONCINE. Its objectives include creating a Venezuelan presence in world film markets, searching out new co-producers, and the establishment of the Venezuelan Film Commission (VFC). The latter has been promoting the country as a huge film set in order to attract film-makers and foreign investors. The varied geography that Venezuela has to offer – tropical rainforest, snowy mountains, flat lands with a myriad of bird species, pristine beaches – was widely admired at the Venezuelan Film Commission stand in Los Angeles in March this year.

The CNAC has also been responsible for signing agreements with Spain, France, Puerto Rico, Canada and Argentina to help improve the local industry. The total budget allocated to CNAC reached a peak of US$ 200 million for 1996. In the past two years, CNAC has approved 10 feature films and 10 short films. The Cinemateca Nacional, the venerable art house, celebrated 30 years with a tribute to one of its founders, film-maker Margot Benacerraf (*Araya, Reverón*). Still looking for a permanent space, the Cinemateca Nacional has stressed the need to encourage and develop the formation of film-makers, given the lack of graduate cinema studies and research institutions, and an absence of investigators in the field of cinema.

During 1996, several films have been completed and others are awaiting to be exhibited, including: **Voice of the Heart** (*La voz del corazón*) by Carlos Oteyza, where love and ecology go hand in hand; **Before Dying** (*Antes de morir*) by Pablo de la Barra, a police thrillers; **Tosca, the Movie** (*Tosca, la pelicula*) by Iván Feo; **Bridal Shower** (*Despedida de soltera*) by Antonio Llerandi; **A Shot in the Back** (*Un tiro en Ia espalda*) by Alfredo Lugo; **Black Hearts** (*Corazones negros*) by Gabriela Rangel; **Cat Trap** (*Trampa para un gato*) by Manuel de Pedro; and **Tokyo-Paraguaipoa** by Leonardo Henriquez.

The Venezuelan box-office is still largely determined by the latest U.S. releases. But a number of co-productions are underway with European and Latin-American countries. Venezuelan film-makers are eager to pursue their associations with whatever country can provide the support and opportunities to crystallise their ever-growing talents.

LUIS SEDGWICK BÁEZ, film buff, has written for several publications, including *Encuadre* (for the past eight years), *Domingo hoy, Imagen, Excelencia.*

Still from TOKYO — PARAGUIAPOA, directed by Leonardo Henríquez

Producers

Bolivar Films
Av. Luis Guillermo Villegas,
Edf. Bolivar Films, Urb. Santa
Eduvigis, Chacao. Apartado postal
62270. Caracas, Venezuela.
Tel: (58-2) 283 4455
Fax: (58-2) 284 1011

Alter Producciones Cinematográficas
Av. Diego de Losada, Qta. Alter No 3
(al lado del IESA). San Bernardino,
Caracas. Venezuela.
Tel: (58-2) 51 4536, 51 7881,
51 1923
Fax: (58-2) 52 7297

Producciones Tango Bravo, C. A.
4ta. Avenida, entre 9a. y 10a.
transversal, Quinta "Turandot",
Los Palos Grandes. Caracas,
Venezuela.
Tel: (58-2) 283 4829
Fax: (58-2)285 9237

35 mm Producciones Cinematográficas
Final Avenida 12, entre 7a. y 8a.
transversal, Qta. Las Lidas,
Altamira Norte, Caracas,
Venezuela.
Tel: (58-2) 261 0250
Fax: (58-2) 261 4076

Nexus Productora Cinematográfica, C. A.
Calle Tiuma, Edf. Tiuna, piso 1,
Boleita Norte. Caracas, Venezuela.
Tel: (58-2) 237 6375
Fax: (58-2) 234 9986
E-mail: Infonenex@nexus.internet.ve

Distributors

Cinematográfica Blancica
3era. transversal de las Delicias de
Sabana Grande
Edf. Banco Banesco, piso 6.
Caracas, Venezuela.
Tel: (58-2) 762 9780, 762 9781,
762 9782
Fax: (58-2) 762 5929

Cines Unidos
Edf. Teatro Las Palmas, Mezzanina,
Av. Las Palmas, La Florida. Caracas,
Venezuela.
Tel: (58-2) 781 7511, 781 7144

Korda Films
3era Av. Las Delicias, Edf. Las
Delicias, piso 5, Sabana Grande.
Caracas, Venezuela.
Tel: (58-2) 762 6384, 762 0338,
762 6030

Roraimex
Av. Las Palmas
Edf. Teatro Las Palmas, piso 6.
Caracas, Venezuela.
Tel: (58-2) 793 0470, 793 7128,
782 9675

Useful Addresses

Asociación Nacional de Autores Cinematográficos (ANAC)
Urb. Avila, Av. San Gabriel,
Qta. Primavera, Alta Florida.
Caracas, Venezuela.
Tel: (58-2) 74 0360, 74 1767,
74 1737
Fax: (58-2) 74 1954

Asociación Venezolana de Exhibidores de Peliculas (AVEP)
Av. Rómulo Gallegos,
Edf. Torresaman, piso 1, oficina 11,
Los Dos Caminos. Caracas,
Venezuela.
Tel: (58-2) 237 0357

Centro Nacional Autónomo de Cinematográfia (CNAC)
Av. Diego Cisneros, Edf. Centro
Colgate, Ala Sur, Piso 2, Los Ruices.
Apartado postal 70102. Caracas,
Venezuela.
Tel: (58-2) 238 1775, 238 1622,
238 1050
Fax: (58-2) 239 4786, 238 5230

Fundación Cinemateca Nacional
Final Av. Este 2. Edf. José Vargas,
piso 14. Apartado postal 17045.
Caracas, Venezuela.
Tel: (58-2) 576 2336, 576 1491
Fax: (58-2) 576 1548, 576 2912

The 1972 annual meeting of the NAMC voiced some concern over this rather narrow and high-brow approach of the Cinema and Film Foundation. Implicitly and explicitly, the delegates pointed out the need to promote the big entertainment pictures, to boost further the impact of the box-office locomotives. By doing so, the NCFF would also make room for the culturally ambitious films, it was argued. The litany of combining the stock exchange with the cathedral – echoing Thomas Carlyle's vision of the publishing house – was invoked to describe the ideal operating profile of the municipal cinemas.

Cinema PR Roadshow

The request of the annual meeting turned into provisional plans for "screening days" for cinema managers to preview a number of up-coming attractions before the autumn season. Then a group of like-minded acquaintances from the seaside village of Drøbak, south of Oslo, got wind of the plans and more or less created the first Norwegian Film Festival out of the air. An NCFF-appointed General Committee oversaw the fledgling festival, two film critics and the programming director of the Oslo cinemas guaranteed the quality of the 15 international films selected.

It was, agreed everyone who participated, a splendid event. Improvised and overcrowded in a village which could hardly offer lodgings to more than a fraction of the 250 trade and press participants, the Festival enjoyed un-seasonably good weather and the presence of François Truffaut, who came to present *Day for Night* (*La Nuit Américaine*). The five days in Drøbak were all fun and friendly fellowship, even when the distributors and the cinema managers met to thrash it out in eleven-a-side soccer, even when the Danish pastries were reserved for the press.

The Norwegian Film Festival had come to stay – but not in one place. Hosting the Norwegian Film Festival became something of a competitive sport between cinemas in larger towns and cities. The Festival began its cycle of ambulatory existence.

Stuck in a Rut

During the following years the Festival passed through several cities, on the implicit understanding that no-one would be allowed to monopolise the publicity created by the event. A queue system evolved. In 1980 the Festival was booked for the next three years to different communities. . . .

Whatever infrastructure the Festival had was maintained by the Cinema and Film Foundation staff. A co-ordinating committee would be set up in spring with representatives of the host community, a selection committee would be at work picking 10 to 15 foreign films during the summer, participants would register with the NCFF, and then the staff would descend on the host town a few days ahead of the Festival opening. A daily festival newspaper, first mimeographed, later photocopied, had appeared to keep participants up to date in between screenings. Similarly, press conferences had become a professional ritual.

Participation increased slowly. By the time the Festival made its first stop at Haugesund in 1979, the number of accreditations had doubled since Drøbak to around four hundred. But the guests coming to present their films were all Scandinavians. No major film personality of an international calibre had appeared on the scene since Truffaut's visit to Drøbak.

"And the winner is . . ."

The need to professionalise the Festival was becoming obvious. After its second stop at Haugesund in 1981, the town's culture and cinema director Gunnar Johan Løvvik quietly began preparing a bid to make it the permanent base for the Festival. Firm backing from local authorities and a network of business contacts made it possible for Løvvik to outline a development plan. It included expansion of the Edda multiplex theatre, a new culture centre comprising a theatre-cum-cinema auditorium, and increased accommodation capacity, along with more

Liv Ullmann, Karen-Lise Mynster, and Erland Josephson at the press conference for SOPHIE at Haugesund in 1992
photo: Sigurd Moe Hetland

mundane details like access to the municipal printing office for production of the Festival newspaper. The municipality declared itself willing to invest in the theatres, and to provide staff to supplement the NCFF officers who would still be manning key posts in the event.

The plan was launched as a member's proposal at the 1982 annual meeting of the NAMC. In spite of a negative evaluation from the administration and obvious misgivings from the Board, which comprised representatives from three potential rival cities, the debate and vote gave Haugesund a ringing victory. The mayor of Haugesund, formally presenting the proposal, had to compromise in allowing for other cities to make their bid for hosting the Festival at a minimum of three-year intervals. Otherwise, Haugesund's victory was complete. The Festival had found a home.

Two more years were to elapse before the Norwegian Film Festival opened permanently in Haugesund, however. The two largest cities in Norway were already in the pipeline for their shot at hosting the Festival. The Bergen event in 1982 proved to what extent a community could infuse its particular culture and character into the Festival – to the benefit of both parties. And the Oslo event the following year confirmed that it had been a wise decision to let a small city become the permanent base of the Festival.

The Lillehammer Effect

Meanwhile, Løvvik had prepared to turn the former shipping and fishing town into "Norway's Cannes". Turning the festival preparations into a veritable *dugnad,* a traditional community work project, Løvvik managed to harness local enthusiasm in much the same manner which was later to characterise the winter Olympic Games at Lillehammer in 1994. Where else could a politically elected member of the municipal Board of Culture be found driving a hospitality car, or the main-street watchmaker volunteering his time and sailing boat to take festival guests sight-seeing?

One key element in Løvvik's game plan was to attract the press and media. As a professional event, the Norwegian Film Festival can only communicate with the greater audience through the media, was the simple analysis. Making the journalists feel comfortable, and facilitating their work, paid off handsomely in reams of newspaper clippings. Inviting the many fledgling local radio stations to cover the event opened up a whole new range of opportunities for media exposure. The Festival even produced its own daily closed-circuit television programmes just to prove to national telecaster NRK that it could be done – and that the Festival provided interesting programme material.

Amanda, Moore and more

International film-makers had started making their appearances at the Norwegian Film Festival in 1980. When UIP brought Alan Alda to Haugesund in 1981, PR reps got a surprise. The visit created a near-avalanche of press articles, interviews and photographs. Yet it was a mere trifle compared to the headlines when Roger Moore appeared on screen in *A View to a Kill* – and in person in the *Haraldsgata* pedestrian precinct – in 1985.

Moore was joined on stage by Michael Palin and Liv Ullmann, the Festival's new honorary president, for the inauguration of the Amanda awards for film and television merit. Broadcast live on national television, the Amandas greatly strengthened the Festival's image as the central event for film and cinema in Norway, as did the four prizes going to the national box-office hit *Orion's Belt*.

Product Development

After a mandatory detour to Kristiansand in 1986, in compliance with the 1982 compromise, the Film Festival was back in Haugesund in 1987. Meanwhile, it had become a limited company, with two-thirds of the capital provided by the NCFF, one-third by the Municipality of Haugesund. Gunnar Johan Løvvik could formally style himself Festival Director, and by his side he had a Programme Director, responsible for film selection –

Nils Aas with the Amanda that inspired his statuette award *photo: Sigurd Moe Hetland*

Sydney Pollack attending the Norwegian Film Festival in 1993 *photo: Sigurd Moe Hetland*

since 1991 Vigdis Lian. The move helped streamline festival procedures and cut through a lot of red tape.

"I think the Festival has found its form," Løvvik pronounced in an interview in 1988. Yet side-bar events and fringe attractions kept being added to the Festival. The Festival Director's recipe for making something new out of an event is product development. In 1987 Frans Widerberg became the first "Festival exhibiting artist". A Children's FilmFest was added in 1988, to encourage the import, distribution and exhibition of films for "tomorrow's audience". "Meet the Film-Maker", an informal occasion for the audience to meet the people behind the films, became a fixture, as did the silent film concerts. Special events for Canadian and Italian films have paved the way for Ettore Scola to launch a Norwegian Film Week in Rome and for a co-production treaty with Canada. A 1996 manifestation devoted to France may bring further contacts. And "New Nordic Films" has been highlighting recent productions from the north of Europe from 1995.

Along the way, the Festival can also pride itself on having presented films and film-makers of renown, not a few of them well before their major breakthrough: Bille August, Dŭsan Makavejev, Susan Seidelman, Gabriel Axel, Fernando Solanas, Terence Davies, Jerry Zucker, Neil Jordan, Mike Leigh to name but a few. There will be more to come. . . .

NILS KLEVJER AAS is Curator of the Department of Museum and Archives in the Norwegian Film Institute. A writer and lecturer on Norwegian film history, he served on the staff of the NCFF and the Norwegian Film Festival from 1978, being Programme Director between 1987 and 1991.

Guide to Leading Festivals

Amiens

November 8-17, 1996

A competitive festival in northern France, for both shorts and features. There are also retrospectives (Imamura, South Africa, both in 1996), as well as a "Cinémas du Monde" series, which includes works from Africa, Latin America, and Asia. *Inquiries to:* Festival du Film d'Amiens, 36 rue du Noyon, 80000 Amiens, France. Tel: (33) 22 91 01 44. Fax: (33) 22 92 53 04.

Annecy/MIFA

May 26-31, 1997

The long-established international – and competitive – animated film festival in the Savoie region of south-east France, with a useful market (MIFA) to further the sale and distribution of animated films. Also retrospectives and exhibitions. *Inquiries to:* Centre International du Cinéma d'Animation, B.P. 399, 74013 Annecy Cedex, France. Tel: (33) 50 57 41 72. Fax: (33) 50 67 81 95.

Berlin

February 13-24, 1997

Berlin is generally recognised to be the most efficiently-organised of the world's major festivals. In addition to the competitive programme and information section, there is a Retrospective, screenings of all new German films, and of course the Forum of Young Cinema, directed by Ulrich Gregor, where many of the most imaginative films are screened. *Inquiries to:* Berlin International Film Festival, Budapester Strasse 50, 10787 Berlin. Tel: (30) 254890. Telex: 185255. Fax: (30) 25489249.

AWARDS 1996

Golden Bear: **Sense and Sensibility** (U.S.A.), Lee.
Special Jury Prize: **All Things Fair** (Denmark/ Sweden), Widerberg.
Best Director: (*shared*) Yim Ho for **The Sun Has Ears** (China, Hongkong); Richard Loncraine for **Richard III** (U.K./U.S.).
Best Actor: Sean Penn for **Dead Man Walking** (U.S.).
Best Actress: Anouk Grinberg for **Mon homme** (France).
Best Short: **The Arrival of the Train** (Russia).
Lifetime Contribution to the Art of Cinema: Andrzej Wajda.

Cambridge

July, 1997

A film festival in this historic university town can call on considerable local and student interest, and ranks alongside London and Edinburgh as the best festival in the U.K. Now in its 21st year the event is non-competitive and screens both shorts and feature films often in the presence of directors and actors. *Inquiries to:* Tony Jones, Cambridge Film Festival, Cambridge Arts Cinema, 8 Market Passage, Cambridge, CB2 3PF, U.K. Tel: (1223) 578944. Telex: 81574. Fax: (1223) 578929. E-mail: François@Cambarts.co.uk. Website: http//www.WORLDSERVER. PIPEX.con/CAMBARTS.

Cannes

May 7-19, 1997

Cannes, which this year celebrates its 50th Anniversary, remains the world's top festival, attracting the American key independents and personalities as well as entries from the more obscure countries. Cannes includes two major sections: the Competition and "Un Certain Regard". There are also the Directors' Fortnight screenings, as well as the Marché (MIF). The Critics' Week, and innumerable other useful screenings (e.g. the Australian, New Zealand and Scandinavian films). The great advantage of Cannes is that everyone of importance attends the event. *Inquiries to:* 99 boulevard Malesherbes, 75008 Paris, France. Tel: (331) 45 61 66 00. Fax: (331) 45 61 97.60.

AWARDS 1996

Palme d'Or: **Secrets and Lies** (U.K./France). Leigh.
Grand Prix du Jury: **Breaking the Waves** (Denmark), von Trier.
Best Director: Joel Coen for **Fargo** (U.S.A.).

The 6th Brisbane International
Film Festival
31 JULY - AUGUST 10 1997
shorts, fiction features & documentaries
in film, video & multi-media
WORLD CINEMA
ASIA PACIFIC FOCUS
CHAUVEL AWARD
for distinguished contribution to Australian feature filmmaking
THE BIFF FAST FILM
short film competition
RETROSPECTIVES
Entries close 24 May 1997
Year round activities: Cinematheque screenings, Director Showcases and Queensland New Filmmaker Awards
Brisbane International Film Festival, GPO Box 909 Brisbane 4001
Level 3 Hoyts Regent Building 167 Queen Street Brisbane 4001
Phone 617 3220 0333 Facsimile 617 3220 0400
e-mail brisfilm@thehub.com.au website http://biff.thehub.com.au

Best Actor: (shared) Daniel Autueil, Pascal Duquenne for **The Eighth Day** (Belgium).
Best Actress: Brenda Blethyn for **Secrets and Lies** (U.K./France).
Best Screenplay: Jacques Audiard for **A Self-Made Hero** (France).
Special Jury Prize: **Crash** (Canada), Cronenberg.
Caméra d'Or Short: **The Wind** (Hungary), Ivanyi.

Cartagena

March 7-14, 1997

Cartagena is the oldest film festival in Latin America (37 years old in 1997). Cartagena is an old-world town and famous summer resort, and fest screens Ibero-Latin features, shorts and docus, as well as international screenings and a TV & video market. President of the new Latin American Film Foundation, and Nobel Prize winner, Gabriel García Márquez, is one of the festival's sponsors. *Inquiries to;* Cartagena International Film Festival, Baluarte de San Francisco, Calle San Juan de Dios, A.A. 1834, Cartagena, Colombia. Tel: (5) 644 2345, 660 0966. Fax: (5) 660 0970, 660 1037.

16th Amiens International Film Fest
November 8-17, 1996
- Official Selection: Competition full-length and short fiction films / Non competitive "Cinémas du Monde" : documentary and fiction by young directors
- A tribute to Shohei Imamura (Japan) : cinema and TV
- From apartheid to democracy : South African cinema
- Suburbs in European cinema

Amiens International Film Fest
36 rue de Noyon – 80000 Amiens – France
Tel. (33) 22 91 01 44 – Fax: (33) 22 92 53 04

Cartoons on the Bay 2

April 5-9, 1997

A competitive event dedicated to television animation, Cartoons on the Bay will take place every year, in April, between the MIP TV of Cannes and the World Children's Book Fair in Bologna. The Festival is organised by SACIS with the collaboration of RAI. Programmes not admitted to the competition will be presented within the "Show-Case". The other sections of the Festival are: Premieres of various feature-length films and TV programmes; Fairy Tales will be dedicated to the cross-over between animation and other special aspects and areas of communication with imaginative themes (special effects, animatronics, etc.); Planet Italy will be reserved for Italian animation, including new productions, projects, meetings with cartoonists and also retrospective exhibitions. The Golden and the Silver Pulcinella awards will be assigned by an international jury. *Inquiries to:* SACIS, 66 Via Teulada, 00195 Rome, Italy. Tel: 6/37498274. Fax: 6/3701343.

Chicago

October, 1997

Now in its fourth decade, the Chicago International Film Festival is the oldest competitive event in America. It aims to bring the most important international productions to the U.S., as well as acting as a showcase for independent film-makers. Twenty features compete for the Gold Hugo, the festival's grand prix, with separate competitions for shorts, docus, animated and student films. Recent honorees include Tom Cruise, Sophia Loren, Jack Lemmon, Sydney Pollack and Kathleen Turner. *Inquiries to:* Chicago International Film Festival, 415 North Dearborn, Chicago, Illinois 60610, U.S.A. Tel: (312) 644 3400. Fax (312) 644 0784. E-mail: filmfest@wwa.com. Website: http://www. chicago.ddbn.com/filmfest/.

Cinéma Tout Ecran

September 1997

The first and until now the only festival to devote its programming to films of cinematic quality produced by TV. The goal of the event is to help good films cross over from the small to the big screen. There are retrospectives of major directors who have worked in television, as well as a competition with three major prizes. Shorts and symposia make up the festivals. *Inquiries to:* Cinéma Tout Ecran, Maison des Arts de Grütli, 16 rue de Général Dufour, Case postale 53005, CH-1211 Geneva 11. Tel: (41 22) 328 85 54. Fax: (41 22) 329 68 02.

Clermont-Ferrand

January 31-February 8, 1997

The ideal destination for anyone who wants to explore over 200 of the best short films of the year, the volcanoes of the Auvergne and the exquisite cuisine of the region. This growing competitive event (53 countries in 1996, with 110,000 spectators) offers both national and international competitions alongside retrospectives, school programmes, debates and an accessible marketplace for shorts. *Inquiries to:* Clermont-Ferrand Short Film Festival, 26 rue des Jacobins, 63000 Clermont-Ferrand, France. Tel: (33) 73 91 65 73. Fax: (33) 73 92 11 93. E-mail: shortfilm@cirvax.in2p3.fr. Website:http//clrwww.in2p3.fr.CourtMetrage/ClermontFd.html.

MAIN AWARDS 1996

International Festival:
35 Aside (Ireland), O'Donnell.
Fridge (U.K.), Mullan.
National Festival:
La huitième nuit, Breton.
Départ immédiat, Briat.
Une visite, Harel.
L'enfant de La Ciotat, Debrée.

Denver

October, 1997

More than 100 film programmes from around the world make up the 20th Denver International Film Festival for ten days in October. New international features, documentaries, new American cinema and critic's programmes are screened and more than 50 film artists are due to attend the event in Colorado's delightfully spacious and friendly capital. Denver is non-competitive, but presents an achievement award. Also under the Denver Film Society umbrella: WAM! KidzFilmFest in June and Denver Jewish Film Festival in August. *Inquiries to:* DIFF, 1430 Larimer Square, Ste. 201, Denver, Colorado 80202.
Tel: (303) 595 3456. Fax: (303) 595 0956.
E-mail: denver/film@csn.net.
Website: http://www.2.csn.net/denverfilm.

Dutch Film Festival

September 24-October 3, 1997

Long established as an important occasion

DENVER FILM SOCIETY

20th Denver International Film Festival
OCTOBER 16-23, 1997

Celebrating 20 years of challenging, provocative film

Inquiries to:
Denver International Film Festival
1430 Larimer Square, Suite 201
Denver, Colorado 80202 U.S.A.
Phone 303.595.3456
Fax 303.595.0956
e-mail denverfilm@csn.net

during which the entire output of Dutch film-making may be assessed, in the attractive old town of Utrecht. A selection of Dutch features, shorts and television dramas are screened and judged, and there are Golden Calf awards in eleven different categories. Special programmes and retrospectives address various aspects of Dutch film. The Holland Film Meeting, the foreign section of the festival, is for festival directors, film buffs, distributors and critics, national and international. *Inquiries to:* Stichting Nederlands Film Festival, PO Box 1581, 3500 BN Utrecht, Holland.
Tel: (31) 30 2322684. Fax: (31) 30 2313200.
E-mail: NEDFILMFEST@INTER.NL.NET.
Website: http://www.DRU.NL.

AWARDS 1995

Best Film: **Zusje**, Westdijk, Koning.
Best Director: Marleen Gorris for **Antonia's Line**.
Best Actor: Rijk de Gooyer for **Hoogste Tijd**.
Best Actress: Willeke van Ammelrooy for **Antonia's Line**.
Best Short: **Bitings and Other Effects. . .**, Clara van Gool.
Best Documentary Short: **I Have a Problem, Madam**, Schmidt, Doebele.
Best Documentary Feature: **Mother Dao, the Turtlelike**, Monnikendam.
Special Jury Award: Jany Temime.

Edinburgh

August 10-24, 1997

The oldest continually-running film festival in the world, Edinburgh is also one of the most accessible. Emphasis on new films, innovation and excellence in film-making worldwide, U.K. films and young directors, with particularly well-chosen retrospectives and seminars. There's an offbeat sparkle to the Edinburgh selection which is reflected in the enthusiasm of local audiences. The 1996 event marked the festival's 50th anniversary, and again featured the New British Expo, a unique showcase of U.K. film production. *Inquiries to:* The Drambuie Edinburgh Film Festival, 88 Lothian Road, Edinburgh, EH3 9BZ, Scotland. Tel: (131) 228 4051. Telex: 72166. Fax: (131) 229 5501. E-mail: info@deff.demon.co.uk.

ESPOO CINÉ
August 22 - 31, 1997
Tapiola, Finland

now twice as good: TEN thrilling days of best European cinema!

PO Box 95, 02101 Espoo, Finland
tel +358-9-466 599, fax +358-9-466 458

fantasporto
FESTIVAL INTERNACIONAL DE CINEMA DO PORTO
February 7 to 15, 1997
XVII OPORTO INTERNATIONAL FILM FESTIVAL
XIV FANTASY FILM COMPETITION and VI NEW DIRECTORS WEEK
deadline November 30
Each year 200 new feature films/250 media representatives/100.000 spectators
further information please phone 351.2.5508990/1/2 or fax 351.2.5508210
or write to Rua da Constituição 311-4200 Porto-Portugal

18th FESTIVAL DES 3 CONTINENTS

NANTES - NOVEMBER 19 - 26 1996

80 FEATURE LENGTH FICTION FILMS FROM AFRICA, LATIN & BLACK AMERICA AND ASIA IN COMPETITIVE AND NON COMPETITIVE SECTIONS

Tel: (33) 40 60 74 14 - Fax: (33) 40 73 55 22

Espoo Ciné

August 22-31, 1997

Held in the beautiful "garden city" of Tapiola and now in its eighth year, this event showcases a selection of new European cinema, highlights from other continents, and the latest Finnish output of quality. Outdoor screenings, seminars on various topics, retrospectives, horror extravaganza, sneak previews and director guests make this a treat for film-fans. *Inquiries to:* Espoo Ciné, PO Box 95, FIN-02101 Espoo, Finland. Tel: (9) 466 599. Fax: (9) 466 458.

Fajr International Film Festival

February 20-30, 1997

The Fajr festival has flourished as a competitive event and now aims to provide a bridge between Eastern and Western cinemas. Fajr caters mainly for Iranian films, although screenings of international films are on the increase. The

26 FESTIVAL INTERNACIONAL DE CINEMA FIGUEIRA DA FOZ

SEPTEMBER, 1997 — PORTUGAL

FESTIVAL INTERNACIONAL DE CINEMA
DA FIGUEIRA DA FOZ
APARTADO 50 407 — 1709 LISBOA CODEX
TEL: (35) 11 812 62 31 ext. 27 — FAX: (35) 11 812 62 28

15° FESTIVAL INTERNAZIONALE CINEMA GIOVANI TORINO-ITALIA

15th TURIN INTERNATIONAL FILM FESTIVAL

NOVEMBER 14 - 22, 1997

"THE BEST ITALIAN FILM FESTIVAL"
Nanni Moretti

Director:
Alberto Barbera

FESTIVAL INTERNAZIONALE CINEMA GIOVANI

Festival Internazionale Cinema Giovani
Via Monte di Pietà, 1
10121 Torino, Italia
Phone +39-11-5623309
Fax +39-11-5629796
Internet: http://www.webcom.com/ficg
e-mail: ficg@webcom.com

de Silva Associati

festival also plays retrospectives. *Inquiries to:* Farhang Cinema, Dr. Shariati Ave., Gholhak, Tehran 19139, Iran. Tel: (20020) 888 990. Fax: (20020) 267 082

Fantasporto

February 7-15, 1997

The Oporto International Film Festival, now going into its 17th edition, specialises in fantasy and science-fiction films in its official competitive section. This festival also includes the 7th New Directors Week with an official competition, and a retrospective section dedicated to German cinema, with special tributes to the directors Fritz Lang, Hans J. Syberberg and Wim Wenders. A retrospective on John Woo is also expected. Festival director Mario Dorminsky is preparing, with the help of the Portuguese Film Institute, a programme of Portuguese films for the benefit of foreign guests to Fantasporto, including a look at the beginnings of Portuguese cinema. *Inquiries to:* Fantasporto, Oporto Film Festival, Rua da Constitução 311, 4200 Porto, Portugal. Tel: (351-2) 550 8990/1/2. Fax: (351-2) 5508210. E-mail: fantas@caleida.ot. Website: http://www.caleida.pt/fantasporto.

AWARDS 1996

Best Film: **Seven** (U.S.A.), Fincher.
Best Direction: (*shared*) Philip Ridley for **The Passion of Darkly Noon** (U.K.); Kazuyashi Okuyama for **The Mystery of Rampo** (Japan).
Best Actor: Rupert Everett for **Dellamorte dell'amore** (Italy).
Best Actress: Helena Bonham Carter for **Margaret's Museum** (Canada).
Best Screenplay: Andrew Kevin Walker for **Seven** (U.S.A.).
Best Special Effects: **Taxandria** (Belgium), Servais.
Best Short: (*shared*) **Les escarpins sauvages** (France), Poirand; **The Bitch is Back** (Netherlands), Penning.
Special Jury Award: (*shared*) **Taxandria** (Belgium), Servais; **Institute Benjamenta**, (U.K.) Quay.

Festival des 3 Continents

November, 1997

This is the only annual competitive festival in the world for films originating solely from Africa, Asia and Black and Latin America. The festival does not have a paternalistic view of third world countries;

AND THE MOST FANTASTIC FESTIVAL IS...

SITGES

International Fantasy Film Festival

Rosselló 257, 3-E - 08008 Barcelona - Spain. Tel. 34 3 415 39 38 - Fax 34 3 237 65 21

on the contrary, its aim is to present their cultural values in the best possible conditions. *Inquiries to:* Alain and Philippe Jalladeau, Director, Festival des 3 Continents, BP 3306, 44033 Nantes Cedex, France. Tel: (33) 40 69 74 14. Fax: (33) 40 73 55 22.

Festival Internacional de Cinema Fantàstic de Sitges

October, 1997

The 28th edition of Sitges International Fantasy Film Festival presents films from all over the world in its usual sections: Official section, the Festival's core devoted to the Fantasy genre, with films in competition and out of competition; Premiere, a pre-screening of films not necessarily related to the Fantasy genre; Seven Chances, seven films with little chances to be commercially distributed chosen by seven critics; Anima't, a selection of the latest animation trends, and Brigadoon, an alternative space with projections in new formats. *Inquiries to:* Festival Internacional de Cinema Fantàstic de Sitges. Rosselló 257-3 E, 08008 Barcelona, Spain. Tel: (343) 415 39 38. Fax: (343) 237 65 21.

Festival Internazionale Cinema Giovani

November, 1997

This well-organised event takes place in Turin each autumn and focuses exclusively on films made by new directors. There is a competitive section for shorts, features and Italian independents, as well as a section for retrospectives and spotlights. The festival has been recognised as a top-drawer showcase for hot new international talent and dubbed second only to Venice on the crowded Italian festival circuit. *Inquiries to:* Festival Internazionale Cinema Giovani, Via Monte di Pietà 1, 10121 Torino, Italy. Tel: (11) 562 3309. Fax: (11) 562 9796. E-mail: FICG@WEBcom.com. Website: http://www.WEBCOM.COM/FICG.

Flanders International Film Festival • Ghent

- *October 7 - 18, 1997*
- *Regarded as one of the best organized fests of its kind. Some 130 films from all over the world. Over 65,000 spectators.*
- *Highly rated among the guests for its "Burgundian" hospitality.*
- *Strongly appreciated for its backing to the producers and for its promotional platform.*
- *International competition on the creative role of music in film. Grants up to 65,000 $ for the winners.*
- *Applications : until August 10 th simply by forwarding a VHS viewing tape.*
- *Programme deadline date : August 20 th, 97*

• Contact for information

• Flanders International Film Festival

Flanders International Film Festival
Kortrijksesteenweg 1104
9051 GENT • Belguim
T 32/9/221 89 46 • F 32/9/221 90 74
http : www.rug.ac.be/filmfestival/Welcome.html

Paris : Denise Breton 33/1/42 66 20 02
U.S. : Encore Int'l 1/310/246 06 88
U.K. : John Cartwright 44/181/423.19.89

Robert Wuhl, Michael Caine, Gregory von Hausch (Executive Director of the festival), Robert Evans, and Roger Moore at the 1995 Fort Lauderdale event

Figueira da Foz

September, 1997

One of Portugal's most established film events, which celebrated its 25th edition in 1996, the Figueira da Foz Festival focuses on "quality" cinema with a wide range of competitive sections for features, shorts, film values, first films, innovation, environmental values, and films from Asia, Latin America, Africa. Bulwarked by round tables and special publications and with a good international turn-out of stars and directors, it is held early September in an exquisitive Portuguese seaside resort. *Inquiries to:* José Vieira Marques, Director, Figueira da Foz International Film Festival, Post Box 50 407, 1709 Lisbon Codex, Portugal. Tel: (1) 8126231. Fax: (1) 8126228.

AWARDS 1995

Grand Prix (Feature Films) (ex aequo)*:* **Nu Ren Hua** (China), Wang Jin; **Vor lauter felgheit gibt es kein erbarmen** (Austria), Andreas Gruber.

Grand Prix (Images and Documents): **September Songs** (Canada), Larry Weinstein.

Short Film Prize: (ex aequo): **Kymata** (Canada), George Zarkadas; **Picasso Would Have Made a Glorious Waiter** (USA), Jonathan Schell.

Flanders International Film Festival (Ghent)

October 7-18, 1997

Belgium's most prominent yearly film event attracts annual attendances of over 62,000 and focuses on "The Impact of Music on Film." The Ghent Festival is competitive, with grants of up to $130,000, and screens around 150 features and 80 shorts, most without a Belgium distributor. Outside the competitive section, screenings include Country Focus, a Film Spectrum of international titles receiving their world, European or Benelux premieres, as well a tribute to an important film-maker. Deadline for entry forms: mid August. Deadline for prints: October. *Inquiries to:* Flanders International Film Festival-Ghent, 1104 Kortrijksesteenweg, B-9051 Ghent, Belgium. Tel: (32) 9 221 89 46. Fax: (32) 9 221 90 74. E-mail: filmfestival@infoboard.be. Website:http://www.rug.ac.be/filmfestival/Welcome.html.

AWARDS 1995

Best Film: **Cyclo** (France), Tran Anh Hung.

Fort Lauderdale

November, 1997

The Fort Lauderdale International Film Festival features some hundred films from around the world including features, docus, shorts and student films. The festival will honour with Lifetime Achievement Awards outstanding industry leaders in the fields of acting, directing, producing, writing and composing. The popular event (42,000 admissions in 1995) also offers film competition with cash prizes, and a host of gala events on the beaches and waterways of South Florida. *Inquiries to:* The Fort Lauderdale International Film Festival, 2633 East Sunrise Boulevard, Fort Lauderdale, FL 33304, U.S.A. Tel: (305) 563 0500. Fax: (305) 564 1206. E-mail: Brofilm@aol.com. Website: http://www.http://vcn.net/filmfest.

AWARDS 1995

Best Film: **Cold Comfort Farm** (U.K.), Schlesinger.
Best Director: John Schlesinger.
Best Actor: Sean Astin for **The Low Life** (U.S.).
Best Actress: Piper Laurie for **The Grass Harp** (U.K./U.S.).

Gijón International Film Festival

November 22-29, 1996

With a calling card of "the best young cinema worldwide", the 34-year-old Gijón Festival led by director José Luis Cienfuegos. Set in lovely Northern Spain,

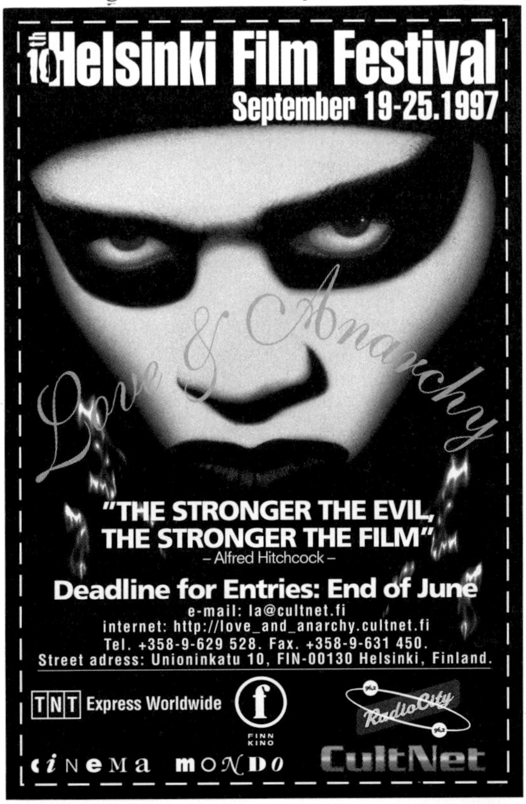

and bidding fair to enter Spain's top five festivals, Gijón features an official competition. *Inquiries to:* Gijón International Film Festival, Maternidad 2, 2º, 33207 Gijón, Asturias, Spain. Tel: (34) 8 5343739. Fax: (34) 8 5354152.

AWARDS 1996

Best Film: **Heavy** (U.S.A.), Mangold.
Best Direction: Michael Rymer for **Angel Baby** (Australia).
Best Actor: Jason Andrews for **Rhythm Thief** (U.S.A.).
Best Actress: Alicia Witt, Renee Humphrey for **Fun** (U.S.A.).
Best Screenplay: James Mangold for **Heavy**.

Göteborg

January 31-February 9, 1997

A genuine success story. Now in its 20th year Göteborg has established itself as not only the best film festival in Norden but as one of the key events in Europe, with almost 103,000 eager and discriminating spectators who warm the cockles of a nervous director's heart with their spontaneous applause. Hotels and cinemas are close to one another. Swedish TV selects one film daily for simultaneous telecasting, a symbol of the prestige which the event carries in Sweden. *Inquiries to:* Göteborg Film Festival, PO Box 7079, S-402 32 Göteborg, Sweden. Tel: (31) 41 0546; Telex: 28674. Fax: (31) 410063. Email: goteborg.filmfestival@mailbox.swipnet.sc. Website: http://www.2datatorgeteduc.goteborg.sc/kultur/filmfest/.

Heartland Film Festival

November, 1997

The Festival was established in 1991 in Indianapolis, Indiana to honour and reward film-makers whose work explores the human journey by artistically expressing hope and respect for positive values of life. $100,000 in cash prizes are awarded to the winners each year. *Inquiries to:* Heartland Film Festival, 613 N. East Street, Indianapolis, Indiana 46202, U.S.A. Tel: (317) 464 9405. Fax: (317) 635 4201. E-mail: HFF@iquest.net. Website: http://www.heartlandfilmfest.org.

Helsinki Film Festival – Love and Anarchy

September, 1997

Nine years old this year and hailed as the most important film festival in Finland, Helsinki aims to promote high quality international films and film-makers to Finnish audiences and distributors. Honouring the "Love and Anarchy" subtitle, the event challenges the limits with a programme of uncompromising and controversial titles from around the world. *Inquiries to:* Helsinki Film Festival, Unioninkatu 10 A 27, SF 00130 Helsinki, Finland. Tel: (358) 0 629 528. Fax: (358) 0 631 450. E-mail: r&a@cultnet.fi,. Website: http://www. love&anarchy.cultnet.fi.

Hong Kong

March 25-April 9, 1997

The usual selection of Asian product and a Hong Kong Cinema Retrospective are included among 200 films and videos on show at various venues. The festival has been recognised as a "showcase" for Asian works and valuable for the West to discover the riches of Chinese cinema. *Inquiries to:* Senior Manager, Festivals Office, Urban Services Department, Level 7, Administration Building, Hongkong Cultural Centre, 10 Salisbury Road, Tsimshatsui, Kowloon, Hongkong. Tel. (852) 2734 2903. Fax: (852) 2366 5206. Website: http://www.asiaonline.net/hkiff.

Independent Feature Film Market

September, 1997

The Independent Feature Film Market (IFFM) is the only market devoted to new, emerging American independent film talent. Since 1979, the IFFM has presented the industry with its first look at such landmark films as: *American Dream, Badlands, Blood Simple, The Brothers McMullen, Clerks, Daughters of the Dust, El Norte, Let's Get Lost, Metropolitan, My Dinner with Andre, One False Move, Poison, Slacker, Stranger Than Paradise, Swoon, The Hours and Times, Roger & Me,* and many others. The IFFM screens over 250 film projects, including Works-in-Progress, and presents over 100 newly copyrighted scripts. *Inquiries to:* The Independent Feature Project, 104 West 29th Street, 12th Floor, New York, New York 10001-5310. Tel: (212) 465-8200. Fax: (212) 465 8525. Website: http://www.ifp.org.

India

January, 1997

The International Film Festival of India (IFFI) is held each year and is non-competitive (recognised by FIAPF). There is a substantial information section, a new competition for features made by Asian women, a comprehensive "Cinema of the World" section, foreign and Indian retrospectives, and a film market, as well as a most valuable panorama of the best Indian films of the year, subtitled in

22nd FESTIVAL DE CINE IBEROAMERICANO DE HUELVA

23rd – 30th November 1996

CASA COLON
Plaza del Punto, s/n
21003 HUELVA

Tels. (959) 210171
210170
Fax (959) 210173

Producer Christophe Rossignon, actress Tran Nu Yen Khe, and director Tran Anh Hung in Hof for the screening of CYCLO

Please contact:
Heinz Badewitz, Director
Lothstraße 28
D-80335 München
FAX: -89 / 123 68 68
Telex: 5 212 042 flmw d

INTERNATIONAL HOF FILMDAYS

Every Last Week in October

JERUSALEM FILM FESTIVAL

Israel's Most Prestigious Cinema Event

July 1997

P.O.B. 8561
Jerusalem 91083, Israel
Tel: 972 2 6724131
Fax: 972 2 6733076

Director: **Lia Van Leer**

English. *Inquiries to:* Mrs. Malti Sahai, Director, Directorate of Film Festivals, Ministry of Information and Broadcasting, Government of India, 4th Floor, Lok Nayak Bhavan, Khan Market, New Delhi 110003, India. Tel: (91) 11 461 5953, 469 7167. Fax: (91) 11 462 3430.

International Film Festival Mannheim – Heidelberg

October 10-18, 1997

A festival for young independent film-makers from all over the world. The event, which gave early recognition to Truffaut, Fassbinder, Kieślowski and Jarmusch, shows features, shorts and documentaries in competition, with DM 30,000 going to the best film, DM 10,000 to the best newcomer, best documentary and for the Rainer Werner Fassbinder Prize, and DM 5,000 to the best short. The festival management awards a Distribution Grant of DM 35,000 to the German distributor who ensures a cinematic release for one of the award-winning films. Sidebars include a new Independent Market Service and a Co-production Conference. *Inquiries to:* Dr. Michael Koetz, International Filmfestival Mannheim-Heidelberg, Collini-Centre, Galerie, D-68161 Mannheim, Germany. Tel: (621) 102943. Fax: (621) 291564.

AWARDS 1995

Best Film: **Keita, l'héritage du Girot** (Burkina Faso), Kouyate.
Most Promising Newcomer: Neil Abramson for **Without Air** (U.S.A.).
Best Documentary: **Scavengers** (Japan), Shinomiya.
Rainer Werner Fassbinder Prize: **Il Verificatore** (Italy), Incerti.
Best Short: **Land Unter** (Germany), Schönborn.

Internationale Hofer Filmtage

October, 1997

Dubbed "Home of Films" by Wim Wenders, Hof is famous for its thoughtful selection of some 40 features. Founded by the directors of the New German Cinema, Hof enjoys a high reputation among German film-makers and American cult figures like Roger Corman, Monte Hellman, John Sayles and Henry Jaglom, all of whom have attended retrospectives in their honour. The real applause should go to the peripatetic Heinz Badewitz, who established the festival 30 years ago! A screening in Hof can often result in a distribution deal. *Inquiries to:* Postfach 1146, D-95010 Hof, Germany: or Heinz Badewitz, Lothstr. 30, D-80335 Munich, Germany. Tel: (89) 1297422. Fax: (89) 1236868.

Istanbul

March 29-April 13, 1997

The only film festival which takes place in a city where two continents meet, the Istanbul International Film Festival, recognised as a specialised competitive event by FIAPF, acts as a valuable showcase for distributors – not just Turkish. Attendances reach 100,000 every year. Now in its 16th year, this dynamic event focuses on features dealing with the arts (literature, music, cinema, dance, etc.) with other thematic sections such as Tributes, selections from World Festivals, "A Country – A Cinema", and a panorama of the Turkish cinema. *Inquiries to:* Ms Hülya Uçansu, Istanbul Kültür ve Sanat Vakfi, Istiklal Cad. Luvr Apt. No. 146, Beyoğlu 80070, Istanbul, Turkey. Tel: (90 212) 293 3133/34/35. Fax: (90 212) 249 7771.

AWARDS 1996

Golden Tulip: **Little Sister** (Netherlands), Westdijk.
Special Jury Prize: Amalia Moutoussi for **A Drop in the Ocean** (Greece).
Best Turkish Film: **80th Step**, Giritlioğlu.

International Tournée of Animation

This feature-length touring showcase of international short animated films is

Turkish director Ömer Kavur, Jean Loup Passek (founder and director of the festival), with Japanese film-maker Kiju Yoshida at the 1996 Festival de La Rochelle

XXVe FESTIVAL INTERNATIONAL DU FILM DE LA ROCHELLE

directed by jean-loup passek **27 JUNE - 7 JULY, 1997**

100 FEATURE FILMS 300 SCREENINGS NON COMPETITIVE

3 MAIN SECTIONS

- Retrospectives devoted to the work of past filmmakers
- Tributes to contemporary directors, in their presence
- Le Monde Tel Qu'il Est (The World As It Is), a selection of unreleased films from all over the world.

Festival International du Film de la Rochelle
16, rue Saint Sabin, 75011 Paris
Phone: (1) 48 06 16 66 Fax: (1) 48 06 15 40

exhibited in over 400 specialised theatres and art centres in the United States and Canada. Since 1985 the Tournée has been on the Top Ten list of the highest grossing speciality pictures. Typically the Tournée includes 15-20 film selections including each year's Academy Award-winner, the prizewinners from the major festivals, and the best new work of independent animators. *Inquiries to:* Terry Thoren, 30101 Agoura Court, Suite 110, Agoura, CA 91301, U.S.A. Tel: (818) 991 2884. Fax: (818) 991 3773. E-mail: animag@aol.com. Website: http//animag.com.

Jerusalem

July, 1997

Lia van Leer, director and founder of the Festival, continues to bring to Jerusalem the finest in international cinema. For 10 days audiences can see the latest features, new documentaries, avant garde, animation, restored classics, retrospectives, Mediterranean and Israeli cinema. Prizes given at the festival are the *Wolgin Awards for Israeli Cinema*; the *Lipper Award for Best Israeli Screenplay*. Two international prizes: *Wim van Leer 'In the Spirit of Freedom'* focus on human rights. *In Pursuit of Peace and Tolerance for Mediterranean Cinema*, initiated by MCM (under the auspices of UNESCO). *Inquiries to:* Jerusalem Film Festival, P.O. Box 8561, Jerusalem 91083, Israel. Tel: (972) 2 724131 Fax: (972) 2 733076.

Karlovy Vary

July, 1997

Now an annual event, Karlovy Vary is one of the oldest film festivals in the world. International features are screened in competition, with an international jury awarding prizes for Best Film, Actor and Actress, as well as a Special Jury Award. There is a major focus on the latest Czech features, and those from the other former communist countries. The 1996 event featured U.S. indies, a retrospective on films about the holocaust, and profiles of Antonin Artaud and John Woo. *Inquiries to:* Film Festival Karlovy Vary Foundation, Panska 1, CZ 110 00 Prague 1, Czech Republic. Tel: (2) 2423 5412, 2423 5413. Fax: (2) 2423 3408.

AWARDS 1995

Grand Prix: **Jízda** (Czech Republic), Svařák.
Special Jury Award: **The Garden** (Slovak Republic), Šulík.
Best Director: Lars von Trier for **The Kingdom** (Denmark/Sweden/Germany).
Best Actor: Ernst Hugo Järegård for **The Kingdom** (Denmark/Sweden/Germany).
Best Actress: Qui Ah-Lu for **Maiden Rose** (China/Hong Kong).
Best Documentary: **In the Garden** (Czech Republic), Vojnár.
Special Lifetime Achievement Prize: Gina Lollobrigida.

La Rochelle

June 28-July 7, 1997

Jean-Loup Passek builds a bright and enthusiastic bridge between past and future cinema with his popular and distinguished festival in this French resort, with some magnificent discoveries (the Francesca Bertini retrospective in 1993, for example), a profusion of new features and thematic programmes. Much more exciting than most competitive festivals! Well over 60,000 admissions in 1996, with the 25th anniversary hoving into view! *Inquiries to:* Festival International du Film de La

Rochelle, 16 rue du Saint Sabin, Paris 75011, France. Tel: (33-1) 48 06 16 66. Fax: (33-1) 48 06 15 40.

Local Heroes

March 9-15, 1997

Launched in 1984, the Local Heroes International Screen Festival brings some of the finest independent films from Canada and around the world, along with their creators, to Edmonton for five days every winter. The festival is non-competitive and is comprised of international screenings (recent guests have included Costa-Gavras, Jiři Menzel and Bruce Beresford), daily industry sessions on the current state of the Canadian film industry, and the best of independent Canadian short films. *Inquiries to:* Local Heroes International Screen Festival, National Screen Institute - Canada, 3rd Floor, 10022 - 103 St, Edmonton, Canada T5J 0X2. Tel: (403) 421 4084. Fax: (403) 425 8098. E-mail: deb-nsi@sopernet.ab.ca. Website: http://www.culturenet.ca/NSI.

The 1997
Mill Valley Film Festival

The Perfect Environment For Film.

For 19 years, the small town of Mill Valley in Northern California (just a shade north of San Francisco over the Golden Gate Bridge) has been the place for a film festival like no other. A festival that captivates audiences and filmmakers alike.

October 2nd-12th

Call The Film Institute of Northern California at 415-383-5256, or surf our site at www.well.com/user/finc

Locarno

August 7-17, 1997

Under its director Marco Müller, Locarno has become a place where world and European premieres are regular occasions, and where serious buyers mingle with creative film-makers – with national and international attendance of 150,000. Eurimages and the Council of Europe have been involved, as well as EFDO and the Foundation "Montecinemaverità" (with its annual budget of 300,000 Sfrs.). Müller can justifiably claim that Locarno is now one of the world's top half-dozen festivals. *Inquiries to:* Festival Internazionale del Film, Via della Posta 6, CH-6600 Locarno, Switzerland. Tel: (91) 751 0232. Fax: (91) 751 7465.

London

November, 1997

The London Film Festival is presented at the National Film Theatre and at cinemas throughout the capital. The programme comprises around 180 features and documentaries, as well as a showcase for shorts. Aside from the British section there is a very strong International selection including the *Evening Standard* Film on the Square, Asia, Africa and Latin America as well as Europe's largest and most influential section of U.S. indies. The festival attracts over 400 U.K. and international press and provides a buyers/sellers liaison office. *Inquiries to:* London Film Festival, South Bank, London SE1 8XT. Tel: (171) 815 1322/1323. Fax: (171) 633 0786. E-mail: jane.ivey.@bfi.org.U.K.

Los Angeles International Animation Celebration

April 1, 1997

This "festival of festivals" is a new concept for the animation industry with more than 1200 films entered in competition and 400 films chosen for exhibition. An international panel of experts presents cash and prizes of more than $100,000 to the best in 15 categories. The festival is open to

20th GÖTEBORG

film festival

31st JANUARY – 9th FEBRUARY 1997

THE LEADING INTERNATIONAL
FILM FESTIVAL IN SCANDINAVIA

XX

1997

SUPPORTED BY THE SWEDISH FILM INSTITUTE

Mail: Box 7079, 402 32 Göteborg, Sweden

Phone: 46 - 31 - 41 05 46 Fax: 46 - 31 - 41 00 63 Tlx: 28674 Fifest S

annecy 97

ANNECY
ANNECY

International Animated Film Festival

26 - 31 mai

- International competition : short films, feature films, TV series, commissioned and advertising films
- International competition for student films and graduation films
- Poster competition «Jules Chéret prize»
- Film tributes, retrospectives and exhibitions
- International film project competition

M I F A

International Animated Film Market

28 - 31 mai

- International youth film programme market : live drama, animation and documentaries
- Animation production and facilities market
- Computer-aided animation and new production technology market
- International encounter of multimedia and interactive audio-visual programmes
- Market for rights and patents for merchandizing

Contact : BP 399, 74013 Annecy Cedex - France - tel (33) 04 50.57.41.72 fax (33) 04 50 67 81 95 films in 16mm, 35mm, and video completed since January 1994. *Inquiries to:* Terry Thoren, Chairman, Expanded Entertainment, Agoura Court, Suite 110, Agoura, CA 91301, U.S.A. Tel: (818) 991 2884. Fax: (818) 991 3773. Telex: 247770 ANIM UR.

Los Angeles International Film Festival

October, 1997

Continuing the tradition started by Filmex, this event is the largest of its kind in the United States. Collaborating with over 30 film and arts organisations, the L.A. FilmFest is each year dedicated to different aspects of film-making. *Inquiries to:* Gary McVey, AFI Festivals, 2021 N. Western Avenue, Los Angeles, CA 90027. Tel: (213) 856 7707. Fax: (213) 462 4049. E-mail: afifest@afionline.org. Website: http://www.afionline.org.

MIFED (Milan)

October, 1997

Long established film market held in the expansive Milan Fair, particularly well attended by buyers and sellers from all over the world. Third (in calendar terms) of the year's big three film markets – preceded by the American Film Market and the Cannes Film Festival – the atmosphere is all business, but Milan is still attractive, even in gloomy October. *Inquiries to:* Mrs Elena Lloyd, E.A. Fiera Internazionale di Milano, Largo Domodossola 1, 20145 Milano, Italy. Tel: (2) 48012912/48012920. Fax: (2) 49977020. E-mail: mifed@fmd.it. Website: http://www.fmd.it.

Mill Valley

October, 1997

The Mill Valley Film Festival presents a wide variety of international programming that is shaped by a commitment to cultural and artistic excellence. This intimate event of unusually high calibre and dedication is set in a beautiful small town just north of San Francisco. The eleven-day, non-competitive festival includes the prestigious Videofest, as well as tributes, seminars and special events. *Inquiries to:* Mill Valley Film Festival, 38 Miller Avenue, Suite 6, Mill Valley, CA 94941, U.S.A. Tel: (415) 383 5256. Fax: (415) 383 8606. E-mail: finc@well.com. Website:http://www. Well.com/user/finc.

Montpellier

October, 1997

A major meeting-place of Mediterranean cinema, the annual Montpellier Festival has a rich programme covering past and present productions. The film competition awards prizes to features and shorts, with at least two pre-production grants for full length fiction films awarded with the help of the Commission of the European Union. *Inquiries to:* Montpellier International Festival of Mediterranean Film, 6 rue Vieille-Aiguillerie, 34000 Montpellier, France. Tel: (33) 67 66 36 36. Fax: (33) 67 66 36 37.

Montréal World Film Festival

August 21-September 1, 1997

Serge Losique has established a major competitive festival in Montréal in late summer, and it is the only such event recognised by FIAPF in North America. There are several categories (Official Competition, Hors Concours section, Latin American Cinema, Israeli Cinema of Today, Panorama Canada, TV films), public attendance is extremely high, and the number of foreign personalities swells each year. Montréal is the ideal location for such an event, with its bilingual facilities and its proximity to all major North American outlets. *Inquiries to:* Serge Losique, World Film Festival, 1432 de Bleury St., Montréal (Québec), Canada H3A 2J1. Tel: (514) 848 3883. Fax: (514) 848 3886. E-mail: ffm@interlink.net. Website: http://www.ffm-montreal.org.

AWARDS 1995

Grand Prix of the Americas: **Georgia** (France/U.S.), Grosbard.

Special Grand Prix of the Jury: **A Moslem** (Russia), Khotinenko.

Best Director: (*shared*) Xie Fei for **A Mongolian Tale** (China); Goran Marković for **Burlesque Tragedy** (Bulgaria/France).

WORLD FILM FESTIVAL
MONTREAL '97
August 21 — September 1

1432, de Bleury St.
Montréal (Québec) Canada H3A 2J1
Tel.: (514) 848-3883 • Fax: 848-3886
URL: http://www.ffm-montreal.org
E-MAIL: ffm@interlink.net

AIR CANADA

Rothmans FILM INTERNATIONAL

Netherlands Film Festival 1997

NEDERLANDS FILM FESTIVAL

24 September to 3 October
Utrecht - the Netherlands

Grand Prix for Dutch Cinema: **The Golden Calf Awards.** The main competition programme comprises all Dutch new feature films, documentaries, short films and tv-drama productions.

Retrospectives, Seminar, live tv-talkshows and the 'Cinema Militans Lecture'.

At the **Holland Film Meeting,** the recent Dutch film and television production is presented for professionals from abroad. The Meeting will be held from Friday 26 to Monday 29 September 1997.
Holland Meets .... is a comprehensive exchange between the film and television industry of the Netherlands and another European country.

**INFORMATION AND CONTACT:
NETHERLANDS FILM FESTIVAL
P.O.BOX 1581, 3500 BN
UTRECHT, THE NETHERLANDS
TEL: (31) 30 32 2684
FAX: (31) 30 31 3200**
**internet: www.nethlandfilm.nl
E-mail: Ned.filmfest@inter.ni.net**

38. NORDIC FILM DAYS LÜBECK
7 – 10 November 1996

LARGEST SCREENING OF NORDIC FILMS IN GERMANY

THE BEST FILMS OF THE YEAR
BIG SHOTS AND NEWCOMERS

Information:
NORDISCHE FILMTAGE LÜBECK
D-23539 Lübeck
Fax +49 451 12-24106

Best Actor: Fabrizio Bentivoglio for **Eroe Borghese** (Italy).
Best Actress: Jennifer Jason Leigh for **Georgia** (France/U.S.A.).
Best Screenplay: Shemi Zarhin for **Passover Fever** (Israel).
Best Short: **The End of the World in Four Seasons** (Canada), Driessen.

Mystfest

June, 1997

The International Mystery Film Festival aims to draw attention to and promote the distribution of films of the mystery, crime and detection genre. Prizes are awarded for the best direction and for the best first or second feature ($10,000). The event is well-attended by local talent (Scola, Verdone, Wertmüller) as well as international directors. *Inquiries to:* Mystfest International Mystery Film Festival, Centro Culturale Polivalente, Piazza della Repubblica 31, 47033 Cattolica (RN), Italy. Tel: (541) 967802. Fax: (541) 967803. E-mail: mystfest@cattolica.net. Website: http://www.cattolica.net.

New York

October, 1997

Now in its 35th year, the New York Film Festival has resisted the temptation to grow into a major market offering hundreds of films, remaining instead a small (under 30 total) selection of feature films and shorts culled from around the world. Attendance has been well over 95% for the past decade, and each selection receives extensive coverage in local, national and even international media. *Inquiries to:* Film Society of Lincoln Center,

70 Lincoln Center Plaza, New York, NY 10023, U.S.A. Tel: (212) 875 5610. Fax: (212) 875 5636.

Nordische Filmtage

November 6-9, 1997

This annual event held in the charming medieval town of Lübeck (north of Hamburg), throws a spotlight on the Scandinavian and Baltic cinema and enables members of the trade, critics, and other visitors to see the best of the new productions. A large documentary section is also featured. *Inquiries to:* Nordische Filmtage Lübeck, D-23539 Lübeck, Germany. Tel: (451) 122 4105. Fax: (451) 12 24106.

Norwegian International Film Festival

August 16-25, 1997

Held in the west coast port of Haugesund every summer, the Norwegian film festival has now become the country's major film event attended by many international visitors along with more than 1,000 representatives from the Norwegian and Scandinavian film world. The festival is run by festival director Gunnar Johan Løvvik and programme director is Vigdis Lian. Honourable President is Liv Ullmann. The "Amanda Statuettes" are presented there, as well as the "New Nordic Film" market. *Inquiries to:* PO Box 145, N-5501 Haugesund, Norway. Tel: (47) 52 734 430. Fax: (47) 52 734 420.

Nyon

April 21-27, 1997

This documentary festival has been recently reorganised with a new title ("Visions du Réel") and a new crew. The aim of the festival is to promote creative documentary cinema, with conferences and forums as well as the International Competition and Swiss panorama. *Inquiries to:* Nyon-Visions du Réel, Case postale 2320, CH-1260 Nyon, Switzerland. Tel: (41) 22 361 60 60. Fax: (41) 22 361 70 71.

Oberhausen

April 23-28, 1997

Now in its 43rd year, Oberhausen still has a just claim to be the world's premier short film festival. There is a wide selection of shorts from all over the world (international and German competition), but also an opportunity to attend various special showcases, symposia and discussions about relevant questions in the media field. *Inquiries to:* Internationale Kurzfilmtage Oberhausen, Christian-Steger Strasse 10, D-46045 Oberhausen 1, Germany. Tel: (208) 825 2652. Fax: (208) 825 5413. E-mail: Kurzfilmtage:oberhausen@ uni-duisburg.de. Website: http://www. uni-duisburg.de/HRZ/IKF/home.html.

Odense

August, 1997

Denmark's only international short film festival invites unusual films with an original and imaginative sense of creative delight – the sort of delight to be found in

We look forward to greeting you again!

HAUGESUND

The NORWEGIAN INTERNATIONAL FILM FESTIVAL

AUG 16 - AUG 23, 1997

It is the aspiration of the Festival to maintain and enhance its particular blend of artistic ambition, business focus and conviviality. Also including 'New Nordic Films' a separate market and a unique opportunity for distributors and others to see the best of new Nordic cinema.

Gunnar Løvvik
Festival Director
Vigdis Lian
Programme Director

PO Box 145 N-5501
Haugesund, Norway
Tel: +47 52 73 44 30
Fax: +47 52 73 44 20

Honorary President:
Liv Ullmann

the works of Hans Christian Andersen. All 16mm and 35mm films can participate. Maximum length 45 minutes running time. *Inquiries to:* Odense Film Festival, Vindegade 18, DK-5000 Odense C, Denmark. Tel: (45) 66 131372, ext. 4044. Fax: (45) 65 914318.

Oulu International Children's Film Festival

November, 1997

The only annual festival of full-length feature films for children in Scandinavia. Event is competitive and screens both recent films and retrospective seasons. *Inquiries to:* Oulu International Children's Film Festival, Torikatu 8, SF-90100 Oulu, Finland. Tel: (81) 314 1735. Fax: (81) 314 1730. E-mail: RAIMO.KINISJARVI OUFILMCENTER. INET.FI. Website: http://www.OUKA.FI/OEK.

Palm Springs

January 9-26, 1997

Palm Springs International Film Festival is a glittering event, screening over 100 films from 25 countries, including U.S. and world premieres. Founded by Congressman Sonny Bono, the festival offers seminars on various aspects of film-making and presents awards to leading film-makers at a black-tie event. The event has grown rapidly since it began in 1990 with only 3 days, to 16 days in 1996. *Inquiries to:* Nortel Palm Springs International Film Festival, PO Box 2230, Palm Springs, California 92263, U.S.A. Tel: (619) 322 2930. Fax: (619) 322 4087. E-mail: filmfest@ix.netcom. Website: http://www.palm-springs.org/filmfest.

Pesaro

June, 1997

The "Mostra Internazionale del Nuovo Cinema" (Pesaro Film Festival) is particularly concerned with the work of new directors and emergent cinemas – in other words, with innovation at every level of the film world. For the past 33 years this Mediterranean resort has been the centre for some lively screenings and debates, and in recent seasons the festival has been devoted to a specific country or culture. The main festival is coupled each year with a special event devoted to a retrospective of Italian cinema. *Inquiries to:* Mostra Internazionale del Nuovo Cinema, Via Villafranca 20, 00185 Rome, Italy. Tel: (39-6) 445 6643-491156. Fax: (39-6) 491163. Website: http://www.ABANET.IT.

Pordenone

October, 1997

Although, to quote Hemingway's *Farewell to Arms,* Pordenone is "not much of a place", for one week each autumn this small Italian town is visited by a devoted group of scholars, collectors, archivists and enthusiasts, who travel from Europe, America, and as far away as Japan or Australia to attend the "Giornate del Cinema Muto," a silent film festival held each year since 1982. Pordenone 1995 explored "non-fiction cinema" and featured a retrospective devoted to the early work of Max and Dave Fleischer, the animators who brought Betty Boop, Popeye and Superman to the screen. *Inquiries to:* La Cineteca del Friuli, Via Osoppo 26, 33013 Gemona (UD), Italy. Tel: (0432) 980458. Fax: (0432) 970542.

Portland

February 13-March 2, 1997

The Portland International Film Festival is an invitational event presenting over seventy films from two-dozen countries. New international features, documentaries and shorts enjoy an audience of up to 30,000 people from throughout the Northwest. Special programmes include classic silents with live orchestra performances, visiting artists, children's programming, an annual Pacific Rim Showcase and, last year, "Cine-Lit", a special selection of new Hispanic language films and symposium on literature. *Inquiries to:* Portland Inter-

XVI
INTERNATIONAL
CHILDREN'S
FILM FESTIVAL
OULU

17-23 NOV 1997

Torikatu 8,
SF-90100 Oulu, Finland
Tel: +358 8 8811293, 1294
Fax: + 358 8 8811290

MISSING SOMETHING?

Back issues of *International Film Guide* are available for most years since the late 1960's. Send us your needs and we will invoice you.

Variety, 34-35 Newman Street, London W1P 3PD, U.K.

national Film Festival, Northwest Film Center, 1219 S.W. Park Avenue, Portland, OR 97205, U.S.A. Tel: (503) 221 1156. Fax: (503) 226 4842. Website: http://www.nwfc.org.

Puerto Rico

November, 1997

The Puerto Rico International Film Festival acclaimed as the fastest-growing film event in Latin America, offers around 100 feature films on six screens, showcasing three sections: International Cinema, Current Spanish Panorama and Best Latin American Cinema (FIPRESCI Award for Best Film in this section). Recent premieres include *Before the Rain, Strawberry and Chocolate* and *Bandit Queen*. *Inquiries to:* Juan Gerard Gonzalez, Puerto Rico International Film Festival, 70 Mayaguez Street, Suite B1, Hato Rey, Puerto Rico 00918, U.S.A. Tel: (809) 763 4997, 764 7044. Fax: (809) 753 5367.

Riminicinema International Film Festival

September, 1997

The first festival in Italy to focus its attention on "displaced wandering film-makers and contaminated cinema", originating from the relationships and the exchanges between different cultures and peoples. Riminicinema takes place every year in Rimini, famous seaside holiday resort and native town of Federico Fellini. Besides the competition open to feature films, awarding the Golden "R" (plus fifteen million lire),and the Silver "R" (plus 5 million lire), the programme includes a competition open to film school students from all over the world, monographs, retrospectives, debates and special events. The Festival also selects a young film-maker for the Federico Fellini Award (20 million Lire). *Inquiries to:* Riminicinema, via Gambalunga 27, 47037 Rimini, Italy. Tel: (541) 26399-22627. Fax: (541) 24227. Telex: 563170 COMRIM I. E-mail: rimini03@nettuno.it.

AWARDS 1995

Golden "R": **Cold Fever** (Iceland), Fridriksson.
Silver "R": **Al-comparss** (Syria), Maleh.
Federico Fellini Award: Emir Kusturica.

Rotterdam

January 29-February 9, 1997

The largest film festival in Benelux, 26 years old, has a reputation for programming innovative, independent new works alongside more commercial productions. More than 100 features have their world, international or European première here. The 1996 festival welcomed 250,000 visits at 1,100 screenings, 1,225 international professionals and 490 journalists from 61 different countries. The festival also hosts the **Cinemart**, the leading co-production market for independent film-makers, producers, financiers and distributors. Rotterdam's Hubert Bals Fund supports film-makers from developing countries. *Inquiries to:* Rotterdam Film Festival, PO Box 21696, 3001 AR Rotterdam, Netherlands. Tel: (31 10) 4118080. Fax: (31 10) 4135132. E-mail: iffr@luna.nl. Website http://www.iffrotterdam.nl.

San Francisco

April -May, 1997

The Western Hemisphere's oldest international film festival, now in its 40th year, continues to rise in importance and popularity. Over 150 films were shown non-competitively (invitation only), while the competitive Golden Gate Awards attracted over 1,800 entries from all over the world. Other awards include the Akira Kurosawa Award for Lifetime Achievement in Directing (Arthur Penn in 1996), and the Satyajit Ray Award given to a film-maker of exceptional promise. *Inquiries to:* San Francisco International Film Festival,

the supportive
film festival

26TH International
Film Festival Rotterdam
29 Jan • 9 Feb 1997

Web site: http://www.iffrotterdam.nl

1521 Eddy Street, San Francisco, CA 94115-4102, U.S.A. Tel: (415) 929 5000. Fax: (415) 921 5032. E-mail: sfiff@sfiff.org.

San Juan Cinemafest

October, 1997

San Juan Cinemafest is an important event in the Latin American circuit. The Carribean Competition accepts both film and video, and an international jury awards the Pitirre Prize in the categories of fiction, documentary and animation. The World Cinema Section shows the best of the latest crop of international cinema. 1995 awards included *Principio y fin* (Caribbean Competition), *I Don't Want to Talk About It* (Film Critics Circle) and *The Dark Side of The Heart* (Prize of the Public). *Inquiries to:* San Juan Cinemafest, PO Box 4543, San Juan, Puerto Rico 00902. Tel: (809) 721 6125, Fax (809) 723 6412.

San Sebastian

September, 1997

Held in an elegant Basque seaside city, San Sebastian remains the most important film festival in Spain in terms of glitter, sections, facilities, attendance, competition, partying and number of films. The city is known for its superb gastronomy, beautiful beaches and quaint streets. The festival usually attracts a number of international celebrities, as well as a wide selection of national and international press, talent, and buffs. The Euskal Media Award (US$200,000) is given by the Basque government as a co-producer grant for the director/producer's next project. *Inquiries to:* San Sebastian International Film Festival, Apartado de Correos 397, San Sebastian 20080, Spain. Tel: (43) 481-212. Telex: 38145 FCSS E. Fax: (43) 481-218. E-mail: ssiff@mail.ddnet.es. Website: http://www.ddnet.es/san-sebastian-film-festival/.

AWARDS 1995

Golden Shell: **Margaret's Museum** (Canada/U.K.), Ransen.
Best Director: Mike Figgis for **Leaving Las Vegas** (U.S.).
Best Actor: Nicolas Cage for **Leaving Las Vegas**.
Best Actress: Victoria Abril for **Nadie Hablará de Nosotras Cuando Hayamos Muerto** (Spain).

International competition
Film school competition
Federico Fellini award
Previews
Monographs
Midnight section
Debates, meetings with filmakers

Riminicinema
via Gambalunga 27
47037 Rimini (Italia)
tel. 0541/26399-22627
fax 0541/24227
telex 550318

Rimini, September 1997

Mostra internazionale del cinema indipendente
RIMINICINEMA

SAN SEBASTIAN

The September Festival.

SAN SEBASTIAN
INTERNATIONAL FILM FESTIVAL

Apartado de correos, 397
Tel: 43-48 12 12
Fax: 43-48 12 18
Internet: http://www.ddnet.es/san_sebastian_film_festival/
E-mail: ssiff@mail.ddnet.es
20080 SAN SEBASTIAN - SPAIN

OFFICIAL SPONSOR
CANAL+ SPAIN

Sydney Pollack (left) at a press conference at the 1996 Rotterdam Film Festival *phot: Andreé Bahhor*

Stockholm

November 5-12, 1997

Since its start in 1990, the festival has established itself as one of the leading media events in Northern Europe. Sections include: Stockholm VIII, a competitive section for directors who have made their first, second or third features; Open Zone, an outlook on where world cinema stands today; U.S. independents; Twilight Zone, films exploring the subcultures of cinema; Northern Lights, a Critic's Week for films from the Nordic and Baltic Countries; and Made in Sweden 1997, a summary of the Swedish films released this year. *Inquiries to:* Stockholm International Film Festival, P.O. Box 3136, 103 62 Stockholm, Sweden. Tel: (46 8) 677 5000. Fax: (46 8) 200 590. E-mail: info@cinema.se. Website: http://www.filmfestivalen.se.

AWARDS 1995

Best Film: **Institute Benjamenta** (U.K.), Quay Brothers.
Best First Film: **Butterfly Kiss** (U.K.), Winterbottom.
Best Actor: John Hannah for **Madagascar Skin** (U.K.).
Best Actress: Catherine Keenan for **Living in Oblivion** (U.S.A.).
Best Screebplay: Chris Newby for **Madagascar Skin** (U.K.)

Sundance Film Festival

January 16-26, 1997

The Sundance Film Festival is widely recognised as one of America's most respected exhibition events of American independent cinema. The dramatic and documentary films presented in the

Independent Feature Film Competition each year are indicators of the current trends prevalent in American independent cinema. *Inquiries to:* Sundance Film Festival, P.O. Box 16450, Salt Lake City, UT 84116, U.S.A. Tel: (801) 328 3456. Fax: (801) 575 5175.

AWARDS 1996

Grand Jury Prize (Dramatic): **Welcome to the Dollhouse**, Solodz.

Grand Jury Prize (Documentary): **Troublesome Creek: A Midwestern**, Jordan, Ascher.

Film-Makers Trophy (Dramatic): **Girls Town**, McKay.

Film-Makers Trophy (Documentary): **Cutting Loose**, Todd, Young.

Audience Award (Dramatic): **Care of the Spitfire Grill**, Zlotoff.

Audience Award (Documentary): **Troublesome Creek: A Midwestern**, Jordan, Ascher.

Taipei

December, 1997

International Film Exhibition Taipei is run every year alongside Taiwan's Golden Horse Awards for offshore Chinese cinema, and is organised by the city's Film Library. *Inquiries to:* Taipei Golden Horse Film Festival Commitee, 7F, No. 45 Chilin Road, Taipei, Taiwan. Tel: (886 2) 567 5861. Fax: (886 2) 531 8966.

Tampere

March 5-9, 1997

The 27th year of one of the leading short film festivals in the world. This event attracts entries from 60 countries and has the tradition of offering an interesting collection from Eastern Europe. The International competition has categories

INTERNATIONAL THESSALONIKI Film FESTIVAL

A FORUM FOR THE YOUNG CINEMA
NOVEMBER 1997
TEL: (301) 3610418 - FAX: (301) 3621023

for short documentary, animation, and fiction films as well as open seminars and debates. *Inquiries to:* Tampere Film Festival, PO Box 305, 33101 Tampere, Finland. Tel: (358) 3 213 0034. Fax: (358) 3 223 0121. E-mail: film.festival@tt.tampere.fi. Website: http://www.tampere.fi/festival/film.

AWARDS 1996

Grand Prix International: **Quiet Harbour** (Poland), Malec.

Special Jury Prize: **The Maiden and Soldier** (Finland), Lillqvist.

Public's Prize International: **A Close Shave** (U.K.), Park.

Telluride

August 29-September 1, 1997

This friendly gathering in a spectacular location in the mountains of Colorado is one of the world's most influential festivals, with the historic mining town of Telluride becoming the Festival as famous directors, players, and critics descend on the Sheridan Opera House and other theatres. The dedication of both organisers and participants to the art of cinema liberates Telluride from the shallow ballyhoo that envelops many film events. *Inquiries to:* The National Film Preserve Ltd., PO Box B1156, Hanover, New Hampshire 03755, U.S.A. Tel: (603) 643 1255. Fax: (603) 6435938. E-mail: Tellufilm@aol.com. Website: http://www.Telluridenm.com/filmfesthtml.

Thessaloniki International Film Festival

November, 1997

This festival, now in its 38th year, is the oldest and most important film event in Greece. Thessaloniki targets a new generation of film-makers as well as high quality independent films made by established directors. The International competition (for first or second features) awards the Golden Alexander (approx. US$ 50,000) and the Silver Alexander (approx. US$ 30,000). Other sections include the Greek film competition, retrospectives, focus on the Balkans, New Horizons and a number of special galas and exhibitions etc. *Inquiries to:* Michel Demopoulos (Director), International Thessaloniki Film Festival, 36 Sina Street, 106 72 Athens, Greece. Tel: (1) 361 0418, 362 0907. Fax: (1) 362 1023. E-mail: filmfestival@comulink.gr.

Toronto International Film Festival

September, 1997

A rich diversity of world cinema is featured yearly with over 250 films in ten days during the Toronto International Film Festival. The event, which last year celebrated its 21st anniversary, offers hundreds of films and film-makers, in a wide range of international programmes – Galas, Contemporary World Cinema, The Edge, First Cinema, Planet Africa, Asian and Latin American Panoramas, Spotlight, Midnight Madness and Perspective Canada – to a large and eager audience. There is also a Sales Office and an industry Symposium. *Inquiries to:* Festival of Festivals, 2 Carlton St., 16th Floor, Toronto, Ontario, Canada M5B 1J3. Tel: (416) 967-7371. Fax: (416) 967-9477. E-mail: TIFFG@TORFILMFEST.CA. Website: http://www.bell.ca/toronto/filmfest.

Tromsø International Film Festival

January 22-26, 1997

Possibly the world's northernmost film event, far beyond the Arctic Circle – this "Winter Wonderland" festival focuses on contemporary art films and documentaries - 35mm feature length films from all continents. *Inquiries to:* Tromsø International Film Festival, Georgernes Verft 3, N-5011

tromsø internasjonale filmfestival •97

Far beyond the Arctic Circle
TROMSØ INTERNATIONAL FILM FESTIVAL
Welcomes you to
the Winter Wonderland
of the Northernmost
Film Festival in the World!
January 22 - 26 1997
Postboks 285 N-9001 Tromsø, Norway • Tel +47 776 20 607 • Fax +47 776 83 570

Bergen, Norway. Tel:(47) 55 322 590. Fax: (47) 55 323 740. Festival Director: Hans Henrik Berg. Fax: (47) 776 83570.

Umeå

September 17-25, 1997

Umeå is an annual, non-competitive event screening some 70 features plus 150 shorts, including a number of Swedish premieres from around the world. Director Thom Palmen's lively programme includes a spotlight on women film-makers, a selection of sneak previews and films for children, as well as a focus on the contemporary cinema of a particular country or genre. The popular "Camera Obscura" section features restored or neglected classics. There are seminars and workshops for festival visitors. *Inquiries to:* Umeå Filmfestival, Box 43, 901 02 Umeå, Sweden. Tel: (46) 90 13 33 88/13 33 56. Fax: (46) 90 77 79 61.

Uppsala

October 21-26, 1997

The only International Short Film Festival in Sweden, Uppsala presents a wide range of film styles and topics. Awards in six categories – Fiction (under 20 mins), Fiction (20-60 mins) Animation, Documentary, Experimental and Children's & Youth films. The festival also includes retrospectives, exhibits and seminars. Special section of international children's and youth films, with an award presented by a special children's jury. *Inquiries to:* Uppsala Short Film Festival, PO Box 1746, S-751 47 Uppsala, Sweden. Tel: (18) 12 00 25. Fax: (18) 12 13 50. E-mail: joost@opuluspress. Website: http://www2.passagen.se/opulus/com/Film/film.htm.

AWARDS 1995

Best Fiction Film: **The Border** (Sweden/Denmark), Parsa.
Best Short Fiction Film: **The Truce** (France), Paulin.
Best Animated Film: **Sortie de bain** (Belgium), Henrard.
Best Documentary: **You Don't Know Trudy Luscher** (Germany), Kley.
Best Experiemental Film: **The People in the House** (Canada), Bourque.
Best Children's/Youth Film: **Dog Thieves** (Finland), Komulainen.

Umeå International Film Festival

September 17 – 24 1997

International Panorama – Exciting new films from all over the world

Camera Obscura – Forgotten, challenging – or just plain obscure!

Document – New and interesting documentaries

Shortfilm Section – Shortfilms from all over the world

Womens Gaze – Different aspects of women's filmmaking

Contact us: Box 43, S-901 02 Umeå, Sweden, Phone +46-90-13 33 88, Fax +46-90-77 79 61

Umeå filmfestival

Valladolid

October , 1997

One of the best organised European fests and the year's most popular Spanish event, Valladolid offers an Official section with features and shorts in competition, special tributes, retrospectives and a competitive documentary section. The 1996 sidebars included a focus on Australian cinema (1975-1995), another on Spanish composer José Nieto and a third on Yugoslavian film-maker Goran Paskaljević. *Inquiries to:* Semana Internacional de Cine de Valladolid, Spain. Tel: (34-83) 305700/77/88. Fax: (34-83) 309835.

AWARDS 1995

Golden Spike: **Someone Else's America** (U.K./France/Germany), Paskaljević.
Silver Spike: **El Callejón de los Milagros** (Mexico), Fons.
Best New Director: (*shared*) Iciar Bollaín for **Hola, ¿estás sola?** (Spain); Tom DiCillo for **Living in Oblivion** (U.S.A.).
Best Actor: Bruno Bichir for **El Callejón de los Milagros** (Mexico).
Best Actress: Antje De Boeck for **Manneken Pis** (Belgium).
Best Cinematography: Mick Coulter for **The Neon Bible** (U.K.).
Jury Prize: **Nelly & Monsieur Arnaud** (France), Sautet.
Best Short: **Surprise!** (Germany), Helmer.

Vancouver

September 26-October 12, 1997

Now in its 16th year, this festival has grown into an event of considerable stature. About 130,000 people attend more than 250 films from all parts of the world, and the Canadian city's natural beauty adds to the hospitality offered guests. Areas of special focus are East Asia, Canada, Documentaries and the Annual Trade Forum. *Inquiries to:* Alan Franey, 410-1008 Homer Street, Vancouver, B.C., Canada V6B 2X1. Tel: (604) 685 0260. Fax: (604) 688 8221. E-mail: viff@viff.org. Website: http://viff.org/viff/.

Venice

September, 1997

The Lido's generous screens offer a permanent revenge to an overflow of Italian films. So far the organisers have resisted all temptations to create an official film market, but the local audience is growing steadily. Great retrospectives plus superb parallel art exhibitions guarantee the pleasure of a visit. *Inquiries to:* La Biennale, San Marco, Cà Giustinian, 30124 Venice, Italy. Tel: (39 41) 521 8860. Fax: (39 41) 520 0569. Telex: 410685 BLE-VE-1.

AWARDS 1995

Golden Lion: **Cyclo** (France/Vietnam), Tran Anh Hung.
Special Jury Prize: (*shared*) **God's Comedy** (Portugal), Monteiro; **L'Uomo delle stelle** (Italy), Tornatore.
Best Actor: Götz George for **Der Totmacher** (Germany).
Best Actress: (*shared*) Sandrine Bonnaire, Isabelle Huppert for **A Judgment in Stone** (France).
Silver Lions: **In the Bleak Midwinter** (U.K.), Branagh; **Maborosi no hikari** (Japan), Koreeda; **Det yani dokhtar** (Iran), Jalili.

Viennale

October, 1997

A "Festival of Festivals", the Viennale presents a line-up of new international films; young cinema and a Children's Film Festival; a Twilight Zone section (midnight

42
VALLADOLID
INTL. FILM FESTIVAL (Spain)
17/25 OCT.'97
P.O. Box 646 • 47080 VALLADOLID
TEL: (34-83) 305700/77/88
FAX: (34-83) 309835

screenings); creative documentaries; world premieres and a selection of recent Austrian films; tribute programmes dedicated to "outsider" directors; and a large thematic/ historic retrospective (*Before the Code: Hollywood 1929-1934* in 1996). *Inquiries to:* Viennale, Stiftgasse 6, A-1070 Vienna, Austria. Tel: (431) 526 59 47. Fax: (431) 523 4172. E-mail: OFFICE@VIENNALE.OR.AT. Website: http://www.VIENNALE.OR.AT.

Vila do Conde

June-July, 1997

Set in a seaside town 25km north of Oporto, this up-and-coming festival, which is gradually currying international recognition, enters its 5th year in 1996 with competitive sections for both Portuguese and international (in fiction, documentary and animation categories) short films. It also runs retrospectives, programmes "Short Films by Great Directors" and will showcase Film Music for its 1997 edition. A Market for shorts is also held. *Inquiries to:* Festival Internacional de Curtas Metragens, Auditório Municipal, Praça de República, 4480 Vila do Conde, Portugal. Tel: (351) 52 641644. Fax: (351) 52 642871.

Kenneth Branagh in Valladolid for a screening of IN THE BLEAK MIDWINTER *photo: Heras*

AWARDS 1996

Grand Prix: **Breathing Lessons: The Life and Work of Mark O'Brien** (U.S.), Yu.

Vue sur les Docs

June, 1997

The Vue sur les Docs International Documentary Festival, along with the International Documentary Market Sunny Side of the Doc, takes place every summer in Marseille. The Market deals with the prospects and economic aspects of the sector and the Festival is a rich showcase for talent, an opportunity for a wide variety of cinematographic styles to be presented to an audience of around 20,000. 100 films are screened, with 15-20 in the International Competition, as well as retrospectives and special sections. *Inquiries to:* Vue sur les Docs, 3 Square Stalingrad, 13001 Marseille, France. Tel: (33) 91 84 40 17. Fax: (33) 91 84 38 34.

AWARDS 1995

Grand Prix: (*shared*) **Mother Dao, the Turtlelike** (Netherlands), Monnikendam; **Nico-Icon** (Germany), Ofteringer.

Prix Procirep: **Lee Millar - La traversée du miroir** (France), Roumette.

Prix Planète Cable: **Une mort programmée** (France), Friedman, Brunet.

Warsaw

October, 1997

Prepared by a dedicated staff of four, this audience-oriented 12-day event has been going strong since 1985. Screens the cream of recent productions by invitation only, attracting around 33,000 spectators. Sections include European Cinema, U.S. indies, World Panorama, plus a selection of new Polish features, all screened non-competitively. *Inquiries to:* Warsaw Film Festival, P.O. Box 816, 00-950 Warsaw 1, Poland. Tel/fax: (22) 644 1184.

Wellington

July 11-26, 1997

Screening an invited programme of around

JULY 1997

Presenting

THE WELLINGTON FILM FESTIVAL

THE AUCKLAND INTERNATIONAL FILM FESTIVAL

PO Box 9544 Te Aro
Wellington 6035
New Zealand
Telephone **+64-4 385-0162**
Fax **+64-4 801-7304**
E-mail **enzedff@actrix.gen.nz**
Website **http://www.enzedff.co.nz**

100 features and 50 shorts, this 27 year old Festival, along with its Auckland sibling, provides a non-competitive New Zealand premiere showcase for a striking diversity of film (and video) styles. An archival component, co-ordinated by Jonathan Dennis, also enjoys considerable prominence. Now in their second decade under the direction of the apparently tireless Bill Gosden, the latest editions played to audiences totalling 49,000 in Wellington and 80,000 in Auckland. *Inquiries to:* Wellington Film Festival, Box 9544, Te Aro, Wellington, New Zealand. Tel: (64) 4 385 0162. Fax: (64) 4 801 7304.

Wine Country Film Festival

July-August, 1997

Set in the heart of Northern California's premium wine country, this event accepts feature films, shorts, documentaries, animation, student films and videos. There are five categories including the independent features, international films, films that have a social comment, films about the arts and films about the environment. Generally non-competitive, but with a short film competition, a new directors prize, and in 1995 a Lifetime Achievement Award to Anthony Quinn. Not surprisingly, the festival also presents special events featuring the culinary arts and the finest of wines. *Inquiries to:* PO Box 303, Glen Ellen, CA 95442, U.S.A. Tel: (707) 996 2536. Fax (707) 996 6964.

WorldFest-Charleston

November, 1997

This annual festival, held in Charleston, South Carolina, offers premieres of independent and international features, shorts and documentaries. The five day event also offers in depth film and video production seminars, from screen-writing to independent feature production. Screenings are held in a restored Eighteenth-century opera house, and a select programme of 25 features are premiered. *Inquiries to:* WorldFest Charleston P.O. Box 838, Charleston, SC 29401, U.S.A. Fax: (713) 965 9960.

Warszawski Festiwal Filmowy ● Warsaw Film Festival

13th edition — October 9 – 20, 1997

P.O. Box 816 , 00-950 Warszawa 1, Poland

WorldFest-Houston

April, 1997

The Houston International Film Festival, 30 years old this year, offers competition for features, shorts, documentaries, student films, TV productions and commercials, music videos and screenplays. Worldfest-Houston is the largest film and video competition in the world in terms of the number of entries received (in 1994, over 4,100 entries from 38 countries). Festival director J. Hunter Todd now operates a new discovery festival programme which automatically enters all winners in more than 200 major international film festivals. They are then eligible for more than $2 million in cash awards. *Inquiries to:* WorldFest-Houston, P.O. Box 56566, Houston, TX 77256. Fax: (713) 965 9960.

11th Wine Country Film Festival

July-August 1997

Competitions:
Short Film
First Feature
Documentary

mail:
Box 303
Glen Ellen
CA. 95442

Tel: 707-996-2536
Fax: 707-996-6964

TWO GREAT FESTIVALS, TWO GREAT CITIES, TWO TIMES A YEAR!

WORLDFEST CHARLESTON
NOVEMBER

WORLDFEST HOUSTON
APRIL

For Poster, Entry Kit and information contact:

Entry Director P.O. Box 56566 Houston, TX USA 77256-6566 or call 713-965-9955 (USA) FAX 713-965-9960 • We're on the Internet • e mail-worldfest @ aol.com

Other Festivals and Markets of Note

Alexandria Film Festival, 9 Oraby Str., Cairo 11111, Egypt Tel: 574 1112. Fax: 768727. *(Competitive, mainly for Mediterranean countries–August/September.)*

America Film Festival, Museumstrasse 31, A-6020 Innsbruck, Austria. Tel: (512) 580723. Fax: (512) 581762. *(Features and docus from North and South America, all Austrian premieres. Non-competitive – June.)*

American Film Market, 10850 Wilshire Blvd, 9th Floor, Los Angeles, CA 90024, Tel: (310) 446 1000. Fax: (310) 446 1600. *(Efficiently-run market primarily for English-language theatrical films. Buyers must be accredited – February.)*

American Independent Feature Film Market, 12th Floor, 104 West 29th, New York, NY 10001, U.S.A. Tel: (212) 243 7777. Fax: (212) 243 3882. *(Showcase for independently produced American films – September.)*

Ann Arbor Film Festival, P.O. Box 8232, Ann Arbor MI 48107, U.S.A. Tel: (313) 995 5356. Fax: (313) 995 5396. *(Presenting experimental films from all over the world – March.)*

Asian American Intl. Film Festival, Asian Cinevision, 37 East Broadway, New York, N.Y. 10002, U.S.A. Tel: (212) 925 8685. Fax: (212) 9258157. *(Showcases works by established and emerging Asian and Asian American filmmakers – July.)*

Asia-Pacific Film Festival, Jalan Menteng Rayano 62, Jakarta 10340, Indonesia. *(Organised by members of the Federation of Motion Picture Producers in Asia-Pacific. Competitive – July.)*

Aspen Filmfest, 110 E. Hallam, Ste. 162, Aspen, CO 81611, U.S.A. Tel: (910) 925 6882. Fax: (910) 925 1967. *(Features, documentaries and shorts – September. Short subject film competition – April.)*

Atlantic Film Festival, P.O. Box 36139, Halifax, Nova Scotia, Canada. Tel: (902) 422 3456. Fax: (902) 422 4006. *(Features, documentaries, shorts and work-shops. Incorporates ScreenScene children's festival – September)*

Auckland Intl. Film Festival, P.O. Box 9544, Wellington, New Zealand. Tel: (4) 3850162. Fax: (4) 8017304. *(A leading showcase of over 100 features and 50 shorts. Twinned annually with the Wellington Film Festival – July.)*

Augsburg Children's Film Festival, Filmbüro Augsburg, Schroeckstrasse 6, 86152 Augsburg, Germany. Tel: (821) 153079. Fax: (821) 3495218. *(New international feature films for children. Competitive – November.)*

Baltimore Film Festival, The Baltimore Film Forum at the Baltimore Museum of Art, 10 Art Museum Dr., Baltimore, Md. 21218, U.S.A. Tel: (410) 8891993. Fax: (410) 8892567. *(Celebration of world cinema including restored classics. Non-competitive. Runs throughout April, in latter half of weeks.)*

Banff Festival of Mountain Films, The Banff Centre, Box 1020, Stn. 38, Banff, AB, Canada T0L 0C0. Tel: (403) 762 6125. Fax: (403) 762 6277. *(International competition for all films and videos related to mountains and the spirit of adventure – November.)*

Bergamo Film Meeting, Via Pascoli 3, 24121 Bergamo, Italy. Tel: (35) 23 40 11. Fax: (35) 23 31 29. *(Useful gathering aimed at the specialist distributors interested in buying quality films for Italy – competitive cash prizes – March.)*

Birmingham International Film and Television Festival, c/o Central TV, Central House, Broad Street, Birmingham B1 2JP, U.K. Tel: (121) 634 4213. Fax: (121) 634 4392. *(Growing provincial festival – November.)*

Boston Film Festival, P.O. Box 516, Hull, MA02045, U.S.A. Tel: (617) 925 1373. Fax: (617) 925 3132. *(Screening about 50 films including American independents, short subjects, documentaries and major studio releases – September.)*

Breckenridge Festival of Film, P.O. Box 718, Riverwalk Center/150 W. Adams, Breckenridge, CO 80424, U.S.A. Tel: (970) 453 6200. Fax: (970) 453 2692. *(Independent U.S. and international fare, with tributes, receptions and educational activities – September).*

Brisbane International Film Festival, P.O. Box 909, Brisbane 4001, Australia. Tel: (7) 3220 0333. Fax: (7) 3220 0400. *(New Australian event, aiming for a strong Asian input – August.)*

British Short Film Festival, Room 313 – BBC Threshold House, 65-69 Shepherds Bush Green, London W12 7RJ, U.K. Tel: (181) 743 8000. Fax: (181) 740 8540. *(Only competitive short film fest in U.K. – September.)*

Brussels Festival of Cartoons and Animated Films, Folioscope, rue de la Rhetorique 19, B-1060 Brussels, Belgium. Tel: (2) 5344125. Fax: (2) 5342279. *(Showcase for the newest, most interesting works in animation – February.)*
Brussels Intl. Festival of Fantasy, Thriller & Science Fiction Films, 144 Avenue de la Reine, 1030 Brussels, Belgium. Tel: (2) 2011713. Fax: (2) 2101469. *(An international selection of thrillers, fantasy & sci-fi films. Competitive – March.)*
Brussels Intl. Film Festival, 50 chaussée de Louvain, 1030 Brussels, Belgium. Tel: (2) 2185333. Fax: (2) 2181860. *(European features – January.)*
Cairo International Film Festival, 17 Kasr El Nil Street, Cairo, Egypt. Tel: (2) 392 3962. Fax: (2) 392 3562. *(Competitive, aimed at showing major international films not usually available at local cinemas – November.)*
Cairo International Children's Film Festival, 17 Kasr El Nil Str., Cairo, Egypt. Tel: 3923 562. Fax: 3938 979. *(Competitive – March.)*
Camerimage, Foundation TUMULT, Rynek Nowomiojski 28, 87-100 Torun, Poland. Tel: (56) 24879. Fax: (56) 27595. *(International event celebrating the art of cinematography, with a competition and many top cinematographers in attendance – November-December.)*
Cape Town International Film Festival, Univ. of Cape Town, Private Bag, Rondesbosch 7700, South Africa. Tel: (021) 23-8257. Fax: (021) 242355. *(Longest established such event in South Africa, non-competitive in structure, progressive in tone – April.)*
Chicago Intl. Children's Film Festival, Facets Multimedia, 1517 W. Fullerton, Chicago, Il. 60614, U.S.A. Tel: (312) 2819075. Fax: (312) 9295437. *(Largest competitive festival for children's films in North America, screening films and videos from 25 countries – October.)*
Chicago Latino Cinema, 600 S. Michigan Ave, Chicago, IL 60605, U.S.A. Tel: (312) 431 1330. Fax: (312) 360 0629. *(Aims to promote awareness of Latino culture through film and video – April.)*
Cinefest: The Sudbury Film Festival, 218-40 Elm Street, Sudbury, Ontario POM 150, Canada. Tel: (705) 6881234. Fax: (705) 6881351. *(Aims to programme the best of*

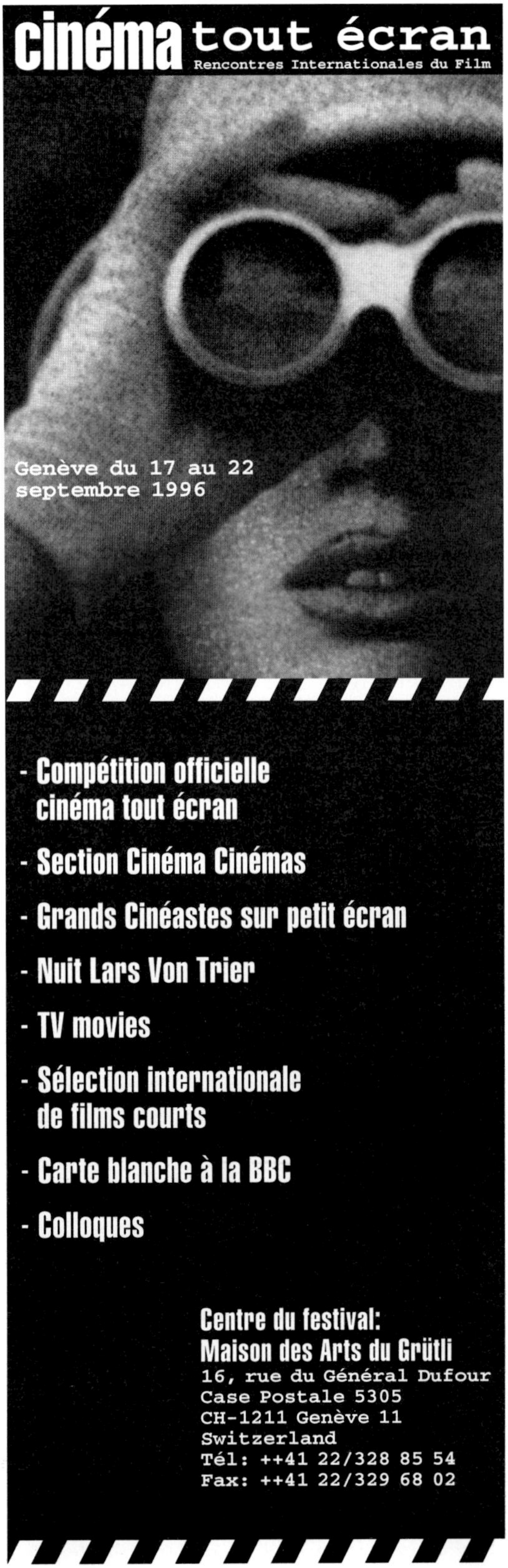

contemporary Canadian cinema – September.)

Cinemagic Festival for Young People, Northern Ireland Film Council, 21 Ormeau Ave., Belfast BT2 8HD, Ireland. Tel: (1232) 232444. Fax: (1232) 239918. *(Children's films in competition – December.)*

Cinema Italien Rencontres D'Annecy, Bonlieu Scene Nationale, 1 rue Jean Jaurès - BP 294, 74007 Annecy Cedex, France. Tel: 50334400. Fax: 50518209. *(Feature films from Italy, with tributes and retrospectives. Competitive – December.)*

Cinema Jove, Jerónimo de Monsoriu, 19, 46022 Valencia. Tel: (6) 3985969/26. Fax: (6) 3985965. *(Feature and especially short film festival with multiple side bars – late June.)*

Cinequest, San Jose Film Festival, PO Box 720040, San Jose, California 95172, U.S.A. Tel: (408) 995 5033. Fax: (408) 995 5713. *(Excellent showcase for independent films from around the world, grants awarded to indie-makers – November.)*

Cinewoman Festival, Cinema City, St Andrews Street, Norwich NR2 4AD, U.K. Tel: (1603) 632 366. Fax: (1603) 767838. *(Mixed programme of features, shorts, documentaries etc. made by women, with workshops and seminars –October.)*

Cleveland International Film Festival, 1621 Euclid Ave., Cleveland, Ohio 44115, U.S.A. Tel: (216) 623 0400. Fax: (216) 623 0103. *(Round-up of new and classic films from all major countries – March.)*

Copenhagen Film Festival, FSI, Vesterbrogade 35, 1620 Copenhagen V, Denmark. Tel: 3325 2501. Fax: 3325 5756. *(Audience-orientated event showing features, previews etc., with a special Gay and Lesbian programme, as well as Spanish and French films – September.)*

Cork Film Festival, Festival Office, Tobin Street, Cork, Ireland. Tel: (21) 271 711. Fax: (21) 275 945. *(Annual and competitive, for documentaries, animation, art films, fiction and sponsored shorts – October.)*

Cracow International Short Film Festival, c/o Apollo Film, ul. Pychowicka 7, 30-364 Kraków, Poland. Tel: (12) 672340. Fax: (12) 671552. *(Poland's oldest international film festival and respected short film showcase – May.)*

Danubefilm Festival, Via delle Mura Aurelie 19, 00165 Rome, Italy. Tel: (6) 632881. Fax: (6) 632897. *(New touring festival*

Modem Festival closes 1 Dec 96
WWW.poptel.org.uk/
acrobat-services/modfest
something continues

which takes place on board a ship on the river Danube and visits Vienna, Bratislava and Budapest – October.)

Deauville Festival of American Films, 36 rue Pierret, 92200 Neuilly-sur-Seine, France. Tel: (1) 46 40 5500. Fax: (1) 46 40 55 39. *(Showcase for U.S. features and independent films – September.)*

Dublin Film Festival, 1 Suffolk Street, Dublin 2, Eire. Tel: (1) 679 2937. Fax: (1) 679 2939. *(Amicable Irish festival focusing on world cinema with special emphasis on Irish film – March.)*

Duisburg Film Week, am König-Heinrich-Platz, D-47049 Duisburg, Germany. Tel: (203) 283-4171. Fax: (203) 2834-130. *(Dedicated to German documentaries – November.)*

Durban International Film Festival, University of Natal, King George V Avenue, Durban 4001, South Africa. Tel: (31) 811 3978. Fax: (31) 261 7107. *(Annual festival devoted to a better understanding of international cinema. Arranges screenings in peri-urban Black areas of the city – July.)*

Emden Film Festival, An der Berufsschule 3, 26721 Emden, Germany. Tel: (4921) 31675. Fax: (4921) 21517. *(Focussing on North-Western European films, particularly from Germany and Great Britain – May.)*

Festival de Genève, Case Postale 5615, CH–1211 Geneva 11, Switzerland. Tel: (22) 321 5468. Fax: 809 9400. *(Screens films featuring up-and-coming actors and actresses – October.)*

Festival of French Cinema, Tel-Aviv Cinémathèque, 2 Sprintzak Street, Tel-Aviv, Israel. *(Screens new French fare, many Israeli premieres, with tributes and retrospectives – April.)*

Festival Intl. du Film Francophone, 175 rue des Brasseurs, 5000 Namur, Belgium. Tel: (81) 241236. Fax: (81) 224384. *(Feature films, shorts and docus from French speaking countries, with retrospectives and first-time directors. Competitive – September.)*

Festival Intl. du Film Juif & Israelien de

Rich Wilkes (LAST CALL) and Ian Hart (CLOCKWORK MICE) at Cinequest 1996

Montpellier, 500 Boulevard d'Antigone, 34000 Montpellier, France. Tel: 67150876. Fax: 67150872. *(Showcases Jewish and Israelian Films. Competitive – November.)*
Festival dei Popoli, Via de Castalani 8, 50122 Florence, Italy. Tel: (55) 294 353. Fax: (55) 213 698. *(Documentaries on social issues, films on history etc., in part competitive – November-December.)*
Festival du Cinéma International en Abitibi-Témscamingue, 215 Avenue Mercier, Rouyn-Noranda, Québec J9X 5WB, Canada. Tel: (819) 762 6212. Fax: (819) 762 6762. *(Competitive for features and shorts held in northwestern Québec – October-November.)*
Festival International Nouveau Cinéma et Vidéo, 3726 Boulevard Saint-Laurent, Montréal, Québec, Canada H2X 2V8. Tel: (514) 843 4725. Fax: (514) 843 4631. *(Seeks to promote experimental films of outstanding quality as an alternative to the conventions of the commercial cinema. Fest also plays in New York – June.)*
Film Art Festival, Cankarjev Dom, Presernova 10, 61000 Ljubljana, Slovenia. Tel: (66) 125 8121. Fax: (66) 212 492. *(Presents work of young European writers and directors, U.S. Independents, documentaries and lesser known cinematography–October.)*
Filmfest DC, P.O. Box 21396, Washington DC 20009, U.S.A. Tel: (202) 274 6810. Fax: (202) 274 6828. *(Celebrating the best in World cinema – April.)*
Filmfest München, Kaiserstrasse 39, D-8000 Munich 40, Germany. Tel: (89) 381 9040. Fax: (89) 381 90426. *(International screenings, TV movies, retrospectives – June.)*
Filmfest Hamburg, Friedensallee 1, 22765 Hamburg, Germany. Tel: (40) 39826210. Fax: (40) 39826211. *(International productions, retrospectives, tributes, focus on Hong Kong, children's films, shorts and a presentation of Hamburg productions – September.)*
Filmfestival Max Ophüls Prize, Mainzerstrasse 8 66121 Saarbrücken, Germany. Tel: (681) 39452. Fax: (681) 9051943. *(Competitive event for young directors from German-speaking countries – January.)*
The Film Festival of the Whole of Sweden, Municipality of Jokkmokk, S-962 85 Jokkmokk, Sweden. Tel: (971) 173 34. Fax: (971) 17201. *(Biennial event focusing on the countryside – May.)*
Films from the South, P.O. Box 125, Blindern, N-003154 Oslo, Norway. Tel: (22) 360718. Fax: (22) 857698. *(Dedicated to the films of Asia, Africa and Latin America – September.)*
Florida Film Festival, 1300 South Orlando Avenue, Maitland, Florida 32751, U.S.A. Tel: (407) 629 1088. Fax: (407) 629 6870. *(Ten days of film premieres, seminars and galas. Competitive – June.)*

THE NASTY GIRL ERMO LADYBIRD, LADYBIRD ANTONIA'S LINE MY OWN PRIVATE IDAHO DON QUIXOTE THE MYTH OF THE MALE ORGASM THE SUMMER HOUSE ED'S NEXT MOVE ANTONIA AND JANE POCO LOCO

HIGHLIGHTED MAVERICKS '95–96
Gus Van Sant
John Waters
Michael Radford
Werner Herzog
Robert Wise
Luis Valdez
Russ Meyer

Cinequest
THE SAN JOSE FILM FESTIVAL VII
JANUARY 30 – FEBRUARY 5, 1997
Ask for Mike or Halfdan
TEL: 408.995.5033 • FAX: 408.995.5713

Picture the Possibilities ....

French Film Festival, 5555 North Tamiami Trl., Sarasota, Florida 34243, U.S.A. Tel: (941) 351 9010. Fax: (941) 351 5796. *(Quality showcase for French cinema; a screening here could lead to national distribution – November.)*

French American Film Workshop, 10 Montée de la Tour, 30 400 Villeneuve les Avignon, France. Tel: 90259323. Fax: 90259324. *(Programmes the best in independent French and American cinema with premieres and retrospectives. Competitive – June.)*

Fribourg Film Festival, Rue de Locarno 8, 1700 Fribourg, Switzerland. Tel: (37) 222232. Fax: (37) 227950. *(Features, shorts and docus from Asia, Africa, and Latin America – March.)*

Fukuoka Intl. Film Festival, c/o Fukuoka City Hall, 1-8-1, Tenjin, Chou-ku, Fukuoka 810, Japan. Tel: (92) 7335170. Fax: (92) 7335595. *(Dedicated to the promotion of Asian film. Non-competitive – September.)*

Gay and Lesbian Film Festival, National Film Theatre, South Bank, London SE1 8XT. Tel: (171) 815 1322/3. Fax: (171) 633 0786. *(Films made by, or about, gays and lesbians – March.)*

Golden Golem - Prague Intl. Film Festival, Dlouha 16, 110 00 Prague 1, Czech Republic. Tel: (2) 2322068. Fax: (42) 2 2322069. *(Panorama of international and Czech features, indies from around the world, with retrospectives and a film market – June.)*

Gramado Cinema Festival, Avenida des Hortensias, 2029, Cap. 9567, 1000 Gramado, R. G. Sul, Brazil. Tel: (54) 286 1501. Fax: (21) 5372898. *(International selection, focusing on films made in the main Latin Language countries – August.)*

Haifa International Film Festival, 142 Hanassi Avenue, Haifa 34633, Israel. Tel: (4) 8386 424. Fax: (4) 8384 327. *(A non-competitive event, including a broad spectrum of new films from around the world, special tributes, retrospectives and other events – September/October.)*

Hawaii International Film Festival, 700 Bishop Street, Honolulu, Hawaii 96813, U.S.A. Tel: (808) 528 3456. Fax: (808) 528 1410. *(Promotes cross-cultural understanding among people.)*

Holland Animation Film Festival, Hoogt 4, 3512 GW Utrecht, Holland. Tel: (30) 312 216. Fax: (30) 312 940. *(Animation from all over the world, competition for applied animation – November.)*

Independent Film Days, Filmbüro Augsburg, Schroeckstrasse 6, 86152 Augsburg, Germany. Tel: (821) 153077. Fax: (821) 3495218. *(International event for docus and indie features, with retrospectives, national focus and a symposium of film students – March.)*

International Animation Festival, c/o The British Film Institute, 21 Stephen St., London W1P 1PL, U.K.. Tel: (171) 255 1444 ext. 101. Fax: (171) 255 2315. *(Held in Cardiff, fest is a biennial event with films, exhibitions and workshops on all aspects of animation – May.)*

International Animated Film Festival – Cinanima, Rua 62, No. 251, 4501 Espinho Codex, Portugal. Tel: (2) 721 611. Fax: (2) 726 015. *(Animation – November.)*

International Animation Festival in Japan – Hiroshima, 4-17 Kako-machi, Naka-hu, Hiroshima 730, Japan. Tel: (82) 2450245. Fax: (82) 2450246. *(Competitive event for animation – August.)*

International Children's and Young People's Film Festival, Deutsches Filmmuseum, Schaumainkai 41, 60596 Frankfurt-am-Main, Germany. Tel: (69) 2123 8835. Fax: (69) 2123 7881. *(New films for children and young people – September.)*

International Cinema Week, Via S. Giacomo alla Pigna 6, 37121 Verona, Italy. Tel: (45) 800 6778. Fax: (45) 590 624. *(Offers a wide panorama of film-makers and genres from a particular country – April.)*

International Documentary Filmfestival Amsterdam (IDFA), Kleine Gartmanplantsoen 10, 1017 RR Amsterdam, The Netherlands. Tel: (20) 6273329. Fax: (20) 6385388. *(Docu films compete for the Joris Ivens Prize. Includes the Forum, a market for international co-financing of docus – December.)*

International Documentary Film Festival, Rua Angola, Olival Basto, 2675 Odivelas, Portugal. Tel: (1) 9388407. Fax: (1) 9389347. *((nternational documentaries – November.)*

International Documentary Film Festival - Munich, Trogerstrasse 46, D-81675 Munich, Germany. Tel: (89) 4703237. Fax (89) 4706611. *(International and German docus. Competitive – April.)*

International Festival of New Latin American Cinema, Calle 23 No. 1155,

32nd KARLOVY VARY INTERNATIONAL FILM FESTIVAL

The most prestigeous cinema event in the Czech Republic

4th - 12th July 1997

- **Two official competitions**
  Feature Films and Documentaries
- **Hors Concours Sections**
  Horizons - The Best of Last Seasons
  Another View
  Forum of Independents
  East of the West
- **Czech Cinema**
- **Retrospectives**
- **Special Programs**

Contact address:
Film-Festival Karlovy Vary Foundation
Panská 1, 110 00 Praha 1, CZ
tel.: ++42-2-24 23 54 12
fax: ++42-2-24 23 34 08

Vedado, Havana, Cuba. Tel: (7) 34169. Fax: (7) 334273. *(Competitive event and market for Latin American and International films – December.)*

International Women's Film Festival, Maison des Arts, Palace Salvador Allende, 94000 Créteil, France. Tel: (1) 49 80 38 98. Fax: (1) 43 99 04 10. *(Features, shorts, animated films all made by women. Annual spotlight on an actress – March.)*

International Festival of Films for Children and Young Adults, Farhang Cinema, Dr. Shariati Ave., Gholbak, Tehran 19139, Iran. Tel: (20020) 888 890. Fax: (20020) 267 082. *(Promotes film and video production for children – October.)*

Ismailia Intl. Film Festival, Culture Development Fund, Ministry of Culture, Opera House Area, El Gezira, Cairo, Egypt. Tel: 3407001. Fax: 3406759. *(Shorts, docus and cartoons. Competitive – July.)*

Israel Film Festival, Israfest Foundation, 6404 Wilshire Blvd., Suite 1240, Los Angeles, Calif. 90048, U.S.A. Tel: (213) 9664166. Fax: (213) 6586346. *(Showcase in U.S. for Israeli features, shorts, docus and TV dramas with an American Film and TV symposium at the Tel Aviv Cinematheque – October.)*

Junior Dublin Film Festival, Irish Film Centre, 6 Eustace Street, Dublin 2, Ireland. Tel: (1) 6777095. Fax: (1) 6778755. *(Showcases the best in world cinema for young people and includes workshops and seminars – November.)*

Kidfilm Festival, USA Film Festival, 2917 Swiss Ave., Dallas, Texas 75204, U.S.A. Tel: (214) 8216300. Fax: (214) 8216364. *(New and classic children's films from around the world – January.)*

Leeds International Film Festival, Town Hall, Headrow, Leeds LS1 3AD. Tel: (113) 247 8389. Fax: (113) 247 8379. *(Retrospectives, premieres and director tributes with a yearly theme – October.)*

Lille International Festival of Short and Documentary Films, 24-34 rue Washington, 75008 Paris, France. *(Competitive for shorts, with additional panorama of recent French production in the field – April.)*

London Jewish Film Festival, National Film Theatre, South Bank, London SE1 8XT, U.K. Tel: (171) 815 1322. Fax: (171) 633 0786. *(June.)*

London Latin American Film Festival, Metro Pictures, 79 Wardour Street, London W1V 3TH, U.K. Tel: (171) 434 3357. Fax: (171) 287 2112. *(Films from Latin American countries – September.)*

Mardi Gras Film Festival, P.O. Box 1081, Darlinghurst, NSW 2010, Australia. Tel: (2) 3324938. Fax: (2) 331 2988. *(Features, docus and shorts that are of interest to, or are made by, gays and lesbians – February.)*

Margaret Mead Film Festival, American Museum of Natural History, 79th St. at Central Park West, New York, N.Y. 10024, U.S.A. Tel: (212) 7695305. Fax: (212) 7695329. *(International docu and ethnographic festival includes shorts and features – November.)*

Melbourne International Film Festival, P.O. Box 296, Fitzroy 3065, Victoria, Australia, Tel: (3) 9417 2011. Fax: (3) 9417 3804. *(The oldest festival in the Southern hemisphere, incorporating international features, animation, documentary and experimental work – July.)*

Miami Festival, Film Society of Miami, 444 Brickell Road, Suite 229, Miami, FL 33131, U.S.A. Tel: (305) 377 3456. Fax: (305) 577 9768. *(Non-competitive, with emphasis on Hispanic cinema – January.)*

Midnight Sun Film Festival, Malminkatu 36 B 102, 00100 Helsinki, Finland. Tel: (358–0) 685 2242. Fax: (358–0) 694 5560. *(Long weekend for film lovers in the Midsummer beauty of Finland, and above the Arctic Circle! – June.)*

Minneapolis/St. Paul International Film Festival (formerly Rivertown), University Film Society, Minnesota Film Center, 425 Ontario Street SE, Minneapolis, MN 55414. Tel: (612) 627 4431. *(Event built up over 15 years by the reliable Al Milgrom. Scores of foreign films (especially Scandinavian) on display – April 11-25, 1997.)*

Muestra de Cine Mexicano, Av. Vallarta no. 2181, S.J. C.P. 44140, Guadalajara, Jalisco, Mexico. Tel: (36) 164023. Fax: (36) 150332. *(Devoted to the promotion of new Mexican and latin American cinema – March.)*

NAT – Annual Film Festival of Denmark, NatFilm Festivalen, Festivalsekretariat, Store Kannikestræde 6, 1169 Copenhagen, Denmark. Tel: (45) 3312 0005. Fax: (45) 3312 7505. *(Offers offbeat retros and tributes from smaller countries. Travels around Denmark – March.)*

New Directors/New Films, The Film Society of Lincoln Center, 70 Lincoln Center Plaza, New York, N.Y. 10023, U.S.A. Tel: (212) 8755610. Fax: (212) 8755636. *(Co-sponsored by the Museum of Modern Art and The Film Society of Lincoln Center, this is a forum for works by new directors – March.)*

New England Film & Video Festival, Boston Film/Video Foundation, 1126 Boylston Street, Boston, MA 02215, U.S.A. Tel: (617) 5361549. Fax: (617) 5363576. *(Festival devoted to films created in the previous two years by students/residents of New England – May.)*

New Orleans Film and Video Festival, P.O. Box 50819, New Orleans, LA 70150, U.S.A. Tel: (504) 5233818. Fax: (504) 5292430. *(International features, workshops and indie film competition – October.)*

New York Exposition of Short Film & Video, New York Expo, 532 LaGuardia Place, Box 330, New York, NY 10012, U.S.A. Tel: (212) 5057742. *(Showcase for cutting-edge indie shorts with sections for animation, documentary, experimental and narrative, highlights from the Oberhausen Intl. Short Film Festival, and panel discussions – November.)*

Northwest Film & Video Festival, Northwest Film Center, 1219 S.W. Park Ave., Portland Ore. 97205, U.S.A. Tel: (503) 2211156. Fax: (503) 2264842, *(Annual survey of new moving image art produced in the U.S. Northwest. Features, shorts and docus – November.)*

Norwegian Short Film Festival, Dronningensgt. 16, 0152 Oslo, Norway. Tel: (22) 47 4646. Fax: (22) 47 4690. *(Local shorts in competition, plus selection of titles from other international festivals – held in Grimstad every June.)*

Osaka European Film Festival, Osaka Station No. 2 Bldg., 11F, No. 14, 2-2-110, 1-chome, Umeda, Kita-ku, 530 Osaka, Japan. Tel: (6) 341 9181. Fax: (6) 341 3166. *(Showcase for the diversity of European cinema including exhibitions – October.)*

Oslo Animation Festival, Dronningens gt. 16, N-0152 Oslo, Norway. Tel: (22) 4746 33/4. Fax: (22) 4746 87. *(Nordic and international animation, with retros and student films. Competitive – April.)*

Österreichische Filmtage, Columbusgasse 2, A-110 Vienna, Austria. Tel: 604 0126. Fax:

602 0795. *(Annual survey of new Austrian features, documentaries, TV, avant-garde, and video productions – June.)*

Palm Springs International Short Film Festival, P.O. Box 2230, Palm Springs, CA 92263, U.S.A. Tel: (619) 322 2930. Fax: (619) 322 4087. *(Largest competitive shorts festival in North America. Student competiton, international competition, cash awards, seminars, workshops – August.)*

Peñiscola International Comedy Film Festival, Oficina de Turismo, 12598 Peñiscola (Castellón), Spain. Tel: (34) 64 474901/474612. Fax: (34) 64 474007. *Comedy film competition section and tributes in a picturesque Mediterranean resort – June.*

Pia Film Festival, 5-19 Sanban-chu, Chiyoda-ku, Tokyo, Japan. tel: (3) 32651425. Fax: (3) 32655659. *(Aims to nurture new, unique voices and emergent talent in Japanese cinema. Competitive – December.)*

Philadelphia Festival of World Cinema, Intl. House, 3701 Chestnut St., Philadelphia, Penn. 19104, U.S.A. Tel: (215) 8956593. Fax: (215) 8956562. *(Screens features, docus and shorts from over 30 countries, celebrating emerging talent and cultural diversity – May.)*

Polish Film Festival, Piwna 22, PO Box Nr. 192, 80-831 Gdańsk, Poland. Tel/Fax: (58) 313744. *(Showcase for the most recent Polish productions – October.)*

Raindance Film Showcase and Market, 81 Berwick Street, London W1V 3PF, U.K.. Tel: (171) 4373991. Fax: (171) 4392243. *(Showcase for British, North American and European independent films, shorts and docus. This year sees a new multimedia sidebar – October.)*

Riga Film Forum, ICNC "Arsenal", Marstalu Iela 14, Riga, LV, 1047 Latvia. Tel: (2) 221 620. Fax: (2) 882 0445. *(A non-competitive show of experimental, avant-garde film-making – September.)*

Rio de Janeiro Film Festival, Rua Voluntarios de Patria 88, Rio de Janeiro, RJ 22270 Brazil. Tel: (21) 286 8505. Fax: (21) 286 4029. *(Screens over 50 American and European features – September.)*

Rouen, Festival du Cinéma Nordique, 22 rue de la Champmeslé, 76000 Rouen, France. Tel: 35 98 28 46. Fax: 35 70 92 08. Telex: 771444. *(Competitive festival of Nordic cinema, including retrospective and information sections – March.)*

San Francisco Intl. Asian American Film Festival, c/o NAATA, 346 Ninth St., San Francisco, Calif. 94621, U.S.A. Tel: (415) 8630814. Fax: (415) 8637428. *(Film and video works by Asian and Asian American artists – March.)*

San Francisco Intl. Lesbian and Gay Film Festival, Frameline, 346 Ninth St., San Francisco, Calif. 94103, U.S.A. Tel: (415) 7038650. Fax: (415) 8611404. *(Focus on gay and lesbian themes – June.)*

Santa Fe de Bogota (Moving Images Market), Calle 26, #4-92, Santa Fe de Bogota, Colombia. Tel: (1) 282 5196. Fax: (1) 342 2872. *(Showing films never exhibited in Latin America before – September.)*

São Paulo International Film Festival, Alameda Lorena 937, 303-01 424 São Paulo, Brazil. Tel: (11) 883 5137. Fax: (11) 853 7936. *(Competitive event with features and shorts from around 30 countries. Emphasis on independents – October.)*

Santa Barbara International Film Festival, 1216 State Street, Suite 170, Santa Barbara, CA 93101, U.S.A. Tel: (805) 963 0023. Fax: (805) 962 2524. *(International showcase for features, docus and shorts. Competitive – March.)*

Screens on the Bay/CD Rom on the Bay, Sacis, Via Teulada 66, 00195 Rome, Italy. Tel: (6) 379 981. Fax: (6) 370 1393. *(Convention – October.)*

Seattle International Film Festival, 801 East Pine Street, Seattle, Washington 98122, U.S.A. *(Unusual Northwest Pacific coast event that has done a great deal to establish Dutch cinema in the States – May-June.)*

Short and Documentary Film Festival, Farhang Cinema, Dr. Shariati Ave., Gholbak, Tehran 19139, Iran. Tel: 265 086. Fax: 678 155. *(July.)*

Shots in the Dark, Broadway Media Centre, 14 Broad Street, Nottingham, NG1 3AL, U.K. Tel: (115) 9526 600. Fax: (115) 952 6622. *(Non-competitive festival of crime and mystery films – June.)*

Singapore International Film Festival, 400 Orchard Road, 24-09 Orchard Towers, Singapore. Tel: 738 7567. Fax: 738 7578. *(Showcases best of Asian and world cinema. Competitive Asian Section – April.)*

Solothurner Film Days, Postfach 1030, CH-4502 Solothurn, Switzerland. Tel: (32) 625 8080. Fax: (32) 623 6410. *(Screenings of all new Swiss films and video productions.)*

South African International Film Festival, Lyle Britton, 139 Smit Street, Braamfontein, Johannesburg 2000, South Africa. Tel: (27 11) 403 7111. Fax: (27 11) 403 1025. *(The largest annual festival in South Africa. Includes a short film competition – September.)*

St. Petersburg Festival of Festivals, 190 Kamennostrovsky Ave, St. Petersburg 197101, Russia. Tel: (812) 238 5811. Fax: (812) 232 8881. *(Features international productions as well as local fare. Non-competitive – June.)*

Sydney Film Festival, P.O. Box 950, Glebe, NSW 2037, Australia. Tel: (2) 660 3844. Fax: (2) 692 8793. *(Broad-based, non-competitive event screening new features and Australian shorts – June.)*

Taormina International Film Festival, Palazzo Firneze, Via Pirandello 31, Taormina, Italy. Tel: (942) 21142. . Fax: (942) 23348. *(Competitive and non-competitive event in Sicily with stress on films by new directors, plus retrospectives and discussions – July.)*

Tokyo International Film Festival, 4th Floor, Landic Ginza, Bldg. II 1–6–5 Ginza, Chuo-ku, Tokyo 104, Japan. Tel: (813) 3563 6305. Fax: (813) 3563 6310. *(New mammoth event with competition and other sidebar events – September-October.)*

Troia International Film Festival, 2902 Setabal Codex, Portugal. Tel: (65) 44123. Fax: (65) 525 681. *(Wide variety of categories in this competitive festival. Held in a summer recreational area on the tip of a peninsula – early June.)*

USA Film Festival, 2917 Swiss Avenue, Dallas, Texas 75204, U.S.A. Tel: (214) 821 6300. Fax: (214) 8216364. *(Eight-day festival featuring new U.S. and foreign independents. Competition for U.S. shorts with cash prizes – April.)*

Valencia Film Festival, Plaza Arzobispo, 2 acc. B., Valencia 46003, Spain. Tel: (96) 392 1506. Fax: (96) 391 5156. *(Competitive section for films made in and around the Mediterranean – October.)*

Vevey Intl. Comedy Film Festival, La Grenette, P.O. Box 325, CH-1800 Vevey, Switzerland. Tel: (21) 9222027. Fax (21) 9222024. *(Comedy films, including retrospectives, Swiss section, open air screenings and cartoons – July.)*

Victoria Commonwealth Film Festival, Box 3035, Victoria B.C., Canada V8W 3P3. *(Focuses on films from commonwealth nations currently under-represented at most North American festivals – April/May.)*

Virginia Festival of American Films, P.O. Box 3697, 104 Midmont Lane, University of Virginia, Charlottesville, Va. 22903, U.S.A. Tel: (804) 9825277. Fax: (804) 9825297. *(Annual event dedicated to the study of American film, with a focus on independent productions, documentaries, short subjects and premieres, as well as panels and discussions – October.)*

Yamagata International Documentary Film Festival, Kitagawa Building, 4th Floor, 6-42 Kagurazaka Shinjuku-ku, Tokyo 162, Japan. *(Biennial event showcasing documentary films from Japan and around the world – October.)*

12º FESTIVAL INTERNACIONAL DE CINE DE MAR DEL PLATA

7 AL 16 DE NOVIEMBRE - ARGENTINA

International Competition
Behind the Camera
Women and Films
Midnight Express
Ibero American Screenings
'96 Argentine Panorama
Retrospectives and Tributes

The Argentine Film Institute (INCAA) has decided to give an additional prize to the film that wins the 12th Mar del Plata International Film Festival's **GOLDEN OMBU** awarded by the International Grand Jury.
This special prize, which consist of **U$S 625.000.-**, will be a capital input to the producer of the winning film, for a feature film in co-production with an Argentine producer.

FUNDACION CINE ARGENTINO
INSTITUTO NACIONAL DE CINE Y ARTES AUDIOVISUALES

Lima 319 (1073) Buenos Aires - Argentina
Tel.: 54-1 383-2622 Fax: 54-1 383-9091
http: //www. incaa. com/

The London International Film School

• Training film makers for 40 years •
• Graduates now working worldwide •
• Located in Covent Garden in the heart of London •
• Accredited by B.E.C.T.U. •
• 16mm documentary & 35mm studio filming •
• Two year Diploma course in film making •
• Commences three times a year: January, May, September •

London International Film School,
Department IG12. 24 Shelton Street, London WC2H 9HP
Tel: 0171 836 9642/0171 240 0168 Fax: 0171 497 3718
Email: lifs@dial.pipex.com Web Page: http://www.tecc.co.uk/lifs/index.html

FILM SCHOOLS

AUSTRALIA

Australian Film, Television and Radio School, PO Box 126, North Ryde, NSW 2113.

AUSTRIA

Hochschule für Musik und darstellende Kunst, Abteilung für Film und Fernsehen, Metternichgasse 12, A-1030 Vienna. Director: Mrs. Hannelore Götzinger.

BELGIUM

Hogeschool voor Audiovisuele Communicatie (R.I.T.S.), Naamsestraat 54, 1000 Brussels. Tel: (32) 2 511 93 82. Fax: (32) 2 502 55 06

Institut des Arts de Diffusion, (I.A.D.), Rue des Wallons No. 77, B 1348 Louvain-la Neuve, Belgium.

Institut National des Arts du Spectacle et Techniques de diffusion (I.N.S.A.S.), Rue Thérésienne, 8, 1000 Bruxelles, Belgium.

Koninklijke Academie voor Schone Kunsten-Gent, Academiestraat 2, B-9000 Gent.

BRAZIL

Universidade de São Paulo, Escola de Comunicacões e Artes, Departamento de Cinema, Radio e Televisão, Av. Prof. Lúcio Martins Rodrigues 443, São Paulo 05508, Brazil. Tel: (5511) 813 3222. Fax: (5511) 8153083.

CANADA

Queen's University, 160 Stuart St, Kingston, Ont K7L 3N6. In its four-year B.A. (Honours) degree programme and three-year B.A. degree programme the Department of Film Studies provides an integrated approach to film criticism, history and production.

Sheridan College, Faculty of Visual Arts, 1430 Trafalgar Road, Oakville, Ontario, L6H 2L1, Canada. Dean: Donald Graves. Intensive and award-winning diploma programmes in: Classical Animation, International Summer School of Animation, Computer Animation, Computer Graphics and Media Arts. Summer workshops available from May to August For further information, please call (905) 845 9430 ext. 2700.

Simon Fraser University, School for the Contemporary Arts, Burnaby, B.C. Canada V5A 1S6. Tel: (604) 291 3363. Fax: (604) 291 5907.

Vancouver Film School, 400-1168 Hamilton Street, Vancouver, British Columbia, V6B 2S2. Tel: (604) 685 5808. Fax: (604) 685 5830. President: James Griffin. VFS is a unique training centre that offers 5 immersion programmes in communication production: Film Production, Multimedia Production, Classical Animation, Computer Animation, and Acting for Film and Television. All programmes have been designed with industry consultation and are taught by industry professionals. Specialising in shorter (1 year) and intensive formats, students create their own graduate productions. For detailed information, please contact the Registrar.

Univ. of Manitoba, 450 University College, Winnipeg, Man R3T 2M8. Basic film-making, screenwriting.

University of Windsor, Ont. N9B 3P4. Film Radio TV.

York University, Faculty of Fine Arts, Film & Video Department, 4700 Keele Street, North York, Ontario M3J 1P3. Offers studies in Film, Video, Screenwriting, and Theory over a 4-year Honours BA or BFA programme. 2-year MFA.

CZECH REPUBLIC

FAMU Film and Television Faculty, Academy of Performing Arts, Smetanovo nábř. 2, CS 116

LOOK & LISTEN & INTERACT!
CINEMA IS ALSO MUSIC.
LISTEN TO CINEMA.

C.A.M. ORIGINAL SOUNDTRACKS from the golden years of Italian and French cinema.
Over 170 titles and 75 composers available on compact disc.
Ask for our catalog. Also available on CD-ROM.

CAM Original Soundtracks VIA COLA DI RIENZO, 152 - 00192 ROME (ITALY) - FAX:(+39-6) 687.4046

65 Prague 1. Tel: (42) 2 24229176. Fax: (42) 2 24230285. Dean: Jan Bernard.

DENMARK

European Film College, DK-8400 Ebeltoft. Tel: (45) 86 34 00 55. Fax: (45) 86 34 05 35. Principal: Kjeld Veirup. Chairman of the Board: Litten Hansen. Annual 32-week course starting September. No special qualifications required (although students must be over nineteen years of age, and must be able to speak and write in English). Short courses, masterclasses and seminars also available during summer months.

The National Film School of Denmark, Vognmagergade 10, DK-1120 Copenhagen K. Tel: (45) 33743430. Fax: (45) 33743435.

EGYPT

Higher Film Institute, Academy of Arts, Gamal EL Din El Afaghani Str., Pyramids Ave., Giza. Tel: 537703. Fax: 5611034.

FINLAND

Taideteollinen korkeakoulu, elokuvataiteenlaitos. University of Industrial Arts, Department of Cinema and TV, Pursimiehenkatu, 29-31, SF-00150 Helsinki.

FRANCE

Institut de Formation et d'Enseignement pour les Métiers de L'Image et du Son, 6 rue Francœur, 75018 Paris. Chairman: Jean-Claude Carrière. Director: Christine Juppé-Leblond.

Conservatoire Libre du Cinéma Français (C.I.C.F.), 9 quai de l'Oise, 75019 Paris. Tel: 40 36 19 19..

GERMANY

Deutsche Film- and Fernsehakademie Berlin GmbH, DFFB, Pommernallee 1, 1000 Berlin 19. Director: Prof. Reinhard Hauff. Four-year course dealing with theories of film-making, film-history, and all aspects of practical film and television production; script-writing, direction, camerawork, editing and special effects. Students make films and videos and are encouraged to gain experience in as wide a variety of techniques as possible.

Hochschule für Fernsehen und Film, Frankenthaler Strasse 23, D-81539 München. President: Prof. Dr. Helmut Oeller. Approx. 200 students, 50 staff. Four-year course providing instruction in the theory and practice of film and television. Facilities provide for work in 16 and 35mm as well as video equipment. Studies are free. Two-step admission process; ask for details in January each year. Studies begin each Autumn.

Hochschule für Film und Fernsehen "Konrad Wolf", Karl Marx Strasse 33/34, 14482 Potsdamm. Rector: Prof. Dr. Dieter Wiedemann.

HONG KONG

Hong Kong Academy for Performing Arts, School of Film and Television, 1 Gloucester Road, GPO Box 12288, Wanchai, Hong Kong. Dean: Mr. Don Zirpola. Tel: 2584 8626/8679. Fax: 2802 4372.

HUNGARY

Szinbáz-es Filmmiivészeti Föiskola, Vas u. 2/c, 1088 Budapest. Rector: Péter Huszti. General Secretary: Lászlo Vadász.

INDIA

Film and Television Institute of India, Law College Road, Pune 411 004, India. Director: John Shankaramangalam. Chairman: Mahesh Bhatt. India's premier film school imparts training in five diploma courses: Motion Picture Photography, Audiography, Film Editing, Production Management (Film & TV), Art Direction (Film & TV), and a Post Diploma course in Film Direction. All the courses are of two years duration with an intake of ten students for each course. Training is also given for a short-term six month course in Acting (Film & TV) with an intake of twenty students. The Television wing gives in-service training to employees of Doordarshan, the Indian National Television Network.

IRELAND

European School of Animation, Senior College, Ballyfermot, Dublin 10. Tel: (353) 1626 9421. Fax: (353) 1 626 6754.

ISRAEL

Department of Film and Television, Tel Aviv University, Tel Aviv.

Sam Spiegel Film & Television School - Jerusalem, 4 Yad Harutzim St, Jerusalem. Director: Renen Schorr.

ITALY

Centro Sperimentale di Cinematografia (C.S.C.), Via Tuscolana 1524, 00173 Rome. Director: Angelo Libertini.

Instituto di Storia del Cinema e dello Spettacolo, Universitá di Torino Facoltá di Magistero, Via San'Ottavio 20, 10124 Torino.

JAPAN

Nihon University College of Art, Asahiganoka 2-42, Nerimaku, Tokyo, 176. Head of Film Department: Professor Toru Otake.

NETHERLANDS

Nederlandse Film en Televisie Academie, Ite Boeremastraat 1, 1054 PP Amsterdam. Managing Director: Richard Woolley. 260 students, 60 staff. Four years.

POLAND

Państwowa Wyższa Szkola Filmowa, Telewizyina c Teatralna, im Leona Schillera, ul. Targowa 61/63, 90 323 Lódz. Tel: (42) 743943. Fax: (42) 748 139.

ROMANIA

Academia de Teatru si Film, str. Matei-Volevod nr. 75-77 sect. 2

cod 73226, Bucharest. Dean: Stere Gulea.

RUSSIA

Vserossuyski Gosudarstvenni Institut Kinematografi (VGIK) (All-Union State Institute of Cinematography), ulitsa Vilgelma Pika 3, Moscow 129226. Fax: (95) 187 7174.

SERBIA & MONTENEGRO

Fakultet dramskih umetnosti (pozorišta, filma, radija i televizije), Bulevar umetnosti 20, 11070 Belgrade. Tel: (381 11) 135 684. Fax: (38 11) 130 862.

SPAIN

University of Valladolid, Cátedra de Historia y Estética de la Cinematografica, 47002, Valladolid. Tel: (983) 423611. Fax: (983) 423007. Director: Sr. Dr. Francisco Javier de la Plaza.

SWEDEN

Department of Film Studies, University of Stockholm, Filmhuset, Borgvägen 1-5, Box 27062, S-102 51 Stockholm.

Dramatiska Institutet (College of Theatre, Film, Radio and Television), Borgvägen, Box 27090, S-102 51 Stockholm. Head of School: Kjell Grede. Formed in 1970, the Institute is intended to provide instruction in production techniques for theatre, film, radio and television. The Institute is equipped with film and TV studios, 10 editing rooms for 8, 16 and 35mm, and 4 video editing rooms with S-VHS,2 video editing rooms with Light Work, 1 on-line editing room with M II, sound mixing studios and portable video equipment.

U.K.

Bristol University, Department of Drama, Film and Television Studies, Cantocks Close, Woodland Road, Bristol BS8 1UP. Tel: (0117) 928 7838. Fax: (0117) 928 8251.

University of Derby, Kedleston Road, Derby DE22 1GB. Director of Studies: John Fullerton. MA/FT/PT in Film with Television Studies. BA(Hons) – subject to validation.

University of Westminster, Harrow School of Design and Media, Northwick Park, Harrow, HA1 3TP.

London International Film School, 24 Shelton Street, London WC2H 9HP. Principal: Martin M. Amstell. The School offers a practical, two-year Diploma course to professional levels, accredited by the British film technicians' union – B.E.C.T.U. Approximately half each term is devoted to film production and half to practical and theoretical tuition. All students work on one or more films each term and are encouraged to interchange unit roles termly to experience different skill areas. Facilities include two cinemas, two shooting stages, two rehearsal stages and fifteen cutting rooms. Equipment includes 16mm and 35mm Panavision, Arriflex and rostrum cameras, Nagra recorders, Steenbeck editing machines and U-matic video. Tuition is by permanent and visiting professionals. Entrance requirements: a degree or an art or technical diploma. Lesser qualifications accepted in cases of special ability or experience. All applicants must submit examples of their work and be proficient in English. New courses commence each January, April and September.

Middlesex Polytechnic, Faculty of Art and Design, Cat Hill, Barnet, Herts EN4 8HT. Tel: (0181) 368 1299.

National Film and Television School, Station Road, Beaconsfield, Bucks, HP9 1LG. Tel: (01494) 671234. Fax: (01494) 674042. Director: Henning Camre.

Newport Film School, Faculty of Art and Design, Gwent College of Higher Education, Clarence Place, Newport, Gwent NP9 0UW.

Northern School of Film and Television, Leeds Metropolitan University, 2-8 Merrion Way, Leeds LS2 8BT. Tel: (113) 283 3193. Fax: (113) 283 3194.

University of Westminster, School of Communication, 18/22 Riding House Street, London W1P 7PD. M.A. in Film and Television Studies; advanced level part-time course (evenings and weekends) concerned with theoretical aspects of film and TV. Modular credit accumulation scheme. Postgraduate Certificate normally awarded after one year (40 credits), Postgraduate Diploma after two years (70 credits), M.A. after three years (120 credits, including research thesis). Modules offered: Authorship and Mise-en-Scène, Structuralism and Genre, Realism and Anti-Realism. The Film and TV Audience; Film, Culture and Society; Hollywood 1900-1940, British Cinema 1927-1947, British TV Drama, The Documentary Tradition, Public Service Broadcasting, TV Genres and Gender, Psychoanalysis and Cinema, Third World Cinema, Soviet Cinema of the 1920's and 1930's, Production Studies, Issues in British Film Culture, Modernism and Postmodernism, Women and Film Narrative, European Cinema since 1945, Techniques of Film Art. No practical component. Course leader: Dr Robert E. Peck.

Royal College of Art, Department of Film and Television, Kensington Gore, London SW7 2EU. 35 students.

The Surrey Institute of Art and Design, Farnham Campus, Falkner Road, Farnham, Surrey GU9 7DS. Tel: (01252) 722 441.

University of East Anglia, School of English and American Studies, Norwich NR4 7TJ.

University of Stirling, Film and Media Studies, Stirling FK9 4LA. Head of Department: Professor P.R. Schlesinger.

URUGUAY

Escuela de Cinematografia, Chucarro 1036, CP 11300 Montevideo. Tel: 776389. Fax: 494572.

U.S.A.

Information on the many thousands of U.S. film courses is contained in the *American Film Institute's Guide to College Courses in Film and Television* which can be ordered at Publications, The American Film Institute, 2021 North Western Avenue, Los Angeles, California 90027.

FILM ARCHIVES

Note: each year we write to all Archives listed in this section. Those who respond will usually find most of the data they submit included in their entry. We can no longer print suspect data year after year without confirmation from the appropriate archive.

ARGENTINA

Cinemateca Argentina, Corrientes 2092, 2nd floor, 1045 Buenos Aires. Tel: (54-1) 953 3755/953 7163. Fax: (54-1) 951.8558. Executive Director: Mrs. Paulina Fernandez Jurado. Established in 1949. Stock: 11,700 film titles, 6,100 books, collection of film periodicals, 352,000 film stills, 6,600 film posters. The collection of micro-filmed clippings holds files on individual films, and on foreign and Argentine film personalities. The library is open to researchers and students. The Cinemateca operates one film theatre with daily screenings.

AUSTRALIA

Archives office of Tasmania, 77 Murray Street, Hobart, Tasmania, Australia 7000. Tel: (02) 491 411. Fax: (02) 492 816. State Archivist: Ian Pearce. Stock: 1,500 titles relating to Tasmania.

National Film and Sound Archive, McCoy Circuit, Acton, Canberra A.C.T. 2601. Tel: (61-6) 209 3111. Fax: (61-6) 209 3165. Director: Ron Brent. Deputy Director: Ray Edmondson. The Archive has assembled a collection of more than one million items including discs, audio and video tapes, films, photographs, cylinders, piano rolls and artefacts, and a further one million items of documentation.

State Film Archives, Library and Information Service of Western Australia, Alexander Library Building, Perth Cultural Centre, Perth, WA 6,000. Tel: (619) 427 3310. Film Archivist: Robin Faulkner. Stock: 1,800 film titles.

AUSTRIA

Österreichisches Filmarchiv, A-1010 Vienna, Rauhensteingasse 5. Film stores and theatre; Laxenburg, Altes Schloss. Tel: 5129936. Fax: 513 5330.

Österreichisches Filmmuseum, A-1010 Vienna, Augustinerstr. 1. Tel: 533 70 54-0. Fax: 533 70 56 25. Directors: Peter Konlechner and Prof. Peter Kubelka. Stock: app. 10,000 film titles, and an extensive library.

BELGIUM

Cinémathèque Royale, 23 rue Ravenstein, 1000 Brussels. Tel: (2) 5078370. Fax: (2) 513 1272.

BRAZIL

Cinemateca Brasileira, Caixa Postal 12900, 04092 São Paulo. Tel: 577 4666. Fax: 577 7433. Director: Thomaz Farkaz.

Cinemateca do Museu de Arte Moderna, Caixa Postal 44, CEP 20021, Rio de Janeiro, RJ. Tel: (021) 2102188. Telex: 21-22084 FTVRBR. Director: João Luiz Vieira.

BULGARIA

Bulgarska Nacionalna Filmoteka, ul. Gourko 36,1000 Sofia. Tel: (359 2) 87 37 40, 87 13 92. Fax: (359 2) 87 60 04.

CANADA

La Cinémathèque Québécoise, 335 boul de Maisonneuve est. Montréal, Québec H2X 1K1.Tel: (514) 842 9763. Curator: Robert Daudelin.

Conservatoire d'Art Cinématographique de Montréal, 1455 de Maisonneuve West, Montréal, Québec. Director: Serge Losique.

National Archives of Canada, Visual and Sound Archives, 344 Wellington Street, Room 1036, Ottawa, Ontario, K1A 0N3. Tel: (613) 9966009. Fax: (613) 995 6575. Director: Betty Kidd.

CHINA

Cinémathèque Chinoise, 25B rue Xin Wai, Beijing. Tel: 2014316. Telex: 22195.

CZECH REPUBLIC

Národní filmový archiv, Malešicka ul, CS-1300 00 Praha 3. Tel and Fax: 894501. Curator: Vladimir Opéla.

DENMARK

Det Danske Filmmuseum, Gothersgade 55, DK-1123 Copenhagen K. Director: Ib Monty. Stock: 18,000 film titles, 48,000 books, 350 periodicals subscribed to, 1,950,000 film stills, 18,000 posters, 158-seat cinema used for three daily screenings and for researchers and students. The Museum also publishes a magazine, "Kosmorama", and a year book.

EGYPT

National Archive of Egyptian Film, c/o Egyptian Film Centre, City of Arts, Pyramids Road, Giza, Egypt. Tel: 585801/5850897. Fax: 585701 Curator: Abdel Ghani Daoud.

FINLAND

Suomen elokuva-arkisto, Pursimiehenkatu 29-31 A, P.O. Box 177, SF-00150 Helsinki. Tel: (358) 0 615400. Fax: (358).0.615 40 242. Director: Matti Lukkarila. Stock: 7,200 feature film titles, 19,000 shorts and advertising film (spots), 18,000 video cassettes, 18,500 books, 140 magazines (currently subscribed), 9,500 dialogue lists and scripts, 326,000 different stills, 110,000 posters and 41,000 documentation files. The archive arranges regular screenings in Helsinki and eight other cities.

FRANCE

Cinémathèque Française, 29 rue du Colisée, 75008 Paris. President: Jean Rouch.

Cinémathèque de Toulouse, rue de Faubourg Bonnefoy 12, 31500 Toulouse, France. Tel: (33) 61 48 90 75. Fax: (33) 61 58 19 79. President/Curator: Guy-Claude Rochemont.

Cinémathèque Universitaire, UFR d'Art et d'Archéologie, 3 rue Michelet, 75006 Paris.

Institut Lumière, 25 rue du Premier-Film, 69008 Lyon. Tel: 78 78 18 95. President: Bertrand Tavernier.

Musée du Cinéma de Lyon, 69 rue Jean Jaurès. 69100 Villeurbanne. Tel: 7853 27 69. President: Paul Génard. Stock: 1,600 film titles, 1,000 film stills, 50 posters.

Service des Archives du Film du Centre National de la Cinématographie, 7 bis rue Alexandre Turpault, 78392 Bois d'Arcy Cedex. Tel: 30 14 80 00. Fax: 34 60 52 25.

GERMANY

Arsenal/Kino der Freunde der Deutschen Kinemathek, Welserstrasse 25, 10777 Berlin. Tel: (30) 213 6039. Fax: (30) 218 4281. The nearest equivalent of Britain's NFT. Programming: Ulrich and Erika Gregor , Milena Gregor. The Freunde also run a non-commercial distribution of about 800 films, most of them from the International Forum, the independent second main programme of the Berlin Film Festival, organised by the Freunde.

Bundesarchiv-Filmarchiv, Fehrbelliner Platz 3, 10707 Berlin. Tel: (49-30) 86811. Fax: (49-30) 868 1310.

Deutsches Filmmuseum Frankfurt am Main, Schaumainkai 41, 60596 Frankfurt am Main. Tel: (69) 212 38830. Fax: (69) 212 37881. Director: Prof Walter Schobert. Deputy Director and Film Archive: Claudia Dillmann.

Deutsches Institut für Filmkunde, Schaumainkai 41, 60596 Frankfurt am Main. Tel: (69) 961 2200. Telefax: (69) 620060. Director: Dr. Gerd Albrecht. Administrative Director: Helmut Possmann. Stock: 4,200 film titles, 54,000 books, 260 periodicals, 1,000,000 film stills, 30,000 posters, 16,000 dialogue lists, 5,000 scripts. Also programmes, newspaper clippings, advertising material.

Münchner Stadtmuseum/Filmmuseum, St. Jakobsplatz 1, D-80331 München. Tel: (49) 89233 22348. Fax: (49) 89 233 239 31. Director: Dr. Jan-Christopher Horak. Founded in 1963, this municipal film archive runs a daily cinema programme. Film archive holds approx. 5,000 titles, including many restored silent German film classics, New German cinema, and the Orson Welles Collection. Estate holdings from G. W. Pabst, Dr. Arnold Fanck etc. Library holds over 6,000 film books, 10,000 film periodicals.

Stiftung Deutsche Kinemathek, Pommernallee 1, 14052 Berlin. Tel: 30307234. Fax: 3029294. Director: Hans Helmut Prinzler. Stock: 8,000 film titles, 1,500,000 film stills, 15,000 posters, 60,000 film programmes, 10,000 scripts etc. The Kinemathek's library of books and periodicals is amalgamated with that of the Deutsche Film-und-Fernsehakademie-Berlin, in the same building.

HUNGARY

Magyar Filmintézet, Budakeszi ut 51b, 1021 Budapest. Tel: (36 1) 1767106. Director: Vera Gyürey. Stock: 7,022 feature titles, 8,713 short films, 3,756 newsreels, 13,224 books, 3,710 periodicals, 2,708 scripts, 5,381 manuscripts, 143,159 stills, 15,365 posters. The institute, besides housing the archive, also does research into the history of the cinema, particularly the Hungarian cinema, and encourages the development of film culture in Hungary.

Szinház-és Filmmüvészeti Főiskola, Vas utca 2/c, Budapest 1088. Tel: (361) 1384 749. Fax: (361) 1294 790. Rector: Péter Huszti. General Secretary: Lajos Tiszeker.

ICELAND

Kvikmyndasafn Islands (Icelandic Film Archive), Laugavegur 24, 101 Reykjavík. (Postal: P.O. Box 320, 121 Reykjavík.) Tel: 10940. Fax: 627171. Nearly 400 titles in the collection, documentaries being the larger part of it. Numerous sources of information regarding Icelandic films and the national film history.

INDIA

National Film Archive of India, Ministry of Information and Broadcasting, Government of India, Law College Road, Poona 411 004, India. Tel: 331 559. Director: Suresh Chabria. Stock: 12,922 films, 1069 video cassettes, 20,935 books, 152 periodicals, 21,403 scripts, 7,287 pamphlets/folders, 136,273 press clippings, 97,989 stills, 3,236 slides, 6,410 wall posters, 6,252 song booklets, 1,858 disc records, 153 audio tapes, 1,957 micro films, 42 microfiches, 209 pre-recorded cassettes.

IRAN

National Iranian Film Archive, Baharestan Square, Tehran. Tel: 324 1601. Director: Mohammad Hassan Khoshnevis.

ISRAEL

Israel Film Archive/Jerusalem Cinémathèque, PO Box 8561, Jerusalem 91083, Israel. Tel: (972) 2 724 131. Fax: (972) 2 733 076. Director: Lia van Leer. Stock: 18,000 prints – international, Israeli, Jewish film collections. Books, periodicals, stills, posters and scripts. Israeli and Jewish film documentation and educational programme for school children and adults. Permanent exhibition of early cinema apparatus and cinema memorabilia. Organisers of the Jerusalem Film Festival.

Tel Aviv Cinémathèque (The Doron Cinema Centre), 2 Sprintzak Street, Tel Aviv. PO Box 20370, Tel Aviv 61203. Tel: (03) 6917181-8. Fax: (03) 6962841. Director: Alon Garbuz. Stock: 12,000 video cassettes, 5,000 books, periodicals, stills, posters, scripts. 1,500 screenings yearly, various activities, lectures and seminars for the general public, and special morning educational programmes for schools.

ITALY

Cineteca del Friuli, 26 via Osoppo, 33013 Gemona del Friuli (Udine). Tel: (0432) 980458. Fax: (0432) 970 542. Established in 1977, this excellent Italian archive conceived the idea for the Pordenone Silent Film Festival, and organises regular screenings. Stock: 2,000 film titles, 3,000 newsreels, 10,000 books.

Cineteca Italiana, Via Palestro 16, 20121 Milano. Tel: 799224. Sec. General: Gianni Comencini.

Cineteca Nazionale, Via Tuscolana n. 1524, 00173 Rome. Tel: 722941. Fax: 7211619. Director: Angelo Libertini.

Museo Internazionale del Cinema e dello Spettacolo, Casella Postale 6104, 00195 Rome. Tel: 370 0266. Fax: 397 33 297

JAPAN

Kawakita Memorial Film Institute, (Japan Film Library Council), 18 Ichibancho, Chiyoda-ku, Tokyo. President: Masayo Okada (Mrs.).

National Filmcenter, 7-6, 3 chome, Kyobashi, Chuoku, Tokyo. Curator: Masaioshi Ohba.

LATVIA

Riga Film Museum, P.O. Box 391, Kraslavas str. 22. LV1047, Riga. Tel: (0132) 220282.

LUXEMBOURG

Cinémathèque Municipale de la Ville de Luxembourg, 19 rue de la Chapelle, L-1325 Luxembourg. Tel: (352) 4796-2644. Fax: (352) 4593 75. Curator: Fred Junck.

MEXICO

Cinemateca Luis Buñuel, Calle 5, Oriente 5, Apdo. Postal 255, Puebla, Pue. Curator: Fernando Osorio Alarcon.

Cinemateca Mexicana, Museo Nacional de Antropologia, Calzada M. Gandhi, México 6, D.F. Director: Galdino Gomez Gomez.

Cineteca Nacional, Av. Mexico-Coyoacán 389, Col. Xoco 03330 Mexico. Tel: 688 8814. Telex: 1760050 RTCME. Director: Mario Aguiñaga. Mexico's main film archive, sup-ported by the Federal government. Deputy Director: Alberto Zuckermann. Stock: 5,600 films, 100,000 stills, 4,000 posters, 5,000 books, 1,300 scripts and 6 film theatres.

Direccion General de Actividades Cinematograficas UNAM, San Ildefonso 43 Centro, 06020 Mexico, D.F. Tel: (525 7) 04 37 00. Fax: (525 7) 02 45 03. General Director: Biol. Ivan Trujillo Bolio. Stock: 16,000 film titles, 203,060 stills, 6,179 posters, 83,479 lobby cards, 9,739 books, 2,182 original scripts, 37 subscriptions to film periodicals, 5 film theatres and 200 apparati dating from 1880 to 1969.

NETHERLANDS

Stichting Nederlands Filmmuseum, Vondelpark 3, 1071 AA Amsterdam. Tel: (020) 5981 400. Fax: (020) 6833401. Director: Hoos Blotkamp. Deputy Director: Eric de Kuyper.

Audiovisual Archive of the Netherlands Government Information Service, PO Box 20.009, 2500 EA The Hague, Tel: (3170) 3564106/4110. Fax: (3170) 3647756. Head: Mr Robert Egeter-van Kuyk.

NEW ZEALAND

The New Zealand Film Archive, P.O. Box 11-449, cnr. Cable Street and Jervois Quay, Wellington. Tel: 3847647. Fax: 382 9595. Telex: 30386.

NORWAY

Henie-Onstad Art Centre, 1311 Hovikodden, Oslo. Director: Per Hovdenakk.

Det Norske FIlminstituttet, Militærhospitalet, Grev Wedels plass, Postboks 482, Sentrum, 0105 Oslo 1. Tel: (47 22) 428740. Fax: (47 22) 332277. Telex: 11619. DIrector: Erling Dale. Curator: Nils Klevjer. Head of Cinémathèque: Kjell Billing. Stock: 13,000 film titles, 15,000 books, 130 periodicals and a large collection of stills and posters. Also over five hundred pieces of early cinema apparatus and a fine theatre for screening films. The cinémathèque of the film institute is run in co-operation with the organisation "The Friends of the NFI".

SOUTH AFRICAN NATIONAL FILM, VIDEO AND SOUND ARCHIVE

The aims of this Archive are the acquisition, preservation, storage, adaptation and supply of available films, video and sound material of archival value, with specific reference to South Africa. Further, to provide an information service with regard to film, video, sound material and photographs.

It is a division of the State Archives of the Department of Arts, Culture, Science and Technology.

Private Bag X236
PRETORIA
0001
South Africa

Fax +27 12 3445143

PANAMA

Cinemateca del GECU, Universidad de Panama, Apartado 6-1775, El Dorado, Panama. Tel: (507) 223 9324. Fax: (507) 264 2737. Stock includes films, books, periodicals, film stills and posters. It has a small theatre with three daily screenings. Director: Roberto Enrique King.

POLAND

Filmoteka Narodowa, ul. Pulawska 61, 00-975 Warszawa. Tel: 455074. Fax: 455074. Telex: 813640.

Muzeum Kinematografii, Pl Zwyciestwa 1, 90312 Lódź. Tel: 740957.

PORTUGAL

Cinemateca Portuguesa, Rua Barata Salgueiro 39-1200 Lisboa. Tel: 546279/547732. Fax: 3523180. Director: João Bénard da Costa.

RUSSIA

Gosfilmofond of Russia, Belye Stolby, Moskovskaia oblast. Tel: 546 05 16, 546 05 13.Telex: 411700 LASTI 007913.

SOUTH AFRICA

South African National Film, Video and Sound Archives, Private Bag X236, Pretoria 0001. Enormous variety of 35mm and 16mm footage, video and sound material as well as stills, scripts, books, posters and other material. The Archive is a State controlled organisation, dedicated to the classification and preservation of all items relating to the film, video and sound industries.

SPAIN

Filmoteca Española, Carretera Dehesa de la Villa, s/n. 28040 Madrid. Tel: 549 00 11. Fax: 549 73 48. Director: José María Prado.

Filmoteca de la Generalitat de Catalunya, Diputació 279-281, Barcelona 08007. Tel: 488 1038. Fax: 487 4192. Director: Antoni Kirchner. Stock: 9,000 film titles, 10,500 books, 8,000 videos, 1,000 magazine titles, 3,500 stillls, 30,000 photographs. Three daily screenings in Cinema Aquitània. Publishes monographs and brochures.

Biblioteca de Cinema "Delmiro de Caralt", Rambla de Catalunya, 81 pral. 08008 - Barcelona. Tel: (343) 215 1069. Fax: (343) 487 "50 76.

SWEDEN

Asta Nielsen Filmmuseum, Vapenkroken 29, S-226 47. Lund. Established in 1946 by G.D. Postén, Head of the Film History section at the Dept. of History, University of Lund. This is one of the biggest, private, non-commercial international collections of published, written materials on motion pictures and the film industry. Included in the collection are stills, programmes, books, magazines, posters, historical materials, etc. with the emphasis on the silent screen. Also the most complete collection of material on Asta Nielsen.

Cinemateket, Svenska Filminstitutet. Filmhuset, Box 27126, S-102 52 Stockholm. Tel: (46-8) 665 1100. Fax: (46 8) 6611820. Curator: Rolf Lindfors. Head of Documentation: Margareta Nordström. Stock: 15,700 film titles, 40,000 books, 250 subscriptions to periodicals, 1,500,000 film stills, 31,000 posters, and unpublished script material on 7,200 foreign films and 1,800 Swedish films.The collection of microfilmed clippings holds 52,000 jackets on individual films, 15,500 jackets on film personalities and jackets on general subjects classified by the FIAF scheme. Cinemateket has two theatres and four daily screenings in Stockholm. A selection of the yearly programme is also shown in Göthenburg and Malmö.

SWITZERLAND

Cinémathèque Suisse, 3 Allée Ernest Ansermet, 1003 Lausanne. Tel: 3310101. Fax: 3204888. Curator: Hervé Dumont. Stock: 25,000 titles (300,000 reels), 260 apparati, 35,000 posters, 300,000 film references, 15,000 books, and 1,000,000 stills. Three projections each day.

THAILAND

The National Film Archive of Thailand, 4 Chao Fa Road, Bangkok 10200. Tel: 282 0170/282 1847. Director: Penpan Jarernport.

TURKEY

Turkish Fllm and Television Institute, 80700 Kislaönü-Besiktas, Istanbul. Tel: (212) 266 1096. Fax: (212) 211 6599. Director: Prof. Sami Sekeroğlu. The Institute is a science and art centre which is engaged in education, research and archiving on cinema and television. Stock: 6,000 film titles, 3,500 video titles. Library of books, periodicals, newspaper clippings and photos available to researchers. Price list available upon request

U.K.

Imperial War Museum, Lambeth Road, London SE1 6HZ. Tel: (0171) 416 5000. Fax: (0171) 4165379. Keeper of the Film and Video Archive: Roger Smither. Deputy: Paul Sargent. Stock: over 40 million feet of actuality film relating to conflict in the Twentieth Century, from Britain and other countries. Viewing facilities for students and researchers *by appointment only*; public film screenings.

National Film and Television Archive, 21 Stephen Street, London W1P 1LN. Tel: (0171) 255 1444. Fax: (0171) 580 7503. Curator: Clyde Jeavons. Deputy Curator: Anne Fleming. Stock: 275,000 film and television titles, over 5,000,000 black-and-white stills, 700,000 colour transparencies, 18,000 posters, 2,500 set-designs. Viewing service for students and researchers, production library for film-makers.

The Scottish Film Archive, Scottish Film Council, 74 Victoria Crescent Road, Dowanhill, Glasgow G12 9JN. Tel: (0141) 334 4445. Fax: (0141) 334 8132.

URUGUAY

Cinemateca Uruguaya, Lorenzo Carnelli 1311, Casilla de Correo 1170, Montevideo. Tel: 482460, 494 572. Fax: 494 572. Curator: M. Martinez Carril.

U.S.A.

Academy of Motion Picture Arts and Sciences, Centre for Motion Picture Study, Academy Film Archive, 333 South La Cienega Blvd., Beverly Hills, California 90211. Director: Michael Friend. Curator: Daniel Woodruff.

American Cinematheque, 1717 N. Highland Ave. (at Hollywood Blvd.), Hollywood 90028. Executive Director: Barbara Zicka Smith. A viewer supported arts organisation dedicated *exclusively* to the public exhibition of film and video. State-of-the-art theatres, galeries and gathering places (including a café and bookstore) scheduled to open in 1995. Meanwhile, regular film and video programming for the public is underway now at the new Directors Guild theatre complex in Hollywood.

American Film Institute/National Center for Film and Video Preservation, John F. Kennedy Center for the Performing Arts, Washington, DC 20566. Archivist: Susan Dalton.

George Eastman House/ International Museum of Photography and Film, 900 East Avenue, Rochester, N.Y. 14607. Tel: (716) 271 3361 Fax: (716) 271 3970. Senior Curator of Film: Dr. Paolo Cherchi Usai.

Harvard Film Archive, Carpenter Center for the Visual Arts, Harvard Univ, 24 Quincy Street, Cambridge, MA 02138. Tel: (617) 4954700. Curator: Vlada Petrić. Films (16mm and 35mm); 4,000 titles, including the Film Study Center collection (Robert Gardner, Producer/Director).

The Library of Congress, Motion Picture, Broadcasting and Recorded Sound Division, Washington, DC 20540. Tel: (202) 707 5840. Fax: (202) 707 2371. Telex: 64198. Chief: Devid Francis.

Museum of Modern Art, Department of Film and Video, 11 West 53rd Street, New York, NY 10019. Tel:(212) 708 9602. Telex: 62370. Chief Curator: Mary Lea Bandy. Curators: Adrienne Mancia, Larry Kardish. Stock: 12,000 film titles, 2,500 books, 250 periodicals, 4,000,000 film stills. The excellent research and screening facilities of the department are available to serious students only by appointment with the supervisor, Charles Silver; 1,000 of its films are available for rental, sale, and lease. Stills Archive open by appointment with Mary Corliss.

National Museum of Natural History/Human Studies Film Archives, Rm E307, 123 Smithsonian Institution, Washington DC 20560. Tel: (202)357-3349. Fax: (202) 357 2208. Director: John P. Homiak.

Pacific Film Archive, University Art Museum, 2625 Durant Avenue, Berkeley, California 94720.

UCLA Film and Television Archive, 302 East Melnitz Hall, University of California, 405 Hilgard Avenue, Los Angeles, CA 90024. Tel: (310) 206 8013. Fax: (310) 206 3129.

The Wisconsin Center for Film and Theater Research, 816 State Street, Madison, Wisconsin 53706. Tel: (608) 264 6466. Fax: (608) 2646472. Head of Archive: Maxine Fleckner Ducey.

Jugoslovenska Kinoteka, Knez Mihailova 19, 11000 Belgrade. Tel: 622 555, 550 471 (Archive). Fax: 622 587, 555 015 (Archive). Director: Radoslav Zelenović Head of Archive: Stevan Jovičić. Programme Director: Dinko Tucaković.

Stock Footage Libraries

The following is a listing of the major U.S. independent stock footage libraries.

Archive Films/Archive Photos, 530 West 25th Street, New York, NY 10001. Tel: (212) 620 3955. Fax: (212) 645 2137. Archive Films/ Archive Photos is a leading historical image library with more than 14,000 hours of stock footage including newsreels, TV news, Hollywood feature films, silent films, documentaries, and vintage industrial and educational films. In addition, it represents special collections such as The March of Time, The RKO/Pathe Library, The Prelinger Collection of American Life, Culture and Industry, and The Gaumont Newsreel, among others. All footage in Archive's collection has been transferred to time-coded screening video cassettes for screening purposes, and catalogued shot-by-shot on a computer database. Archive has its own in-house film-to-tape transfer facility and can provide footage on a variety of digital formats. Archive licenses its footage through offices in New York, London, Paris, Cologne, Stockholm, Milan, Amsterdam, and Tokyo. Archive Photos has over 20,000,000 photographs, engravings and drawings spanning 3,000 years of world history and growing daily with up-to-the-minute news and celebrity photos.

Film Bank, 425 South Victory Blvd, Burbank, CA 91502. Tel: (818) 841 9176. Fax: (818) 5674235. President: Paula Lumbard. Film and video stock footage library.

Producers Library Service, 1051 North Cole Avenue, Hollywood, CA 90038. Tel: (213) 465 0572. Fax: (213) 465 1671. Houses more than 5 million feet of 35mm colour film from the 1950's to the present, 1 million feet of 16mm colour film from the 1940's and 1950's, and more than 1 million feet of 35mm black-and-white film from the 'teens through the 1940's; it represents stock footage from the productions of ABC Circle and Orion, specialises in Hollywood history and has direct access to stock footage from all Hollywood studios.

Sherman Grinberg Film Libraries, Inc., 630 Ninth Avenue, New York, NY 10036. Tel: (212) 765 5170. Fax: (212) 262 1532. Also, 1040 North McCadden Place, Hollywood, CA 90038. Tel: (213) 464 7491. Fax: (213) 462 5352.

FILM BOOKSHOPS POSTERS & RECORDS

Australia

Electric Shadows Bookshop,
City Walk, Akuna Street, Canberra, ACT 2601. Tel: (61) 62488352. Fax: (61) 62471230.

Readings Records and Books,
P.O. Box 482, South Yarra 3141. Tel: (03) 867-1885.

Soft Focus,
P.O. Box 508, Hawthorn, Victoria 3122.
Free catalogue available listing movie books, magazines, posters, and memorabilia.

Canada

Theatrebooks,
11 St. Thomas Street, Toronto, M5S 2B7. Tel: (416) 922-7175. Fax: (416) 922 0739.
Founded first as a source of theatre, opera, and dance books. Theatrebooks has since 1982 also developed a first-class film book collection. Worldwide mail order is handled.

Lux,
5220 boul. St-Laurent, Montréal.
Large stock of European movie posters. Open daily 10 a.m. to 4 p.m.

France

Atmosphère, Librairie du Cinéma,
10 rue Broca, 75005 Paris. Tel: 43 31 02 71. Fax: 43 31 03 69.
Atmosphère offers a wide range of film publications, with a large stock of stills, postcards, posters of new and old movies, of all origins and sizes. Also back issues of magazines. Open every day except Sunday, from 2 p.m. to 8 p.m. Atmosphère sets up shop during the Cannes Festival, too.

Cinédoc,
45-53 Passage Jouffroy, 75009 Paris.
Posters, books, stills, pressbooks, magazines, etc.

Ciné-Folie,
14 rue des Frères-Pradignac, 06400 Cannes. Tel: 93.39.22.99.
Stills, books, posters, postcards.

Cinémagence,
12 rue Saulnier, 75009 Paris. Tel: 42.46.21.21. Fax: 42.46.20.20.
Stills, posters, magazines, books. Mail Order service. Free catalogue.

Contacts Champs Elysées,
24 rue du Colisée, 75008 Paris. Tel: (1) 43.59.17.71. Fax: (1) 42.89.27.65.
Cinema bookshop established 40 years ago in the area of the Champs Elysées close to the film production companies. Amply stocked with French and foreign-language books on technique, theory, history, and director monographs. Also magazines. Reliable mail order service. Free "new acquisitions" list. Open year round.

Le Réverbère,
4 rue Neuve, 69002 Lyon.

Germany

Buchhandlung Walther König,
Ehrenstr. 4, 50672 Köln. Tel: (221) 20 59 60. Fax: (221) 205 9640.
Offers a comprehensive catalogue of international titles in the film department, also useful antiquarian section.

Buchhandlung Langenkamp,
Beckergrube 19, D-2400 Lübeck. Tel: (0541) 76479.

H. Lindemanns Book Shop,
Nadlerstrasse 4 + 10, D-70173 Stuttgart 1. Tel. (711) 233 499. Fax: (711) 236 9672.
Photography and film literature.

Sautter & Lackmann,
Filmbuchhandlung, Admiralitätstr. 71/72, 20459 Hamburg. Postfach 11 04 31, 20404 Hamburg. Tel: (40) 37 31 96. Fax: (40) 36 54 79.
Books, posters, programmes, videos, rare items etc.

Marga Schoeller Bücherstube,
Knesebeckstr. 33, D-10623 Berlin. Tel: (030) 8811122. Fax: (30) 881 8479.
One of the fabled literary haunts of western Europe, Marga Schöller's shop is justly proud of its film book selection.

contacts
Librairie du Cinéma
24, RUE DU COLISEE 75008 PARIS
TEL. (1) 43 59 17 71

A PARIS
La meilleure librairie du CINEMA,
internationalement Vôtre,
avec des livres et des revues du monde entier.
Tél. : (1) 43 59 17 71 - Fax : (1) 42 89 27 65

ATMOSPHERE

10 Rue Broca, 75005 Paris

Métro: Censier. Tél: +33 (0) 1 43 31 02 71.

Fax: +33 (0) 1 43 31 03 69

Open daily: 11 am / 7 pm.

Credit cards welcome. Please Note New Address

LIBRAIRIE DE CINEMA

Verlag für Filmschriften Christian Unucka,
Am Kramerberg 7A, D-85241 Hebertshausen. Tel: (08131) 13922. Fax: (08131) 10075.
Books, posters, programmes, stills, postcards, videos, rare items, etc.

Italy

Libreria dello Spettacolo,
via Terraggio 11, 20123 Milan. Tel: (02) 864 51730.
"Il Leuto",
via Di Monte Brianzo 86, 00186 Rome. Tel: (06) 656 9269.

Spain

El Espectador,
Consejo de Ciento 475 bis, 08013 Barcelona. Tel: (93) 231 65 16.
Specialising in cinema and video books, magazines, etc.
Filmoteca Española, Cine Doré,
Santa Isabel 3, Madrid.
Well-stocked bookstore dealing with movie topics.
R. Seriña,
Calle Aribau 114, Barcelona 11.
A specialist collection of books, photos, magazines, press books, posters and programmes on sale to the public in Spain and abroad.

Sweden

The Pic's,
Placehuset Brunnsparken, S Hamngatan 2, 411 06 Goteborg. Tel/Fax: (31) 151412.
Film and music posters, photos and postcards, t-shirts. Postal service available.

Switzerland

Filmbuchhandlung Hans Rohr,
Oberdorfstr. 3, CH-8024 Zurich. Tel: (01) 251 36 36. Fax: (01) 251 33 44.
In its long-established existence, Hans Rohr has offered an efficient and reliable service when it comes to dealing with mail order inquiries for literally any film book or magazine in print.
Librairie du Cinéma,
9 rue de la Terrassière, CH-1207 Genève. Tel: (022) 736.8888. Fax: (022) 736 6616.
Immaculate display of posters, books, stills, film postcards, soundtrack CD's, and videos. A veritable treasure trove for the movie buff. Closed Monday mornings.

U.K.

The Cinema Bookshop,
13-14 Great Russell Street, London WC1. Tel: (0171) 637.0206. Fax: (0171) 436 9979.
Fred Zentner's film bookshop close to the British Museum has succeeded by virtue of prompt and friendly service, and an eye for rare items.
The Cinema Store
Unit 4b, Orion House, Upper St. Martin's Lane, London WC2H 9EJ. Tel: (171) 379 7838. Fax: (171) 240 7689.
Fine selection of mags, toys and models, laser discs, posters etc. in Paul McEvoy and Neil Palmer's well-stocked and friendly store, recently moved to brighter new premises in central London. Mail order catalogue £1.

READ & LISTEN & INTERACT!

CINEMA IS ALSO MUSIC.
LISTEN TO CINEMA.

C.A.M. ORIGINAL SOUNDTRACKS from the golden years of Italian and French cinema.
Over 170 titles and 75 composers available on compact disc.
Ask for our catalog. Also available on CD-ROM.

CAM Original Soundtracks **VIA COLA DI RIENZO, 152 - 00192 ROME (ITALY) - FAX:(+39-6) 687.4046**

NATIONAL FILM THEATRE BOOKSHOP

Europe's definitive supplier of books on cinema, television and media

national FILM theatre NFT

A wide range of art-house videos
Specialist mail-order service world-wide
Foreign imports and periodicals

bfi on the South Bank

Telephone enquiries welcome 0171-815 1343

Open daily 10.00am-9pm
NFT Bookshop, National Film Theatre,
Southbank, Waterloo, London SE1 8XT

THE REEL POSTER GALLERY

First Floor, 22 Great Marlborough Street,
London W1V 1AF
Tel: (+44) 0171 734 4303
Fax: (+44) 0171 734 4260

Original Vintage Film Posters

Fully archived, colour illustrated catalogues are available.
Four catalogue subscription £25 within EC; £30 non-EC.

Cox, A.E.,
21 Cecil Rd., Itchen, Southampton SO19 2HX. Tel: (01703) 447989.
This long-established dealer specialises in books, magazines, and ephemera on both theatre and cinema. A catalogue (Stage & Screen) of out-of-print items is published four times yearly.

Film Magic,
The Business Centre, Colne Way, Watford, Herts.
Mail order service for colour and black-and-white stills of film and TV stars, plus books, magazines and posters.

Greenroom Books
11 Bark Lane, Addingham, Ilkley, West Yorkshire LS29 0RA. Tel/Fax: (01943) 830 497.
Mail order service for books on the performing arts.

MOMI Shop,
Museum of the Moving Image, South Bank, London SE1 8XT. Tel: (0171) 928 3535.
Visitors to the National Film Theatre now have a comprehensive bookshop in the foyer, to complement the stock of posters, postcards, toys and videos available at the MOMI shop.

The Reel Poster Gallery,
22 Great Marlborough Street, London W1V 1AF. Tel: (0171) 734 4303. Fax: (0171) 734 4260.
London's first gallery dedicated to original vintage film posters. An extensive yet selective stock includes posters pf all genres, from Westerns to science-fiction, and Hollywood classics to cult titles, seen through the eyes of artists from various countries.

Anne FitzSimons,
62 Scotby Road, Scotby, Carlisle, Cumbria CA4 8BD. Tel: (01228) 513815.
A useful source for second-hand and out-of-print books on the cinema, as well as the theatre, puppeteering, etc. Private premises. Postal only.

58 Dean Street Records,
58 Dean Street, London W1V 5HH. Tel: (0171) 437 4500, 734 8777.
Specialising in soundtracks, original cast shows (incl. imports), personalities, and nostalgia. Over 7,000 titles both current and deleted items; LP's, cassettes, and CD's. (Mail Order service).

David Henry,
36 Meon Road, London W3 8AN. Tel: (0181) 993 2859.
Mail-order business – catalogues on request.

Ed Mason,
Shop 5, Chelsea Antique Market, 253 King's Road, London SW3. Tel: (0171) 352 6338.
Large and carefully-assembled stock of memorabilia from the silents to the 1980's. Plus stills, pressbooks, posters. Customers served by post.

Flashbacks,
6 Silver Place, (Beak St.), London W1R 3LJ. Tel/Fax: (0171) 437 8562.
Most impressively stocked establishment which, in London's

THE GRADUATE (1967). Original British poster 30 × 40 inches available through the Reel Poster Gallery

BRIEF ENCOUNTER (1945). Original Italian poster by Alfredo Capitani. Courtesy of the Reel Poster Gallery

Samuel French Bookshops in conjunction with the Directors of America presents John Frankenheimer and Robert Wise signing their books at Showbiz Expo, Los Angeles, 1995. *photo: Kate-Lesli Hay*

West End, caters for those interested in movie ephemera – posters, stills, pressbooks – from many countries and every period of cinema history. Also extensive Mail Order service. (No catalogue issued, but individual requests responded to. Monday to Saturday 10.30-19.00).

Zwemmer, A.,
80 Charing Cross Road, London WC2. Tel: (0171) 379 7886.
Large selection of new and out-of-print film books, from early film-making to digital video. Mail order inquiries.

Movie Boulevard,
3 Cherry Tree Walk, Leeds LS2 7EB. Tel: (0113) 242 2888. Fax: (0113) 243 8840.
Welcome north of England addition to the ranks of shops specialising in soundtracks, videos, laserdiscs and memorabilia. Headed by the enthusiastic Robert Wood.

U.S.A.

Applause,
211 West 71 Street, New York, NY10023. Tel: (212) 496 7511.
Now one of the few – and certainly the only uptown – film and showbiz bookstores in Manhattan.

Cinema Books,
4753 Roosevelt Way NE, Seattle, Washington 98105. Tel: (206) 547-7667.
Fine selection of film books and magazines, with space also devoted to TV and theatre. Mail Orders welcome.

Cinemonde,
138 Second Avenue North, Suite 106, Nashville, Tennessee 37201. Tel: (615) 742 3048. Fax: (615) 742 1268.
Installed in a capacious gallery in Old Nashville, Cinemonde may well be the world's premier poster store for movie buffs. Items are immaculately displayed and stored, and the colourful catalogue is a collector's item ($15 incl. airmail costs). In addition, Cinemonde has a search service in San Francisco (1932 Polk St., San Francisco, CA 94109. Tel: (415) 776 9988. Fax: (415) 776 1424) for hard-to-find vintage posters, headed by the movie poster consultant for Sotheby's, New York.

Dwight Cleveland,
P.O. Box 10922, Chicago, Illinois 60610-0922. Tel: (312) 523 9152. Fax: (312) 525 2969.
Buys and sells movie posters.

Collectors Book Store,
Dept 10, 1708 N. Vine Street,Hollywood, California 90028. Tel: (213) 467-3296. Fax: (213) 467 4536
Offers a superlative range of posters, stills, lobby cards, TV and film scripts.

Samuel French's Theatre & Film Bookshop,
7623 Sunset Boulevard, Hollywood, California 90046. Tel: (213) 876-570. Fax: (213) 876 6822.
The world's oldest and largest play publisher (est. 1830) operates a separate film bookshop. Complete range of new movie books available: directories, reference, writing, acting, biography, screenplays, etc. 3,000 titles and growing! Worldwide mail order service. Note that French's also have a store at 11963 Ventura Blvd, Studio City, California 91604. Tel: (818) 762-535. Gwen Feldman and Jim Fox prepare some meticulous catalogues that include more data than most similar efforts.

SAMUEL FRENCH BOOKSHOPS

PLAYS, and BOOKS on FILM, THEATRE and the MOTION PICTURE INDUSTRY

EVERYTHING FOR THE FILMMAKER, PRODUCER, ACTOR & FILM BUFF

WORLDWIDE MAIL ORDER VISA, MC, AM EX, Discover
FILM BOOKS CATALOGUES on request

7623 Sunset Blvd., Hollywood, CA 90046
phone (213) 876-0570 • fax (213) 876-6822
email: samfrench@earthlink.com

NEW TITLES WE STRONGLY RECOMMEND:
*ZEN AND THE ART OF SCREENWRITING: **Insights and Interviews*** by William Froug ($18.95 paper)
*IN THE BLINK OF AN EYE: **A Perspective on Film Editing*** by Walter Murch ($12.95 paper)
RAYMOND CHANDLER IN HOLLYWOOD by Al Clark ($19.95 paper)
*AFRICAN-AMERICAN SCREENWRITERS NOW: **Conversations With Hollywood's Black Pack*** by Erich Leon Harris ($16.95 paper)
*MAKING MOVIES WORK: **Thinking Like A Filmmaker*** by Jon Boorstin ($19.95 paper)

BESTSELLERS:
*MAKING A GOOD SCRIPT GREAT – **Second Edition*** by Linda Seger ($12.95 paper)
*DEALMAKING IN THE FILM AND TELEVISION INDUSTRY: **From Negotiations Through Final Contracts*** by Mark Litwak ($26.95 paper)
COMEDY WRITING STEP BY STEP by Gene Perret ($13.95 paper)

Gotham Book Mart,
41 West 47th St., New York, NY 10036. Tel: (212) 719 4448.
This famous literary bookshop in mid-Manhattan, established in 1920, is the only New York city bookstore offering new, used and out-of-print film and theatre books. Also an extensive stock of 'quality' film magazines dating from the 1950's to the present.

Larry Edmunds Bookshop,
6644 Hollywood Blvd., Hollywood, California 90028. Tel: (213) 463 3273. Fax: (213) 463 4245.
The stills collection alone is a goldmine for any film buff. Back numbers of movie annuals, posters, lobby cards and largest collection of new and used books in the world. Magazines always available.

Limelight Film and Theatre Bookstore,
1803 Market Street, San Francisco, California 94103. Tel: (415) 864-2265.
Roy A. Johnson runs this lively store for film and theatre books. Collection includes plays, screenplays, biographies, history

IFG's Book of the Year, published by Richard Cohen Books, London.

and criticism of films and film and television technique.

Movie Madness,
1222 Wisconsin Avenue NW, Washington DC 20007.
Posters, etc. available at this tiny store adjacent to the Key (one of Washington's best repertory cinemas).

Jerry Ohlinger's Movie Material Store Inc.,
242 West 14th Street, New York, NY 10011. Tel: (212) 989-869.
Jerry Ohlinger's emporium stocks a wealth of stills from the 1960's through the 1990's, specialising in colour material. Posters are also plentiful and there are some magazines as well.

The Most Comprehensive Array of Collectible Movie Memorabilia in the World.

COLLECTORS BOOK STORE

Movie Stills • Posters • Movie Magazines
Movie & TV Scripts

1708 N. Vine Street, Hollywood
CA 90028 (213) 467-3296

(at Hollywood & Vine – since 1965)

BOOK REVIEWS

After years of research, Kevin Brownlow's monumental biography of **David Lean** (Richard Cohen Books, London) has arrived like a tombstone on reviewers' desks. Slimmed down by Adrian Turner, the book remains compulsive reading, the finest product of Brownlow's love for cinema since *The Parade's Gone By* some thirty years ago. Its sources are impeccable, Lean himself spoke for hours to Brownlow before he died, and the balance between biographical detail and film analysis is well struck. If every director could enjoy such treatment...

Trusting the teller rather than the tale remains the watchword for many publishers. **Fellini on Fellini,** edited by Costanzo Costantini (Faber, London), however, transcends at a bound the average interview book. Fellini is witty and lubricious by turns, confronting every question with relaxed good humour and reflecting on his life, his colleagues, and his films with perspicacity – and not a jot of weariness. **Almodóvar on Almodóvar,** edited by Frédéric Strauss (Faber, London) suffers by comparison, but the Spanish maestro talks in great detail about individual themes and sequences.

James Howard's potted biography of **Michael Powell** (Batsford, London) cannot add much to what we already know from Kevin Macdonald's works and of course Powell's voluminous autobiography. The well-reproduced pictures compensate for the whirlwind haste of the text. Jack Cardiff, a distinguished craftsman who photographed *The Red Shoes, Black Narcissus* and other Powell movies, has written an engrossing memoir: **Magic Hour, The Life of a Cameraman** (Faber, London). Anecdotal in a controlled kind of way, *The Magic Hour* tells more about the life than the technique of one of Britain's finest cinematographers.

An unexpected jewel in the year's crown of film literature is **Letters, Inventing the Cinema,** by Auguste and Louis Lumière (Faber, London). A veritable blizzard of correspondence between these French pioneers and their suppliers and clients, the book charts the very fabric of primitive cinema. Even more arcane, and sumptuously produced, is **Light and Movement, Incunabula of the Motion Picture, 1420-1896** (published by Giornate del Cinema Muto of Pordenone, and available outside Italy through BFI Publishing). Printed in four-colour and on fine paper, it's a goldmine for pre-cinema devotees. Julian Fox's **Woody, Movies from Manhattan** (Batsford, London) offers a competent if *faux-intime* survey of Allen's career, no mean feat in the shadow of Eric Lax's biography and Stig Björkman's interview book published in 1994.

One picture may not replace a thousand words, but Brian Hamill's shots of **Woody Allen at Work** (Abrams, New York) bear eloquent testimony to the director's relationships with his actors and technicians, and also include a majority of the best stills ever taken of Allen's films. This is an album produced with the intelligence and splendour one associates with Abrams.

Useful Flow of Screenplays

Once again Faber and Faber published an invaluable selection of illustrated screenplays during the year. **Trainspotting and Shallow Grave,** by John Hodge, come in a single volume, and it's a relief to find that behind the vernacular doric of the former film lies some shrewdly written, coherent dialogue. And when *Shallow Grave* is recognised as one of the finest debuts in British film history, this screenplay will be treasured. Mike Figgis's **Leaving Las Vegas** (from the novel by John O'Brien) is a beautifully-modulated script, and the Afterword features notes on certain scenes and their gestation.

In films where the action and the visuals predominate over dialogue, however, the Faber screenplays are less illuminating: both **Fargo,** by Ethan Coen and Joel Coen, and **From Dusk Till Dawn,** by Quentin Tarantino, fail quite to capture the mood and look of their respective films. **Dead Man Walking,** written and directed by Tim Robbins, achieves a perverse balance of sympathies in its scrutiny of a criminal prior to execution, and its characterisations are taut as a whiplash.

One of the most articulate sound engineers in the world is Walter Murch, whose association with Francis Coppola is legendary. **In The Blink of an Eye, A Perspective in Film Editing,** by Walter Murch (Silman-James Press, Los Angeles) comprises lectures given by Murch on various topics relating to craftsmanship in the cinema, and should be inspired reading for students at colleges everywhere.

In an impoverished year for genre studies, Ian Cameron and Douglas Pye's **The Movie Book of the Western** (Studio Vista, London) rekindles memories of *Movie* magazine and the early 1960's. The essays cover nearly all the landmark directors and Westerns, and although the type is too small to read easily, this is a book to dip into when reviewing the classics of a genre that has refused to ride away into the sunset.

Various guides to national cinemas have appeared in the past year. The impeccable design of **Mexican Cinema,** edited by Paulo Antonio Paranagua (BFI Publishing) mirrors the Centre Georges Pompidou series from which it has been translated, and accompanied a revelatory season of Mexican films at the National Film Theatre. In that original French series, under the overall guidance of Jean-Loup Passek, both **Le Cinéma Turc** and Freddy Buache's **Trente Ans de Cinéma Suisse** furnish the film buff with profiles, data, and critical appreciation on lesser-known film territories. Roy Armes's **Dictionary of North American Film-makers** (London), printed usefully in French and English, treads altogether new turf as far as Anglo-Saxon scholarship is concerned. The wealth of detail assembled by Armes makes his book indispensable for good libraries.

Ginette Vincendeau, now one of Britain's most distinguished film academics, has without doubt laboured hard to make the **Encyclopedia of European Cinema** (Cassell/BFI Publishing, London) an essential tool for libraries and enthusiasts of what used to be called, quaintly, "the foreign film." The national entries prove excellent, the biographical ones slightly less so. Film festivals have their place, as do technical innovations and genres. How sad that such a book appears twenty years after its time, in a decade where Hollywood cinema rules the roost.

Two of the Nordic countries have published illustrated filmographies. **Filmen i Norge, Norske kinofilmer gjennom 100 år** (Ad Notam Gyldendal, Oslo) takes its place among the most honourable and engaging books published for the centenary. Loving attention has been given to the smallest detail of what constitutes a comprehensive filmography of the 568 features made in Norway between 1908 and 1995. The illustrations are impeccably reproduced, and the text laid on the page in inviting fashion. It would have been useful to have a sufficient introduction or *vade mecum* in English and French, but to deny the success of a book that has reached tens of thousands of readers in Norway would be churlish indeed.

Admirable too are volumes 1 and 2 of the Finnish national filmography, **Suomen Kansallisfilmografia** (Edita/Finnish Film Archive, Helsinki). Running from 1907 to 1941, these tomes give comprehensive coverage to each film produced in the period. Once complete, this series will serve as a monumental to the scholarship and devotion of Kari Uusitalo, the editor-in-chief.

Angus Finney has performed a creditable job of recreating a chaotic episode in recent British film history, namely the rise and fall of Palace Pictures. **The Egos Have Landed** (Heinemann, London) revels in the unsubtle, often unsavoury business methods of Nik Powell and Steve Woolley, without quite deciding if the duo's accomplishments added up to anything more than a couple of good movies and a lot of bad debt.

A final commendation for some recent entries in the BFI Film Classics series (BFI Publishing, London): **Queen Christina,** by Marcia Landy and Amy Villarejo (the feminist reading), **An Actor's Revenge,** by Ian Breakwell, and in particular Jim Kitses's **Gun Crazy,** which stands as a passionate rediscovery of one of Hollywood's finest Z-movies. And applause of course for John Boorman and Walter Donohue's series, **Projections** (Faber, London), which has now reached its sixth stanza and continues to corral some fascinating items written by film-makers themselves.

Peter Cowie

MAGAZINES

The following list amounts to a selection only of the world's hundreds of film publications. Editors wishing to receive a free listing must send sample copies (preferably opening a sample subscription for us). Address: IFG, Variety, 34-35 Newman Street, London W1P 3PD, U.K.

AMERICAN PREMIERE

8421 Wilshire Blvd., Penthouse; Beverly Hills, CA 90211, U.S.A. Bi-monthly industry magazine, free to members of the Academy of Motion Picture Arts and Sciences.

ANIMATION JOURNAL

AJ Press, 2011 Kingsboro Circle, Tustin, California 92680-6733, U.S.A. The only peer-reviewed scholarly journal devoted to animation history and theory. Quarterly.

ANIMATION MAGAZINE

Terry Thoren, Agoura Court, Suite 110, Agoura, California 91301, U.S.A. International guide to the animation industry in a new eye-catching format. Bi-monthly.

AUDIENCE

P.O. Box 215, Simi Valley, CA93062-0215, U.S.A. Billed as an "informal commentary on film", this witty, well-informed bi-monthly features articles and reviews, both recent and retrospective.

AVANT PREMIERE

Case Postale 5615, 1211 Geneva 11, Switzerland. Colourful monthly with lengthy reviews of new releases, as well as a pullout brochure on Swiss production and distribution.

BIANCO E NERO

1524 via Tuscolana, 00173 Rome, Italy. Italian yearly that boasts a reputation for scholarship second to none in its country.

CAHIERS DU CINEMA

Editions de l'Etoile, 9 passage de la Boule Blanche, 75012 Paris, France. Celebrated French journal now enjoying a second lease of life after a long spell in the wilderness.

CHAPLIN

Box 27 126, S-102 52 Stockholm, Sweden. Edited by FilmhusFörlaget AB, a subsidiary to the Swedish Film Institute. Covers Swedish and international cinema by Sweden's foremost film critics. Now more appealing than ever. Bi-monthy.

CINE & MEDIA

Rue du Saphir 15, 1040 Brussels, Belgium. Multilingual (French, English and Spanish) bi-monthly published by the International Catholic Organisation for Cinema and the Audiovisual, with reports from all continents.

CINEASTE

Suite 1601 200 Park Avenue South, New York, NY 10003, U.S.A. Perhaps the finest anti-establishment movie magazine, never afraid to tackle controversial issues and never prone to Hollywood worship. Interviews are especially good in *Cineaste.*

CINE-BULLES

4545 avenue Pierre-de-Coubertin, CP 1000, Succursale M. Montréal, Canada H1V 3R2. Remarkable and informative Québécois quarterly that may just be the best in Canada.

CINE-BULLETIN

Swiss Film Centre, P.O. Box, Neugasse 6, CH-8031 Zürich, Switzerland. Serious Swiss monthly in French and German with box office and films in production.

CINECRITICA

Via Yser, n.8-00198 Rome, Italy. Dense Italian quarterly focussing on world cinema.

CINE CUBANO

Calle 23, no. 1115 Apdo. 55, Havana, Cuba. Vital information on all Latin American cinema, unfortunately only in Spanish.

CINEFANTASTIQUE

P.O. Box 270, Oak Park, Ill. 60303, U.S.A. An enthusiastic, well-written, beautifully produced monthly with a special emphasis on horror, fantasy and s-f films.

CINE-FICHES DE GRAND ANGLE

Rue d'Arschot 29, B-5660 Mariembourg, Belgium. Monthly review of new films and videos.

CINEMA & CINEMA

1 via Battibecco, 40123 Bologna, Italy. Respected quarterly.

CINEMA & VIDEO INTERNATIONAL

Via Tevere 46B, 00198 Rome, Italy. Monthly for audiovisual professionals in English and Italian.

CINEMA JOURNAL

University of Texas Press, Box 7819, Austin, Texas 78713-7819, U.S.A. Essays concerned with the study of the moving image from diverse methodological perspectives, with information on upcoming events and research opportunities.

CINEMA NOVO

Apartado, 78, 4002 Porto Codex, Portugal. Bi-monthly Portuguese magazine dealing with international and Portuguese topics.

CINEMANIA

Fran Via 32, 2°, 28013 Madrid, Spain. Upmarket monthly with news, interviews, reports, feature articles and TV and video coverage.

CINEMA NUOVO

PO Box 362, 70100 Bari, Italy. Polemical, academic Italian quarterly with excellent articles.

CINEMA PAPERS

116 Argyle Street, Fitzroy, Victoria, Australia. Excellent large-format Australian bi-monthly, packed with information and pictures, useful for anyone monitoring the industry in Oz.

CINEMATECA REVISTA

Lorenzo Carnelli 1311, Casilla de Correo 1170, Montevideo, Uruguay. Bright magazine with international slant published by Cinemateca Uruguaya. Ten times a year.

CINEMATHEQUE

P.O. Box 20370, Tel Aviv 61203, Israel. Fine monthly Israeli magazine (with summary in English) dwelling on seasons at the Tel-Aviv Cinémathèque but also reporting on world festivals etc.

CINEMAYA

B 90 Defence Colony, New Delhi 110 024, India. Informative, elegant magazine, published quarterly in English since 1988, on all aspects of the Asian film industry. Is the official journal of NETPAC (Network for promotion of Asian Cinema).

CINEMAZERO

Piazza Maestri del Lavorò 3, 33170 Pordenone, Italy. Serious Italian bi-monthly covering international cinema, with festival news and book reviews.

CINESITH

142 Abeyratne Mawatha, Boralesgamuwa, Sri Lanka. Sri Lanka's only serious film magazine focuses on national and international cinema with special reference to Asia.

CITY ENTERTAINMENT

6/F, Flat A, Tung Nam Bldg, 475-481 Hennesssy Road, Causeway Bay, Hongkong. Glossy, indispensable Hongkong monthly for anyone interested in Chinese cinema. In Chinese.

CLASSIC IMAGES

P,O. Box 809, Muscataine, IA52761, U.S.A. Formerly "Classic Film Collector," a good source for film buffs eager to enlarge their library of movies. Monthly.

CULTURE AND CINEMA

18 Safa Alley, Kushk St., Saadi Ave., Tehran, Iran. Monthly magazine featuring Iranian cinema.

DIRIGIDO POR

Rbla de Cataluña, 108 3. 1, Barcelona 08008, Spain. This handsomely-produced Spanish monthly throws the spotlight each issue on a particular genre, studio or director of international renown.

DOX

PO Box 100534, 45405 Mulheim an der Ruhr, Germany. An independent magazine on documentary film, film-making and viewing. Interviews, international news, festival reports and industry profiles. Bi-monthly.

EKRAN

1000 Ljubljana, Miklošičeva 38, Slovenia. Provides critical evaluation and topical consideration of Slovene and foreign films. Bi-monthly.

EL REFUGIO

José Granda 460, Lima 27, Peru. South American monthly with reviews and features on world cinema.

EMPIRE

1st Floor, Mappin House, 4 Winsley Street, London W1N 7AR, U.K. Glossy fanzine monthly with profiles, reviews and behind-the-scenes reports. Excellent photos.

ENFOQUE

Publicaciones y Audiovisuales, Linterna Mágica Ltda., Casilla 15, Correo 34, Santiago, Chile. Occasional quarterly taking an in-depth look at the Chilean/Latin American markets and new-releases.

ENTERTAINMENT HERALD

Corrieres 2817 3-A 1015, Buenos Aires, Argentina.

ENTERTAINMENT MARKT

Stahlgruberring 11a, 81829 Munich, Germany. Bi-weekly business magazine that covers the German video, CD-ROM and computer games market.

EURO-MOVIES INTERNATIONAL

News-Movies, SCP, San Gaudencio 7, Sitges, 08870, Barcelona, Spain. Spanish and Latin American panorama, with reviews, festival news and television section.

FANTASTIC

Gran Via de les Corts Catalanes 132, 2°, 08014 Barcelona, Spain. Monthly, dedicated to s-f films, with articles and photographs. Reaches 146,000 readers an issue.

FARABI FILM QUARTERLY

55 Sie-Tir Ave., Tehran 11358, Iran. Quarterly periodical issued by the Farabi Cinema Foundation, with the aim of upgrading film culture in the country.

FATAL VISIONS

P.O. Box 133, Northcote 3070, Victoria, Australia. Irregular but lively title dedicated to horror, sci-fi and sexploitation flicks with interviews, reviews and a Chinatown beat.

FILA 7

Avda. de la Sierra 6. 2° D, Aptdo. de Correos 55, 28700 San Sebastian de los Reyes, Madrid, Spain. Monthly consumer-oriented, with features and photographs. Its sister publication, *Fila 7 Video*, features video, television and new technology.

FILM

Pulawska 61, 02595 Warsaw, Poland. Popular Polish monthly with international slant.

FILM

(Yeonghwa), Motion Picture Promotion Corporation of Korea, 34-5, 3-ga, Namsan-dong, Junggu, Seoul. South Korea's only serious film magazine, packed with information. Bi-monthly.

FILMHÄFTET

Box 101 56, 100 55 Stockholm, Sweden. Egghead monthly with features on international directors, retrospectives, and Scandinavian television.

FILM INTERNATIONAL

P.O. Box 11365-5875, Tehran, Iran. Quarterly publication which not only focuses on Iranian films and film-makers, but also on issues regarding third world cinema. In English.

FILMJOURNALEN

Finlandssvenskt filmcentrum, Nylandsgatan 1, 25700 Åbo, Finland. Passionate Swedish-language quarterly focusing on Nordic and Finnish cinema.

FILMKULTURA

Solymár u. 8, 1032 Budapest, Hungary. Essays and reviews on Hungarian and international cinema. Six times a year.

FILMMAKER MAGAZINE

110 West 57th Street, New York, Ny 10019-3319, USA. Tel: 212-581-8080. Fax: 212-581-1857. Aimed at independent film-makers, this quarterly offers interviews, news and sound advice.

FILMVILAG

Pozsonyi út 20, H-1137 Budapest, Hungary. Monthly with reviews and interviews.

FILMS IN REVIEW

P.O. Box 589, New York, NY 10021, U.S.A. Compact bi-monthly journal, reviewing notable new releases with interviews, retrospective articles and television/video reports.

FILM & DOBA

Halkova 1, 120 72 Prague 2, Czech Republic. The principal Czech film monthly.

FILM APPRECIATION

The National Film Archive of the R.O.C., 4th Floor, 7 Ching-tao East Road, Taipei, Taiwan R.O.C. Taiwan's premier serious film journal, published as a bi-monthly. Focus on the cinematic output of Taiwan, Hong Kong and mainland China, as well as from Chinese communities overseas.

FILM EN TELEVISIE + VIDEO

Haachtesteenweg, 35, B-1210 Brussels, Belgium. Extensive reviews of major new film and video releases, profiles and interviews, festival news.

FILM BULLETIN

Postfach 137, CH-8408 Winterthur, Switzerland. Informative, straightforward look at international cinema, with useful Swiss material also. Bi-monthly.

FILM COMMENT

Film Society of Lincoln Center, 70 Lincoln Center Plaza, New York, NY 10023, U.S.A. Informative, feisty, and usually uncompromising articles as well as interviews on wide-ranging international topics. New video and even occasional laserdisc sections. Still the best U.S. bi-monthly on the cinema.

FILM CRITICISM

Allegheny College, Box D, Meadville, PA 16335, U.S.A. Scholarly essays on film history, theory and culture. Quarterly.

FILM DOPE

74 Julian Road, Nottingham NG2 5AN. Not so much a magazine, more a part-work film dictionary, this irregular British quarterly is to be welcomed for its exhaustive research.

FILMIHULLU

Malminkatu 36, FI-00100 Helsinki, Finland. Finnish film and TV magazine with perverse, rather old-fashioned critical approach, appearing eight times a year.

FILM HISTORY

John Libbey and Co. Ltd., 13 Smiths Yard, Summerley Street, London SW18 4HR, U.K. Articles on the historical development of the motion picture, in a social, technological and economic context. Quarterly.

FILM JOURNAL INTERNATIONAL

The Sunshine Group, 244 West 49th Street, Suite 200, New York, NY 10019, U.S.A. Monthly magazine covering international exhibition.

FILM LITERATURE INDEX

Film and Television Documentation Centre, State University of New York, 1400 Washington Avenue, Albany, NY 12222, U.S.A. The most comprehensive international index to the journal literature of film and television.

FILM MONTHLY

P.O. Box 11365-5875, Tehran, Iran. The leading Iranian film magazine, published since 1982, mainly focuses on domestic film industry and international cinema. In Farsi.

FILM NA SWIECIE

Polish Federation of Film Clubs, Plocka 16/34, 01138 Warsaw, Poland.

FILM QUARTERLY

University of California Press, 2120 Berkeley Way, Berkeley, California 94720. Publishes readable discussions of issues in contemporary film, TV and video, substantive film reviews and interviews, and analyses of independent, documentary, avant-garde and foreign films.

FILM REPORT

3rd Floor, 123 Jami St., Hafez Ave., Tehran, Tehran, Iran. Reviews and features on the latest releases.

FOTOGRAMAS

Gran Via de les Corts, Catalanes 133, 2°, 08014 Barcelona, Spain. Glossy monthly, packed with colourful articles and photographs, also video reviews and television film listings. Circulation: 220,000 per month.

GRIFFITHIANA

Cineteca del Friuli, 26 via Osoppo, 33013 Gemona del Friuli (Udine), Italy. Italian quarterly devoted exclusively to the study of silent cinema and animation. Each issue is a miracle of scholarship and devotion.

HOLLAND ANIMATION NEWSBRIEF

Hoogt 4, 3512 GW Utrecht, The Netherlands. Quarterly newsletter from the Holland Animation Foundation.

HONG KONG FILM MAGAZINE

601 Van Ness Avenue, Suite E3728, San Francisco, California 94102, U.S.A. Quarterly focusing on the Hong Kong cinema scene, featuring news, reviews and interviews. In English.

IMAGEN

Casilla 1733, La Paz, Bolivia. Magazine of the Bolivian New Cinema Movement.

IMAGENES DE ACTUALIDAD

Consell de Cent, 304, 2.º, 1.ª, 08007 Barcelona, Spain. Glossy, well presented international magazine with strong Hollywood bias. Monthly.

IMMAGINI & SUONI

FIAIS, Casella postale 6306, 00195 Rome, Italy. Published by the International Federation of Film Archives. In French and Italian.

THE INDEPENDENT FILM/VIDEO GUIDE

EFLA, 45 John Street, New York, NY 10038, U.S.A. Quarterly index to the works exhibited by non-commercial film-video show-cases in New York City and New York State.

INTERFILMS

Valportillo Primera 16, Poligono Industrial Alcobendas, Alcobendas 28100, Madrid, Spain. Monthly film magazine for consumer.

INTERNATIONAL DOCUMENTARY

1551 South Robertson Boulevard, Suite 201, Los Angeles, CA 90035, U.S.A. The only publication to focus exclusively on non-fiction film and video. Presents new work and ideas in the documentary field with informative articles, reviews and interviews. Published ten times a year.

ISKUSSTVO KINO

9 ul. Usievicha, 125319 Moscow, Russia. Chunky, theoretical, most authoritative Russian film monthly.

JUMP CUT

P.O. Box 865, Berkeley, California 94701, U.S.A. Published only once or twice a year, this tabloid contains an extraordinary amount of closely-woven text.

KINEMA

Fine Arts (Film Studies), University of Waterloo, Waterloo, Ont. N2L 3G1, Canada. A journal of history, theory and aesthetics of world film and audiovisual media. Twice yearly.

KINETOSCOPIO

El Palo No. 53-24, Apdo. Aereo 8734, Medellin, Colombia. Bi-monthly covering international and Latin American cinema, Colombian directors and festival news.

KINO: GERMAN FILM + INTL. REPORTS

c/o Holloway, Helgoländer Ufer 6, 10557, Berlin, Germany. Excellent quarterly devoted to both German cinema and international festival reports. Features reviews, interviews and credits.

KINO

Chelmska 19/21, 00-724 Warsaw, Poland. Culturally inclined Polish monthly designed to promote European cinema, with interviews, reviews and essays.

KOSMORAMA

The Danish Film Museum, Gothersgrade 55 Dk1123-Copenhagen K, Denmark. One of the most beautifully-designed and lovingly-edited of Nordic film magazines. Quarterly.

LA STRADA

P.O. Box 432, 33101 Tampere, Finland. Finland's largest film magazine, this quarterly is provocative and entertaining, with lots of news and reviews. In Finnish.

THE LIMITED EDITION

The Score Company, Linzer Str. 5, 53604 Bad Honnef, Germany. Quarterly devoted to soundtracks and the art of film scoring.

LITERATURE/FILM QUARTERLY

Salisbury State University, Salisbury, Maryland 21801, U.S.A. Scholarly quarterly with film and book reviews, interviews and articles. Manuscripts inivited for submission.

THE MAGUFFIN

177 Simpson Street, East Melbourne 3002, Australia. Scholarly newsletter focusing on the films of Alfred Hitchcock. Intelligent and jargon-free.

MEDIAFILM

Haachtsesteenweg 35, B-1210 Brussels, Belgium. Serious Belgian quarterly, with extensive reviews, analysis and focus on directors. Quarterly.

MEDIASUD

Maison de la presse, Tahar Djaout, 1 rue Bachir Attar, Place du 1er Mai, Algiers. New Algerian film publication.

MEDIUM

Postfach 50 05 50, Frankfurt am Main, Germany. Highbrow German publication covering film, radio, T.V., and the press. Bi-monthly.

MOVIELINE

1141 South Beverly Drive, Los Angeles, CA 90035, U.S.A. Intelligent, irreverent and refreshingly candid Hollywood monthly. Great interviews.

MUSIC FROM THE MOVIES

1 Folly Square, Bridport, Dorset DT6 3PU, U.K. Informative quarterly devoted to all aspects of film music and its composers, with articles, interviews and soundtrack reviews.

NICKEL ODEON

Bárbara de Braganza 12, 28004 Madrid, Spain. Important new quarterly from Spain, very well illustrated and researched. First issue offers an in-depth look at Spanish cinema.

THE NIGHTINGALE REPORT

45 Barclay Road, Toronto, Ontario M3H 3EZ, Canada. Fortnightly newsletter aimed at Canadian film and television industry. News and comprehensive listings.

NUOVO CINEMA EUROPEO

Via delle Cinque Giornate 15, 50129, Florence, Italy. Chunky bi-monthly report on Italian film industry, in English with Italian summary. Includes industry news, such as box-office, markets and foreign sales.

NZ FILM

P.O. Box 11-546, Wellington, New Zealand. News from the New Zealand Film Commission, a twice yearly round-up of the country's film industry.

ONFILM

P.O. Box 6374, Wellington, New Zealand. A film, television and video magazine for New Zealand, with location reports and a production survey.

PHOTOGRAPH

No 20, 19th Alley, Gandhi Ave., Tehran, Iran. A monthly magazine by the Young Iranian Cinema Society.

PICTURE HOUSE

5 Coopers Close, Burgess Hill, W. Sussex RH15 8AN. Admirable quarterly devoted to the cinema buildings of the past.

POPULAR CINEMA

(Dazhong dianying), 22 Beisanhuan donglu 22, Peking, China. Leading mainland Chinese monthly, also carrying pieces on Hongkong, Taiwan and foreign cinema.

POSITIF

19 Villa Croix Nivert, 75015 Paris, France. In-depth interviews, articles, all immaculately researched and highly intelligent. By a clear margin, this is Europe's best film magazine. New large format.

PREMIERE

151 rue Anatole France, 92534 Levallois-Perret Cedex, France. France's familiar movie monthly, packed with information, reviews and filmographies.

PREMIERE

1990 South Bundy Drive, Suite 250, Los Angeles, CA 90025, U.S.A. Diluted in size and scope since its launch seven years ago, but still has its finger on the pulse of Hollywood and retains a huge circulation.

PREMIERE U.K.

Mappin House, 4 Winsley Street, London W1N 7AR, U.K. Glossy monthly with in-depth personality profiles and stylish photography, reviews.

PRO CINEMA

Str. Luterană 11, et. II, sector 1, Budapest, Romania. New Romanian monthly covering mainstream European and Hollywood fare. Plenty of colour pics and interviews.

PRODUCER

162-170 Wardour Street, London, W1V 4LA, U.K. Welcome voice for the independent British producer.

QUADERNI DI CINEMA

Via Benedetto Varchi 57, 50132 Florence, Italy. Wide-ranging Italian bi-monthly, striving to match cultural politics with an enthusiastic appreciation of film.

RECTANGLE

CAC Voltaire, Rue Général-Dufour 16, 1204 Geneva, Switzerland. Only film magazine in the Suisse romande, and admirably poised between the theoretical and researchist approach to the cinema, with a fresh and lively layout.

RIVISTA DEL CINEMATOGRAFO

Via Giuseppe Palombini, 6-165 Rome, Italy. Important Italian monthly.

SEGNOCINEMA

Via G Prati 34, Vicenza. Glossy Italian bi-monthly packed with profiles, reviews and photographs. September issue lists complete guide to all titles released the previous season.

SIGHT AND SOUND

British Film Institute, 21 Stephen Street, London W1 1PL, U.K. Apart from its reference guide to most films released in the U.K., this once-celebrated magazine is still a pale shadow of its former authority. Slight improvement in the past year.

SKRIEN

p/a Filmmuseum, Vondelpark 3, 1071 AA Amsterdam, The Netherlands. Excellent Dutch magazine that appears with regularity and enthusiasm. Bi-monthly.

SOUNDTRACK!

Astridlaan 171, 2800 Mechelen, Belgium. Excellent quarterly for film music collectors.

SPECIAL EFFECT

B/4, Balgachia Villa, Calcutta 700 037, India. Formerly *Magic Lantern*, this Indian film quarterly mixes interviews and reviews with insightful comment, and surveys different trends in Indian cinema.

STARS

Rue d'Arschot 29, B-5660 Mariembourg, Belgium. Quarterly publication giving actors' biographies and filmographies.

STUDIO MAGAZINE

116 bis, avenue des Champs-Elysées, 75008 Paris, France. Glossy, beautifully designed monthly with reviews, articles and interviews.

TALKING PICTURES

3 Glengarry Road, East Dulwich, London SE22, U.K. Quarterly booklet with interviews, reviews and articles on film culture in the U.K. Mainstream film and book reviews are also a regular feature.

24 IMAGES

3962, rue Laval, Montréal, QC H2W 2J2, Canada. Exceptionally attractive French/Canadian quarterly, witty and well-informed.

VE CINEMA

Hil Yayinlari, Cagaloghi, Istanbul, Turkey. Quarterly published in Turkish.

VERTIGO

7-9 Earlham Street, London WC2H 9LL, U.K. New quarterly for independent British film-makers and audiences. A forum for critical debate.

VIDEO MAKER

Oasis Publishing, Media House, Boxwell Road, Berkhamsted, Herts, England. Film and video monthly that concentrates on the craft of making your own films.

WELTWUNDER DER KINEMATOGRAPHIE

Postfach 100 274, D-10562 Berlin, Germany. Fascinating, well-researched new title, with detailed articles on the past, present and future of cinematography and the technical art of film-making. Yearly.

WIDE ANGLE

The Johns Hopkins University Press, Baltimore, Maryland 212180, U.S.A. Scholarly thematically arranged journal. Wide range.

WORLD SCREEN

China Film Press, 22 Beisanhuandonglu, Beijng 100013, China. Monthly primarily devoted to new/classic features from around the world, with artist profiles and events.

Z FILMTIDSSKRIFT

Teatergt 3, 0180 Oslo 1, Norway. Enthusiastic quarterly with a focus on film theory and history, both Norwegian and international. Now with useful summaries in English.

ZOOM

Bederstrasse 76, Postfach, 8027 Zürich, Switzerland. Swiss monthly highlighting new releases, with interviews and good festival coverage. In German.

National Organs

ACADEMIA

Sagasta 20, 3° drcha., 28004 Madrid, Spain. Excellent quarterly with articles, news and opinions of members of Spain's Academy of the Arts and Cinematographic Sciences.

AFC NEWS

GPO Box 3984, Sydney NSW 2001, Australia. Monthly, with regular production and multimedia reports, industry statistics, funding approvals and Australian films at international markets and festivals and awards won.

CINEMA, CINEMA

Ministère de la Culture Française, avenue de Cortenbur 158, 1040 Brussels, Belgium.

FEPACI NEWS

01 BP. 2524 Ouagadougou 01, Burkina Faso. Monthly newsletter of the Pan-African Federation of film-makers.

FILM CANADA YEARBOOK

Cine-communications, Box 152, Station R, Toronto, Ontario M4G 3Z3, Canada. Comprehensive directory of the Canadian film industry for over a decade.

ISRAEL FILM CENTRE INFORMATION BULLETIN

Ministry of Industry and Trade, 30 Agron Street, Jerusalem, Israel. Yearly review of Israeli film industry and catalogue of Israel films.

KINO

Export-Union des Deutschen Films, Türkenstr. 93, D-80799 München. Information on new German features (in production and already released), and selected personalities of the German film industry. Published three times a year in English, French, Spanish and German, with a yearbook also available.

Trade and Technical

AMERICAN CINEMATOGRAPHER

ASC Holding Corp., Box 2230, Los Angeles, CA 90078, U.S.A. Glossy monthly on film and electronic production techniques.

IMAGE TECHNOLOGY – JOURNAL OF THE BKSTS

67-71 Victoria House, Vernon Place, London WC1B 4DA, U.K. Covers technologies of motion picture film, television and sound at professional level. Ten times yearly.

BLICKPUNKT-FILM

Stahlgruberring 11a, 81829 Munich, Germany. Strong on box-office returns and marketing, this German weekly also covers the video and T.V. market.

BOXOFFICE

6640 Sunset Blvd, Suite 100, Hollywood, California, 90028-7159, U.S.A. Business monthly for the Hollywood and movie theatre industries.

CINEINFORME & TELE

Grand Via 64, 28013, Madrid, Spain. 35-year-old monthly that covers Spanish and international film, video and TV development.

CINEMA D'OGGI

Viale Regina Margherita 286, 00198 Rome, Italy. Fornightly. Interviews with producers.

CINEVIDEO 20

Apartado 2016, 28080 Madrid. Features technologies of film, video, computer, studio facilities, satellite and cable for a Spanish readership.

ECOMONO PRESS ACTING NEWS

Via Belluno 1, 00161 Rome, Italy. Comprehensive weekly reports on Italian film starts. Four market issues have English translations.

LE FILM FRANÇAIS

90 rue de Flandre, 75947 Paris Cedex 19, France. Lightweight weekly with news, reviews, box-office and production schedules.

FILM-ECHO/FILMWOCHE

Marktplatz 13, 65183 Wiesbaden, Germany. Doyen of the German trade. Weekly.

FILM JOURNAL

Pubsun Corp., 244 West 49 Street, New York, NY 10019, U.S.A. Monthly magazine aimed at U.S. exhibitors.

FILM OG KINO

Kongens gate 23, 0153 Oslo, Norway. Wide-ranging and well-illustrated. Covering new releases in cinema as well as national and international trade matters and festival reports.

GIORNALE DELLO SPETTACOLO

Via di Villa Patrizi 10, 00161 Rome, Italy. Box-office data, legal requirements, technical information etc.

THE HOLLYWOOD REPORTER

5055 Wilshire Boulevard, Los Angeles, CA 90036-4396, U.S.A. Daily.

MONITEUR DU FILM

36 rue des Frambosiers, 1180 Brussels, Belgium. Monthly.

MOVIE/TV MARKETING

Box 30, Central Post Office, Tokyo, 100-91 Japan. Monthly from Japan – in English.

MOVING PICTURES INTERNATIONAL

151-153 Wardour Street, London W1V 3TB, U.K. European-orientated bi-monthly trade paper published in London, with daily editions at numerous festivals.

MÜNCHEN FILM NEWS

Kaiserstrasse 39, 80801 Munich, Germany. A monthly put out by Munich's Informationbüro Film containing festival reports, films in production, personalities and other news concerning the Munich film scene. Specials in English.

SCREEN INTERNATIONAL

33-39 Bowling Green Lane, London, EC1R 0DA, U.K. Weekly, U.K.-oriented trade organ.

VARIETY

5700 Wilshire Boulevard, Suite 120, Los Angeles, CA 90036. The world's foremost newspaper (daily and weekly) of the entertainment business.

VARIETY'S ON PRODUCTION

5700 Wilshire Boulevard, Suite 120, Los Angeles, CA 90036, U.S.A. New technology and facilities for film, television and commercial production.

Index to Advertisers

YES

ORDER NOW!

THE CAM CATALOG ON CD-ROM

Just fax us this coupon with your credit card details and/or fax us to obtain a free brochure containing CAM soundtracks on CD.

For only $95.00 (shipping charges included).

☐ Yes, please mail me the **CAM ORIGINAL SOUNDTRACKS CATALOG** on **CD-ROM**. My mailing address is as follows (please allow 6-8 weeks for delivery):

NAME

STREET ADDRESS

CITY/STATE

ZIP/COUNTRY

TEL. NO.

☐ I wish to pay with my credit card. Below are the details.

☐VISA ☐MASTERCARDS ☐EUROCARD ☐AMEX ☐DINERS

Credit Card Number Exp

Cardholder Name Signature

CAM® Original Soundtracks

VIA COLA DI RIENZO, 152 - 00192 ROME (ITALY) - FAX:(+39-6) 687.4046